HEALTH PSYCHOLOGY

AN INTERDISCIPLINARY APPROACH TO HEALTH

Deborah Fish Ragin

Montclair State University

PEARSON

Boston   Columbus   Indianapolis   New York   San Francisco   Upper Saddle River
Amsterdam   Cape Town   Dubai   London   Madrid   Milan   Munich   Paris   Montreal   Toronto
Delhi   Mexico City   Sao Paulo   Sydney   Hong Kong   Seoul   Singapore   Taipei   Tokyo

For Luther, Remi and Chrissy:

To your health

Editor: Susan Hartman
Editorial Assistant: Laura Barry
Marketing Manager: Nicole Kuntzmann
Marketing Assistant: Shauna Fishweicher
Senior Production Project Manager: Patrick Cash-Peterson
Manufacturing Buyer: Debbie Rossi
Cover Designer and Administrator: Joel Gendron
Editorial Production and Composition Service: TexTech International
Interior Designer: TexTech International
Photo Researcher: Martha Shethar

Credits from other sources that are reproduced within this text, with permission, appear on the appropriate page.

This is a special edition of an established title widely used by colleges and universities throughout the world. Pearson published this exclusive edition for the benefit of students outside the United States and Canada. If you purchased this book within the United States or Canada you should be aware that it has been imported without the approval of the Publisher or the Author.

Many of the designations by manufacturers and seller to distinguish their products are claimed as trademarks. Where those designations appear in this book, and the publisher was aware of a trademark claim, the designations have been printed in initial caps or all caps.

25668188

10 9 8 7 6 5 4 3 2 1

Prentice Hall
is an imprint of

ISBN 10:   0-13-256857-8
ISBN 13: 978-0-13-256857-9

CONTENTS

PREFACE

The field of health psychology has changed considerably over the past several decades. The change largely reflects a better understanding of the factors that influence health. Traditionally, the study of individual, community, or even regional health involved an examination of individual physiological and behavioral factors, as well as the effects of familial or cultural practices. Today, with those elements as the foundation, we have added the following additional health outcome determinants to our study of the field of health psychology: physical environment, health systems, and health policy. Rather than rely on formulistic determinations, health psychologists have come to understand health as a dynamic process represented by the interaction of biology, human behavior, physical and social environments, health systems, and health policy. In essence, the field of health psychology increasingly has taken a social ecological approach to the study of health and well-being.

Health Psychology presents a social ecological perspective, an approach consistent with the changes and developments in the field of health psychology. The ecological model allows us to expand on our discussion of the biological, psychological, and sociological factors traditionally associated with health psychology. Using this model we now include in greater depth, a review and analysis of the impact of cultural, environmental, spiritual, and systems factors on health and health outcomes. The expanded perspective encourages, and in fact requires, that we consider the role of related fields such as anthropology, biology, economics, environmental studies, medicine, public health, and sociology. Many health psychologists contend that it is only through the lens of an interdisciplinary approach to health that we come to understand how health affects the individual on a mental and emotional level, and how the individual responds to the challenges.

The expanded model of health evident in the social ecological model is also more consistent with the new definition of health proposed by the American Psychological Association's (APA) Division of Health Psychology. Members of the Division, and an increasing number of health psychologists, believe that a more comprehensive and integrated approach to health psychology will enable us to arrive at a better understanding of the role of each factor in determining health outcomes.

Consistent with an interdisciplinary approach to health, one that gives equal weight to the physiological, emotional, psychological, environmental, and systems contributions to overall individual well-being, we introduce several topics in this text not typically covered in health psychology. For example, we introduce and explore in greater detail than many texts the global nature of health. Comparing the health outcomes of people with the same illness in different countries allows us to see the impact of difference environments and health systems on health status. We also devote a chapter to HIV/AIDS, the pandemic of the twentieth century to explore how determinants such as individual behaviors and lifestyles, social environments, health systems, and health policy promote or inhibit the spread of the disease. At the same time, we can explore the vital contributions of health psychologists to research on HIV/AIDS and to mental and physical health care for persons with the disease.

Departing from the format of some health psychology textbooks, this text does not include a separate chapter on biological systems. Rather, we incorporate in each chapter a section on the physiological systems relevant to that issue. For example, when discussing emotional health and well-being, we devote a section of the chapter to a discussion of the biological systems and neurotransmitters that are essential to understanding the body's response to emotions. Likewise in the chapter on cardiovascular health, we review the heart and its components as well as the circulatory system prior to discussing specific cardiovascular diseases or their treatments.

Several features are included in this text to underscore the point that health is an integral part of our lives. First, each chapter begins with an *opening story* that poses a scenario or problem for consideration. The opening stories highlight a central concept in the chapter and draws readers into the main topic of the chapter. Stories summarize current events that pertain to or impact health and allow the reader to apply the concepts in the chapter to real life situations. For example, the chapter on Cancer begins with a story on the association between cell phone use and brain tumors.

Second, each chapter ends with a *Personal Postscript* that encourages students to reflect on the main concepts of the chapter and to apply them to actual or likely life events. Personal postscripts are designed especially for a college-aged audience. They propose situations and offer advice or solutions to situations commonly encountered by college students that pertain to health. Finally, the postscripts bring the chapters "full circle," allowing students to reflect again on the applied aspects of the health issues presented in the chapter.

Third, the chapters include special "*boxes*" that explore selected material in depth without disrupting the flow of the text. It is ideal for students and instructors who seek more in-depth information on a topic introduced in the text. At the same time, the information in boxes can be omitted by readers who are less interested in the detailed topic.

Fourth, and central to the social ecological model, one chapter is dedicated to the role of health systems and health policy which also identifies career opportunities in health policy. Students are presented with various ways in which health psychologists can provide research and direct service to health policy institutions that affect the health of individuals, communities, regions, and countries.

Fifth, a sample of actual survey and health instruments used in medicine and health to measure mental, emotional and physical health are included. The instruments provide students interested in health research with real examples of valid instruments that can serve as templates for their own research. Students interested in applied work in health psychology will find the instruments a good resource for future use.

Finally, the chapters conclude with *Important Terms,* concepts, and procedures common in health and health related fields. Terms are highlighted and defined in text and itemized at the end of each chapter to remind students of the important concepts to remember in each chapter.

SUPPLEMENTS

Pearson Education is pleased to offer the following supplements to qualified adopters.

Instructor's Manual (0205004717) Prepared by Catherine Deering (Clayton State University), the instructor's manual is a wonderful tool for classroom preparation and management. Corresponding to the chapters in the text, each of the manual's 13 chapters contains lecture launchers, chapter outlines, extramural assignments, classroom demonstrations, and in-class student activities.

Test Item File (0205004725) Prepared by Michelle Loudermilk (Fayetteville Technical Community College), the test item file provides instructors with a bank of over 1,500 readymade multiple choice, short answer, true/false, and essay questions.

PowerPoint Presentation (0205004733) Prepared by Karla Felix (Brooklyn College), the PowerPoint Presentation is an exciting interactive tool for use in the classroom. Each chapter pairs key concepts with images from the textbook to reinforce student learning.

ACKNOWLEDGMENTS

If it takes a village to raise a child, it also takes one to create a textbook. A number of people have given generously of their time, talents and knowledge, and evidenced great patience over several years to assist me in writing and producing this book. I am very grateful for the encouragement, support and assistance of two wonderful executive editors at Pearson, Susan Hartman and Jeff Marshall. Their strong support of my work and critical input was appreciated throughout this process. I am especially indebted to Jeff who, from the beginning, supported my desire to write a health psychology text that was consistent with my interdisciplinary view of health and who monitored the process carefully.

It has also been a pleasure to work with a wonderful group of editorial assistants, development editors, and a production team who through their professionalism and with plenty of patience guided me through the process and taught me about the world of publishing. A talented production team managed by Patrick Cash-Peterson worked to meet deadlines and to transform the manuscript into a visually impressive and professional end product. Among other tasks too numerous to mention, Susan McNally did an outstanding job with production, Patrick Cash-Peterson provided valuable advice and assistance specifically when selecting the photos for the book, and Melinda Alexander handled the time consuming job of permissions and research with incredible patience and enthusiasm. Finally Maheswari PonSaravanan's careful attention to detail helped transform the manuscript into its final, finished form. A host of editorial assistants assumed a number of tasks of which I probably know only a few. My sincere thanks to Laura Barry, Kara Kikel, Mary Lombard, Aaron Talwar and Amy Trudell for their editorial support.

I also wish to thank the many reviewers for their valuable comments and suggestions during the preparation of the manuscript. Included in that list are: Carole Baker, Todd Doyle, Karla Felix, Caren Ferrante, Tamara Fish, Timothy Hedman, Dave Holson, Michelle Loudermilk, Rafaela Machado, Cruz Medina, Meg Milligan, Christina J. Ragin, Luther M. Ragin, Jr., Renee Michelle Ragin, Sarah Riddick, Sangeeta Singg, Guido G. Urizar and Gary Winkel. A special thanks to Lynne D. Richardson, the late Shelly Jacobson, and my colleagues at the Mount Sinai School of Medicine, Department of Emergency Medicine for their support and assistance in our research on health care which shaped my current perspectives of health.

Finally, my greatest debt is to my husband, Luther M. Ragin, Jr. and our two daughters, Renee Michelle and Christina, without whose support and assistance I could not have written this text.

ABOUT THE AUTHOR

Deborah Fish Ragin earned her A.B. in Psychology and Hispanic Studies from Vassar College in 1978, and her Ph.D. in Psychology from Harvard University in 1985. Dr. Ragin has served on the faculty several universities as an Assistant Professor in Community Health Education at Hunter College at the City University of New York, as an Assistant Professor at the Mount Sinai School of Medicine's Department of Emergency Medicine (New York City). Currently, Dr. Ragin is an Associate Professor of Psychology Montclair State University, and an Adjunct Associate Professor at the Mount Sinai School of Medicine. Her professional service includes a five year appointment as an American Psychological Association's (APA) Representative to the United Nations, where she focused on global efforts to address the psychosocial impact of HIV/AIDS, and serving as president of the APA's Society for the Study of Peace, Conflict and Violence (Division 48 Peace Psychology). Dr. Ragin is the author of numerous articles on HIV/AIDS, domestic violence, health care disparities.

Chapter One

An Interdisciplinary View of Health

Chapter Outline

Chapter Objectives

After studying this chapter, you will be able to:

1. Identify three ancient cultures that contributed to our current concept of determinants of health.
2. Identify Hippocrates and explain the mind–body connection in health.
3. Identify the role of health policy as a determinant of health in three civilizations.
4. Describe how religion influenced beliefs about health and illness.
5. Identify the four domains of health as defined by the American Psychological Association Division of Health Psychology.
6. Identify and describe four current models of health.

OPENING STORY: HOW WOULD YOU DESCRIBE WINSTON'S HEALTH?

Winston describes himself as an "average high school senior." He is the captain of his school's varsity baseball team, he helps coach his younger sister's little league softball team, he writes for his school newspaper, and he is applying to college. Yet most people who know him think Winston is exceptional. He performs all of his academic and extracurricular activities well while managing health flare-ups caused by multiple sclerosis.

Multiple sclerosis (MS) is a persistent neurological disease with episodes that can last for long periods of time. It is caused by damage to the nerve fibers in the body. The damage disrupts normal neurological functions and can cause a variety of symptoms including fatigue, headaches, light-headedness, soreness on various parts of the body, and blurred vision (Kunz, 1982). Some people with MS also report mental and emotional problems, including mood swings or depression.

Winston was diagnosed with MS at age 16, after numerous episodes of fatigue, blurred vision, and weakness in his arms and fingers. Now, at age 18, Winston says he has learned to manage his disease. He takes medication to control the symptoms but can have occasional flare-ups. Still, Winston does not let his condition stop him from participating in the activities he enjoys. He attends every varsity baseball practice and game. When he feels unable to play, he asks the team's designated hitter to take his place. And, when fatigued, he still cheers loudly from the dugout.

He even manages to maintain his sense of humor about his illness. Once, while warming up before a game, Winston noticed his vision was blurry. His coach insisted he rest for the first several innings. Eventually, Winston convinced the coach he was ready to return to the game. But, as he walked to the plate, he turned and jokingly asked, "Coach, which pitcher should I focus on, the one on the left or the one on the right?"

In spite of the difficulties, when asked about his health, Winston always responds the same: "I'm great. I'm doing well, and my health is excellent."

Would you agree?   ∎

Not everyone would agree with Winston's characterization of his health. For some, having a disease or illness, by definition, is inconsistent with being in "excellent health." Others might label Winston's health status as "fair" because he takes medicine for his illness and at times is unable to perform specific activities. Finally, people who consider Winston to be in "good health" may contend that even though he has a *chronic illness*, here meaning an illness that is persistent and that lasts over time (see Chapter 3, Global Communicable and Chronic Disease), he appears to manage well with the help of medication. In addition, he appears to be coping well emotionally. Winston's positive attitude and his efforts to remain active would suggest, in their opinion, overall good health.

What explains the difference in opinions about Winston's health? Different theories about what constitutes health, which are shaped in part by historical and cultural factors, have contributed to our current views on health. We review some of these theories briefly in this chapter and return to them throughout the book. Briefly, some people believe that health is determined by a person's *physiological state*, here meaning a person's ability to physically perform his or her daily functions without limitations, restrictions, or impediments. Such beliefs may derive from theories that propose that an individual's health is defined by the presence or absence of disease, dysfunction, or other abnormal biological changes in the body (Chapter 6, Emotional, Health and Well-Being) (Wade & Halligan, 2004). Others believe that health is defined not only by a person's physical functional status but also by that person's attitude about the illness and his or her overall mental and emotional state. For these people, health is a holistic concept. We define ***holistic health*** as a state of being, influenced by physiological, psychological, emotional, and social factors. ***Hippocrates***, a Greek physician and philosopher, is often credited as the first to acknowledge the connection between emotions and health (Salovey, Rothman, Detweiler, & Steward, 2000). Yet, we will see here and in Chapter 6 (Emotional Health and Well-Being) that many other cultures also believed that physical health was integrally linked to emotional and mental health. In fact, a review of the history of health will reveal that health is an evolving concept that has been shaped by science, culture, and history (Boddington, 2009).

For the moment, Winston's characterization of his own health appears to be consistent with the holistic approach. When describing his health, he considers his physiological condition, including his ability to perform tasks (especially favorite activities such as baseball), and his level of satisfaction with his life. Using a holistic definition, it may be easy to see why Winston describes his health as excellent.

History shows that for centuries scholars have identified many different primary or contributing factors that influence health outcomes. We call these factors ***determinants of health***. We will see that some determinants are universal, while others appear to be specific to a culture or time.

In this chapter we will also see that, currently, health researchers propose five principal determinants of health: individual physiology and behaviors (such as diet, exercise, and use of alcohol), family and cultural traditions (diet, social customs, and belief systems), physical environmental conditions like those suggested by Figure 1.1 (such as clean water and safe neighborhoods), health systems (health care delivery organizations), and health policies (regulations that promote or protect the health of communities). Some even include a sixth determinant, spiritual well-being.

Many health psychologists explain individual outcomes using either a holistic model that includes physiological, psychological, emotional, and social determinants or a social ecological model that includes the same four determinants but adds physical and psychological environments, health systems, and health policy. In the opening story we noted that Winston's concept of health was consistent with a holistic health perspective. He assessed his physical, emotional, and social well-being, all of which he believed were excellent.

Although we explore the social ecological model later in the chapter, for the moment it is important to note that it is perhaps the only model that includes health systems and health policy as health determinants, determinants that were introduced by earlier civilizations as important health factors.

We will begin our overview of health and well-being by exploring health determinants identified in earlier civilizations, such as those in the Indus Valley and ancient China, Egypt, and Greece. As we progress forward in time, we will compare these early beliefs and practices with the healing practices of Native American and southern African cultures where ***botany***, here meaning the study of plants and plant life, were important to their health practices. We conclude the historical review by examining the impact of spiritual beliefs on health in Western Europe during the Middle Ages and afterward during the Renaissance.

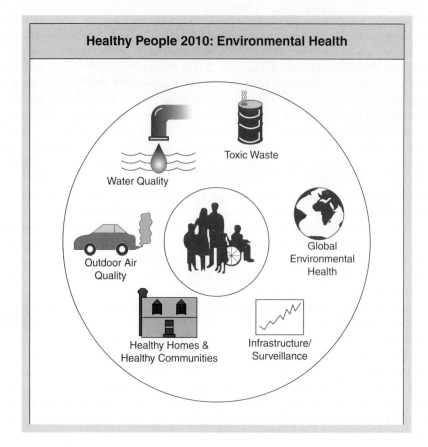

FIGURE 1.1   Environmental Determinants of Health. Known pollutants and other environmental factors that can influence health status.

Source: http://www.healthypeople.gov/document/images/environment.jpg

In Section II, we review three of the current models used by health psychologists: the biopsychosocial model, the wellness model, and the social ecological model. All three and others are explored in greater depth in Chapter 6, Emotional Health and Well-Being. Here, however, we focus on three to complete the historical time line of changes in the definition and determinants of health.

Finally, in Section III we review current research that explores the role of biological (physiological), social (including family and community), and environmental factors, as well as health systems and the health policies on individual health outcomes. We then explore the contributions of health psychologists in explaining and changing individual health outcomes.

After reading this chapter you will be able to summarize the changes over time and across cultures in the concepts and determinants of health. You will be able to compare and contrast the earlier views of health with current and modern concepts and to describe the research that supports or refutes the current perspectives.

SECTION I. A BRIEF HISTORY OF HEALTH

It is tempting to think that our current beliefs about health reflect new knowledge, based partly on new research findings. But history shows us that many civilizations pioneered some of the "modern" concepts of health that we embrace today beginning in the third century BCE (before common era). From written records, public works (infrastructure), and even art, we can glimpse the health beliefs and practices of earlier civilizations and link them to the health outcomes of their populations.

Health Practices in Early Civilizations

UNDERSTANDING HEALTH THROUGH HEALTH POLICY   There are many health behaviors that we take for granted. For example, today most people accept that clean water and sanitation are essential to prevent illness and to maintain good physiological health. But did you know that the Egyptian and Indian civilizations also considered clean water and sanitation important health determinants? The notions of health in these civilizations may differ, but they both established and maintained public water delivery systems that enhanced the health of their populations.

For example, archeological records from the Indus Valley region in the second millennium before the common era (2000 BCE) revealed evidence of bathrooms and sophisticated public and private drainage systems as shown in Figure 1.2. Located in an area known presently as Pakistan, the Indus Valley civilization consisted of more than 100 well-ordered and structured towns and villages that appeared to be administered by a centralized form of government. The ruins from the largest cities in the Indus Valley, Harappa and Mohenjo-daro, also revealed large water reservoirs constructed on the outskirts of the communities to collect and store clean water for personal consumption (Misra, 2001). Ancient Greek aqueducts that transported water, which were later adopted and enhanced by the Romans, as shown in Figure 1.3, are evidence that these cultures also understood the health implications of clean water (Picket & Hanlon, 1990).

FIGURE 1.2   Indus River Valley Civilization Drainage System. An example of an indoor drainage system in a private home in the Indus River Valley.

Source: http://www.sewerhistory.org/images/w/wam/moh_wam13.jpg

FIGURE 1.3   Roman Aqueduct. The Pont du Gard in Nîmes, France, is the tallest of all the Roman aqueducts.

Water, drainage, and sewer systems are examples of infrastructure constructed usually as a result of a policy issued by a ruler or other governing authorities charged with protecting the water supply for its citizens. For example, *health policies* that provided access to clean water ensured that civilizations as diverse as the Indus Valley and ancient Greece and Rome would have less exposure to contaminants that could cause illnesses. The policies were a determinant of health in these civilizations.

To put the early policy works into perspective, consider this: The aqueducts and drainage systems of earlier civilizations are similar to the extensive sewer, drainage, and water supply systems we find in many modern cities today. Centuries from now the remnants of our current systems may be interpreted by later civilizations as evidence of our belief that the structures and policies that provide access to clean water to inhabitants are two important determinants of health.

In essence, artifacts such as the ruins of earlier civilizations are one way we learn about health beliefs and practices that predate modern beliefs.

UNDERSTANDING HEALTH THROUGH PHILOSOPHY AND MEDICINE   Many people credit Hippocrates, a Greek physician, with proposing an association between the mind and the body that affects health. His views about the mind–body connection are represented in his *humoral theory*, a topic we discuss more fully in Chapter 6, Emotional Health and Well-Being.

But Hippocrates was not the first to link emotional and physiological health. For example, researchers have often noted that the mummification process and rituals used by the Egyptians in the third millennium BCE revealed a sophisticated knowledge of the body and the circulatory system. In Egyptian culture, however, a person's health was influenced not only by anatomical systems but by scientific and spiritual beliefs as well. And ***Daoist philosophy*** (developed in ancient Chinese civilizations) determined that the harmonic balance of yin and yang, the environment and the energy or life force, called ***Qi*** (pronounced "chi"), were essential determinants of health. As we will see in Chapter 6, Emotional Health and Well-Being, Daoist philosophy greatly influences Chinese traditional medicine, a form of medicine that is practiced by many today as complementary to or in lieu of modern Western medicine.

Hippocrates' theory of a mind–body connection that influenced health was challenged by other Greek philosophers. For example, in 500 BCE, some Greek philosophers proposed the ***Aesculapian theory***, which held that illnesses had spiritual origins and required spiritual intervention, ritual cures, and mediation by priests. Still others supported the ***Cnidian theory***, which stated that illnesses were associated with physical diseases and were unrelated to mental, spiritual or emotional well-being (Chambers, 2001; Metzer, 1989). Table 1.1 provides a brief time line of these and other changing concepts of health.

What is interesting is that concepts of health like the three proposed by different Greek philosophers also appear over time and in other cultures. For example, like the Cnidians, Galen (Rome) in 200 CE and Descartes (France) in 1600 CE proposed that health is a disease that affected only the body, disassociating the body from influences of the mind or emotion. But, like Hippocrates, Galen, a noted philosopher and physician, also believed that humors could cause illnesses. According to Galen, the diseases that caused imbalance were located in the organs and not, as Hippocrates suggested, in the body fluids. Clearly, Galen's view was more consistent with a physiologically based concept of health and illness.

In comparison, other civilizations, such as the pre-Columbian cultures that include the Mayans and Aztecs (1400 CE), the more than 1,000 Native American cultures in North America (1300 CE), and African cultures such as the Khoisan (southern Africa) and the Yoruba and Dahomey (western Africa, 1500–1600 CE) linked the spiritual health of individuals with their physiological health, treating both using natural herbs and plants from their environments (Bucko & Cloud, 2008; De Smet, 1998).

We explore Native American, southern and western African, and other traditional health practices in Chapter 6, Emotional Health and Well-Being. The important point here is that prior to the 16th century there were a variety of concepts about health. Some, like Galen, believed health to be affected largely by physiological states. Others, like the ancient Egyptian, Indian, Chinese, Native American, and African cultures, examined the roles of emotional, spiritual, or environmental determinants as contributors to individual health status. We will see shortly that some Western concepts of health include many of the same determinants.

UNDERSTANDING HEALTH THROUGH PHARMACOLOGY   Early and later civilizations also demonstrated knowledge of health through botany, the study of plants and plant life. For example, artifacts from the Zulu and the Khoisan of southern Africa (vanWyk, 2008) and the Chinese and Indian cultures in Asia, as well as the Native American and pre-Columbian cultures we referred to previously, demonstrate the extensive knowledge of the ***materia medica***, also called the medicinal properties of plants. Plants provided the tools to address the physical, mental, emotional, and spiritual health of members of these cultures. Consider this: Moerman (1998), studying the medical practices of the Native American cultures, found that many tribes used over 4,000 plants to treat in excess of 25,000 different medical—here meaning physiological—illnesses.

TABLE 1.1	Concepts of Health		
Era	**Year**	**Culture**	**Concept of Health**
Before common era (BCE)	2600	Egypt, Old Kingdom	Health influenced by anatomical, scientific, and spiritual beliefs. Sophisticated knowledge of body's circulatory system.
	500	Greece	Three views of health: 1. *Aesculapian theory:* Illness required spiritual intervention and ritual cures 2. *Cnidian theory:* Illness linked to physical disease 3. Hippocrates' *humoral theory:* Connection between mind and body shapes health
	250	Ancient China	Three determinants work together: *harmonic balance of forces *nature's five elements *an energy or life force
Common era (CE)	200	Rome (Galen)	Health rooted in diseases caused by bad air or body fluids that impair bodily activities
	500–1400	Middle Ages, Europe	Disease as God's punishment
	750–1260	Islamic cultures	Holistic approach to health integrating anatomy, spirituality, and culture
	1400	Pre-Columbian civilizations	Heath determined by spiritual forces but could be remedied by herbal or physical treatments
	1600	Descartes (France)	Separation of mind and body: diseases affected body
	1880	Koch (Germany)	Bacteria cause disease
	1890	Freud	Health influenced by emotions and mind
	1930s	Flanders and Dunbar	Psychosomatic medicine linking biological, behavioral, psychological, and social contributors to health
	1948	World Health Organization (WHO)	A state of complete physical, mental, and social well-being and not merely the absence of diseases or infirmity

Yet, the same plants were used to address over 15,000 spiritual and emotional health ailments as well. Similar discoveries of the use of *materia medica* were found in Mesoamerican cultures, including the Mayan and Aztec cultures (Cruz-Coke, 2007).

How do we know that plants were used as health aids? You may remember that at the beginning of the section we stated that some cultures maintained written records of their health beliefs and practices while others recorded their practices in art or other artifacts.

Specifically, some accounts of the use of medicinal herbs have been maintained in written records in China and India (De Smet, 1998). But, the use of medicinal herbs in some cultures is also documented in artwork, such as sculptures, paintings, and other artifacts. For example, historians have identified and decoded many depictions of medical practices and health remedies in sub-Saharan African art found in Ghana, Nigeria, the Republic of Congo, and Burkina Faso, to name a few (De Smet, 1998). In some cases the art depicts health procedures such as craniotomies (a cut into the skull, usually to gain access to the brain). In others, the works depict a process such as extracting bark from a tree. In some cultures, tree bark is used to prevent the growth of bacteria or to ease pain (see Figure 1.4).

FIGURE 1.4 *Ghanaian Men Gathering Medicinal Tree Bark.* An example of West African artwork that depicts a health practice and the use of botany as *materia medica*.

UNDERSTANDING HEALTH THROUGH RELIGION Over the centuries, spirituality has been included as one of several factors that contribute to health (Chambers, 2001; Cruz-Coke, 2007; Falagas, Zarkadoulia, & Samonis, 2006; Yeo, 2003; Zuskin et al., 2008). Beliefs about spirituality, religion, and their impact on health are well documented in Egyptian, Islamic, pre-Columbian, African, and North American cultures.

It should not be surprising, therefore, that religion also shaped the concept of health in Western European cultures, especially during the Middle Ages (500–1500 CE). Briefly, approximately 500 CE marked the beginning of the decline of the Roman Empire. We must note that, prior to the Middle Ages, the Roman Empire actively participated in extensive trade with other civilizations in Northern Africa (including Egypt), India, and China. Through trade, these cultures shared goods and knowledge. At about 500 CE, however, the Roman Empire began its decline. During this time the peoples of Western Europe reduced their trade, exchange, and contact with other civilizations and suffered deterioration in their infrastructure and a weakened economy. The self-imposed isolation from other cultures led to what some historians characterize also as a cultural decline (once referred to as the "Dark Ages") that lasted approximately 1,000 years.

BOX 1.1   Artifacts: A Roadmap to Health Practices When Written Records Are Not Available

What happens to the knowledge possessed by earlier cultures when there are no written records? Fortunately, historians interested in the health practices and behaviors of earlier civilizations have found a way to extract information about the health beliefs in such cultures through art.

Take, for example, African art objects. Carvings and other works of art produced by some African cultures are interesting because of the level of detail depicted in the work, the artist's skill in reproducing images or people, and the material used to create the piece. Over the past 40 years, **ethnopharmacologists**, researchers who study the medicinal practices of different cultures, have discovered an added benefit of the works. The artwork also contains a wealth of information about health practices and medicines used at the time. The discovery is helping health researchers understand the concepts of health in different cultures.

One example of the health practices evident in art is seen in the pendants displayed in Figure 1.5. At first the pendants appear to be ornamental pieces of jewelry. But ethnopharmacologists discovered the pendants serve two purposes. They are decorative and ornamental pieces, but in certain Ethiopian societies, they are also functional: they are ear cleaners! Without knowledge of a culture or its past medical practices it is easy to mistake the pendants as ornamental jewelry with little functional value.

Current research also suggests that some African art depicts procedures, such as extraction of teeth, caesarean sections, or craniotomies. Others depict activities such as removal of tree bark or cassava root: two ingredients used in some medicines (see Figure 1.4).

Through research we are learning that the artistic record is yet another way that earlier civilizations recorded health practices and reflected their concept of health.

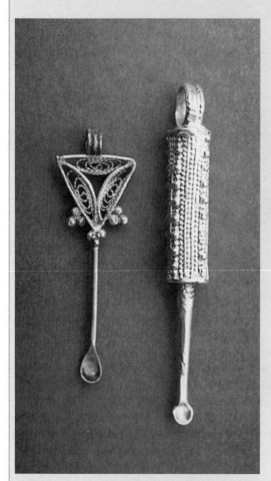

FIGURE 1.5   Pendants: Decorative and Purposeful Ear Cleaners. These pendants serve two purposes: decorative jewelry and practical medicinal use.

During the Middle Ages, Rome also experienced a significant loss of population. One reason for the population decline was a successive wave of *pandemics*, or communicable diseases that affected large numbers of people across a geographic region (see Chapter 3, Global Communicable and Chronic Disease). Two pandemics in particular, the first and second *plagues of Justinian* (541–542 CE and 588 CE, respectively), resulted in the death of millions of inhabitants.

What caused the plagues? We now attribute them to a recurrent bacterial infection that remained in the population for over 200 years (Allen, 1979). Influenced by the religious doctrine of the time, however, many people embraced the view that the plague and other diseases were caused by demons. In essence, sickness was a sign of God's punishment for the sins committed by the sufferers (Burton, Smith, & Nichols, 1980). Consistent with these beliefs, the Church—specifically the priests—became responsible for healing the spiritual afflictions that were thought to be the source of the disease.

It is important to point out that the belief that illnesses were caused by spiritual ill health is not uncommon. Many of the cultures described earlier in this chapter held similar beliefs. In Europe, however, the religious beliefs of the time stressed that diseases were punishments from God.

Near the end of the Middle Ages (approximately 1347–1350 CE), Europe experienced a third major pandemic, the *haemorrhagic plague*, also referred to as the "Black Death." This plague was, by far, the most deadly. It accounted for more than 25 million deaths across the continent. To put the number into perspective, the Black Death is believed to have killed approximately one-third of the population of Western Europe in just two years, from 1348–1350 CE (Slack, 1989).

Any illness responsible for at least 25 million deaths is an important event when examining the historical accounts of health. Yet, the haemorrhagic plague is also significant because of the change in health beliefs that occurred at approximately the same time. The plague struck just as Western Europe was about to experience a *Renaissance*, or cultural rebirth. The Renaissance prompted a move away from the belief that illnesses were a punishment for evil and a return to the scientific exploration of the human body.

Consistent with the revised theory, scholars and physicians during the Renaissance suggested that diseases were the result of environmental, not spiritual, factors. Thus, to help control the haemorrhagic plague, local municipalities in Western Europe instituted a number of health policies to control the outbreak. For example, local administrators isolated and quarantined many people diagnosed with the disease. In addition, buildings and houses were fumigated, and entire towns were burned in an effort to kill the germs and the animals, especially rodents, assumed to carry the disease (Duncan & Scott, 2005; Christensen, 2003; Slack, 1989).

Isolations, quarantines, fumigation of communities, and sophisticated water disposal and water collection systems are all examples of health policies, regulations designed to protect the health of the community and thereby of individuals. Sometimes the policies protect individuals from initial contact with the diseases. Other times, the policies that helped contain diseases also served to minimize their impact on the population. Using health policy and environmental controls to reduce health risks is evidence that by the early 1500s CE, Western Europe embraced the belief that better controls on environmental conditions and health policy together would have a positive impact on health outcomes.

Health Practices in the United States

The Renaissance also introduced a period of maritime exploration. Voyagers set out from Europe to discover and colonize "new worlds." In the process, however, they brought with them contagious diseases that had deadly consequences for both the carriers and those who came in contact with them.

As in the case of the pandemics in Europe, some contagious diseases could decimate the entire population of a region. For the colonizers of new territories like the Americas, outbreaks of yellow fever, smallpox, and other contagious ailments were particularly problematic because they could threaten the viability of new colonies. For this reason, by the early 1800s, shortly after the founding of the new United States of America, major cities such as Philadelphia, New York, Boston, and Washington adopted public health policies to protect their citizens and the new nation (Harvard University Library Open Collections Program, 2008; Means, 1975). Once again, health policies became important determinants of health outcomes for individuals as well as entire communities.

Summary

What can we learn about health from a brief review of ancient concepts of health and the history of health practices? We realize that many cultures established systems, built infrastructures, and made use of their natural resources, such as herbs and plants, to protect and enhance the health of their citizens. By examining diverse cultures, we also see the range of beliefs about health. While some cultures treated health holistically or ecologically, others chose to focus almost exclusively on only one or two factors. We see that discoveries in the medical sciences, specifically anatomy, advanced our understanding of epidemiology, the study of the origins and spread of disease. Such discoveries contributed to the development of the health models that are used by health psychologists today.

Finally, we learned that, throughout history, health policies have played a critical role in changing the environmental conditions that affect individual health status. By reviewing history we see that the five determinants of health—individual physiology and behaviors, social environments (family, communities, cultures), physical and psychological environments, health systems, and health policies—have defined health throughout the centuries.

SECTION II. DEFINING HEALTH TODAY

Early Holistic Concepts

MIND–BODY CONNECTION AND HEALTH   Current concepts of health appear to have much in common with the holistic perspectives suggested by earlier cultures. Not surprisingly, psychologists have contributed to the current evolution in the definition of health. One well-known contributor is Sigmund Freud, the "father of psychoanalytic psychology."

Some may think it odd to see a reference to Freud in a book on health psychology. But, when Freud proposed that physiological illnesses can have psychological causes, he reintroduced the relationship between the mind and body and its effects on health outcomes. This time, however, research on the mind–body association and health resulted in the development of a new field: *psychosomatic medicine*. Much like the concepts of health espoused centuries before, psychosomatic medicine examines the relationships among the physiological, psychological, social, and behavioral influences on an individual's health status. In essence, the determinants of health that define psychosomatic medicine include all but two of the factors thought to be influential centuries ago: environment and spiritual forces.

Freud's research on psychosomatic causes of illnesses was largely nonreplicable because he based his theories on his clinical work and intuitions. Fortunately, empirical studies by other pioneers in the field, including Cannon and Washburn and Dunbar (Dunbar, 1943; Kimball, 1981), which suggested an association between personality types and disease, supported the link between the mind–body and health (Kimball, 1981).

In spite of some empirical support, psychosomatic diseases increasingly were viewed as invalid or false. They became associated with chronic complaints that were more psychological than physiological. The increasing emphasis on physiological causes of illness in the 20th century, together with the prevailing popular view that psychosomatic illnesses were contrived, led to a decline in support for the mind–body connection and health.

WORLD HEALTH ORGANIZATION MODEL OF HEALTH In 1948, the World Health Organization (WHO, 1948) introduced another definition of health, one that integrates the physical, emotional, psychological, and social determinants. According to WHO (WHO, 1992), health is "a state of complete, physical, mental and social well-being and not merely the absence of disease and infirmity." In other words, health is more than just a disease. It includes a person's functional ability, psychological well-being, physiological status, and social health. Does this sound familiar? Although not identical to the concepts of health espoused by the earlier civilizations, WHO's definition includes emotional and mental health as factors in overall well-being. Some of these determinants were in the opening story as well.

Building on WHO's definition are three additional models that also explore the physiological, psychological, sociological, and, for some, environmental determinants of health. They include the *biopsychosocial model*, the *wellness model*, and the *social ecological model* (sometimes referred to simply as the *ecological model*) of health. We briefly review each model to provide the foundation for the theoretical framework of the field of health psychology.

We begin, however, with the biomedical model: a model that is central to the practice of medicine in Western cultures and, according to some, a core component of some holistic health models as well.

Models of Health and Well-Being

BIOMEDICAL MODEL The late 19th century (1880s) marked a return to the theory that germs, rather than sins or spiritual forces, caused diseases. The renewed belief was supported by research by Robert Koch, a German scientist who was the first person credited with discovering that specific bacteria can be linked to specific diseases (see Figure 1.6). Koch's work lead to the development of the *biomedical model* of health, which purported that illness is defined as a dysfunction of the body caused by microorganisms and resulting in illness or disability (Engel, 1977). The clear association between bacteria and disease once again placed a greater emphasis on physiological factors as the principal determinant of health. While few would challenge the theory that microorganisms can cause diseases, the more relevant question is whether microorganisms can also explain nonphysiological causes of illnesses. Most health researchers now agree that the biomedical model's emphasis on physical causes of illnesses overlooks the critical contributions of emotional, social, and environmental factors on health. Newer health theories account for some if not all of these factors.

FIGURE 1.6   Robert Koch. Koch was the first to link bacteria to specific diseases.

BIOPSYCHOSOCIAL MODEL   An odd-sounding name to be sure, the biopsychosocial model was one of the first 20th-century models to reintroduce a holistic theory of health in which multiple factors, not just physiology, explained health outcomes.

Engel (1977) proposed the *biopsychosocial model* in 1972 to explain outcomes not adequately accounted for by biological factors alone. Engel suggests that biological factors (*bio*) in addition to psychological influences (*psycho*), including emotions, *social* support, and personal traits (Lazarus & Folkman, 2002; Ryan & Deci, 2000), as well as sociological (social) factors such as family, culture, and community also strongly affect overall well-being and health outcomes.

Can emotions really affect our physical health? Research on the relationship between stress and illness offers some of the clearest evidence of the association between emotional (stress) factors and adverse physiological outcomes. For example, research by Rabin and colleagues (1989) suggests that emotions such as stress have an impact on physiological health by affecting the immune system and by influencing health behaviors. Recent studies also report an association between other emotions, such as depression, and heart disease. Interestingly, some researchers even draw connections among depression, heart disease, and death (Glassman & Shapiro, 1998; Schulz, Martire, Beach, & Scheier, 2005). We explore the relationship between stress and physical health in greater depth in Chapter 6, Emotional Health and Well-Being. Thus, current research supports the link between the mind (emotions) and body that was suggested by earlier civilizations and by individuals such as Hippocrates and Freud. Yet, we know, even from our limited review thus far, that health is a complex state influenced by more than just the mind and the body. The biopsychosocial model was the first modern model to address the physiological, psychological, and social determinants of health.

CHALLENGES TO THE BIOPSYCHOSOCIAL MODEL   In spite of its broader focus, some health psychologists criticize the biopsychosocial model for being too "bio-centered." According to these critics, the model places biological determinants at the core of the concept of health. Specifically, Armstrong (2002) notes that in this model, psychological and sociological factors are "add-ons" to explain outcomes that cannot be explained using physiological factors alone. Thus, rather than offering a balanced perspective that gives equal weight to biological, psychological, and sociological determinants of health, the biopsychosocial model is criticized for being at its core a biological model.

A second critique suggests that the model overlooks environmental factors known to influence health and well-being. Part of the problem here may be the definition of *environmental*. For some, social environmental variables such as family, community, and culture represent environmental determinants of health. For others, however, they do not. For example, some researchers who study the effects of environments on health focus on air and water quality, toxic waste sites, or other pollutants as the principal physical environmental determinants of health status. Indeed, many would agree that poor air quality can cause breathing and other respiratory problems that may result in adverse health outcomes (see Chapter 4, Theories and Models of Health Behavior Change). The point here is that, for many researchers, environmental determinants of health refer to the physical not social environment, and the biopsychosocial model does not address physical environmental determinants of health.

Finally, the biopsychosocial model does not account for the effects of perceived quality of life or spirituality on health status. As we will see in the following section on the wellness model, current research suggests that quality of life and spirituality are important psychological and emotional factors that also affect health outcomes for some.

WELLNESS MODEL   Not to be confused with *well-being,* which is defined as one's overall state of health, the wellness model adds two health determinants not commonly found in other models: spirituality and ***quality of life***. Recall the concepts of health in earlier civilizations that included spirituality as a core determinant. In some respects the wellness model is suggestive of those earlier beliefs with one caveat. In the wellness model, spirituality refers to an individual's perspective on the meaning of life and the impact of their values on their overall well-being (Mullen, McDermott, Gold, & Belcastro, 1996). It is not intended to have religious connotations (see Figure 1.7).

FIGURE 1.7   Tengka Tengah Zaharah Mosque, Malaysia. Religious practices may entail behaviors that contribute to stress abatement and better health outcomes.

An example of spirituality's contribution to health and well-being in the wellness model is evident in research that suggests that spirituality may enable one to experience peace and tranquility even during stressful events. In other words, it helps to abate stress. Consider this: Research suggests that reducing stress is important for maintaining good physiological health. If spirituality serves to reduce stress and create peaceful environments for some, then we may reason that spirituality abates stress for some individuals thereby directly contributing to their overall well-being (Bosswell, Kahana, & Dilworth-Anderson, 2006; Poage, Kitzenberger, & Olsen, 2004; Reid & Smalls, 2004).

One additional point should be made regarding spirituality and stress. Some spiritual beliefs encourage individuals to adopt behaviors that lead to healthier outcomes. For example, an individual may refrain from drinking alcohol or smoking cigarettes because of spiritual beliefs. Avoiding alcohol and cigarettes are, themselves, ***health-enhancing behaviors***, that is, behaviors that will increase one's positive health status (Poage et al., 2004; Reid & Smalls, 2004). We explore the role of health-enhancing behaviors more fully in Chapter 5, Risky Health Behaviors.

Other contemporary examples of spiritual beliefs that are integral to health beliefs and practices are found in the traditional medical practices of many Native American tribes, in ***curanderismo***, a religious and cultural belief system that informs health and wellness among many Latin American cultures, and among the Suku, a group in the Republic of the Congo in Africa. When addressing a physiological health concern, it would not be uncommon in these cultures for the healer to attend to the emotional and spiritual health of his or her "patient." All three cultures consider spirituality to be a core component of health (Avery, 1991; Bourgeois, 1980; De Smet, 1998). We review this concept more fully in Chapter 6, Emotional Health and Well-Being.

Finally, the wellness model is the only model that includes the psychological concept of quality of life as a determinant of health. In the wellness approach, an individual's perceived satisfaction with life will affect his or her overall well-being. Satisfaction is influenced by psychological as well as physiological states. Remember Winston from our opening story? Most likely, Winston believes he has a very good quality of life. Although he has MS, Winston has a positive psychological state that undoubtedly helps him cope with his physical limitations.

Not everyone enjoys a good quality of life, however. Consider a different scenario. A young man has been a star athlete in basketball since his junior varsity days in middle school at age 12. As a college student, he was widely recognized as an outstanding player who was destined for a career as a professional basketball player. A sudden accident permanently damaged his spinal column, paralyzing him from the hips down. The accident ended his life dream to play professional ball and confined him to a wheelchair. For weeks after the accident he was depressed and despondent. While he has learned to be largely self-reliant with respect to his daily functions, he never speaks of basketball and forbids others to raise the subject with him. How would you rate this former athlete's quality of life?

The biopsychosocial model and the wellness model identify specific psychological, sociological, and spiritual factors that, researchers suggest, influence health outcomes. Yet, according to current research, there are still other critical determinants of health.

SOCIAL ECOLOGICAL MODEL   We traced the evolution of the definition of health through three models. In the process we found that, with the exception of the biomedical model, most definitions of health included both physiological and nonphysiological determinants, including biology, emotions, psychological states, social factors, quality of life, and spirituality. Can there be anything else? There is, according to the social ecological or ecological model.

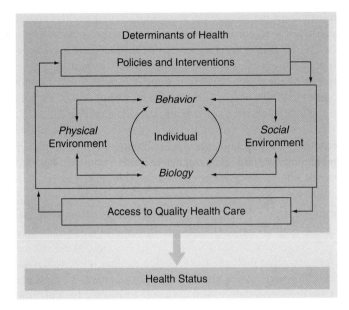

FIGURE 1.8 A Social Ecological Model of Health. The social ecological model suggests five determinants of health, including access to health care systems and health policies.

As depicted in Figure 1.8, the ecological model includes five major determinants of health. The individual (biology and behavior) and the social environment created by family, community, and cultural practices comprise the first two. Uniquely, the ecological model includes three new dimensions. First is the ***physical environment***, which includes factors such as housing conditions, neighborhood sanitation, cleanliness, safety, and a physical space free of toxicity or pollutants. Second is the ***health systems***, defined here as the health care delivery organizations that provide access to care. Finally, health policy, as we saw earlier in the chapter, made up of the regulations that promote or protect the health of individuals in the community.

Refer back to the environmental health photo in Figure 1.2. Like the photo, the ecological model suggests that an individual's physical setting can contribute to or inhibit good health outcomes. Waste products from manufacturing plants and vehicles affect air and water quality, essential elements for life. The role of the physical environment on health may be easy to grasp when considering environmental pollutants. But the model also addresses the physiological and psychological consequences of negative environmental factors such as crime and violence. Consider this: Is there a relationship between a neighborhood's high rates of crime and childhood obesity? Researchers seem to think so. Several studies have shown that children raised in neighborhoods perceived to be unsafe due to crime and violence are at greater risk for obesity than those in "safer" environments (Boehmer, Lovegreen, Haire-Joshu, & Brownson, 2006; Regan, Lee, Booth, & Reese-Smith, 2006; Weir, Elelson, & Brand, 2006). The cause? Safety concerns make parents or other caregivers less likely to allow children out of doors, limiting opportunities for physical activity. What is more, by remaining inside, children also increase their likelihood of consuming high-calorie, high-fat foods, further compounding problems of weight gain and obesity. A fuller discussion of the effects of physical environments on health is presented in Chapter 4, Theories and Models of Health Behavior Change, and Chapter 5, Risky Health Behaviors.

Finally, the ecological model is perhaps the only model that proposes that health systems and health policy also determine health. Let's examine this by way of another example. An individual's ability to obtain timely medical attention and to receive needed medical care may determine whether that person's health concern will be resolved quickly with minimal long-term impact or become a protracted problem requiring longer-term treatment. Yet, as we will see in Chapter 12, Health Care Systems and Health Policy, systems and policy may contribute to a delay in access to care or limit one's ability to obtain needed health care. The ecological model proposes that any system that controls access to care or that prescribes the type of care available will, by definition, determine an individual's health outcomes.

Defined in this way, it is apparent why health systems and health policy should be included in a discussion of the determinants of health. Yet, they are absent in most other models.

APPLYING THE SOCIAL ECOLOGICAL MODEL TO HEALTH PSYCHOLOGY   With four models and at least five different determinants, how do we decide which model(s) best characterizes health?

Remember, in psychology there are often multiple theories that explain a phenomenon. The same is true for the discipline of health psychology. Yet, new directions in the field may help determine which models are most applicable to our current concepts of health. In 2002, the American Psychological Association's Division of Health Psychology redefined the field, acknowledging the central role of health systems and policy on health status. Now, when characterizing health psychology, the division describes the field using four principal domains: the individual, the family/community, health systems, and health policy. The new definition is consistent with Joseph Matarazzo's 1980 reconceptualization of the field in which he describes health psychology as:

> the aggregate of the specific educational, scientific, and professional contributions of the discipline of psychology to the promotion and maintenance of health, the prevention and treatment of illnesses, and the identification of etiologic and diagnostic correlates of health, illness, and related dysfunction, and to the analysis and improvements of the health care system and health policy formation. (Matarazzo, 1980)

Put simply, Matarazzo acknowledges the traditional role of health psychologists as professionals who focus on health promotion, disease prevention, and health maintenance at the individual and the family/community level. But he sees two additional functions. First, he identifies an investigative role for health psychology, exploring the causes (*etiology*) and the related consequences of illnesses. Second, Matarazzo sees health psychologists as analysts, capable of identifying problems and recommending solutions that help improve the health care system and that improve health policy.

What is more, Matarazzo and the APA's revised description lend support to the ecological model of health because both include individuals, society, health systems, and health policy as determinants of health. Furthermore, Matarazzo's definition may also include environmental determinants because the environment is often an etiology of health outcomes.

Again, we caution, however, that the study of any field of psychology rarely contains only one explanatory theory. Thus, the ecological model remains one of several currently in use.

SECTION III. CURRENT VIEWS ON DETERMINANTS OF HEALTH: A HEALTH PSYCHOLOGY PERSPECTIVE

The models used by health psychologists highlight the role of some determinants on health outcomes. But, as we indicated, "individual determinants" or "environmental determinants" can mean many things. In this section, we explore the specific components of the health determinants from a health psychology perspective. We will identify their contributions to health status and identify ways in which health psychologists can change determinants in order to improve health outcomes.

Individual/Demographic Influences

We return to Winston and the opening story to illustrate the role of individual/demographic influences on health. We noted in the story that Winston plays baseball for his high school team. We did not mention that he joined the team in his sophomore year in high school. And, in the first week of practice, Winston collided with another teammate while running to home plate. He fell and hit his head on the field. Winston complained of dizziness and fatigue several hours after the incident. And when Winston complained again several weeks later about dizziness and fatigue, his coaches thought the symptoms were related to his accident.

Health psychologists interested in understanding what factors contribute to an individual's health outcome may review Winston's story and ask whether his health condition is due to his accident, or whether it is due to genetic makeup, familial (inherited) factors, or even environmental factors. Like his coaches, health psychologists may be tempted to conclude initially that his recurrent symptoms were due to his behavior—a collision with a teammate. While unintentional injuries such as a collision or head injury can cause short- or long-term health consequences (see Chapter 5, Risky Health Behaviors), we know from the opening story that Winston's problems were not due to the injury. Rather, the determinants of Winston's health problem appear to be genetic, familial, and even environmental, all factors that contribute to MS.

We noted in the opening story that MS results from damage to the body's nerve fibers. We review the function of the body's nerve fibers in Chapter 6, Emotional Health and Well-Being. For the moment, it is sufficient to know that nerve fibers transmit neurochemical messages throughout the body. The fibers are encased in a ***myelin sheath***, a coating that protects the fibers from damage and helps speed message transmission. Damage to the myelin sheath exposes the fibers to damage, which could slow or impede message transmission. The interruption of message signals to or from the spinal column or to the brain could result in an impairment of motor movements or other body functions and result in the symptoms reported by Winston.

One cause of erosion to the myelin sheath is genetic. Researchers have established that multiple sclerosis is a complex trait whose onset is due, in part, to the interaction of several genes (Compston, 2000; Handel et al., 2010; Rasmussen & Clausen, 2000).

In addition to genetic factors, demographic characteristics also help determine when a person is most likely to be affected by the disease. You may have seen the term *demographic variables* in a statistics or research methods class. Demographics may be fixed characteristics, such as gender or race/ethnicity. But demographics can also be characteristics that are subject to change, such as age, socioeconomic class, level of education, and occupation. For example, MS is considered the most common neurological disease affecting young adults (Ramagopalan,

Knight, & Ebers, 2009). Consider this: The usual onset for MS is between 20 and 40 years of age. In addition, women are somewhat more likely to be affected by the disease than are men (Kunz, 1982). Can an individual's characteristics really affect his or her health? In the following chapters we explore this question more fully when examining chronic illnesses such as cardiovascular disease, arthritis, and cancer. We will see that, in fact, diseases such as cancer or cardiovascular disease can affect people differently based on some characteristics, including their genetic makeup, their gender, and sometimes their race or ethnicity.

What does this mean for Winston? First, study findings suggest that Winston's health problem may be rooted in a genetic abnormality. In other words, Winston's genetic composition may make him susceptible to MS. We also note that the fact that MS is associated with young adults increases the likelihood that, with a prior susceptibility to the disease, Winston, at 16, could show signs of the illness. Admittedly, he is on the younger end of the estimate age of onset. Yet estimated age at onset of an illness is just that: an estimate. The illness can occur at slightly earlier or slightly later ages. Table 1.2 includes a sample of factors that can determine health outcomes.

Family/Cultural Influences

We inherit many observable traits from family members: eye color, hair color, facial features, and even handedness. Is it likely, therefore, that we might also inherit a susceptibility to specific illnesses? Scientists seem to think so. As we noted earlier current research on MS points conclusively to a familial link to the illness. Research by Sadovnick, Baird, and Ward (1988) established that individuals with *first-degree relatives*, here meaning parents, siblings, or grandparents, with MS were 15 to 35 times more likely to develop MS than were individuals without such a family history.

Genes also have been found to play a role in the transmission of many other diseases. For example, asthma and some forms of coronary artery disease, sometimes referred to as heart disease, tend to run in families. Genetics, therefore, can also be a *familial determinant of health*.

Other familial determinants of illnesses may be rooted in our behaviors. Just as there are genetic factors that occur in families, there are also health behaviors or practices that are common to family members. Consider this: In past generations it was not uncommon to find several smokers within one family. In fact, smoking could be thought of as an activity in itself or something done in conjunction with other activities such as bowling, card games, or even fishing. Researchers studying MS now suggest that smoking behaviors may be another factor that increases susceptibility to the disease (Handel et al., 2010). In this instance, a health behavior may increase the risk of a disease that also has a genetic determinant. As we will see in later chapters, there are a number of health behaviors that increase the risk of illnesses. For example, eating high-fat, high-calorie foods increases the risk of cardiovascular disease (see Chapter 9, Cardiovascular Disease), of obesity, and of Type II diabetes (see Chapter 3, Global Communicable and Chronic Disease). Some of these behaviors are attributed to individual behaviors, while others, such as dietary practices, may also be associated with family practices, much like smoking.

Thus, to effectively change behaviors that contribute to health problems, psychologists may need to be mindful of and address familial and cultural health beliefs and practices that shape behaviors. In other words, people in the professions may need to borrow some techniques

TABLE 1.2	Factors That Influence Health in an Ecological Model
Determinant of Health	**Factors**
Biological	Genetics Immune system Nutrition Physiology Gender Age
Psychological	Coping strategies Personality Pessimism/optimism Risk-taking behaviors Response to stress
Sociological	Cultural beliefs Diet Ethnicity Socioeconomic class Social support networks Concept of health Spiritual beliefs
Environmental	Air/water quality Neighborhood safety Neighborhood cleanliness
Health systems	Accessible health facilities Health insurance Medical specialists Emergency care options Affordable care Treatment options Long-term care options
Health policy	Mandated health plan Water/sewage disposal systems Safety legislations Workplace safety regulations

of medical anthropologists and explore the behaviors and culture of their populations before attempting to change behaviors. As Hippocrates noted:

> Whoever wishes to investigate medicine properly, should proceed thus . . . the mode in which the inhabitants live, and what are their pursuits, whether they are fond of drinking, and eating to excess, and given to indolence, and are fond of exercising and labor, and not given to excess eating and drinking.

Are familial risk factors another possible determinant of Winston's condition? It is impossible to determine from just the information presented in the opening story. While research suggests that a family history of MS may increase susceptibility to the illness, we have no information to suggest that any of Winston's first-degree relatives have the disease.

Physical Environmental Influences on Health

We noted earlier that the term *environmental determinants* can have more than one meaning. It can refer to physical entities such as air, water, land, or neighborhood. Yet, it can also imply social conditions, as in a "hostile environment," a "threatening environment," or a "friendly environment."

The physical environmental conditions that could impair or enhance health outcomes are readily identifiable in many communities. For example, it is easy to detect the strong odors produced from water treatment plants, or the smell of exhaust from a bus depot that houses a fleet of public buses. Physical environmental determinants of health are important contributors to an individual's health because they may introduce contaminants that create or exacerbate health problems. Yet, they may pose greater problems for health psychologists when attempting to improve the health status of an individual or a community. When the cause of a heath condition is rooted in environmental determinants of a physical nature, psychologists may resort to health policy interventions rather than just individual behavior changes to improve outcomes.

Consider this: We now know that secondhand smoke presents a hazard to all people, including nonsmokers, and many individuals attempt to reduce their exposure to such smoke. An impractical strategy for avoiding secondhand smoke is to teach individuals to leave an environment in which people are smoking. This is impractical for two reasons. First, it may be impossible for an individual to leave the site. For example, if smoking is permitted in the workplace, it may not be feasible for an employee to leave the worksite to avoid inhaling a secondhand smoke. Second, such a strategy encourages smokers to continue their behavior with the expectation that people who do not like the unhealthy habit will accommodate the smoker at their own expense.

Instead, health policy regulations put in place by local and national policy regulators (thanks in no small part to research on secondhand smoke conducted by many health researchers) ban smoking in many public places. We explore the issue of health policy and smoking more thoroughly in Chapter 13, Health Psychologists' Role: Research, Application, and Advocacy. For now it is important to note that, in such instances, the work of health psychologists on environmental determinants has focused on policy initiatives that benefit large populations rather than selected or targeted individuals.

Returning to our example of Winston and MS, here, too, researchers have found a possible environmental link to MS. Several studies confirm that insufficient exposure to ultraviolet (UV) light may increase risks of susceptibility of MS (Handel et al., 2010; van der Mei, Ponsonby, & Dwyer, 2003). Specifically, studies that examine population occurrences of MS suggest that this disease is more prevalent in people who live farthest from the equator. In other words, in geographic regions where exposure to UV light is reduced, researchers found higher incidences of MS. When interpreted together, the results of these MS studies suggest that genetic factors (individual determinant), smoking behaviors (individual/behavioral determinant), and physical environmental conditions (UV light) account for 75% of the prevalence of MS cases in European study samples (Handel et al., 2010).

What do these studies suggest about a possible environmental determinant of MS for Winston? We cannot tell. Not knowing where Winston lives, and without additional studies to corroborate such findings, we can only note that environmental factors such as UV light may contribute to susceptibility to MS.

Social Environmental Influences on Health

Social conditions in the environment that affect health are more challenging to identify and address because they depend, in part, on an individual's perceptions of an environment. We have no research to suggest that social environmental factors may contribute to the development of MS; therefore, we will examine the impact of social environmental determinants on other health issues.

Consider this: When walking in an unfamiliar neighborhood where the residents are of a different ethnic group, one individual may perceive the residents of the community as hostile while another may not. Some researchers have explored the perception of racism or of a racist environment on health outcomes. Several studies suggest that environments that are perceived to be racist can foster high stress levels in some individuals that result in adverse health conditions such as high blood pressure and other heart conditions (Albert et al., 2008; Barksdale, Farrug, & Harkness, 2009; Cooper et al., 2009). Here, too, when addressing such social environmental conditions, psychologists may turn to health policy to address the multiple causes of the problem. We explore social environmental determinants more fully in Chapter 5, Risky Health Behaviors and Chapter 9, Cardiovascular Health.

Health Systems/Health Policies Influences

Lately health psychologists have come to recognize the role of health systems in enhancing or inhibiting good health outcomes. We explained earlier that any system that regulates an individual's access to health care, by definition, regulates that person's health outcomes. As such, it is a determinant of health.

We explore more fully the effects of health systems on an individual's health status in Chapter 12, Health Care Systems and Health Policy. For the moment, however, we need to emphasize two points. Access to timely, quality health care appears to be a significant contributor to good health outcomes. But it appears that both individual and systems factors affect access to health care. With regards to individuals, we will see in the coming chapters that factors such as employment status, income, and sometimes age or gender may influence an individual's likelihood of seeking health care or of securing the means of access to care. In such instances, a health psychologist may work specifically with individuals to promote the benefits of access to care and to change beliefs about the need for health care.

Research comparing health policies suggests that universal health care, a system that provides free or greatly subsidized access to care, ensures better overall access to care and results in improvements in health status (Lasser, Himmelstein, & Woolhandler, 2006; National Health & Hospitals Reform Commission, 2009; Siddiqi, Zuberi, & Nquyen, 2009). We also explore the concept of universal health care and its application in other countries more fully in Chapter 12, Health Care Systems and Health Policy. For the moment, it is important to note that, while there are many different types of universal systems of care, all share one common element: The systems ensure that all persons seeking medical or mental health services will receive care without regard to their income or economic status. Health psychologists who explore the effects of health systems and health policy on outcomes will devote their attention largely to health policy issues that apply to large segments of society. Interestingly, the benefits of universal access to care have become a major political and policy issue once again in the United States in 2009–2010, just as they were in 1994, 1968, and even earlier.

Again, we return to Winston and ask: How could access to health care, health care systems, or health policy affect Winston's health status? Consider this: Without access to health care, Winston's condition could have been untreated or misdiagnosed. Either outcome could have resulted in incorrect treatment that could hve affected Winston's ability to play baseball or to pursue his studies. In other words, untreated or misdiagnosed illnesses can limit an individual's ability to perform his or her usual daily activities or preferred activities. Winston was able to obtain the needed health care to identify the problem and adopt behaviors that allow him to manage his disease while enjoying his favorite activities. Without such care, baseball could have been an unrealized dream.

Summary

This is an exciting time to explore the field of health psychology. Evolutions in the concept of health, new developments in science and medicine that explain pathways to disease and illness, and the work of health psychologists on the many determinants we have discussed suggest that there is still much to learn about the factors that affect and shape our health. This growing field also offers individuals interested in health psychology opportunities to work in many different settings on a wide array of interdisciplinary issues.

Consider this: Health psychologists can be found in research settings in hospitals, medical laboratories, academia, pharmaceutical companies, and a host of other research-related environments. If one is interested in applying research to help individuals change behaviors and improve health status, health psychologists can fit easily into community-based health centers, medical centers with outpatient health programs, and even in private physician's offices where allied health services are offered. Health psychologists interested in specific populations are often found in school settings, senior citizen centers, and nursing homes, where attention to health and health behaviors is an ongoing concern.

Finally, if one is interested in the health issues of a community or larger populations, health psychologists can and do contribute to health policy work through local and national departments of health responsible for creating, monitoring, and maintaining health policy, as well as international agencies that monitor and address global health problems.

Personal Postscript

After reading the chapter, how would you describe your health? Maybe the following scale would help. While rating yourself, see how many determinants of health you can identify in the scale.

1. In general would you say your health is:
   Excellent
   Very good
   Good
   Fair
   Poor

2. For how long (if at all) has your health limited you in each of the following activities?

Activity	Limited >3 months	Limited <3 months	Not limited at all
The kinds or amounts of vigorous activities you can do, like lifting heavy objects, running, or participating in strenuous sports			
The kinds or amounts of moderate activities you can do, like moving a table, carrying groceries, or bowling			
Walking uphill or climbing a few flights of stairs			
Bending, lifting, or stooping			
Walking one block			
Eating, dressing, bathing, or using the toilet			

3. How much bodily pain have you had during the past four weeks?
   None
   Very mild
   Mild
   Moderate
   Severe
   Very severe

4. Does your health keep you from working at a job, doing work around the house, or going to school?
   Yes, for more than three months
   Yes, for three months or less
   No

5. Have you been unable to do certain kinds or amounts of work, housework, or schoolwork because of your health?

    Yes, for more than three months

    Yes, for three months or less

    No

6. For each of the following questions please check the box for the one answer that comes closest to the way you have been feeling during the past month.

Activities	All of the time	Most of the time	A good bit of the time	Some of the time	A little of the time	None of the time
How much of the time, during the past month, has your health limited your social activities (like visiting with friends or close relatives)?						
How much of the time, during the past month, have you been a very nervous person?						
During the past month, how much of the time have you felt calm and peaceful?						
How much of the time, during the past month, have you felt downhearted and blue?						
During the past month, how much of the time have you been a happy person?						
How often, during the past month, have you felt so down in the dumps that nothing could cheer you up?						

7. Please check the box that best describes whether each of the following statements is true or false for you.

Description	Definitely true	Mostly true	Not sure	Mostly false	Definitely false
I am somewhat ill.					
I am as healthy as anybody I know.					
My health is excellent.					
I have been feeling bad lately.					

Source: Adapted from Ware and Sherbourne (1992) as cited in MacDowell (2006).

Important Terms

Aesculapian theory   7
biomedical model   13
biopsychosocial model   13
botany   3
chronic illness   2
Cnidian theory   7
curanderismo   16
Daoist philosophy   7
determinants of health   3
ecological model   13
ethnopharmacologist   10
etiology   18

familial determinant
   of health   20
first-degree relatives   20
haemorrhagic plague   11
health-enhancing
   behaviors   16
health policy   6
health systems   17
Hippocrates   3
holistic health   3
humoral theory   6
materia medica   7

multiple sclerosis (MS)   2
myelin sheath   19
pandemics   11
physical environment   17
physiological state   2
plagues of Justinian   11
psychosomatic medicine   12
Qi   7
quality of life   15
Renaissance   11
social ecological model   13
wellness model   13

Research Methods

Chapter Objectives

After studying this chapter, you will be able to:

1. Identify and describe the five classic indicators of health.
2. Explain proximal and distal causes.
3. Identify and describe nonexperimental research designs.
4. Explain the relevance of nonexperimental designs for health research.
5. Identify and describe experimental designs.
6. Explain the relevance of experimental designs for health research.
7. Describe intervention studies.
8. Explain the relevance of intervention studies for health research.
9. Identify historical events leading to the establishment of the Nuremberg Code of Conduct, the Declaration of Helsinki, and the U.S. National Research Act.
10. Describe IRBs, their role, and their function.
11. Identify and explain the two principal violations of research ethics in the Tuskegee study.
12. Identify and explain the psychological harm to participants in the Stanford prison experiment.
13. Explain the concept of "research without informed consent."

OPENING STORY: HEALTHY VOLUNTEER DIES IN ASTHMA STUDY

"On July 19 [2001], after investigating the death of a previously healthy [research study] volunteer, the United States **Office for Human Research Protections (OHRP)** *suspended nearly all federally funded medical research involving human subjects at Johns Hopkins University. The death has been described as 'particularly disturbing' because 24 year old Ellen Roche was a healthy volunteer who had nothing to gain by taking part in the study"* (Savulescu & Spriggs, 2002).

What caused the death of a healthy research study participant? The following facts may help answer the question.

In 2001, a Johns Hopkins researcher was conducting a study to identify the reflex that protects healthy people from developing asthma (Savulescu & Spriggs, 2002). The researcher needed healthy, nonasthmatic participants for the study who would be given **hexamethonium***, a drug that induces a mild asthma attack (Johns Hopkins University, 2001). Ms. Roche, a technician employed by Johns Hopkins, was asked by a Johns Hopkins doctor to consider volunteering for the study. She agreed but died after participating in the study for about a month. She suffered pulmonary (lung) complications, blood pressure irregularities, and kidney failure, resulting from her participation in this study. Unfortunately for Ms. Roche, the investigator was unaware of several research findings published in the 1950s and 1960s that identified hexamethonium as a toxic substance. In addition, the researchers also appeared unaware that the Food and Drug Administration (FDA), the agency that approves the sale and distribution of drugs for humans, withdrew the drug for human use almost 30 years earlier* (Office for Human Research Protection, 2001). ∎

The OHRP, a federal agency that monitors research involving human subjects, conducted an investigation of the Johns Hopkins study after learning of the death of Ellen Roche. According to the OHRP, the death of a study participant or any injury or illness to a participant as a result of his or her involvement in an approved research study is an ***adverse event*** requiring investigation. The OHRP's investigation revealed that hexamethonium was one probable factor in Ms. Roche's death. In addition, the OHRP discovered that the researcher failed to report that, prior to Ms. Roche's death, two other asthma study participants had become ill as a result of their participation. The earlier illnesses did not result in death, but the failure to disclose the initial adverse events was further evidence of a serious breech of research procedure.

The death of a research participant is an alarming event to any researcher. But there were two additional reasons that health researchers in particular were concerned about the events in the Johns Hopkins study. First, by not reporting the first two adverse events, the researchers exposed all participants in the study to a similar risk of illness or other injury. All researchers who use human subjects in their experiments must take care not to use techniques or procedures that could harm or injure the volunteers. One could argue that Ms. Roche's death may have been prevented had the earlier events been reported and investigated.

Second, the errors committed by the Johns Hopkins researchers could have jeopardized subsequent asthma research. Scientists continue to search for more effective means of controlling or possibly curing asthma. Adverse events like those that occurred in the Johns Hopkins study could have delayed or suspended this vital work. The Johns Hopkins researchers certainly considered the potential benefits of the study and drug for asthma sufferers. But in the process they appeared to have overlooked the warning signs that signal potential risks to participants.

All research involving human subjects must balance the potential benefits of the study with the potential harm to participants. For this reason, studies that involve human subjects must be reviewed, approved, and monitored by local or national research review boards. The job of the review boards is to protect the health and welfare of human subjects and to ensure that investigators comply with the code of conduct for research with human subjects.

We need to point out that the overwhelming majority of studies conducted, including those in health psychology, are safe. The research review boards help to ensure participants' safety. Yet, accidents do happen. In this chapter we highlight four historic studies or events that demonstrate the adverse consequences that can occur when the health and welfare of study participants are overlooked. The Johns Hopkins study is one recent and notable example.

We begin in Section I with a review of research terms. The review will introduce, or reintroduce for some, research methodology and concepts needed for our discussion of research ethics later in the chapter. It will also serve as a guide to understanding the research procedures used in other studies presented throughout the text. We then continue in Section II with a discussion of some of the research methods used often by health psychologists. By the end of Sections I and II you will be able to identify and define the five classic measures used to describe the health of a population, explain distal and proximal causes of illnesses, and describe nonexperimental, experimental, and quasi-experimental study designs and their relevance for health psychology research.

Finally, in Section III, we examine the rules regarding the ethical conduct of research involving human subjects. Using the research terms and methods that we learned in Sections I and II, we examine two studies, the Tuskegee Syphilis Study and Philip Zimbardo's Stanford prison experiment, and identify the violations of research methods and ethics in each case.

SECTION I. MEASURING HEALTH

Borrowing from Epidemiology

Health psychology borrows some concepts from the field of epidemiology. ***Epidemiology*** is the study of factors or determinants of health status among population groups and the use of that knowledge to help control the spread of health problems in the population (Centers for Disease Control [CDC], 2004b). The word *epidemiology* derives from three Greek words: e*pi*, meaning "among"; *demos*, meaning "people"; and *logos*, referring to a scholarly discipline or study.

Epidemiologists, or people who study the determinants and distribution of diseases, are like detectives. In fact, they can be thought of as "medical detectives." When studying the causes of a health problem, epidemiologists attempt to determine the origins of a disease by identifying and examining the first or earliest known human infected as well as the agent that caused the infection. A crucial second component of their work is determining the risk posed by the disease to current and future populations. Thus, one application of epidemiological research is to inform us about the origins of a disease, its impact on prior generations, and its potential risk to people at present and in the future.

MORTALITY VERSUS MORBIDITY   Two measures that describe the health of a population are mortality and morbidity. *Mortality* refers to death. For example, mortality data on the number of deaths due to heart disease could be used to describe the cardiovascular health of people over 65 years of age in a specific geographic area. On the other hand, *morbidity* refers to diseases that may contribute to mortality. Take diabetes, for example. Diabetes is a disease that will not cause death but that can cause a number of health problems that lead to death. The number of people with diabetes, therefore, could be a morbidity statistic that also describes the health of a population.

Epidemiologists and other health researchers use two types of data when reporting mortality and morbidity statistics, *raw data* and *rates*. When measuring mortality, the raw data are the total number of deaths for a defined population. For example, Figure 2.1 shows infant mortality data for seven Western industrialized countries. The raw data present the actual number of infants (children 0 to 12 months of age) who died in each of the seven countries in 2003, the last year for which statistics are available for all seven countries.

According to the data, the United States reported the largest number of deaths for infants one year of age or younger (28,428) with France second at 3,325. Finland reported only 176 deaths, the fewest number of infant deaths for children of this age (United Nations, 2006).

Using raw data to compare the infant mortality statistics of the seven countries is a little like comparing apples and oranges. When using raw data we cannot determine whether the number of infant deaths represents a large or small percentage of the infant population in each country. In other words, the raw data on infant mortality do not adjust for differences in the total number of infants in 2003 in each country. Consider this: Using just the raw data, we would conclude that the United States had 8.5 times more infant deaths than France and a whopping 161.5 times more deaths than Finland. Does this mean that U.S. infants are 8.5 times more likely to die than infants in France and 161.5 times more likely to die than infants in Finland? Not really.

To compare mortality statistics across two or more countries we must adjust for the difference in the size of the populations. For this type of comparisons we use rates.

To understand the likelihood of infant deaths in the United States versus France and versus Finland, we compute the *mortality rates* for infant deaths using the formula: total number of infant deaths/total population of infants × 1,000. The formula allows us to convert the raw data on infant mortality in Figure 2.1 to *infant mortality rates* for the same seven countries. The rates express the number of infant deaths for every 1,000 infants born in the country.

Using rates we see that although France reported the *second highest* raw number of infant deaths in 2003 (Figure 2.1), they actually had the *third highest* infant mortality rate: 4.40. In fact, France's rate is comparable to Denmark's, a country with the *third smallest* raw number of infant deaths. France's rate of 4.40 deaths per 1,000 infants also compares favorably with the other European countries in the group. By comparison, the United States and Canada had the highest infant mortality rates among the group in 2003 at 7.0 and 5.4 deaths for every 1,000 infants born, respectively.

To summarize, the raw infant mortality statistics present the total number of infant deaths. But, if we want to understand the magnitude of a health problem—here meaning infant deaths—in comparison to other countries, we must use mortality rates rather than the raw data.

In some instances, the infant mortality statistics also provide information on the health of other members in the community. For example, the infant mortality data also serve as basic

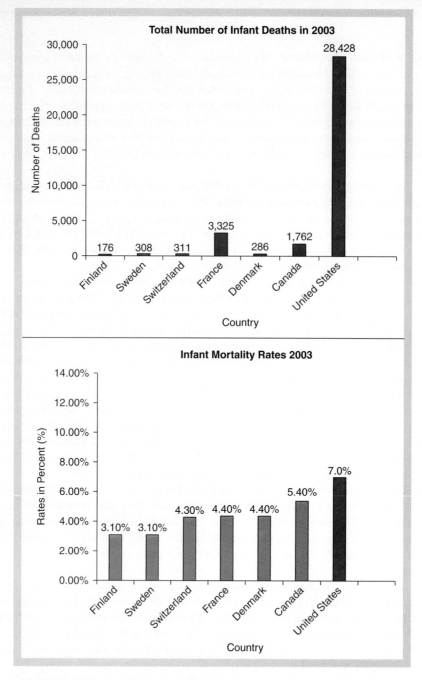

FIGURE 2.1 Number of Infant Deaths Versus Infant Mortality Rates in Seven Industrialized Countries. According to the raw data, the United States and France have the highest number of infant deaths (children 12 months of age or younger), but when compared to the total population of infants (mortality rates) United States and Canada have the highest rates of infant mortality.

Source: United Nations (2006).

indicators of the health of a community or region. Consider this fact: In 1997, the three leading causes of death for infants in the United States were birth defects, disorders related to premature births, and sudden infant death syndrome (SIDS) (CDC, 1999; Ebrahim & Atrash, 2006). But researchers note that two principal causes of birth defects are a lack of prenatal care for the mother and the mother's use of substances (cigarettes, alcohol, or illegal drugs) while pregnant. In other words, the two main causes of infant deaths cited here are linked to maternal health factors. Thus, infant death rates may be indicators of maternal health as well as the overall health of the infant (CDC, 1999; Ebrahim & Atrash, 2006).

INCIDENCE, PREVALENCE AND RELATIVE RISKS

Incidence   Three other statistics provide a gross measure of the health status of a population: incidence, prevalence, and relative risk. *Incidence* refers to the number of new cases of a disease in a specific population for a given time period. We can examine how quickly a disease is spreading through a population by examining the number of new cases, or incidence, of a disease. A helpful example is the rapid increase in the incidences of HIV cases in Ukraine. In 1994, Ukraine reported a total of 183 cases of HIV. But in 1998, just four years later, they reported over 8,112 new cases. The rapid increase in new cases earned Ukraine the distinction of having the "fastest growing HIV infection rate in Eastern Europe" (Ministry of Health, Ukraine, 2000; UNICEF, 2004).

Prevalence   In comparison, *prevalence* is the total number of cases (old and new) of a specific disease in a population, also for a given time period. Current estimates place the prevalence of HIV cases in Ukraine at approximately 360,000 cases as of 2004 (UNAIDS, 2004). Remember, here we are looking at the total number of cases, not just new cases. The 8,112 new incidences of HIV in 1998 and the approximately 360,000 total prevalence of HIV as of 2004 measure the impact of HIV/AIDS on the Ukrainian population using the actual number of cases.

As with the raw infant mortality data, the raw data on incidence and prevalence of HIV in Ukraine are useful when describing the spread of the disease within a country. But, to understand the magnitude and severity of HIV in Ukraine, and to make meaningful comparisons between Ukraine and other countries, we must convert the raw data to *incidence rates* and *prevalence rates*.

As of 2005, Ukraine reported an HIV prevalence rate of 1.4%. (HIV incidence rates for Ukraine were not reported after 1998). This means that 1.4% of all adults in Ukraine were infected with HIV. Comparing the Ukrainian prevalence rate to the 1.0% global prevalence rate for HIV, we find that the Ukrainian rate exceeded the global rate by 0.4%. Admittedly, 0.4% is a small difference. But remember, Ukraine reported only 183 total HIV cases prior to 1994, a prevalence rate of much less than 1.0%. The point here is that the HIV prevalence rate in Ukraine rose quickly in just 10 years—from less than 0.5% (183 cases) to 1.4% (360,000 cases). Stated simply, the incidence and prevalence rates show us that Ukraine experienced a rapid spread of HIV infection.

Relative Risk   Finally, we use *relative risk* to express the risk to individuals of acquiring a specific disease. Relative risk helps to estimate the risk of acquiring a disease by persons who are members of the exposed group. It compares the risk to members of the exposed group with the risk of acquiring the same disease by persons who are not members. In Ukraine, intravenous

TABLE 2.1	Calculating Rates	
Rate	**Definition**	**Sample Calculation**
Mortality	Number of deaths (cause specific or general) in a total population for a specific period	$\dfrac{\text{Automobile fatalities 2005}}{\text{U.S. population in 2005}} \times 100{,}000^a$
Morbidity	Specific illnesses that may contribute to death in total population for a specific time period	$\dfrac{\text{Hypertension in 2005}}{\text{U.S. population in 2005}} \times 100{,}000^b$
Incidence	The number of new cases of a disease in the population for a specific time period	$\dfrac{\text{New HIV Cases in 2004}}{\text{Ukrainian population in 2004}} \times 100{,}000^c$
Prevalence	The number of all current cases of disease in the population for a specific time period.	$\dfrac{\text{All HIV cases in 2004}}{\text{Ukrainian population in 2004}} \times 100{,}000^d$
Relative risk	The number of cases of the disease in an exposed group compared to the number of cases of the disease in a nonexposed group	$\dfrac{\text{HIV cases of drug users in Ukraine}}{\text{HIV cases of non–drug users in Ukraine}} \times 100{,}000^e$

[a] Expressed as automobile fatality rate in the United States per 100,000 people in 2005
[b] Expressed as hypertension rate in United States per 100,000 people in 2005
[c] Expressed as Incidence rate of HIV in Ukraine per 100,000 people in 2004
[d] Expressed as prevalence of HIV in Ukraine per 100,000 people in 2004
[e] Expressed as relative risk of drug users in the Ukraine for contracting HIV per 100,000 people

drug users (IVDUs) are believed to be at higher risk of contracting HIV than non–intravenous drug users (non-IVDUs). Briefly, the practice of sharing syringes to inject illegal drugs increases the likelihood that IVDUs may contract HIV from previous needle users who may be infected with the disease. Because of this practice, IDVUs in Ukraine are considered members of a group with a high risk of exposure to HIV. Using the number of HIV cases among IVDUs and non-IVDUs, Ukrainian health officials calculated that the relative risk to IVDUs of contracting HIV is 60.1%. This means that an IVDU in Ukraine has a 60.1% greater chance of contracting HIV than a non-IVDU.

In sum, measures of mortality, morbidity, incidence, prevalence, and relative risk are five classic measures of the health of a population. They are, however, only rough measures of the health of the community. For a further explanation of the health status of individuals or of a community we turn to more specific measures.

PROXIMAL VERSUS DISTAL CAUSES OF ILLNESS

Proximal   Two measures that help explain individual or community health problems are *proximal* (or *precipitating*) and *distal* (or *predisposing*) causes of health and illness. Proximal and distal causes may include individual, situational, or environmental factors. Consider this example: In December 2006, 71 people in five states (Delaware, New Jersey, New York, Pennsylvania, and South Carolina) reported gastrointestinal problems (diarrhea, bloating, or nausea due to problems in the stomach or intestines) shortly after eating at a Taco Bell restaurant in four of the five states listed above. Epidemiologists and health officials found that the proximal cause for the gastrointestinal problems of the 71 patients was the *E. coli 0157:H7 bacterium*. It appears that several shipments of shredded lettuce from a food manufacturing plant were unknowingly contaminated with E. coli. The lettuce was shipped to the Taco Bell restaurants in Delaware, New Jersey, New York, and Pennsylvania, and was consumed by the customers who became ill (CDC, 2006). After further investigation, the CDC determined that the contamination resulted from poor hygiene or poor food preparation procedures at the processing plant that supplied lettuce to the Taco Bell restaurants in the four states.

You will notice, however, that the fifth state, South Carolina, was not included in the delivery. If the contaminated lettuce, the proximal factor, was not delivered to South Carolina, why was a related case of E. coli discovered there? In one word: travel. A resident of South Carolina dined at a Taco Bell restaurant in one of the four affected states before returning home. The "medical detective" work of the epidemiologists helped to tie the incident of E. coli in South Carolina to the proximal environmental cause in the other 70 cases by probing into the recent travels of the South Carolina resident.

Distal   To explain distal causes of an illness, researchers may need to examine factors or events that predate the illness by months or perhaps years. For example, heart disease in adults is an illness that could have several distal causes. One cause could be a congenital problem, or a problem present at birth, such as an *atrial septal defect*—sometimes called a hole in the wall of the heart—which often is undetected at birth. And, if left undetected, the defect may develop into hypertension (high blood pressure) in adolescents or adulthood. Thus, a child born with an atrial septal defect may be predisposed to developing heart related problems such as *hypertension* (see Chapter 9, Cardiovascular Disease) as an adolescent or adult. For this reason, atrial septal defect could be considered a distal factor that could cause heart disease in later years.

Summary

Five classic measures—mortality, morbidity, incidence, prevalence, and relative risk—enable health researchers to describe the health status of a population in general terms. Proximal (or precipitating) and distal (or predisposing) factors help explain the timing of an illness as well as the probable cause. In Section II we review some of the research methods used by health psychologists to analyze the cause of diseases and to predict their future occurrences.

SECTION II. METHODOLOGY

We sometimes refer to methodology as the research design segment of a study. The word *design* suggests a creative process. Here researchers can use their creativity to craft interesting and unique studies that test research hypotheses. There is just one caveat: A creative study must adhere to a few fundamental principles of research design.

In this section we will briefly review selected research designs focusing on the methods used most often by health psychologists. In the process you will see how the health concepts used by epidemiologists are married to the research techniques and methods used in psychology to produce studies of interest to both epidemiologists and health psychologists. You may want to return to this section as a reference guide when reading about research studies in this and subsequent chapters.

There are two general types of research methods in psychology, *nonexperimental* and *experimental studies*. We will begin with an overview of two types of nonexperimental studies used frequently by health psychologists, qualitative and correlational studies (see Table 2.2).

TABLE 2.2	Sample Research Methods for Health Psychology Research		
Design	**Purpose**	**Statistic**	**Pros (P) and Cons (C)**
Nonexperimental			
Qualitative	Explore phenomenon in context	Minimal or no statistical data. Analyze content of responses	(P) In-depth analysis of response. (C) Cannot examine cause–effect relationships
Case	In-depth exploration of person, place, situation	Minimal or no statistical data. Analyze content of responses	(P) In-depth exploration of rare/unique events. (C) Cannot examine cause–effect relationships
Focus Groups	Gather information. Generate insight. Explore decision making. Encourage interactions	Minimal use of descriptive data. Analyze content of responses	(P) Generate new information, insights. (P) Interactive approach. (C) Cannot examine cause–effect relationships
Correlational Studies	Describe relationship between two variables	Pearson Correlation Coefficient (r). Range $= -1.00$ to $+1.00$	(P) Identifies relationship between two variables. (C) Cannot determine casual relationship

TABLE 2.2	(Continued)		
Design	**Purpose**	**Statistic**	**Pros (P) and Cons (C)**
Experimental			
Experimental Studies	Detect cause–effect relationship between variables.	Central tendency (mean, median, mode) Student's T, Analysis of Variance (ANOVA) Multiple Analysis of Variance (MANOVA) Linear, multiple, or logistic regression (R^2)	(P) Causal explanation of effects of one or more variables on outcomes (P) Direct control of causal variables (C) Not suitable for all studies (C) No in-depth analysis
Intervention Studies	Measure effect of intervention usually with pre-post-test format	Central tendency (mean, median, mode) Student's T, Analysis of Variance (ANOVA) Multiple Analysis of Variance (MANOVA) Linear, multiple or logistic regression (R^2)	(P) Direct measure of effectiveness of intervention (P) Causal explanation of effects (C) Not suitable for all studies (C) No in-depth analysis
Quasi-experimental			
Quasi-experimental	Detect cause–effect relationship between two variables with limitations	Central tendency (mean, median, mode) Student's T, Analysis of Variance (ANOVA) Multiple Analysis of Variance (MANOVA) Linear, multiple or logistic regression (R^2)	(P) Limited cause–effect relationship (P) Control of some causal variables (C) Pre-existing conditions may not be controlled
Intervention Studies	Measure effect of intervention usually with pre-post-test format	Central tendency (mean, median, mode) Student's T, Analysis of Variance (ANOVA) Multiple Analysis of Variance (MANOVA)	(P) Measure intervention effect on single group (P) Limited subject variance due (C) Limited inference of causality without control groups

Afterwards, we will review experimental studies including quasi-experimental methods. By the end of this section you will be able to: distinguish between nonexperimental, experimental, and quasi-experimental studies; to define qualitative, correlational, intervention, pre-post-test, and clinical trial studies; and to describe the types of research questions that each of these methods addresses.

Qualitative Studies

One factor researchers consider when designing a study is the type of data to be collected. In Section I, we described morbidity, mortality, incidence, prevalence, and relative risks: examples of *quantitative data* that characterize numerically the health status of a community. By comparison, proximal and distal data yield contextual rather than numeric information. They provide explanations about an outcome, not just numbers. The purpose of proximal and distal data is to explain the occurrence of the problem rather than to count the number of occurrences.

Qualitative studies, like qualitative data, are used when the goal of the researcher is to gather largely nonstatistical data that help to explain a behavior or outcome in the environment in which it occurs (Salkind, 2006). Qualitative studies in health psychology, therefore, provide rich, contextual data that allows for an in-depth exploration and analysis of the health issue. But, as we will see shortly, there are benefits and drawbacks to qualitative studies.

In qualitative studies, researchers use the context in which the health event occurred to explore a phenomenon and to identify factors that contribute to an outcome. Consider this: When exploring the proximal causes of the gastrointestinal problems of the 71 Taco Bell customers discussed in Section I, researchers collected information from the customers about their behaviors immediately preceding the illness. Here the critical information came in the form of a brief history of customers' recent travels and eating behaviors—that is, nonstatistical data. For example, researchers may have asked the 71 customers what they ate for breakfast or where they ate before going to a Taco Bell. They may have asked, also, whether they went to Taco Bell with friends or family and whether their friends and family also became ill. Using the customers' histories, the researchers then analyzed the responses searching for common factors that linked all 71 E. coli sufferers. In this case, there were two commonalities: All 71 customers ate at Taco Bell and all ate shredded lettuce. Undoubtedly some of the data obtained in the investigation were numerical, but other information, such as what was consumed and other related behaviors, was nonnumerical.

CASE STUDIES   Researchers in the Taco Bell investigation most likely used a qualitative research design called a *case study* to obtain data. Consistent with other forms of qualitative research, case studies allow for an in-depth analysis of rare or unique events. For example, case study methods are used often by epidemiologists when investigating new outbreaks of diseases. The West Nile virus outbreak in the United States is one recent example in which a case study approach was used to investigate the occurrence of a new health problem that affected many communities.

The first case of West Nile virus in the United States occurred in 1999. Some of the people infected with the virus showed symptoms of *encephalitis,* a severe inflammation of the spinal cord and the brain. Epidemiologists used the diagnosis of encephalitis, other medical tests, and descriptions obtained from patients about the events leading up to their illnesses to build a case study of each infected patient. For patients who were unconscious or too ill to respond, family and friends provided the needed information. Researchers then compared the case studies of patients with similar symptoms to identify commonalities and to link the common symptoms to a likely cause. Using medical records, researchers were able to diagnose the then unknown virus as the West Nile virus, a disease that was first reported in Egypt and France in the 1950s and 1960s (CDC, 2004e).

FOCUS GROUPS   Another type of qualitative study commonly used by health researchers is a *focus group*. Focus groups serve four main functions: to gather information, to generate insight, to explore a decision-making process, and finally to encourage interactions that create new insights (Salkind, 2006). The groups are facilitated by a moderator. The job of the moderator is to pose questions for discussion and to ensure that all participants are able and encouraged to contribute.

Participants in a focus group usually have one or more characteristics in common, characteristics that are central to the research question or topic. For example, researchers could convene a focus group of first-year college students to explore new students' perceptions of stress during their first semester. Not all first-semester college students experience stress. But in focus groups a researcher can obtain information from the students who do as well as those who do not report feelings of stress in order to generate insight into the factors that contribute to stress.

The in-depth information obtained from focus groups may identify new causes of stress that are unknown to the investigator. Alternatively, the group format can provide a forum for an exchange of ideas or experiences that may generate new insight into the causes of stress. Thus, unlike case studies, focus groups yield in-depth information but from a group of people simultaneously rather than from people individually.

INTERVIEWS   Finally, some research requires structured as well as unstructured responses to specific questions. For example, the ***one-on-one interview*** is a data collection technique that can allow for a range of responses according to the type of questions posed. Using ***closed-ended questions***, here meaning those questions offering a forced choice response, such as "yes" or "no," researchers can obtain succinct responses to specific questions. In addition, however, one-on-one interviews may also contain ***open-ended questions***, here meaning questions yielding descriptive responses that allow study participants to provide additional information that may offer important details about the person's health behaviors. Open-ended questions also allow respondents to construct and deliver their own answers without regard to the length of their response.

An example of an open-ended question is: What is the reason for your visit to the doctor's office today? Answers to this question may vary based on the participants' reasons for seeking medical care, the choice of words used to describe their illness or injury, and the level of detail they provide when responding.

In essence, qualitative studies often use nonstatistical research tools to obtain information about an event in context. But sometimes a researcher requires a more quantitative answer to questions. In such cases, we turn to analytical research methods that use quantitative statistics.

Correlational Studies

We identified methods for describing the health status of a population using, for example, mortality and morbidity data. We also identified methods for explaining a health event using qualitative data. But, when researchers want to do more than simply describe a health status or an event, they use analytical research methods. For example, researchers may want to examine the relationship between two variables that affect health outcomes, such as diet and exercise. By "relationship" we mean simply determining whether two variables share something in common. If they do they are correlated (Salkind, 2006). One way to examine the relationship between two variables is through correlation research.

Correlational studies use the *Pearson correlation coefficient (r)*, a statistic that describes the strength of the relationship between two variables. The correlation coefficient is expressed numerically as a value ranging from +1.00 to −1.00. Correlations can be strongly positive ($r = +1.00$), strongly negative ($r = −1.00$), or totally unrelated, thereby showing no correlation ($r = 0.00$).

Examples of correlations are presented in Figure 2.2 and Figure 2.3. We borrow the results from a study by Bourne (2009) on the relationships between health-seeking behavior and health insurance and between poverty and health insurance. Bourne conducted a *retrospective analysis*, here meaning analyzing data from an existing database, using statistics on health behaviors in Jamaica over 19 years, between 1988–2007. Bourne found a significant *positive correlation* between ownership of health insurance and health-seeking behaviors. In other words, in the record data from Jamaica during the 19-year period captured, people with health insurance were significantly more likely to seek health care when needed if they also had health insurance. In this instance a positive correlation is demonstrated because an increase in the percentage of people seeking health care is associated with an increase in the percentage of people with health insurance. Note, however, that a positive correlation could result if as one variable goes down the second variable also decreases in value. Put it this way: To demonstrate a positive correlation, both variables must move in the same direction, either both increase in value or both decrease in value.

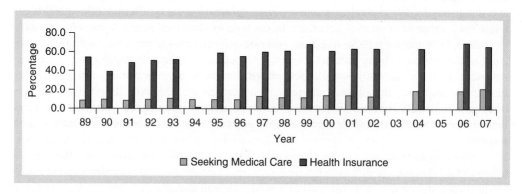

FIGURE 2.2   Percent of People Seeking Medical Care by Percentage with Health Insurance. Bourne's study suggests that people who seek medical care correlates positively with people with health insurance.

Source: Bourne, 2009.

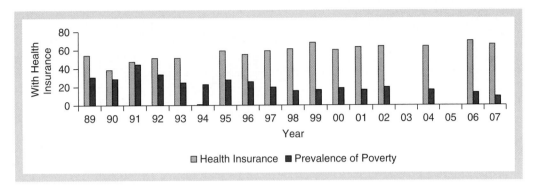

FIGURE 2.3   Percent of People with Health Insurance, by Prevalence of Poverty. Bourne's data suggests that a decrease in the prevalence of poverty is negatively correlated with health insurance.

Source: Bourne, 2009.

An interesting additional result in the same study indicated that health insurance ownership was related to poverty. In Figure 2.3, Bourne demonstrates that the greater the prevalence of poverty among the population, the less likely they are to have health insurance. In essence, as the prevalence of poverty decreases over years, the likelihood of health insurance ownership increases. In a ***negative correlation***, as one variable decreases the other increases.

When using correlation data, the strength of the relationship between the variables is expressed by the correlation coefficient. Although the strength of a correlation between two variables is expressed also by the *p*-value of the statistic, researchers often use the following guidelines to help identify potentially weak, average, or strong correlations. As a general rule of thumb, coefficients between $r = 0.21$ and $r = 0.39$ represent a weak correlation. Coefficients between $r = 0.40$ and $r = 0.59$ suggest moderate correlations, and coefficient values of $r = 0.60$ and above usually are considered high or strong correlations.

One correlation used often as a gross measure of health status is the relationship between a person's height and weight. Using a growth chart, shown in Figure 2.4, physicians examine the relationship between height and weight for children to determine whether a child's growth in feet and inches corresponds to an increase in weight that is appropriate given their height (Adams et al., 2007; Hu et al., 2000). In other words, physicians expect to see a positive correlation between children's weight gain and their growth in height. A negative correlation, one in which height increases but weight does not, could suggest health problems such as malnourishment or other physiological problems that threaten the infant's chances of survival. For infants, therefore, the correlation between height and weight is a gross measure of good health status.

We must mention one major limitation with this elegantly simple form of descriptive data. You may remember from your statistics class that correlation does not imply causality. For example, height and weight may be correlated, but we cannot conclude that an increase in height causes an increase in weight or vice versa. Thus, one limitation of correlational studies is the

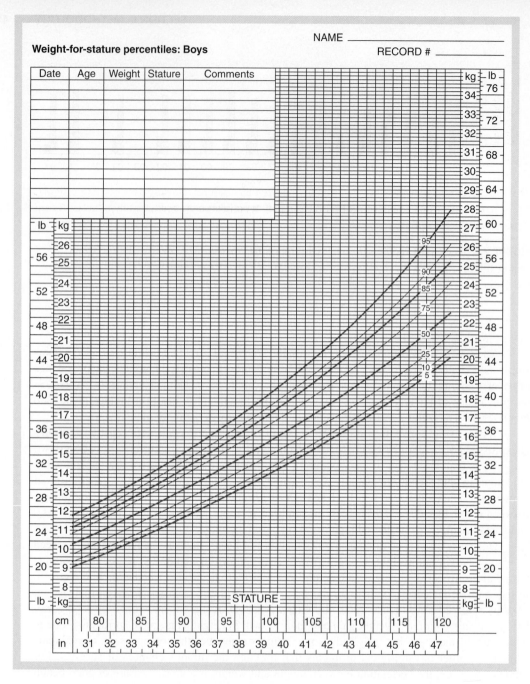

FIGURE 2.4 Boys' Growth Chart: Weight versus Height Centers for Disease Control (2000). An example of a common positive correlation showing the relationship between height and weight Published May 30, 2000 (modified 11/21/00).

Source: Developed by the National Center for Health Statistics in collaboration with the National Center for Chronic Disease Prevention and Health Promotion (2000). http://www.cdc.gov/growthcharts

inability to demonstrate a ***cause-and-effect relationship*** between the variables. Researchers who want to explore causal relationships between variables often turn to experimental research methods.

Experimental Studies

When researchers want to explore whether there exists a cause-and-effect relationship between two variables they construct an experimental research study. For example, a researcher may ask, "Does exercise affect stress levels?" To determine whether there is a relationship between exercise and stress, a researcher first restates the question as a null hypothesis or as a research hypothesis. A ***null hypothesis*** is an objective extension of the question that assumes no relationship between exercise and stress. In this case, the null hypothesis would be: There is no effect of exercise on stress.

We must point out, however, that in most published research studies, it is more common to see a ***research hypothesis***, that is, an objective extension of the question but one that assumes a relationship between the two variables. Using the same example of exercise and stress, the research hypothesis would be: There is a relationship between exercise and stress. In experimental studies, the researcher poses the null or the research hypotheses to determine whether and how changes in one variable, in this case exercise (the cause), affects the outcome of another variable, stress (the effect).

There are a number of key concepts in an experimental design. Experimental psychology textbooks discuss many of them in great detail. For our purposes, however, we limit our discussion to just four concepts: independent versus dependent variables, experimental versus control groups, random sampling, and longitudinal versus cross-sectional studies.

INDEPENDENT VERSUS DEPENDENT VARIABLES   One advantage of experimental research designs is that the investigator can limit or control many of the variables to be studied. The variable that the investigator manipulates or controls is called the ***independent variable***. In our example of the effects of exercise on stress, the independent variable is exercise. By carefully selecting the independent variables to include in a study, researchers can examine the effect of each variable on the study's outcome. Experimental studies may have multiple independent variables. For simplicity, however, our example has just one independent variable, exercise. Note, however, when designing a study on the effects of exercise on stress, researchers must define the type or types of exercise they include in the study.

A study's outcome variable is called the ***dependent variable***. Returning to our example of the relationship between exercise and stress, the dependent variable in this case is stress because the amount of stress experienced is assumed to be influenced by the amount of exercise (independent variable). After the variables have been identified and defined, researchers must develop a method for measuring participant's level of stress after performing the exercises.

EXPERIMENTAL VERSUS CONTROL GROUPS   Experimental research includes at least two groups of study participants, one control group and at least one experimental group. The ***experimental group*** is the test group. They receive a special treatment or condition. Again, referring to our example of exercise and stress, an experimental group's treatment could consist of 30 minutes of free swim three times a week. The ***control group***, however, would not receive the special condition or treatment. They may receive some form of treatment but nothing that would affect the dependent variable, stress. For example, participants in the control group might be placed in a room for 30 minutes with reading materials about swimming.

RANDOM SAMPLING   One goal of psychology researchers is to explain human behavior. Specifically, one goal of health psychology researchers is to explain the health behaviors or health outcomes of individuals or groups. Therefore, even though researchers conduct studies on small samples of people, the real goal is to generalize the results of their study to other groups in an effort to explain human behavior.

It is rarely possible to test a research hypothesis or question on an entire population. Consider this: If a researcher were interested in examining the frequency of accidents and injury to left-handed people, would the researcher be able to test the entire population of left-handed individuals? Clearly not. Consequently, research studies test hypotheses using a subset of a population rather than the full population.

When experimenters select a sample of participants from a population they wish to study, they must ensure that all eligible subjects have an equal and independent chance of participating. In addition, they must ensure that they are picking a sample that is representative of the population. Consider this: If a study on exercise and stress among college students were conducted at your college, researchers would need to advertise the study in such a way that all eligible students at your college would have an equal chance of participating in the study if they so desired. What methods could a researcher use to notify all eligible students? In some colleges, the campus newspaper is one way to disseminate information. For others, campuswide e-mails that are widely read would provide all students with an opportunity to participate.

When all eligible persons have an equal chance of participating, researchers can be reasonably assured that their recruitment procedures sought and most likely obtained a representative sample of the population. For that reason, researchers emphasize the importance of choosing a *random sample*, a group of people all of whom have an equal chance of participating in the study and who will be representative of the population to be studied. A truly random sample minimizes the possibility that the individuals chosen for the study reflect the preferences or biases of the experimenter.

Another issue pertaining to random selection is the *random assignment* of participants to treatment conditions. We mentioned that experimental studies have at least one experimental group and one control group. The experimenter must randomly assign participants to either group. Here, too, the experimenter must choose a process that allows each volunteer to have an equal chance of being assigned to either condition. Ensuring a random selection of participants and a random assignment of participants to study conditions gives the researcher greater confidence that the results are likely to be unbiased with respect to sample selection and assignment of conditions.

LONGITUDINAL VS. CROSS-SECTIONAL DESIGN

Longitudinal   The last of the key concepts in experimental design that we will address is longitudinal versus cross-sectional studies. In *longitudinal study designs*, researchers study a phenomenon over an extended period of time using the same participants. This is a useful design when studying health problems such as stress because stress is affected by a host of individual and environmental variables that contribute to the condition over time (see Chapter 7, Stress and

Coping). A longitudinal study can reveal a pattern of stress that is more reliable and less influenced by episodic changes caused by a specific event. Using the same people over time also helps control variability in the results due to subject factors such as age, ethnicity, or gender.

The disadvantages to using longitudinal studies are that they are time consuming and can be costly. Another factor, attrition, may affect longitudinal studies because participants are "lost" over time or discontinue participation due to lack of interest.

An example of a longitudinal health study is the *Framingham Heart Study*. This study, which began in 1949 in Framingham, Massachusetts, was designed as a detailed epidemiological study of heart disease. Its goal was to investigate the possible factors related to the development of various forms of coronary heart disease and hypertension (Dawber & Kannel, 1966). Within the first four years of the study, researchers were able to identify a number of personal and environmental characteristics associated with heart disease. And, equally as important, the Framingham study demonstrated that a longitudinal study of a health problem provided valuable information about previously unknown factors that contributed to the disease. As incredible as it might sound, this longitudinal study continues even today, some 60 years after its inception. Why? By continuing the study, researchers can examine the offspring of the original Framingham study sample, this time to look for genetic as well as individual and environmental factors that contribute to heart disease.

Cross-Sectional *A cross-sectional study design* is used to study a phenomenon across a wide group of participants. Unlike longitudinal studies, cross-sectional designs require less time because they measure each participant or groups of participants only once, rather than taking multiple measures from the same participants over time. If conducting a cross-sectional version of the Framingham study, for example, researchers would obtain measures of the occurrence of heart disease from many groups of men and women of different ages. But, they would measure each participant only once.

The advantages of a cross-sectional design are shorter duration and less cost. The disadvantage, however, is the use of multiple subject groups, which introduces more variability in the results due to possible individual or subject differences.

Intervention Studies

Intervention studies occupy a unique position in research design. They can be either experimental or quasi-experimental, depending on the study question. We will examine experimental intervention studies first and discuss quasi-experimental intervention studies in the following section on quasi-experimental design.

Intervention studies are used often in research on health issues because they test the extent to which an intervention (a special program, therapeutic treatment, or training) improves health outcomes. Here, improvements can be defined as enhancements in knowledge, attitudes, or behaviors or measurable changes in physical or mental health.

In intervention studies, participants are given a *pretest* or *baseline measure* to assess their knowledge, performance, or physical or mental status before the intervention. The study group is then given an intervention followed by a second assessment that is identical to or much like the first. The experimental group's performance on the first (pre) and second (post) assessment are compared to determine the effects, if any, of the intervention on the dependent variable specified

BOX 2.1   The Framingham Heart Study: A Longitudinal Design

Would you be willing to participate in a longitudinal study that followed you for life for the benefit of science?

It may sound like an unusual proposition, but in 1949 5,127 men and women, ages 30 to 60, agreed to become the first **cohort**, or group, of people to participate in the Framingham Heart Study. Researchers decided to choose Framingham, Massachusetts—hence the name of the study—for two reasons. First, Framingham was the site of a previous, and successful, community-based study. Second, Framingham was close to several major medical research centers (Splansky et al., 2007).

The researchers were primarily interested in identifying the personal habits and traits that contributed to the development of coronary heart disease (see Chapter 9, Cardiovascular Disease). Therefore, when recruiting the sample of eligible participants, researchers obtained baseline, or initial, health measures on each person. Only individuals with no prior history of heart disease were eligible for the study. This was a key **eligibility criterion**. Researchers wanted to ensure that heart disease was not a preexisting condition of any of the participants. After enrolling in the study, each participant was reassessed every two years for the duration of the study. During the first 20-year reassessment period, a number of study participants developed heart disease.

Although important, the fact that some of the over 5,000 individuals developed heart disease was not the most significant finding. Rather, the important discovery was that, for the first time, researchers were able to demonstrate an association between coronary artery disease and individual as well as environmental causes. Specifically, researchers demonstrated that high blood pressure, excessive body weight, high cholesterol (related in part to dietary habits), lack of physical activity, a smoking habit, and diabetes, among other factors, significantly increased the chances of heart disease. And individuals who had two or more of the associated characteristics were at a higher risk of heart disease than those who only reported one such factor (Anderson, Odell, Wilson, & Kannel, 1991; Dawber & Kannel, 1966; Kannel et al., 1964).

These findings may not seem surprising to us today because many of the individual and environmental causes of heart disease are well known. However, one reason we know the risk factors for heart disease is because of the Framingham study. Remember, the Framingham study began in the late 1940s. The first results were published in the 1950s when little was known about the risk factors for coronary heart disease.

The Framingham study continues even today. It monitors some participants from the original cohort and now includes second- and even third-generation offspring of the original group. The information about the heart histories of relatives of the original cohort, including individuals who did and did not develop heart disease, will provide additional information about genetic as well as individual and environmental factors that contribute to heart disease (Splansky et al., 2007). Most important, however, the results of this study have provided valuable information to medical doctors. The findings have assisted and will continue to aid doctors in determining their patients' risk for heart disease—something they could not do without such a detailed, longitudinal study.

TABLE 2.3	Sample Pre-Posttest Design		
Participants	**Phase I**	**Phase II**	**Phase III**
Experimental group	Pretest	Intervention	Posttest
Control group	Pretest	No intervention	Posttest

for the study. Studies that include a pretest followed by an intervention and conclude with a *posttest* are also known as ***pretest-posttest studies***, or ***pre-posttest***, for short (see Table 2.3).

One important consideration for researchers when designing interventions studies is whether to use a control group. We introduced the term *control group* in the preceding section on experimental versus control groups (page 43). Control groups allow the researchers to determine whether the performance of study participants, as measured by the dependent variable, is influenced by the experimental treatment (the intervention). Thus, an intervention study in health psychology that uses an experimental and a control group would enable researchers to determine the effectiveness of the health intervention on participants' health status. As we will see shortly, intervention studies that do not include control groups limit researchers' ability to determine the true effectiveness of the intervention.

Ethical Considerations in Experimental Design

Pre-posttest interventions designs are used also in randomized clinical trial studies. ***Randomized clinical trials*** use one control and at least one experimental group to test the effects of a new medication, a therapeutic approach, or an apparatus as a treatment for a medical or mental illness. The Johns Hopkins study of asthma, discussed in the opening story, was designed as a randomized clinical trial. Ms. Roche, the research participant who died, was assigned to the experimental group.

One caveat to randomized clinical trials should be noted, especially for health psychology research. As we saw in the opening story, research studies that test the effectiveness of new drugs pose clear risks to participants. For this reason, the FDA requires that new drugs undergo several stages of testing, beginning with laboratory tests, followed by tests on laboratory animals, moving on to tests on people only in the later stages of development. The process can take years.

Because of the lengthy process, some researchers and health advocates argue for a different testing procedure for evaluating the benefits of new and potentially lifesaving drugs (Richter & Lindegger, 2000; U.S. Food & Drug Administration, 2007). Their arguments are based, in part, on ethical concerns. For example, health advocates who challenged the use of control groups in pre-posttest studies of new HIV/AIDS drugs contend that control group participants experience a delay in receiving a potentially lifesaving drug, if they receive the drug at all. They claim that the additional time needed to confirm the drug's effectiveness delays the potential benefits for people who need the new drug (South African AIDS Vaccine Initiative, 2007; Strode, Slack, & Mushariwa, 2005; U.S. Food and Drug Administration, 2007).

The ethical arguments pose problems for randomized clinical trial designs. On the one hand, researchers must ensure that the new drugs are effective, are safe, and do not cause life-threatening complications. Such testing takes time. On the other hand, the time needed to

BOX 2.2   The Stanford Three Community Study: An Intervention Study with Three Communities

The Stanford Three Community Study is another example of an intervention study, although shorter in duration than the Framingham study. The Stanford study also examined heart disease; however, its goal was to examine the effect of several types of interventions on risk reduction for heart disease (Meyer et al., 1980). Specifically, Meyers and coauthors (1980) wanted to determine whether mass media campaigns and intensive individualized instruction reduced individuals' risk of heart disease.

To test their hypotheses, the researchers chose three communities in California—Watsonville, Gilroy, and Tracy—that fulfilled the study's eligibility criteria. In the Stanford study, researchers determined that the participants from the three communities should be comparable on three demographic categories: age, ethnicity, and socioeconomic status. In addition, all communities needed to meet eligibility criteria. These three communities were eligible because they had community media (television and newspaper), were in close proximity to Stanford University (the host site for the study), and lacked community-based health education programs.

In the study, researchers obtained baseline information on the health status, health habits, and risk factors for cardiovascular diseases for participants in each of the three cities. One community in the study, Tracy, served as the control site. Residents of Tracy received no intervention, here meaning no mass media and no individualized instruction on cardiovascular health. Residents of Watsonville were assigned to an experimental condition that included both the mass media and individualized instruction. Gilroy residents, the second experimental group, received only the mass media communication intervention. The results of the intervention study suggested that the mass media campaign was successful in changing health behaviors and in lowering the risks for cardiovascular disease.

The results of the Stanford Three Community Study demonstrated the effectiveness of mass media in changing health behaviors and reducing the risk of health disease. By using both experimental and control groups, researchers demonstrated that mass media campaigns, as opposed to just individualized instruction or no intervention at all, helped reduce the risks of heart disease.

In addition, this study demonstrated that researchers could conduct a longitudinal, **community-based study**, like the Framingham Heart Study, to understand the health behaviors that increase the risks of heart disease. Studies like the Stanford study are referred to as community-based studies because they measure the impact of an intervention in the participants' natural environment rather than in a laboratory or other environments constructed for the study.

complete all testing procedures delays the distribution of potentially life-saving drugs. What would you suggest to researchers testing a potentially lifesaving drug for HIV/AIDS?

One way to address the ethical dilemma is through a *pre-post-post-test design*. In this design both the experimental and control groups would receive the actual treatment, although not at the same time. For example, when testing a potentially lifesaving or life-prolonging drug for

Participants	Pretest	First intervention	Posttest	Second intervention	Post-post-test
Experimental group (A)	A	A	A	———	A
Control group (B)	B	———	B	B	B

TABLE 2.4   Sample Pre-Post-Post-Test Design

HIV/AIDS, the pre-post-post-test design for one control and one experimental group could be administered as shown in Table 2.4.

Essentially, the experimental and control groups both get the drug, referred to here as the intervention. The only difference is the timing of the intervention. Here, the experimental (A) and the control (B) groups get the pretest at the same time. The experimental group gets the intervention drug first, and the control group's intervention is delayed. Control group members will receive the intervention only after receiving a pretest and the first posttest. A second posttest is administered after the delayed intervention.

How does the pre-post-post-test design address the ethical concerns while also addressing the need for carefully controlled experimental studies? Put it this way: Using the pre-post-post-test design, researchers ensure that both groups (experimental and control) get the drug. But, with a minimal delay in administering the drug to the control group, researchers can still conduct a drug versus no-drug comparison to test the drug's safety and effectiveness.

Quasi-Experimental Intervention Studies

Up to this point our discussion on research design included independent variables that could be controlled by the experimenter. But, in truth, health researchers cannot control many of the factors that affect the health conditions they wish to study. Variables such as gender, age, or ethnicity are not subject to experimenter control. Thus, when conducting research, health researchers must design studies that take into consideration their lack of full control over the independent variables. The solution is to use a modified methodological approach known as a *quasi-experimental design*.

Although a quasi-experimental design adjusts for the fact that researchers cannot always control each independent variable, the adjustment comes at a price. The inability to control some independent variables means that researchers are not able to demonstrate a direct cause-and-effect relationship between the independent variable and the dependent variable or outcomes. In other words, accommodating life's realities in the quasi-experimental design comes at the price of certainty.

Quasi-experimental intervention studies differ from experimental studies in another respect: They do not include control groups. In some quasi-experimental designs, a control group may be unnecessary if a researcher is interested only in the impact of an intervention on the study participants. In such cases, all participants are assigned to the same condition. However, without a control group, the researcher loses the ability to compare outcomes of the intervention to another group. Absent this comparison, researchers cannot claim a cause-and-effect relationship, nor can they generalize their findings to a larger population.

Summary

Health psychologists may use a number of different research methods to explore the health status or changes in health outcomes of a specific study sample. These include qualitative studies such as case studies, focus groups, and interviews, as well as experimental studies that may rely on pre-posttest, pre-post-post-test, random clinical trials or longitudinal or cross-sectional methodology. Health researchers can also use quasi-experimental designs that employ a modified version of the techniques used in experimental studies. The choice of research methods will be determined by the hypothesis or research questions posed by the researcher and the type of data to be collected.

SECTION III. RESEARCH ETHICS AND POLICY

We began this chapter on research methods with a story describing the death of a research subject in a Johns Hopkins study on asthma. The story illustrated two important points about conducting research. First, all research using human subjects is governed by regulations that define ethical research practices. Second, research volunteers may experience real and severe consequences when researchers fail to follow the regulations.

To understand some of the problems posed by the Johns Hopkins study and to prepare for our discussion on research ethics, we reviewed research concepts and methods in Sections I and II. We can now continue our examination of research ethics and researchers' responsibilities introduced in the opening story.

Reactions to the Word *Research*

What do you think when you hear the word *research*? For some people, the word brings to mind experimenters in white lab coats or research volunteers viewing images projected on screens. Perhaps your views on research were influenced by firsthand experiences, by books, or by movies. Some people associate research with outcomes such as advancements in science or new lifesaving discoveries. Yet others may view research as abuse, involving the mistreatment of subjects or the use of people as human "guinea pigs."

Which view of research is most accurate? The history of research in the United States and other countries provides ample evidence that research has made significant contributions to society. Unfortunately, it is also true that a small number of research studies have caused fatal injury or harm to participants. We begin this section by examining two studies, each of which caused harm to its participants in distinctly different ways. The famous *Tuskegee Syphilis Study*, conducted in the United States from 1932 through 1972, is an example of an egregious breech of research ethics that caused irreparable harm to the medical and mental health of the participants.

By contrast, Philip Zimbardo's *Study of Interpersonal Dynamics* (sometimes referred to as the *Stanford prison experiment*) in social situations caused no physical harm to the participants but raised concerns about the potential of studies to cause psychological or emotional injury. During our discussion of the Tuskegee and Zimbardo studies, we will identify the historical events that lead to the establishment of the codes of conduct for human research. These include the Nuremberg Codes, the Declaration of Human Rights, and the Declaration of Helsinki. You will become familiar with the U.S. National Research Act of 1974 and the Belmont Report. Finally, we will review the three fundamental principles for the protection of human subjects: respect for persons, beneficence, and justice.

The Tuskegee Syphilis Study

The Tuskegee Syphilis Study employed two unethical procedures: deception and disregard for the rights and welfare of human subjects in experiments. This longitudinal study was designed initially as a nine-month investigation to examine the course of syphilis and its impact on neurological functioning. Unfortunately, it evolved into a 40-year experiment following its "volunteers" to their deaths. The volunteers were not informed that the goal of the study was to demonstrate the neurological impact of syphilis on the brain. Nor did they know that the demonstration could be accomplished only by autopsies. To be clear, an autopsy is conducted on an individual after death. Thus, the volunteers in the Tuskegee study were unaware that they were expected to die to fulfill the goals of the study. The details of the deception by government agencies, educational institutions, medical care providers, researchers, local institutions, and individuals are provided in Box 2.3.

Dr. John Heller, the Director of Venereal Diseases at the United States Public Health Service from 1943 to 1948, rationalized the deception employed by members of the Tuskegee study research team by stating that "the [study participants'] status did not warrant ethical debate. *They were subjects, not patient[s], clinical material, not sick people*" (italics added) (Jones, 1981). The Tuskegee study was terminated 40 years later in 1972, four years after the Civil Rights Act of 1968, when it was brought to the attention of the public through a newspaper article in the *Washington Star* and other publications, thereby provoking a public outcry (Jones, 1981; Thomas & Quinn, 1991).

FIGURE 2.5 Veterans Administration Hospital, Tuskegee, Alabama. Site of autopsies for Tuskegee study victims.

BOX 2.3 Syphilis Victims in U.S. Study Went Untreated for 40 Years

. . . the longest non-therapeutic experiment on human beings in medical history . . . (Jones, 1981)

In the late 1920s, a group of researchers wanted to observe the effects of syphilis on different races. Some researchers theorized that untreated syphilis in its *latent*, or non-contagious, stage affects races differently. Some proposed that, for blacks, syphilis affected the cardiovascular system, while others contended that syphilis in whites affected their neurological systems (Jones, 1981; Thomas & Quinn, 1991). Research published in Norway at about the same time demonstrated that untreated syphilis caused cardiovascular damage and not neurological damage in whites. Yet, this finding ran counter to popular theories in the United States at the time.

Concurrent with ongoing research, the Rosenwald Fund designed a demonstration study to improve the health status of and health care delivery to African Americans in rural southern counties in the United States (Parran, 1937). The purpose of the study was to show the feasibility of testing and treating rural African Americans for syphilis. The first stage of the study revealed that approximately 40% of all groups tested in Macon County, Alabama, tested positive for syphilis. Consistent with the treatment goals, the study sought to make the standard treatment for syphilis available to African Americans in rural communities: injections of arsenical compounds and mercury or bismuth ointments that were applied to the skin (Tuskegee Syphilis Study Legacy Committee, 1996). The treatment program was to be a collaborative effort between the Rosenwald Fund and the United States Public Health Service (USPHS).

Unfortunately, 1929–1930 coincided with the beginning of the Great Depression in the United States. Like other philanthropic organizations, the Rosenwald Fund lost its endowment in the economic crash of the 1930s. Without the financial support of the Rosenwald Fund, the USPHS could not afford to conduct the proposed public health program. If, however, the program were redesigned as a scientific experiment, the U.S. government could fund the project. So, in 1932 the USPHS began a research study to document the long-term consequences of syphilis. The goal of the study, however, differed from the goal of the program proposed by the Rosenwald Fund. The USPHS study was not designed to provide medical testing and treatment to rural African Americans; rather, it proposed to study the effects of untreated syphilis, following the study subjects to the "endpoint," in essence, to their death.

The USPHS service enlisted the help of many local and state agencies and individuals to find and recruit rural African American men in Macon County. Included among the organizations that assisted researchers conducting the study were the Macon County Medical Society, the Tuskegee Institute, the Boards of Health in the state of Alabama and in Macon County, the Milbank Memorial Fund, as well as some leaders of local black churches and public schools, and plantation owners (Thomas & Quinn, 1991). Using trusted institutions and individuals as recruitment agents proved very successful for the USPHS study. In the end, 399 men were recruited with another 201 participants serving as the control group.

The approximately 400 experimental and 200 control group participants were not told the true aim of the study. This was the first deception. In addition, they were not told that they tested positive for syphilis. Rather they were told simply that they had "bad blood," a generic term common in the rural South used to describe all forms of general ailments (Jones, 1981). Thus the second deception was inaccurate information given to the men about their health status. In fact, the men did not know that untreated, their illnesses would result in death. With no access to other health care facilities, the men also had no ability to seek alternative care.

When penicillin became available as a more effective treatment for syphilis, the men were not given the new treatment as part of the study. In fact, they were not advised that a new, more effective treatment for syphilis existed. Worse still, the USPHS took measures to ensure that the study participants would not be given penicillin. Ironically, during the course of the study, 50 study participants received letters from their local military draft boards as part of their conscription for military service, requiring them to take penicillin to treat their syphilis infections. Interestingly, through an agreement between the USPHS and the draft board, these 50 men were exempted from the therapeutic treatment and from military service (Jones, 1981).

In 1966 Peter Buxtun, an investigator with the Public Health Service, raised moral and ethical concerns about the Tuskegee study. After several letters to Dr. Brown, the Director of Venereal Diseases at the time, the Centers for Disease Control and Prevention decided to convene a panel in 1969 to review the study. Ultimately the panel decided not to treat the Tuskegee syphilis study participants and to permit the Tuskegee study to continue (Thomas & Quinn, 1991). The Tuskegee study ended in 1972 only after Buxtun reported the study and his concerns to the Associated Press. It then appeared as the front-page story in the *Washington Star* on July 25, 1972. A second newspaper, *The New York Times,* followed with a full-page story the next day.

The final tragedy of this study involves more than deception and the deliberate withholding of lifesaving health care for study participants. The study may have caused physical harm to the participants' spouses and unborn children. Due to imprecise study protocol, it was impossible to ensure that all participants were diagnosed with latent syphilis—a less contagious stage of the disease. In essence, it is likely that many of the participants exposed and infected their spouses, their in-utero children, or both to the disease (Hammonds, 1994).

In retrospect, we should ask the following questions about the Tuskegee study. How could this abuse happen? Two factors contributed to this abuse: placing the quest of knowledge above the well-being of human subject participants and failing to regulate and to monitor the conduct of research involving human subjects.

Who let this happen? Society and the community at large contributed to this outcome. The list of agencies and individuals who recruited people for the study demonstrates that such abuses require cooperation from many individuals. The responsibility was shared by individuals, communities, religious leaders, and government institutions. However, the greatest responsibility lies with those with full knowledge of the design and purpose of the study.

The Tuskegee experiment was not the first use of human subjects as "clinical material, not . . . people." Medical records in the United States document smaller-scale yet no less disturbing abuses of individual rights in the name of research in the early to mid-1800s. For example, in Georgia in the early 1800s, a physician, Thomas Hamilton, conducted tests on African slaves in the United States to find a treatment for heatstroke (Boney, 1967). In one series of experiments, Hamilton placed a stool in a pit approximately three feet deep. He sat one of his slaves on this stool, naked, such that only his head was above ground while Hamilton fed the slave different medications to test treatments for heatstroke (Boney, 1967). During this same time period, another physician, James Marion Sims, a pioneer in the field of gynecology, experimented on slaves by performing over 30 operations to develop a procedure for repairing vesicovaginal fistulas. Each operation was done without the benefit of anesthesia, although anesthesia was widely available.

In retrospect, it seems obvious that the Tuskegee study and the lesser-known medical experiments placed scientific curiosity above the well-being of humans. They exposed all participants to serious risks, including death. If we are able to recognize the risks and danger to "study participants," you might ask why others failed to recognize the same. A thorough analysis of the reasons such practices were permitted is beyond the scope of this book. But in 1946, midway through the Tuskegee experiment, abuse of human subjects in the name of science was brought to the attention of several national and international organizations.

The Nuremberg Code of 1947

Attention to the abuse of human subjects was prompted by discoveries at the end of World War II. Military personnel from the United States and Western European countries released survivors, largely Jews, from concentration camps run by the Third Reich, the ruling government in Germany at the time. The military, largely U.S. and Allied forces that liberated the camps, learned that many detainees of the camps were used as subjects in medical experiments in the name of science. The experiments included studies on procedures to change eye color by injecting chemicals into eye sockets, forced sterilization, and the effects of starvation on the livers of "volunteers." When the experiments were revealed to the world, a U.S. military tribunal convened an international court known as the Nuremberg trials.

THE NUREMBERG TRIALS AND OUTCOMES One purpose of the Nuremberg trials was to try the doctors and other persons responsible for conducting such research. One outcome of the Nuremberg trials was the *Nuremberg Code* of 1947, a list of 10 conditions that regulated the use of human subjects in research (NIH, 2004) (Box 2.4). The Nuremberg Code was the first formal document defining the rules of conduct for research involving human subjects. Later, the Nuremberg Code was incorporated into the Declaration of Human Rights, a document developed and approved by the 51 original signers of the Charter of the United Nations. In 1964, the World Medical Society broadened the scope of the Nuremberg Code and the Declaration of Human Rights by adopting the *Declaration of Helsinki*: Recommendations Guiding Medical Doctors in Biomedical Research Involving Human Subjects (Box 2.5). The documents have been revised several times, most recently in 2000.

In 1953, to monitor research in the United States involving human subjects, the U.S. National Institutes of Health (NIH) established an Institutional Review Board (IRB). The IRB is a system of national and local research review boards responsible for ensuring the protection of

BOX 2.4   The Nuremberg Code of 1947

1. The voluntary consent of the human subject is absolutely essential. This means that the person involved should have legal capacity to give consent; should be so situated as to be able to exercise free power of choice, without the intervention of any element of force, fraud, deceit, duress, over-reaching, or other ulterior form of constraint or coercion; and should have sufficient knowledge and comprehension of the elements of the subject matter involved as to enable him to make an understanding and enlightened decision. This latter element requires that before the acceptance of an affirmative decision by the experimental subject there should be made known to him the nature, duration, and purpose of the experiment; the method and means by which it is to be conducted; all inconveniences and hazards reasonable to be expected; and the effects upon his health or person which may possibly come from his participation in the experiment. The duty and responsibility for ascertaining the quality of the consent rests upon each individual who initiates, directs or engages in the experiment. It is a personal duty and responsibility which may not be delegated to another with impunity.

2. The experiment should be such as to yield fruitful results for the good of society, unprocurable by other methods or means of study, and not random and unnecessary in nature.

3. The experiment should be so designed and based on the results of animal experimentation and a knowledge of the natural history of the disease or other problem under study that the anticipated results will justify the performance of the experiment.

4. The experiment should be so conducted as to avoid all unnecessary physical and mental suffering and injury.

5. No experiment should be conducted where there is an a priori reason to believe that death or disabling injury will occur; except, perhaps, in those experiments where the experimental physicians also serve as subjects.

6. The degree of risk to be taken should never exceed that determined by the humanitarian importance of the problem to be solved by the experiment.

7. Proper preparations should be made and adequate facilities provided to protect the experimental subject against even remote possibilities of injury, disability, or death.

8. The experiment should be conducted only by scientifically qualified persons. The highest degree of skill and care should be required through all stages of the experiment of those who conduct or engage in the experiment.

9. During the course of the experiment the human subject should be at liberty to bring the experiment to an end if he has reached the physical or mental state where continuation of the experiment seems to him to be impossible.

10. During the course of the experiment the scientist in charge must be prepared to terminate the experiment at any stage, if he has probable cause to believe, in the exercise of the good faith, superior skill and careful judgment required of him that a continuation of the experiment is likely to result in injury, disability, or death to the experimental subject.

Retrieved from the Office of Human Subjects Research (http://ohrs.od.nih.gov/guidelines/nuremberg .html)

BOX 2.5   Excerpts from the World Medical Association Declaration of Helsinki

WORLD MEDICAL ASSOCIATION DECLARATION OF HELSINKI

Ethical Principles for Medical Research Involving Human Subjects

Adopted by the 18th WMA General Assembly, Helsinki, Finland, June 1964, and amended by the

29th WMA General Assembly, Tokyo, Japan, October 1975

35th WMA General Assembly, Venice, Italy, October 1983

41st WMA General Assembly, Hong Kong, September 1989

48th WMA General Assembly, Somerset West, Republic of South Africa, October 1996

and the 52nd WMA General Assembly, Edinburgh, Scotland, October 2000

Note of Clarification on Paragraph 29 added by the WMA General Assembly, Washington 2002

Note of Clarification on Paragraph 30 added by the WMA General Assembly, Tokyo 2004

A. INTRODUCTION

1. The World Medical Association has developed the Declaration of Helsinki as a statement of ethical principles to provide guidance to physicians and other participants in medical research involving human subjects. Medical research involving human subjects includes research on identifiable human material or identifiable data.

2. The Declaration of Geneva of the World Medical Association binds the physician with the words, "The health of my patient will be my first consideration," and the International Code of Medical Ethics declares that, "A physician shall act only in the patient's interest when providing medical care which might have the effect of weakening the physical and mental condition of the patient."

3. In medical research on human subjects, considerations related to the well-being of the human subject should take precedence over the interests of science and society.

4. The primary purpose of medical research involving human subjects is to improve prophylactic, diagnostic and therapeutic procedures and the understanding of the aetiology and pathogenesis of disease. Even the best proven prophylactic, diagnostic, and therapeutic methods must continuously be challenged through research for their effectiveness, efficiency, accessibility and quality.

5. Medical research is subject to ethical standards that promote respect for all human beings and protect their health and rights. Some research populations are vulnerable and need special protection. The particular needs of the economically and medically disadvantaged must be recognized. Special attention is also required for those who cannot give or refuse consent for themselves, for those who may be subject to giving consent under duress, for those who will not benefit personally from the research and for those for whom the research is combined with care.

6. Research Investigators should be aware of the ethical, legal and regulatory requirements for research on human subjects in their own countries as well as applicable international requirements. No national ethical, legal or regulatory requirement should be allowed to reduce or eliminate any of the protections for human subjects set forth in this Declaration.

B. BASIC PRINCIPLES FOR ALL MEDICAL RESEARCH

1. Medical research involving human subjects must conform to generally accepted scientific principles, be based on a thorough knowledge of the scientific literature, other relevant sources of information, and on adequate laboratory and, where appropriate, animal experimentation.

2. Appropriate caution must be exercised in the conduct of research which may affect the environment, and the welfare of animals used for research must be respected.

3. The design and performance of each experimental procedure involving human subjects should be clearly formulated in an experimental protocol. This protocol should be submitted for consideration, comment, guidance, and where appropriate, approval to a specially appointed ethical review committee, which must be independent of the investigator, the sponsor or any other kind of undue influence. This independent committee should be in conformity with the laws and regulations of the country in which the research experiment is performed. The committee has the right to monitor ongoing trials. The researcher has the obligation to provide monitoring information to the committee, especially any serious adverse events. The researcher should also submit to the committee, for review, information regarding funding, sponsors, institutional affiliations, other potential conflicts of interest and incentives for subjects.

4. Medical research involving human subjects should be conducted only by scientifically qualified persons and under the supervision of a clinically competent medical person. The responsibility for the human subject must always rest with a medically qualified person and never rest on the subject of the research, even though the subject has given consent.

5. Physicians should abstain from engaging in research projects involving human subjects unless they are confident that the risks involved have been adequately assessed and can be satisfactorily managed. Physicians should cease any investigation if the risks are found to outweigh the potential benefits or if there is conclusive proof of positive and beneficial results.

6. Medical research involving human subjects should only be conducted if the importance of the objective outweighs the inherent risks and burdens to the subject. This is especially important when the human subjects are healthy volunteers.

7. Medical research is only justified if there is a reasonable likelihood that the populations in which the research is carried out stand to benefit from the results of the research.

8. In any research on human beings, each potential subject must be adequately informed of the aims, methods, sources of funding, any possible conflicts of interest, institutional affiliations of the researcher, the anticipated benefits and

(continued)

potential risks of the study and the discomfort it may entail. The subject should be informed of the right to abstain from participation in the study or to withdraw consent to participate at any time without reprisal. After ensuring that the subject has understood the information, the physician should then obtain the subject's freely-given informed consent, preferably in writing. If the consent cannot be obtained in writing, the non-written consent must be formally documented and witnessed.

9. When obtaining informed consent for the research project the physician should be particularly cautious if the subject is in a dependent relationship with the physician or may consent under duress. In that case the informed consent should be obtained by a well-informed physician who is not engaged in the investigation and who is completely independent of this relationship.

10. Research on individuals from whom it is not possible to obtain consent, including proxy or advance consent, should be done only if the physical/mental condition that prevents obtaining informed consent is a necessary characteristic of the research population. The specific reasons for involving research subjects with a condition that renders them unable to give informed consent should be stated in the experimental protocol for consideration and approval of the review committee. The protocol should state that consent to remain in the research should be obtained as soon as possible from the individual or a legally authorized surrogate.

C. ADDITIONAL PRINCIPLES FOR MEDICAL RESEARCH COMBINED WITH MEDICAL CARE

1. The benefits, risks, burdens and effectiveness of a new method should be tested against those of the best current prophylactic, diagnostic, and therapeutic methods. This does not exclude the use of placebo, or no treatment, in studies where no proven prophylactic, diagnostic or therapeutic method exists.

2. At the conclusion of the study, every patient entered into the study should be assured of access to the best proven prophylactic, diagnostic and therapeutic methods identified by the study.

3. In the treatment of a patient, where proven prophylactic, diagnostic and therapeutic methods do not exist or have been ineffective, the physician, with informed consent from the patient, must be free to use unproven or new prophylactic, diagnostic and therapeutic measures, if in the physician's judgement it offers hope of saving life, re-establishing health or alleviating suffering. Where possible, these measures should be made the object of research, designed to evaluate their safety and efficacy. In all cases, new information should be recorded and, where appropriate, published. The other relevant guidelines of this Declaration should be followed.

human subjects in research studies. The NIH defines research as "any systematic investigation designed to develop or contribute to generalizable knowledge" (NIH, 2004), and "human subjects" are defined as living individuals from whom researchers propose to obtain information (data) through intervention with the person (NIH, 2004).

The American Psychological Association (APA) joined the efforts to protect the rights of volunteers in research by establishing codes of ethical standards for psychologists. The 1958 version of the APA standards for ethical behaviors for psychologists cautioned that conducting research with serious after effects is possible only when the participant or someone authorized to speak on that person's behalf is fully informed (Committee on Ethical Standards of Psychologists, 1958). A revised code of conduct added that psychology researchers were required to show respect for the rights and dignity of individuals, concern for others' welfare, and social responsibility to human subjects in experiment (American Psychological Association, 1992). While the guidelines are not legally binding, they are enforceable by the APA and, if breached, can lead to loss of membership.

In spite of the guidelines, however, occasionally a study is conducted that does not adhere to the rules. The Johns Hopkins asthma study is one example. Another is the Zimbardo Stanford prison experiment.

Study of Interpersonal Dynamics (Stanford Prison Experiment)

As early as 1964, over 51 countries, including the United States, endorsed the code of conduct for use of human subjects in research. But in 1971 Philip Zimbardo designed a two-week study on interpersonal dynamics (Haney, Banks, & Zimbardo, 1973; Zimbardo, 1973) and sought to determine whether social contexts can influence, alter, shape, or transform human behavior (Haney & Zimbardo, 1998). Zimbardo's intent was to contribute to the then current research by examining the role of institutional environments in influencing the behaviors of persons.

Briefly, 24 male Stanford University students volunteered to participate in Zimbardo's Stanford prison experiment. They were randomly assigned to one of two roles, prison warden or prisoner. Prisoners were assigned to live in a mock prison for the full two weeks while wardens worked eight-hour shifts "guarding" the prisoners for the duration of the study. The two-week study was terminated after only the sixth day due to the prisoners' demonstrable and extreme psychological trauma and to the increasingly hostile and abusive behavior of the wardens. Box 2.6 provides more detail.

In essence, Zimbardo's research question was answered in just six days. "Bad" social contexts or environments can alter the behavior of otherwise "good" people and, apparently, quicker than he thought. How is it possible that two studies, one ongoing (Tuskegee) and another just beginning (Zimbardo), were conducted at the same time that the world was enacting regulations for the ethical conduct of research with human subjects? There are two possible explanations. First, the Zimbardo study was a social psychological study. Specifically, Zimbardo examined the effect of conformity expectations on people in institutional settings. The intent of the research and its design did not initially raise concerns about the potential harm to research participants, perhaps because there were few if any perceived risks of physical harm. In addition, some contend that Zimbardo's study was relevant to understanding human behavior given the events of World War II and the atrocities performed in the concentration camps. His study appeared to suggest that individuals may come to perform hostile or abusive behaviors when placed in a social context that permits or encourages such behaviors.

BOX 2.6 The Social Power of Groups and Conformity: The Stanford Prison Experiment

Picture this scenario: A group of college students volunteer for a two-week research study exploring the effects of social contexts on human behaviors. The study takes place in a mock prison. Half of the students are randomly assigned to play the role of prison warden, and the other half are assigned the role of prisoner. The prisoners live in a mock prison for the full two weeks while the wardens work daily eight-hour shifts for the duration of the study. The "wardens" are permitted to make up their own rules for keeping order among the prisoners with one exception: Physical abuse is not permitted. Suddenly, after only six days, the investigator ends the study. What do you think caused its abrupt halt?

Perhaps the following background information will help answer the question. In 1971, Philip Zimbardo designed a study to determine how social contexts can influence, shape, or transform human behavior. Specifically, Zimbardo questioned whether a "bad situation" can cause otherwise "good" people to act in ways inconsistent with their usual behavior. Zimbardo's Stanford prison experiment (SPE) was to test the research question. He converted the basement of Stanford's Psychology Department into a prison for the experiment. He then recruited 24 male Stanford University students to participate in the study. All students were screened to ensure they were physically and psychologically healthy with no history of criminal behavior. Zimbardo wanted to ensure that all participants were, in fact, "good" people (Zimbardo, 2007). After the screening, the 24 participants were randomly assigned one of two roles, prison warden or prisoner. Zimbardo played the role of the prison supervisor.

To make the experiment as realistic as possible, Zimbardo arranged for the participants assigned to the prisoner group to be "arrested" by the Palo Alto police department and brought to the mock prison at Stanford at the beginning of the study. The "prisoners" were processed using some of the same procedures used in an actual prison. They were given identity numbers, stripped naked, and deloused (Zimbardo, 2007).

Unexpectedly, on the second day of the experiment, the prisoners staged an unplanned rebellion. The prison wardens, determined to end the rebellion, chose to deal harshly with the "dangerous prisoners." Within four days, prison wardens were observed becoming verbally and psychologically abusive toward the prisoners. For example, some wardens punished the prisoners by chaining their legs, repeatedly disrupting prisoners' sleep at night, and making prisoners engage in humiliating activities billed as "fun and games" (Zimbardo, 2007).

By the fifth day of the experiment five of the student prisoners were allowed to end their participation because they suffered from extreme stress. In actuality, all prisoners had experienced psychological stress, trauma, and emotional breakdowns. The prisoner's changed emotional state was evident in their attitudes and demeanors. They became very compliant to the warden's hostile and abusive treatment.

Does this additional information provide clues that explain the abrupt termination of the study? There is one additional point. Zimbardo, the investigator and prison superintendent, initially did not realize the impact of the situation on the prisoners and the wardens. In fact, Zimbardo candidly confessed that he, along with visitors to the study while in progress, including colleagues, parents of the "imprisoned" college students, and a prison chaplain, did not question the impact of the study or the effect of the study on the student prisoners. So why did Zimbardo terminate the experiment?

Zimbardo credits a close friend who also visited the prison as the person who identified the study's dangers. After reviewing the friend's comments, Zimbardo realized that the mock prison environment had a profound affect on all participants, an impact far greater than either he or his colleagues imagined. In just six days a mock prison environment converted the 24 Stanford students into either hostile and abusive wardens or submissive, compliant, and stressed prisoners. The impetus for the change was the prisoners' rebellion, an act perceived as a threat to the wardens' authority. The response was an excessive use of power to dominate and suppress the powerless, in this case the prisoners.

Zimbardo's study found that a "bad" environment can have a profound impact on individuals. Even Zimbardo was affected. His inability to see the destructive effect of the mock prison setting on both groups of study participants was due, in part, to his role as the prison superintendent. The role conflicted with the investigator's responsibility to uphold the ethical standards of research.

The results of Zimbardo's study were indeed shocking. Yet, the investigator's decision to end the study and his candid assessment of the dangers posed by his work serves as an example of the ethical standards of researchers. Zimbardo did not intend to cause psychological injury to his study participants. But, when the injuries became apparent to him, he terminated the study. Today, Institutional Review Boards (IRBs) would not permit such a study. In the absence of IRBs, however, Zimbardo's actions are commendable.

The rationale for continuing the Tuskegee study for decades after the adoption of the Nuremberg Code is less clear, but may be linked to the U.S. regulations. Although in 1966 the NIH established policies for the protection of human subjects, the policies were not binding. They were elevated to the status of regulations, an enforceable set of codes, only in 1974, after the Tuskegee experiment and its abuses had been exposed nationally.

Following the public exposure of the Tuskegee experiment, the U.S. Senate Committee on Labor and Human Resources held hearings. Two of the outcomes from these hearings included the "National Research Act of 1974 that required the (then) Health, Education, and Welfare Department to [formalize and regulate] its policy for the protection of human subjects to [establish] the National Commission for the Protection of Human Subjects of Biomedical and Behavioral Research" (NIH, 2004).

The second outcome was the commission's final report, *The Belmont Report: Ethical Principles and Guidelines for the Protection of Human Subjects of Research*, published in 1979. The **Belmont Report** identified three fundamental, ethical principles for the protection of human subjects:

1. *Respect for persons*: Recognizing the dignity and autonomy of individuals and requiring special protection for people with diminished capacity.
2. *Beneficence*: Requiring researchers to protect individuals further by maximizing the potential benefits and minimizing the potential harm or injury to them as research participants.

3. *Justice*: Requiring the fair and just treatment of participants, including the absence of bias in selection for or exclusion from research.

The new federal regulations, in addition to the Institutional Review Boards required at all major medical, academic, and other research centers, signaled the desire of the U.S. government and researchers to prevent the atrocities that occurred in Macon County, Alabama, as well as the debatable research ethics in Palo Alto, California, at Stanford University.

It is tempting to conclude here with the hope that no other abuses since then have been or will be committed. Unfortunately, in 1993, then U.S. Energy Secretary Hazel O'Leary discovered, in the Energy Department archives, records of U.S. government experiments involving the use of radiation on U.S. residents from 1945 through the early 1980s (Tisdall, 1993). Ms. O'Leary noted that due to a "culture of deception" these activities remained hidden in files. The experiments included over 200 underground nuclear tests conducted in the United States between 1963 and 1990. Eighteen of these experiments occurred during the 1980s. While the records confirm the tests, no information is available at present that explains the reasons for the tests or the need for their secrecy (Tisdall, 1993).

The main point here is that research abuses demonstrate the need to establish regulations and regulatory bodies that protect the health and well-being of study participants. Today, the vast majority of research studies are safe. Federal, state, and local regulations concerning the use of human subjects are effective in preventing research that will not protect the study participants. It is not true, however, that occasionally studies that are not in compliance with the regulations do take place. Yet, as we noted previously, many good and ethical studies are conducted and contribute to our understanding of health-enhancing and health-promoting behaviors. Therefore, at the conclusion of this chapter, we suggest ways to ensure that you can participate safely in research studies, should you desire.

Research without Informed Consent

Does this section title seem confusing? We reviewed several extreme examples of abuses in research with human subjects, some of which pertained to the conduct of research on individuals without their informed consent. In fact, we just reviewed a number of regulations and codes that specified the need for informed consent. What is left to say?

The World Medical Association (WMA) in 1964 (revised as of 2000) stated that research is permissible on individuals from whom it is not possible to obtain consent *only if* the physical or mental condition that prevents research subjects from giving informed consent is a necessary characteristic of the research population (WMA, 2000). In essence, the WMA states that in limited instances, research on persons who are unconscious or have ***diminished mental capacity***, here meaning individuals who are unable to understand the research design and to give consent responsibly, is permissible if the persons' condition is due to their medical or mental illness and is a qualifying condition (eligibility criterion) for the study population. For example, when suffering a cardiac arrest a person instantly becomes unconscious. If researchers developed a drug to reverse the almost always fatal outcomes of cardiac arrests, they would not have an opportunity to obtain the consent of an unconscious cardiac arrest patient, someone who in this case is also a potential study participant, before testing the drug's effectiveness in reversing the fatal effects of a cardiac arrest. Emergency medical research on incapacitated persons is one example of a potentially lifesaving technique that must be tested on an eligible individual without his or her consent. To this end, the WMA developed broad guidelines for the conduct of this type of emergency medical or mental research with the expectation that individual countries would provide more specific regulations for such research.

In 1996, the United States established new regulations that state that emergency medical research may be conducted without informed consent if all of the following conditions have been met: The patient is experiencing a life-threatening condition for which existing treatments are deemed either unsatisfactory or unproven; further evidence is needed to determine an experimental treatment's safety or efficacy; the participant is incapable of consent due to his or her medical condition; intervention is necessary before an authorized representative can be consulted; and researchers have observed a number of special protections including "community consultation" (Schmidt, Delorio, & McClure, 2006). Many of these conditions can be demonstrated easily. The condition of "community consultation," however, is more problematic because the definition of "community" and its role and authority in decision making is a hotly debated proposition (Ragin et al., 2007).

Summary

National and international research studies have exposed a host of problems relating to the ethical conduct of research. Many of the problems have been addressed through the establishment of regulatory bodies, such as Institutional Review Boards, the National Commission for the Protection of Human Subjects of Biomedical and Behavioral Research, and the World Medical Association of the World Health Organization. Regulations including the Nuremberg Code, *The Belmont Report: Ethical Principles and Guidelines for the Protection of Human Subjects of Research,* and U.S. federal regulations governing research without informed consent also were devised to guard against the abuse of human subjects. These governing bodies and regulations are effective but not fail proof, as we have seen. Therefore, the responsibility for the ethical conduct of research begins with the researcher.

Personal Postscript

RESEARCH STUDY NEEDS VOLUNTEERS: SHOULD YOU VOLUNTEER?

The next time you see a notice asking for volunteers for a study you might hesitate. After reading this chapter and learning about the Tuskegee study, Zimbardo's social contexts and human behavior, the Johns Hopkins study, the U.S. radiation experiments, and other abuses you might wonder whether it is safe to participate.

While there is some risk involved in all experiments, the vast majority of studies pose little physical or psychological risks to participants. This chapter highlighted four studies that entailed risk to the participants. But, when considering the total number of studies conducted each year it becomes clear that such risks are rare. Nevertheless, there are some precautions every potential study participant should take before agreeing to volunteer for any study.

First, be sure to read the informed consent form carefully. The consent form should explain in clear terms the activities required of each participant, as well as the risks and benefits of participating.

Second, be sure to ask questions if anything is unclear. The researcher is responsible for ensuring that all study participants understand the information presented in the consent form as well as the tasks to be performed.

Third, sign the consent form only if you understand the tasks involved and have had a chance to ask any questions you have about the study.

Fourth, insist on receiving a copy of the consent form. The experimenter should provide this automatically; but, if not, remember to request a copy.

Fifth, study participants may discontinue their involvement *at any time* and *for any reason*. This, too, should be written in the consent form because it is a right of all study participants, regardless of the nature of the study.

Finally, if interested, request a copy of the results of the study when they are available. Researchers rarely share the raw data but can make available summaries of the main findings. Be patient, though. It may take several months or even years before results are ready and can be disseminated to the public.

Participating in a research study can be fun and informative, but do follow the steps outlined for your protection.

Important Terms

adverse event   29
atrial septal defect   35
baseline measure   46
Belmont Report   61
case study   38
cause-and-effect
    relationship   43
closed-ended questions   39
cohort   46
community-based study   48
control group   43
correlational studies   40
cross-sectional study
    design   45
Declaration of Helsinki   54
dependent variable   43
diminished mental capacity   62
distal cause of illness   35
E. coli 0157:H7 bacterium   35
eligibility criterion   46
encephalitis   38
epidemiology   30
experimental group   43
experimental study   36
focus group   39

Framingham Heart Study   45
hexamethonium   29
hypertension   35
incidence   33
incidence rates   33
independent variable   43
infant mortality rate   31
intervention study   45
latent stage   52
longitudinal study design   44
morbidity   31
mortality   31
mortality rates   31
negative correlation   41
nonexperimental study   36
null hypothesis   43
Nuremberg code   54
Office for Human Research
    Protections   29
one-on-one interviews   39
open-ended questions   39
Pearson correlation
    coefficient (r)   40
positive correlation   40
posttest   47

predisposing factor   35
pre-post-post-test design   47
pre-posttest design   48
pretest-posttest design   49
pretest   45
prevalence   33
prevalence rates   33
proximal cause of illness   35
qualitative study   38
quasi-experimental design   49
quantitative data   38
random assignment   44
random sample   44
randomized clinical trial   47
rates   31
raw data   31
relative risk   33
research hypothesis   43
research without informed
    consent   63
retrospective analysis   40
Study of Interpersonal
    Dynamics (Stanford
    prison experiment)   50
Tuskegee Syphilis Study   50

Chapter Three

Global Communicable and Chronic Disease

Chapter Objectives

After studying this chapter you will be able to:

1. Define epidemics and pandemics.
2. Define communicable, recurring, and chronic diseases and give three examples of each.
3. Compare the health consequences of communicable diseases in developed versus developing countries.
4. Compare the health consequences of chronic diseases in developed versus developing countries.
5. Explain the role of chronic diseases in assessing quality of life.
6. Identify and describe the mission of three international health organizations.
7. Explain how health policy contributes to individual health outcomes.
8. Explain the effects of individual health outcomes on the family, community, society, and country.

OPENING STORY: MAN WITH DRUG-RESISTANT TUBERCULOSIS CAUSES INTERNATIONAL HEALTH SCARE

Andrew Speaker probably did not intend to cause an international health incident when traveling by plane in May 2007. He just wanted to attend his own wedding in Greece and then fly to Rome for his honeymoon. But Mr. Speaker faced a major obstacle. He was under medical care for **pulmonary tuberculosis,** *and he was advised not to travel (Markel, Gostin, & Fidler, 2007).* **Tuberculosis (TB)** *is a communicable disease that can be spread when TB germs, sometimes called* **bacilli,** *are propelled from a contagious person's cough, sneeze, talk, or spit, sending the TB germs airborne to other persons sharing the same airspace (CDC, 2007b; World Health Organization, 2007b).*

Mr. Speaker was first diagnosed and treated for pulmonary TB in March of 2007, but the treatment was ineffective. Why? It appears that Mr. Speaker had an extremely drug-resistant form of tuberculosis. His form of TB was resistant to the primary and secondary antibiotics used normally to treat TB. Given the seriousness of his illness and the highly contagious nature of the disease, on May 10, 2007, public health authorities advised Mr. Speaker to avoid travel and to obtain special treatment (Markel, Gostin, & Fidler, 2007). Specifically, the Centers for Disease Control and Prevention (CDC) recommended that Mr. Speaker consider isolation or quarantine to prevent spreading the disease to others (CDC, 2007b).

With a wedding and bride-to-be waiting, Mr. Speaker decided not to follow medical and public health advice. Instead, he left two days earlier than planned to attend his wedding in Greece (Markel et al., 2007). Traveling by air, Mr. Speaker flew from Atlanta, Georgia, to Paris, France, on May 12 and then on to Greece. U.S. public health officials were unable to contact Mr. Speaker until May 22, when they eventually located him on his honeymoon in Rome, Italy. They again advised him not to travel and urged him to report to Italian health authorities. The U.S. health officials did not want Mr. Speaker to expose more people to his highly contagious illness. Unfortunately, on May 24, Mr. Speaker decided once again to disregard the health official's advice. He flew from Prague in the Czech Republic to Montreal, Canada. By this time, U.S. public health officials had placed Mr. Speaker's name on a health surveillance list: a procedure that would first detain Mr. Speaker when he attempted to reenter the United States and then notify public health officials. At least that was what should have happened.

What really happened? Mr. Speaker reentered the United States without being detained, and public health officials were not notified. When Mr. Speaker finally contacted health authorities, he was ordered to go to Bellevue Hospital in New York City. At Bellevue, federal officials found it necessary to hold Mr. Speaker in federal isolation for treatment. The last time such an order was issued in the United States was in 1963 to detain a person suspected of having smallpox (Markel et al., 2007). Meanwhile the Centers for Disease Control and Prevention (CDC) and other public health officials in several countries were sufficiently concerned about the health of the airline passengers who were on the same flights as Mr. Speaker that they contacted passengers they felt were most at risk for contagion and recommended that they be tested and evaluated for TB.   ■

Mr. Speaker's case illustrates one of the many reasons why health is considered a global issue (see Figure 3.1). International travel is one way in which communicable diseases such as TB can be transported to different countries. When traveling with a contagious disease, individuals risk infecting other persons during their journey. During his trip, Mr. Speaker not only put fellow Americans at risk of contracting an extremely drug-resistant strain of TB, he exposed French, Czech, Italian, and Canadian citizens as well. Multiple national and international exposures to TB complicate efforts to control its spread and can create an international health crisis.

It might sound incredible, but in spite of Mr. Speaker's travels to five countries while infected, his case caused only a minor international health incident. Make no mistake: The Canadian, Czech, French, and Italian governments were extremely concerned, and not at all pleased, to learn that the United States was unable to detain Mr. Speaker. But for the moment it appears that other travelers were not infected with Mr. Speaker's active and contagious strain of TB. Thus, one reason Mr. Speaker's case is seen as a minor incident is because health officials believe they managed to contain the potential damage.

FIGURE 3.1 Andrew Speaker. An international threat of tuberculosis was prompted by Mr. Speaker's "unauthorized" international travels.

Source: ABC/Associated Press (2007).

The same cannot be said about the avian bird flu in 2005 or the "swine flu" in 2009. In 2005, the world became aware of a health crisis involving a virus that was transmitted from birds to humans. Between 2005 and 2006, more than 200 people in 13 different countries contracted the virus. As of 2006, six human deaths had been attributed to the avian bird flu (CDC, 2006). And, unlike the TB scare in 2007, most governments were unaware of the virus until incidences of the disease were reported among their populations. By the time health officials learned of the widespread impact of the avian flu, people in China and other countries in Southeast Asia, Northeast Africa, the Middle East, and Europe were becoming ill from the virus. The delay in notifying health officials allowed the virus to spread.

By comparison, Mexican authorities acted more quickly and with fuller disclosure when discovering incidences of a deadly "swine flu," known medically as Type A/H1N1 influenza, in April 2009. Within weeks of the flu's detection, Mexican health officials reported 81 deaths (rising to over 97 documented deaths shortly thereafter) in addition to thousands of incidences of illness thought to be associated with the A/H1N1 virus.

The warning about A/H1N1 came none too soon. Within days of notifying the World Health Organization, an international health organization that coordinates and at times implements global health policy (see Section II, Global Health Organizations, page 93), 11 additional countries also reported incidences of the disease. Some, like the United States, even reported deaths associated with the illness. The H1N1 flu, unlike Mr. Speaker's TB incident, was an international health crisis because people in many different noncontiguous countries contracted the disease. The countries then braced for the impact of the illness on their citizens.

Mr. Speaker's TB problem, the avian bird flu, and the A/H1N1 flu demonstrate that contagious diseases can and do travel across borders. Their ability to infect large numbers of people in many countries can create global health problems of concern to many health professionals including psychologists. But, interestingly, global health problems give health psychologists an opportunity to study and test the effects of different health determinants in a variety of cultures such as individual and cultural behaviors, environment, health policy, and health systems on individual health outcomes.

In this chapter, we explore the impact of each of the determinants of health on the health status of people in countries around the world. We will pay particular attention to changes in health outcomes of people in economically prosperous nations, here referred to as *developed countries*, versus those in less economically advantaged, or *developing countries*.

We begin Section I with a brief review of nine of the most famous communicable diseases in history and explain their effects on communities. We continue with a discussion of childhood viral illnesses and the disparities in health outcomes for children who contract childhood infectious diseases in developed versus developing countries. We conclude Section I by explaining the role of childhood immunizations as an effective tool for improving health status, specifically mortality and morbidity rates, among children worldwide.

BOX 3.1   A 21st-Century Pandemic?

It came as a shock to many. Was it really possible that the world was confronting a 21st-century global health scare that could become a pandemic? The World Health Organization, an international health organization, seemed to think so.

The exact origin of the disease and its progression is still unknown. But, at present, it appears that residents in a small town in Mexico or in the United States (a point debated by some Mexican and U.S. health officials; Lacey, 2009) became infected with Type A/H1N1 Influenza, a type of flu commonly found in pigs. Because of its prior association with pigs, the new disease was nicknamed the "swine flu."

Epidemiologists realized that while the A/H1N1 Influenza was common among pigs, it was now spreading to humans as well. At first, the disease was communicated from animals to humans. As the illness spread, however, the method of transmission changed. Within a few short weeks, health researcher observed that the disease could be passed by humans to other humans, a process referred to as *human-to-human transmission*. Contact with an infected animal was no longer necessary.

When WHO officials realized the new danger of H1N1, they became concerned. Like other influenzas that are passed from person to person, the H1N1 was now capable of spreading quickly through a population. In fact, within weeks, more than eight countries reported actual or suspected cases of the flu. In response to the escalating threat, WHO issued a Phase 4 global threat warning to notify all countries of the potential of an imminent global health crisis; the threat level was elevated to Phase 6 by late June 2009 (see Figure 3.2).

The story worsened with each passing day. As of June 1, 2009, 62 countries were reporting a total of more than 17,410 confirmed cases of A/H1N1 virus. The United

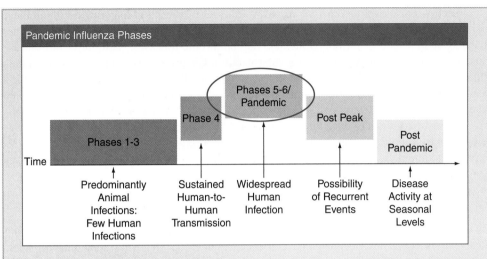

FIGURE 3.2 Pandemic Influenza Phases. By late June 2009, the H1N1 virus reached Phase 6 of the WHO influenza phases.

Source: WHO (2010a).

States accounted for 51.5% (8,975) of the cases but only 10% (15) of the deaths. By comparison, only 28.8% (5,029) of the global cases of H1N1 were officially reported in Mexico, the site of origin of the disease (WHO, 2010b). Yet Mexico was responsible for more than 84% (97) of the deaths. The statistics made some wonder about the actual number of cases of A/H1N1 in Mexico. With more than 84% of deaths due to the flu, some researchers suggested that the over 5,000 cases of H1N1 in Mexico may not reflect the total number of people infected.

On the other hand, differences in infection and death rates for H1N1 led some epidemiologists to speculate that people in the United States and other countries had contracted a less severe strain of the flu than individuals in Mexico. The reason for the difference in severity could not be explained. Some speculated that better access to medical care may have reduced both the intensity and duration of the flu in the United States and other countries, while others suggested the possibility of a different strain of flu in Mexico versus other countries.

Equally uncertain is the final effects of the flu. The H1N1 flu is a new variant of Type A influenza. As such, there is no way to predict the likely course of the disease, its duration, the number of people to be affected, or the estimated mortality rates. One thing we do know, however: On average over 36,000 people die from complications associated with the seasonal Type A influenza every year. It is too soon to determine whether the 2009 outbreak of H1N1 will result in mortality rates that are similar to or that exceed the average outcomes for annual flu outbreaks.

Section I also explores ***chronic diseases***, illnesses that result in lingering health problems and that limit an individual's daily functioning. In this section, we examine two chronic illnesses: diabetes and chronic respiratory illnesses. (Other chronic illnesses, including heart disease, cancer, and arthritis, are explored in greater detail in Chapters 9 through 11). Again taking a global health approach, we explore the impact of chronic illnesses on populations in developed versus developing countries to illustrate the role of socioeconomic status and access to health care (a health systems determinant) on mortality rates and other health outcomes.

In Section II we introduce three international health organizations that provide health systems and health policy assistance to countries unable to provide such services themselves. We explore the international organizations' roles in addressing the specific health promotion and health maintenance needs of the region.

By the end of Sections I through III you will be able to distinguish between chronic and communicable diseases and describe the global consequences of each, explain how individual behaviors, demographic factors (such as socioeconomic status), access to health care, and health policy result in different health outcomes, and finally compare the health of people living in developed versus developing countries.

Finally, in Section IV we explore the economic consequences of poor health. In this section we examine ways in which an individual's health status can adversely affect his or her immediate family, in addition to the well-being of the community, society, and the nation.

SECTION I. GLOBAL HEALTH PROBLEMS

Communicable Diseases: Human-to-Human Transmission

EPIDEMICS AND PANDEMICS   History shows us that for centuries communicable diseases have caused severe illness and death throughout the world. Table 3.1 identifies four of the most recent major global diseases over the past 600 years based on historical records (between 1347 CE to the present). Each of these diseases was transmitted by humans to other humans.

The first documented communicable disease occurred in 430 BCE in Greece. The origin of the disease, commonly referred to as the ***Athenian plague***, is unclear, but its effects were indisputable. After suffering a number of symptoms including fever, inflammation of the eyes, tongue, or throat, gastrointestinal symptoms such as diarrhea or vomiting, as well as rashes covering the entire body, the victims usually died within seven or eight days of contracting the disease. To this day, archeologists and epidemiologists dispute the name of the disease. Some liken it to the ***Ebola virus*** (Holden, 1996), an often fatal disease that spreads quickly between people. Others claimed that it was more similar to ***glanders***, another fatal disease that spread from animals to humans that was eradicated in the early part of the 20th century (Eby & Evjen, 1962).

Historians likewise have been unable to estimate accurately the number of deaths attributed to the Athenian plague. Some contend that the plague resulted in death to thousands in the city of Athens. When diseases affect large numbers of a population within a geographic area, epidemiologists call the disease an ***epidemic***, from the Greek words *epi* meaning "upon" and *demos* meaning "people." The Athenian plague is an example of an epidemic. Diseases that spread though large geographic regions of the world or occur worldwide are called ***pandemics***. Again,

TABLE 3.1	Major Epidemics/Pandemics				
Time	**Name**	**Location**	**Cause**	**Symptoms**	**Outcomes**
1347–1350 CE	Haemorrhagic plague (Black Death)	Europe, Asia, and Middle East	Movement of military and trade	Fever, diarrhea, pustules	Death toll >137 million
1816 CE– present	Cholera	India, Russia, Europe, North America, South Asia, Africa	Trade and commerce	Diarrhea, severe dehydration, kidney failure	Death toll >1 million
1918 CE	Influenza	France, U.S., and Sierra Leone	Movement of trade	Unspecified	Death toll >40 million
1980 CE– present	HIV/AIDS	U.S., Africa, Asia, Europe	Risky sexual behavior	Lesions, pneumonia, cancer	Death toll >2 million

the origin of this word is Greek, derived from the words *pan* meaning "all" and *demos* meaning "people." All diseases listed in Table 3.1 were considered pandemics because of their impact on multiple populations and millions of people across many global regions.

Perhaps the best-known pandemic is the ***haemorrhagic plague***. Commonly called the ***Black Death***, it decimated villages throughout Europe, Asia, and the Middle East for approximately three years, from 1347 to 1350 CE. An estimated 25 million people died during the first two years of the plague. Unfortunately, there were seven reoccurrences of the Black Death, the last of which occurred in the 18th century. Together the eight episodes of the plague were responsible for the deaths of over 137 million people.

The most recent addition to the list of deadly pandemics that affected tens of thousands worldwide is the ***HIV/AIDS virus***. Although we discuss HIV/AIDS more fully in Chapter 8, HIV and AIDS, one point is worth making now. While the origins of HIV/AIDS continue to be disputed, the method of transmission is indisputably through human contact. High-risk sexual behaviors, including multiple sex partners and unprotected sex, and the sharing of hypodermic needles by intravenous drug users (IVDUs) are the primary means of transmission.

In summary, the pandemics listed in Table 3.1 were transmitted by people through war, commerce, travel or, in the case of HIV/AIDS, high-risk behaviors. All are effective methods for spreading diseases between people and over great geographic distances.

TUBERCULOSIS (TB)   We began this chapter with a story about Mr. Speaker, a man with an extremely drug-resistant strain of TB. Tuberculosis fits the definition of a communicable disease because it can be transmitted from one living organism to another. The transmission can be direct (from person to person) or indirect (through environmental agents such as air) and may involve direct contact with another person's saliva, nasal secretions, or feces (CDC, 2007b).

TB is not a new illness. In fact, archeologists found evidence of tubercular decay in Egyptian mummies as early as 2400 BCE (National Tuberculosis Center, 1966). It was a common ailment also in ancient Greece in 570 BCE (Daniel, 2006).

More recently, however, health records indicate that the United States and Europe experienced major TB epidemics in the 18th and 19th centuries. We describe the history and treatment of TB in the United States in Section III of this chapter. For the moment, however, we call attention to current trends in global versus national TB rates that, once again, illustrate the importance of a global perspective on health. At present, the United States enjoys one of the lowest TB infection rates in the world. Yet, as the opening story with Mr. Speaker suggests, the disease still poses problems even in the United States. WHO's data on worldwide TB rates report an increase in the incidence of TB from 2000 through 2005. The higher rates appear to be due to three factors: drug-resistant strains of the disease (like Mr. Speaker's illness); HIV/AIDS—a disease that weakens the immune system, making people with HIV/AIDS more susceptible to other infections (see Chapter 8, HIV and AIDS); and an increase in the number of refugees due to wars, famines, and natural disasters (WHO, 2008d).

Researchers have shown that a person with an ***active case of TB***, here meaning someone who is untreated or ineffectively treated, can infect, on average, one person per month. At that rate, a contagious individual can infect 10 to 15 persons per year. Once infected, a person may become sick with active TB bacteria within a year (Caminero Luna, 2003; WHO, 2007b). By comparison, a person with a ***latent case of TB*** will test positive for the bacteria but will not show signs of illness, will not be sick, and cannot communicate the disease to others.

The TB rates shown in Figure 3.3 indicate that current TB incidence rates differ by country. Eastern, Southern, and Southeastern Asia, as well as sub-Saharan Africa, have experienced increased incidences of TB over the past five years. The increase in TB in Africa has been linked to an increase in the rates of HIV/AIDS in the region.

Reasons for the increase in TB rates in Asia are less clear. There as in Africa, HIV/AIDS may be associated with the increase in TB rates. Half of all of the new cases of TB in Asia appear to occur principally in six Asian countries: Bangladesh, China, India, Indonesia, Pakistan, and the Philippines (WHO, 2008d).

How do the TB rates in the United States compare to the global statistics? The good news is that TB rates in the United States are not increasing. But health officials report another troubling statistic. Recent data show a slower reduction in the rates of TB in the United States relative to other developed countries over the past four years. What does that mean? Specific statistics may help. The CDC reported that the average decline in TB rates in the United States for 1993 through 2002 was 6.6% per year. In other words, there were 6.6% fewer TB cases each year in the United States between 1993 and 2002. From 2003 through 2006, however, there were only 3.1% fewer cases of TB per year. The slower reduction means more cases of TB in the United States during 2003 through 2006.

There are several possible reasons for the slower decline of TB in the United States. Health officials suggest that one reason for the decline may be related to immigration. In the United States, foreign-born residents have higher rates of TB than do U.S.-born residents. In 2006, the prevalence rate for TB for foreign-born persons in the United States was 22.0 cases per 100,000 people. For U.S.-born residents, however, the prevalence rate was only 2.3 per 100,000 persons (CDC, 2007b), approximately one-tenth the rate for foreign-born residents. Thus, the data seem to suggest that immigration plays a role in slowing the decline of TB rates in the United States.

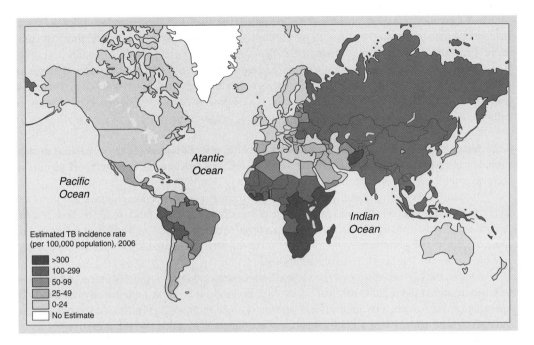

FIGURE 3.3   Estimated Number of New Tuberculosis Cases, 2006. Global incidence of tuberculosis shows that the highest rates of tuberculosis occur in sub-Saharan Africa, with significant rates reported also in eastern Europe and throughout Asia.

Source: CDC, 2009d.

At this point you may be wondering why global and U.S. TB rates are relevant to health psychologists. Put it this way: The TB statistics are relevant to health psychologists who study the health status of communities, especially if their work involves immigrant communities. For example, in examining the community health indicators of immigrant communities, these statistics suggest that researchers and health providers should include measures of TB risk to obtain a complete profile of community health status.

Equally as important, health psychologists who work to reduce TB rates in the United States could use the statistics to identify groups of people at greatest risk for contracting TB. They could design intervention, prevention, and treatment programs tailored specifically to the higher-risk groups to maximize likelihood of successful health outcomes. The statistics suggest that one high-risk group is certain immigrant populations.

CHILDHOOD VIRAL DISEASES   Measles, mumps, rubella, chicken pox, diphtheria, whooping cough, and polio: Do these diseases sound familiar to you? Most children in developed countries like the United States are medically protected from such *childhood viral diseases*. In fact, few would recognize names like whooping cough or mumps, and fewer still would come in contact with such diseases

But, for millions of other children, the same diseases often lead to serious illness or death. In this section we examine three childhood diseases that continue to pose health problems for the global community: measles, chicken pox, and polio (see Box 3.2). We examine childhood viral diseases as part of our study of health psychology because the diseases have one thing in common: They are all preventable. Preventable illnesses are of special interest to health psychologists because they suggest an opportunity to improve health outcomes through changes in individual behaviors or through improving access to health care. And, as we will see in Chapter 4, Theories and Models of Health Behavior Change, one goal of health psychologists is to motivate individuals to adopt behaviors that will improve their health status.

Measles, Chicken Pox, and Polio   *Measles* is a viral infection most commonly found in children. It can result in respiratory illness and even death. For that reason, it is the most serious of the preventable childhood infections (Kunz, 1982).

In many developing countries, children who are merely exposed to the measles virus are likely to contract the disease. And in many cases the disease will be fatal. In 2005, over 90,000 people in Africa—mostly children—and more than 126,000 people in Southeast Asia died of measles. But in the same year fewer than 2,000 deaths were attributed to measles in Europe and in North, Central, and South America combined.

Due to the high mortality rate associated with measles in developing countries, its prevention is considered the highest medical priority for children. It is given high priority especially in emergency settings such as natural disasters or refugee camps. WHO statistics show that, in emergency settings, 25% of all child deaths are attributed to measles (WHO, 2006).

Chicken pox, or the *varicella zoster virus*, as it is known in the medical community, is an uncomfortable but rarely serious illness when contracted during childhood. Before 1995, approximately 90% of U.S. children experienced and successfully overcame chicken pox by age 10. As with many other childhood diseases, a person who has the disease is immune for life. Thus, by age 10, over 90% of children in the United States were effectively immune from contracting the chicken pox a second time.

Finally, *poliomyelitis*, referred to commonly as *polio*, is a highly contagious viral disease that damages cells in the spinal cord and specifically attacks the muscle-controlling nerves (Wilson, 2005). While polio results only in flulike symptoms for over 90% of people who contract the illness, approximately 2% experience more severe manifestations such as partial or full paralysis of the arms or legs.

During the first half of the 1900s, the United States experienced many waves of polio, often referred to as polio epidemics. The most serious epidemic occurred in 1916, followed by a succession of epidemics occurring from 1930 through 1960. The numbers of people affected by polio during that time exceeded 400,000 (Wilson, 2005).

The statistics on measles, chicken pox, and polio may seem unreal. For example, when was the last time you heard of someone dying of measles? In fact, when was the last time you remember hearing that someone even contracted the measles? The extremely low rate of measles and other childhood communicable diseases in the United States is no accident. Incidences of childhood viral illnesses are infrequent in the United States primarily because children with access to health care receive vaccines that *immunize* them against the diseases. *Vaccines* are medicines that contain a small amount of the virus (dead or live) from the disease in question.

To prevent children from contracting measles, scientists developed a vaccine made, in part, from the dead measles virus. Introducing a controlled amount of a virus to the body encourages the body's immune system to build *antibodies*. We explore the body's immune system more fully

BOX 3.2   Do These Viral Infections Sound Familiar?

How many childhood illnesses have you had? What about your friends? Chances are, not many. Incidences of measles, polio, and now even chicken pox in the United States are very low. Childhood immunization programs in the United States have made such diseases a rare occurrence. For that reason, we present a brief summary of three diseases that are uncommon in the United States but that still occur at alarmingly high rates in developing countries.

Measles

Measles is a viral infection seen most commonly among children. Early symptoms usually include a fever and a rash that appears first on the face and neck, eventually spreading to other parts of the body. The symptoms last approximately 10 to 12 days.

The illness itself is not as dangerous as the likely complications. Pneumonia, severe diarrhea leading to dehydration, or encephalitis (a dangerous inflammation of the brain) are the more serious complications and can lead to death (WHO, 2006a). Measles is especially fatal for children five years of age or younger who are malnourished, have weakened immune systems, or have vitamin A deficiencies.

Chicken Pox

More uncomfortable to children than dangerous, chicken pox is characterized by an itchy rash that often turns into a blistering pox and, when ruptured, secretes a small quantity of pus. Children who catch chicken pox often complain of fever in addition to the uncomfortable itchy sensation from the blisters.

Prior to 1995, the United States reported approximately 4,000 cases of chicken pox per year, mainly among children. In those years, parents sometimes purposely exposed their noninfected children to others with active cases of chicken pox so that noninfected children would catch the essentially harmless disease as a child. However, for adults who were never exposed to chicken pox, the disease is not as benign. Approximately 10% of adults in the United States are susceptible to chicken pox and can suffer complications that can include respiratory diseases such as pneumonia.

Polio

Like chicken pox and measles, polio is a viral disease. Unlike the other two, however, polio can be a crippling disease. The effects of the disease can vary from a mild, flulike infection, including fever, nausea, and fatigue, to partial or total paralysis of the arms or legs.

When thinking of polio, many recall Franklin D. Roosevelt, the 32nd president of the United States. President Roosevelt contracted polio in 1921 at the age of 39. His case demonstrates that older people afflicted with polio experience more severe symptoms, such as paralysis, than do children.

Thanks to the effectiveness of a vaccine discovered by Jonas Salk and eventually administered worldwide, polio is considered largely a disease of the past, at least in the United States.

in Chapter 8, HIV and AIDS. But, briefly, antibodies are proteins that identify and destroy bacteria and viruses that are foreign to the body. The immune system then retains some antibodies to recognize and destroy the virus if an individual becomes exposed to it at a later time. By teaching the body to recognize and destroy a controlled amount of the virus, vaccines are able to protect or immunize the vaccinated individual from future occurrences.

Effectiveness of Vaccines   How effective are vaccines in preventing the spread of childhood viral illnesses? We noted that, for the United States, measles is a rare occurrence. Now consider this: In 1995, a new vaccine was introduced in the United States to add to the arsenal of childhood vaccines. Today, two administrations of the varicella zoster virus vaccine protects 95% of children from the disease (Chaves et al., 2007; Tugwell et al., 2004). In addition, by vaccinating children to protect them from chicken pox, we reduce the exposure risks for adults who are more likely to develop serious and sometimes fatal complications.

The success of vaccine programs in the United States is due in part to public health regulations that strongly recommend that, by age six, children should have received all vaccines for measles, mumps, rubella, chicken pox, diphtheria, whooping cough, polio, and other infectious diseases usually contracted in childhood.

Is it a coincidence that public health officials chose six years of age to mandate immunization of children? Not at all. In the United States, children are required to attend school starting at age six (or age five in states that require children to attend kindergarten). Thus, hundreds of children spend five days a week acquiring knowledge and sharing germs in a common space. Unvaccinated children in such an environment could easily spark a mini-epidemic of childhood illnesses. To protect the health and well-being of all children, their families, and the community, most local and state health policies require that children be immunized before starting school.

To summarize, a goal of U.S. health officials is to reduce the incidences of childhood diseases and to minimize the chance of children experiencing illness or death associated with serious diseases such as measles. Consequently, for children in the United States, Europe, or other developed countries with established immunization programs, measles and other serious childhood diseases are rare occurrences.

It is worth repeating that one reason why developed countries can state and achieve such goals is because childhood viral illnesses are preventable. Vaccines have been proven effective not only in preventing children from becoming seriously ill or disabled but also in protecting the health and well-being of a community. Yet, as we see from the changes in polio statistics worldwide (see Box 3.3), not all children are vaccinated.

What would prevent someone from vaccinating a child to protect against a serious or potentially fatal disease? Health psychologists ask this question often to understand the factors that influence an individual's decision to obtain health-enhancing or health-sustaining treatments. In the case of childhood illnesses, we noted that cultural or religious beliefs (individual, family, cultural factors), fear of the consequences of vaccines (individual factors), the cost of vaccines (affordability, a demographic factor), access to health care (health systems factor), and vaccine programs (a health policy factor) all determine the likelihood that a child or an adult may contract a contagious viral infection. We explore the factors that influence health behaviors from a health psychology perspective more fully in Chapter 4, Theories and Models of Health Behavior Change.

BOX 3.3   The Effectiveness of Vaccines in Preventing Contagion

We can understand the beneficial impact of vaccines by examining an incident in 2003 when polio vaccines were suspended in Nigeria. Until 2003, polio was thought to be under control in all regions of the world. However, a new outbreak of polio was reported in seven west and central African countries: Burkina Faso, Cameroon, the Central African Republic, Chad, Ghana, Nigeria, and Togo (see Figure 3.4). The source of the outbreak appeared to be Nigeria, where the government suspended its polio immunization campaign in the northern part of the country. The reason for the suspension is unclear. What is clear is that the change in Nigeria's national immunization policy appears to be the principal cause of the resurgence of polio that now affects eight countries in Africa. Nigeria's changed health policy is a good example of the effect that health policy may have on individual health outcomes.

The proven effectiveness of vaccines is one reason why international aid organizations such as the World Health Organization (WHO) and the United Nations Children's Fund (UNICEF) have placed a high priority on global immunization programs for children. An equally compelling reason to prioritize childhood immunizations is the minimal cost. For less than U.S.$1.00 per child, international aid agencies could vaccinate all children, five years of age or younger, to control and eventually to eradicate childhood infectious diseases. Over 345,000 deaths in 2005 due to measles could have been prevented if children, especially those in developing countries, had been immunized against the disease. The cost for such a program would have been $345,000, a minor sum for most developed countries.

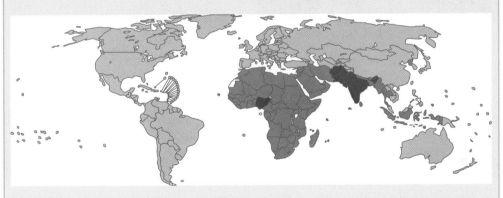

FIGURE 3.4   Wild Polio Virus, 2008. Endemic polio is shown in dark green; light green indicates certified polio free; medium green is neither certified free nor involved with endemic polio.

Source: WHO, 2009c.

BOX 3.4   In the Wake of Hurricane Katrina

Hurricane Katrina, the Category 5 hurricane that severely flooded and damaged New Orleans and the Gulf Coast of Mississippi, is a recent example of a natural disaster that created the perfect conditions for a cholera outbreak.

Katrina destroyed the water levees that protect New Orleans from the Gulf of Mexico and Lake Pontchartrain. Massive amounts of water flooded into the city when the levees failed, disrupting the city's infrastructure, causing major damage to sewer systems, and contaminating water supplies as well as other systems (see Figure 3.5). Raw sewage and other waste products flowed into the waters that flooded streets and neighborhoods, especially in the Lower Ninth Ward and Chantilly, two neighborhoods in New Orleans.

Once the storm ended, many health workers braced for an outbreak of cholera. Why? The scarcity of clean drinking water and the contaminated water in streets and homes meant that people were exposed daily to microorganisms (see Chapter 1, An Interdisciplinary View of Health) that increased their risk of infections. Fortunately, no major outbreaks of cholera were diagnosed. There were, however, over 140 cases of diarrhea and more than 289 cases of other infectious diseases reported in the first days after the storm (CDC, 2005). The point is that while most developed countries, like the United States, worry about outbreaks of cholera only in the event of natural disasters like Hurricane Katrina, developing countries face the potential for cholera outbreaks with regularity.

FIGURE 3.5   Hurricane Katrina Aftermath. A view of Canal Street flooded due to damage to the levees.

Recurring Diseases

A second type of communicable disease is recurring diseases such as cholera, malaria, and dracunculiasis, sometimes called "guinea worm" (see Box 3.6). These particular diseases present special challenges to the global health community because they are transmitted to humans from insects or bacteria that breed in unsanitary environmental conditions. In other words, for many recurrent diseases, environmental conditions are a predisposing factor (see Chapter 2, Research Methods) that contributes to the disease.

CHOLERA   Like measles, very few people contract *cholera* in developed countries The reason for the low rates of infection in developed countries is health policies at the local and national levels that ensure safe, clean water for the majority of the population (see Chapter 1, An Interdisciplinary View of Health).

Vibrio cholerae bacteria cause the intestinal infection that we call cholera. The bacteria are usually found in contaminated food or water or in human fecal matter. An individual who eats contaminated food, drinks contaminated water, or is in contact with human fecal matter infected with the bacteria can contract cholera (WHO, 2008c). Approximately 80% of the time, cholera causes mild or moderate symptoms that usually include diarrhea and stomach cramping. In 10 to 20% of the cases, however, diarrhea can be so sudden and severe that it causes severe dehydration, kidney failure, or death.

Cholera is closely linked to poor environmental management and unsafe water conditions. Therefore, countries with limited water treatment facilities, such as Mexico, the Dominican Republic, Costa Rica, and Thailand, encounter frequent problems with water contaminants. In some instances, travelers to these and other countries are warned not to drink the water.

Even developed countries, however, may experience a disruption of water sanitation systems that jeopardize the water supply. Hurricane Katrina (see Box 3.4) damaged water treatment systems and prompted concern by health officials about a potential outbreak of cholera in the United States.

In essence, cholera is a preventable disease; but, like vaccinations for childhood viral illnesses, it is best addressed through health policy interventions. And, as we indicated in Chapter 1, An Interdisciplinary View of Health, local, regional, or national governments are best equipped to develop the health policies that provide the environmental and safety systems needed to ensure safe water supplies.

MALARIA   Mosquitoes! For many people the word *mosquito* conjures annoying images of insects that leave irritating welts after biting and an itchy sensation that can take days to subside. For others, the word *mosquito* is linked to insect sprays or other repellants that help avoid the irritating bites or welts.

Hot, humid weather and large bodies of stagnant water offer an ideal breeding ground for mosquitoes. And, in countries with extensive hot or humid seasons, as well as large bodies of stagnant water and large populations of mosquitoes, these insects can be more than just annoying: They can mean death if they carry the *malaria* virus.

How does a mosquito become a carrier of the virus? The process begins with a parasite called *plasmodium*. The plasmodium parasite infects humans, but then it is transmitted from person to person with the aid of the female *anopheles mosquito* (WHO, 2007a). When the anopheles mosquito bites an infected person, it injects a small amount of fluid that causes the skin irritation associated with mosquito bites. It then withdraws a small amount of blood from the infected person. The anopheles mosquito then moves on to its next victim. When biting the next victim, some of the blood from the first person is injected into the newly bitten person along with the fluid. In this way, the anopheles mosquito transmits malaria from one person to another.

Over 90% of the deaths from malaria occur in sub-Saharan Africa, where children disproportionately are the victims. Although hot, humid, tropical climates are the preferred breeding grounds for mosquitoes, in truth any area with favorable breeding conditions for mosquitoes is a potential

BOX 3.5   Combating Malaria

In 1998 a Roll Back Malaria campaign supported by WHO proposed and implemented three strategies to combat and control the spread of malaria: drug treatments, repellant-treated mosquito nets, and education. The drug treatment approach has become more successful with the discovery of a new drug called **artemisinin**. When combined with a second antimalarial medicine, artemisinin is far more effective in controlling the illness than previous drug treatments. Currently, over 40 countries have changed their health policies and adopted the new combination drug treatment regimen (WHO, 2005b).

The second strategy, sleeping under mosquito nets treated with insect repellant, effectively reduces the number of mosquito bites and therefore the number of persons infected with malaria. Because mosquitoes are most active from dusk to dawn, individuals are most at risk for being bitten at night and while sleeping. The simple solution of sleeping under treated nets further reduces mosquito's access to unsuspecting sleeping victims (Malaria No More, 2010).

The third and final strategy introduced by Roll Back Malaria is a global education campaign. The aim of the third strategy is to teach mothers, shopkeepers, and other village residents in malaria-infested areas to recognize the symptoms of malaria and to treat malaria with the combination drug therapy ACT (WHO, 2005b).

Like cholera and measles, malaria is treatable but only with concerted national and in some cases, international efforts.

malaria region. For this reason, high rates of malaria infection have been reported in Southeast Asia as well as in Central America and northern South America. Like cholera, malaria is preventable. Antimalaria medication widely available in the United States in addition to precautions such as mosquito repellants, protective clothing, and protective bed nets sprayed with repellant help to reduce the risk of contracting malaria (see Box 3.5).

PARASITES   The U.S. Food and Drug Administration (FDA) frequently warns us of the danger of eating raw or undercooked meats or pork. These warnings are really meant to protect us from consuming meat products that are contaminated with the **cestodiasis parasite** commonly known as **tapeworm**.

The cestodiasis parasite lives in the intestines of animals such as cattle or pigs. People can be infected with the parasite if the meat they consume from cattle or pigs is not cooked long enough or at a high enough temperature to kill the organism. Infected beef may contain the parasite **taenia saginata**, whereas the parasite found in contaminated pork is called **taenia solium**. When consumed, either parasite is capable of causing diarrhea, abdominal pain, and weight loss. In severe cases, the parasite can cause brain damage when left untreated. It is important to point out that the taenia solium parasites found in pigs are not related to the agents that cause the A/H1N1.

Chronic Diseases

Until recently, health researchers believed that communicable diseases, like TB, cholera, and malaria, were the principal health problems for developing countries. On the other hand, chronic

BOX 3.6   Dracunculiasis (Guinea Worm)

Not all parasites are as easy to detect and treat as the cestodiasis or tapeworm. For example, some developing countries continue to struggle to combat an extremely painful and debilitating parasite known as ***dracunculus medinensis***, or ***guinea worm***. Like the cestodiasis, the guinea worm is contracted when a person consumes a contaminated substance. Because the guinea worm lives in contaminated water, a person can contract this parasite when drinking water that contains **copepods**, or small crustaceans that contain the larvae of the guinea worm (CDC, 2004a). If consumed, the copepods die, but the larvae continue to live. The larvae will grow in the host (in this case a person) for approximately 12 months until they become adult worms.

After maturing, the female worms leave the host site, here meaning the human body. But the process by which the worm leaves the body is the painful and debilitating part of the disease (CDC, 2004a; WHO, 1999, 2009a). To leave a host's body, the female worm forms a blister on the skin of the host, usually on the lower leg or foot. The worm ruptures the blister when it exits, causing an open wound in the skin. The rupture causes a burning pain so intense that most infected persons try to relieve the discomfort by placing the blistering part of the body in water. While the water certainly relieves the discomfort for a moment, it also puts the worm once again in water, the preferred environment to exit the body and to reinfect others. To speed the process, some individuals help the worm exit by pulling the worm as it exits in water. The female worm once again deposits a fresh supply of larvae. The cycle then begins again for another individual (see Figure 3.6). Regardless of how it exits, extracting the worm is a slow and painful process.

For approximately 58% of people infected with the guinea worm, the process of the worm leaving the body is so debilitating that they are unable to walk for a month afterwards.

There is good news, however. The guinea worm is rarely life threatening. Most people are able to resume normal functioning after recuperating from the process. In addition, through concerted efforts by international aid organizations, guinea worm disease has been reduced by 99.7%. In 1986, global estimates of guinea worm disease totaled 3.5 million cases. As of 2005, fewer than 11,000 cases of the disease were reported worldwide (Hopkins, 2006). It is now one of two diseases targeted for full eradication by international health organizations.

How will the organizations eradicate the remaining cases? Remember that the disease is caught through contaminated water. By providing clean, safe drinking water to the approximately 20 countries in Africa and Asia where the disease is most prevalent, eradication of the guinea worm may be achievable in the very near future.

(continued)

FIGURE 3.6   Extracting a Guinea Worm. Extracting the guinea worm is a painful process than can render a person immobile for up to one month.

diseases, here defined as long-term (three to six months or longer) complex illnesses that can be controlled but not cured, were thought to be the main health concerns for developed countries like the United States (Australian Institute of Health and Welfare, 2002; O'Halloran, Miller, & Britt, 2004). Because of such views, chronic diseases were given the nicknames "*diseases of affluence*" and the "*western disease*" (Ezzati, Vander-Hoorn, & Lowes, 2005; McKeowan, 1988). But we now know that chronic and communicable diseases are widely prevalent in all countries. As we will see, the high rates of cardiovascular disease (chronic disease) in developing countries and the prevalence of HIV/AIDS and TB (communicable diseases) in developed countries demonstrate that diseases do not discriminate based on a country's economic status.

Chronic diseases include illnesses such as arthritis, asthma, cancer, chronic heart disease, chronic renal disease, chronic respiratory diseases, depression, diabetes, osteoporosis, stroke, and others (see Table 3.2). The symptoms associated with chronic diseases vary according to the illness. Yet, one thing is common across all illnesses; the symptoms may occur intermittently or they may be continuous and worsen over time.

Earlier in the chapter we introduced childhood and other infectious diseases, some of which can be fatal, that affect millions of people each year. But it may surprise you to know that the leading causes of death *worldwide* are chronic diseases, not infectious diseases. This is true for both developed as well as developing countries. Statistics from WHO underscore this fact. Of the 58 million total deaths worldwide in 2000, approximately 35 million (or 60%) were due to chronic illnesses. To put this is perspective, 35 million deaths due to chronic diseases is more than double the number of deaths from all infectious diseases worldwide, including HIV/AIDS

TABLE 3.2	Estimated 10 Leading Causes of Death in 2000 (Chronic Diseases Are in Bold)					
2000 Rank	Leading Causes of Death Worldwide		Leading Causes of Death: Developed Countries		Leading Causes of Death: Developing Countries	
1	Ischaemic Heart	12.4%	Ischaemic Heart	22.6%	Ischaemic Heart	9.1%
2	Cerebrovascular	9.2%	Cerebrovascular	13.7%	Cerebrovascular	8.0%
3	Lower respiratory infection	6.9%	Trachea, bronchus, and lung cancer	4.5%	Lower respiratory infection	7.7%
4	HIV/AIDS	5.3%	Lower respiratory infection	3.7%	HIV/AIDS	6.9%
5	Chronic obstructive pulmonary disease	4.5%	Chronic obstructive pulmonary disease	3.1%	Perinatal conditions	3.6%
6	Perinatal conditions	4.4%	Colon and rectal cancers	2.6%	Chronic obstructive pulmonary disease	5.0%
7	Diarrheal diseases	3.8%	Stomach cancer	1.9%	Diarrheal diseases	4.9%
8	Tuerculosis	3.0%	Self-inflicted injury	1.9%	Tuberculosis	3.7%
9	Road traffic accident	2.3%	Diabetes	1.7%	Malaria	2.6%
10	Trachea, bronchus, and lung cancer	2.2%	Breast cancer	1.6%	Road traffic accident	2.5%

Source: Anderson & Chu, 2007.

(WHO, 2005c). What is more, 80% of the deaths due to chronic illnesses occurred in developing countries (WHO, 2005a). In fact, five times as many people will die in developing countries from cardiovascular diseases (a chronic illness) than will die from HIV/AIDS (WHO, 2005a).

The difference in mortality rates due to chronic illnesses in developed versus developing countries illustrates differences in individual outcomes for the same illness. Health psychologists and other researchers have determined that one probable explanation for the disparity in outcomes is lack of access to health care. Research shows that people with infrequent or irregular medical care have a higher mortality rate associated with chronic illnesses than people with a regular source of care or medical treatment (Beaglehole et al., 2007; Unal, Critchley, & Capewell, 2005). Thus, higher death rates due to chronic illnesses in developing countries could be caused, in part, by an individual's inability to afford health care or to a nation's inability to provide medical care to its neediest citizens.

It is important to note, however, that lack of access to medical care is a problem in developed countries as well. In such instances, however, it is usually lower-income or poor individuals who experience such outcomes.

CAUSES OF CHRONIC DISEASES   Researchers almost unanimously agree that there are three principal causes of chronic illnesses: unhealthy diets, physical inactivity, and tobacco use (Strong, Mathers, Epping-Jordan, & Beaglehole, 2005). In other words, the main determinants of chronic illnesses are the choices people make about their diets, their activities, and their habits. We add to these principal determents two *confounding factors*, here meaning variables that do not cause but may exacerbate the problem, socioeconomic class (specifically income) and race/ethnicity. In this section, we explain the causes and the confounding factors for chronic illness by examining two prevalent chronic diseases in the United States, diabetes mellitus and chronic respiratory diseases. We will explore other chronic illnesses, specifically cardiovascular diseases, arthritis, and cancer, in greater depth in Chapters 9 through 11.

DIABETES MELLITUS   *Diabetes mellitus* is a chronic disease that occurs when the pancreas, an organ below the stomach, does not produce enough *insulin*, here meaning a hormone that controls the blood sugar levels in the body, or when the body cannot use the insulin it produces. There are two types of diabetes. *Type 1 diabetes* is usually genetic in origin. The cause of Type 1 diabetes is the body's failure to produce insulin. In the United States only 5 to 15% of Americans have Type 1 diabetes (American Diabetes Association, 2007).

The second type of diabetes, formerly called *adult-onset diabetes*, is now referred to simply as *Type 2 diabetes*. This is the most common form of diabetes both in the United States and worldwide. In the United States, approximately 20 million people have been diagnosed with the illness. Worldwide, approximately 90% of all incidences of diabetes are classified as Type 2.

Type 2 diabetes is caused by insulin resistance or the inability of the body to use insulin properly. Individuals with Type 2 diabetes could have a family history of diabetes that would predispose them to a greater likelihood of the disease (see Chapter 2, Research Methods). However, researchers have determined that the largest single contributor to its onset is unhealthy diets. In addition to poor dietary habits, however, Type 2 diabetes rates are increasing because of the increasingly *sedentary lifestyles* of people in Western industrialized countries.

Researchers generally agree that we can reduce the incidences of chronic health problems, like diabetes, through relatively small changes in lifestyles and health behaviors. Specifically, reducing the consumption of foods with high concentrations of saturated fats and salt, increasing consumption of fresh fruits and vegetables, and increasing physical activity would help prevent many types of chronic illnesses (WHO, 2005c).

Furthermore, some researchers suggest that the dietary habits of Western cultures, like the United States, increase the risk of chronic illnesses. Western diets have an abundance of high-processed foods and foods with a high fat, high calorie, but low fiber content. Unsure about this claim? Try this exercise. Next time you have lunch at a fast food or other restaurant with friends count the number of high-fat, high-calorie items on the menu. To help you in this process, be sure to include the following: pizza, hamburger or cheeseburger, French fries, onion rings, cheese steak sandwiches, and nachos with cheese. The highly processed, high-fat items are excellent examples of foods to limit or avoid to reduce the likelihood of developing chronic health problems (Scott, 2007; WHO, 2005c) later in life. When consumed in excess, such foods contribute to the increasing obesity rates in the United States, a precipitating factor for diabetes mellitus.

We now know that it is never too soon to address dietary habits. Consider this: In 2003, the American Academy of Pediatricians, a professional organization for medical doctors in the United States who treat children from infancy to age 18, acknowledged the link between obesity, caused largely by eating habits and sedentary lifestyles, and diabetes. Later that same year, the academy asked pediatricians to include screenings for obesity as part of their annual or biannual checkups of patients. The aim was to monitor and address the increasing rates of obesity in American children (Wartik, 2003, see Figure 3.7). Their fear: if left unchecked, obese children will be more likely to develop diabetes as adolescents, a previously uncommon phenomenon.

Diabetes and Lifestyle Choices   What do we mean by sedentary lifestyles? Television viewing and leisure use of computers are examples of sedentary behaviors. When done in moderation, they are relaxing activities that may be part of a balanced regimen of active and passive behaviors. However, researchers are finding that the amount of time children and adolescents engage in such sedentary activities is increasing over time (Nelson et al., 2006; Sothern, 2004). For example, in a longitudinal study of adolescents' activities between 1999 and 2004, Nelson and colleagues (2006) found that girls and boys show a decrease in physical exercise that begins in

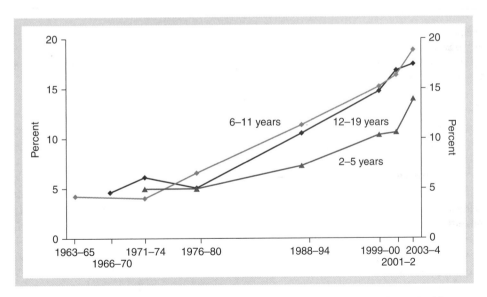

FIGURE 3.7 **Trends in Child and Adolescent Overweight.** Between 1963 and 2004 incidences of overweight have increased almost 400% for children and adolescents 6–11 years and 12–19 years of age, and almost 300% for children 2–5 years of age.

Source: Centers for Disease Control (2009c).

early adolescence and continues well into the late adolescent years. At the same time, however, they note an increase in leisure computer use, a sedentary behavior.

Nelson and colleagues' (2006) findings are supported by research by Kahn and colleagues (2008) that similarly show a decrease in adolescent physical activity after age 13 for both boys and girls.

Diabetes Diagnosis   Diabetes can go undetected and undiagnosed for considerable periods of time. Why is this possible? Symptoms of diabetes can be nonspecific and easily overlooked. For example, a frequent need to urinate or an extreme thirst may not be associated at first with diabetes. In addition, some symptoms are nonspecific. Unusual weight loss, increased fatigue, and irritability may signal the onset of diabetes. Yet they could also be warning signs of some forms of cancer (American Diabetes Association, 2007).

The most reliable method for detecting diabetes is through a blood test. But consider this: Unless a person has a reason to suspect that symptoms may be early warning signs of diabetes, he or she may either overlook the symptoms or fail to mention them to his or her physician. Lack of awareness of the symptoms of diabetes or a lack of access to health care for testing can delay diagnosis and treatment. Delays in treatment, or nontreatment of diabetes, can lead to health complications including blindness, amputation of extremities (arms or legs), or kidney failure, which can also lead to death.

We stated earlier that Type 2 diabetes is preventable. Thus, we might be tempted to assume that anyone who contracts the disease has only him- or herself to blame. While such a conclusion may be accurate when individuals have access to nutritious foods or balanced diets and health care, it is less accurate when explaining the incidences of diabetes among individuals in developing countries with limited resources and less opportunities to obtain care. For diabetes, therefore, national or regional health policies that ensure access to health care offer preventive or early detection options that can reduce the onset or adverse consequences of diabetes. Here again, health policy can play a crucial role in an individual's health outcome.

CHRONIC RESPIRATORY DISEASES   *Chronic respiratory diseases* are a class of chronic illnesses that affect the airways and damage lung function over time. Examples of chronic respiratory diseases include asthma, chronic obstructive pulmonary disease (COPD), respiratory allergies, and occupational lung diseases such as mesothelioma (see Table 3.3).

Like other chronic diseases, the cause of chronic respiratory disease can be both biological and environmental. For example, a biological cause of *asthma*, a partial obstruction of the airways that can cause wheezing or impair breathing, may be a family history of asthma that predisposes an individual to experiencing asthma-like symptoms or to having the illness (see Table 3.3). On the other hand, environmental triggers such as cigarette smoke and animal fur may cause an irritation of the airways that also results in asthma. Cigarette smoke is the most significant contributor to respiratory ailments, specifically asthma (National Heart, Lung & Blood Institute, 2009). This is true for individuals who smoke, as well as for individuals exposed to secondhand smoke on a regular basis (Gergen et al., 1998).

COPD and Access to Care   Obtaining an accurate estimate of the incidences of asthma or other chronic illnesses is difficult. Respiratory diseases can be difficult to detect or diagnose

TABLE 3.3	Common Chronic Respiratory Diseases
Disease	**Defined**
Asthma	Partial obstruction of the airwaves (lungs) that causes episodic attacks of wheezing and difficulty breathing. Attacks can be triggered by allergies to pollen, mites, house dust, or other agents
Chronic obstructive pulmonary disease	Damage to the airways (lungs) caused by irritants such as tobacco smoke, pollution, chemical fumes, or dust. COPD causes coughing, mucus, sneezing, shortness of breath, chest tightness, and other symptoms
Respiratory allergies	A physical response or hypersensitivity to foods, plants, animal hair, or other elements based a misdirection of the body's immune system.
Mesothelioma	A form of cancer of the lungs that develops in the lining of the chest cavity, caused principally from inhaling asbestos fibers that cause irritation and damage to the lungs.

Source: CDC, 2004f.

accurately. Take, for example, ***chronic obstructive pulmonary disease (COPD)***. Underdiagnosis of respiratory diseases such as COPD is common due to the difficulty of diagnosing the disease but also to a lack of access to regular medical care. Falagas, Vardakas, and Paschalis (2007), and Scott (2007) note that in developing countries, less than half (44.6%) of the people suspected of having COPD receive a pulmonary function test, a basic test that measures how well the lungs take in and expel air. Of those, fewer than 24% received an official diagnosis confirming COPD. For individuals in developing countries, making repeat visits to doctors, being tested, and receiving the results of tests is a costly and time-consuming process that many cannot afford, especially when testing for a long-term and debilitating, but not necessarily fatal, disease.

In case this sounds a little shortsighted, consider another example. In developed countries it is not uncommon for an individual to postpone seeking treatment for what appears to be a minor cough. You may know of someone who feels this way. A person with a minor cough may postpone seeking medical care even when the cough worsens and causes a heavy feeling in the chest. That person's rationale for not seeking treatment may be that the cough is not serious; he or she can still perform daily tasks; or the person cannot afford the time off from work or school to seek treatment. All three factors are cost factors that an individual considers when determining whether to seek treatment. The cost factors may be similar regardless whether the individual lives in a developed or a developing country.

BOX 3.7   Do Cockroaches Cause Asthma?

Researchers have known for some time that there are higher incidences of asthma in inner cities in the United States, especially in crowded multifamily dwellings. They also knew that one probable cause of the high asthma rates is an infestation of cockroaches (Eggleston, 1999; Eskenazi, Bradman, & Castorina, 1999; U.S. Environmental Protection Agency, 2007). Some propose that by reducing or eliminating the cockroach problem one might hope to reduce the incidences of asthma associated with it. To that end, health officials have used pesticides, chemical solutions that repel cockroaches to prevent cockroach infestations. But pesticides have a side effect for humans: They can irritate the airways of asthma sufferers and can cause asthma attacks.

Researchers were aware of the adverse effects of pesticides on asthmatics. What they did not realize, however, is that cockroaches were capable of developing an adaptive response to the pesticides. Research by a high school student, Yi Chen Zhand, winner of an Intel-Westinghouse Science scholarship, revealed that cockroaches produce droppings in response to the pesticides. Their droppings include an irritant that triggers an asthma attacks in humans. We now know that, in the "war" to rid apartments of cockroaches, the insects fight back by producing droppings that trigger asthma attacks in humans.

WHO placed the number of deaths due to chronic respiratory disease in 2005 at approximately 4 million worldwide (WHO, 2005c), approximately three times the number of deaths due to diabetes. In the United States alone approximately 120,000 Americans died of complications associated with COPD in 2000 (NHLBI, 2009).

In developed countries, chronic illnesses such as diabetes or chronic respiratory diseases will interfere with a person's daily functioning but rarely lead to immediate death. In fact, the long-term nature of most chronic illnesses leads many to view chronic diseases as less threatening to one's health than infectious diseases. But remember, as we noted at the beginning of the section on chronic diseases, more deaths are attributed to chronic illnesses worldwide than to infectious diseases, a fact that should encourage us to reconsider the impact of chronic diseases on individual or community health outcomes.

SOCIOECONOMIC CLASS, RACE/ETHNICITY, AND CHRONIC DISEASES   Socioeconomic class and race/ethnicity are two confounding factors that contribute to chronic illnesses. Yet many researchers contend that socioeconomic class and race/ethnicity are indirect contributors to chronic illnesses because they primarily affect lifestyle choices and access to care. These factors, in turn, are most directly linked to chronic illnesses.

Research conducted by the WHO and the Institute of Medicine (IOM), a U.S.-based institution that examines health care systems and access to care, demonstrate the effects of race/ethnicity and socioeconomic factors on health care outcomes as shown in Box 3.8. Briefly, the findings suggest that individuals in the lower socioeconomic groups (people who, by income levels, would be considered poor, working poor, or lower middle income; see Chapter 6), are less

BOX 3.8   Health Care Disparities in the United States

Do individuals experience differences in health care treatment in the United States, based on their socioeconomic status or race/ethnicity? Some researchers think so.

Sonel and colleagues (2005) designed a study to examine this question for patients with coronary or heart-related illnesses. A total of 400 hospitals participated in a program called CRUSADE, which stands for "Can Rapid Risk Stratification of Unstable Angina Patients Suppress Adverse Outcomes with Early Implementation of ACC/AHA Guidelines?" Hospitals in the CRUSADE study agreed to provide data for Sonel and colleagues (2005) to determine whether there were differences in medical care for heart patients of different ethnic/racial or socioeconomic classes. Specifically, Sonel and colleagues reviewed the medical records of over 43,000 patients, of whom approximately 84% were white and 13% were African American, to determine whether African Americans and whites received different types of treatment for largely similar heart-related illnesses when seeking care in hospitals.

Their results revealed significant treatment differences between whites and African Americans in the sample. In general, Sonel and colleagues (2005) found that African American patients were more likely to be in poorer health and to have less access to health care. Specifically, African Americans were more likely to be younger than the white patients and to be female. Healthwise, African Americans were more likely to have a diagnosis of hypertension (high blood pressure), to have a confirmed diagnosis of diabetes, and to have a history of smoking and of heart disease. With respect to access to health care, African American patients were less likely to have health insurance through either a health maintenance organization (HMO) or other private insurance. They were more likely to be self-insured or have no insurance and less likely to have a cardiologist as their primary care physician at the hospital.

Sonel and colleagues' study demonstrates clear differences between African Americans and whites in health status and access to health care. But do the differences extend to the types and quality of health treatment? The answer to that question also appears to be yes. When examining the type of treatment given to African American versus white patients, Sonel and colleagues found that while African Americans were as likely as whites to receive the standard treatment, such as aspirin, for acute coronary (heart) problems, they were 20 to 40% less likely to be given the newer, more resource-intensive treatments.

Why is there such a difference? One study alone cannot address that question. However, an earlier study suggests that ethnicity plays a role. Whittle, Conigliaro, Good, and Lofgren (1993) examined the rates of four types of cardiovascular procedures on African American and white patients in a Veterans Administration (VA) Hospital. By choosing a VA hospital, the researchers controlled for the possible confounding effect of income or insurance on the likelihood of the procedure being performed because veterans' care is funded by the government. Yet here, too, the researchers found that African American patients were 1.38 to 2.2 times *less* likely to receive the more invasive surgical

(continued)

procedures to address their cardiovascular illness than were whites. Now, with income and insurance not a factor, the only remaining factor appears to be ethnicity.

Studies like these have prompted the Institute of Medicine, a U.S. research and policy organization, to caution and advise U.S. health care providers about the continuing problems of disparities in health care in the United States due to race/ethnicity and socioeconomic class.

able to obtain quality health care when needed than are individuals in the middle and upper middle socioeconomic groups (IOM, 2002). In addition, Adler and colleagues (1994) demonstrate that an individual's socioeconomic status is linked to the likelihood of chronic and infectious diseases and to higher rates of morbidity and mortality due to the diseases. Specifically, the lower one's socioeconomic class, the higher the likelihood of contracting a chronic illness.

Equally alarming, however, is that even when there is no disparity in socioeconomic status, researchers found inequities in health care based on ethnicity and race (Kelley et al., 2005; Ibrahim et al., 2003). As Adler and colleagues (1994), Kelley and colleagues (2005), and the IOM report (2001) state, an individual's heath outcomes will be affected by a country's economic status (developed versus developing), by the individual's own socioeconomic class, and by his or her race/ethnicity.

Measures of Life Expectancy, Quality of Life, and Chronic Illnesses

We mentioned in Chapter 2, Research Methods, that mortality rates are a gross measure of the health of a nation. In general, countries and communities with higher life expectancies are believed to have a healthier population because longevity is an indication of healthier living conditions. Now, however, we can use more precise measures to assess the overall health of a population by estimating the effect of chronic illnesses on overall well-being.

The *Disability Adjusted Life Expectancy (DALE)* is a new method of measuring a population's health status that calculates health by adjusting for *quality of life*. Here, *quality of life* is defined as the number of years of good, fully functioning ability.

It is important to point out that the DALE estimates the number of years of healthy, unimpaired functioning, not life expectancy. As such, some health researchers question its usefulness as a measure of the health status of a population because it measures healthy function and not mortality. For some illnesses, however, health impairments are morbidity factors (see Chapter 2, Research Methods) that contribute to mortality. Hence the DALE may measure an individual's *overall life expectancy*.

In addition to estimating an individual's number of years of fully functioning health, the DALE also measures a population's likely productivity based on the health of its population. Consider this: Using the DALE, WHO estimates that developed countries lose about 9% of their population's productivity to disability, whereas less developed countries lose approximately 14%. In essence, the DALE serves as a measure of overall health that also helps to predict a country's likely economic health based on its most valuable resource: the health of its workforce.

BOX 3.9 Calculating Disability Adjusted Life Expectancy

To calculate the adjusted life expectancy using the Disability Adjusted Life Expectancy (DALE), we determine first the number of years the person is expected to live under completely healthy conditions, that is, without impairment. Life expectancy data, sorted by country and gender (published by United Nations 2007; see Table 3.4), provide the vital statistics needed for the first part of the calculation.

TABLE 3.4 Life Expectancies by Birth Year: Top 40 Countries by Descending Overall Longevity

Country Overall	Total 2005–2010
Japan	82.6%
Hong Kong (People's Republic of China)	82.2%
Iceland	81.5%
Switzerland	81.7%
Australia	81.2%
Spain	80.9%
Sweden	80.9%
Israel	80.7%
Macau (People's Republic of China)	80.7%
France (metropolitan)	80.7%
Canada	80.7%
Italy	80.3%
New Zealand	80.2%
Norway	80.2%
Singapore	80.0%
Austria	79.8%
Netherlands	79.8%
Martinique	79.5%
Greece	79.5%
Belgium	79.4%
Malta	79.4%
United Kingdom	79.4%
Germany	79.4%
U.S. Virgin Islands	79.4%
Finland	79.3%
Guadeloupe	79.2%
Channel Islands	79.0%
Cyprus	79.0%

(continued)

TABLE 3.4 (Continued)	
Country Overall	**Total 2005–2010**
Republic of Ireland	78.9%
Costa Rica	78.8%
Puerto Rico	78.7%
Luxembourg	78.7%
United Arab Republic	78.7%
South Korea	78.6%
Chile	78.6%
Denmark	78.3%
Cuba	78.3%
United States	78.2%
Portugal	78.1%
Slovenia	77.9%
Worldwide	**67.2%**

Source: United Nations (2007). World Population Prospects: The 2006 Revision Highlights.

Using Table 3.4, we can take, as an example, an individual from Martinique. The overall life expectancy in Martinique is 79.5 years. Using the information in Table 3.4 and the DALE, we can calculate the adjusted life expectancy of an individual in Martinique if we know that person's current health status, that is, his or her current illnesses. For this exercise, assume that a Martinique man contracted cancer at age 60. We compute the number of years of expected ill health (that is, less than fully functional health) based on his current health status and the severity of any current illness. For cancer, some would estimate a loss of five years due to ill health while undergoing treatment. We subtract five years from the overall life expectancy for a Martinique man according to Table 3.4 (79.5 years) to obtain an adjusted life expectancy of 74.5 years.

Country	Overall Life Expectancy	Years of Expected Ill Health	Adjusted Life Expectancy
Martinique	79.5 yr	5 yr	74.5 yr

To review, chronic illnesses are the leading causes of deaths worldwide. For this reason alone, health care providers and health psychologists should include healthy lifestyles and their impact on chronic illnesses as an important determinant of an individual's health status. Surprisingly, many do not. In Part III of this book, we devote three chapters, Chapters 9 through 11, to three of the leading chronic health illnesses in the United States in an effort to refocus needed attention on the impact of chronic illnesses on overall well-being.

SECTION II. GLOBAL HEALTH ORGANIZATIONS

We indicated that a country's health needs are usually addressed by local or national health care systems or policy organizations within countries. In some countries, however, local or national governments do not have the personnel, financial, or material resources to meet even the most basic health care needs of their population or to establish policies to do the same. In such cases, *global health organizations* help bridge the gap between needed and available health resources. We examine the contributions of global health organizations in this section because health care systems and health policy are two important determinants of individual health outcomes.

In this section, we focus on three organizations that provide health services and assistance to the international community: the World Health Organization, the Federation of Red Cross and Red Crescent Societies, and Médecins Sans Frontières (Doctors without Borders).

World Health Organization (WHO)

Throughout the chapter we have presented facts and statistics on global health issues published by the *World Health Organization (WHO)*. It should come as no surprise, therefore, that WHO is considered one of the leading international health policy organizations.

WHO is a UN specialized agency created in 1948 to help attain the highest standard of health for all people (WHO, 2010c). In 2005, WHO identified three new health goals consistent with their aim to improve global health standards: Improve detection and management of emerging threats to health, reduce tobacco use, and increase healthy eating habits to prevent the onset of chronic diseases (WHO, 2005a). Referred to as the Millennium Development Goals, these goals address the need to attend to communicable (emerging threats) and chronic health issues. You may have noticed that the goals are similar to some of the objectives espoused by health psychologists. Thus, another reason to examine WHO's work is the common goals of both fields.

WHO promotes its health goals using a three-step process. It assesses the health needs of a population, it develops policy initiatives, and, to a limited extent, it implements the policies in targeted regions of the world. One example of WHO's needs assessment work is shown in a publication entitled *Preventing Chronic Diseases: A Vital Investment* (WHO, 2005c), considered the most authoritative source of information on chronic illnesses worldwide. *Preventing Chronic Diseases* has led some health providers to reclassify chronic illnesses as an important, perhaps even critical, unmet need in all countries.

Second, WHO formulates and adopts policy initiatives aimed at eliminating specific health problems. This is a critical role because, as we have indicated, some countries do not have the resources to develop and adopt health policy initiatives themselves. For example, 25% of countries worldwide have no mental health legislation to address the needs of persons with depression, schizophrenia, bipolar disorder, or other illnesses (WHO, 2005d). To respond to the health needs of people with mental illnesses, WHO developed programs to assist countries in adopting mental health legislation for their citizens.

Third, the organization plans for and implements policy changes at the national, subnational (regional), and individual level. Consider this: In response to the recurrent problem of malnutrition, WHO developed a high-protein food that, when given to children suffering from the disease, decreases mortality rates due to malnutrition (see Box 3.10).

Finally, WHO examines the *macroeconomic impact of ill health* on individual nations and on the world. What does this mean? We explored this briefly when explaining the uses of the DALE

BOX 3.10   Policy to Practice: The Problem of Malnutrition

WHO and other international agencies have had plenty of opportunity to test the effectiveness of a new treatment for malnutrition. A new, ready-to-use, peanut butter paste that replenishes the body's lost minerals and protein appears to reverse the debilitating effects of malnutrition within 48 to 72 hours if administered in time.

The ready-to-use therapeutic food, more commonly called RUTF, has been successful in treating severely malnourished children by resulting in rapid weight gain (WHO, 2009b).

Just what is in this "miracle" food? The ingredients are quite common: whole milk, sugar, vegetable oil, peanut butter, and mineral vitamin mix (Manary, 2005). In fact, the ingredients are so common they can be obtained and stored by any individual at home.

In addition to reversing the effects of severe malnutrition, RUTF is easy to transport and maintain. It can be packaged for individual use and requires no special storage or refrigeration. In fact, RUTFs can be stored for three to four months in hot and remote areas such as Ethiopia, the Sudan, or other countries with similar climates and lack of electricity. The successful treatment of malnutrition coupled with the easy portability and storage of this lifesaving food are two reasons why it has been used so extensively. To date, ready-to-use foods have been most effective in treating cases of extreme malnutrition among children in refugee camps.

RUTFs are so successful in reversing severe malnutrition that WHO is considering revising their policy, which currently restricts the use of ready-to-use foods to extreme cases of malnutrition. Now they are considering using the same emergency food as preventive measures for underweight children. If the food is used before children reach the extreme state of malnutrition, WHO may be able to significantly reduce one morbidity risk factor for children.

in assessing worker productivity. There are several ways to calculate the effect of an individual's ill health. For much of this chapter we have focused on the impact of illness or disease on either the individual, his or her family, or the immediate community. However, another reason that countries establish national health policies is to help sustain the economic health of the country. Countries realize that highly contagious or chronic diseases can reduce the number of able-bodied workers. A reduction in the workforce reduces the quantity of products produced, and a reduction in the quantity of products will reduce the country's ability to export goods for sale to sustain its own citizens. For example, WHO calculated that the Russian Federation, China, and India could lose between $200 and $550 billion in national income between 2005 and 2015 due to the impact of three chronic diseases on their eligible workforces: heart disease, stroke, and diabetes (WHO, 2005c).

How does one person's illness affect a country's productivity? In truth, one sick person would have little if any impact on a country's economy. A number of people suffering from the same or related illnesses, however, would affect productivity. In essence, WHO recognizes that individual health affects more than just the individual. It has the potential to affect the economic health of a country as well.

The Federation of Red Cross and Red Crescent Societies

The *Federation of Red Cross and Red Crescent Societies* was established as an international committee to provide relief to wounded soldiers. The founders believed that any organization that provides medical care to soldiers wounded on the battlefield should be a neutral entity in war and therefore free from attacks by either side.

The federation began as a collection of smaller, unaffiliated organizations. In 1919 the smaller organizations banded together to form an international organization known then as the League of Red Cross Societies. Renamed in 1991, the federation currently consists of over 180 societies.

The federation's mission is to provide assistance to individuals irrespective of nationality, race, religious beliefs, class, or political opinion and to improve the lives of people by mobilizing the power of humanity. The federation focuses on four key areas: promoting humanitarian principles and values, disaster response, disaster preparedness, and health care in communities. However, the federation is probably best known for its work in the area of disaster relief.

Remember our discussion earlier in the chapter about Hurricane Katrina? To use the federation's familiar tag line, "The Red Cross was there." The federation provided temporary shelter, meals, and general assistance to the thousands of people displaced by Hurricane Katrina. The goal was to provide for individuals' basic needs including food, shelter, and emergency health care.

Another recent example of the relief assistance provided by the federation is the aid provided to thousands of people injured and displaced by the tsunami that destroyed parts of Indonesia and Southern Thailand in December 2004. The tsunami killed approximately 110,000 people and left hundreds of thousands of others homeless.

Thus, in contrast with WHO, the federation focuses on providing emergency medical and humanitarian aid to people as a result of a natural or a man-made disaster. It does not address policy issues.

Médecins Sans Frontières (Doctors Without Borders)

Médecins Sans Frontières (MSF) shares some of the goals of the Federation of Red Cross and Red Crescent. Like the federation, MSF is an international humanitarian organization that provides emergency aid to persons in need. Specifically, however, MSF responds to the medical care needs of people affected by armed conflict (wars), epidemics, and natural or man-made disasters and to persons who have no access to health care. It was founded in 1971 as a nongovernmental organization to provide emergency medical assistance to people in need and to document the plight of the people it served. Currently, MSF is based in 19 countries.

MSF is known throughout the world for its work in establishing emergency feeding stations in famine-stricken areas such as East Africa or among refugees in countries affected by war or civil conflicts. Recently, MSF has been at the forefront of the effort to use the ready-to-use peanut butter paste (RUTF) to combat malnutrition, an effort also spearheaded by WHO as mentioned earlier (Doctors Without Borders, 2006).

In addition to feeding stations, MSF provides medical care. While this work often falls under the category of immediate care, MSF also assists the trained health care providers in each region or country to support their existing efforts to provide care and to train them to improve the quality of care available. In this way MSF endeavors to help develop the in-country personnel resources needed to provide long-term and sustained medical care once MSF departs. In essence, MSF provides both immediate and long-term health care systems.

WHO, the Federation of Red Cross and Red Crescent, and Médicins Sans Frontières supply some of the basic health and humanitarian services that are unavailable or unaffordable in developing as well as some developed countries. In essence, they provide the basic health systems infrastructure unavailable in some regions of the world.

SECTION III. HEALTH POLICY

National Policy: Global Implications

At first glance, this section may seem redundant. After all, we have discussed national health policy throughout the chapter. For example, we explained the benefits of U.S. national childhood immunization policies on families and communities and examined the effect that termination of such policies has on the health of an entire nation or region. And through our opening story about Mr. Speaker, we saw how one individual's efforts to circumvent national health policy can set the stage for a potential national or international health crisis. In each of these instances, it is easy to see the benefits to individuals and to the community of having a national health policy.

But national policies can have a negative effect as well. One criticism of national health policies is that in some instances national policies prioritize the health of the community over the rights of the individual. The isolation and containment policies to limit the spread of TB in the 19th and 20th centuries in the United States serve as good examples.

Isolation and Containment for TB and HIV/AIDS

In the late 19th and early 20th centuries, local and federal agencies in the United States identified TB as a contagious disease that posed a public health threat to the population (Snider, 1997). To prevent the risk of infection of whole communities, several states constructed *sanatoriums*, lodgelike facilities to isolate and treat TB patients. The primary goal of the treatment centers was to contain the spread of the highly contagious TB disease by preventing individuals with the disease from interacting with noninfected persons. A second goal was to treat TB patients before returning them to their communities. Local and state governments could and often did force TB patients to reside in a sanatorium, sometimes for as long as a year, before returning to their homes. In essence, local and national health policy prioritized the public health and welfare of the population by treating and forcefully isolating (if necessary) individuals with TB, sometimes against their will.

The first sanatorium of record in the United States was opened in 1885 in Lake Saranac, New York (Davis, 1996). Later, other states constructed similar treatment sanatoriums. By the 1950s, over 800 sanatoriums were operating in the United States, serving over 70,000 patients (Davis, 1996; Snider, 1997). The screening and isolation of TB patients, in addition to a rise in the socioeconomic conditions of the U.S. population, jointly helped reduce the prevalence of TB (Binkin et al., 1999).

More recently, in 1986, Cuba used a similar containment strategy for HIV/AIDS. When HIV/AIDS was first detected in Cuba, the Ministry of Health isolated individuals who tested positive for HIV to treat them and their sexual partners. The aggressive policy of isolation, containment, and treatment of HIV-positive individuals helped reduce the prevalence rate in Cuba to 0.1% by 2001 (AMFAR, 2006). When compared with a global HIV rate of 1.0%, Cuba' prevalence rate for HIV was, essentially, negligible (see Chapter 2, Research Methods).

Containment and isolation policies always raise concerns about the rights of the individual. For example, you may have had a few questions about Mr. Speaker's rights when reading in the opening story that the United States activated its forced containment policy. Yet the policies of isolation and containment as practiced in two very different countries suggest that, in some cases, a government may believe that it is its duty to protect the health and well-being of communities first when responding to the health problems of an individual.

In spite of the benefits of public health policies that protect the community, we cannot deny that such policies carry a cost for the individual. In Mr. Speaker's case, in the cases of U.S. TB patients in the 19th and 20th centuries, and in the case of HIV-positive individuals in Cuba, the individual may not be free to determine whether or how to address his or her health issue.

SECTION IV. THE ECONOMIC CONSEQUENCES OF POOR HEALTH

Who Is Affected?

When thinking about health and illness, we often focus on the sufferer, the person afflicted with the illness. That is a sensible place to start. But consider for a moment an individual's health from another perspective. Suppose a 40-year-old man is the major wage earner for his family, a wife and three children. His work in a textile factory, together with his spouse's income as an assistant in a local bakery, provides them with enough money to buy a small but adequate house for themselves and their three children and to pay for daily necessities. This income does not allow enough, however, to afford health care insurance.

Suddenly, the man suffers a stroke. After several weeks of medical care and daily exercise, he is able to move about without assistance, but he cannot return to his old job. His job required manual labor: lifting and transporting heavy containers. Unable to do the same job and unable to find a less physically demanding job, he is now unemployed.

The man's wife takes a second job to make up for the loss of earnings, but her two jobs still pay considerably less than her husband's old job at the factory. What is more, working two jobs the woman finds that she is often exhausted and more prone to catch colds and other minor viral infections.

Seeing the desperate economic condition of the family, the oldest son decides to leave school in the 10th grade to find work and help the family. Because he is a talented student, the family hoped the son would study engineering at a university near them. With a degree in engineering, the son could have helped support his family. Perhaps he can return to school in the future. For now, however, he is needed at home to provide additional economic support for his family.

This is a sad but all too common story in many parts of the world. One person's illness can have a domino effect on the health and well-being of an entire family. It is easy to see the physical costs of the illness on the man and on the economic stability of the family. Less easy to see is the effect his illness has on his emotional state as he sees his wife and son work harder to compensate for his limitations or the emotional and health strains experienced by other family members.

One clear impact of the changed financial circumstances on the wife is her need to work two jobs. The additional responsibility is clearly more demanding physically. But there are emotional health costs as well. With less time at home, she has less time to devote to her role as the primary caregiver of the younger children. The story could go on. We could look at each of the younger children to assess the impact of the changed circumstances on their physical and emotional health, but the likely effect is clear. One person's illness can affect an entire family. The family's well-being is jeopardized by this economic downturn, and as a result the family can easily slip into poverty, and into poor family health.

Individual Health and Community Outcomes

The family certainly suffers from the ill health and loss of productivity of one of its members. But so does the community. We noted previously that communities, and in some cases whole countries, can be adversely affected when large numbers of their working-aged population are compromised by ill health. To illustrate this point, we consider the case of workers in Lesotho, a landlocked country in South Africa (see Figure 3.8). Lesotho, a country the size of the state of Maryland, has little industry to employ its people or to help them earn an income. As a result, many travel into South Africa, an hour's journey by local transport, to find jobs as domestic workers, day laborers, or other similar type jobs.

Currently, Lesotho has an HIV/AIDS prevalence rate of 40%, meaning that 4 in 10 adults are infected with the disease. In some cases whole communities have been affected, leaving

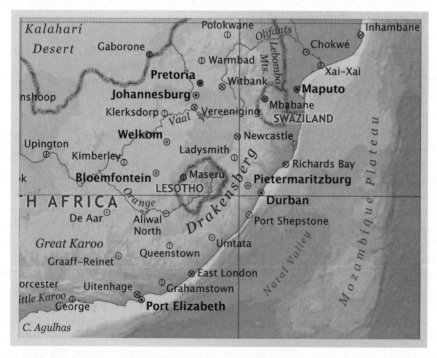

FIGURE 3.8   South Africa and Lesotho. Lesotho, a landlocked country surrounded by South Africa, reports an adult HIV infection rate of 40%.

Source: World Site Atlas.

children and grandparents as the principal wage earners. In essence, in Lesotho almost half of a generation of adults, 20 to 40 years of age, is becoming ill and dying at an alarming rate. Their illnesses and diseases devastate not only the family but the community and the country as well. The young adults would have assumed roles in their communities as employed laborers but also as local organizers for social events, such as fundraisers to raise money for irrigation ditches, or as the coach of a local soccer team. Now, the same adults are unable to work or volunteer. As a result, businesses fail or relocate to countries with a larger supply of workers, and community life becomes a shadow of its former self.

The loss to Lesotho's workforce can be measured in the country's economic profile. The loss to Lesotho's families and to their community is much harder to quantify.

Summary

Many would agree that access to health care should be the right of all individuals. Yet we have been reading about many instances in which, unfortunately, this is not the case. In both developed and developing countries, large segments of societies are unable to obtain health care due to a host of individual, community, systems, and policy factors. The lack of access to health care leads to poorer health outcomes and more costly health care.

It may not be immediately obvious how a health policy positively impacts individual's health. In fact, most often the impact may be indirect. Yet health policies that ensure access to clean water and air and safe neighborhoods or that provide direct medical care benefit each individual in the society.

Personal Postscript

DO GLOBAL HEALTH POLICIES AFFECT YOU?

Simply stated, yes! We may not be aware of the ways in which global health policies affect us given the vast and well established health care systems and infrastructure in the United States, but they do.

First, most developed countries are members of the World Health Organization. U.S. representatives to WHO help shape the policy decisions and plan the health activities and projects to be undertaken throughout the world. The effects of these policies are more evident in less developed countries, but even developed countries must continue to strive toward the Millennium Goals of 2012 to provide health care for all, both here and abroad.

In addition, organizations like the Federation of Red Cross and Red Crescent and Médecins Sans Frontières send their aid workers to assist in disasters and to provide needed medical care in all countries, even in the United States. The Red Cross and Médecins Sans Frontières were two of the many aid organizations that provided valuable assistance to the residents of New Orleans in the aftermath of Hurricane Katrina. Assistance also poured in from Europe and Latin America, in part because nations around the world see it as their responsibility to help provide for the health and well-being of others, regardless of their nationality.

Remember also that diseases and illnesses can cross borders. Throughout history we have seen the effects of epidemics and pandemics that, by definition, do not respect borders. More recently, we have experienced the effects of HIV/AIDS, the avian flu, and the A/H1N1 (swine) influenza, which have caused illness and death to thousands globally including the United States. So another reason to be mindful of global health policy is to safeguard and protect your own health as well as others.

Important Terms

active TB   72

adult-onset diabetes   84

anopheles mosquito   79

antibodies   74

artemisinin   80

asthma   86

Athenian plague   70

bacilli   66

Black Death   71

cestodiasis parasite   80

chicken pox   74

childhood viral
    diseases   73

cholera   79

chronic diseases   70

chronic obstructive pulmonary
    disease (COPD)   87

chronic respiratory
    diseases   86

copepods   81

confounding factors   84

developed countries   68

developing countries   68

diabetes mellitus   84

Disability Adjusted Life
    Expectancy (DALE)   90

diseases of affluence   82

dracunculus medinensis   81

Ebola virus   70

epidemic   70

Federation of Red Cross
    and Red Crescent
    Societies   95

glanders   70

global health
    organizations   93

guinea worm   81

haemorrhagic plague   71

HIV/AIDS virus   71

human-to-human
    transmission   68

immunization   74

insulin   84

latent TB   72

macroeconomic impact of ill
    health   93

malaria   79

measles   74

Médecins Sans Frontières
    (MSF)   95

overall life expectancy   90

pandemic   70

parasites   80

plasmodium   79

poliomyelitis   74

Polio   74

pulmonary tuberculosis   66

quality of life   90

sanatorium   96

sedentary lifestyle   84

taenia saginata   80

taenia solium   80

tapeworm   80

tuberculosis (TB)   66

Type 1 diabetes   84

Type 2 diabetes   84

vaccine   74

varicella zoster virus   74

vibrio cholerae   79

western disease   82

World Health Organization
    (WHO)   93

Chapter Four

Theories and Models of Health Behavior Change

Chapter Objectives

After studying this chapter you will be able to:

1. Accurately define *expectancy value theory, social cognitive theory, the theory of planned behavior, health belief model,* and *the transtheoretical model of behavior change.*
2. Name and describe the key concepts of each theory and model.
3. Identify one contribution of each theory and model to understanding human health behavior.
4. Define social marketing.
5. Explain the four *P*s of marketing and their role in shaping behaviors.
6. Identify the five components of the ecological model.
7. Describe the factors that limit access to health care.
8. Explain the effects of limited access to care on individual health outcomes.
9. Define health policy.
10. Explain the goal of health policy initiatives for individual health behaviors.

OPENING STORY: EDDIE'S DILEMMA

Eddie is a 28-year-old single man who began smoking when he was 13 years old. He wanted to look mature like his older brother, who also began smoking as a teenager.

Eddie now smokes 20 to 30 cigarettes a day. He calls himself a "social smoker" because he smokes with his friends either after work or at social events. Recently he met Sarah, someone whose company he really enjoys. Sarah does not smoke. In fact, she detests the smell of cigarettes. After months of encouragement from Sarah, Eddie decided to stop smoking. On New Year's Day, Eddie threw away all the cigarette packs in his home and car.

For 11 days Eddie managed without a cigarette. On the 12th day he attended a birthday party for a friend. Many of his friends from work were at the party also. When one friend offered Eddie a cigarette, Eddie accepted without hesitation. He has continued smoking ever since.

On occasion, Eddie tells himself he should stop smoking. Perhaps it is more accurate to say that Sarah tells him he should stop smoking. But he quickly dismisses the suggestion when he remembers his attempts to stop on New Year's Day. He remembers feeling fidgety and irritable on the fourth day without cigarettes. He dreads the thought of experiencing withdrawal symptoms once again, a sign that Eddie was physically addicted to cigarettes. In addition, he recalls the daily struggles to resist the temptation to smoke when his other friends who smoke were with him and their constant criticism of his efforts to quit.

Eddie's friends do not understand his desire to stop smoking and think that Sarah is being unreasonable when she makes Eddie choose between smoking and spending time with her. Unlike Sarah, they are not supportive of Eddie's efforts to change behaviors. Eddie commented recently to one friend that he feels like a yo-yo: Sarah pressures him to stop smoking while his other friends entice him to smoke.

Sarah understands his dilemma, but she is growing increasingly intolerant of Eddie's smoking habit. She never thought she would have a close relationship with a smoker and questions whether she can continue even now.

Now what? What if you were Eddie? What factors would support or undermine your efforts to quit smoking?   ■

The opening story identifies several social factors that influence Eddie's smoking behaviors. Without a doubt, friends, peer groups, and family all influence individual health behaviors (Hoffman, Sussman, Unger, & Valente, 2006). But our health behaviors are also shaped by other factors, including our attitudes about behaviors, our knowledge of the health consequences of our behaviors, our environment, and our access to health care.

A number of theories and models in psychology explain human behavior. Some are designed specifically to identify factors that explain or predict health behaviors while others were intended to explain general behaviors. In this chapter we will examine five theories or models employed by health psychologists to explain a range of health behaviors: expectancy value theory, the theory of planned behavior, the health belief model, social cognitive theory, and the transtheoretical model of behavior change. Expectancy value theory (EVT), the theory of planned behavior (TPB), and the social cognitive theory (SCT) were developed originally to explain general human behavior. They have been adapted for use in health psychology to explain health behaviors. Others, including the health belief model (HBM) and the transtheoretical model of behavior change (TTM), were developed specifically as health behavior models. We will also examine a technique called social marketing which, although not a model, has been found to influence behaviors including health behaviors. Finally, consistent with the research in this field, we will explore blended models, that is, a combination of several models designed to improve our ability to explain or predict health behaviors.

By the end of Section I you will be able to describe each of the five theories or models used frequently in health psychology to explain health behaviors. Section II introduces social marketing and its contribution to promoting behavior change. By the end of that section you will be able to define and explain social marketing and its contribution to shaping health behaviors. You also will be able to describe blended models.

In Section III, we discuss an ecological approach to health by explaining the relative contributions of the individual, cultural or social networks, environment, health systems, and health policy on individual health outcomes. By the end of the section, you will be able to give examples of how each of these factors contributes to individual health outcomes. Finally, Section IV concludes the chapter with a discussion of the challenges to sustaining healthy behaviors.

While reading this chapter you will want to remember one thing: The theories and models included were developed and tested primarily in Western, developed countries. Their usefulness as global theories or as universal models of health behaviors is still being explored.

SECTION I. THEORIES AND MODELS OF HEALTH BEHAVIOR CHANGE

Expectancy Value Theory (EVT)

Fishbein's *expectancy value theory (EVT)* is one of three theories originally developed to explain human behavior. Health psychologists adapted the EVT to explain health behaviors. The EVT states that two forces motivate behavior, the anticipated or expected outcome of the behavior and the value assigned to the outcome (Fishbein & Ajzen, 1975).

According to the EVT (see Table 4.1), every behavior has a consequence. Individuals anticipate these consequences and assign a positive or negative value to the outcomes (Palmgreen, 1984). The anticipated consequence of a behavior and the value assigned to it are based on an individual's past experiences with the behavior and its outcome. These influence the decision to engage or not to engage in similar behaviors in the future (Borders, 2004; DelBocca, Darkes, Goldman, & Smith, 2002). In essence, the EVT describes a cognitive process whereby individuals assess their behaviors and evaluate the consequences based on the values they assign to the consequences.

We can examine the EVT using Eddie as a test case. In the opening story, Eddie is evaluating his smoking behavior and the consequence of smoking based on the value that he assigns to the consequence. Initially, Eddie enjoys smoking, especially "social smoking." Thus, he assigns a positive value to smoking. Based on this information, the EVT might predict that Eddie would continue smoking.

We see from the story, however, that Eddie's decision about smoking is not quite that simple. There are two additional factors that influence Eddie's smoking behavior, his peer groups and their views on smoking. Unfortunately, the EVT is designed to explain only one behavior. EVT can explain Eddie's smoking behavior independent of group influences but cannot evaluate

TABLE 4.1	Theories and Models of Behavior Change		
Author	**Theory/model**	**Defining features**	**Limitations**

Fishbein & Ajzen, 1975	Expectancy value theory (EVT)	Two forces motivate behavior:
		    Anticipated/expected outcome
		    Value assigned to outcome
			Cannot explain effects of multiple factors on behavior

Bandura, 1977	Social cognitive theory	Individuals learn from cognitive assessment and consequences of behavior using four cues:
		    Direct experiences
		    Vicarious experiences
		    Persuasory learning
		    Inferred learning
		Self-efficacy is critical to learning
			Reciprocal determinism (RD):
			    Behavior viewed in context of environmental factors, personal factors, and behaviors
			No way to test RD

Ajzen & Fishbein, 1980	Theory of reasoned action	Behaviors determined by intentions
		Intentions influenced by two factors:
		    Attitudes about behavior
		    Subjective norms
			Cannot explain spontaneous, involuntary, habitual behaviors

Ajzen (1985)	Theory of planned behavior	Behaviors determined by intentions
		Intentions influenced by three factors:
		    Attitudes about behavior
		    Subjective norms
		    Perceived behavioral control
			Self-efficacy (perceived behavioral control) strongest predictor of behaviors
			Does not explain spontaneous or habitual behaviors

Rosenstock, Strecher, & Becker (1988)	Health belief model	Motivational factors that influence health behaviors and health care seeking are:
		    Perceived severity
		    Perceived susceptibility
		    Perceived benefits
		    Perceived barriers
		Self-efficacy added as fifth factor
			Self-efficacy accounts for many behavioral outcomes

TABLE 4.1	(Continued)		
Author	**Theory/model**	**Defining features**	**Limitations**
Prochaska & DiClemente (1983)	Transtheoretical model of behavioral change	Change is a process that includes: Precontemplation Contemplation Preparation for action Action Maintenance Recidivism explains setbacks	Fails to weigh effects of factors other than individual in process of change

the effects of the second factor, peer groups, on the target behavior (Borders, 2004). As we indicated earlier, social influences affect behaviors, and these, too, must be considered.

Because the EVT cannot account for the effects of peer groups on Eddie's smoking behavior, it similarly cannot explain the impact of the negative or positive values of the group on Eddie's behaviors (Williams, Anderson, & Winett, 2005). For Eddie, there are negative outcomes associated with smoking and negative outcomes associated with not smoking. The outcomes are rooted in the values of each of the peer groups. For example, Sarah detests smoking. Therefore, one negative outcome associated with smoking is the loss of Sarah's company. On the other hand, Eddie's friends enjoy smoking. Eddie's friends represent a negative outcome associated with not smoking.

The EVT's inability to account for more than one factor that also influences behavior is a limitation of the theory. To address this limitation, Herrnstein (1970) and later Borders (2004) proposed adding the concept of matching law to EVT. The ***matching law*** states that decisions to engage in a specific behavior are influenced, in part, by reinforcements for the intended behavior as well as reinforcements for alternate behaviors (Herrnstein, 1961). If the reinforcement for an alternate behavior is greater than the reinforcement for the intended behavior, then the likelihood is greater that an individual will perform the alternate behavior.

How could EVT with matching law explain Eddie's behavior? Consider this: Eddie's intended behavior is smoking. One alternate behavior is spending time with Sarah. The reinforcement for spending time with Sarah is that Eddie enjoys her company. If Eddie determines that the reinforcement he feels from time with Sarah outweighs the reinforcement from smoking, then, according to the EVT with matching law, he will choose the alternate behavior, spending time with Sarah.

Research studies often test the explanatory power of theories. Their results are used either to support or to refute the theory in whole or in part. Research testing the EVT has produced findings that do both. For example, Finch and colleagues (2005) tested the EVT's ability to explain weight loss. They tested whether highly favorable outcome expectations would promote weight loss. Using a randomized clinical trial design (see Chapter 2, Research Methods) with 349 largely white (89.1%), female (86.7%) participants, Finch and colleagues (2005) found that positive expectations alone were not sufficient to predict weight loss. Similar studies examining the EVT's ability to predict othere health behaviors such as physical activity among adults showed mixed findings (Rovniak, Anderson, Winett, & Stephens, 2002; Sallis, Hovell, & Hofsteller, 1989).

The mixed results from studies testing the EVT do not provide strong support for the theory. Yet specific concepts introduced by this theory have been adopted and are incorporated in other models (Bandura, 1977; Fishbein & Ajzen, 1975). For example, social learning theory and the theory of planned behavior include values and expected outcomes as determinants of an individual's intention to engage in specific behaviors (Bandura, 1977; Fishbein & Azjen, 1975). In essence, while researchers question whether EVT with matching law adequately explains behaviors, they accept that some concepts included in EVT are important determinants of behavior.

Social Cognitive Theory (SCT)

LEARNING PROCESSES   Albert Bandura's *social cognitive theory* (*SCT*, originally *social learning theory*) proposes that cognitive processes are critical to the acquisition and regulation of behaviors (Bandura, 1977). Bandura contends that individuals learn from the consequences of their behaviors. He calls this concept *learned behavioral consequences*. Consequences are communicated through "response information" cues that are acquired in one of four ways. First, information can be acquired through *direct experiences*, that is, an individual engaging in a behavior that results in a specific behavioral outcome. Consider this example. A person who touches a hot stove and withdraws the hand in pain will learn through the direct experience that a hot stove causes pain. The experience of touching a hot stove resulted in a negative association. The behavior of touching the stove together with the negative outcome conveys information to the person about the behavior. By linking behaviors with informational cues, Bandura links direct learning with our cognitive process. The pairing occurs as a conscious effort by the actor. It is not automatic.

Information also comes in the form of *vicarious experiences*. Here, Bandura characterizes the learning that occurs as a result of observing the outcomes of another individual. We will return to our example of touching a hot stove. In vicarious experiences we may witness someone else touching a stove that we know to be hot. We may see the other person withdraw his or her hand quickly from the stove and cry out in pain. We learn through the other person's experience that the hot stove causes pain. There is no need to repeat the same act to determine the outcome. Like direct experiences, vicarious experiences also require cognition because the person observing the behavior deduces that similar behavioral outcomes would accrue to him or her if engaging in the same behavior.

Persuasory learning is the learning that occurs from the judgments expressed by others about specific behaviors. Persuasory learning requires no action on anyone's part. It is a wholly cognitive learning process. We may not ever witness the behavioral outcomes, yet we acknowledge and accept them as valid based on the credibility and/or authority of those rendering the judgment. For example, we may never experience or see firsthand the lung cancer that resulted from long-term smoking behavior, but we credit the judgment of the experts who tell us that lung cancer is a possible outcome from smoking.

Finally, *inferred learning* is learning derived from a person's own knowledge. The application of logic or rules allows an individual to posit an outcome without having to engage in the act. As with persuasory learning, inferred learning requires no action. Rather, our cognitive process of deduction allows us to derive a set of probable behaviors and their corresponding behavioral outcomes based on our knowledge of both the behaviors and our application of rules.

SELF-EFFICACY   Self-efficacy is a fifth and critical component of Bandura's theory. *Self-efficacy* is defined as a person's conviction that his or her actions will produce the expected outcomes. It is related to the concept of outcome expectancies. While the term *outcome expectancies* refers to our expectation of positive or negative outcomes resulting from our performance (Williams et al., 2005), self-efficacy characterizes our judgment about our ability to perform a specific task. According to Bandura, our strong belief in our ability to perform a behavior will increase the probability of performing the behavior. Conversely, serious doubts about the ability to perform a specific behavior will almost certainly result in the behavior not being performed. Bandura contends that efficacy expectations vary on three dimensions: magnitude, referring to the level of difficulty; generality, pertaining to the level of mastery needed to accomplish a specific task; and, strength, here meaning strength of the expectation, which will be weak or strong (Bandura, 1977).

Does self-efficacy help explain Eddie's behaviors in the opening story? It may be difficult to determine based on the information presented. Initially Eddie's self-efficacy about ending his smoking habit was high, as evidenced by the fact that he attempted and successfully stopped smoking for 11 days. In the story, Eddie's reluctance to try to stop smoking for a second time is attributed to the negative sensations of nicotine withdrawal and the negative reinforcement of his close friends. It is also possible that Eddie now perceives the task as very difficult, a perception that may lower his overall self-efficacy to try again to quit. Eddie is aware that he failed to stop smoking once before and may believe that he lacks the level of mastery needed to accomplish his goal.

The self-efficacy concept in Bandura's SCT is compelling and appears to be an important factor in determining behaviors. It has been used in a number of studies that report strong correlations between self-efficacy and behavioral outcomes. For example, Shiaw-Ling and colleagues (2006) tested three theories to determine which best predicted the reproductive health intentions of adolescent diabetic women. They found self-efficacy to be one of the best predictors of intention to use birth control. Similarly, Luszczynska and Schwarzer (2003) reported the strong effects of self-efficacy when predicting women's intentions to conduct breast self-examination.

RECIPROCAL DETERMINISM   Overall, Bandura's theory offers an interesting approach to understanding human behaviors and specifically health behaviors. The principal problem with Bandura's SCT is the inability to test a concept he calls *reciprocal determinism*. Another key concept in the SCT reciprocal determinism states that behavior must be viewed in the context of environmental events (*E*) and personal factors (*P*) that influence behaviors (*B*) (Kohler, Grimley, & Reynolds, 1999) as shown in Figure 4.1. Bandura proposes that each of these variables interact significantly with the other two. Unfortunately, the simultaneous interaction of all

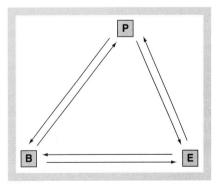

FIGURE 4.1   Reciprocal Determinism in Social Cognitive Theory. Bandura's reciprocal determinism explains behavioral outcomes as a product of the interaction between the person, the environment, and the behavior itself.

Source: Bandura (1986).

three variables makes it almost impossible to isolate one of the variables, such as environment, to test its effect on the other two.

In essence, the social cognitive theory of behavior is compelling conceptually but difficult to test. On the other hand, the concept of self-efficacy, which has been supported in subsequent research and included in many theories and models of health behaviors, appears to be central to behavioral outcomes.

Theory of Planned Behavior (TPB)

The *theory of planned behavior (TPB)* proposed by Ajzen (1985) builds on an earlier theory known as the *theory of reasoned action (TRA)* (Ajzen & Fishbein, 1980). We include a brief review of TRA because it is the foundation for TPB and because some studies continue to test the predictive validity of TRA.

THEORY OF REASONED ACTION   Briefly, TRA states that an individual's behavior is determined by his or her intentions. Intentions, however, are influenced by two factors, attitudes about the behavior and subjective norms, as shown in Figure 4.2.

Consider this example. Seeing a traffic light at an intersection change from green to yellow, a motorist must decide either to continue through the intersection or to slow to a stop anticipating the red stoplight. If the motorist decides to continue without stopping at the light then, according to TRA, that motorist's behavior is preceded by the intention to continue through the light regardless of the changing signal. The intention is based on a belief about the likely outcome of the behavior (Madden, Ellen, & Ajzen, 1992). One likely outcome the motorist may anticipate is safe passage through the intersection. TRA proposes that the behavior and the expected outcome are determined by two factors, the motorist's attitude about performing the action and the subjective norm associated with the behavior. A positive attitude about the behavior of continuing through the changing traffic light means that the motorist associates the decision to proceed with a positive outcome such as saving time or safe passage through the light (Kohler, Grimley, & Reynolds, 1999). A negative attitude about proceeding might be based on an expectation of a negative outcome such as getting a traffic ticket or having a traffic accident. Thus, a negative attitude would lead to a decision to stop at the light.

The second factor influencing both intentions and behaviors, according to TRA, is *subjective norms*. Here the authors are referring to the motorist's belief about what others would think about his or her behavior. The concern here is not what others, in general, think. What matters is the opinion of people who are important to the motorist. This might include family members, close friends, or perhaps her or his employer.

Do people really base their behaviors on the thoughts and beliefs of people close to them? Theories like TRA suggest that an individual's behavior is shaped by the opinions of close friends or family members. But, at other times, individuals engage in behaviors that are inconsistent with the attitudes or values of their closest associates. For example, in many cases illegal drug use or acts of theft are not supported or valued by an individual's friends. To account for behaviors that are at odds with the values and beliefs of one's social group, TRA proposes that we must consider a person's motivation to comply with the expectations of the social group. For example, if the motorist's friends think that refusing to stop when a traffic light changes to red is acceptable or even "cool," *and* if the motorist cares about the group's approval, it is likely that the

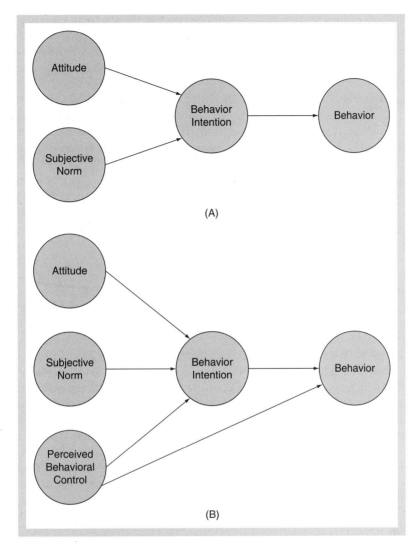

FIGURE 4.2   Models: Theory of Reasoned Action (A) and Theory of Planned Behavior (B). The theory of planned behavior adds, in effect, a self-efficacy component to help explain behavioral outcomes.

Source: Madden, Ellen, & Ajzen (1992).

motorist will adopt this behavior. If the motorist does not strongly seek the approval of the group or is not inclined to comply with the subjective norms of the group pertaining to driving through red lights, then the motorist will be less likely to adopt this behavior (Kohler, Grimley, & Reynolds, 1999).

SIMILARITIES BETWEEN EVT AND TRA   We mentioned earlier that researchers have applied some of the concepts introduced by the expectancy value theory (EVT) to explain human behavior. A closer examination reveals similarities between the EVT and the TRA. The EVT identifies anticipated outcomes and values as determinants of human behaviors. The TRA identifies attitudes and subjective norms as the principal factors influencing behaviors. Yet attitudes and behaviors reflect values, and values are influenced, in part, by the subjective norms of an individual's peer groups.

It seems intuitive that attitudes about a behavior will affect the likelihood of performing the behavior. If we dislike a behavior, we may be less likely to repeat that act. Similarly, if our group's subjective norms are inconsistent with a specific action, we are less likely to perform that act. In many instances, a group's approval or disapproval of a person's behavior often influences that person's choice of behaviors.

Researchers continue to test the predictive validity of the TRA but, as was the case for the EVT, support for the TRA is mixed. In most instances, research supporting the TRA focuses on the ability of the theory to predict the intention to act but not the actual behavior (Poss, 2001). For example, Ross and colleagues (2007) tested the TRA's ability to explain African American men's intention to obtain information about prostate cancer. Their findings suggest that both attitudes and subjective norms were important predictors of the intention to seek information. They did not indicate whether the men actually obtained the information. Similarly, Boyd and Wandersman's (1991) study of condom use by college undergraduates revealed that the intention to use condoms was associated with behavioral and normative beliefs. But here, too, research did not reveal whether the targeted behavior was performed.

Other criticisms of the TRA include the association among subjective norms, behavioral intentions (Johnston, White, & Norman, 2004), and their effects on volitional acts, a subset of behaviors that are under a person's direct control. If, according to the TRA, intentions determine behaviors, then the theory cannot explain addictive, habitual, or involuntary behaviors. This is a major omission because addictive, habitual, and involuntary behaviors occur frequently in most humans. Consider this: Few people who engage in addictive behaviors do so to obtain the negative outcomes often associated with those behaviors. For example, smokers who are addicted to nicotine do not intend to put themselves at higher risk for lung or throat cancer. Nor do they intend to allocate ever-increasing amounts of their disposable income to sustain their habit.

Likewise, the TRA is unable to explain behaviors that are largely habitual, like brushing one's teeth in the morning before leaving for work or school or other hygiene habits that are done without prior thought. Spontaneous behaviors also cannot be explained using this theory because intent assumes some level of thought and purposefulness, which is, by definition, the opposite of spontaneity.

THEORY OF PLANNED BEHAVIOR   To address these omissions, Ajzen proposed the Theory of Planned Behaviors (TPB). The TPB includes the concept of *perceived behavioral control* (Azjen & Madden, 1986) to account for nonvolitional actions. The TPB suggests that peoples' belief that they possess the resources and the opportunities needed to perform a behavior is directly related to their perceived control over their behavior. The greater the perceived behavioral control, the greater the likelihood that the behavior will be performed.

The concept of perceived behavioral control presented here is quite similar to Bandura's concept of self-efficacy, that is, the belief that one has the ability to achieve the intended behavior. Some research that tests the TPB suggests that the revised theory predicts both intentions and adherence to new health behaviors. For example, in a study of adherence to treatment regiments for diabetes and hypertension among South Africans residing in a rural region called the Western Cape, the TPB variables of attitude, perceived behavior control, and subjective norms were the strongest predictors of behavioral outcomes (Kagee & van der Merwe, 2006). Similarly, TPB was strongly associated with self-management of arthritis among rheumatoid arthritis patients (Strating, Schuur, & Suurmeijer, 2006), and regulation of sugar intake in Tanzania (Masalu & Astrom, 2003). What is important to note in all of these studies is the role of self-efficacy in explaining or predicting behaviors. In all three studies, self-efficacy was cited as a critical factor that, together with attitudes and subjective norms, boosts the predictive value of this model.

The theory of reasoned action and the theory of planned behavior identify two constructs—attitude and subjective norms—that contribute to explaining human behavior. The models also rely heavily on self-efficacy as a determinant of behavior. But, to explain spontaneous, habitual, or unplanned behaviors, we must turn to other models and theories.

Health Belief Model (HBM)

A model designed to examine the motivational factors specifically associated with health behaviors is the ***health belief model (HBM)***. Irwin Rosenstock introduced the health belief model in 1974 to understand why and under what conditions a person uses preventive health services. Examples of preventive health services include annual physical examinations, sometimes referred to as well-care medical visits, or annual dental examinations. Understanding the factors that motivate people to prevent, detect, and diagnose diseases is the first step toward the goal of predicting, promoting, and assisting people in changing health behaviors (Rosenstock, 2005). The health belief model seeks to explain the preventive health behaviors of persons who believe they are healthy and who attempt to maintain that status by preventing disease or by detecting disease in its earliest, asymptomatic stages (Rosenstock, 2005). The goal coincides with the public health goals of prevention, early detection, and disease control. As such, the HBM was considered a useful tool for the field of public health.

The central concepts of HBM derive from work by Kurt Lewin (1935), a social psychologist. Drawing from Lewin's theory, the HBM attempts to explain and predict an individual's health behavior using the individual's own subjective frame of reference. For this reason, the HBM is considered a psychosocial model. The subjective focus of this theory is evident in the five key concepts used to explain health behaviors: perceived susceptibility, perceived severity, perceived benefits, perceived barriers, and cues to action. A sixth concept, Bandura's self-efficacy, was added to the model when it was determined to be a critical component of barriers to act (Bandura, 1982, 1977). Perceived susceptibility and perceived severity together contribute to the perceived threat of a disease, whereas perceived benefits and perceived barriers directly affect the likelihood that a person will take action against the disease.

PERCEIVED SUSCEPTIBILITY AND PERCEIVED SEVERITY   *Perceived susceptibility* is the degree to which an individual feels at risk for catching a disease or illness. It is measured on a continuum. For example, a person may deny any possibility of contracting a disease. Conversely, a person may concede that contracting a disease is possible but highly unlikely. Finally, a person may concede a high probability of catching a disease and feel that they are in imminent danger (Rosenstock, 2005).

Consider for the moment the probability of farmers in Des Moines, Iowa, contracting the avian influenza A virus (avian flu) introduced in Chapter 3, Global Communicable and Chronic Disease. Avian flu was identified first in Hong Kong. It was the first known case of animal-to-human transmission of influenza A virus, spread from infected poultry. At its onset, the avian flu accounted for six deaths and 12 illnesses (CDC, 2005). Initially, poultry farmers in Des Moines, Iowa, may not have perceived themselves susceptible to the avian flu from Hong Kong given the distance between Hong Kong and Des Moines. Reasonably, therefore, Des Moines farmers may have perceived their susceptibility to avian flu as low to nonexistent.

When avian flu was detected in poultry in China, Greece, Turkey, and England, the Des Moines farmers may have reassessed their susceptibility to the virus. The spread of the virus to other countries, some a long distance from Hong Kong, changed the statistical probability of contracting the disease among people who raise or handle poultry. Des Moines farmers may have conceded the possibility of contracting the disease given its spread to other countries. Still, the farmers may have determined that their risk of catching the disease remained low because Iowa is an ocean away from all of the affected countries. But when avian flu was detected in New York State, the farmers probably perceived a marked increase in their susceptibility to the disease.

Perceived severity or the perception of the seriousness of a disease also varies by person; it is a subjective value. Perceived severity is shaped, in part, by two factors, a person's emotional response to the illness and the perceived impact of the disease on the person's life. For example, for some individuals the possibility of suffering irreversible loss of sight in one eye due to glaucoma may be a frightening prospect. Yet the fact that the loss of sight is limited to one eye may be reassuring. For others, however, loss of sight, whether in one eye or two, could be emotionally devastating and could signal a major change in lifestyle or behaviors.

The perceived severity of a disease, however, refers to more than just the impact of the disease on the infected person. Severity could include the effect of the disease on people's daily functioning or on their responsibilities for their family. In some cases, the physical limitations caused by the disease may be less disruptive than the impact of the disease on the person's familial responsibilities. When combined, a perceived high susceptibility to, and a perceived high severity of, the disease should result in a strong perceived threat of the disease, perceptions that should lead to action.

PERCEIVED BENEFITS AND PERCEIVED BARRIERS   The HBM proposes that individuals also calculate the *perceived benefits* and *perceived barriers* to health behaviors. Perceived benefits and perceived barriers help individuals transition from potential to actual behavior change. When calculating the perceived benefits of a health behavior, individuals consider the physical benefits of performing the behavior as well as the psychological benefits of preventing the onset of an illness or of controlling its effects. Here the influence of social psychology is evident again. The perception of benefits is highly subjective. Consider the benefits of testing to determine whether one has been infected with the HIV virus. For many individuals, knowing one's HIV status may be a psychological benefit, especially if the individual does not have the disease. Knowledge may relieve worry.

However, some of the behaviors required to produce the benefit may present barriers. Consider this: Health care workers in southern Africa thought that knowing one's HIV/AIDS status would be seen as a benefit for villagers in rural areas. The increased incidences of HIV/AIDS throughout southern Africa led many villagers in rural areas to be wary of the disease.

Consequently, health care workers thought that knowing one's HIV/AIDS status would be seen as a benefit for villagers. They surmised that an HIV test would provide reassuring information for those who tested negative and give those who tested positive an opportunity to obtain early counseling and treatment. Instead, researchers discovered that, for the villagers, testing triggered an unanticipated barrier: stigma (Pendry, 2001). In some villages, individuals who were tested for HIV were suspected of having the virus even before the results were known. Thus, villagers who were tested were ostracized by their community whether or not they tested positive for HIV. Some individuals were ostracized even by family members, who feared that the village would generalize their reactions to the entire family regardless of whether they sought testing. In this case, the anticipated benefit of screening to determine one's HIV/AIDS status was outweighed by the barrier of certain stigma for the individual and his or her family (Mills, 2006).

Similar barriers to testing have been reported in other countries. In studies among HIV-positive gay and bisexual men and of heterosexual African men and women in England, as well as among HIV-positive women in the United States, respondents also cited a fear of ostracism in their communities as a deterrent to HIV testing (Abel, 2007; Dodds, 2006). Thus, a community's social norms can create a psychological barrier that prevents some individuals from performing a beneficial health behavior in order to prevent certain stigma.

It is important to note that, in some instances, society's stigma may be triggered by the behavior that lead to the disease rather than the disease itself. Consider this: Many societies discourage specific behaviors, including multiple sex partners, sex in exchange for money or goods, or illicit drug use. It just so happens that these are the same behaviors that increase risks of contracting HIV/AIDS. It is possible, therefore, that society's reaction is directed at the behaviors that cause HIV/AIDS, consistent with their values, rather than the disease iteself.

Do the HBM concepts really explain our health behavior process? Can the HBM predict a person's likelihood of using preventive health services? The answer is an equivocal "sometimes." In a review of 29 studies testing the explanatory power of the HBM, Janz and Becker (1984) found strong evidence to support three of the four principal constructs of this model. Perceived barriers were found to be the strongest of the four constructs in explaining both preventive health behaviors and "sick role behaviors," that is, behaviors of people diagnosed with an illness and who are receiving medical treatment. Perceived susceptibility explained only preventive health behaviors, and perceived benefits explained only sick role behaviors. Perceived severity explained little in the way of behaviors (Janz & Becker, 1984).

In sum, health benefits, real or perceived, may be negated by barriers. We define barriers as any impediment, real or perceived, that prevents an individual from performing beneficial health behaviors. Barriers include tangible factors such as money, time, and effort, as well as psychological factors such as stigma or a loss of social standing among one's peer groups.

CUES TO ACTION   The fifth variable in the HBM, *cues to action*, prompts an individual to act when several conditions are met: The person perceives he or she is susceptible to a disease, the person views the disease as serious, or the person positively views the benefits to action and identifies few if any barriers to action.

There are several types of cues. A cue could be a tangible or visible factor such as a physiological reaction or symptom of illness. Psychological prompts such as concern on the part of the susceptible person or by family or friends also motivate action. Finally, environmental cues such as an advertisement or other stimulus external to the individual may also evoke action.

SELF-EFFICACY   Perceived benefits, barriers, susceptibility, and severity provide the analytic framework for deciding on a healthy course of action. But health-enhancing behaviors assume that a person feels he or she can perform the behavior successfully. Hence, Bandura's self-efficacy was added to the HBM.

Recent studies provide additional support for the role of self-efficacy and perceived barriers in explaining health behaviors. Findings from longitudinal studies by Walter and colleagues (1992, 1993, 1994) suggest that self-efficacy is crucial for adolescents when attempting to use health-enhancing behaviors. Specifically, Walter and colleagues (1993, 1992) examined factors associated with AIDS risk behaviors among over 1,000 New York City high school students, grades 10 and 11, testing the role of perceived benefits, barriers, susceptibility, and severity of HIV/AIDS and the role of self-efficacy in engaging in preventive HIV/AIDS risk behaviors. Specifically, the studies sought to measure the intention of students to use condoms when engaging in sexual intercourse. Condom use was considered a perceived benefit for HIV/AIDS prevention because it reduces the risk of contracting the disease.

High school students in the studies were presented with an eight-week educational intervention program designed to impart knowledge, teach skills, and build confidence (self-efficacy) in negotiating safer sexual behaviors. Pre- and posttests (see Chapter 2, Research Methods) measured the effectiveness of the intervention in reducing intentions to engage in risky sexual behaviors linked to HIV/AIDS. Walter and colleagues (1992, 1993) found that students readily accepted the benefits of condom use in reducing the risk of HIV/AIDS. They even believed that the skills-building exercises that taught them to negotiate safer sexual behaviors (also a benefit) could be effective. However, the study revealed that students believed their self-efficacy in negotiating safer sex would be compromised severely if they consumed alcohol or used other substances before any attempt to negotiate about sexual behaviors. In addition, students believed that other socioenvironmental factors, including perception of friends' behaviors and the student's personal values about the preventive behaviors, would mitigate their ability to practice safer sex. In essence, Walter and colleagues (1993, 1992) demonstrated that self-efficacy is important for performing a behavior, but it can be undermined by substance use, by attitudes about the behaviors, and by the perceived subjective norms of the peer group.

The findings by Walter and colleagues (1992, 1993) were replicated by Naar-King and colleagues (2006) in their study of the relationship between substance use and the decreased use of condoms. They reaffirmed the role of self-efficacy in influencing behaviors associated with unprotected sexual behaviors.

Other studies that support the role of self-efficacy as a predictor of health behaviors include women's perceived severity, perceived susceptibility, or self-efficacy with respect to osteoporosis and colon and breast cancer (Dassow, 2005); women's intention to use hormone replacement therapy to control the physiological and emotional effects of menopause (McGinley, 2004); and women's dietary behaviors (Lea, Crawford, & Worsley, 2006; Schwarzer et al., 2007).

The findings from recent studies that highlight the role of self-efficacy do not negate the importance of the four HBM concepts of perceived severity, perceived susceptibility, perceived benefits, and perceived barriers for explaining health behaviors. They do suggest, however, that self-efficacy is an essential component for action but one that is vulnerable to psychological and socioenvironmental factors.

TESTING THE HBM   It seems only fitting that we use Eddie's case once again to test the HBM as a predictor of health-seeking behaviors. In the opening story, Eddie does not consider the health consequences of smoking. He does not consider his susceptibility to illnesses associated with smoking or the severity of such illnesses. Therefore, when applying the HBM to Eddie, we focus on the perceived benefits and perceived barriers of smoking cessation and on Eddie's self-efficacy. For Eddie, not smoking will result in both benefits and barriers. In the story, Eddie perceives that Sarah's support and friendship are the only benefits if he stops smoking. By comparison, the barriers to ending his smoking behaviors include the lost companionship and support of his other friends and the physical discomfort of withdrawal symptoms. At this point, it appears that the barriers outweigh the benefits.

Finally, Eddie's self-efficacy seems to be diminishing. His failed effort to stop smoking, in addition to the discomfort he experienced during that time, seem to suggest a waning belief in his ability quit for a second time. If using the HBM to assess Eddie's behavior, we might conclude that Eddie will not stop smoking. However, this is an incomplete test because the health consequences of smoking are not included in this assessment.

Taking stock of the theories to date we notice a pattern. Each theory identified factors that contribute to the likelihood of performing a health behavior. Notice also that the theories borrow or adapt concepts from other theories. This is a common practice. Rather than discard a theory entirely, researchers may borrow concepts from existing theories in an effort to build a stronger model to explain human behavior. As we continue with this chapter, you will see more examples of the practice of "borrowing" concepts to strengthen models.

Transtheoretical Model of Behavioral Change (TTM)

Prochaska and DiClemente's (1983) *transtheoretical model of behavioral change (TTM)* is a model that explains change as a process, not an event. This is an important distinction that differentiates the TTM from other models. The TTM asserts that change takes place over time. The developmental process of change described in the TTM leads us to classify this model as a stage model. Each stage of change is completed before moving to the next or more advanced level.

Prochaska and DiClemente (1983) contend that people must progress through five stages in order to obtain successful behavioral change: precontemplative, contemplative, preparation for action, action, and maintenance. Essential to this model is an accurate assessment of a person's readiness for change. According to TTM, a major reason that programs and individuals fail to attain their stated health behavior goals is that programs misjudge individuals' level of readiness for change. Recidivism, a sixth level, is included to reflect the process of failure to maintain the new behavior.

PRECONTEMPLATIVE STAGE   The *precontemplative stage* is best characterized as the "not-ready-for-change" stage (see Figure 4.3). Individuals at the precontemplative stage are engaged in an unhealthy or risky health behavior but are not thinking about changing their behaviors. For example, we may encounter numerous print advertisements or radio or television announcements about a health behavior that pertains to us. Our friends or family members may even talk with us about changing our behavior. For the most part these messages will go "over our heads." We do not attend to or process the information. In fact, we may become defensive when hearing the message repeatedly.

Think about Eddie again. Before meeting Sarah, he was in the precontemplative stage of behavior change. He was not thinking about changing his smoking behavior. In fact, he enjoyed

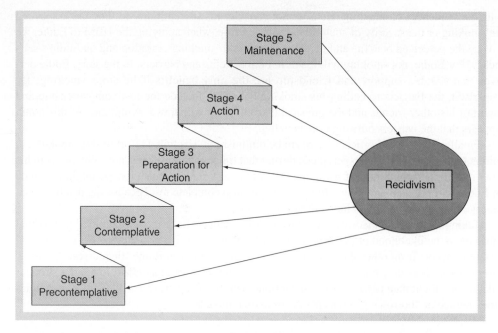

FIGURE 4.3 **Stages of the Transtheoretical Model of Behavior Change.** The TCM's stagewise process of behavioral change addresses well-documented lapses in new behavioral regimens (recidivism) and methods for reinitiating the change process.

the behavior. He may have been aware of the dangers of smoking, as are some individuals in this stage. But, if Eddie or others in the precontemplative stage are aware of the health consequences of their behaviors, the consequences have not prompted them to change behaviors.

CONTEMPLATIVE STAGE   The *contemplative stage*, the second stage in TTM, signals the beginning of the change process. In this stage the person is thinking about change, although no action is involved. For example, people in this stage may begin to pay attention to commercials that address their behaviors. They also may listen more carefully to comments about their behavior by family members or friends. Finally, individuals in this stage may seek information about their health condition or behaviors.

Think about Eddie again. When he began listening to Sarah's comments about smoking he was in the contemplative stage of TTM. He was receptive to her comments and considered her advice. But, as is the case for many people in this stage, the disadvantages of not smoking were barriers to change. Thus, Eddie also contemplated the missed companionship and his friends' lack of support for his efforts to stop smoking. In essence, individuals in the contemplative stage weigh the benefits of the changed behavior against the barriers to change.

PREPARATION FOR ACTION   If successfully transitioning through the contemplative stage, an individual will move to the third stage, *preparation for action*. The third stage signals a readiness to change behaviors. When preparing for action, an individual plans the activities needed to effect change. For Eddie, preparations included selecting the day he would stop smoking and deciding how to dispose of his supply of cigarettes in his home and car. Eddie chose to stop smoking on New Year's Day. He decided to put all packs of cigarettes in the garbage. In retrospect, we see that Eddie also should have developed a strategy for refusing cigarettes from friends and perhaps a plan to avoid his favorite smoking hangouts.

For other health behaviors, the preparation for action stage may involve more detailed plans. For example, if the planned behavior change involves a new diet, a person might specify the number of meals to be consumed each day. The person might plan the time of day each meal would be eaten as well as the types and quantity of foods to prepare. Finally, the person might plan either to prepare the meals at home or to purchase them, as many weight-loss programs sell prepared meals to participants as an essential part of their programs.

ACTION   The fourth stage is the *action stage*. This is, as the name suggests, the time to enact the plan and to perform the new health behavior. Prochaska and DiClemente (1983) note that stage four is a highly active stage because an individual must work diligently to adhere to the new behaviors. The action stage requires constant monitoring and attention to the new behavior. It also requires active resistance against old behaviors. The action stage usually lasts about six months before an individual will transition to the fifth stage, maintenance.

Eddie successfully entered the action stage. He even managed to stop smoking for 11 days. But he fell far short of the six months needed to solidify his new behavior. Eddie encountered difficulties when offered a cigarette by a friend. With no strategy for refusing cigarettes when offered, Eddie returned to his old behavior apparently without much forethought.

MAINTENANCE   Maintenance is the fifth stage. In theory, the *maintenance stage* requires far less active monitoring and attention to the new behavior than the action stage in part because, by this time, an individual has adopted the new behavior. In practice, however, the maintenance stage is not static. In fact, many longitudinal studies of health behavior change report inconsistent adherence to the new behavior by their study participants after about six months, or the beginning of the maintenance stage (Swardh, Biguet, & Opava, 2008; Tsiros et al., 2008; Woodgate & Brawley, 2008). Alternatively, some also report that participants have regressed back to their old health behaviors. In the TTM, the regression to old behaviors is called recidivism.

RECIDIVISM   *Recidivism* is, according to Prochaska and DiClemente (1983) is part of the process of change, although it is not a formal stage. During recidivism, individuals may revert to the action stage, where they restart the new behavior and again try to adhere to the plan. They may return to the preparation for action stage where they may revise the plan for action or construct a new plan. Alternatively individuals may revisit the contemplative stage, reconsidering the need for change but not acting on their thoughts. Finally, a person may return to the precontemplative stage. Frustrated or discouraged about the inability to sustain the new behavior, an individual may abandon all thoughts and efforts to change.

Prochaska and DiClemente's TTM proposes that people approach the process of change from different starting points. For example, one person may plan to lose weight by thinking about the amount or type of food he eats. Another person may begin with a detailed plan to eliminate the offending foods and substitute them with high-fiber, low-fat foods. Still another may forego a thorough preplanning and make decisions about her food consumption prior to each meal. The different approaches to change suggest that individuals have different levels of motivational readiness (Kohler et al., 1999). Prochaska and DiClemente contend that successful behavioral outcomes are more likely when people, and programs, carefully consider a person's level of readiness for change.

The novel aspect of TTM is that it accounts for individuals' successes, near successes, and failures when changing behaviors. Again, we turn to Eddie as an example. According to TTM, Eddie worked through the precontemplative, contemplative, preparation for action, and action stages. His 11-day adherence to his new behavior, however, means that he did not reach the maintenance stage before showing recidivism.

DECISIONAL BALANCE AND SITUATIONAL SELF-EFFICACY The concept of stages and processes of change are two of the four core constructs proposed in TTM. Prochaska and DiClemente include two others, *decisional balance* (pros and cons) and *situational self-efficacy*. These concepts may look familiar since they appeared in earlier models. The theory of reasoned action (TRA) proposed pros and cons in decision making using the concepts of behavioral outcomes and values. Rosenstock (2005) also introduced pros and cons into the health belief model (HBM) through perceived benefits and perceived barriers. According to the TTM, a person also calculates the pros and cons of engaging in a new behavior when undertaking a change process. This process begins in the contemplative stage and may continue through the preparation for action stage. The TTM proposes that, like the HBM, when the benefits outweigh the cost, there is a good likelihood that a person will adopt and maintain the new behavior.

Many theories and models endorse the importance of self-efficacy, a person's belief that he or she can perform the intended behavior. So too does the TTM. In this model, self-efficacy influences the likelihood that an individual will be effective in planning and performing the new behavior. The study by Naar-King and colleagues (2006) reported earlier in this chapter used the TTM to test students' likelihood of using condoms when engaging in sexual behaviors. Their findings revealed that self-efficacy mediated the relationship between stages of change and unprotected sexual behaviors. In essence, self-efficacy was the best predictor of use of condoms, not stages of change.

Other studies provide stronger support for the TTM as a predictor of health behaviors. The TTM has been used in health behavior programs to address issues of alcohol, drug abuse, and HIV prevention for adolescents (Harlow et al., 1999; Migneault, Pallonen, & Velicer, 1997; Prochaska et al., 1994). Furthermore, a study evaluating the predictive validity of the TTM for monitoring dietary fat in African American women confirms the usefulness of the TTM in explaining health behaviors (Hargreaves et al., 1999). Two studies by Hargreaves and colleagues (1999) determined that the TTM successfully separated 382 participants into three groups: subjects who were not trying to limit dietary fat (precontemplators), noncompliant participants (contemplators or recidivists), or compliant participants (action). Hargreaves and colleagues (1999) used the outcomes to design an eating styles questionnaire to place participants into groups that corresponded to the appropriate TTM stages. Dietary plans then could be designed to address the specific needs of each group based on their TTM stage.

Although the TTM can be effective when used in health behavior programs, research studies stress the importance of self-efficacy in combination with the TTM when predicting health outcomes. Self-efficacy, in addition to attitude toward the behavior, subjective norms, barriers to action, and readiness for change, seems to be a strong predictor of behavior change.

SECTION II. SOCIAL MARKETING: A TECHNIQUE TO PROMOTE BEHAVIOR CHANGE

Many of the theories presented so far address motivation for change. The motivations were either internal within the individual or external, such as friends, family values, or societal expectations. Social marketing explores another type of external motivation for behavior change: the market-place.

Definition

Social marketing may seem like a strange topic to include in a health psychology textbook. The name suggests something more appropriate for business or advertising. Yet many would agree that commercial marketers are quite effective in influencing the behaviors of a target audience.

Social marketers aim to influence behaviors, also, with one exception. They aim to influence health behaviors. Thus, social marketing uses commercial marketing techniques to change behaviors for a social good. For this reason it is appropriate to include social marketing in our discussion of theories and models that explain changes in health behaviors.

Consider this example of commercial marketing. Do you know someone who owns a cell phone? Why did that person decide to purchase the phone? Many times, cell phone owners speak of their "need" to have a phone on their person. Notice we place the word *need* in quotations. Truthfully, for most people, a cell phone is not a needed item. By using marketing techniques, however, product manufacturers have convinced their target audience of just the opposite. In fact, today, many people cannot remember a time when they did not own a cell phone. Undoubtedly, cell phones facilitate immediate contact between individuals (they are convenient), but this hardly rises to the level of "need." Cell phone marketers have reshaped their audiences' perceptions such that many people perceive the desire for quick communication as a "need." In this way commercial marketers have changed both behaviors and attitudes about communication.

Similarly, social marketing aims to effect a change of attitudes and behaviors. In social marketing, however, the goal is to encourage an audience to adopt an intangible idea or a belief that will lead to behavior change. In almost all cases, the intended change will improve health outcomes. To effect change, social marketing uses commercial marketing principles to plan, execute, analyze, and evaluate a program "designed to influence the voluntary behavior of target audiences in order to improve their personal welfare and that of their society" (Andreasen, 1995). Thus, the goal of social marketing is to produce social change by causing outcomes that will benefit the individual and, by extension, the society.

Social marketing programs have been used as a technique in a number of health promotion programs, including enhancing environmental preservation behaviors in Canada (McKenzie-Mohr, 2000); encouraging energy reduction in the United States (Geller, 1989); implementing oral rehydration programs in Kenya (Kenya et al., 1990); establishing programs to counter childhood diarrhea in India (Bentley, 1988); improving mother-to-child nutrition in Senegal (Aubel, Touré, & Diagne, 2004); and encouraging condom use to promote safer sexual behavior in Myanmar, the Russian Federation, Bulgaria, Haiti, Cuba, Cameroon, Colombia, Turkey, and the United States (Cohen et al., 1999; UNAIDS, 2001), as well as implementing effective intervention programs on high blood pressure (hypertension), also in the United States (National Heart, Lung and Blood Institute, 1986).

Social marketing campaigns are favored among some health researchers because they emphasize results. They have been effective in fostering sustained behavior change because they follow a pragmatic program plan. The plan includes careful selection of an activity to be promoted, careful identification of barriers to the activity, a strategy to overcome the barriers, a pilot test of the strategy, and an evaluation of the impact of the program once implemented (McKenzie-Mohr, 2000). Notice that, once again, the concept of barriers to action and self-efficacy reappear in another model. Like other theories, social marketing borrows constructs from existing theories and integrates them with four marketing principles—*promotion*, *product*, *place*, and *price*—to produce change. The four principles are known as the "four *P*s."

The Four *P*s

PROMOTION   Effective promotion requires the selection of a target audience who is the intended recipient of the message. The process is referred to as *market segmentation*. Commercial marketing analysts know that a message designed to appeal to a broad-based audience may create awareness of the message but may not produce behavior change. Therefore, a successful message promotion strategy must appeal to the specific demographics or behavioral characteristics of a target group to attract and retain their attention and to motivate them to initiate the intended behavior.

Kelly and colleagues' (1991) work on HIV/AIDS prevention with gay men is a good example of market segmentation. To promote the idea of safer sexual practices to reduce the transmission of HIV/AIDS, Kelly and colleagues trained 39 men identified as the opinion leaders among gay men in two small southern U.S. communities. The role of the trainees was to become behavior change endorsers to their social network. The leaders were chosen because they reflected the demographic mix of the target audience (gay men) and because they were identified by the target group as leaders within that network.

The leaders received training in the epidemiology of HIV, high-risk behaviors, protective behaviors that can reduce HIV transmission, and misconceptions about the risks. As part of the training, role-play activities taught leaders the elements of successful health promotion messages and encouraged them to practice effective delivery of such messages. Once trained, they were to engage their social network groups in discussions about HIV/AIDS precautionary behaviors.

PRODUCT   Unlike commercial marketers, social marketers do not have a tangible product to sell. They are not encouraging the purchase of a bar of soap or a new car. Rather, in social marketing, the product is the desired outcome. A desired outcome may be stopping a behavior like domestic violence (Ragin et al., 2000) or stopping littering in parks. At other times, social marketing may be used to modify behaviors such as dietary habits to improve nutrition (Samuels, 1993). To reinforce the behaviors, however, the social marketers must associate an intangible concept with a tangible symbol that evokes the concept. The symbol serves as a reminder of the target behavior. Logos or slogans work well for this purpose.

Consider again Kelly and colleagues' (1991) study. The trained leaders needed a way to begin conversations with their social groups. Walking up to a group of acquaintances and saying, "I learned some interesting information about HIV/AIDS prevention," would not necessarily catch the interest of a group intent on enjoying a night out in a club. Instead, Kelly designed a logo for HIV/AIDS precaution in the shape of a traffic light. In the logo, a red light represented high-risk behaviors, yellow was linked to moderate-risk behaviors, and green indicated behaviors with a low risk of contracting HIV/AIDS. The traffic light was fashioned into a lapel pin, and leaders were instructed to wear the lapel pins when going to their social clubs. In addition, posters with the logo were displayed prominently in the same clubs. As anticipated, the lapel pins and the posters prompted club patrons to ask about their meaning. The questions allowed the leaders to explain the analogy of the stoplight to the precautionary behaviors for HIV/AIDS (Kelly et al., 1991). The traffic light lapel pin and posters were tangible symbols that were linked to the intangible product of protective sexual behaviors to reduce the risk of HIV/AIDS infection.

PLACE   Once motivated to adopt a new behavior, the target audience needs to know where to obtain the product, materials, or services to assist them in performing the new behavior. For example, condoms are the materials in Kelly and colleagues' (1991) study that enable the precautionary behavior of safer sex. But the audience needs to know where to obtain the condoms. The place that distributes the product is called the ***distribution channel*** (see Figure 4.4). Place in social marketing is a location for gaining access to the tools needed to perform the new behavior.

Earlier theories suggest that a good distribution channel is one that minimizes barriers to gaining access to the product. A place frequented by the target audience is an ideal distribution channel because it requires little time or effort and does not involve new behaviors. Although Kelly and colleagues' (1991) study did not specify a distribution channel, we can suggest possible places based on the study sample. Kelly and colleagues' study included white gay men who were, on average, 29.1 years of age, who resided in small towns in either Mississippi or Louisiana, and who frequented a specific nightclub in their respective towns. For this group, the

FIGURE 4.4   Publicly Accessible Condom Dispenser. Example of a distribution channel.

researchers could have chosen a site within the nightclubs for distribution. Alternatively, they could have chosen a store or pharmacy in each town frequented by the targeted community.

PRICE   Finally, social marketing, like the health belief model, includes a calculation of the price for adopting the new behavior. This includes the tangible costs associated with performing the new behavior such as monetary costs, time, or distance, as well as the intangible costs, which may include the emotional or social price of the new behavior. We saw in the health belief model that the price of adopting a new behavior, such as HIV testing, may be perceived as too great and may present barriers to action due, in part, to social stigma.

In Kelly and colleague's (1991) study, selecting a pharmacy as a distribution channel could have posed similar problems for the participants. Consider this: Purchasing condoms from a store close to one's home or place of work may expose the target audience member to comment or observation by other members of the community. The comments could evoke a social stigma. And, as we saw earlier with HIV testing in rural communities in southern Africa, the fear of stigma may present insurmountable barriers to performing the health enhancing behavior. Conversely, choosing a pharmacy some distance from the target audience's place of work or home may cost participants valuable time. Put another way, the distance to the distribution channel may be perceived as too far to make it an effective place to acquire the needed materials.

Thus, when designing a social marketing program, planners must anticipate the unanticipated costs to participants and identify methods for overcoming or avoiding such barriers. Again, in Kelly and colleagues' (1991) study, one way of overcoming potential barriers to obtaining condoms from stores would have been to place condoms in a vending machine in the nightclubs. The audience could purchase the product without notice or comment.

Blended Models

Social marketing programs offer a technique for "selling" an audience on a need and a procedure for obtaining health behavior change. The theories and models discussed earlier in this chapter offer an explanation for why change occurs or fails to occur. When combined, a model or theory of behavior change together with the social marketing process set forth a compelling argument for expected behavior change and a technique for realizing such expectations. The transtheoretical model of behavior change (TTM), when paired with social marketing techniques, is one example of a *blended model* that may guide a target audience through the anticipated behavior change.

This blend was tested in a retrospective analysis of a study of public access to defibrillators to prevent deaths due to cardiac arrests (Ragin et al., 2005a). The details of this study are presented in Box 4.1. The goal of the study was to test the effectiveness of automated external defibrillators (AEDs), devices used to return the heart to its normal rhythm after a cardiac arrest, when used by trained laypersons in selected communities. Specifically, the study tested whether laypersons in a community could be trained to provide immediate care to out-of-hospital cardiac arrest victims. Such assistance would shorten the medical response time to victims and improve their chances for survival.

Results of this study showed that a community layperson could be trained to use AEDs effectively. But the study also demonstrated that the response to cardiac arrest victims was best in settings where the community already demonstrated a readiness for change (Ragin et al., 2005a). Put another way, communities that were already in the preparation for action stage were

BOX 4.1   Cardiac Defibrillators in the Community: A "Blended Model" Approach to Behavior Change

You may have seen automatic electronic defibrillators (AEDs) on television or in a movie. An AED is a small machine, about 11 inches by 13 inches, with two detachable paddles. It is used to provide emergency medical treatment when a person suffers a sudden cardiac arrest. In sudden cardiac arrest, a person experiences an abnormal heart rhythm that results in the failure of the heart to pump blood to other organs (Becker, 1996; Eisenberg, 1995). This type of heart failure always results in an immediate loss of consciousness (see Figure 4.5).

When using an AED on a cardiac arrest victim, the technician places the detachable panels on the victim's bare chest. The defibrillator then sends an electric current to the victim's heart via the panels to jolt the heart back into a normal rhythm. This procedure buys valuable time until the person can receive professional medical care.

AEDs have been proven effective in reducing deaths due to sudden cardiac arrests when used by trained medical personnel or trained emergency responders. But the majority of cardiac arrests occur away from medical personnel, usually in private homes, parks, or other public places. And, approximately 95% of all out-of-hospital cardiac arrests result in death. The problems: how to get immediate assistance to out-of-hospital cardiac arrest victims and how to train laypersons to provide that assistance using AEDs.

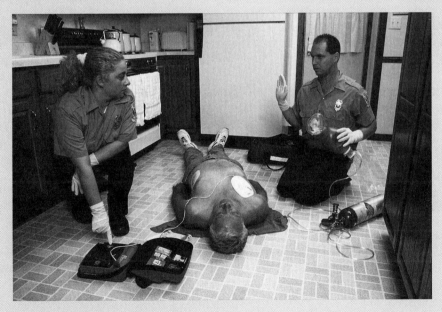

FIGURE 4.5   Automatic Electronic Defibrillator. Here, an AED is administered to a cardiac arrest victim.

(continued)

This was the goal of an international study of Public Access to Defibrillation (PAD): to determine whether community volunteers could be trained to respond to sudden cardiac arrest victims in their communities using AEDs. From a medical perspective, the key to providing a rapid response to sudden cardiac arrests victims is the number of AEDs available and the number of people trained to use them (Valenzuela et al., 2000). However, because the community plays a crucial role in the implementation and outcome of the program, the key to the PAD programs, from a social science perspective, is not equipment or training but rather changing a community's behavior toward the health condition (Ragin et al., 2005a). In social marketing terms, therefore, the product was a new community response to cardiac arrest. So how do we change a community's health response?

The Public Access to Defibrillation (PAD) Trials Study investigators in New York City needed to design a process to inform and instruct the target community about the new medical emergency response system for cardiac arrests. The program they designed resembled a social marketing approach to behavior change, although it was not originally planned with social marketing concepts in mind. The NYC PAD Trials investigators recruited 59 residential buildings and two museums to participate in the study. From the 59 buildings, the Investigators recruited 351 volunteers who agreed to be trained to use the AEDs and to respond to calls to assist cardiac arrests victims.

In addition, the investigators developed an eight-step implementation process to introduce the new emergency activation system at the participating sites. Essentially, the investigators needed to teach the community a new response to a medical emergency. Included in the eight-step process was a detailed information campaign. The researchers developed and disseminated brochures and posters designed to educate the community about the PAD Trials study and about cardiac arrests. The materials described the signs and symptoms of cardiac arrests, introduced the new emergency response system, alerted residents to the availability of trained volunteers on-site, and instructed residents on ways to contact the volunteers in their buildings in the event of a cardiac arrest or a suspected arrest. Additional information was delivered to residents through on-site information sessions. The sessions provided residents with information about the product (their new response to arrests) and the materials (the new response system), promoted the system through written and oral communication methods, and explained how and where to activate the new system (place).

The good news is that residents were able to activate the emergency response system established by the PAD Trials investigators. The disappointing news is that the residents called the on-site trained volunteers for only 25% of the cardiac arrest incidences.

When reviewing these findings, the NYC PAD Trials investigators determined that limitations in their project design accounted for the low activation rate. First, the investigators noted that the informational materials were designed for the general PAD audience. While some of the written materials were available in Spanish, Chinese, and Russian in addition to English, investigators acknowledged that the content of the materials was the same in each language. They did not change the content to reflect the cultural or behavioral practices of the different linguistic or cultural groups. In other words, they did not use market segmentation to design their informational brochures. The "one-size-fits-all" message may have contributed to the low response rate by residents.

A second problem pertained to the residents' level of preparedness for change. In the PAD Trials study some building sites activated the new medical response system, and others did not. Of the sites that activated, 70% already had a dedicated emergency response system specifically for medical emergencies prior to their participation in the PAD Trials Study. By comparison, of the nonactivated sites, fewer than half (43.5%) already had a dedicated medical emergency system. The investigators concluded that the sites with preexisting medical emergency response systems may have responded at a higher rate because they were at a higher level of preparedness for change. If, by using the transtheoretical model of behavioral change, investigators could have designed a special message, a training and implementation procedure for the sites without the preexisting medical emergency systems might have increased their likelihood of activation.

most able to use and implement successfully the new behavioral response introduced by the social marketing techniques.

Finally, it is important to distinguish social marketing approaches from social advertising. Social marketing includes a message and a program. Social advertising includes a message but no program. Social marketing campaigns for condoms sponsored by UNAIDS throughout Africa, Asia, and eastern Europe all include programs to distribute condoms and monitor their use (UNAIDS, 2001). Public service announcements for childhood immunizations in the United States also are supported by immunization centers to serve the demand for immunization created by the message. A limited ban on lobster traps, however, that requests that fishers voluntarily refrain from catching lobsters, is a social advertising campaign because it includes no programmatic support for the message.

While social marketing approaches can be successful for promoting health behavior change, they are somewhat less successful than commercial marketing for three reasons. First, commercial marketers have the advantage of immediate gratification. For example, immediately after buying a cell phone, individuals can show it to their friends, receive calls, make calls, and try the new features. But after beginning a new program of behavior change using social marketing techniques, people must wait for the reinforcing positive outcomes of that change. Thus, they must delay gratification.

Second, the appeal of having a tangible object, and not a symbol, should not be underestimated. A symbol is a tangible reminder of the goal of the health program, but the goal of the program is not the symbol. Finally, commercial marketers have the advantage of impulse. An attractive, well-promoted garment or piece of jewelry that can be acquired easily may lead to an impulsive purchase, one executed without planning or careful thought. But, social marketers cannot rely on impulse. The process of behavior change requires planning and sustained action over time. While some people may begin a behavior change process on an impulse, long-term maintenance or compliance with the new behavior is always subject to review, alteration, and possible discontinuation of the target behavior.

SECTION III. THE ECOLOGICAL APPROACH TO HEALTH: FACTORS THAT INFLUENCE HEALTH BEHAVIORS

As much as we like to think of ourselves as independent, making our own decisions and shaping our own outcomes, the truth is that many of our behaviors are shaped by external factors or factors outside of our control. The previous sections explored the impact of some of these factors, including social groups, group norms, and commercial marketers. As mentioned at the beginning of this chapter, however, individual health behaviors are also shaped by other community, environmental, and health systems and health policy determinants.

David Marks summarized this view when he noted that "historical, cultural and [economic] determinants of individual behavior are . . . robust and resistant to change" (Marks, 2002). This is not to suggest a pessimistic view of an individual's ability to choose or effect change. Rather, Marks's view is consistent with the social ecological health model: Individual health outcomes are influenced by factors that include but are not limited to the individual. In this section we review factors that influence individual health outcomes, including the individual, cultural and social networks, the environment, health systems, and health policy contributions.

Individual Factors

Earlier in the chapter, we explored the impact of social norms on an individual's behavioral intentions and decisions when reviewing theories and models used to explain health behavior change. What we did not emphasize is that some social norms are shaped by individual factors or characteristics that are either beyond our control or difficult to change. For example, each culture or group adopts a set of social norms associated with gender. As we will see shortly, gender is one of several individual-level variables that affect health but that are largely outside of our control. Others include age, income, and ethnic group or culture (Cockerham, 2001). Gender norms are shaped by society and may vary by family, cultural heritage, and country of origin. There are, however, some similarities with respect to gender roles and health behaviors across cultures, as demonstrated by research.

GENDER AND HEALTH-SEEKING BEHAVIORS   Health-seeking behaviors, defined here as actions taken to obtain guidance or assistance with health-related issues, have a direct impact on the quality of an individual's health status. Yet research shows that gender influences a person's health care–seeking behaviors. What is more, this appears to be a cross-cultural phenomenon. For example, VanDervanter and colleagues (2005) found that, among adolescents, boys were significantly less likely to use health care services than were girls, even when participating in intervention programs designed to increase preventive health care–seeking behaviors among adolescents.

In their study, VanDervanter and colleagues (2005) assigned adolescents to one of four groups. Half of the males were assigned to an all-male control group, while the other half were assigned to an intervention group for males that received guidance on seeking medical care. Similarly, half of the females in the study were assigned to an all-female control group, while the other half were placed in an intervention group for females only that was identical to the male intervention group. VanDervanter and colleagues found a significant increase in health care utilization for females who received the intervention when compared with females with no intervention. But, there was no difference in care-seeking behavior for males in the intervention versus the control group. What is more, the results also indicated that while males did not perceive specific barriers to gaining access to care, they did not perceive benefits to seeking care (VanDervanter et al., 2005).

Difference in health care–seeking behavior by gender appears to occur for adults as well. Work by Gili and colleagues (2006) on the cancer-screening behaviors of adult sons and daughters of people diagnosed with colorectal cancer illustrates this point. Research shows that the offspring of parents with a confirmed diagnosis of colorectal cancer are at highest risk for contracting the same form of cancer. Despite this known risk, Gili and colleagues study showed that male offspring were significantly less likely than females to seek a screening test to detect early stages of colorectal cancer.

Why does there appear to be a gender difference in health care–seeking behaviors? Sanden, Larson, and Eriksson (2000) suggest that men in their study consistently ignored health symptoms thinking (perhaps hoping) that the symptoms would go away if ignored. Additional reasons men give for delaying health care include not recognizing the symptoms and believing that they appear weak or nonmasculine if seeking medical care (Chappele, Ziebland, & McPherson, 2004). In fact, a number of studies that report a gender difference in health-seeking behaviors attribute the difference to gender socialization. For men, the social norm states that seeking health care is antithetical to masculine normative behaviors (Galdas, Cheater, & Marshall, 2005; Sobralske, 2006). Thus, some research suggests that there is nothing about gender per se that shapes health behaviors. Rather, the gender socialization process in many cultures subtly discourages health-seeking behaviors among men.

One additional example of the gender difference in health-seeking behaviors is seen in research examining workplace absences. While statistics show that, in general, women tend to have longer life expectancies, studies suggest that women also report more frequent absences from work due to sickness than do men (Bratberg, Dahl, & Risa, 2002; Cockerham, 2001). Think about it: Greater longevity but more absences due to illnesses suggests that health-seeking behaviors such as taking "sick days" to recuperate or to obtain medical care are more common and likely to be more socially accepted for women than men.

MULTIPLE IMPACTS OF HEALTH-SEEKING BEHAVIORS   As we saw earlier, some studies report that gender is only one of several variables that influence health-seeking behaviors. Consider culture (Galdas et al., 2005; Richards, Reid, & Watt, 2002). In cultures that place a strong emphasis on masculine behavior or what is sometimes referred to as "machismo" (Bashour & Mamaree, 2003; Sobralske, 2006), both culture and gender are thought to contribute to the lower rate of health-seeking behaviors among men.

And, a study by Britto and colleagues (2001) found that three factors—gender, age, and ethnicity—contributed to health-seeking behaviors. Britto and colleagues report that girls, younger students, and white students all were significantly more likely to report seeking medical care from nurses, dentists, medical clinics, or private physician offices than were boys, older students, and minorities respectively.

KNOWLEDGE AND HEALTH-SEEKING BEHAVIORS   Finally, researchers have shown that individuals' knowledge about risky or unhealthy behaviors also affects their health-seeking behaviors. Separate studies examining adolescents' and adults' knowledge of the risks associated with smoking and smoking behaviors support this fact. In a study examining adolescents' beliefs about smoking "light" cigarettes, Kropp and Halpern-Felsher (2004) found that adolescents believed they were at significantly lower risk for lung cancer, heart attacks, and deaths due to smoking-related diseases when smoking "light" versus regular cigarettes. In addition, adolescents thought it would be far easier to quit smoking when using "light" versus regular cigarettes (Kropp & Halpern-Felsher, 2004).

The belief that "light" cigarettes lower risks associated with smoking suggests that such smokers also would be less likely to seek help to stop smoking because they think their behavior puts them at less risk that other smokers. There is just one problem. "Light" cigarettes do not reduce the risk of smoking-related illnesses. Misinformation about the apparent advantages of "light" cigarettes is due, in part, to cigarette manufacturers' marketing campaigns that promote "light" cigarettes as a healthy alternative to regular cigarettes. Research refuting that claim is widely available (National Cancer Institute, 1996, 2001); however, adolescents are either unaware of this information or have not changed their views in spite of research results.

Some adult smokers also hold erroneous beliefs about smoking. Cummings and colleagues (2004) assessed adult smokers' beliefs about the health risks of smoking and the benefits of smoking filtered and low-tar cigarettes. Of the 1,046 adults surveyed, these researchers found that adult smokers who were the most misinformed about the risks of smoking were 45 years of age or older, smoked ultralight cigarettes, believed they would stop smoking before experiencing a serious health problem, never used medication to stop smoking, or were smokers with lower levels of education. Such misperceptions would make it unlikely that such individuals would seek assistance to stop smoking and would support the proposition that multiple factors affect health-seeking behaviors.

Clearly, individuals need correct information about the health risks associated with their behaviors to effect change. But sound knowledge alone does not guarantee that individuals will adopt health-enhancing behaviors. Consider this: If individuals always did what was in their best health interest based on knowledge of the risks, their behaviors would be highly predictable and consistent. No doubt you can think of several people who are very knowledgeable about the health risks of, perhaps, smoking or consuming a high-fat diet but who show no signs of changing their behaviors. In addition, cross-cultural research on views about smoking and the dangers of secondhand smoke in the United States and in Burkina Faso also shows that individuals often override their knowledge about risks in order to continue engaging in unhealthy behaviors (Halpern-Felsher, Biehl, Kropp, & Rubinstein, 2004; Halpern-Felsher & Rubinstein, 2004; Ouedraogo, Ouedraogo, Ouoba, & Sawagodo, 2000).

At other times, individuals may have extensive and accurate knowledge about a health issue but are still unable to change behaviors. For example, Lando and Labiner-Wolfe (2006) conducted a focus group to assess individuals' interest in having nutritional information posted on quick-service restaurant menus and billboards. They found that while focus groups members indicated an interest in having the nutritional information displayed—a health-seeking behavior, of sorts—study participants indicated they would not consistently use the information when eating at the restaurant. The study suggests that knowledge does not always translate into behaviors and is not always sufficient to override intended behaviors.

More recent studies suggest a complex relationship between nutrition information (including caloric information) and food choices. For example, Tandon and colleagues' (2010) study of fast-food selections that mothers make for themselves and for their children revealed that when mothers were provided with nutritional and caloric information about food items on a McDonald's menu, mothers ordered, on average, foods with 102 fewer calories for their children than did mothers without such information. Interestingly, there was no such difference when mothers ordered for themselves. The calorie content of foods ordered by mothers for themselves was similar regardless of whether mothers had the menu with the caloric information.

Still, another study found that calorie count information, while helpful, may not provide enough information to result in a reduced-calorie meal. Roberto and colleagues (2010) examined the food-choice behaviors of study participants in a restaurant diner when assigned to one of three conditions: menu with no caloric information, menu with calorie labels only, or menu with caloric labels and with recommended daily calorie intake for the average adult (calorie plus). Their findings were both predictable and surprising. These researchers reported that study participants in both of the calorie label conditions (calorie only and calorie plus) consumed on average 14% fewer calories than individuals in the no-caloric-information condition. In addition, participants in the calorie-plus condition consumed on average 250 fewer calories than participants in either of the other conditions.

The surprising finding, however, was that individuals in the calorie-label-only condition reported consuming more calories after the study dinner than did participants in the no label or the calorie-plus conditions.

What do these findings suggest? First, as noted in other studies, information (knowledge) alone does not always result in changed behaviors. Tandon and colleagues (2010) demonstrated that a mother may apply the new knowledge when addressing the nutritional needs of her child but not when making food choices for herself. Similarly, Roberto and colleagues (2010) showed that, in some settings, limited knowledge (calorie label only) may result in short-term but not longer-term behavior change. In addition, Roberto and colleagues' study suggests that knowledge (information) may be maximally effective when placed in context. Calorie-count information together with the recommended average calorie intake for adults lead to changes in both short- and longer-term food choices for adults in the calorie-plus condition.

Finally, research shows that, in some instances, knowledge about a health issue may be secondary to practical social, socioeconomic, or cultural barriers. For example, in a study of knowledge, attitudes, and beliefs about sickle cell anemia in children in east Africa, researchers found that 75% of caregivers of children with sickle cell anemia knew that the disease was hereditary and 55% knew the symptoms associated with the disease (Macharia, Shiroya, & Njeru, 1997). Researchers then examined five individual factors to determine which best predicted caregivers' health-seeking behaviors for their child: education, monthly income, occupation, religion, and family size. Only family size best predicted attitudes and behaviors. Why would family size affect the likelihood of seeking care for sickle cell anemia? Simply put, a parent may be well educated about the illness but may encounter time, logistic, or even economic barriers when caring for the special needs of one of several children in the family.

Cultural and Social Networks

Studies of immigrant populations in the United States, as well as studies of health-seeking behaviors in other countries, further demonstrate how culture may influence health care behaviors. We explore the role of culture and traditional medicines on health behaviors more fully in Chapter 6, Emotional Health and Well-Being. For the moment, however, it is important to note that in studies of barriers to health care access for Latino children in the United States, researchers have learned that a preference for home remedies, folk medicine practices, use of *curanderos* (cultural healers; see Chapter 6, Emotional Health and Well-Being), and parents' alternative beliefs about the causes of disease all affect the likelihood that parents would seek medical care for their children as well as the type of care sought (Flores & Vega, 1998).

Research by Barrett and colleagues (1998) similarly reveals cultural differences in health-seeking behaviors among the Hmong from Southeast Asia. For the Hmong, the concept of illness and wellness differs from Western medicine. A person who has an illness but is **asymptomatic**, here meaning without noticeable symptoms, is not considered ill according to Hmong beliefs. As one interviewee from the study stated, older Hmong believe that either you are sick and you die or you are well (Barrett et al., 1998). Thus a person with diabetes or high blood pressure, diseases that may be free of symptoms in the early stages but that may be fatal if not treated, may not be considered to be sick in the Hmong culture. Clearly, different perceptions of illness, alternative forms of treatment, and alternate sources of care among some cultural groups will influence a person's likelihood of seeking health care.

PEER GROUPS AND HEALTH-SEEKING BEHAVIORS   The theories we reviewed earlier noted the effect of peer groups on individual health behaviors using the construct of subjective norms. There is an extensive literature on the impact of peer groups on adolescent health, and we examine some of that work in Chapter 5, Risky Health Behaviors. For the moment, we note that much of that work focuses on the effects of peer groups on encouraging or discouraging substance use, including cigarettes, alcohol, and drugs, as well as risky sexual behavior (Mosbach & Leventhal, 1988). For example, studies testing the social cognitive theory (see page 106) to explain smoking behavior among adolescents find that adolescents are influenced by models of smoking in their environments. Poulsen and colleagues (2002) reported that the daily smoking behaviors of students in 48 Danish schools were associated with exposure either to students or to teachers who smoked on the school grounds. And, once again, Eddie's experience may be helpful in understanding this phenomenon. His role models for smoking were his older brother, who also began smoking as a teen, and his closest friends.

Interestingly, however, similar findings appear not to apply for African American adolescents. For example, a study of the smoking behaviors of white and African American adolescents revealed that having a close friend who smoked predicted initiation into cigarette smoking for white adolescents, but this finding was not true for African American adolescents (Greenlund, Johnson, Webber, & Berenson, 1997; Hoffman, Sussman, Unger, & Valente, 2006; Urberg, Degirmencioglu, & Pilgrim, 1997).

Other studies point to the effect of **acculturation**, or adoption of the behaviors and values of a majority group, on health behavior. Studies examining the role of acculturation on health behaviors suggest that individuals who are influenced by the norms and behaviors of the dominant cultural group in their communities attempt to imitate the same health behaviors (Bethel & Schneker, 2005). Specifically, studies report a significant association between the degree of acculturation to Western culture and use of substances, including cigarettes, alcohol, and marijuana (Bell, Ragin, & Cohall, 1999; Trinidad, Unger, Chih-Ping, & Anderson, 2005). In general, the research shows that the more an adolescent attempts to acculturate to the dominant culture, in this case Western culture, the greater the likelihood of experimenting with substances, including cigarettes, alcohol, and drugs.

MEDIA AND HEALTH-SEEKING BEHAVIORS   Earlier in this chapter, we discussed the impact of media and advertising on health behaviors. We made the point that mass media advertisements can effectively shape behavior. In fact, they can shape both positive and negative health behaviors. An example of the role of the media in shaping positive health behaviors can be found in Ogata Jones, Denham, and Springston's (2006) study of breast cancer screening among younger versus older women. In a sample of 284 participants, these researchers found that older women responded more positively to mass media appeals to obtain breast screening exams than did younger women. The younger group responded best to personal communication.

Conversely, there are a host of examples of the media's role in encouraging negative health behaviors. The role of media in promoting cigarette smoking is well known (Braun et al., 2007). Perhaps less well known is the role of cigarette manufacturers in promoting tobacco use among the U.S. military.

Joseph, Muggli, and Pearson (2005) documented a 10-year campaign by cigarette manufacturers to promote tobacco use among U.S. military personnel. According to this study, the military is an ideal target audience for cigarette manufacturers because of the volume of people, the availability of a target audience already preselected by socioeconomic class, the common culture of the military, and the promise of a carryover of the product (cigarettes) to the civilian market—in effect, free advertising to a secondary group. The example of marketing to the military is also an excellent illustration of the benefits of market segmentation when promoting a product. The military is one of the cigarette manufacturers' most loyal customers.

Physical Environment

We acknowledged that other people, values, cultures, and social norms are external factors that affect health. Another type of external factor is the environment, here meaning the physical environment. We can examine the relationship between individual health outcomes and the environment by examining the health consequences to individuals caused by environmental contaminants and changes to the environment. Before proceeding, however, it is important to state that, in many instances, the environmental contaminants that adversely affect individual health are caused by human behaviors that changed or altered the environment.

For more than 45 years the U.S. government has lead or supported national and international efforts to become better stewards of the environment. Nationally, the United States has enacted federal regulations to protect two vital national resources, air and water. The Clean Air Act of 1970 established National Ambient Air Quality Standards (NAAQS) designed to protect both the environment and the health of the public (Environmental Protection Agency, 2007a). In 1977, the U.S. government followed with the Clean Water Act. The Clean Air Act and the Clean Water Act regulate the quantity, type, and frequency of pollutants that can be released by industry into the air and water, respectively. Both the Clean Air and the Clean Water Acts are administered by the U.S. Environmental Protection Agency (EPA). While the primary goal of these acts is to protect the valuable environmental resources, they also ensure clean water and air for human consumption.

Internationally, 37 developed nations (the United States withdrew its support) have similarly adopted measures to protect the environment by adopting the Kyoto Protocol. The protocol is an international agreement among nations to reduce greenhouse gas emissions. Greenhouse gasses are natural and artificial substances in the atmosphere that help warm Earth's surface by trapping heat. Examples of greenhouse gasses include water vapors, carbon dioxide, methane, and ozone; these may be produced by the burning of fossil fuels like coal. In essence, the Kyoto Protocol represents a global effort to reduce the production of greenhouse gasses and to minimize the global climate changes that appear to be occurring at an increasingly rapid and potentially dangerous rate (EPA, 2007b). Thus, the Clean Air and Clean Water Acts and the Kyoto Protocol are examples of efforts to correct harmful effects on the environment due, in part, to humans.

SUPERFUNDS   Work in the United States to address *Superfund sites* is another example of the impact of environmental pollutants on human health. In 1980 Congress created the Superfund, a program administered by the federal government to clean up *hazardous waste sites*. The term *hazardous waste sites* refers to land and water sites that contain toxic chemicals or other substances that pose a current or future threat to human health or to the environment.

Superfund sites are created usually from dumping toxic waste products from various industries onto land or into waterways. The toxic substances seep into the soil, the water, and often the underground water systems that supply drinking water to residents in nearby communities. As a result, the sites contain contaminants. The EPA estimates there are tens of thousands of abandoned hazardous waste sites throughout the United States.

For three decades, a host of human health problems has been linked to Superfund sites. In states such as New York, Massachusetts, New Jersey, California, and others, health problems associated with such sites included lung and breast cancer, leukemia, blood-borne illnesses, excessive bleeding, skin rashes, and bronchitis and other respiratory diseases, as well as some unknown illnesses. Without a doubt, Superfund sites created by people contaminated natural resources. These actions not only created hazardous environmental conditions but posed and continue to cause serious health consequences to all individuals. Current efforts to remove the toxic substances in the land and water left by industry are an important step in controlling the adverse health outcomes causes by contaminated environments.

Health Systems

Access to health care in the United States has received considerable attention from local and national government agencies, particularly in the past 18 years. In fact, limited access to care is one of the factors contributing to the current crisis in the U.S. health care system. Access to care is defined as having the means to afford health care or having a person responsible for one's medical care needs. Presently, there are 44 million Americans who are either uninsured or *underinsured*, meaning that their health care insurance does not adequately cover their medical needs (Institute of Medicine, 2000). Chapter 12, Health Care Systems and Health Policy, reviews the impact of health care systems on individual outcomes in some detail.

For now, however, we emphasize several health system–related problems that have been shown to inhibit health-seeking behaviors. The inability to pay for needed medical care at the time of service can cause individuals to postpone care for otherwise treatable illness, usually resulting in more serious health problems. For example, uninsured or underinsured individuals often postpone seeking care when first needed. The delay in care means that these individuals are three times more likely to experience adverse health outcomes and more than four times more likely to experience *preventable hospitalizations*, meaning hospitalizations for conditions that could have been treated in a physician's office or in an outpatient visit (Institute of Medicine, 2000).

Another limitation to seeking or obtaining care is access to a medical care provider. Individuals who do not have a primary care provider responsible for their care are also more likely to delay needed treatment. When unable or unwilling to delay care, some individuals without regular care may seek medical treatment from emergency service centers such as hospital emergency departments (EDs).

But, contrary to popular belief, the frequent users of emergency medical service for routine care issues are individuals who are dissatisfied with their health care options, not those with limited or no access to care. A nationwide study examining the reasons why patients sought care from EDs illustrates this point. In their study of 28 hospital emergency departments nationwide, Ragin and colleagues (2005b) identified five main reasons why patients sought emergency medical treatment: a medical emergency (95.0%), preference for the ED (88.7%), convenience (86.5%), affordability (25.2%), and limitations of insurance (14.9%). Few people consider an emergency department a convenient source of care, and fewer still think of it as a place where they prefer to go for care. So, what do these results mean?

Ragin and colleagues (2005b) reported that for some individuals, the hospital—although not necessarily the ED—was their regular source of care. For others, however, the affirmative preference for hospital EDs may reflect their negative assessment of the quality of care available in other community health care settings. Thus, the 88.7% of persons who "preferred" the emergency department may suggest that the quality of care available in their community is inadequate, not that there is a dearth of service.

Ragin and colleagues (2005b) also found that 86.5% of people cited convenience as a reason for seeking emergency care. To understand that statistic, consider this: Many individuals with primary care physicians report waiting two to three weeks for an appointment for routine care. And, when needing emergency medical care, some individuals report waiting several hours or days because the primary care provider cannot accommodate an emergency visit or because the office is closed. The restricted hours of service, even for emergencies, is considered inconvenient. Such limitations are not the case in hospital emergency departments; hence they are more convenient. In addition, at many primary care practices, appointments for nonemergency health care visits are available only during business hours, usually between 9:00 AM and 5:00 PM on Mondays through Fridays. Individuals unable to take time from work or other family commitments to schedule medical visits during these times often postpone medical care.

Thus, when care is unavailable or inconvenient, people often choose one of two options: Find alternative sources of care, such as hospital emergency departments, or forego care entirely. The first choice is expensive, and the second often leads to more serious health problem in the near future (see Chapter 12, Health Care Systems and Health Policy).

The Institute of Medicine's (2000) report on access to health care emphasizes additional factors such as socioeconomic status, ethnicity, and limitations of insurance as further barriers to care. Their study found that poor and minority groups in the United States are more likely to have limited access to adequate health care. As a result, these groups have poorer overall health outcomes than others in the United States (Bentacourt, 2006; Institute of Medicine, 2000).

We make one additional observation: Insured individuals may also face limitations of care. Many individuals opt to enlist in health insurance plans offered by health maintenance organizations (HMOs), a network of health care providers who have been preapproved to offer health care services to any patient who is a member of the organization. We review health care systems, including HMOs, more fully in Chapter 12, Health Care Systems and Health Policy. For now, however, we briefly note that even individuals who are members of HMOs encounter limitations of service.

HMOs define the type and frequency of service available as well as the providers authorized to provide the services. These restrictions can and often do present conflicts for patients and care providers who may want or need care that is denied by the HMO. Individuals who can pay for the added care are not greatly affected by the regulated services. For others, however, such limitation means limited treatment options even though they are insured.

In sum, health care systems offer affordable options that improve access to care for many. However, here, too, the restrictions in type of service and authorized providers will have an impact on an individual's health outcomes.

Health Policy

Health systems regulate the type of services available to their members. Health policy, however, involves another form of regulation: government regulations intended to improve the overall health of a community, region, or nation. Smoking bans and new restrictions on the types of foods available in school vending machines in some U.S. states are examples of two new health policies at the national and state levels designed to improve health outcomes.

SMOKING AND HEALTH POLICY   In 1998 the U.S. federal government banned smoking on all domestic airline flights (GPO, 2008). Two years later, U.S. Federal Law 106-181, section 252.3, extended this ban to include international travel on U.S. carriers (Pan, Barbeau, Levenstein, & Balbach, 2005). The smoking ban on airplanes was one of the earliest in a series of smoking regulations designed to limit exposure to *secondhand smoke*. Since that time, broader smoking restrictions have been enacted in a total of 27 states. Some states also regulate or restrict smoking in restaurants, movie theaters, and the workplace. This, too, is an example of health policy, but at the state level.

Health policies that restricted smoking venues were supported by the health research literature that demonstrated the dangers of secondhand smoke to nonsmokers. *Secondhand smoke* is defined as the smoke from cigarettes, cigars, and pipes that is inhaled by people who themselves are nonsmokers. Health policy experts were able to demonstrate that environmental tobacco smoke is a carcinogen, an agent that causes cancer in humans (Environmental Health Information Services, 2000). In fact, tobacco smoke is so potent that the EPA cannot identify a safe level of exposure to secondhand cigarette smoke that would result in no harm to an individual (Environmental Health Information Services, 2000).

To put this in perspective, environmental tobacco smoke is the third leading cause of preventable deaths due to heart disease in the United States (Glantz & Parmley, 1991). These data, combined with studies specifically linking secondhand smoke to death due to heart disease in women and poorer health outcomes for asthmatics, have convinced policy makers that secondhand smoke is a health hazard to the public (Eisner et al., 2005; Kaur et al., 2004). Such conclusions led to health policy aimed at improving the outcomes of a population, the primary goal of health policy initiatives.

Remember Sarah, Eddie's girlfriend in the opening story? She clearly dislikes smoking. Perhaps her dislike was based, in part, on her knowledge of the adverse consequences of secondhand smoke.

NUTRITION AND HEALTH POLICY   New policy initiatives in New York City and other urban areas have targeted the dietary habits of schoolchildren. Consider this: Michael Bloomberg, mayor of New York City from 2002 to the present, banned soda, candy, and sugary snacks from vending machines in New York City schools, citing recent statistics on childhood obesity and

BOX 4.2   "Taking Candy from Children?"

Yes, it is true. In the summer of 2003, New York City's schools chancellor, Joel Klein, announced new restrictions on items sold in school vending machines and new standards for school lunches. The new regulations eliminated candy, soda, and juices consisting of less than 100% fruit from vending machines in schools (see Figure 4.6) (Goodnough, 2003). What is more, school lunch menus were revised significantly. More fresh or frozen vegetables and fruits were added to menus, and the number and quantity of high-fat foods were decreased. Items such as macaroni and cheese and potato salad were eliminated from lunch menus entirely. And students' favorites, chicken nuggets and cheese pizza, would be served in smaller portions.

The changes in school lunch menus and vending machine offerings were prompted by a study of obesity and diabetes conducted by New York City's Department of Health and Mental Hygiene and the Department of Education. City departments collected survey data on the height, weight, age, and gender of the city's elementary schoolchildren in kindergarten through fifth grade. The results of the survey, reported in 2003, revealed that 43% of the city's school-aged children in grades K–5 weighed more than the recommended weight for their height and age. While 19% of children were considered overweight, fully 24% were determined to be obese. This represents an increase of 4% in the number of obese school-aged children in New York City from 1996 to 2003 (Perez-Pena, 2003).

FIGURE 4.6   Vending Machines in Public Schools. The items in school vending machines can enhance or undermine efforts to improve the nutritional diets of children and adolescents.

(continued)

> The obesity statistics are even more alarming when compared with national statistics for school-aged children. In that study, 34% of school-aged children nationwide were found to be overweight, of whom only 16% were determined to be obese (Wang & Beydoun, 2007).
>
> New York City's decision is an example of a government health policy implemented to change the nutritional behaviors, and hopefully the health outcomes, of thousands of children. The goal of the policy is to reduce the amount of fatty foods consumed by children in school lunches and from vending machines. The unstated goal, however, may be far more significant. If New York City can succeed in influencing or changing the dietary preferences of elementary school-aged children through the new policies, it may be able to influence later eating behaviors. It is a step in the direction of controlling and possibly reducing childhood obesity or diabetes.

juvenile diabetes (see Box 4.2). The new health policy for the New York City public schools was intended to remove from schools all foods and beverages thought to contribute to the possible development of obesity or diabetes in children and adolescents.

SECTION IV. CHALLENGES TO SUSTAINING HEALTH BEHAVIOR CHANGE

Looking back on this chapter, you may think it is a wonder than anyone manages to initiate or sustain health behavior change. In this chapter, we identified a host of individual, cultural and social network, environmental, health system, and health policy influences on health behaviors. These factors, singly or in combination, challenge our ability to adopt healthy behaviors. We may be aware of the obvious influences on our behaviors by family members and friends. But other factors, such as advertisements or environmental influences, may be more difficult to detect. In this section we consider two additional challenges to maintaining healthy behaviors.

Short- versus Long-Term Adherence

The transtheoretical model of behavior change (TTM) identified short- and long-term behavior outcomes. Eddie's 11 days of abstinence from smoking is an example of a short-term outcome. Yet research shows that the average duration for new health regimens is about six months. During these six months, the individual performing the changed behavior may encounter a number of challenges. These include challenges to one's needed self-efficacy to perform the behavior, temptation from environmental influences to return to the old behavior, and emotional or psychological dependence on the old behaviors. In the opening story, Eddie encountered all of these challenges when trying to quit smoking. One or several of these factors may have resulted in Eddie's decision to return to his previous behavior.

How could Eddie maximize the likelihood of sustained behavioral change? For some behaviors, efforts to change require a change in lifestyle, also. For Eddie, changing his group of friends, his preferred activities, and the emotional satisfaction he derived from smoking with his friends could make him more successful in his smoking cessation efforts. But radical changes in lifestyles often result in limited long-term success.

In addition, after several months of adherence to a new behavior we may believe that the old behavior is no longer a risk or temptation. We may think that we have the situation under control. How many times have you heard someone who has stopped smoking say, "I think one won't hurt me." The question is not whether one cigarette would "hurt" but whether that person can stop after just one. Individuals struggling with smoking cessation say that the notion that one can smoke just one cigarette is often incorrect. One cigarette is the prelude that leads them back to their original behavior. According to the TTM, recidivism back to the old behaviors is due to diminished adherence to the new health behaviors.

The Appeal of Unhealthy Behaviors

Health psychologists face an uphill battle with the marketing savvy of producers of less healthy or risky products. The advertising agencies are excellent psychologists. Through their careful research on targeted populations, they have crafted marketing messages that are very persuasive. For example, the concepts of product, promotion, price, and place all come together to determine that the best placement for the single bars of chocolate candy in a supermarket is at the checkout counter: the place where you wait rather impatiently before totaling and paying for your groceries. No doubt the time it took to shop combined with the smell of the various foods in the store is guaranteed to stimulate the appetite. One chocolate bar, packaged attractively for just one person, would help pass the time while standing in line and would take care of the growl in the stomach at the same time. And although few people enter grocery stores to buy a candy bar, the convenience of the single-serve candy in the checkout line satisfies a "need." It therefore provides immediate gratification for this immediate "need."

Personal Postscript

BE ALERT, BE AWARE: INCREASE YOUR ABILITY TO IDENTIFY TARGETED ADVERTISEMENTS

If you are female and a teen or young adult, a new ad for Camel cigarettes has been designed especially for you! At least that is what the manufacturers intend. The manufacturers of Camel cigarettes realized that few women smoked their brand. Thus they developed a new ad campaign targeted to young women and teenage girls to increase their likelihood of buying and smoking Camel cigarettes.

How does this work? The ad depicts a box of Camel cigarettes in shades of pink and yellow. Pink is a color associated with females. The use of pink and other pastels is intended to appeal to a female sense of esthetics. Next, the company chose a tag line "light & luscious," again words that resonate with a female audience more than a male audience. And they call their new product "Camel No. 9." This name just might happen to make the target audience (females) think of perfumes with a similar sound, like Chanel No. 5 or Chanel No. 19. The product name, the colors, and the tag line all are designed to attract the attention of females and to increase their interest in this new product.

Would the ad attract your attention?

Important Terms

acculturation   130
action stage   117
asymptomatic   130
blended models   122
contemplative stage   116
cues to action   113
decisional balance   118
direct experiences   106
distribution channel   121
expectancy value theory
     (EVT)   103
hazardous waste sites   132
health belief model   111
inferred learning   106
learned behavioral
     consequence   106
maintenance stage   117
market segmentation   120

matching law   105
outcome expectancies   107
perceived barriers   112
perceived behavioral
     control   110
perceived benefits   112
perceived severity   112
perceived susceptibility   111
persuasory learning   106
place   120
precontemplative stage   115
preparation for action stage   116
preventable hospitalization   132
price   120
product   120
promotion   120
recidivism   117
reciprocal determinism   107

secondhand smoke   134
self-efficacy   107
situational self-efficacy   118
social cognitive theory
     (SCT)   106
social learning theory   106
social marketing   119
subjective norms   108
Superfund sites   132
theory of planned behavior
     (TPB)   108
theory of reasoned
     action (TRA)   108
transtheoretical model of
     behavioral change
     (TTM)   115
underinsured   132
vicarious experiences   106

Risky Health Behaviors

Chapter Objectives

After studying this chapter you will be able to:

1. Identify the six priority risky health behaviors.
2. Define unintentional injuries.
3. Identify six factors that contribute to motor vehicle accidents.
4. Describe the effect of violence on individuals and communities.
5. Describe the health consequences of cigarette smoking.
6. Identify and describe the health consequences of illegal and prescription drugs.
7. Identify and describe factors that influence substance use.
8. Define risky health behaviors.
9. Identify the factors that influence risky health behaviors.
10. Define eating disorders.
11. Explain the health consequences of anorexia, bulimia, and obesity.

OPENING STORY: DISTRACTED TO DEATH

Gillian Sabet, a class president at her high school, was driving herself, her boyfriend, and three other teenage passengers to their school prom. According to a Cable News Network (CNN) story, Gillian's mother reported that, while driving to the prom, one of the four passengers asked for a piece of chewing gum. Gillian had a pack of gum in the driver seat pocket. As she reached for the gum she diverted her eyes from the road for the briefest of moments and lost control of the car (Lawrence, 2007). Gillian and her boyfriend were killed in the accident. The three other passengers survived.

Accidents involving teenage drivers do not always make the news, but this accident was different. Gillian Sabet, the 16-year-old driver, was not drunk, had not used drugs, and was not speeding. But she was distracted. ■

This story seems incredible. How is it possible that a very brief distraction—a quick glance to find a pack of gum—could result in a fatal accident? After all, many people do other things while driving: change CDs, change the radio station, look for coins to pay tolls, or reach for something to drink. They do not end up in an accident or dead. Why was Gillian's outcome different?

Gillian's situation included several factors that, when combined with the distraction of looking for gum, may have led to the accident. One factor appears to be inexperience. Most U.S. states require would-be drivers to be at least 16 years of age and to obtain a *learner's permit*, a precursor to an actual license, before they can operate an automobile. You may remember from your own experience or that of your friends that a learner's permit allows a new driver to practice driving skills in real settings provided he or she is accompanied by a licensed driver.

Gillian may have obtained both her learner's permit and her driver's license within one year: a nice accomplishment! But such an accomplishment may have a few disadvantages. Being licensed to drive at age 16, Gillian probably had little actual driving experience. Studies of automobile accident rates involving teenagers show that *newly licensed drivers*, that is, drivers licensed for less than one month, and teenage drivers with little experience behind the wheel are less able to detect and avoid oncoming hazards than are more experienced drivers (Committee on Injury, 2006). What is more, researchers in Nova Scotia, Canada, found that more driving experience usually means fewer automobile accidents. The Nova Scotia study showed that the rate of automobile crashes for newly licensed teenagers decreases by more than half, from 120 accidents per 10,000 drivers to 50 per 10,000 drivers, after just 18 months of driving experience (Mayhew, Simpson, & Pak, 2003). At age 16, Gillian may have had fewer than 18 months of driving experience. It is possible that with more experience, Gillian could have recovered from the hazards posed by a momentary distraction.

A second potential contributing factor to the accident is a driver's age, a factor that is related to inexperience. Age and inexperience are *correlated variables* or, as we explained in Chapter 2, Research Methods, variables that covary. In this case the two variables, driver's age and inexperience, are negatively correlated. As age increases, we find that driving inexperience decreases. Remember, in the opening story Gillian was only 16, and studies show that adolescents

16 to 19 years of age have the highest auto-mobile accident rate of any age group (Committee on Injury, 2006).

The presence of other teenage passengers is a third potential contributing factor to accidents. Notice that we specify *teenage* passengers. What difference does the age of the passengers make? According to some researchers, it may mean the difference between life and death. Studies suggest that teenager passengers are more likely to engage in behaviors that may distract a driver (see Figure 5.1). We saw in the opening story how a minor distraction can prove fatal. Yet research suggests that teens often engage in greater distractions, such as "fooling around," when another teen is at the wheel. Adolescents explain that fooling around behaviors include yelling, arguing, dancing, or wrestling while in a car. The behaviors may involve the driver or just other passengers (Centers for Disease Control, 2006; University of California, Agriculture and Natural Resources, 2007). But, even a driver who does not participate in fooling around is prone to be distracted by the action.

FIGURE 5.1 Teenage Driver with a Teenage Passenger and a Cell Phone Spells Distracted Driving.

Source: www.attorneygeneral.gov

As for speeding, here, too, research suggests that adolescent passengers contribute to the likelihood of this risky behavior. A report by the Committee on Injury (2006) suggests that teen drivers are more likely to speed in the presence of male teenage passengers regardless of whether the driver is male or female. Why do male teenage passengers influence a driver's speed? That is not clear. Perhaps teen drivers are inclined to try to impress or show off their driving skills when males are present. But because most teenage drivers lack experience or well-developed skills, they may overestimate their actual abilities.

Thus, whether distracted, speeding, or just inexperienced, statistics on the rates of automobile accidents by adolescents show that drivers 16 to 17 years of age have a 40% increased risk of motor vehicle accidents when accompanied by one other teenage passenger. The risk doubles when two adolescent passengers are present and nearly quadruples with three or more teens are present (Committee on Injury, 2006). Gillian was traveling with four other teenage passengers. You compute the risk rate.

So, what factors contributed to Gillian's fatal accident? It is impossible to say with certainty, but it appears that her assumed inexperience, her age, the distracting request for chewing gum, and the presence of four other adolescents combined to contribute to the fatal outcome.

Gillian's story is tragic, but you may be wondering how automobile accidents relate to a chapter on risky health behaviors. After all, most health psychology textbooks begin chapters on risky health behaviors with topics such as substance use, sexual behaviors, eating behaviors, exercise, or mental and emotional health. We will examine many of the same topics. But we begin with automobile accidents to highlight one often overlooked fact: ***unintentional injuries***, injuries resulting from accidents or unplanned events, are a leading cause of injury and death among children ages 1 to 14, among adolescents ages 15 to 24, and among adults ages 25 to 44 (see Table 5.1, Department of Health and Human Resources, 2001).

One common cause of unintended injury is automobile accidents. In fact, for adolescents 16 to 20 years of age, the leading cause of death is injury resulting from automobile accidents (National Highway Traffic Safety, 2005a). Risky behaviors such as speeding, drinking and driving, and driving without a license are common causes of motor vehicle accidents for both adolescents and adults.

All of the risky behaviors mentioned previously adversely affect health. What is more, all of the behaviors and hence the health consequences stemming from such behaviors are preventable. They represent, therefore, a category of health behaviors of interest to health psychologists. You may recall from Chapter 4, Theories and Models of Health Behavior Change, that one goal of health psychologists is to encourage individuals to change the behaviors that lead to preventable injury or illness. Therefore we begin this chapter on risky health behaviors with a discussion of unintentional injuries, one of the six priority health risks identified by the Centers for Disease Control (CDC). We follow our discussion of unintentional injuries by exploring the five other CDC priority health risks: cigarettes, substance use, risky sexual behavior, physical inactivity, and unhealthy dietary behaviors (Grunbaum et al., 2002). We will explore each of the six risky behaviors by examining the behavioral ***antecedents***, or factors that influence the behaviors; the frequency of the behavior across age groups; and the long-term health implications of the behaviors. Finally, we will identify and discus relevant theories developed by psychologists and other health researchers that may explain the antecedents of risky health outcomes.

Three important points before we begin: First, a number of risky health behaviors that begin during adolescence continue into adulthood. For this reason, much of the research on risky health behaviors focuses on adolescents (Brender & Collins, 1998; Kulbok & Cox, 2002). We include in this chapter many studies that examine adolescent health risks in order to explore the origins and possible causes for such behaviors for adolescents as well as for adults.

Second, the concepts of risk and risky behaviors need clarification. The World Health Organization (2002) defines *risk* as the probability of an adverse outcome or the occurrence of an event that raises that probability. Likewise, we define a *risky behavior* as an action that increases the probability of an adverse outcome. Note, however, that the presence of a risk factor or risky behavior does not always lead to an adverse health outcome.

Finally, many studies tend to group together individuals who engage in a risky behavior once (or episodically) with repeat or frequent risk takers. They dichotomize adolescents as individuals who either never engaged in a risky behavior or ever engaged in such behaviors, even if only once (Blum et al., 2000; Kulbok & Cox, 2002). The never-versus-ever dichotomy seems a bit extreme. It does not distinguish between experimental risk taking among adolescents that occurs only once or rarely versus behavior that continues over time or is habitual (He et al., 2004). Clearly, the probability of an adverse event resulting from a risky behavior will be greater

TABLE 5.1 Leading Causes of Death by Age Group in the United States, 1997	
Group	**Number of Deaths**
Under 1 year	
Birth defects	6,178
Disorders related to premature births	3,925
Sudden infant death syndrome	2,991
1 to 4 years	
Unintentional injuries	2,005
Birth defects	589
Cancer	438
5 to 14 years	
Unintentional injuries	3,371
Cancer	1,030
Homicide	457
15 to 24 years	
Unintentional injuries	13,367
Homicides	6,146
Suicides	4,186
25 to 44 years	
Unintentional injuries	27,129
Cancer	27,206
Heart disease	16,513
45 to 64 years	
Cancer	131,743
Heart disease	101,235
Unintentional injuries	17,521
65 years and older	
Heart disease	606,913
Cancer	382,913
Stroke	140,336

Source: U.S. Department of Health and Human Services (2001).

among frequent rather than infrequent risk takers. With this point in mind, we further define risky health behaviors as only those behaviors that adolescents engage in repeatedly and over time.

SECTION I. UNINTENTIONAL INJURY AND VIOLENCE

Motor Vehicle Accidents

We began the chapter with a story about an accident involving a teenage driver because it is an example of unintentional injuries that are frequently the result of risky behaviors. Teenage drivers have the highest rate of automobile accidents and the highest rate of deaths due to motor vehicle accidents of any age group. Consider this fact: There are almost 12 million adolescent drivers in the nation. They make up just 6% of the total number of drivers but account for almost 14% of the fatalities due to automobile accidents (National Highway Traffic Safety, 2005a).

Why do younger adolescents have higher accident rates? Earlier we identified three reasons: inexperience, driver's age, and distraction. Clearly, driver's age is uniquely associated with adolescents. Many times, inexperience also plays a role. Other contributing factors to automobile accidents include nighttime driving, failure to use seat belts, type of vehicle driven, and unlicensed drivers (Committee on Injury, 2006; Williams, 2003). In the following section we briefly explore the impact of the first three on unintentional injuries: the effects of nighttime driving, failure to use seat belts, and type of vehicle.

NIGHTTIME DRIVING   Even experienced drivers agree that nighttime driving is challenging because driving hazards are poorly illuminated when dark. For adolescents, however, the usual hazards of nighttime driving often are combined with risky behaviors such as speeding, drinking alcohol, or driving with other teenage passengers (Simons-Morton, Lerner, & Singer, 2005; vanBeurden, Zask, Brooks, & Dight, 2005).

The higher rate of nighttime accidents and fatalities among adolescents is one reason for a health policy instituted in United States and Canada, as well as other countries, for teenage drivers. Specifically, the United States and Canada have adopted a ***graduated license law (GDL)*** that issues first-time adolescent drivers a ***provisional driving license***, a license that limits adolescents to driving only under specific conditions (Sibbald, 2007). The restrictions vary by state (in the United States) and country but many include a prohibition from driving at night or with other teenage passengers, among other restrictions (Goodwin, Wells, Foss, & Williams, 2006). In effect, the provisional license provides a test period, an opportunity for the new driver to establish an accident- or incident-free driving record. And, to date, studies suggest that provisional licenses for adolescents have been effective. Current findings show that the provisional or graduated licenses have helped reduce adolescent automobile accidents and other driving-related incidences by 9% to 41% (Goodwin et al., 2006; Ulmer et al., 2000).

SEAT BELTS   Why are seat belts used by approximately 81% of drivers in the United States (NHTSA, 2006)? The Automobile Association of American offers one possible motive: Seat belts save lives. Put another way, researchers have shown that seat belt use reduces the number of fatal injuries due to automobile accidents. And such outcomes are not limited to the United States.

A study by El-Sadig and colleagues (2004) provides strikingly clear evidence for the health enhancing effect of automobile seat belts in the United Arab Emirates (UAE) in the Middle East.

El-Sadig and colleagues (2004) examined the severity of injuries sustained by adults in automobile accidents before and after seat belt legislation was passed in the UAE in 1999. Before the seat belt legislation, 54% of adults in automobile accidents died after reaching the hospital. El-Sadig and colleagues found that, after the new legislation, the fatality rate associated with automobile accidents dropped to 17% after hospitalization. At the same time, the percentage of minor injuries pre- versus postlegislation increased from 42% to 77% (El-Sadig et al., 2004). Thus, the study showed that seat belt use did decrease mortality rates in the UAE due to automobile accidents. And although the rates of minor injuries sustained in accidents increased, the injuries were not life threatening.

Additionally, the study demonstrated that seat belt laws, a health policy regulation, did improve an individual's health outcomes. In essence, requiring individuals to use seat belts as a matter of law also requires them to adopt a behavior that improves their health outcomes in the event of an auto accident.

TYPE OF MOTOR VEHICLE   Unlike automobiles, motorcycles do not come with seat belts. In fact, they come with little more than the seat, the motor, the wheels, and a steering device. The structure of a motorcycle—no doors, cushions, or airbags—provides motorcyclists little protection from the impact of other motor vehicles in an unavoidable collision (see Figure 5.2). The lack of protection

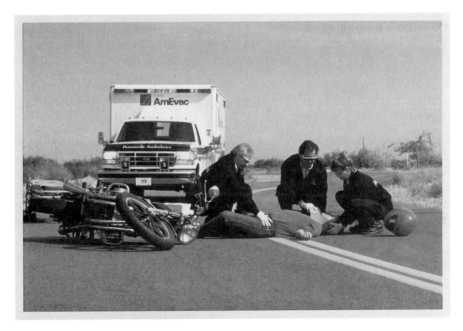

FIGURE 5.2   Stabilizing a Motorcycle Accident Victim. Motorcycle riders have the highest rate of fatal motor vehicle injuries.

may be one reason why fatal motor vehicle injury rates are higher for motorcycle riders than for all other forms of motorized travel (Beck, Dellinger, & O'Neil, 2007). The high frequency of fatalities among motorcycle riders also may explain why emergency department physicians sometimes call motorcycle riders "organ donors."

We stated that motorcycle riding is risky. And one behavior that increases the probability of unintentional injuries for motorcycle riders is riding without a helmet. How do we know that helmets reduce fatalities in motorcycle crashes? Consider this: In 1997, Arkansas legislators repealed, or withdrew, the state's adult helmet law, which required all adult motorcyclists to wear helmets when riding. Coincidentally, as in the UAE example, a group of researchers designed a study to compare motorcycle fatality rates before and after the change in the law. Remember, however, that in this case, the law changed from requiring helmets, a health-enhancing behavior, to allowing cyclists to ride helmet free, a risky or compromising behavior. The result? Researchers found a significant increase in the number of motorcycle fatalities after the law was repealed. Before the repeal, 39.6% of motorcyclists died as a result of motor vehicle accidents compared with 75.5% after the repeal (Bledsoe et al., 2002). Not surprisingly, the number of severe but not fatal head injuries also increased after the law was repealed (Bledsoe et al., 2002). In this example, the repeal of a health policy resulted in poorer health outcomes and underscored the health-enhancing role of wearing helmets when riding motorcycles.

What is the point of the statistics on unintentional injuries due to automobile and motorcycle accidents? Simply this: Risky behaviors such as driving while drunk, fooling around in cars, failing to use seat belts, and riding motorcycles without helmets, can increase the chance of motor vehicle injuries or death (see Table 5.2) . The risky behaviors are also wholly preventable, and so are the adverse consequences they cause.

There is some hopeful news, however. Driving is, perhaps, one of the few health behaviors in the current chapter for which repeated practice lessens risky outcomes. Unfortunately, practiced behaviors do not reduce the rates of other unintentional injuries, as we will see in the following sections.

Violence

High school and college administrators in the United States struggle to explain the frequent and apparently random incidences of shootings on school grounds and campuses across the nation. Shootings in high schools in Columbine, Colorado (1999); Jonesboro, Arkansas (1998); San Diego, California (2001); and most recently on college campuses in Blacksburg, Virginia (2007), and DeKalb, Illinois (2008) are indications of a national violence problem caused, in part, by emotional or psychological health issues of the initiator or shooter. We will discuss emotional health more fully in Chapter 6, Emotional Health and Well-Being. Here, however, we will explore briefly the unintentional and preventable injuries that result from violence.

The term *violence* refers to a broad concept that includes many different behaviors. For example, most would agree that *homicide*, or the killing of another person, is a violent act. So, too, is a *physical assault*, a physical confrontation with another person that could include hitting, shoving, kicking, or other physically aggressive behaviors. *Violence* can also be defined more broadly as the intentional use of force against another person, a community, or even against oneself. According to this definition, suicide is also an act of violence (Corso et al., 2007).

TABLE 5.2	Motor Vehicle–Related Health Behaviors among Adolescents

Percentage of high school students who rarely or never wore seat belts,* motorcycle helmets,[†] or bicycle helmets,[††] by sex, race/ethnicity, and grade—United States, Youth Risk Behavior Survey, 2001

Category	Rarely or Never Wore Seatbelts			Rarely or Never Wore Motorcycle Helmets			Rarely or Never Wore Bicycle Helmets		
	Female	Male	Total	Female	Male	Total	Female	Male	Total
Race/Ethnicity									
White	9.7	17.7	13.6	26.4	37.1	33.6	81.1	85.5	83.6
Black	12.2	20.3	16.1	32.1	51.1	44.6	90.4	90.9	90.7
Hispanic	11.3	17.7	14.5	51.1	58.0	55.3	86.9	90.6	88.9
Grade									
9	10.8	19.4	14.9	30.0	39.9	36.5	80.4	86.0	83.3
10	10.3	16.6	13.3	30.2	36.9	34.7	81.5	85.0	83.5
11	9.7	17.5	13.6	33.9	44.0	40.8	86.2	87.7	87.1
12	9.4	18.6	13.9	25.7	42.3	36.1	85.1	87.1	86.3
Total	**10.2**	**18.1**	**14.1**	**30.1**	**40.9**	**37.2**	**82.6**	**86.3**	**84.7**

*When riding in a car driven by someone else.
[†]Among the 25.3% of students who rode motorcycles during the 12 months preceding the survey.
[††]Among the 65.1% of students who rode bicycles during the 12 months preceding the survey.

Source: Youth Risk Behavior Survey, June 28, 2001, Table 2.

Examples of unintentional injuries resulting from violence are, unfortunately, easy to find. Disputes, angry exchanges, or acts of theft may lead to violence and unintentional acts that injure or kill. And, as the school shootings remind us, violent acts often appear suddenly and with little or no warning. Each year in the United States, more that 2.2 million injuries and over 50,000 deaths are attributed to violence (Corso et al., 2007).

Counting the number of individuals injured or killed is one way to measure the cost of violence. Yet we can also assess the effects of violence by examining the psychological impact on its victims and observers. Consider this: In a CDC Youth Risk Behavior Surveillance System (YRBSS) Survey, adolescents were asked how often they carry weapons to school. The survey revealed that 27.6% of high school students reported carrying a weapon to school, and 5.1% report that the weapon was a gun (see Table 5.3).

Clearly a weapon is not an essential school supply. Yet some students believe that weapons are essential to protect them from unwanted confrontations en route to and from school or even while at school. Thus, the psychological impact of living in a violent or potentially violent environment leads some adolescents to carry tools that may increase the chances of violent confrontations. The act of carrying a weapon suggests a willingness or intention to use a weapon perhaps as a first recourse.

TABLE 5.3	Violence-Related Behavior among Adolescents					

Percentage of high school students who carried a weapon* by sex, race/ethnicity, and grade—United States, Youth Risk Behavior Survey, 2001

	Carried a Weapon			Carried a Gun		
Category	Female	Male	Total	Female	Male	Total
Race/Ethnicity						
White	5.1	31.3	**17.9**	1.0	10.2	5.5
Black	8.6	22.4	**15.2**	1.1	12.2	6.5
Hispanic	7.4	26.0	**16.5**	1.6	8.0	4.8
Grade						
9	7.4	33.7	**19.8**	1.0	13.3	6.8
10	5.4	28.4	**16.7**	1.0	9.0	4.9
11	5.9	28.1	**16.8**	1.8	9.6	5.7
12	5.3	25.6	**15.1**	1.2	8.3	4.7
Total	**6.2**	**29.3**	**17.4**	**1.3**	**10.3**	**5.7**

*For example, a gun, knife, or club, on ≥1 of the 30 days preceding the survey.
95% confidence interval.

Source: Mortality and Morbidity Weekly Report, June 28, 2002, Table 6.

The CDC Youth Risk Behavior study also revealed a gender difference in the likelihood of carrying weapons to school. They report that males were much more likely to carry weapons than females (29.3% versus 6.2%) and also far more likely than females to carry guns (10.3% versus 1.3%) (MMWR, 2002). It may be no coincidence, given these numbers, that to date all initiators of high school or college mass shootings have been males. Clearly, carrying a weapon will not necessarily decrease incidences of violence. Nor will it increase a person's perception of a safe environment at school. While some students carry a weapon to counter unwanted confrontations, others, fully 6% of students in the survey, stated that when concerned about their safety at school they chose to be absent. Staying home from school also will not increase a person's perception of safety in his or her environment, although it will increase the risk of poor academic performance.

Carrying a weapon and absenting oneself from school are two reactions to violence in the community, here defined as the school community. Both demonstrate fear or apprehension of violent encounters regardless of whether a person has firsthand exposure to violence. And both can lead to emotional or psychological health problems as a result of exposure to or fear of injury due to violence.

DOMESTIC VIOLENCE Generally, the term *domestic violence* describes actions by one person in a relationship intended to control or dominate another. The actions can be physical, sexual, or emotional and may include acts of intimidation or threats.

Early research on domestic violence focused primarily on a physically abusive relationship between two persons, for example, spouses or intimate partners (Daughtery & Houry, 2008; Duterte et al., 2008; Marcus, 2008). Today, the term is used more broadly to describe abusive relationships between family members or others sharing a living space. It also includes *elder abuse*, here meaning the physical or emotional maltreatment of older persons; *child abuse*, usually the physical mistreatment of a child by an adult; and *emotional abuse*, meaning psychological intimidation and trauma that can include physical acts. In fact, studies examining the psychological state of both the victim and the abuser explain the lasting psychological impact of such abuse (Lee, Pomeroy, & Bohman, 2007; Ragin et al., 2002; Ward, Martin, & Distiller, 2007). For example, several studies show that children and adolescents exposed to (although not the target of) domestic violence in the home experience psychological trauma due to witnessing the violence. They are also at greater risk for physical violence later in life at the hands of an abusive partner (Bagley & Mallick, 2000; Cold et al., 2001; Silverman, Reinhertz, & Giaconia, 1996; Whitfield, 2003; Whitfield et al., 2003).

Another group of studies points to the likelihood of children who, when abused by their parents, becoming abusive as adults (Capaldi & Clark, 1998; Worley, Walsh, & Lewis, 2004). Even when a child is not raised in an abusive environment, researchers suggest that a pattern of aggressive behavior in childhood is predictive of aggressive behavior in adulthood. A recent study by Temcheff and colleagues (2008) found that, for males, childhood aggression represented a stable behavioral style that links male peer aggressive behavior to violence toward their spouse and children.

DATING VIOLENCE   New research on the aggressive and abusive behavior between individuals who are not in committed relationships, known as *dating violence*, has prompted researchers to look more broadly at interpersonal violence. Consider this: The YRBSS high school study revealed that just under 10% of females reported being physically hurt in some way by their dating partner (MMWR, 2002). This statistic suggests that abusive relationships may often go undetected in the early stages of a relationship, a much earlier starting point for interpersonal violence than suspected.

Although health professionals are increasingly attentive to issues of domestic violence in research and in practice, it is unlikely that we will know the true prevalence rates of interpersonal and domestic violence in the United States. For many who experience acts of physical or psychological aggression, domestic abuse is an embarrassing experience. The victim's shame often prevents him or her from disclosing the experience. Still others fear the threats of retaliation by their abuser in the event that they reveal the truth.

Fortunately for the victims and the community, increased media attention to domestic violence through television, radio, and print ads provides information and tangible assistance to people exposed to domestic abuse (see Figure 5.3). Confidential hotlines, counseling services, and domestic violence shelters provide a range of services to help an individual with his or her psychological, physical, and material needs. In addition, many hospital emergency departments screen for and identify patients whose injuries were obtained as a result of domestic violence. Working together with social services and domestic violence shelters, medical facilities in many major urban cities can offer domestic violence victims the option of immediate protection from domestic violence, usually by placement in a domestic violence shelter. Such shelters offer the victims a safe haven from further abuse.

FIGURE 5.3   Domestic Violence Prevention Announcement.
Research suggests that domestic violence prevention should be taught early.

Unfortunately, such services are not universally available. Domestic violence shelters in the United States are often fully occupied. And, in developing countries, shelters may be either fewer in number or considered an unlikely option for women who depend economically on their spouses or family members for survival (Belknap & Cruz, 2007; Khan & Hussain, 2008; Morgaine, 2007).

SUICIDE   A second form of violence that affects the whole community is *self-inflicted injuries*. The most widely recognized form of self-injury is *suicide* or attempted suicide. Suicide is the 11th leading cause of death in the United States. However, this statistic blurs an important distinction among gender, age, and ethnic groups regarding prevalence rates of suicide.

A Centers for Disease Control (CDC) study reports that deaths due to suicide are more prevalent among males than females. It is the 8th leading cause of death among males but only the 16th leading cause of death for females (CDC, 2005a). In fact, among adults the highest suicide rates are recorded for men 75 years of age or older. Older males commit suicide at a rate of 37.4 per 100,000 people. In comparison, the highest suicide rate for women is 8.0 per 100,000 and occurs among the 40- and 50-year-old age groups (CDC, 2005b).

The fact that males commit suicide at a higher rate than females may be news to some. But more surprising may be the fact that suicide rates for older adults are considerably higher than for younger adults. Individuals 65 years of age or older commit one suicide for every four attempts, a ratio of 1:4. Young adults, however, report one suicide for every 100 to 200 attempts, for a ratio of 1:100–200 (Goldsmith, Pellmar, Kleinman, & Bunney, 2002).

When we are comparing suicide rates among ethnic groups, statistics show that the prevalence rate for suicide among Native American and Alaskan Natives is almost twice as high as for other ethnicities. Suicide is the second leading cause of death for Native Americans and Alaskan Natives, affecting primarily adolescents and adults ages 15 to 34 (Goldsmith et al., 2002).

The high suicide rates for males, specifically older males, Native Americans, and Alaskan Natives should prompt us to ask why the rates are much higher for these three demographic groups. Researchers can only speculate based, in part, on information obtained from attempted suicides among individuals from the same group. Such studies find that physical and mental health problems, socioeconomic problems, or family and individual crises all contribute to high male suicide rates both in the United States and globally (WHO, 2010b). For Native Americans and Alaskan Natives, a number of societal problems appear to be linked to suicide.

Frequently cited societal concerns for these groups include extreme poverty, poor education, and a lack of employment options, in addition to social isolation and years of cultural marginalization (LeMaster, Beub, Novins, & Manson, 2004; Olson & Wahab, 2006; Yellow Horse Brave Heart, 2003).

We noted that suicide or self-injury is a form of violence that affects more than just the individual. It affects families and entire communities as well. Suicidal acts can cause psychological or emotional health problems for the victim's social network. As such, although the primary recipient of injury is the individual, the impact of the act has a residual effect on others.

Suicide is also a global health issue. Here, too, we find pronounced differences in suicide prevalence rates, this time between developed versus developing countries (WHO, 2010). WHO reports that suicide rates are highest in western and eastern Europe, the Soviet Union, China, and Japan while the African continent and the South Pacific report the lowest rates (see Figure 5.4). Thus, the studies suggest that a country's economic status, along with individual and societal factors, are important determinants of suicide rates.

In sum, the statistics on all forms of unintentional injuries, including motor vehicle accidents, violent behaviors, and self-injury, demonstrate that, for individuals between the ages of 1 and 44, unintentional injuries pose the greatest health risks. Intervention programs and health policies designed to reduce the adverse consequences of unintentional injuries are growing in number. But, as the recent incidences of school shootings show, this is a continuing problem.

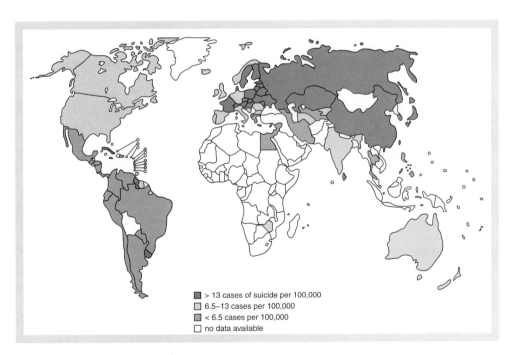

> 13 cases of suicide per 100,000
6.5–13 cases per 100,000
< 6.5 cases per 100,000
no data available

FIGURE 5.4 Map of Suicide Rates (per 100,000 most recent year available as of 2007).

SECTION II. SUBSTANCE USE AND ABUSE: INFLUENCE OF CULTURE, AGE, AND GENDER

In the previous section we examined the impact of unintentional injuries and violence on health outcomes. In the current section we examine the effects of substance use, which some may consider a form of intentional injury, on health outcomes. Users of substances such as cigarettes, alcohol, and illicit drugs may not consider the use of such agents as intentional acts of injury. But the volitional use of such substances can adversely affect health outcomes, thereby causing injury and harm to the user.

Cigarettes

Each day, more that 1,500 teens between the ages of 12 and 17 begin smoking. Is it any wonder, therefore, that more than 70% of adult smokers report that they began smoking before age 18 (Breslau, Fenn, & Peterson, 1993; Klein, Thomas, & Sutter, 2007; Tucker, Ellickson, & Klein, 2002).

Why is smoking, particularly the early onset of smoking, a problem? Consider this: Smoking was the primary or contributing cause of death for over 440,000 adults in the United States in 2000 (U.S. Department of Health and Human Services, 2000). It remains the leading preventable cause of death and the leading cause of death due to disease in the United States (American Cancer Society, 2006). In fact, smoking causes more deaths than AIDS, alcohol, automobile accidents, cocaine, fires, heroin, homicides, and suicides combined (see Tables 5.4 and 5.5) (Dodgen, 2005). But what leads teens to begin smoking, often at such early ages? And why do they continue?

There is no shortage of theories in psychology to explain why adolescents experiment with cigarettes and other substances or why they continue. In this section, we examine some of the social and intrapersonal factors that influence substance use. We then examine five groups of theories that offer explanations about early and habitual adolescent substance use.

TABLE 5.4	Actual Unintentional Deaths in the United States, 2000
Cause of Death	**Number (%)**
Tobacco	435,000 (18.1%)
Poor diet/physical inactivity	400,000 (16.1%)
Alcohol	85,000 (3.5%)
Motor vehicle	43,000 (1.8%)
Firearms	29,000 (1.2%)
Illicit drug use	17,000 (0.7%)

Source: Mokdad, Marks, Stroup, & Gerberding (2004).

TABLE 5.5 Cigarette-Related Deaths

Annual deaths and estimates of smoking-attributable mortality (SAM), United States, 1997–2001

Cause of Death (ICD-10* code)	Male Deaths	Male SAM	Female Deaths	Female SAM
Malignant Neoplasms				
Lip, oral cavity, pharynx (C00–C14)	4,973	3,686	2,525	1,182
Esophagus (C15)	9,037	6,533	2,854	1,625
Stomach (C16)	7,403	2,052	5,223	600
Pancreas (C25)	13,984	3,078	14,774	3,431
Larynx (C32)	3,017	2,499	816	596
Trachea, lung, bronchus (C33–C34)	89,912	79,026	63,181	44,810
Cervix uteri (C53)	—	—	3,989	491
Kidney, other urinary (C64–65)	7,169	2,790	4,454	222
Urinary bladder (C67)	8,025	3,764	3,841	1,054
Acute myeloid leukemia (C92.0)	3,447	791	2,919	299
Total	**146,967**	**104,219**	**104,576**	**54,310**
Cardiovascular Diseases				
Ischemic heart disease (I20–I25)	262,968	54,629	256,871	32,172
Other heart disease (I00–I09, I26–I51)	70,368	13,006	92,173	7,937
Cerebrovascular disease (I60–I69)	64,074	8,543	101,873	8,893
Atherosclerosis (I70–I71)	5,444	1,439	9,276	759
Aortic aneurysm (I71)	9,635	6,203	6,185	3,046
Other arterial disease (I72–I78)	4,188	547	5,585	805
Total	**416,677**	**84,367**	**471,963**	**53,612**
Respiratory Diseases				
Pneumonia, influenza (J10–J18)	27,389	6,170	34,748	4,702
Bronchitis, emphysema (J40–J42, J43)	9,455	8,586	8,594	6,922
Chronic airway obstruction (J44)	48,644	39,563	47,769	35,511
Total	**85,488**	**54,319**	**91,111**	**47,135**
Perinatal Conditions				
Short gestation/low birthweight (P07)	2,435	230	1,980	187
Respiratory distress syndrome (P22)	688	25	468	17
Other respiratory (newborn) (P23–28)	891	44	640	31
Sudden infant death syndrome (R95)	1,603	224	1,082	152
Total	**5,617**	**523**	**4,170**	**387**

(continued)

TABLE 5.5	(Continued)			
	Male		**Female**	
Cause of Death (ICD-10* code)	Deaths	SAM	Deaths	SAM
Burn deaths	—	530	—	388
Secondhand smoke deaths				
Lung cancer	—	1,130	—	1,930
Ischemic heart disease	—	14,406	—	20,646
Total	—	15,536	—	22,576
Total	—	259,494	—	178,408

*International Classification of Diseases, Tenth Revision.

Source: MMWR, July 1, 2005.

SOCIAL NORMS AND ENVIRONMENTAL FACTORS   In Chapter 4, Theories and Models of Health Behavior Change, we noted that product manufacturers are skilled in promoting and selling their products to their intended audiences. For example, marketing and promotional materials used by cigarette manufactures help promote smoking at an early age. Advertisements that promote smoking as a *socially normative behavior*, here meaning a behavior widely accepted by a society, appear to target an audience that includes children and adolescents. If such a claim seems unlikely, consider this: Cartoon characters, smoking logos, and items with the cigarette logos embossed on them are particularly popular with younger audiences. It is not uncommon to find cigarette manufacturers placing logos on jackets, cigarette lighters, water bottles, and even candy cigarettes. Although the ads and products may be intended for adults, chances are that children also find them quite appealing (Sargent et al., 1997).

One example of a popular and effective ad created to promote cigarette use is the Joe Camel cartoon, a caricature depiction of a camel used to advertise Camel cigarettes in the 1970s and 1980s. Joe Camel's 1950s attire—complete with a leather jacket, jeans, sunglasses, and a Harley-Davidson motorcycle—captivated younger audiences. In fact, even children readily identified Joe Camel. In a study by Fischer and colleagues (1991), approximately 30% of 3-year-olds were able to match the Joe Camel cartoon figure correctly with the cigarette, and more than 91% of 6-year-olds were able to correctly pair the image of Joe with the product. Surprisingly, children were more successful in identifying Joe Camel than they were in correctly identifying Mickey Mouse, a Walt Disney cartoon character designed especially for children.

Similarly, when comparing adolescents' and adults' ability to recognize and identify the Camel advertisements, adolescents in grades 9 through 12 were significantly better at the task than adults. Not surprisingly, adolescents also found the ads to be more appealing than did adults (DiFranza et al., 1991).

The Camel campaign with Joe Camel was so successful that Camel product manufacturers saw a 31% increase in their share of the illegal children's cigarette market (DiFranza et al.,

1991). Returning to our question of what explains the early initiation of adolescents into smoking, one possible explanation is the direct and indirect marketing to young audiences. Clearly the marketing strategy appears to have been "effective advertising for future smokers" (Klein & St Clair, 2000; Klein, Thomas, & Sutter, 2007).

SOCIAL ROLE MODELS   If children and adolescents find cartoon cigarette advertisements attractive and appealing, would they also be attracted to actors who smoke in movies? Research suggested that smoking on "the silver screen" has a ***direct*** and an ***indirect effect*** on adolescent smoking. By indirect effect, we mean smoking behavior that is influenced or mediated by a secondary factor. In this case, the secondary or ***mediating factor*** is peers who smoke. Studies suggest that, indeed, teens exposed to smoking by actors in movies are more likely to associate with peers who smoke. And, the teens who associate with other teens who smoke are themselves likely to begin smoking (Wills et al., 2007).

Research also suggests that teen smoking rates increase when the on-screen smoking is done by an adolescent's favorite movie star (Tickle et al., 2001). In a 2004 study of the impact of on-screen smoking on adolescents, Distefan, Pierce, and Gilpin (2004) found that, among adolescent girls who never smoked, the on-screen smoking behavior of their favorite actor strongly predicted smoking initiation. Nonsmoking boys were not as affected by the actions of their favorite on-screen actors, suggesting a gender effect of smoking models on later smoking behaviors.

In essence, research shows that manufacturers of cigarettes and cigarette products seem to have attracted the attention of a young audience. The effective marketing may have encouraged children and adolescents to view smoking as a desirable or even an expected behavior. In addition, the studies suggest that adolescent smoking behavior can be encouraged by exposure to individuals who model smoking behaviors. Movie actors who smoke on-screen constitute one example of a model. Peers who smoke also serve as models.

CULTURE AND GENDER   Adolescents also credit their family members as smoking models. In fact, many adolescents report that their first experience with cigarettes usually occurred in the presence of friends or older siblings who smoke (U.S. Department of Health and Human Services, 1994). Remember Eddie from the opening story in Chapter 4? His brother and his friends helped to create a smoking culture that he found very appealing and difficult to avoid.

Similarly, cultural practices also influence smoking patterns. Global statistics on smoking show that currently China and India are homes to the largest number of tobacco consumers (Paharia, 2008). Thus, China and India are nations in which smoking is a common or normative behavior. By comparison, smoking rates in the United States have declined over the past 40 years. In 1965, 42% of American adults (18 years of age or older) smoked. Presently, approximately 21% of all adults in the United States smoke, a rate that is half that of the 1965 statistic (National Center for Health Statistics, 2006). Similar declines have been reported for adolescent smoking rates, again in the United States. In 2005, approximately 23% of adolescents reported smoking, the lowest level in 15 years (CDC, 2008d).

To what do we attribute differences in smoking rates across cultures? While it is possible that, for some cultural groups, smoking behaviors are part of their traditions, it is more likely that the extensive health promotion campaigns in the United States, designed to decrease smoking rates over the past 30 years, have changed the culture of smoking in the United States. Now, in many places in the United States, smoking behaviors are the exceptions rather than the norms.

In spite of the recent declines in U.S. smoking rates, researchers have noticed striking differences in smoking rates for adolescents by ethnicity and by gender. When comparing adolescent males who are regular smokers, that is, individuals who smoke 10 or fewer cigarettes each day, white males (5.3% of sample) were significantly more likely to report smoking up to 10 cigarettes each day than were Hispanic (1.8%) or African American males (1.1%). The data from the same survey revealed similar differences in smoking rates by ethnicity for female adolescents. White females were significantly more likely to smoke 10 or fewer cigarettes (4.0%) than African American females (0.7%). Similar demographic differences were found for adults also.

Some researchers contend that ethnic differences in smoking reflects an ***acculturation*** process, here meaning the effort to change one's attitudes, values, or behaviors to adopt the attitudes, values, and behaviors of a dominant ethnic group (Burnam, Telles, Karno, & Hough, 1987). Indeed, acculturation may explain the smoking behaviors of some groups. For example, Bethel and Schenker (2005) found that in the United States more acculturated Hispanic women reported higher rates of cigarette use than did less acculturated Hispanic women or men. A review of the literature by Bell, Ragin, and Cohall (1999) reveals similar findings on the impact of acculturation on cigarette smoking and other risky behaviors for adolescents.

In sum, existing studies suggest that perceived social norms, culture, and gender influence smoking initiation and general smoking behaviors. One way to test the relative importance of these factors is by examining theories that assess the role of such factors on these risky health behaviors.

THEORIES OF SUBSTANCE USE   As noted earlier, research on substance use behavior tends to focus on adolescents. Examining early onset of such behaviors helps to identify and assess the factors that contribute to substance use behaviors in the short and the long term. Studies suggest that environmental factors (such as product advertisements, and movie and television images of actors who smoke) as well as social and cultural factors (such as attitudes and behaviors of family and friends) all contribute to adolescent smoking patterns (Pederson & Lefcoe, 1987; Petraitis, Flay, & Miller, 1995). But can we say that these factors *cause* adolescents to initiate smoking behavior?

There is no shortage of theories that attempt to explain the cause-and-effect relationship of individual, environmental, social, and cultural factors on smoking among adolescents; there are far too many to review in this chapter. Fortunately, Petraitis and colleagues (1995) offer an easy and succinct summary of the theories using five central categories: cognitive-affective theories; social learning theories; conventional commitment theories; personality trait theories; and integration theories.

Cognitive-Affective Theories   According to Petraitis and colleagues (1995), one group of theories that can be used to explain substance use is best described as ***cognitive-affective theories***. These theories propose that three factors influence the likelihood of substance use: an adolescent's positive attitudes about substance use, the endorsement of substance use by others, and an individual's decision that the benefits of substance use outweigh the costs. Eddie, for example, was struggling to decide whether the benefits of smoking with his friends outweighed the cost of losing his girlfriend, Sarah. And, as you may have suspected, Azjen's theory of reasoned action and theory of planned behavior (1985) are included in this first group of theories, along with Rosenstock's health belief model (2005; see Chapter 4, Theories and Models of Health Behavior Change).

Social Learning Theories   *Social learning theories*, including Bandura's social cognitive theory (1986) as well as Akers's social learning theory (1996), comprise the second category. Here, substance use is explained as a behavior rooted in the attitudes and beliefs of the adolescent's role models, close friends, and parents (Petraitis, Flay, & Miller, 1995). Social learning theories contend that, by observing the context in which role models use, for example, cigarettes, and the consequences of their use, adolescents form attitudes about smoking and the perceived likely consequences of their decision to smoke.

Conventional Commitment Theories   Third are the *conventional commitment theories*, which view adolescents' level of attachment to conventional social institutions, such as the family, schools, religious institutions, or other structured systems, as buffers against substance use. In this case, *buffers* are the factors that protect an adolescent from initiating substance use behaviors. Conventional commitment theorists claim that weak bonds to structured systems will lead to a lack of commitment to the social norms of the institutions that help guide behavior. The weak bonds lead to a greater likelihood of involvement with other adolescents with similar weak ties, which can lead to "deviant" behaviors (Jessor, Donovan, & Costa, 1991; Kandel, Smicha-Fagan, & Davies, 1986).

What is meant by deviant behaviors in this instance? Consider this example: Members of one family neither smoke nor drink alcohol. The youngest child in the family has a weak attachment to the family and associates with other adolescents who similarly have weak familial attachments. At one point the group of adolescents begins to smoke and drink alcohol. The resulting substance use behaviors of the adolescent are inconsistent with, hence deviant from, the behaviors of the family. It is important to point out that, according to conventional commitment theorists, the adolescent's behavior is not brought about by a desire to rebel but rather by an absence of close personal ties to the institution, in this case the family.

Personality Trait Theories   The fourth category is *personality trait theories*. According to these theories, the individual characteristics of the adolescents and their social settings may influence the timing and occurrence of substance use. Thus, generalized stress and generalized low self-esteem (Kaplan, Martin, & Robbins, 1984; Kumpfer & Turner, 1990–1991) may explain more about the likelihood of substance use than conventional commitment or social normative beliefs. Trait theorists hold that an individual's method of coping with highly stressful environments, rather than that person's commitment to institutions, the behavior of his or her role models, or his or her own views of the behavior, may shape the decision to smoke.

Integration Theories   Finally, Petraitis's fifth category consists of *integration theories*, which include elements of each of the four categories mentioned above. Included in this group is the problem-behavior theory (Jessor et al., 1991), which examines early substance use behavior in the context of other problem behaviors that may occur. Jessor and colleagues suggest that adolescents who exhibit one problem behavior, such as substance use, are prone to engage in other problem behaviors also. Therefore, according to problem behavior theory, early substance use is just one of a number of risky behaviors that must be studied in context. Other theories included in this category are the peer cluster theory (Oetting & Beauvis, 1987; Petraitis et al., 1995), which focuses on the role of peers in influencing substance use, and the model of vulnerability (Sher, 1991), which suggests a genetic or biological determinant of substance use.

So, which theory best predicts early substance use? There is no definitive answer. What is clear, however, is that individual (age, ethnicity, and gender), social (peer influences, cultural norms as seen through family), societal (media), and biological factors all contribute. And given the differences in smoking behaviors by demographic groups, one single theory may not apply to all. Instead, different theories may be needed to explain the substance use behaviors of different populations.

Alcohol

Cigarettes are one of two legal substances in the United States that can cause serious health consequences (see Table 5.6). Another such substance is alcohol. In the United States, only adults 21 years of age or older are legally allowed to purchase and consume alcohol. And, in addition to being legally able to consume, some studies suggest that moderate consumption of alcohol can be beneficial to one's health. For example, some types of red wine contain *plant phenolics* or chemical compounds that serve as *antioxidants* that protect against some forms of cardiovascular diseases and cancer (Klatsky, 2007; Lopez-Velez, Martinez-Martinez, & DelValle-Rebes, 2003). If alcohol is legal and can have health-enhancing consequences, why, then, do we include alcohol in the chapter on risky health behaviors?

Alcohol itself is not the problem. Rather, it is the way we use alcohol, specifically the excessive consumption or the abuse of alcohol, that makes it risky. For example, excessive alcohol consumption and the use of alcohol by adolescents 20 years of age or younger has been linked to a number of illnesses and death (Irving & Schweiger, 1991; Merlin, Jager, & Schulenberger, 2008). Therefore, in this chapter we focus on the misuse of alcohol and its impact on individual and community health outcomes when viewing it as a risky health behavior.

EXCESSIVE CONSUMPTION OF ALCOHOL   Researchers suggest that *excessive alcohol consumption* is the third leading cause of preventable deaths in the United States (McGinnis & Foege, 1993). Specifically, current statistics show that approximately 75,000 people in the United States die each year in deaths related to excessive alcohol use (CDC, 2008e). To understand what constitutes excessive consumption, however, we must first define nonexcessive or "standard" consumption. According to the CDC, a standard drink of alcohol is defined as one that contains approximately 0.5 ounces (1.2 tablespoons) of pure alcohol (CDC, 2008e), the same amount contained in 12 ounces of beer, 8 ounces of malt liquor, 5 ounces of wine, or 1.5 ounces of an 80-proof distilled liquor such as rum, bourbon, or vodka.

To define excessive consumption, health researchers examine the amount of alcohol consumed by calculating the number of alcoholic drinks consumed in a single setting as well as the average number of drinks consumed on a daily basis (see Table 5.7). Excessive alcohol consumption may also be characterized as heavy drinking or binge drinking. In general, *heavy drinking* is defined as consuming five or more drinks in a day (Schoenborn & Adams, 2002), whereas researchers consider five or more drinks in a single setting or within two hours to be the definition of *binge drinking* (MMWR, 2004; Schoenborn & Adams, 2002) (see Figure 5.5).

TABLE 5.6	Substance Use: Perceived Benefits and Short- and Long-Term Health Consequences		
Substance	**Method of Use**	**Perceived Benefits**	**Short- and Long-term Health Consequences**
Cigarettes	Smoked (oral)	Suppresses appetite	Cancer of lungs and esophagus Emphysema Other respiratory problems Yellowed/stained teeth
Alcohol	Drink (oral)	Mild euphoria Reduces anxiety Induces relaxation Some types protect against cardiovascular disease, cancer	Impaired judgment Impaired coordination Cirrhosis of liver Gastrointestinal problems Heart disease or stroke Cancer of mouth, throat, liver, prostate Fetal alcohol syndrome (infants)
Marijuana	Smoke (oral)	Euphoria Giddiness Sedation Tranquility	Impaired coordination Impaired vision Increased anxiety Interference with short-term memory
Cocaine/Crack	Sniff (nasal) or smoke (oral)	Prolonged stimulation Euphoria	Increased temperature, heart rate, blood pressure Irregular heart rhythms Excessive nose bleeds Gastrointestinal problems
Heroin	Inject	Short-term euphoria Long-term drowsiness, relaxed state	Severely impaired coordination Impaired mental functioning Collapsed veins Liver disease Depressed respiratory system

TABLE 5.7	Defining Alcohol Consumption	
Category	Women	Men
Moderate drinking	1 or fewer drinks per day	5 or fewer drinks per day
Heavy drinking	2 or more drinks per day	5 or more drinks per day
Binge drinking	4 or more drinks within two hours	5 or more drinks within two hours

Source: Adapted from Centers for Disease Control (2008b).

Excessive drinking, including binge and heavy drinking, poses serious health risks to the consumer and to others. For the consumer, excessive consumption has been linked to gastrointestinal problems, heart disease, strokes, and cancer of the mouth, throat, liver, and prostate (CDC, 2008a; MMWR, 2004). It is responsible for serious liver diseases, including inflammation and scarring of the liver, known as *cirrhosis*, a disease that prevents the liver from functioning properly to remove waste products from the body. Cirrhosis can lead to liver failure, a fatal outcome (CDC, 2008a). Finally, excessive alcohol consumption also contributes to neurological

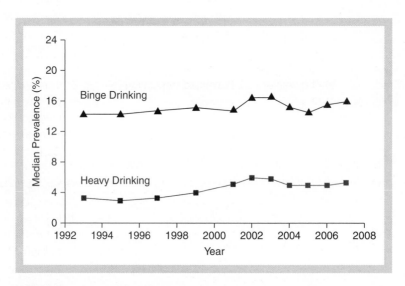

FIGURE 5.5 Prevalence of Binge Drinking and Heavy Drinking among Adults in the United States, 1993–2007.

Source: CDC (2008c).

and psychiatric problems and a greater likelihood of involvement in other risky behaviors such as risky sexual behaviors. And this just describes the risks to the excessive drinker.

Alcohol abuse also affects family members, friends, and communities. Consider this: In 2004 alcohol was implicated in 39% of all deaths due to traffic accidents, totaling 16,500 people (National Highway Traffic Safety Administration, 2005b). What is more, almost 2,000 of the 16,500 deaths were children ages 14 and under (National Highway Traffic Safety Administration, 2005b). Put another way, approximately 2,000 children died in traffic accidents caused by someone who consumed excessive amounts of alcohol.

Excessive drinking also exposes family members to increased risk of violence, such as intimate partner violence and child abuse. Alcohol abuse is cited in 66% of cases of intimate partner violence and is also a primary factor in incidences of child maltreatment (CDC, 2008a; Famularo, Kinscherff, & Fenton, 1992; Miller, Maguin, & Downs, 1997).

Finally, alcohol abuse by pregnant mothers can cause *fetal alcohol syndrome*, a condition that causes physical and mental abnormalities in the developing fetus. It may result in abnormal facial features, growth deficiencies, and problems with the central nervous system. Children born with fetal alcohol syndrome carry these problems throughout life.

In sum, excessive alcohol use can cause a host of health problems to the consumer, the family, and the community. More to the point, current statistics on the rate of alcohol consumption in the United States and in other countries show that we have reason to be concerned about alcohol abuse. Consider this: A CDC survey from 1997–1998 reports that almost two-thirds of U.S. adults 18 years of age or older currently drink alcohol (Schoenborn & Adams, 2002). The troubling part of their findings is that 5% of the same adults described themselves as heavy drinkers, having five or more drinks in a given day on a regular basis. Fully 20.5% of adults reported that they had five or more drinks in a day at least once in the 12 months preceding the survey (Schoenborn & Adams, 2002).

As disconcerting are recent studies suggesting an increase in alcohol consumption by adults. Previous studies suggested that higher alcohol consumption was associated with specific demographic and behavioral characteristics, including whites males, married individuals, those with higher educational attainment and higher income, and smokers (Moore et al., 2005). However, recent research by Keyes, Grant, and Hasin (2008) suggests that the gender difference in alcohol consumption cited in earlier studies is diminishing. Their study examined rates of alcohol use, binge drinking, and alcohol dependency in four groups of adults: those born between 1913 and 1932, between 1933 and 1949, between 1950 and 1967, and between1968 and 1984. Of the over 42,000 interviews collected, Keyes and colleagues discovered that among older adults, or those in the 1913 to 1932 and 1933 to 1949 birth years, males were still more likely than women to report excessive alcohol use, binge drinking, and alcohol dependency. The younger adult cohorts, or those born between 1950 and1967 and 1968 and 1984, however, reported a much smaller difference in excessive alcohol use by gender. In other words, younger women were more heavily represented among the excessive alcohol group than were older women. These findings are consistent with reports of heavy drinking and binge drinking on college campuses by both men and women.

A second study by Moore and colleagues (2005) shows another trend. Whereas earlier studies found that adults usually consume less alcohol as they age, Moore and colleagues' (2005) study revealed that alcohol consumption rates remained higher than expected for older adults in his study.

What do these data show? They indicate that alcohol consumption patterns are changing. The reason for the change is unclear. Some researchers suggest social and environmental factors may account for the shift in consumption patterns, but this is yet to be tested. What is clear, however, is that rates of alcohol use are increasing among women and among older adults, two groups previously unrepresented in the alcohol abuse category (see Table 5.8).

THEORIES OF ALCOHOL USE   The five groups of theories introduced in the previous section to explore early cigarettes use can also be used to explain early and sustained use of all substances, including alcohol. We will not repeat the theories here. We will note, however, two interesting points. First, like the research on cigarettes, research on alcohol also suggests that many factors contribute to excessive alcohol consumption behaviors. Studies suggest that peers (Andrews, Tildesley, Hops, & Li, 2002; Cavanagh, 2007—social learning theorists and integrationists), stress (Harrell & Karim, 2008; Jukkala et al., 2008—personality trait theorists), and social institutions (Delucchi, Matzger, & Weisner, 2008; Wallace et al., 2007—conventional commitment theorists) all influence alcohol consumption. More recently, studies suggest that health policy can also influence drinking behaviors.

Recent work by Harvard researchers Nelson, Naomi, Brewer, and Wechsler (2005) on the effect of state health policies on binge drinking on college campuses underscores the point. Nelson and colleagues found that colleges located in states with more stringent restrictions on alcohol consumption reported the lowest level of adult binge drinking in general and lower binge drinking rates on college campuses. The finding seems to suggest that health policy at the state level can moderate drinking behaviors of college students as well as adults (Nelson et al., 2005).

A second potential explanation for alcohol consumption patterns is found in the work by Denise Kandel. Kandel proposed that substance use is progressive. Specifically, she proposed a *gateway theory* of substance use, suggesting that adolescent substance use begins with legal substances, that is, substances that are legal for adults (Kandel, Yamaguchi, & Chen,1992). She suggests that when adolescents first experiment with substances they begin with cigarettes or alcohol. If continuing, adolescents will then progress to marijuana followed by other illicit drugs. Even with alcohol, Kandel and her colleagues claim that adolescents almost always begin with beer or wine, the drinks with the lowest alcohol content per ounce. For this reason, Kandel has labeled cigarettes and alcohol the "gateway drugs" because, according to her theory, cigarettes and alcohol "open the gate" for experimentation or regular use of other drugs.

Kandel's theory is supported by longitudinal data from studies in the United States and in Israel (Adler & Kandel, 1981; Kandel, Kessler, & Marguiles, 1978; Kandel, Simcha-Fagan, & Davies, 1986; Yu & Williford, 1992). However, recent studies suggest that the gateway theory may not explain patterns and progression of substance use equally well for all populations. For example, Beenstock & Rahav (2002) found that cigarette smoking among a sample of Israeli adolescents did lead to marijuana use, but marijuana use did not lead to "harder" drugs. Similarly, Ginzler and colleagues (2003) found another exception to the theory among homeless youth in the United States. Still others suggest that there may be a progression from one drug to the next but not as predicted by the gateway theory. For example, some researchers suggest that among college students marijuana, an illicit drug, may in fact be a gateway drug for cigarettes, not the other way around (Tullis, Dupont, Frost-Pineda, & Gold, 2003).

Why all the fuss about the gateway theory and progression of substance use? Put it this way: If true, the gateway theory could inform policy to reduce or halt illicit substance use among

TABLE 5.8   Substance Use by Adolescents in the United States

Percentage of high school students who drank alcohol and used marijuana, by sex, race/ethnicity, and grade—United States, Youth Risk Behavior Survey, 2001

Category	Lifetime alcohol use[1]			Current alcohol use[2]			Episodic heavy drinking[3]		
	Female	Male	Total	Female	Male	Total	Female	Male	Total
Race/Ethnicity									
White	79.6	80.7	**80.1**	48.3	52.6	**50.4**	30.5	37.7	34.0
Black	69.7	68.4	**69.1**	30.6	35.0	**32.7**	7.5	15.1	11.1
Hispanic	80.1	81.6	**80.8**	48.8	49.5	**49.2**	28.7	31.4	30.1
Grade									
9	72.0	74.5	**73.1**	40.0	42.2	**41.1**	23.0	26.2	24.5
10	76.9	75.6	**76.3**	43.5	46.9	**45.2**	26.3	30.1	28.2
11	79.3	81.4	**80.4**	45.1	53.6	**49.3**	26.1	38.5	32.2
12	85.5	84.7	**85.1**	53.9	56.6	**55.2**	31.8	42.0	36.7
Total	**77.9**	**78.6**	**78.2**	**45.0**	**49.2**	**47.1**	**26.4**	**33.5**	**29.9**

[1]Ever had ≥1 drinks of alcohol.

[2]Drank alcohol on ≥1 of the 30 days preceding the survey.

[3]Drank ≥5 drinks of alcohol on ≥1 occasions on ≥1 of the 30 days preceding the survey.

Category	Lifetime marijuana use[4]			Current marijuana use[5]		
	Female	Male	Total	Female	Male	Total
Race/Ethnicity						
White	39.2	46.4	**42.8**	20.6	28.4	**24.4**
Black	34.3	46.7	**40.2**	16.0	28.2	**21.8**
Hispanic	39.7	50.0	**44.7**	22.4	26.8	**24.6**
Grade						
9	28.6	37.3	**32.7**	16.5	22.6	**19.4**
10	37.5	46.1	**41.7**	21.5	28.3	**24.8**
11	42.6	51.7	**47.2**	21.4	30.2	**25.8**
12	48.9	54.2	**51.5**	21.8	32.3	**26.9**
Total	**38.4**	**46.5**	**42.4**	**20.0**	**27.9**	**23.9**

[4]Ever used marijuana.

[5]Used marijuana ≥1 times during the 30 days preceding the survey.

Source: MMWR, 2002.

adolesents. For example, health policy advocates and health researchers could use the theory to support limitations on cigarette promotions aimed at adolescents, arguing that such limitations would also significantly reduce the likelihood that adolescents would experiment with or use other substances. Without sound evidence of a progression, researchers must independently examine the antecedents and consequences of each substance.

Illegal and Prescription Drugs

An entire chapter could be devoted to a discussion of the use of *illicit*, that is, illegal drugs, as well as their health consequences. But because this chapter is intended as an overview of risky health behaviors, we will have to content ourselves with just an overview. Here we examine five of the most commonly used illegal drugs in the United States: marijuana, crack/cocaine, heroin, methamphetamine, and MDMA (methylenedioxymethamphetamine), called also ecstasy. In this section we will briefly define each of the drugs and discuss their health consequences and their frequency of use and abuse. And, as with earlier sections, we will conclude by examining theories that attempt to explain drug abuse.

We also include in this section recent research on abuse of *prescription drugs*. Prescription pain medication is fast becoming a drug of choice for many, including adolescents. In 2005, the National Survey on Drug Use and Health (Substance Abuse and Mental Health Services Administration, 2005) reported an increase in the number of persons who report using prescription pain relievers for nonmedical purposes. In fact, the rate of increase for unauthorized use of pain medication exceeded that reported for marijuana, the most frequently used illicit drug. As such, abuse of prescription drugs is a growing problem for health professionals.

MARIJUANA   Known by many names, including pot, weed, grass, ganja, and cannabis, among others, *marijuana i*s the most commonly abused illicit drug worldwide (WHO, 2000). Marijuana is a mixture of the flowers, stems, seeds, and leaves of the hemp plant (NIDA, 2006b), which are combined and smoked as a cigarette or cigar or used in a pipe.

Individuals who use marijuana report a variety of sensations when smoking the drug, depending on the person and the setting. The most common short-term sensation is one of euphoria and giddiness. Such reactions are commonly associated with drugs known as *stimulants*, or drugs that excite the nervous system. With marijuana, however, the excitation is often followed by feelings of sedation and tranquility, sensations often associated with drugs known as *depressants*, or agents that relax and quiet the nervous system. Other more specific short-term effects of marijuana include dizziness or trouble with coordination and with basic motor movements (NIDA, 2002).

What causes the alternate feelings of euphoria and sedation? Marijuana, like other drugs, interacts with the brain's communication system by tapping into the brain's neural activity and interfering with the way the brain sends, receives, and processes information through the nerve cells called *neurons* (NIDA, 2007a). We explain the body's communication system in Chapter 6, Emotional Health and Well-Being. Briefly, to send messages between cells, the body relies on *neurotransmitters*, or chemical substances manufactured in our bodies. Marijuana contains a chemical structure that is similar to some of our body's natural neurotransmitters. Because of this similarity, marijuana is able to mimic *dopamine*, one of the body's neurotransmitters that regulates, among other things, our sensation of pleasure (NIDA, 2007a). Specifically, marijuana floods the body with dopamine. The buildup of dopamine in the system intensifies and prolongs feelings of euphoria. Because euphoria is a pleasurable sensation to many, marijuana's effect often leads to an intense desire to repeat the experience (NIDA, 2007a).

The long-term consequences of marijuana are not as pleasurable as the short-term impact. Regular users of marijuana may experience a variety of permanent health problems, including damage to the brain's short-term memory capabilities, increased risk of heart attack due to elevated blood pressure, a weakened immune system, sexual dysfunction, and an increased risk of cancer (Friedman, Newton, & Klein, 2003; Mittleman, Lewis, & Maclure, 2001; Pope, Gruber, & Hudson, 2001; Zhang, Morgenstern, & Spitz, 1999).

Sound incredible? Consider this additional adverse consequence: Marijuana contains between 50 and 70% more *carcinogens*, or substances that are known to cause cancer, than cigarettes (Hoffman, Brunnemann, & Gori, 1975). The increased carcinogens, in addition to marijuana smokers' tendency to inhale more deeply and retain the smoke in their lungs longer than cigarette smokers, makes them more susceptible to cancers than cigarette smokers (NIDA, 2006b).

Marijuana is a popular drug in the United States and globally. The number of users worldwide totals approximately 141 million people (UN International Drug Control Programme [UNDCP], 1997). The highest rates of marijuana use are reported among three developed countries: the United States, Canada, and Australia. In the United States, an estimated 14.6 million to 21 million adults use marijuana (NIDA, 2006b), approximately 10% of the adult population (WHO, 2000a). Lower rates are reported in Canada (7.4% of its adult population or about 1.8 million) as well as in other developed countries in Europe.

As for adolescents, recent statistics show a decrease in marijuana use in the United States in younger adolescents in the 8th and 10th grades but no real change in frequency of use among 12th graders.

COCAINE/CRACK   *Cocaine* and its less refined version, *crack*, are two powerfully addictive illegal substances. They are derived from the leaves of the coca plant found typically in the South American countries of Bolivia, Colombia, Ecuador, and Peru (WHO, 2000a).

Did you know that cocaine was not always a banned substance? For many thousands of years, coca leaves were chewed by indigenous people. As we noted in Chapter 1, An Interdisciplinary View of Health, indigenous cultures were knowledgeable about the benefits and the medicinal effects of plants in their environments. Until the early 1900s, cocaine was also an ingredient in medicines and beverages in many developed countries. For example, cocaine was a common ingredient in cough remedies in the United States. Even the soft drink Coca-Cola included cocaine as one of its ingredients until 1901. Coca-Cola's slogan, "It's the real thing," was a reference to the fact that one of the ingredients in the beverage before 1901 was small quantities of coca extract (Cohen, 2006). When the "secret" ingredient was removed in the early 1900s, the producers substituted caffeine and sugar for the banned substance. Today, cocaine is no longer found in beverages, but it remains an ingredient in some prescription medicines. In spite of the new regulations, the United States and other developed countries have reported a surge in cocaine use since the 1970s. This time the surge is due to the illicit use of the drug.

Two forms of cocaine are most prevalent in the United States. The powdered form, hydrochloride salt, is a processed form of the drug that has been neutralized by an acid to produce a powdery substance. It is usually inhaled through the nostrils or mixed with water for injection. Crack, an alternate form of cocaine, has not been neutralized and therefore remains in a rock crystal form that is most often heated and smoked (NIDA, 2006a).

In either form, cocaine causes a continual or prolonged feeling of stimulation and euphoria. The reason for the prolonged euphoria is again related to a chemical interference with the body's communication system. Both cocaine and crack block the body's ability to reabsorb the excess dopamine produced by the system. Thus, like marijuana, the excess dopamine in the system means that the body continues to feel euphoric and stimulated.

As with marijuana, the temporary good feeling from cocaine comes with a price: dilated pupils; increased temperature, heart rate, and blood pressure; irregularities in heart rhythm; and heart attacks. As we will see in Chapter 9, Cardiovascular Disease, prolonged elevation of heart rate and blood pressure puts an individual at high risk for *cardiac arrest*, a condition in which the heart immediately ceases to function and the individual becomes unconscious (see Chapter 4, Theories and Models of Health Behavior Change). It is a potentially fatal condition if a person does not receive immediate medical care. In addition, repeated cocaine use can lead to *seizures*, a sudden change in brain activity. Other symptoms associated with the prolonged use of cocaine include excessive nosebleeds, chronic runny nose, and gastrointestinal problems, including abdominal pain and nausea (NIDA, 2006a).

Unlike marijuana, few individuals argue that cocaine is a natural and therefore healthy substance. Their views may be shaped, in part, by the fact that cocaine has been the cause of many drug-related deaths. New York, Michigan, Massachusetts, Texas, and Pennsylvania are just some of the states that reported high rates of cocaine-related deaths in 2003 and 2004 (NIDA, 2006a).

Overall, reports on the frequency of cocaine use in the United States show that the demand for cocaine has fallen since its peak in the 1980s and 1990s (WHO, 2000a). However, among adolescents, rates of cocaine use are increasing, especially among younger teens. Data obtained from middle and high school students, grades 8 through 12, in 2005 show that, while only 3.7% of 8th graders reported using cocaine in any form, by the time the students reach the 12th grade cocaine use had increased to 8%. Increased cocaine use has been reported also among young adults 21 through 25 years of age.

There are few reliable statistics on the rate of cocaine use in Europe and other developed countries. Some reports suggest a small increase in cocaine use in Europe generally and in Mexico, specifically among adolescents (WHO, 2000). In general, however, cocaine use is not as rampant internationally as it is in the United States.

HEROIN   *Heroin* is a natural substance that is extracted from the seedpod of a poppy plant found most commonly in Asia (NIDA, 2010), including Afghanistan. Heroin has a number of alternative names also, such as smack, H, horse, and junk.

There is a distinct difference in the short- and long-term effects and the adverse consequences associated with heroin as opposed to marijuana or cocaine. In the short term, heroin gives its users an initial feeling of euphoria. But that is followed shortly by a drowsy state in which the user seems to alternate between low-level wakefulness and drowsiness. This "nodding" period lasts for several hours.

In the long term, heroin causes a host of health problems, including collapsed veins due to repeated use of the veins to inject the drug, higher risks of infectious diseases including HIV/AIDS, infection of the heart lining and valves, as well as liver disease. Since heroin acts as a depressant, it slows the system and depresses *respiration*, or breathing. Such effects can lead to death.

Like cocaine, heroin use reached a peak in the United States in the 1980s and 1990s. Similar trends in heroin use were found internationally also in England and other parts of Europe (WHO, 2000a). However, current statistics report a decline in heroin use since the 1990s.

METHAMPHETAMINE   *Methamphetamine*, or meth, another illicit drug classified as a stimulant, is one of the most highly addictive substances in the arsenal of recreational drugs. It is a naturally occurring substance found in many substances, including the acacia tree found in Texas. Like cocaine and marijuana, methamphetamine is known by a number of names, including speed, tina, and ice (NIDA, 2006c).

Meth is a potent drug that can damage the central nervous system (NIDA, 2006c). Like cocaine, meth releases high levels of dopamine into the system. As we noted before, high levels of artificial stimulants increase heart rate and blood pressure and cause irregular heart beats. Meth also causes *hyperthermia*, a condition in which the body absorbs or produces too much heat. In addition, it also contributes to *convulsions* and can cause emotional or psychological conditions including anxiety, confusion, insomnia, and irritability. Finally, chronic use of meth has been associated with permanent structural changes in the brain in the areas associated with memory and emotion (NIDA, 2006c; Zickler, 2007).

Recently researchers and drug enforcement agencies in the United States learned that individuals could easily manufacture meth using ingredients found in over-the-counter cold remedies such as Sudafed and Contac. The chemical substances ephedrine and pseudoephedrine can be extracted from these nonprescription cold remedies to provide some of the ingredients needed to produce meth. In 1983, the U.S. and Canadian governments passed a series of laws that prohibited the possession of ingredients and equipment to produce methamphetamine. In spite of these laws, however, meth continues to be produced and is now used as a recreational drug of choice (UCLA Integrated Substance Abuse Program, 2006).

METHYLENEDIOXYMETHAMPHETAMINE (MDMA)   Also called *ecstasy* and the club drug, *methylenedioxymethamphetamine (MDMA)* is one of several recreational drugs popular with teens and adults and is frequently used in nightclubs and bars.

MDMA users report a very intense and intoxicating stimulation or "high" from the drug, which carries several side effects. Like the other drugs, however, MDMA also carries health-compromising side effects. MDMA interferes with the body's ability to regulate its own temperature. Thus, users often complain of extreme thirst. The drug's effect on body temperature, however, can lead to complications with the liver, kidneys, and cardiovascular system.

Of all the drugs mentioned to date, there are far fewer MDMA users in the United States than users of other drugs. Still, the statistics show that approximately 450,000 people reported using MDMA in 2004, while an additional 600,000 reported a first-time use in the same year. The numbers may not be comparable to other drugs in part because MDMA is the newest recreational drug available.

PRESCRIPTION MEDICATIONS   For some time, research on drug use focused almost exclusively on illicit or illegal drugs. Illegal drugs are often associated with crime, and the crime statistics they generate allow researchers to track, report, and measure illegal drug use behaviors. Abusers of prescription drugs, however, are less likely to generate crime statistics and therefore are less visible to researchers.

The term *prescription drugs* refers specifically to medication prescribed by a doctor to treat a specific medical condition. The drug is intended for use solely by the individual to whom it is prescribed. Prescription drugs are used illegally if they are used for nonmedical purposes or used by people other than the person for whom the drug was prescribed.

There are three types of commonly abused prescription medications. *Opioids*, or drugs that treat pain, comprise one type. Such medicines include morphine- and codeine-based treatments. Depressants, used to relax or calm the central nervous system, include barbiturates and benzodiazepines such as Valium or Xantax. Finally, stimulants are designed to increase attention and enhance energy.

Precise statistics on the number of people abusing prescription drugs are difficult to obtain for two reasons. First, prescription drugs are obtained from licensed medical professionals. Doctors may not be aware that their prescriptions are being used for other-than-intended purposes. Individuals who are misusing prescription medicines have no incentive to reveal their true intent to their doctor and would jeopardize their ability to obtain drugs in the future if they admitted to abusing their prescribed medication. Second, doctors who prescribe medicines for nonmedical purposes risk punishment and possibly loss of their medical license. Because it is neither in the abusers' nor the doctors' interest to admit to misusing prescription drugs, statistics on prescription drug abuse capture only those individuals who encounter medical or legal problems as a result of their actions. Yet, even with the limitations in reporting, a staggering 6 million persons were found to abuse prescription drugs in the United States. The most commonly abused prescription drug appears to be pain medication or opioids (NIDA, 2006d).

SECTION III. RISKY SEXUAL BEHAVIORS

Is there a link between substance use or abuse and risky sexual behavior? Absolutely! For several decades researchers have reported that alcohol and drug abuse lowers inhibitions against engaging in risky sexual behaviors (Walters et al., 1992, 1993). In fact, many researchers who examine the risky health behaviors of adolescents and young adults explore the correlations between substance use and sexual behavior. Therefore, it seems appropriate to follow our discussion of substance use with a discussion on risky sexual behaviors.

Defining Risk

Early in the chapter we distinguished between risk and risky health behaviors. We further refine the definitions here for application to sexual behaviors. The term *risky sexual behaviors* describes a category of actions that increase an individual's likelihood of adverse consequences such as acquiring *sexually transmitted diseases (STDs)*—infectious diseases spread by sexual acts, usually through intercourse or through oral sex (see Table 5.9). Having sexual intercourse with multiple sex partners or not using a condom when having sex are two risky behaviors that increase the risk of adverse events.

Before proceeding, we need to make one observation. Sexual behavior is a normal part of adolescent development and of adult behavior. As we explained in the section on alcohol, it is not sexual behaviors per se that increase the risk of adverse consequences. Rather, our focus here is on the *risky* sexual behaviors that can cause negative outcomes for at least one of the participants. Specifically we focus on early initiation of sexual behaviors, engaging in sexual behaviors

TABLE 5.9	Selective Summary of Sexually Transmitted Diseases		
STD	**Cause**	**Symptoms**	**Untreated outcomes**
Chlamydia	Bacteria Chlamydiatrachomatis	Asymptomatic in women	Damage to women's reproductive organs
Herpes	Herpes simplex virus	Pain, itching in genitals Fever, headache Blisters, ulcers on genitals	Recurring bouts of blistering
Genital warts	Human papilloma virus (HPV)	Warts	Complication for pregnancy
Gonorrhea	Gonococcus bacterium	Painful urination Discharge from penis or vagina Discomfort in lower abdomen *Or* asymptomatic	Sterility Infection of joints, skin, bone
Tricomonas	Trichomonas		None, just discomfort
Syphilis	Treponema pallidum bacterium	Chanker sore on genitals, mouth, or rectum Fever, headache, loss of appetite Swollen glands Skin rash	Paralysis Senility, insanity Death

Source: Adapted from Kunz (1982).

without protection against diseases, multiple sexual partners, and combining substance use and sexual behavior.

Early Initiation Behaviors

Researchers suggest that the early onset, or beginning, of sexual activity may indicate problems in an adolescent's life. Integration theorists, who support a problem behavior approach to risky health behaviors (Jessor et al., 1991), believe that early initiation of sexual behaviors may be a symptom of emotional, psychological, or social problems for teens (Biglan, Metzler, & Wirt, 1990; Lowry, Holtzman, & Truman, 1994; Stanton et al., 1997). For example, some studies have found that sexual intercourse in early adolescence is associated with poor family relationships and lack of close relationships with friends or teachers (Anteghini, Fonseca, Ireland, & Blum, 2001), a perspective shared also by conventional commitment theorists. The early sexual behaviors may reflect emotional health problems and other troubled relationships for the teens.

Early sexual behaviors also increase health risks by decreasing the probability that teens will be well informed about protective health behaviors that could minimize risk to themselves or their partner. For example, research shows that African American adolescents engage in sexual behavior earlier than many other ethnic groups. Of the 6.6% of students who report beginning sexual activity before age 13, significantly more adolescents were African American (16.3%) than were Hispanic (7.6%) or white (4.7%; Grunbaum et al., 2002). Yet the same study reports that white students were significantly more likely to receive instruction about HIV/AIDS prevention (91.1% of students receiving instruction) than were Hispanic (86.1%) or African American (80.5%) students. Thus, the adolescents most likely to engage in early sexual behaviors are the worst informed about safer sexual practices. In this case, early initiation may lead to adverse consequences because of lack of knowledge.

What are the consequences of early initiation in the absence of health-protective information? Consider this: African American females have significantly higher levels of HIV and STD infections than other ethnic groups (CDC, 2001; Spitalnick et al., 2007). The study by Spitalnick and colleagues suggests that, for African Americans, early initiation of sex combined with poorer access to health education increases the probability of adverse consequences, in this case HIV/AIDS.

Health-Protecting Behaviors

While it is true that adolescents who are sexually active at earlier ages may be less well-informed than those who wait, it is not always the case. Two studies help illustrate the point. In the first study, Dutch researchers examined perceptions about sex and AIDS, knowledge and attitudes about sexual diseases and sexual risks among over 11,000 Dutch adolescents. Their results showed that sexually active adolescents knew how to protect themselves from contracting HIV/AIDS. They were less clear, however, about protecting themselves from other STDs (Vogels, van der Vliet, Danz, & Hopman-Rock, 1993). Fortunately for the study participants, condoms—the agent that helps protect against HIV/AIDS—also helps prevent other STDs. But their lack of awareness of the dual benefit of condoms suggests that adolescents do not understand the method of transmission for and the risks associated with STDs. Thus, adolescents may need assistance in applying their knowledge appropriately.

A related study on sexual behavior and prediction of condom use among 1,049 U.S. students also revealed a high level of knowledge of HIV/AIDS and STDs and the protective properties of condoms. But, of the 266 sexually active teens, only 29% reported using a condom for protection against HIV/AIDS or other STDs. Once again, research suggests that knowledge does not always inform behavior. The study revealed that the single best motivator for students to use condoms appeared to be the perception of condom use among their peers (social norms) and the absence of risk-taking behavior in general. In this case, peer behaviors, not knowledge about HIV/AIDS or STDs, encouraged protective behaviors (Brown & DiClemente, 1992).

The main point of these studies is that knowledge does not always change behaviors. Indeed, if this were true, none of us would engage in unhealthy behaviors because we would automatically adopt the health-protective behaviors consistent with our knowledge. Clearly, this is not the case.

It is important to state also that the consequences of risky sexual behaviors have changed. Between the 1940s (after the discovery of penicillin for syphilis) and the early 1980s, the cost for engaging in risky sexual behaviors was either an STD or an unplanned pregnancy, or both. Now, however, risky health behaviors can lead to HIV/AIDS, a fatal illness. Consequently, current generations of adolescents and adults have to consider the new and more deadly consequence of their experimental behavior. The change in health outcomes for the same behavior means that health psychologists and health providers also must change their strategies. Rather than encouraging individuals to practice safer sexual behavior to minimize the spread of disease, we now need to encourage safer practices to reduce the risk of death due to STDs and to encourage the prevention or reduction of risky sexual behaviors.

Multiple Sexual Partners

Several studies document the relationship between multiple partners and STDs. For example, in a three-year study involving more than 1,250 young men each year, Dariotis and colleagues (2008) found that STDs and positive chlamydia tests were more prevalent among men with multiple sexual partners. A similar result was reported for men and women in an earlier study by Finer, Darroch, and Singh (1999). These researchers report that the number of sexual partners among men and women is one important predictor of contracting a sexually transmitted disease.

For adolescents who adhere to family or cultural social norms, having multiple sex partners may also increase the risk of stigma from their social groups. Hence, in this instance, social stigma can inhibit multiple sex partners, a health-enhancing behavior that could reduce the risk of contracting an STD. Absent such social norms, however, efforts to discourage multiple partners may compete unsuccessfully with the perception that such behaviors signal a socially successful lifestyle.

Substance Use and Sexual Behavior

We noted earlier that using alcohol and drugs can lower one's sexual inhibition. Some contend that with lowered inhibitions comes an increased likelihood of engaging in high-risk sexual behaviors.

Studies suggest that both adolescents and adults indicate that substance use will undermine even the most confident individual's ability to negotiate safer sexual behavior. In an intervention study designed to teach adolescents in grades 10 through 12 strategies to negotiate safer sexual behaviors, adolescents reported they would not be able to use the strategies learned in the eight-week intervention sessions if they drank alcohol or used drugs immediately before a sexual encounter (Walter, 1992, 1993). The main point here is that alcohol and drug use may compromise judgment and decision-making skills even when a person has demonstrated an ability to exercise sound judgment normally. The impaired judgment puts the individual at higher risk for adverse health outcomes. This is true whether the behavior involves sexual behavior or driving a motor vehicle.

Teenage Pregnancies

It is probably true that, in a limited number of cases, female teenagers intended to become pregnant as a result of sexual behaviors. In most instances, however, a pregnancy is a surprising and unexpected outcome. Therefore, teenage births qualify as an adverse outcome.

Beginning in 1991, U.S. statistics on children born to adolescents showed a steady decline for teens 15 to 17 years of age. The decline was reported for each of the major ethnic groups in the United States: African Americans, Asians, Hispanics, Native Americans, and whites. Now preliminary data show that the trend in declining birthrates is changing. It is still the case that the birthrates for young adolescents, 10 to 14 years of age, remain low (90.6 births per 1,000). But in 2005 rates for births to teens 15 to 19 years of age rose by 3.0%. This increase represents the first significant increase in birthrates to teenagers since 1991 (Hamilton, Martin, & Ventura, 2007).

What does the increase in births to teens mean? Assuming, as we did before, that most adolescents do not intend to become pregnant at an early age, an increase in birthrates represents an increase in risky health behaviors.

SECTION IV. EATING DISORDERS

Smoking, alcohol and drug use, risky sexual behaviors, and excessive dieting share a common factor for many adolescents: a desire to conform to the social norms of their peer groups. But for many adolescents the pressure to conform to an idealized thin body image, or to emulate popular fashion trends and model-like looks, leads to another adverse outcome: eating disorders.

Much of the early research on eating disorders described the problem as a "culture-bound syndrome" rooted in the cultural values and conflicts in Western societies (Prince, 1983). Indeed, the majority of the early research cites examples of high rates of eating disorders occurring most often in the United States and other Western countries, including England, Italy, the Netherlands, Sweden, and Switzerland, among others (Hoek, 1991; Lacey & Dolan, 1988; Norring & Sohlberg, 1988; Rathner & Messner, 1993; Willi & Grossman, 1983). More specifically, researchers have linked Western culture's idealized thin body type to anorexia nervosa, one of the more prevalent eating disorders in Western societies. Current research suggest that in Western countries approximately 0.3% of young women are diagnosed with anorexia nervosa, and another 1% are reported to be bulimic (Hoek & van Hoken, 2003). Yet, as we will see in this section, current fashion trends and cultural norms are just two of the likely explanations for eating disorders. Psychological disorders, socioeconomic class, pressures to acculturate to the dominant society, and, for some, family dysfunction may also contribute to the outcome. In this section, we examine four types of eating disorders that are linked to weight: anorexia, bulimia, binge eating, and obesity. We also explore the role of family and culture as possible determinants of eating disorders.

Anorexia Nervosa

What effect does the intense focus on weight have on the physical and psychological health of the individual? In one word, lots!

It may be challenging to think that there are health risks associated with being underweight. After all, much of the research on nutrition and weight in health psychology focuses on the complications resulting from overweight and obese outcomes (Annals of Internal Medicine, 2008). But failing to provide the body with the nourishment needed to function can also have significant negative consequences. Some of the adverse effects are evident in individuals diagnosed with *anorexia nervosa*, an eating disorder.

ANOREXIA DEFINED   To be clear, anorexia nervosa is more than just an eating disorder. More accurately, anorexia is a psychological disorder that is characterized by a severe disturbance in eating behaviors (Patel, Philips, & Pratt, 1998). The causes of the psychopathology underlying anorexia are thought to include biological factors, environmental factors (family dynamics, cultural and social pressures), or developmental factors (struggle for self-control, autonomy, identity) (Haller, 1992; Yager, 1998). No single cause best characterizes the origins of anorexia.

Psychologically, a person who is anorexic has an intense fear of gaining weight that prevents her or him from consuming the nutrients needed to gain or maintain a body weight needed for normal body function. That person's fear of gaining weight, together with an unrealistic body image (imagining her- or himself to be fat), and, for women, *amenorrhea*, or the cessation of menstruation, are the primary criteria for diagnosing this condition.

Psychologists believe that an anorexic's misperception of her or his appearance is due, in part, to poor self-esteem. The origins of poor self-esteem may be within the individual or rooted in a dysfunctional family life. Negative family relationships, a mother's distorted perception of body size, a mother's body shame, or an individual's perception of parental disapproval all may contribute to anorexia (Bennington, Tetsch, Kunzendorf, & Jantschek, 2007; Hudson, Hiripi, Pope, & Kessler, 2007).

The psychological disorders associated with anorexia indicate that treatment for the disease requires more than just medical attention. Rather, an anorexic must address the psychological and emotional problems that led to the extreme weight loss and the inability to accurately perceive her or his deteriorating health conditions. (We explore some of the social and familial contributions to anorexia later in this section.) Health psychology and clinical psychology are two disciplines well suited to addressing the complex needs of anorexics.

Physically, by depriving the body of food, anorexics also disturb many biological functions. For example, with significant weight loss, the body reduces the production of two hormones needed for reproduction. In women, a significant loss of weight can signal the body to reduce the production of *estrogen*, a hormone associated with reproduction. Similarly, in men, significant weight loss can signal a decreased production of the male hormone *dehydroepiandrosterone (DHEA)*. Other significant physiological changes may include bone loss, extreme sensitivity to cold, bloated stomach, yellowed skin, and thinning hair.

It is important to note that while most cases of anorexia are reported by women, men can also develop this and other eating disorders. In fact, in some studies, men comprise between 10 and 25% of the study sample of anorexics (Garfinkel et al., 1996; Hoek & van Hoeken, 2003; Hudson et al., 2007). Some researchers note that men who develop eating disorders are more likely to report dissatisfaction with their body image or to show heightened preoccupation with body image and weight due to their profession. Male wrestlers and jockeys are two examples of professions in which men pay increased attention to weight and body image (Mickalide, 1990; Olivardia, Pope, Mangweth, & Hudson, 1995; Walsh, 1997)

Bulimia

A second type of eating disorder is *bulimia*, a disorder characterized by binge eating, or the excessive consumption of food. Feelings of guilt or depression often follow binge eating which leads to *purging*—vomiting, fasting, or using laxatives to eliminate the food consumed.

BOX 5.1   Anorexia Taken to the Extreme

In 2006, a 5'8" Brazilian model, Ana Carolina Reston, died at age 21 (see Figure 5.6). She weighed only 88 pounds. By all accounts, Reston died of multiple organ failure, septicemia, and urinary infection (Phillips, 2007). It is also true that she was diagnosed with anorexia nervosa, an eating disorder that is characterized by a dangerously low body weight, a fear of gaining weight, unrealistic assessment of weight, and amenorrhea (Lock & Fitzpatrick, 2009).

Eighty-eight pounds is considered by medical standards to be dangerously underweight on a 5'8" frame. Put it this way, using the old weight charts, women who are 5'8" generally weigh between 126 and 167 pounds. The weight range includes women with small body frames as well as women with medium or larger frames. Thus, according to the old weight charts, Reston weighed only 70% of the lowest acceptable body weight for her height.

If we calculate Reston's weight using the new *body mass index (BMI)*, which measures the proportion of body fat to height, she scored a 13.4. Putting this into perspective, a body mass index (BMI) of 18.5 or less is considered underweight and unhealthy. Normal BMI weight

FIGURE 5.6   Ana Carolina Reston. A Brazilian fashion model, Ana died of complications associated with anorexia nervosa.

for all heights and frames is represented by a range between 18.5 and 24.9. Whether using the old weight scales or the new BMI scales, Ana Carolina Reston was dangerously underweight.

BULIMIA DEFINED   Bulimics are not as easily identified because, unlike anorexics, they do not appear dangerously underweight. Yet the psychological causes of bulimia can be just as deeply rooted and difficult to get at or treat as for anorexics. In addition, bulimics are also susceptible to negative physiological and psychological health consequences. Consider this: The repeated purging after eating causes an imbalance in the body's electrolytes, necessary elements in the body's fluids containing salt and sugar and other elements that stimulate electric charges. In addition, frequent regurgitation of food, causes the acidic gastric juices in the stomach to travel in reverse, that is, up through the *esophagus*, the tube connecting the stomach and the mouth. You may know that the body's normal digestive process rarely causes gastric juices to enter the esophagus. Therefore, repeated regurgitation that forces the juices of the stomach to reverse and enter the esophagus can cause damage to the lining of the esophagus. In addition, the repeated presentation of the juices into the mouth can also cause damage to tooth enamel, which can result in tooth decay. Frequent vomiting also causes damage to the *colon*, a part of the intestines critical for eliminating waste from the body. Finally, if continually irritated by regurgitation, the colon and esophagus can develop tears or ulcers, a painful outcome that further compromises eating and digestive behaviors.

Psychologically, bulimics, like anorexics, are masking underlying problems with their eating disorders. Researchers continue to explore the psychological causes of bulimia. For the moment, however, the consensus seems t ̣ be that family function or dysfunction, self-esteem, emotional problems, and, to a limited extent, psychopathology, may contribute to the development of bulimia (Bennington et al., 2007; Bruce & Steiger, 2005; Hudson et al., 2007). But, as we will see shortly, the complex emotional, psychological, and physical health problems of bulimia also make it a relevant topic for health psychologists.

Obesity

We briefly mentioned obesity in Chapter 2, Research Methods, when identifying the growing number of public health policies to address obesity in children and adolescents in the United States. Studies report that *obesity*, defined as an excessive amount of fatty tissue that exceeds healthy limits, is on the rise in the United States among both adults and children. Currently, researchers suggest that approximately 27% of U.S. adults are obese, and an additional 34% are overweight (Mehler, Lasater, & Padilla, 2003; Mokdad et al., 1999).

Obesity may be caused by genetic, environmental, cultural, or psychological factors. For example, new studies investigating a possible genetic determinant of obesity show that pregnant mothers who are diagnosed with diabetes have a higher likelihood of giving birth to babies of higher birth weights who are later found to be obese (Dabelea, 2007). This is an interesting finding to be sure but, even if true, genetics would account for a very small portion of the current cases of obesity. Instead, it appears that most incidences of obesity are related to cultural culinary practices, family eating behaviors (Holt, Warren, Wallace, & Neher 2006), and environmental cues such as fast-food restaurants that promote high-fat, high-calorie foods.

Another contributing factor to obesity is the sedentary lifestyles of both children and adults. Research has established that adults and children receive less exercise at home and at school (Miles, 2008; Molnar, Gormaker, Bull, & Buka, 2004). For children, fewer opportunities to exercise result in more indoor activities that include less movement and possibly more snacking. Similarly, many schools have reduced the number of physical education classes, which compounds the reduction in opportunities to exercise.

The situation is not much better for adults, who also have increasingly sedentary lifestyles. A longitudinal study examining the relationship between adult workers and obesity revealed that job position, stress, and extended and nighttime work hours contribute to increased obesity rates among American workers (Caban et al., 2005). The growing rate of obesity is one reason why some employers now offer discount memberships to gyms or include exercise or fitness rooms in the workplace. The message is clear: Exercise is important to health maintenance. While environmental factors appear to be one of the primary contributors to obesity, health psychologists are also exploring the role of the individual in creating such outcomes. Specifically, health psychologists are examining the issues of self-control and feelings of insecurity and inadequacy as psychological factors that may contribute to increased food consumption. Thus, in some instances, obesity, like anorexia and bulimia, may be caused by emotional or psychological disorders that are well suited to the work of health psychologists.

There are many potential health hazards associated with obesity, far too many to review here (see Table 5.10). Briefly, however, obese individuals are at increased risk for type 2 diabetes (see Chapter 3, Global Communicable and Chronic Disease); hypertension, also called high blood pressure; coronary disease (see Chapter 9, Cardiovascular Disease); and chronic health conditions such as arthritis (see Chapter 10, Chronic Pain Management and Arthritis) (Mehler et al., 2003; Zanella, Kohlmann, & Ribeiro, 2001).

Binge Eating

Although usually thought of as a symptom of bulimia, binge eating is also a distinct form of disordered eating. *Binge eating*, as distinguished from bulimia, does not entail the compensatory behavior of purging to avoid weight gain (Hilbert & Tuschen-Caffier, 2007). However, many researchers support the notion that, like bulimia, binge eating may be introduced in part to help

TABLE 5.10	Health Complications Caused by Obesity

Obesity-Associated Health Problems

Resulting from the metabolic effects of enlarged fat cells and visceral fat

Type 2 diabetes

Hypertension and dyslipidemia (low HDL-cholesterol levels and high triglyceride levels)

Cardiovascular disease (coronary artery disease, stroke, heart failure, and atrial fibrillation)

Cancer (in men: liver, stomach, pancreas, esophagus, multiple myeloma, rectum, and gall bladder; in women: uterus, kidney, cervix, pancreas, esophagus, gall bladder, breast, liver, ovary, colon, and rectum)

Gastrointestinal disease (GERD, erosive gastritis, gall bladder disease, gall stones, cholecystectomy, and nonalcoholic steatohepatatitis)

Kidney disease (kidney stones, chronic renal disease, and end-stage renal disease)

Endocrine changes (hyperinsulinemia and insulin resistance, disturbed menstrual cycles, and altered cortisol metabolism)

Infertility (the polycystic ovarian syndrome)

Obstetrical risks (Caesarean section, hypertension, stillbirth, and neonatal mortality)

Resulting from increased body mass

Bone and joint diseases (osteoarthritis and hospitalization for back disorders)

Pulmonary disease (sleep apnea, pulmonary embolism, and sleep-disordered breathing)

Social stigmatization

GERD = gastroesophageal reflux disease; HDL = high-density lipoprotein.

Source: Annals of Internal Medicine (2008).

regulate negative affect or negative emotional states (Chua, Touyz, & Hill, 2004; Hilbert & Tuschen-Caffier, 2007).

Current research supports the view that individuals, again largely women, who engage in binge eating do so in response to either negative events or negative emotional states. Yet researchers differ as to the specific intent of the behavior. For example, Peterson and colleagues (2010) suggest that binge eating is evidenced most often by women as a form of harm avoidance, whereas Svaldi, Caffier, and Tuschen-Caffier (2010) suggest that women who binge eat do so to suppress their emotion, most likely a negative emotion. Finally, Chua and colleagues (2004) propose that such disordered eating is caused by negative moods; that is to say, the eating behavior is a response to negative emotions.

Whatever the cause or the intent, the outcome is the same. Binge eating disorder results in increased weight gain and is a contributing factor for obesity.

Eating Disorders in Context

We mentioned at the start of the section that one contributing factor to eating disorders is cultural norms: the pressure to adopt and to emulate standards of beauty in the prevailing culture. But, as we have noted throughout the text, cultures may differ, and such difference can affect health outcomes. Here, once again, we see the role of culture as it influences body image and indirectly contributes to behaviors, sometimes unhealthy behaviors, that affect health.

While it is true that, as noted before, early research focused on the aesthetic preference for and perceived attractiveness of thinness by Western, here meaning European and American, cultures (Greenberg & LaPorte, 1996), recent findings suggest that perceived preference for "thinness" and the associated eating disorders that accompany efforts to achieve the ideal body image are evident also in other cultures. For example, research in Asia suggests that eating disorders are on the increase in China, Hong Kong, Japan, South Korea, and Singapore (Mellor et al., 2009; Miller & Pumariega, 2001). Here, as in Western cultures, changes in societal norms are thought to contribute to the increasing rates of disordered eating (Chisuwa & O'Dea, 2010).

Research in the United States also illustrates the role of culture on body image and eating behaviors. While general studies have shown that eating disorders are less prevalent among ethnic minority groups in the United States, the findings also suggest an association between acculturation to Western culture and abnormal eating attitudes and behaviors (Pate, Pumariega, Hester, & Gardner, 1992; Pumariega, 1997). Consider this: Many studies suggest that, in general, African Americans have a greater acceptance of larger body proportions, are less enamored of thinness, and express lower rates of body dissatisfaction than whites (Ashley, Smith, Robinson, & Richardson, 1996; Schrieber et al., 1996). However, recent research by Abrams, Allen, and Gray (1993) found an increase in disordered eating among African Americans who were more assimilated into white U.S. culture. Similar findings have been reported for Latino women in the United States (Chamorro & Florez-Ortiz, 2000; Robinson et al., 1996).

Summary

In this chapter we explored the definition of risky health behaviors and the factors that shape adverse outcomes associated with these behaviors. We explained the effects of unintentional or accidental behaviors, unplanned behaviors, purposeful behaviors, environmental or culturally induced behaviors, and psychopathological behaviors on health outcomes. We explored theoretical explanations for risky behaviors and reviewed the advantages and disadvantages of strategies designed to limit or eliminate high-risk behaviors that lead to adverse health outcomes. And we included a brief overview of disordered eating and its impact on health outcomes. While disordered eating may appear to be unrelated to other types of risky health behaviors, we include it here because eating disorders can jeopardize an individual's physical and psychological outcomes.

Personal Postscript

CALCULATED RISK: COMPARING THE HEALTH BEHAVIORS AND HEALTH OUTCOMES OF YOUR CLOSE FRIENDS AND YOU

It is quite possible that when reading about risky behaviors in this chapter you thought about family members or friends who sometimes engage in one or more of the risky behaviors identified. It is possible, also, that your friends or family members have not experienced negative outcomes as a result of their behaviors. If that is the case, they are quite lucky. Not everyone has the same luck.

Health outcomes vary according to the individual. One person may escape the dangers associated with binge drinking or years of cigarette smoking, yet another person may have a bad experience after just one episode. How do you know which experience you will have? The problem is that you have no way of knowing.

So what do you do? Do you gamble and follow your friend's example, expecting the same positive outcome, or do you choose a more careful approach? One thing may help you decide. Rather than talking with your closest friends about their risky health behaviors, talk with another group of people about the same age, people with whom you have little regular contact. Listen to their views on, say, binge drinking, or smoking marijuana. Someone from the "new" group may offer a different opinion or a new way of thinking about risky behaviors. Then consider the new information before making a final decision. Different perspectives sometimes help inform our final choices.

Then talk with your friends again. Studies with adolescents show that many overestimate their friends' involvement in risky health behaviors, with regard to type of behavior and frequency. A candid conversation with a friend or an acquaintance might help distinguish between boastful behaviors rooted in fiction and true confessions rooted in fact.

Important Terms

Emotional Health and Well-Being

Chapter Objectives

After studying this chapter you will be able to:

1. Identify and define four major models of health and well-being.
2. Compare and contrast the concept of well-being in the four models.
3. Define *positive psychology*.
4. Identify three studies that demonstrate the beneficial effects of positive affect on health.

5. Identify and explain two criticisms of the positive psychology movement.
6. Describe three major forms of traditional medicine.
7. Compare and contrast traditional versus modern medicine.

OPENING STORY: ANGELITA

Miguel was getting worried. For the past three months his wife, Angelita, seemed inexplicably sad. Usually cheerful, talkative, and energetic, Angelita had become increasingly quiet and weepy. She complained of frequent headaches and spent hours alone in her garden. The only activity she seemed to enjoy was cooking. For example, when cooking her favorite foods from her hometown of La Paz, Mexico, Angelita could be heard singing for hours. But during dinner, she would become quiet. She would feel her stomach begin to "churn" and then excuse herself from the table.

Miguel encouraged Angelita to see her doctor. He hoped that a physical exam would uncover the problem. Angelita's doctor, however, found no viral or bacterial infection and no other physical explanations for the headaches. The doctor believed that Angelita's symptoms were rooted in emotional problems but was uncertain of the cause. He suggested that she come back in one week if there was no improvement in her condition, and he would refer her to someone who could help address what he suspected were emotional problems.

Angelita decided not to return to her doctor. She believed that because he had no idea what was wrong he could be of no help. Instead, she phoned her mother, Carmen, and told her about her current health problems. Carmen, who still lived in La Paz, convinced her daughter to come to Mexico for a week of rest and relaxation. In truth, Carmen wanted Angelita to see the village **curandero***, a traditional healer who practiced a form of medicine called* **curanderismo***, found in many Latin American countries. Curanderismo is a holistic approach to health that treats a person's material, spiritual, and psychic health in addition to his or her physical needs (Trotter, 2001). Carmen believed that* curanderismo *was preferable to modern health practices, especially when dealing with emotional or other nonphysical health issues.*

Carmen notified the curandero*, and, as is the custom, the* curandero *agreed to visit Angelita at home. He came the day after Angelita arrived and spent several hours talking with her. Angelita remembered that the* curandero's *father was the village healer when she was a child. Since that time it appears that the healing gift, referred to as "el don," was passed to the son. After talking with Angelita, the* curandero *gave her an herb tea to drink and rubbed a salve over her temples and forehead. He said he would return to check on Angelita in two days.*

On his second visit, the curandero *brought more herbs and made another tea. He then asked Angelita about her adjustment to her new home and neighborhood in Nashville, Tennessee. When he learned that Angelita could not find in Nashville the same herbs and spices used for cooking and for teas that she used in Mexico, he gave her extra to take with her when she returned. He also gave her a small pillow filled with strong scents.*

Within a week of returning to Nashville, Angelita began feeling better. She seemed happier and appeared more energetic, much like her "old" self. And because she no longer complained of headaches she was more social, no longer needing long periods of solitude. Angelita called her mother to report the changes, and Carmen immediately relayed the news to the curandero*. The* curandero *replied simply that Angelita needed to reconnect spiritually to her home and culture. And because he had given Angelita herbs from Mexico he believed that her spirit would be more content while away from her native country.* ∎

Traditional medicines, like *curanderismo,* may have originated several millennia ago, but they are still used throughout the world today. And, as we saw in the opening story, some people use traditional medicines in addition to or in lieu of modern, here meaning Western, medical approaches. Recall that Angelita sought the assistance of the *curandero* only after seeking assistance from her doctor in Nashville. Her mother, however, preferred to use *curanderismo* as a first or only option.

Using traditional medicines, also known as "folk medicines," the *curandero* determined (or diagnosed, if you prefer) that Angelita's physical symptoms were caused largely by spiritual and emotional health problems, a longing for the familiar. Yet Angelita's doctor in Nashville, who uses modern medical techniques, also concluded that her problem was not physical in origin. In fact, if pressed, the doctor might have suggested that Angelita was suffering from a bout of homesickness, a type of ***psychosomatic illness*** with emotional or psychological underlying causes. Thus, both traditional and modern medicinal practitioners concluded that Angelita experienced an emotional health problem, even though they differed somewhat as to the cause. The opening story introduces one theme of the current chapter: the contrasting and complementary practices of traditional versus modern medicine. We will explore the similarities and differences between both forms of medicine, focusing specifically on their treatment of emotional health issues.

The opening story also illustrates the effect of emotional factors on overall health outcomes. Specifically, Angelita's story reminds us that emotions contribute to our physical state. Thus, in this chapter we also explore the role of emotional health on overall well-being. In the process we will identify the contributions of health psychologists to understanding and addressing emotions as a health factor.

We begin our exploration of emotional health by examining four models used currently in research and practice in the field of health psychology: the biomedical model, the biopsychosocial model, the wellness model, and the ecological (sometimes called social ecological) model. The models were developed and tested in the 20th century largely in Western cultures and therefore represent a modern view of health.

In Section II, we explore a new topic called positive psychology. Positive psychology proposes that to understand human outcomes we must identify and examine all contributing factors, positive as well as negative. Included in this concept is a focus on health-enhancing emotional factors that can lead to good health outcomes. According to this view, the positive emotions, experiences, and personal characteristics that contribute to healthy outcomes have been largely overlooked in psychology. Proponents of positive psychology suggest that if we omit the study of "normal" healthy states, we cannot fully understand health.

Finally, in Section III, we explore a sample of traditional medicines, including Chinese traditional medicine, folk medicines that include *curanderismo* and *sangoma,* as well as a brief overview of Native American healing practices. Again, our focus when reviewing traditional medicines is principally to understand the similarities and differences between traditional and Western medicines as well as the relationship between emotions and overall well-being as explained by these two perspectives.

After reading this chapter, you will be able to identify and explain four models of health currently used to explain outcomes, to explain the role of emotions on individual health outcomes, to identify the central concepts of positive psychology and its contribution to our understanding of health outcomes, and to contrast the treatment of emotional health in modern and traditional medicines.

Consider two important points before proceeding. First, you will notice that some of the health models use the term ***well-being*** to characterize an individual's overall state of health. As noted in Chapter 1, An Interdisciplinary View of Health, well-being describes the state of the body (physical), the mind (psychological), the spirit, and social relations (emotions). It offers a holistic view of health similar to the ecological model, with one distinction. The ecological model includes physical environmental factors as well as health systems and health policy determinants of health. Because well-being incorporates many of the determinants of health found in the social ecological model, we will use this term rather than *health* to characterize a person's overall health condition (physical, emotional, social, and psychological). When applicable, we will add to this concept the effects of the physical and psychological environment, health systems, and health policy on health outcomes to demonstrate the ecological model.

Second, and equally as important, by using the term *well-being* we are reminded that a thorough study of health integrates the emotional and psychological states of an individual. It further supports the inclusion of health psychologists into the practice of and research on health.

SECTION I. FOUR MODELS OF WELL-BEING

Biomedical Model

The first formal, modern model of well-being, here meaning a model supported by scientific inquiry and empirical study, is the ***biomedical model***. In favor since the early 20th century, the biomedical model proposed that health is the absence of disease or dysfunction. Using this definition as a starting point, *disease* was defined as an abnormality, specifically a dysfunction of or deviation in a body organ or other body structure (Engel, 2002; Wade & Halligan, 2004). Thus, according to the biomedical model, a person who is in good health will be free of any abnormal biological changes in or functions of the body, whereas someone in "bad" or ill health will experience a change in the body system or functions. Furthermore, when diseases occur, this model suggests that locating and eradicating the illness will restore a person to good health.

As we saw in Chapter 1, An Interdisciplinary View of Health, a wholly physiologically based concept of health is consistent with some earlier beliefs. For example, the Cnidians in 500 BCE in Greece and the Roman philosopher and physician Galen in 200 CE believed that physical maladies determined an individual's health status. Research suggests that the early views were enhanced and supported by later studies performed in the 1880s by Robert Koch of Germany and by Louis Pasteur of France (Cantor, 2000; Checkland et al., 2008).

In separate, some say rival, studies Koch established that "invisible germs carried contagions." In support of that assertion, Koch identified specific microorganisms that caused diseases such as anthrax and tuberculosis (Tan & Berman, 2008). The irrefutable association between a specific organism and a specific disease convinced many Western scientists that illnesses were indeed caused only by microorganisms.

Pasteur's work, which pioneered the use of vaccines to prevent infectious diseases (see Chapter 3, Global Communicable and Chronic Disease) (Pasteur, Chamberlain, & Roux, in translation by Dasgupta, 2002), further supported the germ theory of disease (see Figure 6.1).

FIGURE 6.1 Louis Pasteur is best remembered for his pioneering work on vaccines to prevent infections.

Thus, it appeared that Koch's discovery of the relationship between microorganisms and disease, and Pasteur's discovery of vaccines that protect individuals from such microorganisms (thereby ensuring good health), explained the origins of illness. These two seminal studies appear to have led to the development of the biomedical model of health (Checkland et al., 2008).

LIMITATIONS OF THE BIOMEDICAL MODEL

To be certain, modern science supports the association between microorganisms and disease, the central tenant of the biomedical model. Unfortunately, the assertion that only physical agents cause illnesses is also a limitation of the model. Other limitations include a problem-oriented approach to health and wellness and a broad, perhaps overbroad, definition of illness. We review each limitation briefly here.

The belief that only physiological determinants cause illness presents, as Engel (2002) suggests, a "culturally specific perspective about diseases," somewhat like a Western culture version of folk medicine. Past and current models of health, in addition to current research, suggest that microorganisms are only one of several factors that influence health outcomes. By focusing on the physical causes of illness, the biomedical model overlooks emotional or psychological determinants that also influence well-being. We explain the specific role of nonphysical factors on health later in this chapter.

A second limitation is the problem-oriented focus of the biomedical model. It proposes that a change in normal bodily functions that results in a deviation from or dysfunction of the body signals a problem to be rectified. But consider this: Would someone with a hearing impairment or someone who is deaf be considered ill because of his or her dysfunctional auditory system? Few people equate dysfunction with a disease-related illness. Indeed, some individuals who are hearing impaired may characterize their limitations as a disability, but few would consider themselves ill. Yet, according to the biomedical model, a dysfunctional auditory system would be considered an illness.

Even the assumption that physical symptoms are clear indications of an illness or disease can be challenged. Let us return to our opening story. Angelita experienced physical symptoms prompting her to seek medical care. But, according to the biomedical model's definition of health, she was not ill. There was no underlying viral or bacteriological disease that caused her symptoms. Still, it was evident that Angelita was not in a state of good overall health. Clearly she was experiencing some type of health problem, just not the sort recognized by the biomedical model.

In addition, consider this: Some illnesses can occur independent of symptoms. Hypertension, a heart-related disease that we will explore in Chapter 9, Cardiovascular Disease, is nicknamed "the silent killer" because it often develops with no observable, here meaning external, symptoms. Similarly, individuals may often be unaware that they have been infected with a deadly human immunodeficiency virus (HIV; see Chapter 8, HIV and AIDS) because it, too, often carries no noticeable external symptoms for the first eight years. Thus, in some cases, external symptoms of an illness can appear without evidence of an underlying disease (like Angelita's problem). In other instances, diseases may indeed be present (like hypertension or HIV), but evidence no identifiable symptoms, especially in the early stages of illness.

To summarize, the biomedical model defines *dysfunctionality* as an illness and interprets physiological symptoms as signs of the illness. But, the biologically based model presents a limited definition of illness that can include a range of dysfunctions not usually classified as an illness. For example, a person who is deaf has a dysfunctional auditory system. Yet, few would determine that a deaf person has an illness. Current research suggests that a more precise and, in some ways, broader definition of health may be more accurate and may include the emotional, psychological, and, for some, spiritual determinants of well-being (Nikelly, 2005).

Let us consider one point before moving on. It is important to restate that a broad definition of health and well-being is not new. Recall that in Chapter 1, An Interdisciplinary View of Health, we briefly reviewed the health practices and beliefs of civilizations including other ancient Greeks (specifically Aesculapius and Hippocrates), as well as Chinese civilizations, Native American healing practices, and the Sans and Yoruba cultures in southern and western Africa. All of these civilizations embraced a holistic or an ecological view of health that included the emotional, physical, psychological, environmental, and for some the spiritual, well-being of the individual.

In more recent times, research by Sigmund Freud in the 1890s reaffirmed a broad concept of health, one that included emotional and psychological factors. Specifically, Freud suggested that many of the physical illnesses described by his patients were, in fact, linked to psychological causes. When the psychological problems were addressed, he noted that the physical symptoms were also resolved without direct treatment. Contemporary health and behavioral medicine furthered Freud's version of the mind–body connection by establishing the field of psychosomatic medicine. This new discipline abolished the separation of the mind and body proposed in earlier versions of Western medicine (Mizrachi, 2001) and reintroduced a holistic concept of well-being. Thus, our brief review of health in Chapter 1 that highlighted examples of holistic and ecological health models set the stage for further exploration of the role of emotions on health in modern and traditional medicines. The biopsychosocial, wellness, and social ecological models are examples of such models.

Biopsychosocial Model

Sometimes referred to as a *holistic health model*, the *biopsychosocial model* proposed by Engel (2002) supports the belief, endorsed by many in health psychology, that well-being is determined by biological (*bio*), psychological (*psycho*), and sociological (*social*) factors. The psychological influences on health include emotions, social support systems, health behaviors, and personal traits (Lazarus & Folkman, 1987, 2002; Ryan & Deci, 2000; Salovey, Rothman, Detweiler, & Steward, 2000), while sociological factors include familial, cultural, and community factors. We examine some of the psychological and sociological factors each in turn.

PSYCHOLOGICAL FACTOR #1: EMOTIONS   We noted earlier that the relationship between health and emotions was proposed many centuries earlier. ***Hippocrates***, sometimes called the father of clinical medicine, is often credited with pioneering the interaction of emotions and health in Western medicine. He believed that an imbalance in any one of four bodily fluids, called ***humors***, could lead to illnesses (Salovey et al., 2000). The important part is that the illnesses he identified were, in fact, emotional. For example, Hippocrates believed that an imbalance of black bile, one type of body fluids, would lead to sadness or melancholy, while an imbalance of yellow bile, another fluid, led to anger. We will see later in the chapter that traditional medicines also defined health in terms of a balance between emotional, physical, social, and environmental forces.

The concept presented by Hippocrates that links health and emotions is supported by current research, although the details have changed considerably. Current studies show that emotions can affect our physiological well-being through two primary pathways, our immune system and our behaviors.

Emotions and the Immune System   Rabin and colleagues (1989) suggest that one way that emotions affect our immune system is through the nerve fibers in our bodies. The fibers connect with the ***central nervous system (CNS)***, the "control center" for our body or, biologically speaking, the brain and the brain stem (see Figure 6.2).

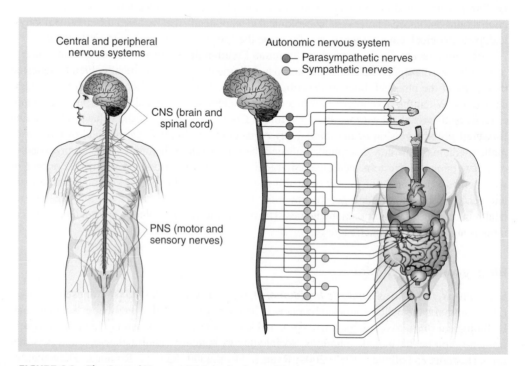

FIGURE 6.2   **The Central Nervous System, Brain, and Brain Stem.**

Source: Human Disease and Condition (2010).

The nerve fibers act like cables carrying information from our *receptors* (skin, muscles, and other sites), to our central nervous system (CNS). It may help to think of the neuron cables as the hardware needed to communicate. The actual message, however, is carried by *neurochemicals* called *neurotransmitters* that travel within the neuron cables. When sending messages from a receptor site—like the skin—to the brain, a neurotransmitter is triggered at the receptor site and passed along from neuron to neuron via the dendrites until the message reaches the processing center of the brain. *Dendrites*, from the Greek word *dendron,* meaning tree, are branchlike

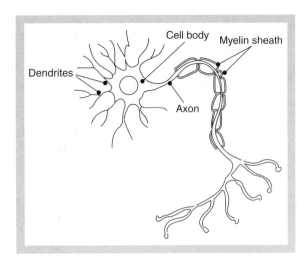

FIGURE 6.3   Structure of a Human Cell.

structures that extend from the cell body and receive the neurochemical message from other cells. Once the message is received, the *axon*, another nerve fiber that extends from the cell body, carries the message to neighboring cells (see Figure 6.3).

The nerve cables that carry messages can be categorized as either afferent or efferent nerve fibers. The *afferent nerve fibers* carry information to the CNS (the brain) from the receptor sites. For example, if a person touches a sharp object, the afferent nerves may send a sensory signal from the fingers (the receptor site) to the brain for processing and interpretation. The *efferent nerve fibers*, on the other hand, carry information from the CNS to the periphery of the body to coordinate the response. Using the same example of touching a sharp object, the brain might send a signal of pain or discomfort to the receptor site (hand) that results in the person withdrawing his or her hand from the sharp object.

Impact of Emotions on Health   Now that we understand the basic structure of the body's neurological communication system, we can examine the effect of our emotions on the communication process and hence on our overall well-being. Perhaps the following research on stress will help demonstrate the effect of emotions on health outcomes (Cohen, Tyrrell, & Smith, 1991, 1993; Dusek & Benson, 2009; Jacobs, 2001; Kiecolt-Glaser & Glaser, 1988; Williams & Williams, 1993). In studies examining the effects of stress on the body's *immune system*, here meaning the body's defense system against illness-producing microorganisms, Cohen (2005) found that stress may influence the production of *hormones*, another type of chemical message released by cells in our body that, in turn, affect the immune system.

How do hormones influence health outcomes? We review stress and the immune systems in Chapter 7, Stress and Coping, and Chapter 8, HIV and AIDS. Briefly, however, *epinephrine* is a stress hormone that helps to suppress the immune system. Suppressing or "turning down" the body's immune system decreases the body's ability to fight foreign or disease-carrying microorganisms and increases the risk of contracting a disease. Thus, if an individual experiences high levels or extended periods of stress, that person's body may increase production of epinephrine and signal the brain to suppress the immune system. A person who contracts a viral or bacterial illness while his or her immune system is functioning at lower levels will be less able to ward off the illness and more likely to show signs of illness.

Applied health psychology research that tests the proposed link between emotions and illnesses similarly reports a correlation between emotions and health. For example, research by Schulz, Martire, Beach, and Scheier (2005) and Schulz and colleagues (2000) tested and established a link between depression and mortality. In their study of approximately 5,200 participants aged 65 or older, individuals with depressive symptoms were 25% more likely to die within six years than were individuals with considerably lower levels of depression (Schulz et al., 2000). In essence, their study suggests that an emotional factor (depression) negatively influences the physiological health of individuals, resulting in an early onset of death. And, in a related study, individuals who were diagnosed with heart disease and who were depressed were significantly more likely to die sooner than were individuals with heart disease with no signs or diagnosis of depression (Glassman & Shapiro, 1998).

Shultz and colleagues (2000, 2005), Glassman and Shapiro (1998), and others are quick to note that they cannot establish through their research that depression definitively causes death. Rather, their research suggests one of two possible explanations for the correlations (see Chapter 2, Research Methods), or relationship, between depression and death. One explanation, as noted previously, is that depression may influence the production of hormones such as epinephrine and other chemicals that suppress the immune system. The suppressed system increases the risk of contracting viruses or other infectious diseases that can lead to mortality. A second possible explanation is that, due to depression, a person may engage in unhealthy behaviors that increase the probability of death. For example, a depressed individual may be more likely to use substances such as alcohol or illegal drugs to cope with the depression. Thus, behavioral factors such as substance abuse, initiated because of depression, could increase the risk of death.

Research on emotions and health show, however, that it is also possible for negative emotions to have positive health consequences. In a review of the research on the health outcomes of negative affect, Mayne (1999) found that in some cases negative emotions can activate the sympathetic nervous system (SNS) and thereby stimulate the immune system.

Negative Emotions, Positive Effects   As Figure 6.2 shows, the *sympathetic nervous system* is part of the *autonomic nervous system (ANS)*, or the part of our body that controls the automatic and involuntary functions that we do not think about but that are essential for living. For example, the ANS controls our heart rate, digestion, and perspiration. Another automatic or involuntary function is the body's physiological response to dangers, emergencies, or foreign organisms that invade the body. The sympathetic nervous system is responsible for mobilizing the body to respond to such dangers. This includes stimulating the immune system. Thus, negative affect, such as fear or fright, can stimulate the immune system to react to danger, possibly resulting in a positive outcome.

We noted that negative emotions can lead to behaviors that negatively affect health. Yet we also find that negative emotions can lead to health-enhancing behaviors. Studies suggest that negative emotions can increase the likelihood that individuals will seek timely medical help. Salovey and colleagues (2000) and Mayne (1999) found that, when experiencing health problems, negative affect such as anxiety or depression may cause a person to perceive his or her physical condition more accurately and therefore increase the probability that that person will seek medical help. Consider this: An individual with a cold may become increasingly anxious if the cold lingers and produces thick mucus. That person's anxiety, a negative affect, may prompt him or her to seek medical care. In comparison, a person with a positive affect may not accurately assess the severity of the health condition or the fact that medical attention is needed. For example, someone with the same symptom—a lingering cold and thick mucus—who feels he or she can "stick it out" with sleep and copious amounts of liquids may not seek assistance. The lack of anxiety and the belief in his or her own skills may prevent that person from accurately assessing the severity of the health problem.

Positive Emotions and Health   If negative emotions can lead to poorer health outcomes, can positive emotions improve health status? We explore this question in depth in the following section on positive psychology. For now, however, it is important to note that some studies suggest such an association. For example, the role of ***positive affect*** on physiological health was demonstrated in a classic study by Cohen and colleagues (1991, 1995). In a laboratory-based study, these researchers exposed participants to a common cold virus to determine whether a person's affect influences disease progression. The study revealed that participants with a positive affect, here meaning positive feelings or emotions, at the time of exposure to the virus developed a less severe form of illness than did participants with a negative affect. Additional research by Moscowitz, Epel, and Acree (2008) found that positive affect can have a greater impact on health. Their research suggests that positive affect can also decrease mortality rates among people with diabetes.

It might be tempting to conclude from the research that people who maintain a positive emotional demeanor will be less susceptible to severe illnesses. But keep in mind that affect is just one of a number of factors that influence health. An individual's physiological state, limitations, or dysfunctions will contribute also to the likelihood of contracting a disease, to the severity of the illness, and to its progression. Emotions, therefore, are just one of several factors that influence physical health.

In sum, current research shows that Hippocrates' initial premise was correct. Our positive and negative emotions do influence our well-being. He was incorrect, however, when characterizing the process by which emotions contribute to health.

PSYCHOLOGICAL FACTOR #2: HEALTH BEHAVIORS   We reviewed a host of health behaviors in Chapter 5, Risky Health Behaviors, and discussed at length their positive and negative impacts on well-being. For example, we noted that while researchers have identified the benefits of consuming moderate amounts of red wine, excessive consumption or abuse of alcohol of any kind can have negative health consequences including gastrointestinal problems, heart disease, stroke, and cirrhosis of the liver (CDC, 2008; MMWR, 2004). We will not repeat the information from Chapter 5 in this section. But it is important to note that here, too, emotions can and often do influence health behaviors. For example, anxiety and depression are cited by some individuals as factors that contribute to their abuse of alcohol or other substances (Jessor, Donovan, & Costa, 1991). Thus, two psychological factors, health behaviors and emotions, can interact to influence health status.

SOCIOLOGICAL FACTOR #1: SOCIOECONOMIC CLASS AND INCOME   In Chapter 3, Global Communicable and Chronic Disease, we identified the barriers to health care posed by lack of access to health insurance or to preventive medical care (Simon, Chan, & Forrest, 2008). What we did not state is that an individual's ***socioeconomic class (SEC)***—or the social and economic group that characterizes that person's social position in society—also greatly affects his or her access to care.

Socioeconomic class is a term developed by sociologists that categorizes individuals according to their positions in society as determined by their parents' level of education and occupation, their family's social status, and their family's income and wealth (Hout, Brooks, & Manzay, 1993; Liberatos, Link, & Kelsey, 1988). When evaluating the impact of socioeconomic class on health, researchers often use a simplified categorization scheme based primarily on household annual income levels: poor (less than $16,000), working class ($16,000 to $35,000), lower middle class ($35,000 to $75,000), upper middle class ($100,000 to $500,000), and wealthy (greater than $500,000) (Thompson & Hickey, 2005).

Without a doubt, SEC, defined here as household income, is a sociological factor that affects health by regulating access to medical care. Put it this way: The ability to pay for health insurance or to pay a medical provider's fee will influence a person's likelihood of seeking health care in a timely manner. Individuals unable to pay for needed health care due to limited income or lack of health insurance may delay seeking care, a decision that could aggravate the health problem. We explain the effect of socioeconomic status (income) on access to health care in greater detail in Chapter 12, Health Care Systems and Health Policy.

In addition to examining the ability to pay for care, studies suggest that people in lower socioeconomic groups may express negative affect more frequently than people in other SECs due largely to social environmental factors (Carroll, Smith, & Bennett, 2002). For example, lower SEC individuals are more likely to experience negative emotions, such as depression, which, as we mentioned already, can trigger illnesses or contribute to mortality (Gallo & Matthews, 2003). In addition, Cohen, Kaplan, and Salonen (1999) note that individuals in lower SEC groups (poor, working poor) experience more stress (most often a negative affect) than those in higher SECs, a condition that can also lead to poorer well-being.

SOCIOLOGICAL FACTOR #2: FAMILY AND CULTURE   Familial and cultural patterns of behavior, including diet and orientation to exercise and sports, also contribute to overall well-being. Take, for example, diet. Research on the nutritional practices of Japanese and Korean Americans reveals that many Asian diets minimize the risk of chronic diseases such as hypertension or digestive diseases (Park, Murphy, Sharmay, & Kolondel, 2005; Yang et al., 2007). Dietary practices in many Asian, specifically East Asian countries include foods high in fiber and low in fats, including fruits, vegetables, and grain products.

Similarly, in a 20-year longitudinal study of deaths of middle-aged men due to chronic obstructive pulmonary disease (COPD; see Chapter 3, Global Communicable and Chronic Disease), researchers found that diets high in fruits and vitamin E decreased the incidences of death due to COPD among the cohort of Finnish, Italian, and Dutch men in the study (Walda et al., 2002). By contrast, as we also noted in Chapter 3, foods with high fat or high calorie content, such as pizza, cheeseburgers, and French fries—favorite American fast foods—are linked to chronic diseases, including heart diseases and diabetes (Scott, 2007; WHO, 2002).

Nutrition and diet are important, but so is exercise. The International Association on the Study of Obesity reports that at least 30 minutes of exercise daily, together with a healthy diet, are required to reduce the risk of chronic diseases (Saris et al., 2003). Yet maintaining a regular exercise regimen is dependent on a number of factors, including past patterns and practices, which are often influenced by family or cultural practices.

To summarize, the biopsychosocial model expands on the definition of health supported by the biomedical model by including psychological, social, and emotional well-being as part of a holistic definition of health. Yet, even with an expanded definition, researchers argue that the biopsychosocial model still places biology at the core of the definition. Thus, they contend that, rather than proposing a truly integrative model of health, the biopsychosocial model simply appends the psychological and sociological determinants of health to the biomedical model (Armstrong, 2002). For this reason we explore other models that offer alternative concepts of well-being that do not place biology at the center of the definition.

Wellness Model

The biopsychosocial model was the first to include psychological and social determinants as contributors to health outcomes. The *wellness model* includes the same psychological, social, and emotional factors included in the biopsychosocial model, but it adds two new dimensions: quality of life and spirituality.

QUALITY OF LIFE   The wellness model defines health according to an individual's assessment of his or her own state of physical, mental, emotional, and spiritual well-being. For example, in a case study by Dinh and Groleau (2008), a Laotian man, Mr. B., summarizes his assessment of his overall well-being using quality of life and spirituality (see Box 6.1). In this study, Mr. B. unwillingly undergoes an emergency amputation of two fingers to protect him from a likely infection. According to the medical doctors on his case, the operation restored him to a state of good physical

---

BOX 6.1   Personal Meaning and Health: One Man's View of Wellness

Dinh and Groleau (2008) examine the case of a 49-year-old married Laotian man, Mr. B., living in Canada. According to their case study, Mr. B. was employed as an operator of heavy machinery at a factory in Canada. While at work, Mr. B. caught his glove in one of the heavy machines. The machine severed part of the middle and fourth fingers on his left hand. He was immediately taken to the nearest hospital where he waited approximately one hour before seeing a surgeon.

Mr. B. asked that his fingers be reattached, but the surgeon indicated that the tendons in his third and fourth fingers were dead and that the remaining parts of his fingers would have to be amputated. The surgeon's decision did not seem logical to Mr. B., who demonstrated that he could move the remaining segments of his middle and fourth fingers. The surgeon was not convinced, and three hours later, despite Mr. B.'s protests and pleas not to amputate, the medical staff prepped him for surgery to remove the remaining segments.

In the months after the surgery, Mr. B. received physical therapy to regain strength and movement in his hand. Doctors considered the surgery a success because it saved Mr. B. from probable infection of the hand and ensured that Mr. B. would regain an overall good state of health. Mr. B. did not share the doctor's point of view. Instead, he believed that the surgery "[took] his life."

(continued)

According to Dinh and Groleau (2008), some Laotians believe that their health depends on the status of 12 souls that comprise a person's life force, known as *H'wen* (Dinh & Gorleau, 2008). The 12 souls correspond to parts of the body. The hands represent one of the souls. When Mr. B. lost his fingers, he lost one of his life forces. Thus, in this case study, Mr. B.'s health, according to the wellness model, was significantly impaired on two fronts, psychosocial and spiritual. First, unable to resume work as a heavy machinery operator, Mr. B. was unable to earn a living and provide for his family. His quality of life was affected by his inability to assume his role as the principal wage earner in the family. Second, the loss of his fingers represented a lost energy force and diminished spiritual well-being.

When explaining his feelings in French, Mr. B could only say he felt "*triste*," or sad. But, when talking with Laotian friends, his wife, or others who understood the Laotian culture, he explained that he felt indignation and felt unworthy of respect.

Mr. B.'s inability to return to his job affected his sense of responsibility and obligation to his family. His feelings of indignation and of being unworthy of respect, however, reflect the influence of Laotian culture—a social influence that impacts his emotional state of health and a spiritual influence consistent with his Buddhist beliefs. Mr. B.'s case demonstrates how spirituality, quality of life, culture, and emotional health all contribute to his assessment of his overall well-being. Not surprisingly, he currently views his overall well-being as poor.

health. But, according to Mr. B., when surgeons removed his two fingers they also took part of his life and his life force. For Mr. B., the operation that Western medical doctors thought of as a life-saving procedure diminished his ***quality of life*** and negatively affected his spiritual well-being.

Similar examples of an individual's perception of wellness that departs from a biopsychosocial concept of health are found in the research literature on total knee replacement surgery, an increasingly common surgery for older adults in many Western cultures. Total knee replacement surgery usually is performed when a person's ***knee osteoarthritis***, a form of arthritis in the knee that can become disabling over time, worsens to the point that surgery is required to relieve the pain or to correct a functional disability (see Chapter 10, Chronic Pain Management and Arthritis). However, research by Toye, Barlow, Wright, and Lamb (2006) shows that, for most patients, a decision to replace a painful knee is rarely explained by painful physical symptoms. Instead, Toye and colleagues (2006) found that a decision to have knee surgery often was based on the patient's feelings of vulnerability because of the unreliable knee, the desire not to depend on others for mobility, and the fatigue associated with an increased effort when performing daily tasks: in other words, quality of life issues. Thus, Toye and colleagues (2006) suggest that decisions to have knee replacement surgery are based on the value placed on mobility, independence, and improved energy levels rather than on pain or discomfort, concepts that may not be considered important in a biomedical or biopsychosocial model of health.

SPIRITUALITY   The wellness model also addresses spiritual health, faith, and religion—topics that are not usually included in psychological research. Some scientists consider ***spirituality*** a pseudoscience or a primitive superstition and therefore not something to be included in rigorous studies that explain individual health outcomes. More recently, however, researchers have been examining the relationship between spirituality and health, suggesting a change among scientists, at least those in the health fields, who believe that spirituality is essential for some individuals to obtain optimal health (Diaz, 1993; Myslakidou et al., 2008; Seaward, 1991).

By spirituality, researchers are not necessarily referring to religious dogma. Rather, many studies examine the impact of an individual's philosophy, values, and meaning of life (Mullen, McDermott, Gold, & Belcastro, 1996). Scientists suggest that the health-enhancing role of spirituality may afford individuals peace and tranquility in the face of stressful events and a sense of meaningfulness that provides them with direction and fulfillment (Perrin & McDermott, 1997). In addition, some spiritual practices promote healthy behaviors. For example, the dietary practices of Muslims and some Christian denominations include abstinence from alcohol; this can be a health-enhancing behavior, particularly for those who may consume alcohol in excess (see Chapter 5, Risky Health Behaviors).

Recent studies examining the relationship between spirituality and well-being among migraine suffers provide additional support for the health-enhancing effects of spirituality. *Migraines* are considered a neurological disorder of unknown origins. The symptoms generally include painful headaches that do not respond to over-the-counter pain medications, nausea, and vomiting. Researchers believe that migraines may be associated with depression and anxiety, suggesting an emotional basis for the illness.

One study examining the impact of spiritual meditation on migraine relief explored the effects of four types of meditation techniques on migraine suffers to determine which, if any, resulted in significantly improved outcomes: spiritual meditation, internally focused meditation, externally focused meditation, and muscle relaxation (Wachholtz & Pargament, 2008). Each of the 83 study participants in the migraine study learned and practiced one of the four techniques for 20 minutes a day for a total of 30 days. The results of pre-post test measures (see Chapter 2, Research Methods) revealed that participants who used the spiritual meditation techniques fared much better than those using any of the other approaches. The spiritual meditation users reported a decrease in frequency of headaches and in negative affect. In addition, they reported an increase in pain tolerance, self-efficacy, and overall well-being (Wachholtz & Pargament, 2008).

In sum, research on the effects of spirituality on well-being suggests that spirituality offers some individuals tranquility in troubled times, guidance on healthy lifestyles and behaviors, and emotional wellness, all of which contribute to well-being.

We need to make one additional point about the role of spirituality. Individuals incorporate spiritual practices into their healing traditions even in cultures where the biomedical model of health is strongly favored. The study with migraine suffers is one example. Consider also the case presented in Box 6.2. Dr. Paul Farmer, a physician, was reminded that, even in Western cultures, individuals combine spirituality with medical science in their efforts to overcome illnesses.

From the research it is clear that spirituality plays a health-enhancing role for many individuals and in many cultures. We will see later that spirituality is also recognized as a central component of well-being in cultures that practice traditional forms of medicine.

Social Ecological Model

The biopsychosocial and wellness models propose that biological, psychological, social, and spiritual health, in addition to perceived quality of life, contribute to overall well-being. Because we

BOX 6.2   Medicine and Spirituality: A Compatible Combination in Western Medicine?

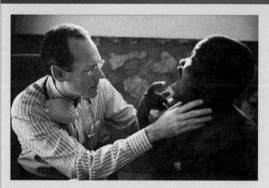

FIGURE 6.4   Dr. Paul Farmer and Patient.
Dr Farmer with a patient in his clinic in Haiti.

Source: UNICEF (2008).

Dr. Paul Farmer is not your "average" doctor. Raised on a boat and in a bus during his childhood, Dr. Farmer's early years accurately could be called atypical. Perhaps his early experience living in nontraditional environments led him to a career caring for the poorest of the poor in Haiti, Peru, Cuba, and Russia (see Figure 6.4).

Dr. Farmer is an infectious disease specialist, someone who studies and treats contagious diseases. Given his special interests, it is not surprising that Dr. Farmer would travel to developing countries (see Chapter 3, Global Communicable and Chronic Disease) where infectious diseases are quite common. But it was during his work in Haiti that he was reminded of the dual presence of medical science and spirituality in Haitian and Western cultures.

One year while treating patients in Haiti for tuberculosis (TB; see Chapter 3, Global Communicable and Chronic Diseases), Dr. Farmer designed a study to test an idea debated by his health care staff. He wanted to understand whether the poor health outcomes of impoverished patients like those in Haiti could be attributed to economic conditions and the inability to pay for care or whether their outcomes were rooted in their belief that illnesses had spiritual origins. In Haiti, some individuals believe that illnesses are sent by enemies through sorcery (Kidder, 2003). Dr. Farmer's staff believed that individuals who believed that illnesses were curses sent by others would be less likely to follow the medical regimen to treat their TB.

To test the idea, Dr. Farmer divided his TB patients into two groups. The medication-only group would receive the necessary treatment for TB, but the medication plus services group would receive the medicine in addition to regular visits from community health workers and cash stipends for child care and for travel by public transport to the nearest village. Dr. Farmer interviewed all of his patients at the beginning of the study and again one year later. Farmer found that few patients in either group admitted believing that TB was sent to them from an enemy via sorcery. In spite of their denial, Dr. Farmer's results suggested otherwise. One year after beginning the study, less than half (48%) of the medication-only group was cured of TB. By comparison, all of the medication plus extra services patients had fully recovered (Kidder, 2003).

As part of the one-year follow-up, Dr. Farmer asked his patients their views on the origins of their disease. He revisited one woman in the medication plus services group who, the previous year, seemed offended at his question about her beliefs in the origin of diseases. At the time, she stated that she knew that TB came from "people coughing germs"

(Kidder, 2003, p. 35). But, one year later, the same woman, now fully recovered from TB, admitted that she knew who sent her the sickness. She vowed revenge on the person.

Realizing that the woman was admitting that she believed in sorcery as a source of the disease, Dr. Farmer asked why she used the medicine to combat the TB. The woman's response illustrates the duality of medical science and spirituality in Haiti and, ironically, in the United States. In Haitian Creole she responded "*Cheri . . . eske-w pa ka kom prann bagay ki pa senp?*" (Kidder, 2003, p. 35). Translated, the woman asked Dr. Farmer, "Honey, are you incapable of complexity?"

The woman's question reminded Dr. Farmer of himself and others he knew in the United States who held similar complex views on faith and medicine. In fact, there are many examples of such complexities in modern medicine. Chapels in hospitals and chaplains in medical centers are but two examples of the complex relationship between faith and health in modern cultures. Many individuals who seek medical care from health care providers in hospitals also call on their faith, which represents their values and belief structures, to guide medical staff and to speed healing and recovery.

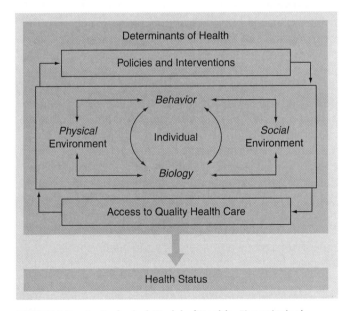

FIGURE 6.5   An Ecological Model of Health. Five principal determinants of health cited in the Social Ecological model include: the individual (biological) and behavioral, social environmental factors, physical environmental factors, health systems (access to quality health care) and health policy.

Source: Adapted from U.S. Department of Health and Human Services, 2001.

have explored the biological, psychological, emotional, and social environmental determinants of health in the previous models, here we focus on three determinants unique to the *social ecological* model: physical and psychological environments, health systems, and health policy.

ENVIRONMENTAL DETERMINANTS The *ecological model* identifies two types of environments. First is a social environment, similar to that proposed in the biopsychosocial model that includes the interpersonal, familial, and cultural factors that affect an individuals' emotional state of well-being. The second environment is a physical space and the perceived quality of that space as a determinant of health (see Figure 6.5).

Physical Environmental Determinants   When exploring environmental influences on health in Chapter 3, Global Communicable and Chronic Disease, we discussed the effects of contaminated environments on overall well-being. We noted that hazards such as toxic waste sites contribute to high incidences of diseases and high infant mortality rates, especially among the poor and working classes. Specifically, we noted that many forms of cancer and severe respiratory illnesses have been linked to toxic waste sites, a physical environmental determinant of ill health.

The effect of the environment on health outcomes is not a new discovery. Sir Edwin Chadwick, an early proponent of the association between environment and health, demonstrated the dangerous consequences of some environments on individual health in England in the mid-1800s. Sir Chadwick's research, summarized in Box 6.3, documented the health consequences of individuals living and working in unsanitary conditions in urban and rural England. In addition, Chadwick also demonstrated that the lower socioeconomic classes, specifically the poor and working classes, were more likely to be exposed to health-compromising environmental conditions than were individuals in the higher socioeconomic classes. Unfortunately, the disparities in living environments for people in the lower SECs are present in most countries even today (Northridge & Sclar, 2003; Schultz & Northridge, 2004; Schultz, Williams, Israel, & Lempert, 2002).

BOX 6.3   Environment, Socioeconomic Class, and Health

"If you trace down the fever districts on a map, and then compare that map with the map of the commissions of sewers, you will find that wherever the commissions of sewers have not been, there fever is prevalent; and, on the contrary, wherever they have been, there fever is comparatively absent" (Thomas Southwood Smith, quoted in Hamlin & Sheard, 1998).

In 1847, Thomas Southwood Smith issued the above statement to explain what we now clearly know about the association between unsanitary environmental conditions and health. However, in the early to mid-1800s this argument met with sharp resistance. Such was the case for Sir Edwin Chadwick, a devout public health advocate. Concerned about the living conditions of the working class and the effects of these conditions on their health, Sir Edwin lobbied the English legislative bodies to examine the public health conditions of the poor and working classes in England. In 1832, England was preparing to revisit the Poor Laws, a set of laws designed to provide equitable assistance to the poor to help improve their standard of living. Chadwick was convinced, however, that no significant improvements could be made unless one also addressed the health status of the working class. He believed that improvements in the health and living conditions of the working class would be necessary to improve their overall well-being.

To this end, Chadwick conducted a survey of adult and infant death rates of the three principal classes in Great Britain in the mid-1800s: the gentry (landowner and aristocrats or professionals), tradesmen or shopkeepers, and finally the wage-earning working class. He summarized his findings in a report entitled *Survey into the Sanitary Conditions of the Labouring [Working] Classes in Great Britain*. Two important statistics included in the survey were a comparison of the mortality rates for adults and the infant death rates among all three classes, as shown below.

Adult Mortality and Infant Death Rates, England, 1842

| Class | Mean Age of Death | | Infant Deaths |
	Urban (London)	Rural (Countryside)	per 1,000 births
Gentry/professional	44 years	35 years	100 deaths
Tradesmen/shopkeepers	23 years	22 years	167 deaths
Wage/working class workers	22 years	15 years	250 deaths

The statistics supported Chadwick's hypothesis: The living and working conditions of the three classes explained much of the disparity in mortality statistics. English wage and working class workers in the 1840s could expect, on average, to live only half as long as individuals in the gentry class. In addition, babies born to parents in the laboring classes were 2.5 times more likely to die before age 5 than were infants born to parents in the gentry or aristocratic classes.

Chadwick argued that the wage-earning and laboring classes lived in the most unsanitary conditions and were exposed to the harshest work environments. He believed that these conditions directly contributed to unusually high early-adult mortality and in high infant mortality rates.

Using these statistics, Sir Edwin convinced the English legislature to pass the Public Health Act and Nuisance Removal and Disease Prevention Act of 1848. But, unsatisfied with the weak content of the act, Chadwick continued to advocate for better health conditions for the laboring class.

The ecological model implicit in Chadwick's work identifies two effects of physical environmental hazards on well-being. First, the model explains the interactive impact of the environment and individuals. In England in the 1800s, many neighborhoods were without sewer and draining systems. The lack of adequate waste disposal systems polluted the environment. The contaminated environment in turn affected the air and water supplies needed by people to maintain health. Thus, in this instance, the physical environmental caused physiological health problems due to actions of individuals on the environment.

Health Systems and Health Policy   Another unique aspect of the social ecological model is its inclusion of health systems and health policy, specifically the regulatory agencies and regulations that define the structure of health care and that regulate its services, as distinct determinants of health outcomes.

Thomas Southward Smith found that the absence of sewers and drainage systems, a health policy decision, was correlated with the frequency of high fevers among residents. Smith's finding is consistent with the studies of Chadwick, who also attests to the relationship between the physical environmental conditions in poor neighborhoods and the poor health outcomes of its inhabitants. Both Chadwick and Smith understood that health policy initiatives could influence

FIGURE 6.6   Water Treatment/Sewage Plant, Houston, Texas.

health status and could either enhance or impair the health outcomes of poorer citizens. Their work supports the role of health policy as a determinant of health (Gee & Payne-Sturges, 2004).

Consider a more current example. In the United States, policy decisions by local or regional governments may result in a solid waste treatment plant being built in or near a residential district. In many instances, such facilities are built in neighborhoods where the majority of the residents either are members of minority groups or belong to the poor or working classes (CERD Working Group, 2008). Residents in such neighborhoods understand that a waste treatment plant could produce unpleasant odors and discharges that could also cause or aggravate respiratory health problems (see Figure 6.6). If, as a result of the new treatment plant, some residents developed respiratory illnesses, it would be incorrect to assume that the residents' own health behaviors caused the illness. Rather, it is equally as likely that the policy decision to locate a waste treatment plant in a specific neighborhood created the conditions for respiratory health problems of the residents.

Psychological Environment and Health   Environment can also be defined as the quality of an individual's physical space as determined by psychosocial variables. For example, overcrowded neighborhoods or communities with high crime rates are psychosocial variables that influence the quality of life and overall well-being.

In Chapter 5, Risky Health Behaviors, we explained how a neighborhood's high crime rate can affect one's health even if an individual is not, him- or herself, a victim. For example, people who perceive that their neighborhood is less safe due to crime will be less likely to engage in outdoor exercise in their neighborhood. Limited access to exercise will have a direct impact on well-being.

High crime rates can also affect emotional health directly. For example, residents in high-crime neighborhoods may be more anxious about leaving or returning home at night and more apt to listen for threatening sounds from the street while at home. Increased anxiety about their safety, even when safely in their homes, may have long-term consequences for well-being, resulting in higher rates of stress and anxiety or greater emotional distress due to concerns for their or their family's safety. We briefly described the effects of stress on well-being in the previous section and explore the issue more fully in Chapter 7, Stress and Coping.

Workplace Environments as Determinants of Emotional Health   Overcrowding and crime are tangible environmental factors that affect psychological health. Yet psychological factors in the environment can also be subtle. One example is the effect of the workplace on individuals' physiological or emotional health. Kawano (2008) conducted a study among nurses in Japan to determine whether working in specific medical services units, such as the operating room, intensive care units, and surgical or internal medicine units, caused higher levels of emotional distress or physical fatigue among the nurses. The results showed that, in fact, nurses in each of the three special units experienced higher levels of emotional distress than their colleges in nonspeciality units. Nurses working in operating rooms reported higher levels of fatigue, while their colleagues in the intensive care units (units that care for patients with critical medical needs) reported higher levels of anxiety. Finally, nurses in surgical or internal medicine units reported higher levels of depression.

These are interesting results, to be sure. But why should one type of medical service cause more fatigue or emotional stress than another? The answer may be clear when we consider what is at stake. The work performed by nurses is vital to returning a patient to overall well-being. And in settings like the operating room or in critical care units, unintentional mistakes can seriously impair a patient's health or even contribute to death, a weighty responsibility for any caregiver. Perhaps, then, the higher levels of anxiety or depression reflect nurses' concern about the consequences of an error, the potential for loss of life, and the likely emotional cost borne by nurses if they were responsible for a mistake resulting in the death of a patient.

Summary

To review, the definition of health has migrated over the past several centuries. The discovery of microorganisms and their role in causing illnesses led modern scientists to focus on the physiological or biological causes of illness and to define health as the absence of disease, as represented in the biomedical view of health. New definitions caused a shift to a more holistic view of health exposed by earlier cultures from a biomedical perspective.

Health psychologists, medical sociologists, and public health experts currently argue for a broader definition of health, best conceptualized as overall well-being. The biopsychosocial model was one of the first models to expand the definition of health by adding social and psychological factors to approximate the concept of well-being. The wellness model contributed a spiritual dimension to well-being and redefined wellness as a person's own assessment, while the social ecological model adds the physical and psychological environmental perspectives as well as the role of health systems and health policy on individual health outcomes.

In sum, concepts of health and wellness have shifted over time, beginning with the concept of wellness as a mind–body connection, moving to a physiologically based determinant of health, only to return once again to a view of health as a holistic or ecological concept. Yet, some health psychologists contend that the definition of well-being is still incomplete. All four models focus on factors that can impair health. Some advocate for a need to examine the positive as well as the negative aspects of well-being in order to provide a balanced perspective of wellness.

SECTION II. POSITIVE PSYCHOLOGY

Positive psychology seems like an odd-sounding "pop" psychology name for a theory. As such, it may be tempting to dismiss the concept as trendy. But, as you will see, it is neither new nor trendy. Positive psychology builds on the wellness model of health and is, according to Seligman (2002), a more complete and balanced perspective of the human experience (Seligman, Steen, Park, & Peterson, 2000). Specifically, positive psychology involves a systematic study of the factors that enhance and maintain an individual's state of well-being.

Defining Positive Psychology

Martin Seligman and Mihaly Csikszentmihalyi (2000) pioneered the concept of positive psychology. In their view, much of psychology over the past 60 years focused on issues of mental illness, damage, or dysfunction (Seligman, 2002). According to some, Seligman suggests that psychology's focus on mental illness positioned it as a science of pathology and weakness rather than a science of health, well-being, and strength (Held, 2005).

Consequently, Seligman and Csikszentmihalyi (2000) proposed to correct what they characterized as an imbalance in the field by identifying and explaining the factors that lead to overall well-being, to thriving communities, and to satisfied individuals and families (Seligman & Csikszentmihalyi, 2000). Seligman, Park, and Peterson (2004) and, later, Peterson and Seligman (2004) proposed that six "virtues," along with 24 signature character strengths that represent positive traits, contribute to life satisfaction and a more meaningful life (Park, Peterson, & Seligman, 2004). The five character strengths most strongly associated with life satisfaction are presented in Table 6.1.

BOX 6.4   Seligman's Classification of Character Strengths

Seligman suggests that individuals who strive to achieve the six universal virtues, here meaning virtues found in many cultures, religions, and philosophical traditions, and the 24 strengths, will live a more fulfilled and happy life. The positive affects that result from a happier and more fulfilled life lead to a greater likelihood of positive, healthy outcomes and overall well-being.

In essence, for Seligman, positive psychology returns the field of psychology to its mission, which is to "make normal people's lives more fulfilling and productive" (Clay, 1977). His work seeks to understand the factors that contribute to such an outcome. Thus, positive psychology moves away from the biomedical concept of health, which focuses on identifying, isolating, and repairing problems, to a more holistic or ecological perspective regarding human potentials, motives, and capacities but one that explains the positive and negative contributions to overall well-being (Seligman & Csikszentmihalyi, 2000; Sheldon & King, 2001).

TABLE 6.1	Character Strengths Most Strongly Correlated with Life Satisfaction
Strength	**Description**
Hope	[Optimism, future-mindedness, future orientation]: Expecting the best in the future and working to achieve it; believing that a good future is something that can be brought about
Zest	[Vitality, enthusiasm, vigor, energy]: Approaching life with excitement and energy; not doing things halfway or halfheartedly, living life as an adventure; feeling alive and activated
Gratitude	Being aware of and thankful for the good things that happen; taking time to express thanks
Curiosity	[Interest, novelty-seeking, openness to experiences]: Taking an interest in all ongoing experiences; finding all subjects and topics fascinating; exploring and discovering
Love	Valuing close relationships with others, in particular those in which sharing and caring are reciprocated; being close to people

Source: Park, Peterson, & Seligman (2004).

Positive versus Negative Psychology?

For some, the term *positive psychology* implies that there is also a "negative psychology." Most likely, Seligman's characterization of some fields of "negative social science and psychology" created the dichotomy that fueled the debate (Held, 2005). Indeed, few would choose to be associated with a discipline within psychology, or any field for that matter, that is characterized as "negative." Although Seligman later rephrased his criticism of other disciplines of psychology in terms that are less stigmatizing, the comparison between positive psychology and other areas within the field continues to cause conflicts about the role and relative contribution of—even the need for—positive psychology as its own discipline.

It would be easy to become enmeshed in a war of words in the characterization of some areas of psychology as positive or negative. But to do so would miss the principal intent of positive psychology, which is to seek and discover an optimal balance between "positive" and "negative" thinking (Seligman, 2002) and to understand psychological phenomenon in its totality

(Carstensen & Charles, 2003). In other words, positive and negative influences contribute to the outcomes, states, emotions, and health of individuals. To understand an individual's end state we need to examine both.

Positive Psychology and Health

After more than 60 years of research using a "disease" model approach to health, Seligman contends that we really are no better at actually preventing negative psychological outcomes or damage than we were when the research began. Rather, he contends that the most effective way to prevent illnesses is to focus on the positive goals of building competencies and on the reinforcing factors that prevent negative events from occurring (Seligman & Csikszentmihalyi, 2000). In this way, positive psychology may be of particular importance to the field of health psychology because it may facilitate a transition from the biopsychosocial to the social ecological approach, which examines the multiple contributions, both positive and negative, to well-being.

So, what are the factors that help build healthier, satisfied, thriving individuals and communities? According to current studies, personal traits such as an individual's subjective sense of well-being, optimism, happiness, self-determination, and positive emotional states contribute to a positive psychology and well-being (Diener, 2000; Myers, 2000; Ryan & Deci, 2000; Salovey, Rothman, Detweiler, & Steward, 2000; Taylor, 1989; Taylor et al., 2000). Like all individuals, thriving and happy people exist in a social context that includes other people, places, and institutions. Therefore, positive psychological states are influenced also by social and environmental factors that include interpersonal relationships, social networks (Cohen, 2004; Ray, 2004; Taylor & Turner, 2001), religion and religious faith (Myers, 2000), and external factors, including socioeconomic status (Coburn, 2004; Wilkinson, 1996).

How do we know that positive psychological states also contribute to our well-being? Consider for a moment the research on *optimism*, here meaning the view that situations and events will work out for the best, however *best* is defined. Studies on the effect of optimism among cancer patients, for example, have found an association between optimism and better psychological and social adjustment to their illness (Lechner et al., 2006). Researchers have also found lower levels of depression or anxiety about the illness itself when patients report high levels of optimism (Bjorck, Hopp, & Jones, 1999; Schnoll, Knowles, & Harlow, 2002). Some cancer patients with an optimistic perspective also believe that they can influence their situation and thereby achieve a better outcome (Folkman & Greer, 2002). If optimism has a direct effect on emotional health, and if positive emotional health can directly influence our physiological states, then we may be correct in concluding that positive psychological perspectives enhance health.

Work by Taylor and colleagues (2000) also demonstrates the positive effects of optimism on indirect health factors that affect well-being. For example, these researchers' study found that optimistic, self-confident people have more social support, here meaning assistance and help from friends, family, or work associates. As we will see in Chapter 7, Stress and Coping, social networks buffer individuals from the effects of negative or stressful situations and enhance their ability to cope with the stressors. Because, as noted earlier, stress can have detrimental physical and emotional effects, factors that minimize stress will enhance health outcomes.

Other studies in the field of behavioral medicine also demonstrate the health benefits obtained from a positive, optimistic state. Ironson and Hayward (2008) and Ironson, Stuetzle, and Fletcher (2006) suggest that optimism, together with active coping strategies and spirituality, predict a slower progression of HIV disease in HIV-positive individuals. A slower progression of HIV may delay the onset of symptoms associated with the illness as well as slow the debilitating effects of the disease itself.

The main point of positive psychology is that we understand only part of our human nature if we focus exclusively on pathology, disorder, or dysfunction. To understand the full human experience and how to make people's lives more fulfilling and satisfying, we need to study the "normal," positive, and productive state of human functioning as well as the disordered or damaged states. As we will see in the following section, for followers of traditional and complementary alternative medicine an understanding of the positive or normal state is also integral to their health beliefs and practices.

Critiques of Positive Psychology

In principle, positive psychology aims to present a more balanced view of the factors that affect outcomes. There are, however, criticisms of the concept. Two issues in particular, the "happiness" approach and the universality of the concept, appear to be the most frequently cited limitations of the positive psychology movement.

HAPPINESS PSYCHOLOGY   Remembering the caution of not becoming embroiled in a war of words, some researchers argue that the principal focus of positive psychology is to study what makes people happy. When stated in this fashion, positive psychology seems insubstantial. However, included in studies on the concept of "happiness" would be research to understand gratitude, forgiveness, awe, inspiration, hope, curiosity, and laughter (Gable & Haidt, 2005). The work of the Truth and Reconciliation Commission in South Africa is one recent example of an application of the positive psychology concept (see Box 6.5).

Widely acclaimed as one of the factors that aided South Africa's peaceful transition and positive development in the aftermath of apartheid, the Truth and Reconciliation Commission's approach to conflict resolution and healing has been praised and emulated around the world (Philpott, 2009). More important, it was integral to forging a new relationship among ethnic groups that would allow the citizens of South Africa to forgive the past and inspire them to work toward building a stronger and more unified country.

If positive psychology is defined simply as what makes people happy, it would seem to have limited application to the work in health psychology. The broader implications of "happiness," as seen through the research and work on forgiveness and emotional and mental health, however, would support the role of this work and the field as part of our understanding of health-enhancing behaviors.

UNIVERSALITY OF POSITIVE PSYCHOLOGY   A more compelling criticism of the field is that the new discipline may not be applicable to some people or cultures in spite of the claims of the universality of positive psychology (Aspinwall & Staudinger, 2003). As Diener and Suh (2000) note, in North American cultures there is a strong psychological pressure to be happy. In fact, Diener and Suh characterize it as an inviolable individual right, particularly in cultures with strong beliefs in individualism and self-determination. Critics argue that if there is no universal belief in the right of individual happiness then positive psychology may not be universal.

BOX 6.5 The South African Truth and Reconciliation Commission: Forgiveness in Post-Apartheid South Africa

The full scope of the atrocities committed under the apartheid government in South Africa may never be known. ***Apartheid***, a social and political policy of racial segregation enforced by the government of South Africa, was finally dismantled in 1992, but not before thousands of South Africans were killed or severely tortured to protect the apartheid system.

Following decades of forced segregation, forced removals from homes and communities, and restrictions on employment and even on education, South Africa's black, colored, and Indian citizens finally won the opportunity to live without the imposition of socially unjust rules imposed under apartheid. As they embarked on the job of forming a new, democratic government, the country faced the daunting task of healing a nation riddled for decades with the racial animus caused by the apartheid system. Central to that task was finding a way to help foster forgiveness between the races.

FIGURE 6.7 Archbishop Desmond Tutu. Chair of South Africa's Truth and Reconciliation Commission, Archbishop Tutu helped guide South Africans through a post-apartheid healing process.

South Africa's Truth and Reconciliation Commission was charged with the responsibility of discovering the truth about the thousands of atrocities committed during apartheid while simultaneously moving the country forward in peace. Archbishop Desmond Tutu, the first black Anglican archbishop in South Africa, headed the commission (see Figure 6.7). With his leadership, the commission pioneered a model by which perpetrators of violence and torture could face their victims. By honestly confessing their crimes, the guilty could seek forgiveness from their victims, while family members of victims could learn the truth about the brutal torture or murder of their loved ones, again from the confessions of the perpetrators of the acts. The act of public confession and contrition was seen as one way to begin the healing process that could allow South Africa's diverse racial groups to survive and to thrive as a nation (Gobodo-Madikizela, 2002, 2003). It was one way to begin to repair the emotional and psychological damage experienced by the nation.

The applicability of positive psychology is also challenged when concepts that are interpreted as positive or that elicit positive connotations in one culture have both negative and positive meanings in another. Take, for example, the concept of "sympathy." In Western cultures, sympathy is a positive emotion suggesting the ability to understand another's position. It is one of several strengths that lead to the six virtues identified by Seligman. Yet, in Chinese culture, sympathy also has a distinctly negative connotation, meaning to commiserate with or to have sympathy with someone's misfortune (Sundararajan, 2005). Thus, a positive concept in one culture can be linked to negative concepts in another. The point here is that the notion that positive characteristics are universally seen as positive in all cultures can be easily challenged by examining the understood meaning of words across cultures.

What is more, Confucianism, an Eastern philosophy that emphasizes human morality and moral development of the individual, proposes that negative emotions play an important role in the development of virtue, the underpinnings of happiness and well-being, according to Seligman (Sundararajan, 2005). In other words, negative emotions are critical for the full development of the individual. In defense, positive psychology does not deny the existence of negative emotions. But it appears that it fails to consider negative emotional development as integral to positive emotions and outcomes.

We close this section with one additional observation. Recently, researchers have re-examined the role of *pessimism* as an adaptive, and hence positive, approach to selected issues or problems. In fact, some contend that pessimism may work to promote problem solving (Aspinwall & Staudinger, 2003). They note specifically that *defensive pessimism*, a coping strategy that keeps disappointments and expectations in check (Norem, 2001), may be adaptive when needed to respond to negative outcomes.

Defensive pessimism may be a particularly advantageous emotion for disenfranchised groups in societies. For such groups, defensive pessimism may help, albeit nominally, to cope with frequent encounters of disappointments and rejections caused, in part, by that group's status in society. For example, minority groups that experience discrimination based on their ethnicity may employ defensive pessimism when involved in social or work settings in the majority culture to minimize the adverse effects of exclusion or other forms of rejection. Thus, while Seligman believes that pessimism is maladaptive (Held, 2005), for some it may be an effective method of coping with a myriad of negative social environmental issues that affect emotional well-being.

In sum, does positive psychology contribute to our understanding of emotional health? It would seem so, in spite of its limitations. No single model or theory will contain all the elements needed to explain behaviors or outcomes. As we indicated in Chapter 4, Theories and Models of Health Behavior Change, models often borrow concepts to build stronger models. Positive psychology could serve as an important additional concept to an existing theory, reminding us that, to understand the full spectrum of human behavior, we need to identify all determinants that contribute to well-being.

SECTION III. TRADITIONAL MEDICINES

Models of health developed by modern societies have identified biology, sociology, psychology, emotion, environments, and health systems and policy as integral to individual well-being. These same factors have also been identified and used in traditional medicines to enhance health outcomes.

Traditional medicine is a term that refers to medical practices, knowledge, and beliefs in cultures whose practices predate those of Western medicine. It includes the use of plant-, animal-, and mineral-based medicines, as well as spiritual techniques to administer to an individual's health needs (WHO, 2003).

Most traditional medicines share four core principles: a belief in a connection among the individual, Earth, and a life or energy force; a belief that a person's state of health reflects a balance or harmony of three connected elements—the individual, Earth, and the energy force; a belief that treatment for a health problem involves the whole individual—physical, emotional or mental, and spiritual; and a belief in the use of herbal remedies or other practices such as ritual chants, acupuncture, bone setting, or smudging, that is, using smoke from burning herbs to cleanse negative energies around a person (Broome & Broome, 2007; Lam, 2001).

In some countries, such as China, Korea, Ghana, and South Africa, traditional and Western medicine approaches are not only widely available, they are often used together to address individual health needs. For example, the South African government integrated the *sangomas*, indigenous healers used by many rural South Africans, into the nation's health care system (Africa First, 2008; IOL, 2004; WHO, 2003). Now South Africans can choose to receive care from either a Western-trained medical doctor or a *sangoma* and have the cost of care paid for or supplemented by the nation's health care system.

It is important to state that the integration of traditional and modern health approaches reflects what individuals have done independently. Remember Angelita from our opening story? She consulted a modern health professional but also accepted the assistance of a *curandero,* one type of traditional healer. One reason people use both health approaches is that they believe that each addresses different health needs. Thus, they seek to maximize the advantages and minimize the disadvantages of each approach. Interestingly, some health care providers also reported consulting both Western medicine and traditional healers for their own health care needs (Bucko & Cloud, 2008; Hon et al., 2005; Lam, 2001; Wong et al., 2006).

Contributions of Traditional Medicine

Would it surprise you to learn that approximately 25% of all modern medicines are made from plants used first by traditional healers (WHO, 2003). This little-known fact is actually taught to children, although they may not be aware of the message at the time. For example, in the Walt Disney movie *Pocahontas,* Pocahontas, the daughter of the chief of the Powhatan nation, gives John Smith, an English settler, ground bark from a willow tree to ease his pain from a gunshot wound. The bark contains **salicylic acid**, an ingredient that controls pain and reduces fever (University of Arkansas, 2007). Pharmaceutical companies, the manufacturers of modern medicines, have developed a chemical equivalent of ground willow bark to relieve similar aches and pain. We call it **aspirin**. Scientists learned to chemically reproduce the same ingredients found in the willow tree used by Native Americans and to mass produce it for general use.

Today, scientists continue to copy and reproduce for mass distribution the medicinal elements found in plants. Take, for example, the plant **hoodia gordonii** (see Figure 6.8). "Hoodia," as it is known in the United States, is a natural plant found in southern Africa used for centuries by the **Sans** people, a nomadic group living in the Kalahari desert of southern Africa. The Sans use hoodia gordonii to suppress appetite. You may wonder why a nomadic group would want to suppress their appetites. Simply put, the Sans hunt for their food. A hunt for a wildebeest or eland large enough for the needs of the tribe may take several days and may require them to be mobile. Hoodia gordonii helps the Sans to sustain their energy while hunting and to minimize hunger so they do not become distracted or too weak to hunt. Like the willow bark, recently the agents found in hoodia gordonii have been chemically reproduced by U.S. pharmaceutical

FIGURE 6.8   Hoodia Gordonii. A natural appetite suppressant agent, hoodia gordonii has been used by the Sans of South Africa for centuries and most recently by dieters in the United States.

companies and are now being sold in the United States as "P57," a diet supplement for people who want to loose weight.

Salicylic acid and hoodia gordonii are just two examples, past and recent, of contributions to modern medicine from traditional medical practices. In the following sections, we explore Chinese traditional medicine (CTM); *curanderismo,* the Mexican folk-healing practice introduced in the opening story; and Native American healing practices, three of the most widely recognized examples of traditional medicines in other cultures. We review them briefly to explore the similarities and differences with modern medicine practices. Keep in mind, however, that the traditional practices included are a small sample of the total number of such practices, even today.

Chinese Traditional Medicine (CTM)

Chinese traditional medicine (CTM), sometimes referred to as *traditional Chinese medicine (TCM)*, is similar to other folk medicines because it is rooted in the philosophy and the belief structure of its culture. As explained in Box 6.6, CTM consists of three main structures that, together with Chinese philosophy and nature, define an individual's well-being: yin and yang, the five elements, and Qi (ch'i).

According to Chinese philosophers, the yin–yang doctrine explains that all things function in relation to two forces, elements, or principles (Quah, 2003). These forces are in a constant state of dynamic balance; continually interacting to maintain harmony. (Harmony is a core concept in Chinese life, Quah, 2003). Thus, yin and yang are complementary forces. Each is needed to complete the other and to achieve and maintain harmony.

The second major structure in CTM is the *five elements*: metal, wood, water, fire, and earth. Each of the five elements is paired with a body organ and a season of the year, demonstrating the close connection between humans and nature. According to this philosophy, a person's health is dependent, in part, on his or her interactions with the physical environment.

The last structure, Qi, is a concept taken from Taoist philosophers. Qi is best understood as a substantial energy force that flows within the body parallel to or as part of the circulation of the blood (Quah, 2003).

TREATING ILLNESSES USING CTM   To individuals unfamiliar with Chinese medicine, the philosophy of three forces that work together to influence health may be clear in concept but not in practice. Consider this: Medical providers trained in CTM are taught to examine both the physiological as well as the psychological contributors to health. Thus, instead of searching only for a proximal physical cause of an illness, health providers will explore the relationship among the

BOX 6.6   Traditional Medicines: An Overview

Chinese Traditional Medicine (CTM)

Yin and yang, the five elements, and Qi are the three principal structures of CTM. *Yin* is associated with passive life-sustaining, conserving energies or latent energies that need to be actualized (Kapke, 2004; Quah, 2003). Yin energies are often associated with darkness and cold (passive, conserving energies) and with water and females (sustaining forces). With respect to the body, yin is associated with specific body organs: the heart, liver, pancreas, kidneys, and lungs. Thus, the yin organs are vital to sustaining life.

In comparison, *yang* energy forces are described as strong forces that cause change. They are the dynamic forces that initiate action. The yang forces are usually characterized as male forces, corresponding to the notion of males as active, assertive, or aggressive (Kapke, 2004). Thus, they are associated with light, fire, heat—all active and potentially destructive forces. In the body, yang is associated with the gall bladder, small intestines, large intestines, and the bladder—organs that transmit, transform, and eliminate nonessential items from the body (Kapke, 2004). According to CTM, our health is optimal when yin and yang forces are in perfect balance. When one or the other is out of balance, however, diseases or other ailments may be present. For example, when yin is out of balance for females, a number of symptoms could appear, including irregular menstrual cycles, irritability, early menopause, or other related problems (D'Alberto, 2006).

The five elements—metal, wood, water, fire, and earth—demonstrate the relationship between human beings and nature. Specifically, these structures emphasize the role of harmony between humans and nature and their effect on well-being. Each element has both yin and yang components. For example, water evidences yin properties when it is cool and nourishing. But water also demonstrates yang energy force when it is destructive. Consider this: In a flood, objects in the path of the rushing water can be dislodged, moved, or destroyed by the pressure exerted by the water (Kapke, 2004). Our interactions with the elements, according to CTM, will affect the balance of yin and yang in our bodies. For example, absorbing too much of the sun's rays will burn yin, the cold energy force, resulting in an imbalance and discomfort.

Finally, *Qi* is an energy source that flows throughout the body, similar to the body's circulatory system. The movement of Qi within the body is influenced by seasons and foods that help to facilitate or to impede its flow.

Curanderismo

Curanderos, or the traditional healers for this form of folk medicine, are believed to have special healing powers. It is a gift (*el don*), not something for which an individual receives formal training, as in Western medicine. Yet, most *curanderos* undergo a period of apprenticeship to learn to use their gift to heal others.

Core to *curanderismo* is spirituality and maintaining harmony and balance with nature (Tafur, Crowe, & Torres, 2009). The central role of spirituality is evident in some of the more common illnesses addressed by the healers. These include *espanto,* an extreme fright believed to be caused by a supernatural force, and *susto,* a fright due to a traumatic experience (Lopez, 2005). Both illnesses are described as "soul loss" in *curanderismo* and require spiritual cures. Researchers note that *espanto* and *susto* often lead to emotional and psychological health problems, including depression, apathy, anorexia, and insomnia (Chesney et al., 2005, 1980). The spiritual causes attributed to what modern medicine considers mental health issues illustrates one contrast between traditional and modern views of health.

One similarity between *curanderismo* and modern medicine, however, is the presence of specialized practices within *curanderismo*. Like modern medical practitioners, *curanderos* may specialize in the types of illnesses they address. For example, herbalists (*yerberos*) focus on the treatment of physical health problems using natural herbs and homeopathic medicines. Thus, stomachaches may be treated with orange leaf tea (*citrus aurantium*), earaches with garlic (*allium sativum*), or sunburns with aloe vera. Illnesses of a spiritual or supernatural origin, however, such as *susto* or *mal de ojo,* the evil eye, would be treated by an *espiritista* who would perform a *limpia* or spiritual cleansing.

Native American Healing Practices

Native American healing traditions were crucial to the survival of the first wave of colonizers to what is now the United States. In spite of this well-known history, it has taken several decades for researchers to document the Native American practices and knowledge of botany to heal both body and mind (Portman & Garrett, 2006).

There are over 500 Native American tribal nations. Thus it is not possible to describe each nation's healing practices in detail. However, there are several core principles that apply to many Native American beliefs and practices. First, there are four constructs that are central to the healing traditions: spirituality, community, environment, and self. The core concepts of spirituality, environment, and life force are similar thematically to *curanderismo* and CTM.

Unique to the Native American practices, however, is a belief in a "circle of life" and in the concept of medicine. The circle of life symbolizes power, peace, and unity (Portman & Garrett, 2006). Each individual holds responsibility for helping to contribute to the circle by living harmoniously with all living elements that are also part of the circle.

With respect to medicines, Native American traditions contend that each person, place, and thing holds medicine within itself. To be certain, Native Americans believe in the healing powers of plants and herbs (or external agents) for holistic health needs. But consider this: Native American health beliefs hold that an event that occurred 10 years ago that made someone laugh and that still makes that person chuckle today when recalling the incident is a form of medicine (Portman & Garrett, 2006). The memory the person holds returns him or her to a state of well-being, if only for a moment. It is a form of temporary medicine.

affected body parts, related areas, emotional states, and environmental factors to discover the source of the disharmony.

Examining relationships among body, emotions, and nature takes time. A complete exploration of the illness and its related causes may require multiple visits to a provider as the CTM provider delves into the patient's emotional health, relationships with others in his or her family, diet, and other aspects of his or her life that may not appear to be the source of the problem but may be related to the disturbance. In this way, the CTM healing process is similar to Angelita's experience with the *curandero* in the opening story.

A principal complaint of individuals who choose the CTM approach for health care is that the process takes longer than when using Western medical methods (Lam, 2001). Still, many prefer CTM for specific ills. Consider this: In a series of focus groups conducted among 29 Chinese residents of Hong Kong, Lam (2001) revealed that many believed that Western medicine is useful if seeking a quick recovery; however, they preferred CTM care when a quick Western medical treatment proved ineffective in curing the disease.

Individuals with access to both forms of medicines believe that there are additional strengths and weaknesses associated with both practices. Western medicine, in addition to being quicker, helps to quickly control symptoms. When confronting contagious illnesses, Western medicine may be preferred for its ability not only to control the symptoms quickly but also to contain the spread of the disease. The disadvantages of Western medicine, according to the Chinese focus group participants in Lam's study, are its inability to completely cure the illness and the strong and unpleasant-tasting side effects of some of the medication.

Among users of both CTM and Western medicine, the advantages of CTM include a more effective cure for illnesses, fewer side effects, and a more effective treatment for chronic illnesses. In essence, users of CTM believe it is a better long-term cure and prefer it as a treatment for the whole person (Hon et al., 2005; Wong et al., 2006). Finally, the fact that many users of CTM indicate that family and friends recommend CTM suggest that family tradition, culture, and sociological factors also influence the choice of medical approaches.

In essence, that there are Chinese respondents who believe that Western medicine is the preferred approach when seeking a quick fix for a medical ailment also suggests a preference for traditional medicines to treat longer-term, chronic illnesses. Consistent with Chinese philosophy, illness represents more than just a physical disharmony. The cure, therefore, must address all elements, including the energy flow and the individual's interaction with the elements.

Curanderismo

The term *curanderismo* comes from the Spanish word *curar,* meaning to heal (Tafur, Crowe, & Torres, 2009). Like Chinese traditional medicine, *curanderismo* originated from cultural beliefs. In this case, the most immediate culture of origin is Mexican. However, anthropologists suggest that *curanderismo* has been influenced by the health beliefs and practices of the Greeks, the Moors (Arabs of northern Africa), the Aztec and Mayan empires (Krassner, 1986), and sub-Saharan African medical practices (Luna, 2003; Morales, 1998), as well as a number of European and Native American cultures (Trotter, 2001). Today, *curanderismo* is an umbrella term that refers to many types of treatments and rituals that, melded together over several centuries, represent a form of folk healing commonly practiced in Mexico (Lopez, 2005). It is, therefore, an evolving form of medicine, continually expanding and incorporating techniques from

TABLE 6.2	Specialties in *Curanderismo*
Specialty	**Function**
Yerberos (herbalists)	Botanical remedies Homeopathic medicines Religious amulets
Partenas (midwives)	Childbirth
Sobadores (masseuses)	Massages General physical imbalances Sprains Bone setting
Espiritistas (spiritualists)	Faith healers Interpersonal relationships Spiritual health Séance

Source: Lopez (2005).

other folk medicines including ***parapsychology***—here meaning psychic experiences including telepathy, clairvoyance, and psychic healing.

Central to the practice of *curanderismo* is the belief that to maintain a healthy body an individual must achieve a balance among biological needs, social-interpersonal expectations, physical and spiritual harmony, and individual and cultural-familial attachments (Vargas & Koss-Chioino, 1992). It is no surprise, therefore, that the *curandero* in the opening story looked to familial attachments and spiritual unrest as possible causes for Angelita's emotional health problems. In sum, good health, as defined by this practice, is more than freedom from illness.

Note also that, in the opening story, the *curandero* used herbs and teas as part of the healing process. Like modern health providers, many healers also have specialties (Torres & Sawyer, 2005). For example, *yerberos* (or *yerberas,* for women) are herbalists who specialize in the use of herbs, homeopathic medicines, and religious amulets, here meaning objects or jewelry intended as protection against evil (Lopez, 2005). Given that the *curandero* in the opening story used herbs as medicinal agents, he may specialize in botanical cures (see Table 6.2).

It is important to note, however, that unlike CTM spirituality plays a central role in the concept of health and healing in *curanderismo*. This is seen most clearly in the common types of illnesses addressed through this folk medicine. For example, there are a number of illnesses that are believed to be supernatural or spiritual in origin (Trotter, 2001). One such illness is *espanto,* often described as a "magical fright" because the cause of the frightened response is linked to supernatural factors. It is also linked with a loss of one's soul and as such is an ailment that is treated with spiritual cures (see Table 6.3).

TABLE 6.3	Commonly Diagnosed Illnesses in *Curanderismo*		
Illness	**Meaning**	**Description**	**Illnesses**
Mal aires (Mal de aire)	Bad air	Cold or hot drafts or other environmental disturbances	Headaches, colds, tuberculosis, digestive disorders, rashes
Mal de ojo	Evil eye	Supernatural or mental illness	Headaches, fever, rashes, death
Envidia	Intense jealousy	Precursor of *mal de ojo*, intense jealousy, or envy	Insomnia, fever, vomiting, restlessness
Susto	Soul loss	Serious fright due to traumatic event, more common in childhood	Depression, introversion, apathy, death
Espanto	Soul loss	Extreme fright due to supernatural causes	Depression, introversion, anorexia, insomnia, hallucinations

Sources: Abril (1977); Alegria, Guerra, Martinez, & Meyer (1977); Lopez (2005).

FIGURE 6.9   Mexican *Curandero.* Shown is a demonstration of acupuncture by a Mexican *curandero* at the University of New Mexico.

Source: Johnson (2006).

In sum, *curanderismo* is a form of traditional medicine that evolved from different cultures and is still evolving today. Spirituality and spiritual forces are central to its healing practices, as is a reliance on botany to address physiological and psychological issues of well-being (see Figure 6.9).

Native American Health Practices

We must state first that there are over 500 different Native American tribal nations. Consequently, we do not imply in our heading that there is a uniform practice with respect to healing and traditional medicines for all Native Americans. Rather, as indicated at the beginning of the section on traditional medicines, here we explore the common themes among the traditional practices of the tribal nations and compare them to *curanderismo* and CTM, described previously.

Native American healing traditions have been described as a practice that involves traditional medicine practitioners, such as medicine men or women, or shamans, and that is intended to restore a person to a healthy state (Chee, 1991). The healing process described, however, is a slow process, similar to the slow cures identified in CTM and *curanderismo*.

General principles that are common to all Native American practices are the belief in a higher power called, among other names, the Creator, the Great Spirit, or Great One; a belief in the interconnectedness of the mind, the body, and the spirit; and the belief that wellness characterizes the state of harmony among the mind, body, spirit, and natural environment (Garrett, 1998; Portman & Garrett, 2006). The importance of spirituality in Native American health beliefs and the unity of mind, body, and spirit are similar to the views expressed in *curanderismo* and come closest to the ecological model.

Not surprisingly, then, central to all Native American healing practices also are four constructs: spirituality (including the creator, mother earth), community (for example, family or tribe), the environment (such as nature, the land) and self (including inner passions, values, and thoughts). It is the balance among the individual, the ecological, and the spiritual that defines, for many Native Americans, "good medicine" (Portman & Garrett, 2006).

Similar to adherents of other traditional health practices, Native Americans believe that a number of forces can cause ill health. Social discord, misuse of traditional practices, and spiritual unrest are but a few of the elements that can disrupt a balance and consequently affect an individual's overall well-being.

There are, however, two interesting differences in the healing practices used in this form of traditional medicine. First is the concept of medicine. While medicinal agents can and do include herbs, teas, or pastes (poultices)—recall the example of Pocahontas earlier in the chapter— Native Americans believe that medicine exists within each individual as well. For example, an experience that caused someone to smile and that continues to evoke the same response years later is considered medicine (Portman & Garrett, 2006). Medicine can also be the peacefulness of a moment. In essence, while external agents are used for their medicinal properties (see Chapter 1, An Interdisciplinary View of Health), experiences, places, and even individuals themselves have the ability to help restore the balance between a person, the mind, the spirit, and nature.

In summary, traditional medicines have existed for centuries. They continue to supply Western medicine with herbal and plant-based medicines, the foundation for many modern medicines used today. They have retained their holistic and for some ecological approach to health, focusing on the well-being of the individual, which includes physical, emotional, social, and spiritual health and harmony with one's environment. They are more consistent with an ecological model of health.

Over time, however, Western medicine's scientific-based approach to health has been refined. It retains the important contributions made by science. Now, Western medicine is broadening its approach to incorporate psychological and emotional health issues into the concept of "health" (see Table 6.4).

Having examined "old" and "new" approaches to health, it may seem that there is nothing more to add. However, the research on stress and coping has established clear links between emotional and physical health and also demonstrates the role of social and psychological environmental factor on overall well-being. We continue the exploration of emotional health in Chapter 7, Stress and Coping.

TABLE 6.4	Comparison of Western versus Native American Medicine	
Western Medicine	**Native American Medicine**	
1. Focus is on pathology and curing disease.	1. Focus is on health and healing the person and community.	
2. Reductionistic: Diseases are biological, and treatment should produce measureable outcomes.	2. Complex: Diseases do not have a simple explanation, and outcomes are not always measurable.	
3. Adversarial medicine: "How can I destroy the disease?"	3. Teological medicine: "What can the disease teach the patient? Is there a message or story in the disease?"	
4. Investigates disease with a "divide and conquer" strategy, looking for microscopic cause.	4. Looks at the "big picture," the cause and effects of diseases in the physical, emotional, environmental, social, and spiritual realms.	
5. Intellect is primary. Medical practice is based on scientific theory.	5. Intuition is primary. Healing is based on spiritual truths learned from nature, elders, and spiritual vision.	
6. Physician is authority who fosters dependence on medication, technology, and so on.	6. Healer is health counselor and advisor who empowers patients with confidence, and awareness of tools to help them take charge of their own health.	
7. Health history focuses on patient and family: "Did your mother have cancer?"	7. Health histories include the environment: "Are the salmon in our rivers ill?"	
8. Intervention should result in rapid cure or management.	8. Intervention should result in rapid cure or management.	

Source: Cohen (2003).

Important Terms

Stress and Coping

Chapter Objectives

After reading this chapter you will be able to:

1. Define *stress* as a stimulus and as a response.
2. Explain the cognitive appraisal process of stressful stimuli.
3. Explain the body's physiological response to stress.
4. Describe the relationship between stress and illness.

5. Identify and describe two cognitive coping strategies.
6. Identify and describe three behavioral coping strategies.
7. Explain the role of positive appraisal in stress and coping.
8. Explain the health psychologist's role in addressing stress and coping.

OPENING STORY: SARAH

Lucinda expected the day would come when her parents would move her grandmother, Sarah, to a nursing home. She just did not expect it to be so soon.

When Sarah was diagnosed with Alzheimer's, Lucinda and her parents knew instantly what to do, or so they thought. They decided that Sarah would live with them. Lucinda remembers her parent's excitement as they rearranged the guest bedroom and sitting room to accommodate her grandmother. But in less than one month the new arrangement led to conflicts and bickering; not with Sarah, but rather between Lucinda's parents.

Susan, Lucinda's mother and Sarah's only child, believed it was the family's responsibility to care for her mother. But Michael, Lucinda's father, argued that Sarah's presence was causing considerable stress on everyone. In truth, Michael was right. The family spent nights listening to Sarah move about the house. Memories of a two-day search for Sarah, who unexpectedly left the house one night while everyone else was sleeping, were still fresh in their minds. For months after the incident, Susan was unable to sleep at night, rising often to check on Sarah.

To add to the challenges, everyone's schedule changed to accommodate Sarah's needs. Lucinda quit her high school cheerleading squad and her job as editor of the school newspaper to care for Sarah after school while her parents worked. Susan stopped accepting consultant jobs after work to be home in the evenings. And Michael reduced his work-related travel to help with some of the caregiving responsibilities. Gone also were the Friday dinner-and-a-movie family nights. Sarah became easily agitated in restaurants and could not sit through an entire movie. As for family vacations, they, too, were a thing of the past.

The changes unexpectedly put a strain on everyone, increasing the amount of tension and bickering over seemingly inconsequential things. After six months of what seemed like endless arguing, Lucinda and her parents sought family counseling. Sarah's presence at the meeting helped the therapist understand the problem quite quickly. It was also easy to see that the solution to the family's problems lay in finding an acceptable arrangement for Sarah's care needs.

After much debate, Lucinda's parents decided to put Sarah in a nursing home that specialized in the needs of Alzheimer's patients. Lucinda and Michael seemed instantly relieved. They returned to their regular schedules and told the therapist that their lives were almost normal again. But new tensions developed in their interactions with Susan. Susan felt guilty about "abandoning" her mother. She visited Sarah in the nursing home daily, even though the visits exhausted her. They were even more difficult when Sarah was having a bad day or struggling to remember Susan's name. For Susan, putting Sarah in a nursing home increased rather than decreased her stress. ■

It may seem that our focus on Susan, Lucinda, and Michael in the opening story is somewhat misplaced. After all, Sarah seems to be the one with the health-related problem.

In truth, however, everyone in the story could be at risk for new health problems after Sarah's arrival. Research suggests that caregivers often experience emotional, mental, and even physical health problems when tending to the needs of persons with terminal or chronic illnesses (Stephens, Norris, Ritchie, & Grotz, 1988; Vitaliano, Zhang, & Scanlon, 2003). Caregivers may neglect their own existing health problems and overlook new or developing issues created by the emotional and psychological demands of their new role (see Figure 7.1; Knussen et al., 2005).

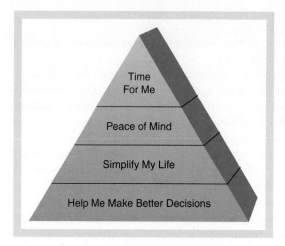

Time
For Me

Peace of Mind

Simplify My Life

Help Me Make Better Decisions

FIGURE 7.1   Caregiver Needs Pyramid. Caregivers may be so preoccupied with their responsibilities that they may ignore the need to tend to their own health.

Source: Wiet (2009).

The opening story with Susan and her family illustrates the problem. The family experienced a number of new challenges and emotional conflicts for a full six months before seeking help.

Because Susan and Michael's problems began when Sarah moved in, it would be reasonable to assume that the conflicts and arguments would subside if not cease altogether when Sarah was relocated to a nursing home. But, as we saw, such was not the case. Again, research offers an explanation for this outcome. Studies suggest that the decision to find alternative health care and living arrangements for a family member who needs special services can exacerbate existing tensions or cause new problems (Gaugler, Mittleman, Hepburn, & Newcomer, 2009). Disagreements about and lack of support for the decision can create guilt, depression, and anxiety in caregivers (Parks & Pilisuk, 1991). For men, the absence of socioemotional support when choosing a nursing facility for family members can cause new tensions and stress. Women, however, tend to cite family conflicts over the decision, rather than the absence of socioemotional support, as the principal reason for increased stress in such situations (Gaugler, Zarit, & Perlin, 1999). Thus, studies suggest that even though Michael and Lucinda supported the decision to place Sarah in a nursing home, Susan's ambivalence and guilt about the decision sparked conflicts with other family members that prolonged stress. If unresolved, the ongoing stress could result in psychophysiological illnesses such as chronic headaches, ulcers, or respiratory infections (Cohen & Williamson, 1991; Kiecolt-Glaser & Glaser, 1995).

The relationship between stress and illness, as shown in the opening story, demonstrates the need for a holistic approach to health. In this example, we find that social environmental stressors also contribute to psychological and physical health problems, making environmental stressors another important determinant of health status.

We begin this chapter by defining *stress* in Section I. In this section we briefly review the seminal works by Walter Cannon (1929) and Hans Selye (1946, 1950) that established a physiological basis for stress. To explain Cannon's and Selye's models of stress we also review the body's physiological response to stressful stimuli, examining the components of the nervous system and the hormones responsible for activating the system when detecting a stressful stimulus. We conclude Section I with an overview of Lazarus and Folkman's transactional model. The transactional model provides another theoretical explanation of stress, examining stress as both a physiological and a psychological process.

In Section II, we explore causes of stress. We pay particular attention to the role of biological determinants, specifically illnesses, social environmental determinants, and psychosocial factors that contribute to stress. We conclude with a discussion of mechanisms and strategies used to cope with stress in Section III. By the end of this chapter you will be able to define stress as a stimulus, a response, and an interaction of both, to explain the body's cognitive, psychological, and physiological response to stressful stimuli, and to explain the role health psychologists can play in assisting individuals in managing daily stressors.

SECTION I. DEFINING STRESS

Undoubtedly you have heard many people talk about a stressful event: a major exam, an important job interview, or specific interpersonal relationship problems with family or friends. The frequent use of the term *stress* suggests that we believe we understand the concept. But do we? We may be very familiar with stressful experiences, but do we understand what causes us to perceive situations as stressful, or do we recognize our natural or acquired strategies for addressing stress?

In the opening story, stress was portrayed as a stimulus, as a response, and as the interaction of both stimulus and response. The ***stressful stimulus***, an event external to the human body that provokes a response, is Sarah. She provokes a response from the family regardless of whether she lives in Susan and Michael's house or in a nursing home. The ***stressful response***, that is, a physical or emotional reaction by an individual to the external stimulus, is the family conflict, discord, guilt, and depression experienced variably by each member of the family.

Finally, the interaction between the stressor and the response, sometimes characterized as the "interplay and feedback" (Lazarus & Folkman, 1984), is portrayed by the interaction of the stressful stimulus, Sarah, with other family members. Consider this: Susan's visits with her mother appear to provoke a stressful response even though Sarah has been relocated to a nursing home. The stress does not dissipate with Sarah's relocation. Rather, Susan's stress stemming from her time with her mother appears to provoke additional conflicts with Michael and Lucinda.

Thus, a thorough study of stress must include the stimulus that prompts the response as well as the response, in order to identify an effective strategy to minimize or abate stress. Consistent with such an approach, we begin the chapter by exploring stressful stimuli and our physiological as well as cognitive and emotional responses to stressful events.

Three Theories of Stress

Three theories, Walter Cannon's "fight-or-flight" theory Hanz Selye's general adaptation syndrome (GAS), and Richard Lazarus and Susan Folkman's transactional model, are considered the principal theories that explain the relationship between stress and illness. Cannon's and Selye's theories focus on the body's physiological response to stressful stimuli while Lazarus and Folkman seek to explain the cognitive appraisal process in response to stress. All three theories demonstrate the relationship between a stressor and a physiological response that can lead to illness. For health psychologists, the relationship between an emotional factor (stress) and health and wellness is fundamental to the field. Therefore, we examine each of these theories.

CANNON'S "FIGHT-OR-FLIGHT" THEORY   One way to define stress is the body's physical or emotional reaction to an external event. Early research in stress, such as Cannon's *fight-or-flight theory*, did just that, focusing specifically on the body's physiological response to stress-inducing stimuli.

Cannon proposed that stress is best understood as the body's biological activation in response to a stress-producing stimuli. Consider the following example: A young woman is walking home from a party late one Saturday night. The walkway is dimly lit. In the distance she can see the shadow of a person behind a building. At one point, as the young woman continues walking, she sees the person emerge from behind the building, look in her direction and retreat, once again, behind the building. How do you think the young woman would respond to the potentially threatening situation?

According to Cannon, in response to the above scenario, the body's biological systems, specifically the sympathetic nervous system and endocrine system, would activate to enable the young woman to exhibit a "fight-or-flight" response to the potential threat.

The Nervous System and Stress   In Chapter 6, Emotional Health and Well-Being, we introduced the nervous system. As we indicated there, there are several noticeable physiological changes that occur when we encounter a stressful event. Some individuals may experience a rapid heartbeat, some might sweat under their arms or on their palms, and others may respond with an increased respiration (breathing) rate. It is also likely that when responding to stressful stimuli, a person's pupils would dilate, and they may experience a sensation of "dry mouth" due to the lack of saliva (see Figure 7.2). Which of these changes do you think were likely to occur to the young woman in our scenario? Which have you experienced when stressed?

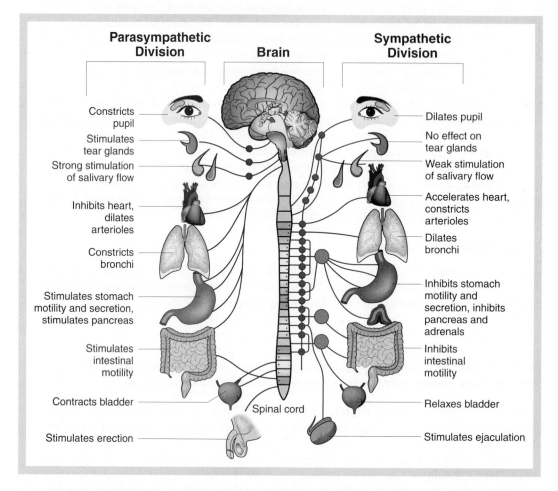

FIGURE 7.2   The Role of the Parasympathetic and the Sympathetic Systems. The sympathetic system activates many organs and processes in response to stressful events, whereas the parasympathetic system returns the body to allostasis.

Source: Prentice Hall, 1995–2002.

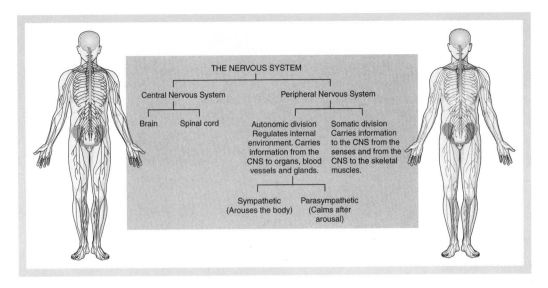

FIGURE 7.3   The Nervous System.

Source: Prentice-Hall (1995–2002).

Physiological responses to stress like those identified above are initiated by a complex communication process that takes place in the ***nervous system***, the body's network of cells that communicate information about itself and its environment. The nervous system consists of two principal parts, the ***central nervous system (CNS)*** and the ***peripheral nervous system (PNS)*** (see Figure 7.3). The central nervous system (CNS) is responsible for receiving and responding to information obtained through our ***sensory receptor sites***, here meaning the parts of the body responsible for initial sensory perception including the eyes, ears, nose, and fingers. The CNS uses the vast structure of nerves in our bodies to coordinate the communication between the receptor sites and the brain, the processing center for our sensory experiences.

The peripheral nervous system (PNS) contains two substructures, the ***autonomic nervous system (ANS)*** and the ***somatic nervous system (SNS)***. We focus our discussion on the autonomic nervous system because it is most relevant when describing the body's response to stress. The autonomic nervous system controls the automatic and involuntary functions that are essential for living. For example, heart rate, digestion, and perspiration are controlled by the ANS.

The ANS also contains two substructures, both of which play a role in our body's response to stress: the sympathetic nervous system and the parasympathetic nervous system. The ***sympathetic nervous system*** is responsible for activating the body's response to danger, emergencies, or foreign microorganisms that invade the body (we explain the role of the ANS with regard to microorganisms more fully in Chapter 8, HIV and AIDS). Thus, when activated, the sympathetic nervous system protects us from external or internal threats. In comparison, the ***parasympathetic nervous system*** takes control once the threat has abated. It is responsible for returning the body to its normal or baseline state, often referred to as ***allostasis***. Specifically, allostasis refers to the body's ability to maintain a "steady state" through changes in both the environment and in the body's physiology (McEwen & Winfield, 2003; Romero, Dickens, & Cyr, 2009).

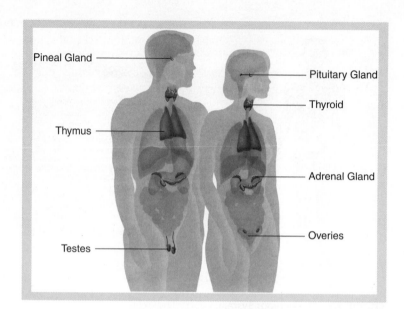

FIGURE 7.4 Major Endocrine Glands. The endocrine glands release hormones in response to stress.

The Endocrine System A second system critical to the body's response to stress is the *endocrine system*, a communication system of the body that sends messages using *ductless glands*, here meaning glands that release *hormones* directly into the body's bloodstream (see Figure 7.4). Hormones, like neurotransmitters (see Chapter 6), are the chemical messages that facilitate the body's communication process.

The endocrine system has many functions, but one of its responsibilities is to respond to stress. To this end, two glands in the endocrine system, the pituitary gland and the adrenal gland, are principally responsible for releasing hormones in response to stress. The *pituitary gland* is adjacent to the *hypothalamus*, a region in the brain that controls basic human needs such as sleep, hunger, thirst, and sex. The location of the pituitary gland suggests that, even though the brain is part of the nervous system, the endocrine and the nervous systems work together when producing and regulating hormones.

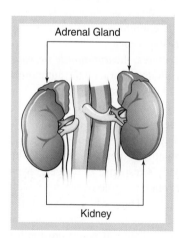

FIGURE 7.5 Adrenal Glands. Adrenal glands (above kidneys) also release hormones in response to stressful stimuli.

The pituitary gland is sometimes nicknamed the "master gland," but this is largely meant to connote the fact that under the direction of the hypothalamus, the pituitary gland produces hormones that stimulate the production of other hormones that play a role in the body's response to stress. For example, the pituitary gland produces *adrenocorticotropic hormone (ACTH)*, a hormone that is responsible for stimulating the *adrenal glands*, located just above each of the kidneys (see Figure 7.5). As we will see shortly, stimulation of the adrenal glands triggers the release of other hormones critical to the stress response.

The adrenal glands consist of two components, the adrenal medulla and the adrenal cortex. The *adrenal medulla* is found in the inner layer of the adrenal glands. When stimulated by the sympathetic nervous system, the adrenal medulla produces *catecholamine*, a class of chemicals that contain *epinephrine* and *norepinephrine*. You may be familiar with another name for epinephrine: *adrenaline*. If this is familiar, then you know that epinephrine (or adrenaline) helps boost the body's energy level. Thus, when epinephrine is released in the body, the sympathetic system is activating the body in response to a stimulant, possibly a stress-provoking event. In fact, epinephrine is linked so closely with stress that it is often used as a physiological index of stress. When the sympathetic nervous system and adrenal glands interact to cause a reaction, we refer to the combined systems as the *sympathetic-adrenal-medullary system (SAM)*.

The *adrenal cortex* is the outer layer of the adrenal glands. The adrenal cortex, when working together with the hypothalamus and the pituitary gland, form the *hypothalamic-pituitary-adrenocortical system (HPAC)*, a system responsible for restoring the body to its baseline steady state. This system, when stimulated by ACTH, activates the adrenal cortex to release one type of hormone, glucocorticoids. *Glucocorticoids* are anti-inflammatory agents that suppress the body's normal reaction to stress, thereby preventing damage to the body's organs (Munck & Guyre, 1986; Munck & Naray-Fejes-Toth, 1994). As shown in Figure 7.2, normal physiological responses to stress may include accelerated heart rate and dilated bronchial tubes (lungs), as well as increased blood pressure. As we will see in Chapter 9, Cardiovascular Disease, prolonged stress on the heart can cause damage to that organ. Therefore, glucocorticoids may play a constructive role in preserving the health of some organs.

In some instances, however, the inhibition of the body's normal stress system response may contribute to illnesses such as chronic infections, major depression, and a clogging of the arteries known as atherosclerosis (see Chapter 9, Cardiovascular Disease) (Calcagni & Elenkov, 2006). Thus, while protecting the body from the effects of the body's normal reaction to stress, the protective agent glucocorticoids may also make the body susceptible to other illnesses.

In sum, Cannon's "fight-or-flight" theory was the first to describe fully the body's biological response to stress-inducing stimuli. Later work by Selye, however, showed that Cannon's discovery of the role of catecholamines and the medulla in stress was only part of the process (Szabo, 1998).

SELYE'S GENERAL ADAPTATION SYNDROME (GAS)   Hanz Selye's work is considered seminal for its identification of the pathways through which stress elicits physiological reactions in organisms, a system that he demonstrated was more complex than that proposed by Cannon (Selye & Fortier, 1950).

Although Selye's research initially characterized stress as either a stimulus or an external agent, he later redefined stress as the organism's response to any form of a "noxious stimulus" (Selye, 1936), which he referred to later as the "stressor" (Selye, 1946). Selye contends that the body responds in the same manner to any stressor (see Figure 7.6). Hence, cold temperatures, surgical injury, or the introduction of intoxicating substances (like drugs or alcohol) would provoke the same three-stage response to the stressor (Selye, 1936).

The three stages of GAS—the alarm stage, the stage of resistance, and the stage of exhaustion—describe, according to Selye, not only the body's response to a stressor but also the process by which illnesses develop as the body tries but fails to cope with the target stressor. In the alarm stage, the organism first experiences shock at the initial and immediate impact of the

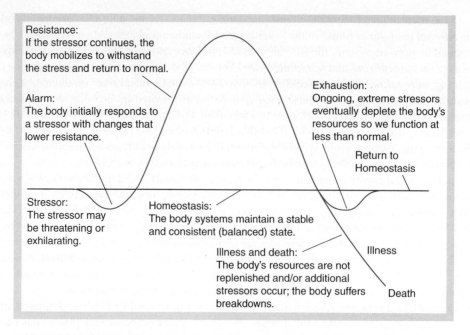

FIGURE 7.6   Selye's General Adaptation Syndrome (GAS). The three stages of GAS triggered during a stressful episode include the alarm stage, the stage of resistance, and the stage of exhaustion.

Source: Hales, 1997.

stress-inducing agent. The initial response to the shock may include a lowering of the body's blood pressure or body temperature (Lazarus & Folkman, 1984). The body then proceeds to the countershock phase *(*still in the alarm stage*)*, in which the organism prepares to respond defensively to the stress-producing agent. It is in the countershock phase that some researchers contend that we see the responses characterized by Cannon as the fight-or-flight reaction. At this point the body may release higher levels of adrenaline and at the same time may increase respiration and blood pressure and activate the sweat glands as the body prepares to respond (look again at Figure 7.2).

The second stage, resistance, is best characterized as the body's increased and sustained resistance to one stress agent. However, it comes at a price. The sustained resistance to one stressor decreases the body's ability to withstand or defend against other agents (Selye, 1946). In essence, while fighting one agent intensely, the body is vulnerable to attack by other stress agents, which could include a range of factors that could lead to illness.

The final stage of GAS is appropriately named the stage of exhaustion. How long an organism can withstand and defend against a specific stress-inducing agent appears to vary as a function of the individual. But, in general, Selye notes that prolonged exposure to stressors can and does cause symptoms similar to those that appear during the alarm stage. Selye notes that, in the final stage of exhaustion, organisms will display the nonspecific systemic reactions that were developed during the adaptation stage but that it could not maintain. Thus, it is in this stage that the disease of adaptation may form, here meaning illnesses that occur as a result of the body's inability to defend against the specific agent or other stressors (Lazarus & Folkman, 1984). Illnesses may include hypertension (high blood pressure; see Chapter 9, Cardiovascular Disease) or gastrointestinal ulcers. Even some forms of allergies may be considered diseases of adaptation (Selye, 1946).

While illuminating an association between stress and illness, Selye's work met with criticism. Most telling is the critique of the theory's inability to explain the role of psychosocial factors on illness. Early research by Mason and colleagues (1976) suggest that the body's hormonal response may differ as a function of a specific emotion and even gender. If so, the belief that all stressors would elicit the same reaction would not be supported.

LAZARUS AND FOLKMAN'S TRANSACTIONAL MODEL (TM) OF STRESS   Work by Lazarus and Folkman addresses some of the psychosocial triggers of stress that critics note are not included in Selye's GAS theory. Lazarus and Folkman (1984) believe that we cannot study a person's response to stress independent of understanding his or her perception of the stress-provoking event. To explain the process, these researchers developed the ***transactional model (TM)***, which proposes that stress is triggered when an external stressor (or event) exceeds a person's personal and social resources to effectively cope with the event. Here, coping includes a person's psychological and emotional resources as well as physiological.

Lazarus and Folkman further note that stress is not a one-time response to a static event. Rather, it involves a person's continuous interactions with, and adjustments to, the event, somewhat like Selye's theory explaining the body's physical interactions and adjustment to the stressor. Recall also the opening story. Sarah's family was responding to new and different stressors each day. But many of the stressors appeared to exceed her family's ability to cope with the new situation.

We can also apply the transactional model to the earlier example of the young woman walking alone along the dimly lit pathway at night. Recall that the woman saw a person emerge from and then retreat behind a building. Instead of asking only how does the body respond to the stressor, Lazarus and Folkman ask, How does the young woman cognitively appraise the stressful event? Equally as important, what does the woman do?

Using the transactional model, we might suggest that, before seeing the shadow, walking at night, alone, along a dimly lit walkway did not exceed the woman's personal or social resources. She was comfortable with the setting and confident of her skills. On seeing the shadow, however, the woman may have reassessed the situation. She may now perceive that the new factor, a person lurking behind a building, potentially poses a threat to her that exceeds her personal resources.

In this situation, the young woman may consider a number of options that will help her minimize the perceived threat. She may begin walking faster and watch for the effect of her faster speed on the person behind the building. Or she may cross the street in another effort to put distance between the threatening situation and herself. Finally, she may take out her cell phone and call a friend to walk with her the remainder of the way home. While considering each possible action, the young woman will reassess the perceived threat. Changes in her behavior and her reassessment are what Lazarus and Folkman mean by "transactions."

Appraisal Process   Lazarus contends that transactions are directed by our ***cognitive appraisal*** of the situation, or the process we use to evaluate the events. Cognitive appraisal involves three components: ***primary appraisal***, the initial assessment of the event and determination of the potential harmfulness; ***secondary appraisal***, an assessment of our resources and determination of how sufficient our resources are to meet the demands of the event; and finally, *cognitive reappraisal*, the reevaluation of the event as it develops. In our scenario, the young woman's cognitive appraisal of the person in the shadows begins with an assessment of the potential harmfulness of the situation (primary appraisal). She will assess the situation to determine whether her resources are sufficient to address the threat (secondary appraisal). And she will reassess the situation (cognitive reappraisal) perhaps more than once to determine if it continues to be as threatening as it seemed at first.

In addition, Lazarus's theory of stress and coping assumes two things. First, he contends that situations or events are not inherently stressful. The stressfulness of a situation depends, in part, on our cognitive appraisal of the event. This means that people will interpret situations differently based on a number of factors, including their prior experiences, their own skills, and their level of confidence in addressing stressful events. Take again the example of the woman walking alone on the dimly lit walkway. She appraised the situation with the person lurking in the distance as stressful—yet another woman may not have. Additionally, consider the situation in the opening story. While Susan's family found the caregiving responsibilities for Sarah stressful, other families may not have. Individual differences, or differences in appraisal, will lead to different interpretations of the same situation and possibly different responses.

Second, an individual may appraise the same situation differently based on his or her mood, health, or motivation. The young woman walking alone at night may have considered the situation stressful primarily because she was aware that her judgment was impaired by the alcohol she had consumed at the party. But had she been returning from her martial arts class, she may have felt less compromised and more comfortable with her resources or ability to handle a potentially threatening individual.

To summarize, we see that stress is both a stimulus and a response. Responses to stress are based in part on our cognitive appraisal of the event. Individuals may differ in their appraisal of a situation and, therefore, may differ in their interpretation of an event as threatening. And, within the same individual there may be differences in the perceived stressfulness of the same situation from one point in time to another, given the individual's own state of mind, mood, or perceived state of health.

Accelerated heart rates, dry mouth, and rapid breathing due to dilated bronchial airways (lungs) are but a few of the physiological changes triggered by the sympathetic system when we cognitively appraise a situation as threatening (look again at Figure 7.2). No doubt the young woman en route home from the party experienced some combination of these symptoms when seeing the shadow of a person lurking behind a building at night.

But suppose, as the young woman in our scenario continues to walk, the person behind the building emerges. Suppose it is a child walking a small dog on a leash. In addition, the young woman observes that the dog seems to pull and jerk the child in different directions. What would happen next as the woman cognitively reappraises the situation? Most likely the young woman would determine that the situation is no longer threatening. Now, with no other apparent threat, the parasympathetic system would activate to return the body to its steady state.

SECTION II. STRESS AND ILLNESS

We now know how our body responds physiologically to stress, but what causes stress? Simply put, everything! It may seem like an exaggeration, but the statement is largely true. Earlier in the chapter we stated that individuals will interpret situations differently. A situation that is stress producing to one may not be viewed as stressful to another. Therefore, any situation has the potential to cause stress to someone. Yet, through research, we know that there are some events that commonly cause stress in spite of individual differences in perception. Commonly reported causes of stress are chronic or prolonged illnesses and psychosocial factors, including events such as the death of a family member, losing a job, or assuming caregiving responsibilities for someone who is unable to care for him- or herself (see this chapter's opening story).

Chronic Illness as a Stressful Stimulant

In Chapter 3, Global Communicable and Chromic Disease, we defined *chronic diseases* as long-term (three to six months or longer) complex illnesses that can be controlled but not cured. Thus, arthritis, diabetes, some forms of heart disease, and migraines are examples of chronic illnesses. Chronic illness requires that the person afflicted, as well as that person's family or others living with him or her, learn to live with the condition over a protracted period of time. It also requires an ongoing adjustment to the challenges and threats presented by the disease, including changes in physical and emotional conditions, pain and pain management, and the inability to perform normal or expected roles (Heijmans et al., 2004). While people learn to manage the disease and its symptoms, studies suggest that the uncertainty and the inability to control disease progression can create anxiety and tensions. In the opening story, Susan, Michael, and Lucinda struggled to cope with Sarah's constant and sometimes unanticipated changes in behavior or ability due to Alzheimer's. The changes caused tensions within the family.

Unpredictable disease outcomes, inability to control disease progression, and the rate of deterioration are commonly reported stressors for most forms of chronic illness (Dunkel-Schetter, Feinstein, Taylor, & Falke, 1992; Nouwen, Gingras, Talbot, & Bouchard, 1997). A study by Heijmans and colleagues (2004) underscores this point (see Figure 7.7). Based on a sample of over 1,300 people diagnosed with one of 10 chronic illnesses (including arthritis, asthma, cancer, diabetes, heart disease, and other illnesses), participants in this study reported being most anxious about the unpredictable consequences of their disease. Specifically, participants who reported concerns about their progressive physical or mental deterioration, the controllability of the disease, or the life-threatening nature of the illness also reported higher levels of stress regardless of the type of illness.

Thus, according to Heijmans and colleagues (2004), individuals with life-threatening or progressive illness report high stress levels when they experience an illness that is less controllable (low control) and contains high levels of disability. Interestingly, individuals whose illnesses are regulated by medical professionals or through self-care and who characterize their illnesses as high in controllability and low in disability also report high stress levels.

At this point it is logical to ask two questions. First, what is unusual about people with chronic illnesses experiencing higher stress than people without such illnesses? And second, why is the higher level of stress a problem?

The fact that an illness may mean a gradual deterioration in physical or mental abilities would cause anxiety and distress in many people. Therefore, stress is not an unusual response to chronic illnesses. And, if elevated stress levels caused no adverse physical consequence, we might not be concerned about their effects. The fact is, however, that prolonged stress can negatively affect health outcomes in anyone but particularly in people with chronic illnesses. Research shows that people with chronic illnesses who also report high stress levels or stressful

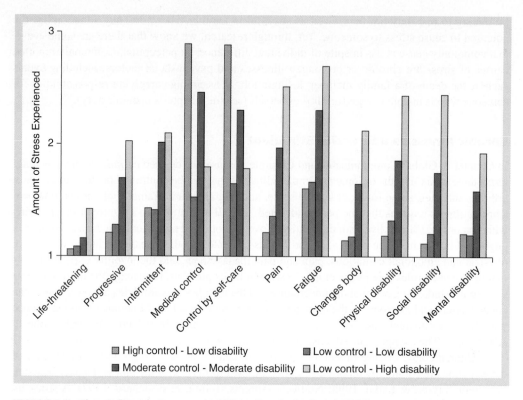

FIGURE 7.7   Chronic Disease Stressors by Diagnosis. The highest levels of stress are reported for illnesses that are highly controllable with low disability as well as difficult-to-control illnesses with high levels of disability.

Source: Heijmans et al. (2004).

environments show poorer overall health outcomes than people with similar diagnoses but with significantly less stress (Ahola et al., 2009; Kershau et al., 2008; Lane, Langman, Lip, & Nouwen, 2009; Manderson & Kokanovic, 2009; Wardle, 1995). In other words, stress can exacerbate an existing health problem, causing further deterioration in health. These findings appear to hold true for many chronic ailments including heart disease, high cholesterol, prostate cancer, and even workplace disabilities.

Stress: A Determinant of Illness

In addition to exacerbating preexisting health concerns, recent research supports the commonly held belief that stressful life experiences can precipitate or cause new physiological illnesses (Arroyo et al., 2004; Skaff et al., 2009; Stanley & Burrows, 2008). There is, however, one caveat: Stressful events are more likely to cause physical illnesses when a person is vulnerable to such illnesses.

Stanley and Burrows (2008) examine the association among stress, illness, and preexisting vulnerabilities through research that shows a relationship between temperament and other inherited characteristics and illness. They cite, by way of example, John Hunter, a Scottish surgeon and scientist in the mid-18th century, who was probably the first to propose specifically that heart ailments could be related to a person's emotional state or personality. Hunter, using himself as an example, suggested that his anxious and argumentative nature (personality) most likely contributed to his experiences of chest pains (Stanley & Burrows, 2008). His supposition was a precursor of the diathesis–stress model of disease.

The Diathesis–Stress (D–S) Model of Disease

Can people be predisposed to illnesses that are then triggered by stress? In Chapter 2, Research Methods, we noted that some people were, in fact, genetically predisposed to illnesses. But the *diathesis–stress (D–S)* model of disease proposes something more. Specifically, it states that an individual's biochemical or organ imbalances can predetermine that person's reaction to environmental stressors and can result in physical symptoms of illnesses (Stanley & Burrows, 2008). In other words, a biological predisposition (see Chapter 2) and an environmental precipitating factor (see Chapter 2) are necessary determinants to cause the onset of a stress-related illness.

The concept of a biological or psychological predisposition to an illness, a diathesis, triggered by an environmental precipitating factor, a stressor, as postulated by the D–S model has been proposed as a possible explanation for psychopathology such as schizophrenia and depression and for physiological illnesses such as chronic pain. Specifically, research by Nuechlerlein and colleagues (1992) suggests that known biological markers for schizophrenia are triggered by an environmental stressor that results in manifestations of schizophrenia. Similarly, research by Banks and Kerns (1996) suggests similar diathesis and stressors may explain the manifestation of depression in response to chronic pain. These researchers suggest that if depression is a reaction to chronic pain, then there may be something unique about some person's psychological experience of living with pain over time that increases the likelihood of developing major depressive symptoms. In this instance depression is the psychological diathesis, and chronic pain represents the stressor.

Physiologically, current research on stress and illness may help explain the general association between stress and illness. Acute stress, meaning sudden and intense responses to a stressful stimuli, or chronic stress, meaning stress that is prolonged over time, can stimulate the release of three hormones: glucocorticoids, cortisol, and catecholamine (Brendgen & Vitaro, 2008). We reviewed the functions of glucocorticoids and catecholamine in the section on the endocrine system in this chapter (see page 223).

We note that *cortisol* slows the body's response to stress. Yet studies also suggest that individuals with biological imbalances or organ system irregularities may produce higher levels of cortisol than those without such imbalances. According to recent findings, elevated cortisol levels in the body contribute to both psychological and physiological health problems. Psychologically, an excess of cortisol is linked to anxiety and depression (Goodyear, Herbert, Tamplin, & Altham, 2000). Physiologically, elevated cortisol levels can suppress the immune system (see Chapter 8, HIV and AIDS), causing psychophysiological health problems, including asthma, chronic headaches, and ulcers (Kiecolt-Glaser & Glaser, 1995; Brendgen & Vitaro, 2008). Once again, if stress can trigger excessive levels of cortisol, which then contributes to specific emotional and physical health problems, we may infer that stress can precipitate illnesses (Mathews & Gump, 2002; Mittleman et al., 1995; Rosengren et al., 2004; Wittstein et al., 2005).

Personality Type, Stress, and Illness

Research on the association between temperament (an inherited quality) and health also led some researchers to propose that personality type may be another predetermining factor for illness. Specifically, early research suggests that individuals with type A personalities are more susceptible to illness, such as heart problems, than those without such characteristics (Friedman & Rosenman, 1959; Hecker, Chesney, & Frautschi, 1988). You may be familiar with the *type A personality* profile: someone who is highly competitive, is high in need for achievement, is impatient, and can appear hostile or aggressive to others. Early research suggested that the behaviors associated with type A personalities (remember, an inherited characteristic) increase the likelihood of heart-related illnesses.

But, consider this: Some work environments, such as the finance industry, including the stock exchange and investment banking, as well as some specialties in law (such as litigation) are highly demanding, competitive, and pressurized environments. Several studies support the view that individuals who work in highly competitive, demanding environments may be at risk for higher frequencies of negative health outcomes related to their work environment. Interestingly, these same environments attract type A personalities. Therefore, it is not clear in such settings whether the environment or the person is the principal factor contributing to illnesses. In other words, if a person who works in one of these competitive and demanding environments develops a heart-related illness, was the illness triggered by the workplace, by their personality type, or by some combination of both?

Recent studies also contend that, if there is any association between personality type and illness, people with *type D* (for distressed) personality characteristics, or people who exhibit generally negative affect (stress, anxiety, hostility, and depression), are more likely to develop heart-related health problems (Denollet, Pedersen, Vrints, & Conraads, 2006; Kupper & Denollet, 2007; Sher, 2005). In other words, research would suggest that distressed emotional states, specifically depression, hostility, and anxiety, are more strongly linked to heart problems than personality type or profession.

BOX 7.1   Can Social Rejection Make a Person Ill? A Test for the Diathesis–Stress (D–S) Model

No one likes to be an "outcast," or rejected from a desired social group. But can such rejection lead to poor physical and mental health? Brendgen and Vitaro (2008) seem to think so, at least with respect to adolescent girls.

Researchers have studied the effects of adolescents' peer networks on a range of factors, including social support, high-risk health behaviors, and emotional and mental health (Brendgen et al., 2001). Building on findings from some of these same studies that suggest that adolescents who are rejected or intensely disliked by their peers are more prone to evidence mental health problems, Brendgen and Vitaro (2008) designed a study to examine the role of peer rejection on physical health. They contend that because peer rejection causes considerable stress among adolescents, the elevated stress would result in high levels of cortisol circulating in the body. Cortisol is a hormone that slows the body's response to stress. However, too much cortisol can cause anxiety and depression and can suppress the body's immune system (see the section on the diathesis–stress model, pg. 229). Therefore, individuals who experience considerable stress as a result of peer rejection may produce excessive levels of cortisol, which may put them at higher risk for negative mental health outcomes, including anxiety and depression, as well as more frequent incidences of physical health problems.

To test this concept, the authors examined several factors: family adversity (including family structure, parental education, socioeconomic status, and parental occupation), self-reported physical health problems, depression symptoms, and peer rejection (peer rating of the students they would be most and least likely to invite to a social gathering). Included also was a measure of ***emotional reactivity***, a teacher-based rating that assessed student's temperament, specifically reaction to and anxiety about a negative event (Brendgen & Vitaro, 2008). For example, teachers assessed the student's likelihood to "get irritated easily" or to "cry easily."

Using a group of 157 high school students in Quebec, Canada, the authors studied girls and boys in grades 7 and 8 over two years. When comparing students, parents' and teachers' ratings, and also students' health profiles, the authors found that adolescents who were emotionally reactive were more likely to report physical health problems. However, Brendgen and Vitaro (2008) found that such results pertained only to adolescent girls who were moderately or highly emotionally reactive. Girls who were less reactive, and adolescent boys regardless of their reactivity level, showed no physical or emotional health problems attributable to peer rejection.

What do these findings suggest? Brendgen and Vitaro's findings seem to suggest a link between emotional temperament and physical health, at least for adolescent girls. Specifically, the findings suggest that girls who are predisposed to highly negative responses to stressful situations (remember, we are defining peer rejection as highly stressful) are at higher risk for overall negative health outcomes. These results seem to suggest support for the diathesis–stress model. Equally important, however, the findings hold implications for health psychologists when addressing the health needs of young adolescent girls. Research has long established that adolescent peer groups can affect the emotional well-being of teens. Now it appears that psychosocial stressors from the same adolescent cohorts can have an impact on the physical health of some adolescent girls as well. Health psychologists, with their ecological health training, are uniquely qualified to address such issues.

Other research examining negative affect and health problems seem to support this claim. Brendgen and Vitaro (2008) conducted a study examining the effects of peer rejection on physical health among 157 middle-school students (grades 7 and 8) to test the theory that high levels of negative emotionality could result in increased stress that, in turn, causes physical health problems. Their results (see Box 7.1) show an association between ***negative emotionally reactive*** adolescent girls, here meaning girls who were prone to respond to stressful events with anger, sadness, anxiety, or depression, and physical and psychological health problems. No significant difference was found for boys regardless of their level of reactivity.

To summarize, consistent with the diathesis–stress (D–S) model, some research suggests that an individual's vulnerabilities (biological or temperamental) may predispose him or her to greater adverse responses to stressful stimuli. Such reactions could result in a greater probability of psychophysiological health problems, such as chronic headaches, asthma, skin disorders, and respiratory infections (Cohen & Williamson, 1991; Kiecolt-Glaser & Glaser, 1995). But the D–S model, which proposes both an individual and an environmental determinant of stress-induced illness, does not explain the relationship between stress and illness in the absence of preexisting vulnerabilities. In such instances, perhaps Lazarus and Folkman's (1984) theory of the effect of daily hassles on health may explain the outcomes. We will explore Lazarus and Folkman's theory in Section III.

Psychosocial Events and Stress

The scenario presented earlier of a woman walking at night helps explain the cognitive process used to interpret a stressful physical stimuli. But what happens when the stressor is a nonphysical event? Consider, again, the case of Sarah in the opening story. Sarah posed no physical threat to the other family members. Yet her story was included in this chapter to illustrate stress as a stimulus, a response, and an interaction of the two.

Sarah's condition caused psychological and psychosocial stressors, here meaning stressors that are both psychological and social in origin, that were capable of producing physical responses. Psychologically, Susan experienced sleep disturbances. And everyone except Sarah exhibited heightened irritability, due, most likely, to the new caregiving responsibilities. Psychosocial stressors included, for example, Susan's ambivalence about putting her mother in a nursing home, contrary to Susan's beliefs about her responsibilities as a daughter to care for her mother, a social construct.

Research suggests that physiological symptoms such as an inability to sleep, atypical eating behavior, and increased irritability are common responses to psychosocial or psychological stress (Epel, Lapidus, McEwen, & Brownell, 2001; Farnill & Robertson, 1990; Haynes, Lee, & Yeomans, 2003; Pawlyk, Morrison, Ross, & Brennan, 2008). For example, Farnill and Robertson (1990) found an association between psychological stress among college students and sleep disturbances. Results from their study with Australian first-year college students showed that the student's perceptions of the new demands of college, together with additional worries about academic performance, independent of actual outcomes, led to an increase in self-reported stress levels and sleep disturbances.

Likewise, research on the association between psychosocial stress and obesity suggests that excessive eating, which can lead to weight gain and obesity, may also be prompted by stress (Epel et al., 2001; Haynes et al., 2003; Strickland, Giger, Nelson, & Davis, 2007). Participants in Strickland and colleagues' study (2007) reported that psychosocial factors, including family responsibilities, workplace issues, and concern about weight, accounted for their tendency to adopt unhealthy eating habits, such as eating frequently or a preference for high-fat and high-calorie foods. In short, stress triggered by psychological or psychosocial causes can cause physiological health problems or behaviors (such as eating behaviors) that can inhibit good health outcomes.

MEASURING STRESS   With so much discussion about stress, it is reasonable to ask, How do we measure stress? Of interest here are methods that assess both the situations that create stressful reactions (stressors) as well as the reactions also referred to as stress. We begin by examining measures that identify stressors.

SOCIAL READJUSTMENT RATING SCALE (SRRS)   The death of a family member, birth of a child, a wedding, a divorce, and major exams are very stressful psychosocial events that could provoke a stressful response. How do we know? For the past 60 years researchers have asked individuals to identify the most and least stressful experiences common to people.

One of the first and perhaps best-known measures of psychosocial stress is the *Social Readjustment Rating Scale (SRRS)* by Holmes and Rahe (1967), also known as the Holmes and Rahe Stress Scale. The 43-item scale includes a list of life events, rank ordered from most to lease stressful, as shown in Box 7.2. Each life event is associated with a *life change unit score*, a measure of the perceived stressfulness of the event on a scale of 100 to 0. Ratings from thousands of participants have produced weighted scores for each psychosocial event, which yielded a rank order of most to least stressful situations that appears to apply to a diverse sample of people. For example, the death of a spouse has a life change unit score (stressfulness score) of 100, suggesting a highly stressful event. Conversely, outstanding personal achievements are assigned a score of 28, or relatively low stress.

BOX 7.2   Holmes and Rahe Social Readjustment Rating Scale (SRRS)

The following items and scores appear on the Social Readjustment Rating Scale (SRRS). In this self-administered format, individuals tally the scores associated with the life events they selected. An interpretation of the total score appears below.

TABLE 7.1   Holmes and Rahe Social Readjustment Rating Scale (SRRS)

Life Event	Life Change Score
Death of a spouse	100
Divorce	73
Marital separation	65
Imprisonment (jail term)*	63
Death of a close family member	63
Personal injury or illness	53
Marriage	50
Dismissal from work (fired at work)*	47
Marital reconciliation	45
Retirement	45
Change in health of a family member	44

(continued)

TABLE 7.1   (Continued)

Life Event	Life Change Score
Pregnancy	40
Sexual difficulties	39
Gain a new family member	39
Business readjustment	39
Change in financial status	38
Death of a close friend	37
Change to different line of work	36
Change in frequency (number)* of arguments	35
Major mortgage (over $10,000)*	32
Foreclosure of mortgage or loan	30
Change in responsibilities at work	29
Child (son or daughter)* leaving home	29
Trouble with in-laws	29
Outstanding personal achievements	28
Spouse (wife*) starts or stops work	26
Begin or end school	26
Change in living conditions	25
Revision of personal habits	24
Trouble with boss	23
Change in work hours or conditions	20
Change in residence	20
Change in schools	20
Change in recreation	19
Change in church activities	18
Change in social activities	18
Minor mortgage or loan (less than $10,000)	17
Change in sleeping habits	16
Change in number of family members	15
Change in eating habits	15
Vacation	13
Christmas	12
Minor violations of law	11

Score of 300+: At risk of illness
Score of 150–299: Risk of illness is moderate
Score of 150 or less: Only slight risk of illness
Words in parenthesis are original text.
Source: Holmes and Rahe (1967).

In a seminal study to determine the relationship between current psychosocial stressors and future illness, Rahe, Mahan, and Arthur (1970) administered their scale to a group of navy sailors just prior to a six-month cruise assignment. The researchers scored each sailor's response to obtain a life change unit score. Rahe and coauthors (1970) then compared the ratings to sailors' health records six months later and found that the sailors with the highest life change unit scores were more likely to be ill six months later than were the sailors with the lowest scores. These authors believe the results of the study suggest a correlation between the number of stressful experiences, the perceived severity of the event, and overall physical health. They suggest that the number and type of stressful events an individual experiences may be a determinant of health outcomes.

The SRRS has been used by researchers to measure the impact of stressful environmental stimuli on health outcomes. It does not negate the association between stress, biological factors, and illness proposed by the D–S model. But the emphasis on the role of psychosocial stressors in the SRRS suggests that environmental factors, here meaning stressful events, may be more likely to trigger health problems than biological or temperamental predispositions.

CRITICISM OF THE SRRS   Criticisms of Holmes and Rahe's scale, specifically wording problems, lack of differentiation between positive or negative events (spouse stops or starts work is one item with one life change score), or an inability to account for individual differences in interpretation or truthfulness, prompted other researchers to refine and improve the original version. For example, some investigators developed scales tailored to specific populations, such as children or college students. Other scales were developed to assess the effect and number of *daily stressors*, defined as incidents that occur as part of one's daily tasks or occupational responsibilities that create stressors or problems.

The critiques notwithstanding, Holmes and Rahe pioneered a method for rating stressful experiences or events to assess a person's likely health risks. Their work, even with the revisions, provides a method for measuring the relationship among psychosocial events, stress, and illness. Furthermore, their work also identifies a role for health psychologists. Recall, again, the opening story with Susan, Michael, and Lucinda. Although the family sought help from a therapist, a health psychologist who addresses health from a holistic perspective could assist the family not only in responding to the stressor but also in addressing their own overall health needs.

Daily Life Hassles and Stress

Holmes and Rahe assume that major life events, positive or negative, will affect health. To that end, each of the 43 items on the original SRRS scale represents an event that most people would agree happens infrequently, if ever. For example, the death of a spouse, divorce, marriage, or marital reconciliation usually are one-time or rare events.

Lazarus and his colleagues offer an alternative interpretation of the effects of stress on well-being. They contend that *daily life hassles* are more likely to cause negative health outcomes than are major events. They propose that major stressful events, like marriages, deaths, or automobile accidents, occur infrequently. As such, major events cannot explain the frequent incidences of stress individuals claim to experience. For example, when was the last time you or your friends suffered a major personal injury? Now, compare that to the last time either you or your friends dropped or

TABLE 7.2	Selected Daily Hassles	
Category		**Example**
Household hassles		Preparing meals Shopping Home maintenance
Health hassles		Physical Illness Concern about medical treatment Side effects of medicine
Time pressure hassles		Too many things to do Not enough time to do all that needs doing Too many responsibilities
Inner concerns		Being lonely Concerns about inner conflicts Fear of Information
Environmental hassles		Neighborhood deterioration Noise Crime
Financial responsibility hassles		Financial responsibilities Concern about owing money Financial responsibilities for someone who doesn't live with you
Work hassles		Job dissatisfaction Dislike of current work duties Problems getting along with fellow workers
Future security hassles		Concern about job security Concerns about retirement Property, investments, or taxes

Source: Lazarus, DeLonges, Folkman, & Gruen (1985).

withdrew from a class. No doubt, major personal injuries occur far less frequently than, say, dropping or changing classes. If stress, a common experience for many, is determined in part by our exposure to stressful events, then events that occur more frequently are more likely to create more opportunities for stress than are the rare but more traumatic major events (see Table 7.2). For this reason, Lazarus and Folkman (1984) believe that the frequently occurring daily hassles of life are more likely to explain the frequent experiences of stress cited by individuals. According to Folkman and Moskowitz (2000), if not managed successfully, such daily hassles can accumulate and can lead to adverse health outcomes over time.

To test this assumption, Lazarus and his research partners developed the Hassles Scale, a 117-item instrument to assess the frequency and level of aggravation associated with daily and usual issues such as "concern about owing money" or "concerns about being lonely." Lazarus then paired the Hassles Scale with an Uplift Scale, a 138-item instrument that listed examples of possible uplifting or positive responses to the hassles. Participants in Lazarus's study were asked to indicate whether they experienced any of the hassles or the uplifting experiences on the two scales over the past month. Lazarus found that while the Hassles Scale was predictive of psychological health, the Uplift Scale was not. In essence, the daily hassles scale supported Lazarus's theory that everyday stressful events, the type encountered as part of one's routine experiences, could, when viewed collectively, predict psychological well-being.

Returning to the example of the opening story, Lazarus and colleagues' (1985) daily hassles theory would propose that, for Susan, Michael, and Lucinda, the daily hassles associated with caring for Sarah may have accumulated to cause high levels of stress for the family. We know from earlier research by Selye (1950) that accumulated stress can result in physiological symptoms and, if uncontrolled, to illnesses.

Additional research by Folkman and Moskowitz (2000) further tested the daily hassles theory of stress by examining coping mechanisms. Coping is an important component for understanding the psychological and physiological impact of stress and by extension on overall well-being. We explore coping with stress in Section III.

High-Risk Behaviors and Stress

To this point, we have identified two factors that can trigger stress indirectly, thereby causing or exacerbating illnesses. Psychosocial factors (illness, death, financial problems) that are largely determined by an individual's social environment can precipitate stress and lead to illness. In addition, chronic illnesses, like heart conditions or diabetes, can be stressors as individuals and their families attempt to manage the sometimes unpredictable course of the disease. In this instance, the illness causes additional stressors that exacerbate the existing illness.

Stressful events or situations may lead to risky or unhealthy behaviors that contribute to poor health outcomes. The research on stress and eating, stress and sexual behaviors, and stress and substance use provide ample evidence of the adverse effect of stress on health behaviors.

STRESS AND EATING   Without exaggeration, there is a large and growing literature that examines the effects of stress on people's eating behaviors. While there is considerable disagreement among researchers about the relationship between the two factors, there is general agreement around some findings. First, researchers tend to agree that, in general, stress influences the amount and type of foods consumed (Baum & Posluszny, 1999; Cartwright et al., 2003; Greeno & Wing, 1994; Wallis & Hetherington, 2004; Zellner et al., 2006). Furthermore, most studies have found that stress causes people to increase their consumption of sweet or fatty foods, rather than bland or salty foods (Grunberg & Straub, 1992; Oliver & Wardle, 1999; Ward & Mann, 2000; Zellner et al., 2006). Finally, researchers generally agree that there is a gender difference in the effects of stress on food consumption. Specifically, women are significantly more likely to increase their food consumption when encountering stressful situations than are men. In addition, women's foods of choice are most often high in fats and calories (Wardle et al., 2004; Zellner, Saito, & Gonzalez, 2007).

There is, however, one caveat in these findings. Even for women, the tendency to reach for the high-fat, high-calorie foods is more prevalent among restrained eaters, or people who report frequently monitoring their diet and food consumption. Researchers suggest that stressful events inhibit the ability of such individuals to exercise control over their eating behaviors. As a result, they select the very foods that they normally avoid for weight loss or health purposes (Zellner et al., 2006).

Occasional lapses in one's diet related to stress may not appear to pose health risks. However, remember that in such circumstances the foods of choice are the high-calorie snacks and high-fat foods. And, as indicated in Chapter 3, Global Communicable and Chronic Disease, unhealthy diets are one cause of obesity, diabetes, heart disease, and other related health problems. When individuals adopt unhealthy eating behaviors in response to stressful events, then stress is considered an indirect cause of negative health outcomes.

Stress, Sexual Behaviors, and Substance Abuse

Other behaviors that may be triggered by stress include unprotected sex and substance use. Studies suggest that high rates of violence in one's neighborhood, repeated exposure to discrimination, and high crime rates can create persistent or chronic stressors. To escape from such environments, or perhaps to manage their effects, some researchers contend that adolescents in such environments may engage in high-risk sexual behaviors such as multiple sexual partners or unprotected sex (Brady, Dolcini, Harper, & Pollack, 2009; Simons et al., 2002). Although such behaviors may temporarily reduce stress, they also increase an adolescent's probability of contracting sexually transmitted diseases (see Chapter 5, Risky Health Behaviors), including HIV/AIDS, or may result in unplanned pregnancies (Bolland, 2003; Brady & Donenberg, 2006; DiClimente et al., 1996).

Other risk behaviors sometimes associated with stress include substance use such as alcohol, cigarettes, or illegal drugs. The practice of using substances in response to stress is common in many cultures, including in the United States. It is even reflected in conversations. Consider this: When having a particularly bad day at work or school, when ending a relationship or experiencing other emotionally upsetting events, it is not uncommon for people to think of having an alcoholic drink in response to the stress to "drown their sorrows" or "cheer themselves up." In fact, the response is so widely accepted by some that the practice is reflected in cartoons and other forms of humor.

Researchers, too, document the common reliance on substances when stressed. A study by Brady and colleagues (2009) showed that the accumulation of multiple stressful events, such as parental divorce or an auto accident, prompted adolescents in their study to turn to substances either to escape or to manage the psychological impact of their experiences.

Interestingly, however, when considering the relationship among stress, substance use, sexual behaviors, and health, even adolescents tend to agree. In response to a questionnaire on stressful life events and healthy lifestyles, adolescents note that a healthy life includes few stressful events (He et al., 2004). This is true regardless of whether teens describe themselves as adhering to a narrow definition of health, one that does not include substance use or sexual behavior, or are following a more broadly defined concept of health, allowing for some use of substances and some sexual behavior. In sum, consistent with Lazarus and Folkman's (1984) daily hassles theory, some adolescents and researchers agree that frequent stressful events may contribute to poor health outcomes by increasing the likelihood of engaging in high-risk health behaviors.

Stress and Catastrophic Events

Lazarus and Folkman's work notwithstanding, there are times when a single and major event produces stress that has an enduring effect on the psychological and physiological health of the individuals. Take, for example, man-made disasters such as the destruction of the World Trade Towers in New York City on September 11, 2001. That catastrophic event, along with the attack on the Pentagon and the crash of United Airlines flight 93, claimed over 3,000 lives and created a stressful environment in New York City as well as the nation for many months. Individuals who witnessed or were directly exposed to the event complained of insomnia, nightmares, and panic attacks, as well as physiological problems such as respiratory distress and chronic respiratory problems for weeks, months, or even years afterwards. Estimates suggest that between 4.7 and 10.2% of the adults in New York City reported some form of health impairment attributable to the stress they experienced from the event. Health professionals have determined that many such individuals were experiencing *posttraumatic stress disorder (PTSD)* (Neria, 2009), an anxiety disorder that occurs after witnessing or experiencing a traumatic event.

PTSD may occur after a single traumatic incident or be the result of multiple exposures to trauma, such as the case with military personnel in combat. Exposure to man-made disasters like the events of September 11 or other events related to conflicts or wars, as well as natural disasters such as tsunamis or hurricanes, can lead to emotional and physiological problems that impair an individual's normal functional ability (Putman et al., 2009). But such experiences can also lead to behaviors that negatively affect health. For example, traumatic events have been cited as one reason for excessive use or abuse of alcohol or drugs by soldiers returning from war.

To review, stress can have both direct and indirect effects on health. As we saw in Section I, stress can directly affect an individual's physiological, emotional, and psychological response to the event. In Section II, we reviewed the direct effects of stress on illness and, conversely, illness as a means of exacerbating stress. We also see that stress can lead to risky health behaviors, such as unhealthy diets, substance use, and sexual behaviors that increase the risk of negative health outcomes. Yet not all encounters with stress result in negative health behaviors or health outcomes. Individuals may employ health-enhancing behaviors to buffer the effects of stress. In the next section, we examine coping mechanisms to reduce the potential adverse consequences of stress.

SECTION III. COPING WITH STRESS

What do you do when nervous? Some people whistle. Others pace, chew gum, listen to music, or exercise. Each of these activities represents ways of *coping*, cognitive or behavioral actions to manage when situational demands exceed our resources (Lazarus & Folkman, 1984).

The concept of coping used here is a logical extension of the theory of stress explained in Lazarus's transactional model. In the model, stress is a process that begins when external factors exceed an individual's personal or social resources. Coping, however, is a process by which an individual applies cognitive or behavioral responses to stressful situations consistent with his or her personal or social resources.

Cognitive Coping

The research on coping suggests two principal types of cognitive coping styles, problem- or emotion-focused versus engagement or disengagement. Problem- or emotion-focused coping includes two levels, problem-focused and emotion-focused.

PROBLEM- OR EMOTION-FOCUSED COPING   When using a ***problem-focused coping*** strategy, an individual will seek information and generate solutions to address the issue or problem encountered. That person's strategy is an active, fact-based, and planful approach to resolving the issue, with little time spent on emotional response. Consider again the scenario presented in the opening story. A problem-focused strategy to address the health care needs of an Alzheimer's patient, like Sarah, as well as the health and well-being of other members of the family, could include identifying the source of the problem and the emotional needs of all involved and seeking a solution that will address everyone's needs as best as possible. The family's decision to seek help from a therapist is consistent with a problem-focused approach to coping with the stressors presented by Sarah's condition. Other problem-focused approaches might include a search of the Internet for information about Alzheimer's or for support groups that might provide assistance to family members.

Conversely, the ***emotion-focused*** approach to coping entails principally seeking solace or support from others for emotional reasons. People who choose the emotion-focused strategy may seek out a family member, friend, or trained professional, such as a health psychologist, to discuss their emotional or psychological pain. They may even obtain a sympathetic audience. In the process, the individual may receive helpful information or guidance; however, that is not the principal intent of his or her interaction. The main goal is to obtain emotional support.

ENGAGEMENT OR DISENGAGEMENT COPING   The second type of coping, ***engagement or disengagement,*** also includes two levels. Engagement represents a hybrid of the problem- or emotion-focused coping approach. It includes both problem solving and emotional support. Thus, an individual who uses an engagement emotion coping approach may initiate conversations about the difficulties of caring for a person with Alzheimer's, perhaps with another person experiencing the same problem. While one outcome of the conversation may be an emotional connection with someone who shares the problem, the goal is to obtain helpful information.

Finally, as the name suggests, the disengagement approach represents a withdrawal from the problem or a denial of its existence. For example, individuals who use a disengagement strategy may attempt to address the needs of a person with a chronic illness or their own needs without seeking treatment or assistance from others. Alternatively, some disengagers may become depressed as a result of the stressors or may turn to substance use (drugs or alcohol) to withdraw from the problems altogether (Helder et al., 2002). Research suggests that, of the four coping styles, the problem-focused approach appears to be the most effective coping strategy for addressing a problem because effort is expended to address and resolve the source of the stress. On the other hand, the disengagement approach is the least effective strategy (Garver, Weintraub, & Scheier, 1989; Lazarus & Folkman, 1984). Withdrawal from a stressful event will do little to

TABLE 7.3	Selected Coping Strategies	
Strategy	**Description**
Problem- or emotion-focused	
Problem-focused	*Principal objective: To find a workable solution to problem*
	Seek information
	Generate solutions
	Have fact-based approach to solutions
	Actively engage
	Have little focus on emotion
Emotion-focused	*Principal objective: To find solace and emotional support*
	Seek comfort
	Share distress and psychological pain
	Look for sympathetic audience
Engagement- or disengagement-focused	
Engagement	*Principal objective: To obtain helpful information and support*
	Seek others to obtain information
	Share emotional burden
	Obtain workable solution
	Look for sympathetic but helpful audience
Disengagement	*Principal objective: To minimize emotional discomfort and stress*
	Address problem without assistance or information
	Withdraw from problem
	Avoid problem or efforts to resolve
	Avoid through substance use
	Deny problem exists

resolve the issue, although it may temporarily abate the sensation of stress. And, as we indicated earlier, when the disengagement approach includes using substances, such a strategy only compounds the problem and increases the risk of negative health outcomes.

Finally, it is important to note that studies on coping also suggest that the coping techniques individuals adopt for a specific illness are related to the coping strategies they use when dealing with everyday life (Helder et al., 2002). In essence, coping strategies appear to be linked to an individual's own disposition toward handling stress of any sort and not just to the health issue or the problem at hand.

Behavioral Coping Strategies

Cognitive responses to stress may be useful for individuals who prefer a cognitive approach to problem solving. But not all people respond to such strategies. Instead, some prefer other methods. Utilization of friends and networks or social support groups is one method of coping. Another includes behavioral coping mechanisms, such as aromatherapy, music relaxation, and humor as response mechanisms to stress. We review all three.

SOCIAL SUPPORT AND THE BUFFERING HYPOTHESIS   What effect do social support networks, here meaning the social groups or the network of friends, family, and other relatives, have on an individual's overall well-being? According to decades of research, social support from individuals and friends has a direct and oftentimes positive effect on health (Broadhead et al., 1983; Cohen & Wills, 1985; Kiecolt-Glaser, Gouin, & Hanstoo, 2009; Putman et al., 2009; Trotter & Allen, 2009).

Much of the early research on the effects of social networks on health indicates that the psychological and material assistance individuals obtain from such networks has a positive effect on overall health and well-being. We explore the benefits of social support groups to specific health issues such as cardiovascular health, pain and pain management, and cancer in Chapters 9 through 11. Here, however, we note that, in addition to numerous studies that show a direct relationship between networks and positive health outcomes, Cohen and Wills (1985) proposed that such support buffers individuals from the potentially pathogenic influences of stress. Put simply, networks protect individuals from the full impact of the stressful event through a variety of ways. And, according to Cohen, a person's involvement in social networks will help to buffer or protect him or her from the full impact of the stressor even if that person received no specific assistance from the network in addressing the stressful situation. Research suggests that the beneficial effects of involvement with a network provides feelings of stability, predictability, and self-worth for the individual (Cohen & Wills, 1985). Thus, while assistance from one's social network directly related to a task is always useful, it is not a necessary criterion to provide a buffer.

It is also the case that just the perception of an available network, without necessarily having consultation or contact with that network, also serves to buffer the individual in stressful settings. Why? According to Cohen and McKay (1984), the support mechanism is mediated in part through one's cognitive assessment of available resources. Thus, the perception that such resources are available may mediate against stress even if no efforts are made to access the help of the network. In essence, Cohen and Wills (1985) suggest, and other researchers have affirmed, that social support networks help to abate stress through direct and indirect support to an individual. Support networks, therefore, are one form of coping with stressors.

AROMATHERAPY AND MASSAGE   *Aromatherapy*, defined as the use of essential oils extracted from plants and herbs to treat disease (Cooke & Ernst, 2000), has been cited often for its stress-abating qualities (Martin, 2001). Some link aromatherapy to the practice of herbal medicine used by the Egyptians, Chinese, and Indians as early as 2500 BCE (see Chapter 1, Interdisciplinary Approach to Health; Cooke & Ernst, 2000; Herz, 2009).

Today, many people endorse aromatherapy as an effective behavioral response to stressful events or stimuli. Yet, recent research findings question the effectiveness of aromatherapy for stress reduction. A number of studies report that this approach is effective only when used in conjunction with massages or music (Cooke et al., 2007; Field et al., 1992; Hur et al., 2007) and not by itself (Howard & Hughes, 2008).

When massages or music is used together with aromatherapy treatments, studies have reported positive health outcomes, such as lower blood pressure, enhanced moods, or reduced anxiety levels. But consider this: Studies show that music or massages, independent of aromatherapy, serve to abate stress. What is more, aromatherapy, when added to these proven behavioral methods, neither contributes to nor detracts from their effectiveness. Such outcomes have led some researchers to conclude that "aromatherapy is effective, even when it isn't" (Vickers, 2000).

MUSIC   The waiting rooms in doctors' offices, elevators in high-rise buildings, and even some supermarkets share a common practice: They often play "background" music. The music is piped in through the intercom and is played at a low volume. In fact, you may not notice the music when you first arrive. After a few moments, however, you may hear the strands of a melody or perhaps hear a bass line or harmony. Why would these unrelated venues all play music softly in the background? The research on stress and music can explain the practice.

With rare exceptions, researchers agree: Music reduces stress and anxiety levels. Studies that examine the effects of music on participant's blood pressure levels, self-reported anxiety levels, self-reported emotional states, or speed and accuracy on performance tasks all reported that music reduced stress-related responses and improved performance (Allen & Blascovich, 1994; Chafin, Roy, Gerin, & Christenfeld, 2004; Labbe, Schmidt, Babin, & Pharr, 2008; Lesiuk, 2008).

Music and Physiological Health   Current research further supports the role of music as a health enhancer for physiological and emotional health. It also suggests that music can benefit individuals indirectly, by enhancing the skills of the health care providers. For example, Nilsson's (2009) study on the effects of music on postoperative coronary artery bypass patients shows a clear link between postoperative music intervention and psychological and physiological well-being. In a controlled study, Nilsson put 20 postoperative coronary patients in a music intervention and bed rest condition, while another 20 postoperative coronary patients received bed rest only. She then measured each patient's plasma oxytocin, a hormone that inhibits sympathetic and hypothalamic-pituitary and adrenal activity during stress and helps to regulate cardiovascular activity (Evans, 1997; Petersson & Uvnas-Moberg, 2007). She also assessed patients' heart rate, blood pressure, and subjective relaxation levels. Results showed that patients in the bed rest with music intervention had higher oxytocin levels and higher subjective relaxation levels than the bed rest only condition. Thus, not only did patients report being more relaxed, their physiological response as determined by their oxytocin levels suggested that they were in fact experiencing a physiological response that would contribute to better heart health outcomes. Music, therefore, had a beneficial effect on both the psychological and physiological health of the study participants.

Music and Emotional Health   Do doctors' offices, elevators, and supermarkets create stressful conditions? Yes, for some people. The wait time in a doctor's office can be stressful as people contemplate the many different ailments imaginable while waiting to speak with the doctor. Elevators, too, can be stressful as some people feel uncomfortable in small enclosed spaces, particularly when the space is crowded with strangers. Finally, supermarkets may not in themselves be stressful, but the process of shopping for groceries while adhering to a budget and managing crowds can create some anxiety.

Are all genres of music equally as effective in reducing stress and anxiety levels? Apparently not. Researchers disagree about whether type of music is an important variable in stress reduction. A study by Chafin and colleagues (2004) suggests that only classical music effectively reduces psychological and physiological symptoms of stress. But Labbe and colleagues (2008) and Leisuk (2008) disagree, indicating that an individual's preferred music genre will be more effective when attempting to lower his or her specific stress and anxiety levels than will classical music (Labbe et al., 2008; Lesiuk, 2008).

A simulated study by Allen and Blascovich (1994) helps put these findings into perspective. These researchers tested the effects of three types of music conditions on stress reduction: no music, experimenter's selected music type, and participant's preferred music type. It is important to note that in this study the participants were all medical doctors who were also trained surgeons.

Because Allen and Blascovich (1994) could not ethically test a surgeon's skill and accuracy in an actual medical procedure, such as an operation, they devised a cognitively challenging mathematical task that they believed presented similar cognitive demands as those encountered by surgeons. They found that music played during the mathematical task could reduce physiological responses to stress in the settings. They also found that the most effective stress-reducing genre of music is the one preferred by the individual. In light of these findings, we might be advised to ask doctors to include their music preference as part of the essential instruments for an operation.

FIGURE 7.8   Relaxing Music. Music can be a health-enhancing behavior as well as an effective stress reduction technique.

HUMOR   Is laughter really the best medicine? According to research on humor, laughter, and physical health, there may be some truth to this saying (McGuire, 1999). Research on humor, defined here as action, speech, or writing that creates amusement, comicality, or fun (Martin, 2001) and on laughter, meaning the behavioral or vocal expression of the humorous experience (Martin, 2001) suggest that there are health benefits to both. For example, Fry (1994) proposed that the physical act of laughing causes changes in the body's physiology, including reduction of muscle tension, increased oxygenation of the blood, and release of ***endorphins***, hormones that enhance positive mood states. Such changes have been linked to positive moods in individuals. As we noted in Chapter 6, Emotional Health and Well-Being, positive dispositions and moods are health-enhancing factors.

BOX 7.3   Rockin' and Rollin' in the Operating Room?

"There I was," reported one fourth-year medical student, "assisting in the operating room. It felt great!"

"What were you doing?" asked his roommate, another fourth-year student.

"Holding the arm of the patient while dancing to the music of Usher. I never knew the head surgeon was so cool!"

In truth very few medical students "dance" with a patient undergoing an operation. But many surgeons do play music in the operating room. The type of music varies according to the doctor's preference.

Without a doubt, the sounds of pop or contemporary music emanating from an operating room during a procedure may be surprising, even shocking to some. After all, an operation is a serious procedure. So many things can go wrong even with simple, straightforward procedures. Yet, research on music, stress, and performance suggest that one way to maximize concentration and improve accuracy is to play background music.

It is necessary to point out that there are a few ethical problems that limit a researcher's ability to conduct a study on the effects of music on a surgeon's performance in an actual operation (see Chapter 2, Research Methods). Therefore, researchers Allen and Blascovich (1994) did the next best thing. They designed an experimental study to test the effects of music on three measures of autonomic reactivity—skin conductivity (sweat), blood pressure, and pulse rate—while participants, in this case surgeons, performed mental arithmetic tasks known to simulate psychophysiological stress.

On the day of the experiment, the participants were placed individually in a room and told to perform the mental arithmetic tasks under three conditions: no music, experimenter-selected music, and surgeon-selected music, here meaning the type of music identified by the surgeon as the music he or she prefers to play when performing medical operations. The results were overwhelming. Blood pressure, pulse rate, and skin conductivity (sweatiness) were highest in the no-music condition, next highest in the experimenter-selected condition, and lowest in the surgeon-selected condition. All differences were statistically significant (Allen & Blascovich, 1994). In addition, the surgeon's speed and accuracy were better in the surgeon-selected music condition than in the other two.

With such outcomes, many people would eagerly ask their surgeons to play music while operating. But what genre of music should they choose? The study suggests that the stress measures are lowest and performance is enhanced when surgeons select the music they most enjoy. Allen and Blascovich (1994) noted that, of the 50 surgeon participants, 46 chose classical music, two chose Irish folk music, and two chose jazz. The type of music is immaterial. What matters is whether the surgeon likes it!

In addition, humor, with or without laughter, also enhances positive moods and moderates stress levels. Research suggests that humor moderates stress in two ways, first as an effective coping response to the stressful stimuli and second as a means of reinterpreting and restructuring the situation so that it is less stressful (Abel, 2002; Lefcourt et al., 1995; Martin, Kuiper, Olinger, & Dance, 1993; Ruch & Carrell, 1998). Consider this scenario: You borrowed your friend's best suit for a very important job interview, which is conducted over lunch. While you are eating, a waiter passes too close to your table and bumps your arm, causing you to spill the contents of your drink on your lap. Stunned, you say nothing at first, thinking only of your friend's reaction when you tell him of the accident. But suddenly the interviewer laughs, as he tells you an amusing story about how he, too, spilled a drink while interviewing with the company's owner, only he spilled his drink on both himself and the boss. The humorous story may help to cope with your immediate response to the problem. Admittedly, however, you will still need to address how best to clean the soiled clothes and hopefully return a stain-free suit to your friend.

A humorous reinterpretation of situations also reduces stress. Consider another scenario: An accountant was told to resubmit her corrected report with no errors because, as her boss indicated, "errors leave a bad taste in my mouth." The employee was upset at her carelessness but as she worked she realized she could not guarantee that the final report was error free. Therefore, she decided to do the next best thing. When she placed her report on her boss's desk she also gave her boss a cup of his favorite mocha latte. When the boss asked why the latte, the employee said, "If you drink the latte while reading the report, there is no chance you will have a bad taste in your mouth."

To summarize, research on coping focuses on effective strategies for controlling distress in response to an external stimulus. Aromatherapy, music, and humor are three of a number of largely behavioral coping strategies used by people to respond to stress-inducing events. They are relevant to our understanding of health and well-being because one role of health psychologists is to assist people in adopting behaviors that will enhance their health outcomes. For example, individuals who encounter stress as a regular feature of their job may need to find and implement effective coping mechanisms on a daily basis. Consider for a moment air traffic controllers. They are responsible for ensuring the safe conduct of airplanes. Similarly, nurses and doctors make decisions that have a direct impact on a person's well-being. Undoubtedly people in both occupations can experience considerable work-related stress. People in such occupations need effective coping mechanisms to effectively perform their jobs and to maintain their own emotional health. Health psychologists can help individuals effectively employ coping strategies to manage the situation and to ensure their overall well-being.

Even people in less high-risk situations need to employ coping mechanisms on occasion. Not sure of this claim? Consider this: You receive an unexpectedly low grade on an exam. Think about the various ways you attempt to reduce your anxiety as the professor hands you the test results with the grade clearly visible.

Positive Affect and Stress

So far, we have defined stress as a negative health factor, something to be controlled, reduced, or eliminated. Yet current research on coping and stress suggests that stress can also be a positive experience. How is it possible that something we have treated as an event to be managed, controlled, or eliminated can be positive? Put it this way: When viewing stress as a negative factor, we are relying on the biomedical model of health in which stress is similar to a disease or illness to be identified, contained, and removed. On the other hand, positive psychology interprets stress as potentially beneficial because a positive affect toward the stressful event may allow for learning or new skill development.

In case this seem counterintuitive, consider the following: Research on the positive outcomes of stress suggest that, during a stressful encounter, a person might learn a new response or acquire a new skill while managing through the situation. These studies suggest that the important factor in such events is not only how one manages the stressful event but also the new skills employed and the new learning opportunities, growth experiences, or even spiritual growth that occurs as a result of the event (Holohan & Moos, 1990, 1991; Nolen-Hoeksema, Larson, & Grayson, 1999; Pargament, 1997; Schaefer & Coleman, 1992).

If you assume a positivist perspective, stressful events may yield two benefits. First, when approaching a stressor with a positive affect, an individual may be buffered or protected from the adverse psychological consequences of stressful events. This implies that the attitude one brings to the situation may help to hold at bay the more negative reactions, such as anxiety, or momentary depression that could result from the problem. Second, a positive affect may help to develop new skills or promote individual growth that will be useful when encountering similar events in the future. Some studies of coping, therefore, focus on *positive reappraisal*, or the use of cognitive strategies to see a situation in a more positive light. An expression often used to characterize positive reappraisal is "the glass is half full," instead of "the glass is half empty."

We can apply the positive reappraisal concept to the opening story. Remember that Susan, Michael, and Lucinda decided to place Sarah in a nursing home. But suppose, rather than opt for the alternative living arrangement, Susan decided to approach the difficulty posed by having Sarah live with them as a challenge to be resolved. For example, we know that Sarah was easily agitated in restaurants. But suppose that at home Susan discovered that Sarah could entertain herself for hours with her Sudoku electronic game board. In fact, Sarah could be so engrossed in the task that she ignored her surroundings and focused only on the game. Using a positive reappraisal, what could Susan do?

One strategy would be to test the effectiveness of the Sudoku game by taking Sarah out with the family for dinner at a small restaurant. Susan may find that the game is sufficient to quiet Sarah, keeping her from becoming agitated by the new surroundings. In the process, the family can enjoy a meal together in a restaurant, one of their favorite family activities.

Research by Folkman and Moskowitz (2000) and Moskowitz, Folkman, Collette, and Vittinghof (1996) also apply the positive reappraisal concept. Specifically, they examine the positive reappraisal strategies of caregivers when managing the daily problems associated with the care and management of AIDS patients. The studies found that AIDS caregivers who were able to set and complete a specific goal each day, regardless how small, felt a sense of accomplishment that helped them manage throughout the day. The goal could be an everyday task such as meeting friends, going to the post office, or having a meal, similar to Susan's goal. The ability to complete one task, regardless of how small, demonstrated their ability to exert control over a situation that sometimes defied control (Folkman & Moskowitz, 2000). The point here is the completed task serves as an accomplishment, something that contains positive meaning.

The short-term impact of positive reappraisal in stressful situations is clear. The individuals experience success. For example, Susan, Michael, and Lucinda's ability to enjoy a meal in a restaurant could reinforce their sense of control over an otherwise uncontrollable or stressful event. And remember that one of the sources of stress as identified by Heijman and colleagues (2004) when dealing with chronic or long-term illnesses is a sense of loss of control associated with the illness.

An interesting additional finding by Folkman and Moskowitz, and one that is particularly relevant to this chapter on stress and health, is that AIDS caregivers in their study who reported small but consistent positive accomplishments also showed better psychological health and adjustment after the death of the AIDS patient than did caregivers who did not use positive reappraisal strategies. Fully three and six months after their caregiving responsibilities ended, AIDS caregivers who demonstrated positive reappraisal strategies were less depressed and had better overall psychological health than non–positive reappraisal strategy caregivers. Thus, positive reappraisal suggests that stress need not be viewed as a negative factor to be controlled and overcome. Rather, positive reappraisal suggests that a positive psychological approach to stress can result in benefits for both the individual and the caregiver and in both the short and long term.

In summary, the original and current research on stress considers the beneficial and the detrimental impacts of stress on health. By examining coping strategies, researchers note first that individual responses to situations will vary. An event that is stressful to one person may not produce the same effect on another. As such, the perception of stress as well as the effectiveness of strategies to cope with stress will vary by individuals.

Second, research on coping also illustrates the advantages of a positive psychological perspective to understanding well-being. We explored the contributions of positive psychology in Chapter 6, Emotional Health and Well-Being. The benefits of a positive affect when encountering otherwise stressful events and positive reappraisal strategies that assist us in interpreting the event are skills that health psychologists may use to help individuals acquire and effectively manage their environments.

Personal Postscript: How Stressed Are You?

Lazarus and Folkman define the daily hassles in life as those little things that can irritate and distress you. We all experience them. Because they are quite common, one way to avoid having such hassles overwhelm us or have a negative impact on our overall well-being is to identify the stressors and then identify, for ourselves, the most effective way to address the problem. This may include the cognitive coping techniques we described, behavioral techniques, or positive reappraisal and positive affect.

To begin the process, included below are items from the Negative Event (Hassles) Scale, a scale adapted from Holmes and Holroyd's Daily Hassles Scale (Holm and Holroyd, 1992). Take a minute to look at the items and determine whether any of the items are occasional, regular, or frequent hassles you encounter. Also think about whether they represent no real hassle, minor hassle, moderate hassle, or considerable hassle. Once you have identified the major hassles, the next task is to consider ways of addressing the problem. Remember, problem-focused coping strategies are best for addressing the stressful stimulus and for enhancing likely overall health outcomes.

SAMPLE OF NEGATIVE EVENTS

Inner concerns

1. Regrets over past decisions
2. Loneliness
3. Fear of rejection
4. Trouble making decisions
5. Concerns about getting ahead
6. Concerns about wasting time

Financial Concerns

1. Not enough money for basic necessities
2. Not enough money for entertainment and recreation
3. Concerns about money for emergencies
4. Concerns about owing money
5. Not enough money for health care

Time Pressures

1. Too many responsibilities
2. Not enough time to accomplish all required tasks
3. Not getting enough sleep

4. Not enough time for entertainment and recreation
5. Concerns about meeting high standards

Work Hassles

1. Job dissatisfaction
2. Hassles from boss or supervisor
3. Don't like current work
4. Don't like fellow workers
5. Problems getting along with fellow workers

Environmental Hassles

1. Pollution
2. Crime
3. Traffic
4. Rising prices of common goods
5. Concerns about news events

Health Hassles

1. Concerns about medical treatment
2. Concerns about side effects of medicines
3. Concerns about health in general
4. Concerns about bodily functions
5. Physical illnesses

Now that you have identified a number of situations that may cause occasional, regular, or frequent hassles for you, the question is what you can do to reduce your stress in responding to them and to cope more effectively. Part of the answer rests in knowing what strategies work best with you and your system. Simply put, one size does not fit all.

Consider this: If one hassle for you is completing work-related tasks according to a time line, you may consider ways in which to make the task less stressful. For example, when working on the task, you may consider playing your favorite music, like the surgeons in Box 7.4. Music helped them relax while doing the procedure and in the process improved both their accuracy and speed in completing the task.

Second, exercise is a known stress reliever. Perhaps you enjoyed exercising in high school or early in your college career. Jogging and swimming are excellent cardiovascular exercises that may help to reduce your stress levels. If, on the other hand, you seek something less intense, yoga, stretching exercises, or meditation may produce the same outcomes for you.

Finally, think about humor. Daily hassles often cause us to lose our ability to laugh. And, as we saw in this chapter, humor can act on both the physiological and psychological factors that contribute to stress. Therefore, consider going to the movies. But be sure to choose a comedy, something with a theme that you find funny. Or attend a comedy club, preferably one that features one of your favorite comedians.

These are just three activities that may help you reduce stress and cope with life's daily hassles. Can you think of others that may work specifically for you?

Important Terms

adrenal cortex   223
adrenal gland   222
adrenal medulla   223
adrenaline   223
adrenocorticotropic hormone
    (ACTH)   222
allostasis   221
aromatherapy   242
autonomic nervous system
    (ANS)   221
catecholamine   223
central nervous system
    (CNS)   221
cognitive appraisal   225
cognitive reappraisal   226
coping   239
cortisol   229
daily life hassles   235
daily stressors   235
diathesis–stress (D–S)
    model   229
ductless glands   222

emotion-focused coping   240
emotional reactivity   231
endocrine system   222
endorphins   245
engagement/disengagement
    coping   240
epinephrine   223
fight-or-flight theory   219
glucocorticoids   223
hypothalamus   222
hypothalamic-pituitary-
    adrenocortical system
    (HPAC)   223
life change unit score   233
negative emotionally
    reactive   231
nervous system   221
norepinephrine   223
parasympathetic nervous
    system   221
peripheral nervous system
    (PNS)   221

pituitary gland   222
positive reappraisal   247
posttraumatic stress disorder
    239
primary appraisal   225
problem-focused coping   240
secondary appraisal   225
sensory receptor sites   221
Social Readjustment Rating
    Scale (SRRS)   233
somatic nervous system
    (SNS)   221
stressful stimulus   219
stressful response   219
sympathetic nervous
    system   221
sympathetic-adrenal-
    medullary system
    (SAM)   223
transactional model (TM)   225
type A personality   230
type D personality   230

HIV and AIDS

Chapter Objectives

After studying this chapter you will be able to:

1. Define HIV and AIDS.
2. Describe the function of T lymphocytes and B lymphocytes.
3. Explain the HIV infection and transmission process.
4. Characterize HIV rates globally and nationally.
5. Describe past and current HIV testing procedures.
6. Explain new developments in HIV treatment and their effects on health outcomes.
7. List and describe limitations to HIV prevention and treatment.
8. Explain the role of psychology in HIV testing and treatment.
9. Define and describe psychoneuorimmunology and its application to HIV.

OPENING STORY: RYAN WHITE: AN AGENT OF CHANGE

Basketball fans were stunned when they heard the legendary Earvin "Magic" Johnson of the Los Angeles Lakers announce on November 7, 1991, that he had the human immunodeficiency virus (HIV), the virus that causes acquired immunodeficiency syndrome (AIDS) (see Figure 8.7). Tennis fans felt a loss when they learned that Arthur Ashe, the first African American man to win Wimbledon and the U.S. and Australian Opens, died of complications related to HIV/AIDS in 1993. And aquatic sports fans soberly absorbed the announcement in 1994 by Greg Louganis, the winner of four Olympic gold medals, that he, too, had HIV. By comparison, few people heard about Ryan White, an adolescent who contracted the disease several years earlier (see Figure 8.1).

*Ryan was not a famous athlete. But like Magic Johnson, Arthur Ashe, and Greg Louganis, his life was irrevocably changed by HIV/AIDS. Ryan was born with **hemophilia**, a rare bleeding disease that prevents blood from clotting normally, turning ordinary scrapes, cuts, and nicks into potentially life-threatening scenarios of excessive blood loss. Hemophiliacs, or people with the disease, also risk damage to their internal organs and possible death due to excessive internal bleeding (National Heart, Lung, and Blood Institute, 2007). To help control the bleeding, hemophiliacs are treated with blood products. Ryan was receiving treatment for his hemophilia when he was diagnosed with HIV in 1984. Apparently, he was given a blood product that was contaminated with the virus. Ryan was only 13 years old.*

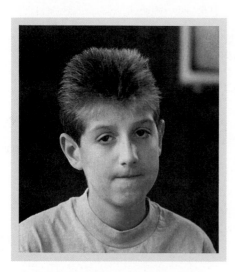

FIGURE 8.1   Ryan White. The first known adolescent infected with HIV from contaminated blood products used to treat his hemophilia.

Source: Health Resources & Service Administration (2009).

In 1984, HIV/AIDS was a rare and relatively unknown disease. At the time, the virus was associated with three groups: homosexual men, intravenous drug users, and Haitians, groups often stigmatized by society. Lack of knowledge about the disease and erroneous assumptions about individuals who were HIV positive caused many to fear or reject anyone with the virus. Ryan's neighbors in Kokomo, Indiana, were no exception. Reacting to Ryan's diagnosis of HIV, the school board in Kokomo banned Ryan from attending school, based on the fear that he would expose other children to HIV/AIDS (AIDSPAC, 2007). Ryan and his mother successfully sued the Kokomo school board. He won the right to return to school, but the family chose to move to Cicero, Indiana, instead: Stigma and isolation by the Kokomo community created an unwelcoming environment for the White family.

Ryan died of AIDS in 1990. That same year the U.S. Congress passed the Ryan White Comprehensive AIDS Resource Emergency (RARE) Act (Public Law 101-381), an act that provides $1.5 billion per year for health care and resources for people with HIV/AIDS (AIDSPAC, 2007). ∎

In the 1980s and early 1990s, HIV was more than an unfortunate, life-threatening disease. It was a stigma. One reason for the stigma was the lack of information about the disease and the populations most at risk. In an effort to quickly inform the public about the disease and to contain its spread, scientists released preliminary information and updates about the virus. Some of the information was found later to be inaccurate. For example, based on preliminary information, people who were diagnosed with HIV were assumed, often incorrectly, to be homosexuals, intravenous drug users (IVDUs), or Haitians. As we will see later in the chapter, the assumption that HIV affected only these three groups obscured the fact that women, children, adolescents, and, yes, even sports celebrities could contract HIV. In addition, it caused adverse emotional and psychological health outcomes for individuals with HIV and others in their social networks. Thus, one role for health psychologists in the early stages of the pandemic was addressing the emotional and psychological health needs of infected individuals and their support groups. By the early 1990s, scientists had discovered that HIV was not associated with high-risk groups; rather it was associated with specific high-risk health behaviors. Scientists learned that HIV was transmitted by direct contact with blood or other body fluids that were contaminated with the virus. But the public, the nonscientific community, seemed to hold fast to earlier information that associated HIV with specific groups.

The revelation in the early 1990s that three sports celebrities—Magic Johnson, Arthur Ashe, and Greg Louganis—had HIV, in addition to more information about the virus, helped change the public's perception of the disease. Slowly, many in the public began to accept that HIV was associated with risky behaviors that exposed individuals to contaminated human body fluids.

Increasingly, the public became aware that women were being diagnosed with HIV, although these cases, like that of Ryan White, were not as well publicized. Included in the count of women with HIV were Amanda Blake (see Figure 8.2), the actress and star of *Gunsmoke*, a popular television series from 1955 through 1975, and actress and model Tina Chow, who died in 1992. Women in the medical profession were also becoming infected, including Lucille Teasdale-Corti, a Canadian physician and international aid worker, and Margrethe Rask, a Dutch physician who worked in Uganda.

The men and women identified here exemplify our current understanding about HIV: It is a disease that can affect anyone regardless of gender, ethnicity, socioeconomic status, or profession. We now know that our health behaviors, not who we are, influence our risk of contracting HIV.

Unlike other contagious diseases such as measles or chicken pox, there is no vaccine to protect individuals from HIV. Currently, the only proven method for controlling the spread of the disease is through behavior change, specifically avoiding risky behaviors that may expose individuals to the virus.

We noted in Chapter 4, Theories and Models of Health Behavior Change, that one goal of health psychology is to improve individual health outcomes by increasing health-enhancing behaviors and decreasing health-compromising behaviors. HIV is an excellent example of a highly infectious and dangerous illness that can be controlled though such behavior change. Thus, over the past three decades, health psychologists have contributed to efforts to control the spread of HIV through research and intervention based on theories of behavior change.

HIV is relevant to psychology also because through HIV we can explore ***psychoneuroimmunology***, a new field that examines mental health (*psychology*) as a cofactor in the progression of diseases involving the central nervous system (*neurology*) and the immune system (*immunology*). Researchers now know that the psychological impact of a positive HIV diagnosis,

FIGURE 8.2   The Cast of *Gunsmoke*. Amanda Blake is in the center of this group photo.

as well as an individual's emotional health in coping with the disease and its progression, affects quality of life and the physical health of HIV-positive individuals.

In this chapter, our discussion of HIV and AIDS will focus on three main topics: the science of HIV, HIV prevalence and human behavior, and psychosocial perspectives on testing and treatment for HIV. In the first section we review the human immune system, focusing on the elements most relevant for understanding the effects of HIV on the body. We also explain the HIV virus. In Section II, we explore the origins of the disease in humans, its symptoms, and its modes of transmission. We examine the prevalence of the disease in the United States and globally, focusing on the role of individuals, health systems, and health policy in contributing to or stemming the spread of HIV. We also dispel some commonly cited myths about the disease. In Section III we discuss new developments in HIV testing and treatment. The focus in this section is on the contributions of health psychology in the posttesting counseling and treatment of people with HIV. We conclude with a discussion of psychoneuroimmunology in Section IV to demonstrate the interaction of psychology, neurology, and immunology on diseases.

SECTION I. THE SCIENCE OF HIV AND AIDS

Definition of HIV and AIDS

HUMAN IMMUNODEFICIENCY VIRUS (HIV)   The acronym HIV is so well known that few people use its full name, ***human immunodeficiency virus***, when talking about the disease. Consequently few people know what the acronym means. Working backward, ***virus*** is a Latin word meaning toxic or poison. When classified as a poison, we know immediately that HIV is harmful to the human body. But the human body comes in contact with many viruses. Influenza is caused by a virus, but it accounts on average for only 36,000 deaths per year in the United States (Dushoff et al., 2006). Similarly, the common cold and chicken pox are caused by viruses. Unquestionably they are uncomfortable illnesses, but they are rarely deadly. HIV, however, always makes individuals susceptible to illnesses that lead to death. For this reason HIV belongs in the category of extremely harmful and fatal viruses.

The word *immunodeficiency* explains HIV's deadly consequences. HIV attacks and renders useless (or deficient) the human body's immune system. It attacks the very system in our bodies designed to fight invading viruses. By suppressing the human immune system, HIV enables other viruses and illnesses to invade the body. As a result, individuals lose their ability to resist or destroy the invading viruses.

ACQUIRED IMMUNODEFICIENCY SYNDROME (AIDS)   Many think that *acquired immunodeficiency syndrome (AIDS)* is a synonym for HIV. In fact, it is not. HIV is the virus that causes AIDS. AIDS, however, is the final and most severe stage of the disease signaled by a collection of infections and illnesses (DiSpezio, 1997).

A person is diagnosed with AIDS when two things occur: First, the individual's immune system is suppressed, making it difficult to resist infections; and, second, his or her white blood cell count falls below 200 cells per microliter of blood, or approximately 200 cells per .0002 teaspoons of blood. We explain the relationship between white blood cells and HIV more fully in the following section. For now, it is enough to note that diminished white blood cell counts suppress the immune system and allow *opportunistic infections*, diseases that invade a weakened or defenseless body to further debilitate it. There are many types of opportunistic infections, but two are often associated with AIDS: *pneumocystic carinii pneumonia*, a form of pneumonia, and *Kaposi sarcoma*, a formerly rare type of cancer.

An individual can be HIV-positive for a number of years and be *asymptomatic*, here meaning showing no symptoms of an illness. But when the body's white blood cells number fewer than 200 cells per microliter, an individual experiences a succession of illnesses, either consecutively or concurrently. The frequent bouts of illnesses will eventually overwhelm the immune system, and the person will die from one of the opportunistic infections. Applying our definition of proximal and distal causes of illness as explained in Chapter 2, Research Methods, the proximal cause of death for someone with HIV could be a major illness such as pneumonia or a minor virus the body could not overcome, like a cold. HIV will be identified as the distal cause of death.

The Human Immune System

When working well, our immune system protects us from a multitude of bacteria, viruses, and microorganisms that are ever present in our world. It does this by protecting our body from foreign substances using *innate*, or *natural, immunity* and by discriminating successfully between our body's own elements and foreign substances using *adaptive*, or *acquired, immunity*. For our purposes we will refer to the two systems as natural and acquired immunity, respectively.

NATURAL IMMUNITY   Our body has several first lines of defense against foreign elements. They include the skin, saliva, urinary tract, and mucus, among others. We cannot review all of the body's natural immunities in this text, so we will explore just one: the human skin.

The skin consists of two layers (see Figure 8.3). First is the *epidermis*, a thin outer layer that contains tightly packed *epithelial cells* and a waterproofing protein called *keratin*. Together they work to repel germs and other foreign matter from the body's surface and to prevent germs from penetrating the skin.

The second layer of skin, the *dermis*, is thicker than the epidermis. It consists of connective tissues that contain blood vessels, hair follicles, and *sebaceous glands*, or glands that secret an

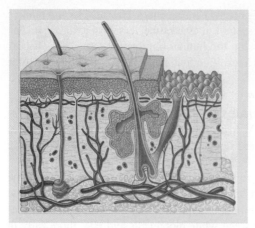

FIGURE 8.3 Human Skin Layers. The human skin contains several layers that protect us from germs as part of our first line of defense.

oily substance. The oils help to maintain the pH balance of the skin and to inhibit the growth of ***microorganisms***, otherwise known as germs. Many microorganisms will be repelled by the skin; however, openings in the skin from scratches, cuts, or punctures will allow microorganisms to bypass the body's natural immunity. If a microorganism bypasses the body's natural immunity, the body's acquired immunity will activate to fight the invading germs (see Figure 8.4).

ACQUIRED IMMUNITY The body's acquired immune system is composed of cells that reside in blood and other body fluids. As the name suggests, the acquired immune system learns to recognize and eliminate microorganisms that are foreign to the body. The learning process is what makes the system adaptive because it must recognize and respond to both new and previously presented foreign substances. Adaptive immunity has four main characteristics as detailed in Table 8.1. The ***self/nonself process*** distinguishes the body's own cells from foreign cells. Second, using ***antigenic specificity***, the body's immune

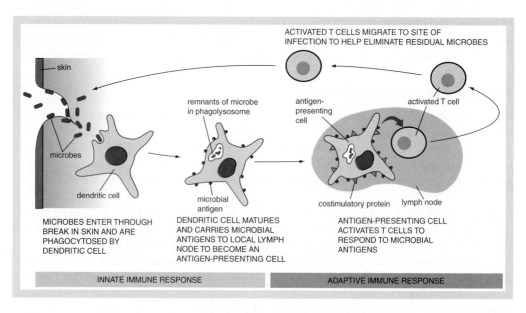

FIGURE 8.4 Natural (Innate) and Acquired (Adaptive) Immune Response.

Source: Bruce, Bray, Lewis, Raft, Roberts, and Watson (2002).

TABLE 8.1   Brief Summary of the Immune System

Two Types of Immunity	Description
Natural (Innate) Immunity	Body's first line of defense against microorganisms Includes: skin, saliva, urinary track, muscles
Acquired (Adaptive) Immunity	Immunity derived from recognizing and defeating microorganisms that the body has experienced before.
Four principal processes	
Self/nonself discrimination	Ability of body cells to distinguish between foreign elements and body's own cells
Antigen specificity	Process of distinguishing among different types of foreign microorganisms and generating a specific immune response to the specific foreign antigen
Diversity	Ability of body to recognize the unique structures of each microorganism
Immunologic memory	Ability to recognize a previously presented antigen when it returns, giving the body the ability to respond more quickly and effectively against foreign microorganisms
Organs and cells	Lymphoid organs (tonsils, lymph nodes, thymus, spleen) that produce white blood cells that fight infection
Main cells	White blood cells or leukocytes that filter microorganisms and help reduce risk of infection
Principal leukocytes	Contain neutrophils and macrophages (phagocytic cells) that collect at the site of an injury of the body to release toxins that produce inflammation and fever that contribute to healing
Polymorphonuclear granulocytes	Comprise 50–70% of leukocytes but appear to play minor role in immune process
Lymphocytes *B cells*	Two types that develop and mature in bone marrow: • B-memory "remembers" prior invading microorganisms and identifies them when representing themselves; faster recognition aids in the process of destroying foreign antigens • B-antibody forms specific antigens to attack invading microorganisms
T cells	Three types born in bone marrow and matured in thymus: • T cytotoxis (T_C), "killer" cells, destroy cells infected with the virus • T helper (T_H) help to produce the cytotoxin that destroys invading virus and assists in the maturation of B cells • T suppressor (T_S) slows the immune system by reducing activity of T_C cells once invading antigens have been eliminated to prevent damage to the immune system

system distinguishes between different forms of foreign *antigens*, here meaning foreign microorganisms that trigger the immune response in the body. Third, the system uses *diversity*, or the ability to recognize the unique structures of each foreign microorganism. Diversity ensures that the system can identify and target specific foreign organisms. The fourth characteristic is *immunologic memory*, or the ability to recognize a specific foreign organism in subsequent exposures.

The four characteristics are one part of the body's immune response. The second component involves the organs and cells that participate in the process. Organs such as the tonsils, the lymph nodes, and the thymus, for example, are called *lymphoid organs* because *lymphocytes*, infection-fighting white blood cells, grow in the organs (see Figure 8.5). Lymphocyte cells can be thought of as the "security patrol" for the body because they search for foreign or infectious microorganisms.

B LYMPHOCYTES   There are two types of lymphocytes. One type, *B lymphocytes* or *B cells*, form in the bone marrow until mature. B cells have two important immune functions. Some B cells are *antibody-producing cells*. They produce cells that attack specific microorganisms. Other B cells are "memory" cells. They encode information that helps them recognize foreign microorganisms encountered and defeated previously.

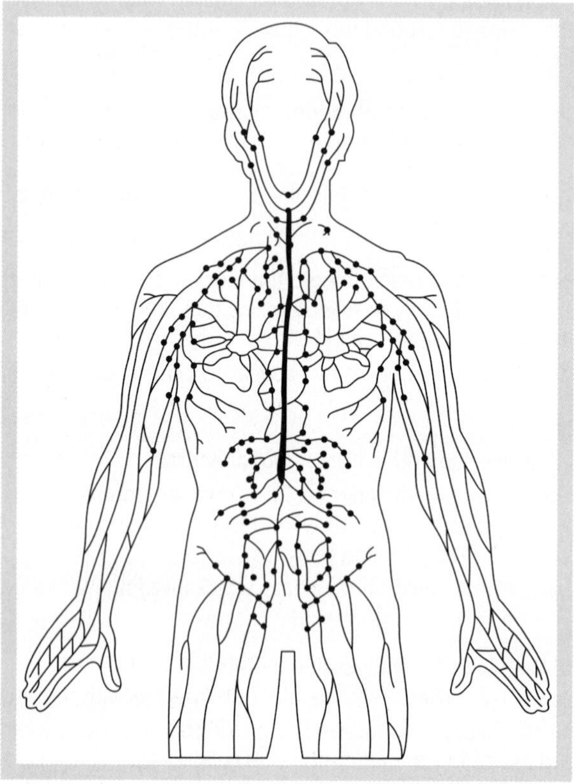

Why is it important for B cells to remember previous foreign organisms? Consider this: In our chapter on Global Communicable and Chronic Disease (Chapter 3), we introduced the concept of vaccines (immunizations). We mentioned that, when vaccinating children against childhood diseases such as chicken pox, a small amount of the virus is injected into the child. A healthy immune system is able to successfully fight and destroy a small quantity of the chicken pox virus introduced to the body for the first time by vaccine. After destroying the foreign organisms, the immune system will "remember" the chicken pox virus so that, when it encounters the same microorganism in larger quantities in the future, it will be able to detect, identify, and eliminate it more quickly and efficiently. In essence, the body's memory of the chicken pox virus ensures that, with rare exception, the body will respond effectively and quickly and protect the child from the effects of chicken pox.

FIGURE 8.5 • Lymphoid Organs of the Human Body. Lymphoid organs (indicated by nodules) produce lymphocytes, the "security patrol" for the body.

Source: Bruce et al. (2002).

T LYMPHOCYTES   A second type of lymphocyte is the *T lymphocytes*, or *T cells*, which form in the thymus (look again at Table 8.1). There are three different types of T cells, all of which perform specific immune functions: T cytotoxis (T_C), T helper (T_H), and T suppressor (T_S). The *T cytotoxis* cell, or *T_C* for short, is known as the "killer" cell. It is responsible for destroying the cells that become infected by a virus. A second T cell is the *T_H* or *T helper* cell, which helps the system by producing *cytokines*, or agents that produce antibodies to fight invading viruses. T_H cells can either help direct the T_C, or 'killer," cells or help activate the B-memory cells.

It is important to point out that with respect to HIV, T_H cells serve another important role for the immune system. The T_H cells display CD4 glycoproteins on the surface of the cell. You may have heard the name CD4 before. As we will see shortly, for HIV-positive individuals the number of CD4 cells is another important measure of the strength of the immune system.

Finally, *T_S* or *T suppressor cells* serve as the "off switch." They help slow the functions of the immune system by sending messages to reduce the activity of the T_C and T_H cells once the immune system has completed its work of destroying the invading cells.

MEASURING THE IMMUNE SYSTEM   There are several ways that health providers measure the strength of an individual's immune system. The number of CD4 cells in the system is one way. Other measures include cell differentiation, cell proliferation, and cytotoxicity (see Table 8.2). Each of these measures can be obtained from a small sample of blood or saliva.

For people who test positive for HIV, the number of **CD4 cells** is a critical measure of the number of T_H cells in the system. CD4 are molecules that bind onto T_H cells, which, as you will recall, initiate the process of identifying and fighting foreign cells. HIV binds onto CD4 cells that serve as the host for the virus. Thus, when the virus begins to reproduce, suppressing the immune system, it also destroys the T cells with the CD4 molecules. The process by which HIV invades and destroys cells is explained in greater detail in the following section.

A normal CD4 cell count, found in HIV-negative and otherwise healthy individuals, ranges from 500 to 1500 cells per microliter of blood (.0002 teaspoon). HIV-positive individuals who are

TABLE 8.2	Selected Methods of Measuring the Health of the Immune System
Measure	**Description**
CD4 cell count	Measures the number of T_H cells that initiate the process for identifying microorganisms. • Normal CD4 cell count: 500–1,500 • Low CD4 count: 200–499 • CD4 < 200 with a positive diagnosis of HIV may be diagnosed as AIDS
Cell differentiation	Percent of $T_{C,H,S}$ cells produced by the body needed to fight infection
Cell proliferation	Rate of multiplication of each T cell type
Cell cytotoxicity	Cell's ability to kill foreign antigens

asymptomatic also may have 500 or more CD4 cells per microliter. When HIV begins to suppress the immune system, the CD4 count will drop to 200 to 499 cells per microliter. A CD4 cell count below 200 cells per microliter indicates that the immune system is severely suppressed. At this point, an individual has advanced to the final stage of illness, a process called *seroconversion* (CDC, 1992).

Cell differentiation measures the degree to which cells divide into the different T cells (T_C, T_H, or T_S). As we noted earlier, each T cell type has a unique function, and each is needed when combating foreign microorganisms. If an immune system does not produce differentiated cell types, or sufficient numbers of each cell type, it may be less able to combat microorganisms.

Cell proliferation refers to the extent to which the cells multiply. Comparable numbers of T_C, T_H, and T_S cells are needed to eliminate viruses. Too little of one type of T cell can diminish the body's effectiveness in combating viruses. Finally, *cytotoxicity* measures the extent to which the body's cells are able to kill foreign organisms.

DNA VIRUSES VERSUS RETROVIRUSES   HIV is a unique virus because it targets and attacks the immune system. It weakens the system, rendering the body unable to defend itself from other infections that lead to death. The repeated exposure to infections and viruses further weakens the immune system and eventually renders the body unable to destroy even minor viral infections.

What makes HIV so distinctive? Simply stated, it is a retrovirus.

Many viruses we encounter are DNA viruses. *DNA* is *deoxyribonucleic acid*, the heredity material present in humans and other organisms. DNA is often called the "human blueprint" because it contains the information needed to construct the cells that comprise our system.

DNA is housed in the cell nucleus, the control center for the activities of the cell, and consists of hundreds of strands packed with information (see Figure 8.6). A DNA virus, however, contains only one strand of DNA. When a DNA virus enters the body, it copies its genetic code onto a *viral RNA*, the agent that helps the virus reproduce. Thus, most DNA viruses are easily identifiable by the viral RNA code they display to the immune system.

HIV, however, is a retrovirus. *Retroviruses* store their genetic information in *RNA* or *ribonucleic acid*. Put another way, the genetic material for HIV is RNA. Unlike a DNA virus that converts into a viral RNA that is easily recognized as a foreign element, the HIV virus does the opposite. The virus converts its genetic RNA into viral DNA. After recoding as viral DNA, HIV inserts itself into the cell nucleus and copies its genetic material onto the host cell's DNA, firmly imbedding itself into the cell (Goldsby, Kindt, Osborn, & Kuby, 2003). Once embedded, the HIV virus has a host that will help it reproduce when the time is right.

Remember, we said earlier that the virus lies dormant for a while, meaning that it does not replicate immediately. Think of it this way: The HIV virus is like a fox, and the body's healthy cells can be compared to sheep. When HIV-fox enters a body full of healthy sheep cells, it attacks one of the sheep. It slowly destroys the sheep and then uses the sheep's wool to disguise itself as just another sheep. The disguised HIV-fox is not recognized by the body as a foreign element. Slowly HIV-fox begins to multiply and invade other sheep.

HIV and the process by which it invades, converts, and destroys healthy human cells present researchers with a unique challenge: how to identify, isolate, and destroy HIV (viral DNA) without killing other human cells necessary for survival. The challenge is one reason why scientists have been unable to effectively isolate and kill the HIV virus.

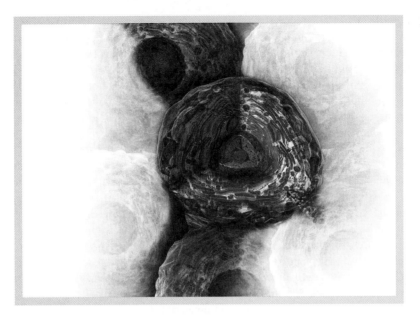

FIGURE 8.6   Cell Nucleus. The cell nucleus is the control center for all activities in the cell.

Summary

We dissected the immune system to briefly explain how it functions. Now, putting it back together, we find that we have two primary components of the human immune system: natural immunity and acquired immunity. Natural immunity is readily visible in the form of skin, saliva, mucus, and other elements. It is the body's first line of defense. Less visible to the naked eye, however, is the acquired immunity. The acquired immune system includes a number of organs and cells. It also contains five types of lymphocytes that serve as the "security patrol" for the body. Each of the five lymphocytes serves a special function. The B lymphocytes can be either specially programmed cells that attack a specific microorganism or "memory" cells that aid the immune system by recognizing foreign microorganisms. The T lymphocytes can be T_C cells that function as warriors, attacking and killing the foreign viruses. They also can be T_H cells that help stimulate other cells, specifically B memory and T_C cells to perform their respective jobs. Finally T lymphocytes can be T_S cells that slow the immune system after activation. Armed with knowledge of the immune system, we are better equipped to study the HIV virus and its effects on the body.

SECTION II. HIV PREVALENCE, HUMAN TRANSMISSION, AND HUMAN BEHAVIOR

When compared with other diseases, HIV in humans appears to be a relatively recent phenomenon. One of the earliest known incidences of HIV was reported in 1977. Dr. Margrethe Rask, a Danish physician, worked for a number of years in Zaire where, it is believed, she contracted the virus (Shilts, 1987). In 1978, reports of an unusual virus began appearing also in some homosexual men in the United States and in Sweden. The early cases were so episodic and puzzling that it took researchers eight years to link the apparently unrelated cases to the same disease and to identify that disease as HIV.

The process of identifying and naming the new virus was not easy. Methods used by epidemiologists and other health researchers, explained in Chapter 2, were employed to investigate the new virus. Teams of researchers sought not only to discover the origins of the disease and to name it but also to determine its likely impact on current and future populations.

In the early days of the disease there were many unanswered questions. For example, initially no one understood why Kaposi sarcoma, a rare skin cancer with flat purplish lesions usually found in Mediterranean and Jewish men 50 to 60 years of age, began appearing in homosexual males, 20 to 30 years of age, who lived in the United States but had never visited the Mediterranean or the Middle East (Shilts, 1987). Other researchers were mystified by incidences of *amoebic dysentery*, an intestinal illness caused by a parasite, which was reported in increasing numbers but appeared to have no known origin. Like the parasitic diseases explained in Chapter 3, Global Communicable and Chronic Disease, amoebic dysentery is usually contracted from consuming contaminated water or foods. But the multiple incidences of amoebic dysentery that appeared suddenly were not due to either contaminated water or food.

After eight years of studying, the scientists were able to link the apparently unrelated cases to the same new disease, HIV. But there were still a host of unanswered questions. For example, how did the disease begin, how many people were affected, and what was the relative risk of the disease to others? Remember, knowing the origins of the disease is interesting, but knowing how to stem the spread of the disease and how to protect others from the disease were the goals of many researchers, including health psychologists.

Origins

Many scientists contend that HIV is linked to a species of chimpanzees known as *Pan troglodytes troglodytes*, found in West Africa (Gao et al., 1999). Gao and coauthors suggest that HIV was probably transmitted from chimpanzees to humans as a result of the animal biting a human or from contact with chimpanzees' HIV-infected blood.

How could a bite from an HIV-infected chimpanzee transmit the virus? Recall that we noted earlier that a break in the human skin caused by a bite will breach one of the body's natural immune systems. Once HIV bypasses the body's natural immunity, the body's acquired immune system must activate to identify and kill the invading microorganism. But, as we also saw in the previous section, the human acquired immune system is no match for the HIV retrovirus. Thus, once the virus bypasses the body's natural immunity, it will certainly impair the body's immune system, exposing it to other infections and illnesses. If scientists are correct, one or several individuals bitten by chimpanzees and exposed to chimpanzee body fluids may explain the origins of HIV in humans.

Just one additional observation before we discuss human-to-human HIV transmission: HIV is not fatal to chimpanzees. The infected primates show no signs of illness or dysfunction from the virus. Thus, while HIV is harmless in one species, it can be fatal in another.

Human-to-Human Transmission

Researchers discovered the human-to-human transmission of HIV through case study analysis of people with HIV, such as Dr. Rask, Magic Johnson, Greg Louganis, Arthur Ashe, and Ryan White. We now know that any activity that results in an exchange of fluids from an HIV-positive person, or that exposes uninfected individuals to contaminated fluids, could result in infection.

Medical studies have determined that HIV is transmitted primary through three routes: sexual intercourse, parenteral (blood-borne) transmission, or perinatal (mother-to-child) transmission (MTCT). Today, sexual transmission accounts for the majority of HIV cases. The virus is carried in semen, vaginal fluids, and blood (saliva is a poor, indeed ineffective, conduit of HIV). As such the virus can be contracted through heterosexual as well as homosexual intercourse. Case study analyses of individuals who tested positive for HIV, such as Magic Johnson and Greg Louganis, helped establish the link between sexual behaviors and HIV infection. And, while earlier studies on HIV emphasized the susceptibility of homosexual men to HIV infection, Magic Johnson's announcement offered a clear and compelling message to the general public that heterosexual men and women were also at risk for contracting HIV.

BOX 8.1 Even Magic Johnson Has It, and He Looks Good

Earvin "Magic" Johnson has everything: five National Basketball Association championships, three Most Valuable Player awards, three National Basketball Association Finals Most Valuable Player awards, a winning personality, and a "magic" smile. What more could he ask for?

Actually, it is what Magic did not ask for. In November 1991 Magic stunned the world when he announced that he was HIV positive. It seemed as if the world stopped and listened. "Sometimes you are a little naïve," he said, "and think that it can never happen to you. You think it can only happen to other people . . . and it has happened but I'm going to deal with it" (American Rhetoric, 2001).

That same November day, after Magic's announcement, the National AIDS Hotline received 40,000 calls, up from its usual 3,800 calls per day. The announcement also spurred an immediate increase in anonymous HIV testing (Gellert, Weismuller, Higgins, & Maxwell, 1992). Other researchers suggest that it created awareness of HIV and perhaps empathy toward people with HIV (Noormohamed, Ferguson, Baghaie, & Cohen, 1994). If Magic Johnson intended to get people's attention about HIV, he succeeded—at least for the moment.

Today, almost 20 years later, Magic looks like the "picture of health." A little heavier than he was in his days as a Los Angeles Laker, Magic is now a business entrepreneur; the principal donor to the Magic Johnson Foundation, which he created in 1991 to

(continued)

FIGURE 8.7   Earvin "Magic" Johnson. Earvin "Magic" Johnson, star athlete and entrepreneur, now devotes time, energy, and resources to HIV/AIDS prevention.

increase awareness of and attention to HIV/AIDS; and a spokesperson for World AIDS Day.

Magic is still strong and active, largely a result of his careful attention to his health and to excellent medical care. Researchers have discovered a combination of medications, sometimes called a "drug cocktail," that, when taken in combination, not only prolongs the life of people with HIV but also improves their overall quality of life. Fortunately for Magic, the cocktail therapy is working well.

Ironically, Magic's success now appears to undermine his message. In spite of the numerous programs and education campaigns to inform the public about the dangers of HIV, Magic's life experiences seem to convey a different message. Current research suggests many men believe that HIV is not such a problem after all. Among males who engage in risky sexual behaviors, researchers note that many are less fearful of HIV now than before. Some males believe that the drug cocktails make HIV a treatable disease rather than a death sentence. With such attitudes, some men may be inclined to continue engaging in the risky sexual behaviors that increase their susceptibility to HIV.

Magic's current health status is a credit to developments in medical research in understanding and treating the disease. But many may still miss the more important message from Magic's experiences. First, Magic contracted a disease as a result of risky sexual behaviors. Heath prevention messages were not effective in changing his behavior to reduce that risk to him. Second, Magic has access to unrestricted and excellent quality health care that provides life-prolonging and health-enhancing HIV medicines. The same may not be true for the average male. Consider this: Research in health psychology shows that lack of access to quality health care is one cause of poor health outcomes (Clauss-Ehler, 2003; Coursen, 2009). It is unlikely that the average male (or female) will have the same access to health care Magic received, either as a member of the Lakers basketball team or in retirement. Finally, while Magic is doing well now, eventually the virus will take its toll. The drug cocktails are a treatment, not a cure. Although difficult to contemplate, as the virus becomes immune to the combination drug therapies, Magic, like other HIV patients, will probably lose his battle with HIV. We should not forget that, at least for now, HIV is a terminal, not a curable, disease.

Until Magic's announcement, many men assumed they were not at risk for HIV because they were not homosexual. Other men assumed that they were at a lower level of relative risk (see Chapter 2, Research Methods) because, among heterosexuals, women reported higher rates of HIV than men. It is true that, due to anatomical differences, women are at greater risk of infection from HIV in heterosexual relationships. But, greater risk for women does not mean that men are risk free. Magic Johnson's case helped illustrate that point and reinforced the fact that unprotected sexual intercourse, a risky health behavior, increases susceptibility to HIV for both men and women, regardless of sexual orientation.

A second method of HIV transmission is *parenteral*, or blood-borne, *transmission*, including blood transfusions similar to the type received by Ryan White and Arthur Ashe. Blood-borne transmissions also include infections from unsanitary needles such as those used by intravenous drug users (IVDUs). Accidental needle sticks, common occurrences among health care workers (Greenblatt & Hessol, 2001), also can result in transmission of HIV if the needle had been used on a patient who was HIV positive.

The third method of infection, *perinatal*, or *mother-to-child, transmission (MTCT)*, occurs when an HIV-positive mother transmits the virus to her child either during birth or possibly through breastfeeding. Early in the HIV disease history, approximately one-third to one-half (35 to 50%) of children born to HIV-positive mothers were thought to have been infected during delivery, a time in which the infant is exposed to a mother's infected blood and other body fluids as it journeys through the birth canal (UNICEF, 2002a, 2002b). Consider this: When Magic Johnson learned he was HIV positive, he immediately became concerned for his wife, Cookie, and one other person. Cookie was pregnant. Both Magic and Cookie faced the real possibility that their unborn child could contract HIV if Cookie tested positive for HIV. Fortunately for the Johnsons, neither Cookie nor baby Johnson was HIV positive. In fact, as of 2005, perinatal transmission rates in the United States have decreased substantially. In 1991, the United States reported that approximately 1,700 infants were infected with HIV at birth, a rate that declined in 2004 to between 96 and 186 infants perinatally infected (McKenna & Hu, 2007).

Until recently, researchers thought that breastfeeding was another possible route of MTCT (Tournoud, Ecochard, Kuhn, & Coutsoudis, 2008). Research on infants in Kwa-Zulu Natal, South Africa, however, suggests that a mother's low CD4 cell count and an infant's low birth weight may be more likely predictors of HIV transmission from mother to child than breastfeeding (Coovadia et al., 2007; Menezes Succi, 2007).

Symptoms of HIV and AIDS

How can you determine if someone has HIV? Will he or she look sick?

By now, many people have seen the HIV education campaigns that attempt to debunk the notion that people with HIV can be identified based on their appearance, their walk, or other obvious outward signs. In fact, individuals who carry the virus often report no noticeable symptoms in the early stages of the disease. One reason is that approximately 15% of HIV-positive people are asymptomatic (Munoz et al., 1995). An additional 25% are unaware during the early stages of the disease that they are infected (Greenwald, Burstein, Pincus, & Branson, 2006). But, for individuals who do experience symptoms, many report flulike ailments, mononucleosis, or frequent rashes that occur 6 to 9 months after the *onset*, or the initial infection. The initial symptoms may disappear after several weeks. What is more, because symptoms in the initial stages of the disease may resemble the flu or other minor viral illnesses, many people mistake the initial HIV symptoms for other common illnesses. For example, Magic Johnson reported that prior to being diagnosed with HIV he thought he had the flu. The point here is that the early onset of HIV is often overlooked because a person is either asymptomatic or presents with very common symptoms that are easily mistaken for other, nonlethal viruses. Thus, the only way to diagnose HIV accurately is through a blood test.

After the onset of HIV, the virus appears dormant. Put another way, there are few if any easily identifiable symptoms of the illness because the flulike symptoms or other external symptoms disappear. While the virus appears inactive, internally the virus is slowly invading the immune system. The dormant period can last 8 to 10 years before symptoms appear that signal significant impairment in the body's immune system. Over time, a number of warning signs will appear. The warning signs are an indication that the body's immune system is beginning to fail. For example, some individuals report a combination of the following symptoms: rapid weight loss; a dry cough; recurrent fevers; profuse night sweats; profound fatigue; pronounced and prolonged swollen glands in the armpits, groin, and neck; diarrhea for more than one week; or white spots or blemishes on the tongue, mouth, or throat (CDC, 2007c). CD4 cell counts during this phase of the disease are often fewer than 500 cells per microliter. A low CD4 cell count, together with a combination of such symptoms, would indicate possible HIV infection.

Two additional factors will signal that an individual has seroconverted from HIV to AIDS, the most severe stage of the disease: a succession of opportunistic infections and a CD4 cell count of less than 200.

In sum, HIV is harmless in the host animal, the chimpanzee. Humans, however, are not as fortunate. In humans, HIV is transmitted through body fluids. Sexual intercourse, which involves an exchange of body fluids, is one way to contract the virus. Blood-borne products and contact with blood-contaminated instruments used by intravenous drug users (IVDUs) or from accidental needle sticks is a second form of transmission. Finally, perinatal or mother-to-child transmission can result in HIV infection in newborns. When infected, individuals may experience three stages of the disease. In the first stage, an individual may be largely unaware of the infection because she or he may be asymptomatic. The infected person may also experience minor, nonspecific symptoms. In the second stage a number of warning signs appear that signal a failing immune system. A reduced CD4 cell count may confirm the assessment. The third and most severe stage is characterized by a succession of opportunistic infections that are debilitating and eventually fatal.

Prevalence of HIV and AIDS: The Effects of Human Behavior and Health Policy

How many people have been infected with HIV? UNAIDS estimates that, as of 2007, 33 million people worldwide had contracted the virus (UNAIDS, 2008a). Of this total, the majority, approximately 30.8 million (93.3%), are adults; 2.0 million (6.1%) are children 15 years of age or younger; and approximately 15.5 million (47.0%) are women or girls (see Table 8.3). These numbers represent a slight decrease in HIV prevalence and incidence rates from the previous year. The current data also show that HIV rates have stabilized, albeit at high rates, in some countries, most notably in southern Africa, including Lesotho, Namibia, South Africa, and Swaziland. At the same time, the rates are on the rise in other countries thought not to be affected in the past, including China, Germany, India, Indonesia, Mozambique, Papua New Guinea, the Russian

TABLE 8.3	Estimated Global versus U.S. HIV Prevalence for 2006	
Category	**Estimated Global Prevalence**	**Estimated U.S. Prevalence**
HIV prevalence: 2006		
Total	33.0 million	1.10 million
Adults	30.8 million (93.3%)	1.05 million (94.9%)*
Women	15.5 million (47.0%)	278,400 (25.5%)
Children under 15 years	2.0 million (6.1%)	56,500**
HIV incidence: 2006		
Total	2.7 million	54,230
Adults	2.3 million (85.2%)	35,730
Children under 15 years	370,000 (14.7%)	18,500***
AIDS deaths: 2006		
Total	2.0 million	
Adults	1.8 million (90.0%)	
Children under 15 years	270,000 (10.0%)	

*Includes persons 25 year of age and older
**Includes persons 24 years of age or younger
***Includes persons 29 year of age or younger
Source: UNAIDS (2008a) and MMWR (2008a, 2008b)

Federation, Ukraine, the United Kingdom, and Vietnam (UNAIDS, 2008a). However, general statistics on the number of people infected with HIV mask important demographic differences in HIV infection rates, as we will see later in this section.

To describe the impact of HIV, researchers report three statistics: HIV *prevalence rates*, or the total number of people infected with HIV; HIV *incidence rates*, or the number of people *newly* infected with HIV; and *mortality rates*, or deaths due to AIDS. Prevalence, incidence, and mortality rates should be familiar measures because they were introduced in Chapter 2, Research Methods. To review, prevalence rate data provide information on the total number of people in a specific population infected with a disease at a specific time, whereas incidence rate data inform us of the rate of growth and spread of the disease, also within a specific population and time frame. Mortality rate measures the rate of death in the population due to the disease, again with reference to a specific time frame.

Prevalence and incidence rates were introduced in Chapter 2 as two gross measures of the health of a population. In the case of HIV, however, not only are these measures gross, they can severely underrepresent the actual rate of spread of the disease. The problem is not the measures or even the tests used to determine a person's HIV status. Rather, the problem lies with individuals' willingness to obtain HIV tests. The stigma associated with being possibly HIV positive, the cost of the test, the lack of access to health care, and the dormant nature of the disease at onset mean that many individuals do not seek testing in the early stages. We noted some of these same barriers to HIV testing in Chapter 4, Theories and Models of Health Behavior Change. Thus, delays in testing for whatever reason result in gross underestimates of the incidence and prevalence of HIV in many regions of the world, including the United States, as we will see shortly.

Among the groups currently reporting a decrease in HIV prevalence is hemophiliacs. You may recall from the opening story about Ryan White that in 1984 hemophiliacs were at high risk of infection for HIV. In 1982 the Centers for Disease Control and Prevention (CDC) reported its first cases of HIV among hemophiliacs. Just one year later, in 1983, the CDC issued a warning that blood products could be infected with HIV and therefore infect persons receiving transmissions. By 1985, approximately 70% of the 10,000 hemophiliacs in the United States were reported to be HIV positive (Blake, 1992).

Realizing that tainted blood products were another source of transmission the U.S. government established that all blood products would be tested and screened. Once instituted, the new health policy had an immediate impact on transmission rates of HIV among hemophiliacs. In 1987, the CDC reported no new cases of HIV among hemophiliacs. And, as of 2007, the CDC reports a total of 198 persons with hemophilia who are also HIV positive and just over 18,000 with AIDS (CDC, 2009b).

THE CHANGING FACE OF HIV/AIDS   Earlier in the chapter we mentioned that in the 1980s many researchers and health practitioners believed that HIV was linked to specific high-risk groups. The groups included homosexual men, intravenous drug users (IVDUs), and Haitians. We also noted that determining an individual's relative risk for HIV (see Chapter 2, Research Methods) based on his or her group category, rather than on individual behaviors, allowed thousands of people to take comfort in the mistaken belief that they could not catch the dreaded new disease because they did not belong to the identified groups. That mistaken belief cost many lives.

It is true that, based on the statistics, homosexual men and IVDUs accounted for the highest rates of HIV in the early days of the disease. However, the risk came from their behaviors, not their status. Remember, HIV is transmitted through an exchange of body fluids. Therefore, homosexual men were logically at high risk given the high probability of open anal sores—a breach of the body's natural immune system—and possible multiple sex partners, which increases the risk of exposure to HIV. Likewise, IVDUs were at high risk because of their tendency to share needles to inject themselves with drugs. Consider this: To extract the last drop of a drug from a syringe, IVDUs will often, after injecting themselves, withdraw a small quantity of blood from their body into the syringe to mix it with the remaining drug and then reinject the drug and blood mixture. The process leaves trace amounts of the drug and blood in the syringe and on the needle. When the syringe is passed to another IVDU, that person inserts a new dose of drug into the now contaminated syringe. If the first IVDU was HIV positive, the second user would be at risk for contracting HIV when injecting the drug with the trace elements of blood from the HIV-positive user into his or her system.

As for Haitians, simply stated, researchers were wrong. In the mid-1980s, many Haitians fled to the United States from their country to escape the poverty in Haiti. Five Haitians in one of the first groups of refugees tested positive for HIV in 1981 (CDC, 1982), but five positive results is too small a sample on which to estimate HIV prevalence rates for an entire country. Some researchers and health professionals appeared to overlook this fact, determining instead that Haitians, as a group, were at high risk for HIV (Pape et al., 2008). The unfortunate mistake of mislabeling a group of people as high risk for a stigmatizing disease such as HIV had—and continues to have—negative consequences for many Haitians.

In essence, linking population groups like Haitians or homosexuals to HIV was and is an inaccurate way of identifying individuals at high risk for HIV. We now know that ***high-risk behaviors***, not high-risk populations, increase susceptibility to HIV.

WOMEN AND HIV   New research shows that incidence rates of HIV are increasing at a faster rate among women than for any other group. In North America, including the United States, Canada, and Central America, women comprised 15% of all HIV cases in 1995. By 2008, the rate increased by 6% to 21% of all cases in North America (UNAIDS, 2008b). But this increase must be kept in perspective. As of the end of 2006 (the last year for which full statistics are available in the United States), the CDC reported that men still accounted for the largest percentage of HIV cases in the United States, an estimated 74.8% of people living with HIV (MMWR, 2008).

How did women recently become so susceptible to HIV? There are two explanations for the change. Initially, the primary mode of transmission of HIV in North America was sexual contact among homosexual men. In other parts of the world, however, transmission of HIV occurred through heterosexual as well as homosexual contact. Thus, while HIV was most prevalent among gay men in the late 1980s and the 1990s in the United States, the high-risk behaviors practiced by some heterosexual couples meant that it was only a matter of time before heterosexuals also reported escalating incidence rate for HIV in the United States (UNAIDS, 200ba, 2008b). Keep in mind, for both groups the risk factor is high-risk sexual behavior, not group identification.

Second, HIV quickly became a risk factor for ***sex workers***, or individuals who earn their living by exchanging sex for food, money, shelter, or drugs (Sagrestano, Rogers, & Service, 2008). The sex trade contributed to a 12% increase in HIV prevalence in Eastern Europe and Central Asia and to a 49% increase in prevalence in Southeast Asia, excluding India (UNAIDS, 2008a, 2008b). In addition, the link between the sex trade industry and drug use also contributed to the spread of HIV to other populations. As we noted in Chapter 2, Research Methods, the rapid increase in HIV rates in Ukraine was due largely to IVDUs.

ADOLESCENTS AND HIV   Consider one final point about HIV prevalence. We mentioned before that HIV can be dormant in an infected individual for approximately 8 to 10 years. Therefore, individuals may be HIV positive long before they realize they are ill or are tested. Today, more than half of the people newly infected with HIV are between the ages of 15 and 24 (United Nations Children's Fund, 2002a). Are adolescents and young adults routinely seeking HIV testing? Not likely. In addition to the asymptomatic nature of the disease, the stigma of HIV and the lack of access to health care present significant barriers to adolescents and to some adults for obtaining an HIV test.

We determine that individuals 15 to 24 years of age are the largest newly infected group of HIV-positive individuals because, when we compare prevalence rates across age groups, we find the highest HIV prevalence occurs among 25- to 44-year-olds. Remembering the 8- to 10-year dormant period for the virus, we can conclude that individuals who are currently 25 to 44 years of age and are newly diagnosed as HIV positive contracted HIV when they were between 15 and 34 years of age.

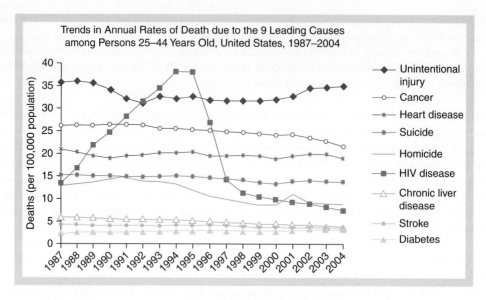

FIGURE 8.8 A Comparison of Leading Causes of Death, 1987–2004. HIV surpassed all other leading causes of death in the United States from 1992 through 1995.

Source: CDC (2009a).

The point here is that adolescents are becoming infected with HIV at increasing rates, and yet many do not realize that they carry the virus. Their lack of awareness of the disease, misunderstandings about the means of transmission, or their inability or unwillingness to be tested means that they may unwittingly contribute to spreading the virus and to furthering the pandemic. Recall that research presented in Chapter 5, Risky Health Behaviors, showed that adolescents are initiating sexual behaviors at earlier ages. Yet they are less informed about the dangers of risky sexual practices. For adolescents, then, the combination of early initiation and lack of information can lead to a potentially fatal outcome for themselves and for others.

HIV/AIDS in the United States: Prevalence and Prevention

When HIV was named as a new disease in 1982, the United States reported the highest incidence rates of HIV worldwide. New York City and San Francisco, California, reported the highest rates in the United States. As a result, in the early 1980s, both cities were labeled *epicenters*, or geophysical foci of the disease. Usually the word *epicenter* describes a place on Earth's surface that corresponds to the focal point of an earthquake. In some respects it is accurate to equate HIV to an earthquake because, like an earthquake, the virus began at a focal point, but its effects radiate outward, infecting and affecting others far beyond the point of origin.

It did not take long for other cities in the United States to begin reporting cases of HIV after the initial discovery. Prevalence rates of HIV and AIDS in the United States grew at an astronomical rate through the 1980s and 1990s, peaking in 1993 at approximately 1,040,000 total cases. At about the same time, the rates of death due to opportunistic infections enabled by

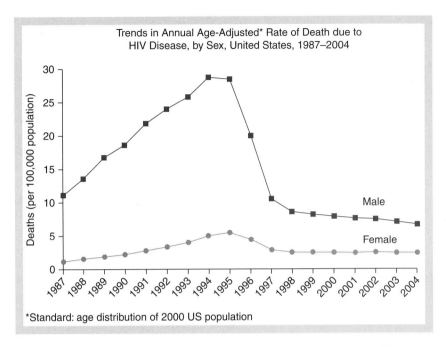

Trends in Annual Age-Adjusted* Rate of Death due to HIV Disease, by Sex, United States, 1987–2004

*Standard: age distribution of 2000 US population

FIGURE 8.9   HIV/AIDS-Related Deaths by Gender. Rates of death from HIV/AIDS show clear gender differences.

Source: CDC (2009a).

the virus also increased. In fact, according to data from the CDC, from 1992 through 1995 the rates of death attributed to AIDS for 25- to 44-year-olds exceeded deaths due to unintentional injuries (see Figures 8.8 and 8.9). Recall that in Chapter 5 we noted that unintentional injuries were the leading cause of death for the 25- to 44-year-old age group for more than 15 years. Yet, during the late 1980s and the early 1990s, HIV/AIDS became the most significant health risk to the U.S. population and the leading indicator of overall health among the population. The severity of HIV dwarfed the effects of other illnesses, at least for a time.

It took the concerted efforts of health care providers, researchers, psychologists, and many community organizations to reduce the incidence and prevalence rates of HIV/AIDS in the late 1990s. Included in this effort were programs, campaigns, and medical interventions designed to enhance knowledge and to increase testing rates of persons who engaged in risky health behaviors. Such efforts combined to dramatically reduce the rates of HIV transmission and the rates of death due to AIDS in the United States. In fact, health practitioners and researchers believed that the efforts were responsible for achieving a new low in HIV incidence rates in the United States.

Recent studies suggest, however, that between 1997 and 2006 HIV incidences rates were underestimated in the United States by as much as 40% (Hale et al., 2008). What does that mean? Simply put, there were far more cases of HIV in the United States during that period than originally estimated. So, current estimates of HIV/AIDS in the United States suggest a far more significant drop in HIV prevalence because the actual number of cases was far higher than realized.

It is likely that people's reluctance to be tested and the lack of awareness of the need to be tested significantly affected researchers' ability to accurately estimate incidences of HIV in the early days of the pandemic.

DISPARITIES IN HIV RATES AND TREATMENT   In the 1980s, many researchers focused on the rates of HIV among gay men and intravenous drug users but missed the escalating rates of HIV in the African American community. Between 1981 and 1983, African Americans comprised 12% of the U.S. population; however, they accounted for 26% of the 3,000 known cases of HIV (MMWR, 1984).

Current statistics show that, when compared with other ethnic groups, African Americans report the largest increase in HIV incidence rates. As of 2006, minorities accounted for approximately 70% of all new AIDS cases in the United States and 45% of all new cases of HIV for the same year (CDC, 2006a; Hale, 2008). To put this in proportion, the HIV rate for African American males is now 18 times higher than for white males. African American women report HIV rates that are six times higher than for white women (Campsmith, Rhodes, Hall, & Green, 2008). In fact, HIV is now the third leading cause of death for African Americans (Sagrestano et al., 2008).

Latinos similarly report higher rates of HIV than whites, although the difference is less dramatic than that between whites and African Americans. HIV rates for Latino males are four times higher than for white males. Female Hispanics report HIV rates that are twice as high as those of white women. HIV is the sixth leading cause of death for Latinos (Sagrestano et al., 2008).

CAUSES OF DISPARITIES: INDIVIDUAL BEHAVIORS VERSUS HEALTH POLICY

Education   There are many possible explanations for the differences in HIV infection rates and outcomes for minorities in the United States, and for African Americans in particular. One possible explanation is misinformation or the lack of information about HIV prevention. In Chapter 5, Risky Health Behaviors, we explored the link between risky sexual behavior and lack of knowledge about HIV and other sexually transmitted diseases (STDs) among African American adolescents. Specifically, we mentioned that, while statistics show that African American adolescents initiate sexual behaviors earlier than adolescents of other ethnic groups, they were less likely to receive information about safer sexual practices (Grunbaum et al., 2002). Thus education, one weapon in the arsenal of HIV prevention, appears to be in short supply, especially for African American adolescents.

In New York City, approximately 80% of the over 1 million public school students are minorities, largely African American and Latino. In response to the growing HIV epidemic (remember that New York City was an epicenter for HIV in the United States) and the lack of knowledge about the disease, the New York City Department of Education mandated a semester of HIV education each year for students in middle and high school. In essence, New York City public school students who remained in the school system from sixth through 12th grade would receive a total of three years of health education focused on HIV/AIDS prevention. Unfortunately, the policy was not well planned or implemented in the schools. Both students and school officials reported that, in fact, students received far less than the mandated three years of HIV prevention instruction due in large measure to poor execution (see Box 8.2).

BOX 8.2   HIV/AIDS Education in Schools: Program in Name Only?

In 1992, the New York City (NYC) Board of Education (now called the Department of Education) instituted a new health policy. All public school students in grades 7 through 12 were to receive one semester of grade-appropriate HIV instruction each year for a total of six semesters of education. The rationale for the plan was simple: Knowledge about HIV and HIV prevention would help decrease the incidence rates of HIV among the NYC adolescent population. Research on HIV prevention certainly seemed to support the notion.

But, as we indicated earlier, the existence of a policy is not enough. One young researcher discovered what happens when there is a disconnect between policy and practice. In 2006, Working In Support of Education (W!SE), a NYC-based nonprofit, challenged the city's high school students to identify an NYC policy in need of revision and propose a solution. Renee Michelle Ragin, then a sophomore at the Bronx High School of Science, chose to take a closer look at HIV/AIDS education in the city's public high schools. Why? One day while surfing the Internet, Ragin found information on the rates of HIV/AIDS among adolescents and young adults. Stunned by the high prevalence rates among her age group and concerned about the quality of HIV/AIDS education she and her peers were receiving in school, Ragin entered the public policy competition to bring to light the disparities in HIV/AIDS education at her school.

Ragin interviewed high school health instructors, hospital clinic administrators, and professors of public health about HIV instruction in the schools. Her findings indicated that, while there was, in fact, a written and standardized (albeit outdated) curriculum for HIV/AIDS instruction, such instruction was offered inconsistently at best, an admission that confirmed Ragin's own experiences. What explained the inconsistent adherence to the new policy? When presented with the materials for HIV instruction, many teachers felt ill equipped to teach the classroom sessions on HIV or were uncomfortable with the material. Others believed it was an important topic that they were willing to teach, but they needed more support to deliver good content and to be helpful to students.

Ragin found that the red flag in the Department of Education's policy was accountability: While the curriculum had been developed and disseminated to all high schools, little was done to ensure that the schools were adhering or were even able to adhere to the policy. Fortunately for Ragin and her classmates, the investigation did not end there. Shortly after the submission of her study, W!SE contacted Ragin because Department of Education officials wanted to meet her and discuss her findings. They were aware of the implementation problems with the HIV/AIDS education policy and wanted to hear about the shortcomings from someone with direct experience and who represented the very audience they targeted.

W!SE went even further, facilitating a meeting between the deputy mayor of NYC and a few students who entered the competition. Renee Michelle Ragin was among them.

Four months later, in December 2006, the NYC Department of Education issued new guidelines for HIV/AIDS instruction, complete with enhanced teacher training, education, and support.

The New York City example demonstrates that health policy can target a specific disease, a specific target group, and specific health-compromising behaviors as part of a plan to improve health outcomes. But, a flawed delivery system, in this case the inconsistent implementation across the school system, created a barrier that limited the effectiveness of the policy designed to change health behaviors and outcomes for adolescents and young adults. Fortunately for New York City and its public school students, the now New York City Department of Education realized the problem and is addressing the barriers to implementation of the health policy.

Peer Influence   We explored the phenomenon of peer influence on risky health behaviors in Chapter 5. We noted that peers are often cited as a significant factor in adolescents' decision to initiate substance use behaviors such as drinking alcohol, smoking cigarettes, or using illegal drugs (Andrews, Tildesley, Hops, & Li, 2002; Cavanagh, 2007; Petraitis, Flay, & Miller, 1995; U.S. Department of Health and Human Services, 1994). It appears that the same holds true for risky sexual behaviors.

Work by Walters and colleagues (1992, 1993; see Chapter 5, Risky Health Behaviors) explores the impact of adolescents' perception of their friends' behaviors on their decision to engage in risky sexual behaviors. Their findings suggest adolescents often misperceive the extent of their friends' involvement in high-risk behaviors or inflate the number of friends involved. Thus, adolescents may justify their own behaviors using their mistaken assumptions about peer risk behaviors. Adolescents' beliefs about friends' behaviors constitute one individual determinant of health that contributes to the risk of contracting HIV. Correcting their misperceptions, therefore, could substantially affect adolescents' risks for contracting HIV.

Health Status   Disparity in individual health status is another individual variable that contributes to higher rates of mortality due to HIV. Our opening story introduced four HIV-positive males who, due perhaps to differences in their health status, showed very different outcomes. They are an example of the diverse impact of the disease.

Two star athletes, Magic Johnson and Greg Louganis, contracted HIV through risky sexual behavior, one through heterosexual contact and the other through homosexual contact. As athletes, they were in excellent physical health prior to becoming infected. Currently, both actively promote HIV prevention messages and experience few limitations due to their disease, although neither continues to compete professionally in his respective sport. It is unclear whether their current health status is due to their robust immune systems, their ethnicity, their access to health care, or to other psychological factors. Yet both are managing their illnesses well with medical care.

Two others, Arthur Ashe and Ryan White, contracted HIV through blood products. Ashe obtained a tainted sample of blood when given a blood transfusion during an emergency brain surgery (CDC, 1993). White was given a contaminated blood product during a routine treatment for his hemophilia. Both Arthur Ashe and Ryan White had preexisting health conditions when they were infected. We know from our earlier discussion of HIV that the virus suppresses the immune system. Because individuals with existing health problems may already have a weakened immune system that puts them at a greater health disadvantage when they become infected, it is possible that Ashe's and White's preexisting medical problems contributed to their poor health outcomes with AIDS more than either their ethnicity, their socioeconomic status, or their access to health care. It is also the case that our lack of knowledge of the disease and lack of effective treatment strategies in the late 1980s and early 1990s contributed to higher death rates due to AIDS. With today's treatment regimen for HIV, people like Ashe and White with preexisting medical conditions that require blood products are able to live longer and manage their illness more effectively.

Access to Health Care   Access to care can be both a health systems and a health policy issue. This is true with respect to HIV/AIDS.

National and international health agencies recognize that one barrier to improving health outcomes for a person with HIV is access to life-prolonging and life-enhancing medications. Health providers know that HIV medications may help slow the progression of the disease and the deterioration in an individual's health, resulting in improved outcomes. Individuals who remain healthy enough to work and conduct other daily functions also are more likely to avoid the downward spiral into poverty for themselves and possibly their families due to missed work opportunities and job loss. Until recently, however, many individuals were unable to obtain the needed medicines because many health insurance companies in the United States would not subsidize the cost of the treatments. Without the subsidy, the full cost of the medicines would be prohibitive for most people. We discuss the impact of health care costs on access to care more thoroughly in Chapter 12, Health Care Systems and Health Policy.

For the moment, an example may help to explain the problem of access to health-enhancing medicines for HIV. Consider this: The cost of HIV medication varies widely depending on the drug, the manufacturer, and the country. In the United States, for example, HIV medications can range from $300 to $2,300 per month. A person who earned $50,000 per year (approximately $4,160 per month) and needed several HIV medications that totaled approximately $2,300 per month could be faced with the decision of spending almost half of his or her monthly income on medicines. If forced to allocate their resources in this way, they would have little money available for other necessary living expenses. Thus, the decision by health care systems not to subsidize HIV medication meant that many people were unable to obtain the new drugs. It is clear that, without access to new HIV medicines, a person would experience a faster deterioration in health and perhaps a much shorter lifespan. In this way it is obvious that a health care systems' decision not to underwrite the costs of some medications is a direct determinant of health.

It is important to note that health insurance companies were not the only factor determining a person's access to medications and thus appropriate care. Pharmaceutical companies that manufacture HIV medicines determine the market price of their product. They contend that the price of the medicines reflects the costs involved for research, development, testing, and marketing the product, all of which are expensive processes. To recoup their expenses and to make a profit, pharmaceuticals may establish a high price for the first several years of the new drug. Thus, the price of medications set by the manufacturer may also limit access to care. In fact, many medical providers have voiced opposition to the price of some drugs, calling the price tags on some medicines unethical. For example, U.S. doctors were shocked and disgusted when, in 2004, one pharmaceutical company increased the price of an essential HIV drug by over 400%. Doctors called the price increase unethical because it prohibited many HIV patients from obtaining the drug. One doctor even equated the new price of the drug to an increase in the price of a gallon of gas from $2.00 to $10.00 (Albert, 2004).

The outrage over the cost of HIV medications in the United States and globally prompted the governments in several countries including Brazil, South Africa, Thailand, and India to challenge current U.S. laws to force pharmaceuticals to lower the costs of HIV medication for the poorest and those most in need. Their proposals to allow governments to purchase *generic drugs*, that is, the same drug copied and manufactured by another producer, would lower the cost of the same, commonly used HIV medication (Harris & Siplon, 2001). The efforts by Brazil and other countries demonstrated an effective use of global health policy to challenge a health system that impeded access to much-needed medical supplies.

There is one other benefit to lower-cost HIV medications. When able to afford the HIV medications and to continue their normal daily functions, HIV-positive individuals reduce the likelihood that their health conditions would become known to the neighbors in their communities, villages, or towns. As we noted before, the stigma of being identified as someone with HIV/AIDS could result in a person not using or adopting the health-enhancing behaviors, like taking the needed medication, to improve their health outcomes. In addition, in traditional communities, a diagnosis of HIV/AIDS can mean certain banishment—another route into poverty.

HIV Prevention/Intervention Strategies That Work

We have identified a number of factors that influence risky health behaviors, contribute to disparate HIV rates, and even inhibit an individual's access to HIV prevention education and medications that might change behaviors and outcomes. But we cannot end the section without acknowledging successful intervention strategies, in the United States and globally, employed to fight HIV. While there are several such examples, we include two—one local and one global—to illustrate the scope of the work on the HIV/AIDS pandemic: the Gay Men's Health Crisis (GMHC) campaign in the United States and the Ugandan HIV/AIDS prevention campaign.

GAY MEN'S HEALTH CRISIS (GMHC) CAMPAIGN   The decreased HIV rates among men, particularly gay men, are credited largely to the aggressive HIV prevention campaign waged by many grassroots and nonprofit organizations in the United States. Central to that effort was a campaign by the Gay Men's Health Crisis (GMHC) that spanned nearly a decade. You may have seen their ads, but, if not, you certainly know their logo: the red ribbon.

The GMHC implemented a successful social marketing campaign (see Chapter 4, Theories and Models of Health Behavior Change) that instructed their audience (largely gay men) about the virus and effective means of prevention and directed them to agencies to obtain testing, counseling, and health care services. The campaign was successful in educating not only gay men but other populations as well. However, it was most effective in decreasing the incidence of HIV/AIDS as well as decreasing the mortality rates due to HIV/AIDS among the target population.

Although the campaign was successful in the 1980s and 1990s, recent studies suggest that HIV/AIDS rates among younger gay men are increasing once again. Between 1999 and 2002, HIV diagnosis among men who have sex with men increased 17% (Easton et al., 2007). In 2006 homosexual males accounted for 53% of all incidences of HIV for that year. The renewed increase in HIV incidence does not suggest that the GMHC campaign was ineffective. Rather, it shows that it was successful during its duration. It suggests to some that social marketing campaigns, while effective, must be maintained to ensure that successive generations hear the same message.

GMAC AND CONDOM DISTRIBUTION   A central message in the GMHC campaign to prevent HIV was condom use. Remember HIV is defined also as a sexually transmitted disease (STD). Thus, some barrier agents that protect against STDs are also effective in preventing the transmission of HIV. Condom use messages were one example of an HIV prevention strategy that, although targeted to gay men, became an effective marketing and promotion message to prevent the spread of HIV among other adolescents and adults who were not the intended recipients of the social marketing campaign. For example, condom distribution campaigns have become commonplace on college campuses, where adolescents and young adults are encouraged to obtain free condoms from their health centers. More controversial, however, are condom distribution programs targeted to middle and high school adolescents. Nevertheless, school districts in several large U.S. metropolitan regions have successfully lobbied to place condom distribution sites in school-based health clinics and in vending machines in girls' and boys' bathrooms across the country.

UGANDAN HIV PREVENTION PROGRAM   Strong leadership by governments such as Uganda also helped reduce the HIV transmission rates. The Ugandan government's program to reduce rates of HIV transmission is particularly noteworthy because Uganda is one of several countries in sub-Saharan Africa that maintain a stable, albeit high, HIV infection rate.

The Ugandan government campaigned to halt the spread of HIV among the most vulnerable population, adolescents and young adults 15 to 24 years of age. It included a large-scale social marketing campaign similar to that developed by GMHC. The campaign initiated by Uganda's president, Yoweri Museveni, not only halted the spread of HIV in Uganda but served as a blueprint for intervention programs that work in Africa, as well as Europe and Asia (see Box 8.3).

Global Epicenters and Global "Hot Spots"

Today, every country is affected in some way by the AIDS pandemic. We noted earlier that worldwide approximately 33 million people are living with HIV or AIDS (UNAIDS, 2008b). The southern region of Africa, including Lesotho, South Africa, and Swaziland, is also considered an epicenter of the disease because their stable yet high HIV infection rates exceed those of many other countries.

Sub-Saharan Africa, currently the region of the world most seriously affected by HIV, has approximately 10% of the world's population but reports an estimated 70% of the world's HIV-positive adults and 80% of the world's HIV-positive children (Harris & Siplon, 2001). The alarmingly high incidence rates of HIV in southern Africa puzzled some researchers who could not explain the large numbers of HIV cases using the three primary methods of transmission: sexual behavior, blood-borne transmission, and perinatal transmission. Recent studies have examined the possibility of ***dual infections***, meaning the presence of one virus causing or greatly increasing the likelihood of another. Specifically, researchers are examining the likelihood that malaria increases the chance of developing HIV or vice versa. Malaria and HIV occur in largely similar geographic regions, areas that have long rainy seasons and large infestations of mosquitoes. What is more, researchers noted that spikes in HIV and malaria rates co-occur after rainy seasons (see Box 8.4). Now there is reason to believe that malaria may increase susceptibility to HIV and vice versa.

Kublin realized that the high HIV transmission rates in southern Africa would mean extremely high rates of risky sexual behavior. There is just one problem. The explanation did not

BOX 8.3   A Surprising Success in Uganda: Declines in HIV Rates and an Example for the World

In the early 1990s, Uganda knew it was in trouble. Reports from ***antenatal clinics***, clinics for pregnant women in urban areas, revealed that at the highest point of infection rates, 25 of every 100 pregnant women tested positive for HIV. Eight years later, in 1998, HIV prevalence rates for men attending STD clinics in urban areas dropped from a high of 46% in 1992 to approximately 30% in 1998 (WHO, 2000b).

Ugandan President Yoweri Museveni realized that HIV rates in Uganda meant one thing: The country's health was in danger. Taking decisive action, President Museveni publically acknowledged the HIV crisis in Uganda. He built an alliance to combat the spread of HIV that included leaders from all sectors of society: religion, education, health care workers, traditional healers, community groups, and government organizations. Together they launched a massive campaign to educate the population about the disease, methods of transmission, and methods of protection. They developed effective social marketing campaigns (see Chapter 4) to raise awareness about the disease and also to direct the population to health centers for testing, treatment, and support.

The campaign's goals were clear: to raise awareness of HIV, to delay the onset of sexual behaviors, to increase access to testing, and to increase the use of condoms among men and women. The campaign to raise awareness and to educate the population about HIV was conducted in schools to reach the adolescent population and on radio to reach the mass population. As of 1998 Uganda reported 100% awareness of HIV/AIDS among the population. Messages that emphasized a delay in the onset of sexual behaviors were also successful. Before 1990, the average age of initiation of sexual behaviors in Uganda was 14 years. In 1995, Uganda reported that 50% of adolescents 15 years of age indicated they never had sex, an increase of 20% just six years prior (WHO, 2002). In addition, as of 1995 statistics reported a two-year delay in sexual initiation for girls until age 16 (Afrol News, 2003). Reported HIV rates in antenatal clinics indicated success as well. Fifteen years into the program, Uganda reports that only 8% of women attending antenatal clinics test positive for HIV, down from almost 30% in 1986.

Finally, using a clever marketing strategy, Museveni's government helped increase condom use and self-treatments for sexually transmitted diseases (STDs). Targeting men seeking treatment for an STD, the government created a special product, "Clear Seven," that contained a 14-day course of treatment for sexually transmitted diseases in addition to condoms and partner referral information. The government aided the distribution of the product by authorizing small retail stores to sell the product and by subsidizing its cost. The "Clear Seven" treatment pack sold for the equivalent of US$1.35. The results are proof of the effectiveness of the campaign. Reported condom use doubled from 32% to 65% and the cure rate for urethritis, inflammation of the urethra in men or women that often indicates a sexually transmitted disease, almost doubled from 46% to 87%.

A powerful message from the government, led by the president, helped stem the spread of HIV in Uganda. It also armed the population with the knowledge and the resources to practice safer sexual behaviors. The message to the world community, however, was just as powerful. Uganda provided a blueprint for fighting HIV that many countries copy today.

BOX 8.4   Is HIV Transmitted by Mosquitoes?

Researchers have been puzzled by the exceedingly high rates of HIV/AIDS in southern Africa. Researcher James G. Kublin has conducted studies on HIV and malaria in southern Africa for a number of years. His knowledge about the customs and traditions of the people in southern Africa led him to question current assumptions about HIV transmission, particularly for the region.

make sense. Many of the cultures in southern Africa observe traditional customs. High levels of sexually risky or permissive behavior are not only inconsistent with the values of the peoples of southern Africa, but Kublin found that they just do not happen. Even if adding other forms of transmission, such as mother-to-child or blood-borne, scientists could not account for the outcomes. Kublin and other scientists began searching for other answers.

One possible explanation for the high HIV rates is linked to the high rates of malaria. In sub-Saharan Africa, Southeast Asia, and Latin America, there is a considerable geographic overlap between the areas most heavily affected by HIV and those vulnerable to malaria (WHO, 2004). But what is the link? Is the anopheles mosquito that transports the malaria virus also a conduit for HIV? After all, the mosquito transports one type of virus. Why not two? While a convenient explanation, scientists discovered that the differences in the structure of the two viruses rule out the temptingly simple explanation. Apparently, HIV will not survive in the anopheles mosquito.

Instead, scientists now propose a dual infection theory: malaria and HIV. Studies show that HIV increases the risk of malaria infection and vice versa. Individuals with suppressed immune systems appear more likely to be infected with malaria in areas with high malaria rates than do those whose immune systems are stronger (Van geertruyden & D'Alessandro, 2007). In addition, laboratory studies suggest that malaria appears to induce replication of the virus (Brentlinger, Behren, & Kublin, 2007), a finding that has been supported by studies of individuals infected with HIV who also contracted malaria (Kublin & Steketee, 2006). These studies support the theory than non–sexually transmitted diseases can affect the spread of HIV (Abu-Raddad, Patnaik, & Kublin, 2006).

The new findings present both good and troubling news to researchers. On the one hand, correcting erroneous assumptions about how HIV is transmitted in regions with high malaria rates is important. It helps health care and health policy workers develop appropriate prevention strategies to reduce the spread of HIV. However, controlling the spread of malaria is and continues to be a challenging health problem. As we saw in Chapter 3, Global Communicable and Chronic Disease, malaria is spread by a natural element—a mosquito. Controlling large infestations of mosquitoes and their impact on the poorest and most vulnerable populations is a daunting task.

The UN Global Fund to Fight AIDS, Tuberculosis and Malaria realizes the pressing health problems posed by all three diseases, especially the dual risks of HIV and malaria. Established in 2002 by UN Secretary General Kofi Annan, the Global Fund was created to promote programs to prevent the spread of HIV, malaria, and TB. Working with governments, private businesses, and communities worldwide, it is an innovate approach to addressing the HIV pandemic and the associated illnesses of malaria and TB.

While southern Africa is currently the world's epicenter, central Africa, Asia, eastern Europe, and the Russian Federation also report alarming increases in the incidences of HIV over the past 10 years. In 2006, eastern Europe and the Russian Federation reported approximately 1.7 million people living with HIV, or almost 1.0% of the population of the region. As we noted in Chapter 2 and earlier in this chapter, intravenous drug use (IVDU) appears to account for the majority of the incidences of HIV in eastern Europe.

South and Southeast Asia, specifically Myanmar, Cambodia, and Thailand, are now considered to be "hot spots" for HIV/AIDS, with more than 600,000 new cases of HIV reported in 2006 (UNAIDS, 2008a, 2008b). While IDVU accounts for some of the transmission rates in these countries, the largest single contributor to the spread of HIV in the region appears to be the sex trade industry and tourism.

GLOBAL HIV/AIDS PREVENTION AND INTERVENTION STRATEGIES   Another global strategy to combat HIV also involves health policy, this time by the United Nations. In 2001, the United Nations convened a special session on HIV/AIDS to develop global health policies to address the HIV pandemic. The United Nations recognized that controlling the spread of the HIV pandemic requires the concerted effort of all countries. To that end, the UN Joint Program on HIV/AIDS (UNAIDS) works collectively with the 180 member nations to promote a global agenda that addresses individual, community, environmental, health systems. and health policy factors that contribute to the spread of HIV. It should not escape notice that the UNAIDS logo includes a red ribbon, the symbol of HIV popularized by the GMHC social marketing campaign.

SECTION III. PSYCHOSOCIAL PERSPECTIVES ON NEW HIV TESTING AND TREATMENTS

Earlier in the chapter we explained HIV testing, treatment, and outcomes from a biological perspective. However, we know that psychological factors affect health at all levels. While new HIV testing techniques could be explained from a purely biological point of view, such an approach would overlook significant psychological factors that contributed to their effectiveness. In addition, as we mentioned previously, a new field, psychoneuroimmunology, is redefining treatment and expected health outcomes for people with HIV. In this section, therefore, we examine new developments in HIV testing, treatment, and outcomes from a psychological perspective.

Testing for and Preventing HIV

In the 1990s, the ***ELISA (enzyme-linked immunosorbent assay) test*** was developed to diagnose HIV. Like other tests of its kind, ELISA identified the presence of HIV antibodies in the body. You may recall that antibodies are produced by the body's immune system in an effort to fight foreign microorganism. A positive ELISA test result means that the HIV virus is present in the body and that the immune system is producing antibodies to destroy the virus or attempt to, in the case of HIV.

In the early years, HIV testing using ELISA was a two-week process, assuming there was no backlog of cases. Imagine the agony. An individual, worried about his or her HIV status, musters the courage to go to a health care provider or clinic for testing. That person prepares him- or herself to answer what seems like a million uncomfortable and embarrassing questions about sexual and substance use behaviors. The individual braces him- or herself for what that person imagines will be disapproving looks from the health care providers and perhaps other patients who may overhear the conversation. After a technician takes a sample of blood, the person is told to return in two weeks for the results.

The two-week wait is agonizing as the individual considers many questions. For example, "Do I really want to get the results? Do I really want to know my status? How will my life change if I have HIV? If I have HIV, can I confide in one of my friends or relatives, and will they keep my secret?" Or "I feel fine now. If I am careful, beginning now, and make sure to use condoms I should be fine, right?"

It should come as no surprise that after two weeks of anguish and questions, approximately 25% of individuals tested for HIV do not return for the results (Downing et al., 1998). What is more, in many states testing is done anonymously. There is no way to identify or contact an individual should he or she not return voluntarily.

Without a doubt, getting tested is an important step in the battle against HIV, but when individuals do not return for the results and to receive treatment, the benefit of testing is lost. Unaware of his or her HIV status, a person with HIV will not obtain the treatment that can slow the progression of the disease and enhance health outcomes. Equally as important, however, an HIV-positive person who is unaware of his or her disease status risks spreading the virus to others, especially if that individual continues the risky behaviors that led to the HIV-positive outcome. Thus, individuals with HIV who do not obtain their test result or seek counseling and treatment pose health risks to themselves as well as their community. HIV follow-up and counseling, therefore, are essential to protect the health of the community.

Now fast forward to 2000. A second individual prepares in much the same way to be tested for HIV. Only this time, after drawing the necessary blood, the technician tells the individual to return to the waiting room. Twenty minutes later a health care provider calls the individual back to the exam room and reads the results. Twenty minutes? Is that possible? Absolutely. New rapid HIV tests allow for almost immediate results. Rapid HIV tests also allow for immediate counseling about the risky health behaviors that prompted concern about HIV. And, equally as important, rapid results allow health psychologists and other health providers to provide immediate posttest counseling to address emotional health needs and to counsel people on important health behavior changes. As we noted in Chapter 6, Emotional Health and Well-Being, an individual's emotional and psychological well-being contributes to physical health outcomes. As such, mental and emotional health counseling complements the physiological response to people with HIV.

POSTTEST COUNSELING   To be clear, in the United States and most developed countries, counseling is a standard part of the HIV testing service regardless of whether the two-week ELISA test or the new rapid test is being used. It is provided to people with positive as well as negative results. For HIV-positive individuals, counseling addresses the predictable emotional turmoil, shock, and despair that often follow the news. It also helps guide the individual to treatment and support networks. When, however, a person tests positive for HIV, the test is almost always repeated immediately. It is important to determine the accuracy of the results as quickly as possible. Remember, the goal is to decrease all barriers to immediate access to care.

Individuals who test negative for HIV also need counseling. Health providers know that, in most instances, a request for HIV testing is an admission that a person has engaged in one or more of the high-risk behaviors that can lead to HIV. And, even if the results are negative, a posttest counseling session provides an excellent opportunity to discuss needed changes in a person's health behaviors. Not surprisingly, health psychologists are well suited to such a role. They can not only encourage individuals to adopt health-enhancing behaviors, they can also assist them in developing plans and strategies to implement the new behaviors. Walter and colleagues' (1992, 1993) work with adolescents and AIDS prevention (Chapter 5, Risky Health Behaviors) serves as an example of a program designed to teach new skills to prevent HIV/AIDS.

An important message for all individuals who obtain a negative HIV test is they were lucky this time, but they cannot assume that their luck will continue if they engage in the same behaviors. Many health providers will recommend a follow-up test in four to six months if an initial test is negative. Assuming no new incidences of risky health behaviors, a second negative result would confirm that an individual is HIV negative.

Unfortunately, in many developing countries the psychosocial component (posttest counseling and recommended behavior change) of HIV testing and care may be missing. The HIV test alone is prohibitively expensive for many nations. The added cost of mental or emotional health counseling for HIV, especially if it means multiple appointments and return visits, may be considered a luxury that neither the medical facility nor the patient can afford. And while rapid HIV testing allows for counseling at the time of testing, economics may again limit or restrict access to the type of health care service in the best interest of individuals. Studies suggest that, while the long-term cost of a rapid HIV test makes it less expensive to perform than the ELISA testing method, the fact remains that for many poorer regions of the United States and for many developing countries, the cost of any type of HIV testing is prohibitive economically (Paltiel et al., 2005).

BENEFITS OF AND BARRIERS TO RAPID HIV TESTS   It seems almost intuitive that the rapid HIV tests are preferable to the ELISA tests: Rapid tests lessen stress and anxiety on the individual. An individual will not have to endure two weeks of uncertainty and the associated toll on his or her emotional and physical health before obtaining the results. The immediate feedback increases notification rates and reduces the 25% attrition rate of individuals who refuse to return (Downing et al., 1998). In addition, rapid results allow for immediate counseling and other psychological services if needed.

Of the four rapid HIV tests available for use in the United States, two can be used in ***point-of-care facilities***, meaning community-based or practitioner's medical offices (Greenwald et al., 2006). Local testing facilities offer several advantages for individuals. In addition to testing within one's own community (Franco-Paredes, Tellez, & del Rio, 2006; Stetler et al., 1998), local testing facilities reduce travel time and the repeated costs associated with multiple visits. You may recall that in Chapter 4, Theories and Models of Health Behavior Change, we noted that travel and economic costs were two barriers to health behavior change, specifically the behaviors involved in seeking health. The rapid HIV tests minimized multiple costs factors in Uganda also; one of the reasons for Uganda's highly successful campaign to decrease HIV rates (Franco-Paredes et al., 2006).

To date, the principal barriers to using the rapid tests for HIV appear to be the cost of the test, a factor that is cited primarily by health care systems. On a per-test basis, rapid tests appear to be more expensive than the older ELISA tests. However, a computer-simulated study revealed that, to the contrary, over time, rapid HIV testing was more cost effective and produced longer survival rates than the original ELISA tests when used with the highest-risk populations, individuals for whom prevalence rates for undetected HIV was approximately 3% (Paltiel et al., 2005). By comparison, the rapid tests were only marginally more cost effective and showed no real improvement in survival rates for groups with HIV prevalence rates of less than 1%. Thus, for high-risk populations or for individuals without regular access to care, rapid tests can result in longer survival rates. One explanation posited for the increased survival rates for the high-risk population is the improved access to care.

Antiretroviral Treatments

We have said it several times, but it bears repeating here: There are no cures for HIV. If prevention programs that aim to limit exposure to HIV fail, the only remaining option is disease management using antiretroviral drugs.

Antiretroviral drugs are medications that slow the progression of HIV. Currently there are 21 different antiretroviral drugs approved for use by the U.S. Food and Drug Administration. However, researchers and medical providers have discovered that three or more antiretroviral drugs, used in combination, dramatically improve the health outcomes of HIV-positive individuals (Cressey & Lallemant, 2007). The three drugs taken together are called a *"drug cocktail."*

More formally, the triple drug combination therapy is known as highly active antiretroviral therapy, or HAART. HAART therapy suppresses the virus's ability to replicate itself. We pause for a moment to recall our discussion earlier in the chapter of the process by which HIV suppresses the immune system. You will recall that the HIV virus, a retrovirus, "sneaks" by the body's immune system by disguising itself as a viral DNA rather than remaining a retrovirus RNA. It then imbeds itself into the healthy cells of the human body. After a dormant period, the HIV begins to replicate and invade other cells using the same disguise to fool the body's immune system.

The antiretroviral cocktails do not stop the virus from invading the body or from imbedding itself into healthy cells. Rather, they slow the rate of progression of the disease. As a consequence, the HIV medications allow the body's immune system to restore (Cressey & Lallemant, 2007). *Zidovudine*, *nevirapine*, and *efavirenz* are three commonly used antiretroviral drugs.

PSYCHOSOCIAL FACTORS IN ANTIRETROVIRAL TREATMENT   Successful management of HIV using antiretroviral treatments is reported in the United States and abroad, especially in countries like Lesotho (in southern Africa) where extreme poverty complicates efforts to treat HIV. As of 2005, the international agency Global Fund to Fight AIDS, Tuberculosis and Malaria had provided antiretroviral drugs to approximately 385,000 individuals throughout the world, especially in the global HIV epicenters of southern Africa and the trouble areas of east Africa and south Asia.

Yet even drug treatments that successfully prevent the virus from replicating are not fail proof. Many difficulties related to HIV are psychosocial in nature. For example, adhering to a daily regime of medications for life presents challenges for most people. Consider this: The antiretroviral drug cocktail must be taken daily at regular intervals without interruption. It is a lifetime commitment. People who do well with such a regimen exhibit good adherence to medication. Yet health maintenance research shows that individuals with long-term illnesses will, at some point, fail to follow a strict medication schedule or will be unable to tolerate the medication side effects. Failure to follow the prescribed regimen for whatever reason is a common cause of ineffective treatment for HIV.

For adolescents, adhering to a daily schedule of medication for life is particularly challenging. The stigma associated with the disease, the need to fit in with their social groups and not appear different, and the plethora of activities that divert adolescents' attention from such a commitment combine to reduce drug treatment maintenance in adolescents.

As with almost all disease-causing organisms, a virus can become resistant to the drugs used to control or destroy it. HIV is no exception. When one or several drugs in the three-drug antiretroviral drug cocktail ceases to be effective in containing the virus, medical providers will change the combination, selecting a replacement from a list of 21 antiretroviral drugs approved for use on HIV. It is also possible, however, that individuals who receive zidovudine or nevirapine as part of their "drug cocktail" may form a resistance to other drugs in the arsenal of antiretroviral drugs, thereby reducing the number of new drugs that can be used as part of the HAART regimen. In essence, several cocktail combinations may be tried before finding one that effectively contains the virus, albeit for a period of time.

Children face a unique problem in HIV treatment, due in part to changes in the effectiveness of antiretroviral drugs as children age and difficulties in diagnosing children younger than 18 months of age in economically disadvantaged areas (WHO, 2005e). Research shows that HAART treatment with children who are severely compromised is not always as effective as it is with adults, even when using the same combination of drugs (Essajee, 1999; WHO, 2005e).

Mother-to-Child Transmission (MTCT) Prevention

We mentioned earlier that infants can be infected with HIV during the birth process. Remember, HIV is transmitted through body fluids, including blood and vaginal fluids. Thus, in normal vaginal deliveries, infants risk exposure to HIV if their mothers are HIV positive.

Many pregnant women without prior access to health care see a medical provider for the first time at or near their time of delivery. With little prior medical treatment and limited knowledge of the pregnant mother's health history, the physician as well as the pregnant woman may be unaware of the woman's HIV status. In fact, some women learn their HIV status at the time of delivery, about the same time they learn that they risk infecting their newborn with a fatal disease. Put another way, while preparing for the birth of a child, a normally happy occasion, some mothers must also grapple with the psychologically and emotionally devastating news that they are HIV positive and that they put their child at risk for contracting the same disease.

Fortunately, researchers discovered a simple and effective way to reduce the transmission of HIV from mother to infants in 66% of cases. Specifically, researchers found that a single dose of nevirapine given to the mother during labor, in addition to a single dose of nevirapine given to the infant within 72 hours of birth, significantly reduces transmission of HIV from mother to child (Ayouba et al., 2003; Guay et al., 1999). In fact, nevirapine is so effective that, when given to Thai women in their third trimester of pregnancy, without an additional dose to the infant, researchers obtained significant reduction in HIV MTCT rates (Lallemant et al., 2004). Additional studies revealed other combinations of antiretroviral drugs, such as nevirapine and zidovudine, produce similar significant reductions in transmission (Lallemant et al., 2004).

In essence, antiretroviral drugs are quite effective in slowing the progression of HIV in positive individuals. But they are also quite effective in preventing newborns from contracting HIV at the point of birth. In sum, antiretrovirals may be the best approach to limit the spread of HIV to a new generation, especially in developing countries.

HIV and Psychological Stress

It is important to point out that the success rate for medical or behavioral health interventions is affected by individual factors as well as an individual's psychological health. Here we refer to the direct effects of the emotional and psychological state of the person infected with the disease as well as the indirect effects on family members and friends who may be affected by the disease. While the direct impact of a serious illness such as HIV may seem intuitively clear, the indirect effects may not. Recall, for example, the opening story in Chapter 7, Stress and Coping. We introduced Sarah, a woman suffering from initial stages of Alzheimer's disease. Sarah was struggling to cope with the symptoms of her illness. So, too, were her immediate family, Susan, Michael, and Lucinda, because Sarah's illness affected their physical, emotional, and social health. The same is true for HIV/AIDS as well as other chronic and life-threatening illnesses. In this section we explore the psychological effects of HIV on people both infected with and affected by HIV.

PSYCHOSOCIAL FACTORS THAT IMPACT HIV   We note that currently, due to the widespread availability of antiretroviral treatments that slow the progression of the virus, HIV is now considered by some to be more like other chronic illnesses such as cancer. Like cancer, the treatment phase of HIV/AIDS in the United States can help prolong an individual's life as long as 20 years postdiagnosis, or almost twice as long as predicted in the early years of the HIV pandemic. As such, research on people with HIV can now examine the psychological impact of the disease on those infected as well as those affected. In general, these study findings mirror results obtained on the psychological impact of other chronic illnesses.

Thirty years of research on the impact of HIV on psychological well-being and, conversely, the effects of psychological status on disease progression show that, with little exception, positive and negative psychological well-being directly affects HIV physiological health status (Chida & Vedhara, 2009). New research on the role of positive psychological factors—such as problem- and emotion-focused coping strategies (see Chapter 7, Stress and Coping) and strong social support networks—shows that such positive emotional states slow the progression of HIV (Chida & Steptoe, 2008; Ironson & Hayward, 2008; Pressman & Cohen, 2005). Conversely, negative psychological factors, such as depressive mood, anxiety, avoidance coping strategies, hopelessness, poor family contact, or unstable partnerships, contribute to increased stress and to HIV disease progression (Ironson et al., 2005; Leserman, 2008). We explore the effects of negative psychological health on physical outcomes related to HIV in greater detail later in this chapter. Here it is sufficient to note that there is evidence that demonstrates the beneficial impact of positive psychological states and the detrimental impact of negative ones.

Psychological distress has also been associated with an individual's health-seeking or health-enhancing behaviors. Research in Australia, the United States, Nigeria, Spain, and other countries suggests that psychological factors affect a person's adherence to the antiretroviral therapy needed to delay the progression of the disease (Adewuya et al., 2010; Gordillo, del Amo, &

Soriano, 1999; Naar-King, Templin, & Wright, 2006; Sternhell & Corr, 2002). Specifically, research by Adewuya and colleagues (2010) found that general psychopathology and poor social support were the strongest predictors of poor adherence to an HIV medical regimen among their study of HIV-positive persons in Nigeria. They suggest that a person's distorted cognitive state or deliberate efforts of self-harm may contribute to the poor adherence. By comparison, Gordillo and colleagues (1999) suggest that the psychosocial factors most strongly associated with poor medical adherence were depression and a self-reported lack of social support.

SOCIAL SUPPORT, HIV, AND PSYCHOLOGICAL HEALTH   Research on other chronic illnesses shows that strong support systems are instrumental in enhancing the health outcomes of the individual with the illness. As we will see in the following three chapters on cardiovascular health, arthritis, and cancer, strong emotional support from family and friends enables the individual afflicted with the disease to cope more effectively with the daily hassles imposed by the illness.

Studies that examine social support and HIV report that here, too, strong support systems are needed. Unfortunately, people living with HIV often report either poorer levels of support or a greater reluctance to reveal their health status and to seek support due largely to the fear of stigma or rejection. Consider this: Studies by Fekete and colleagues (2009a) and by Derlega, Winstead, Oldfield, and Barbee (2003) show that individuals who revealed their HIV status to family or other supportive individuals reported lower psychological distress. As we learned in Chapter 7, Stress and Coping, there is a clear relationship between stress and health, a relationship that is further explained in the following section on psychoneuroimmunology. Yet the same researchers and others report a great reluctance by people with HIV to reveal their health status. Kalichman and colleagues' (2003) study of approximately 330 men and women revealed that both groups selectively disclosed their HIV status. The results showed that friends were perceived as more supportive than family members and therefore were the preferred group to whom to disclose one's HIV status. Among family, however, mothers and sisters were more likely to learn of their family member's HIV status than were fathers or brothers. And, as Fekete and colleagues (2009b) note, the pattern of disclosure is not the same for all ethnic groups. For example, Latino men may be less likely to reveal their HIV status to supportive friends than are Anglos. Interestingly, Fekete and colleagues (2009b) also suggest that Latino men may also be less likely to disclose their HIV status to family members because of fear of stigma. Based on this research, Latino men may have a smaller available support network, an outcome that could increase the psychological and the physiological effects of HIV.

PEOPLE AFFECTED BY HIV/AIDS   Recall again the opening story in Chapter 7, Stress and Coping. Lucinda, Michael, and Susan were the temporary caregivers for Sarah, a person with Alzheimer's. Yet, they, too, experienced a host of psychological and perhaps physiological illnesses in their efforts to assist their family member. Similar health consequences are reported for people who care for people with HIV.

Because we reviewed the impact of chronic illnesses on the caregivers and family members in Chapter 7, we will not review that literature here. Instead, it is sufficient to note that there has been considerably less research conducted on the caregivers and family members of people with HIV. One explanation for the paucity of research in this area is due to the people affected. For example, children constitute one group greatly affected by the disease. In many countries children have lost one or both parents to the disease. In other instances children may serve as caregivers to their ill parents, facing the social stigma and a host of psychosocial issues with little available support to assist them (King, DeSilva, Stein, & Patel, 2009). Yet there is little systematic research on the affects of HIV on this population in part because they are difficult to reach or difficult to recruit due to their protective status as children (see Chapter 2, Research Methods).

Other groups may be equally as difficult to include in studies of individuals affected by HIV due to an effort to avoid or minimize the impact of HIV on their lives. Research by Dageid and Duckert (2008) suggests that, for some South African women, a greater premium is placed on addressing their physical, psychological, or social survival needs. By comparison, they adopt avoidance strategies to minimize the emotional distress associated with caring for people with AIDS in societies with scarce resources and access to health care.

SECTION IV. PSYCHONEUROIMMUNOLOGY

To introduce the final topic, psychoneuroimmunology, we return to Magic Johnson. Magic has been living with HIV for over 18 years, and he appears to be doing quite well. But, as we mentioned, not everyone has the same outcome. Why, scientists wonder, do some people with HIV live long and productive lives with treatment, while others show signs of rapid physical and psychological deterioration, or shorter life spans? The question leads us to explore the relationship among neurology, immunology, and psychology.

Researchers began exploring the relationship between psychology and immunology in 1964, several decades before the HIV/AIDS crisis. The original work by Solomon and Moos (1964) and later work by Solomon (1987) proposed that our psychological states influence and affect our immune functions. This is not a new concept. Remember the work on emotional health and physiological outcomes presented in Chapter 6, Emotional Health and Well-Being.

Solomon and Moos's work complements other studies on immune systems, health, and psychological well-being by examining more closely the role of psychological health on lymphocytes and consequently on physiological outcomes. It is important to note, however, that their work has produced mixed results. For example, studies by Schliefer, Keller, and Meyerson (1984) and by Schliefer, Keller, and Siris (1985) indicate that patients hospitalized with depressive episodes had a decreased number of T and B lymphocytes. Recall that T and B lymphocytes are key components of the acquired immune system that fight and destroy invading microorganisms. A decrease in the number of T and B lymphocytes in depressed individuals could signal a weakening immune system. In their studies, Schliefer and colleagues (1985) found that a psychological trigger—depression—causes a decrease in the number of lymphocytes. As noted previously, decreases in the cells needed to fight foreign microorganisms can impair the work of the immune system, thereby exposing the body to illnesses or infections. What is interesting is that the cause of the decrease in cell numbers appears to be psychological, not physiological.

Social factors that cause emotional distress have also been studied for their possible effects on the immune system. A study by Kiecolt-Glaser, Fisher, and Ogrocki (1987) suggests that individuals experiencing poor marital adjustment or a recent separation from their spouse may experience stress that interacts with the immune system causing some abnormalities in the system. Finally, perhaps one of the clearest findings on the relationship between psychology, neurology, and immunology was shown in work by Locke, Kraus, and Lesserman (1984). Their studies of the effect of life changes on stress show that individuals who expressed fewer psychological symptoms when experiencing multiple life changes had higher levels of killer cell (T_C) activity than did individuals who, experiencing the same multiple life changes, expressed more psychological symptoms. While interesting, the work on the psychological impact on immunology is still considered inconclusive (Gorman & Kertzner, 1990).

Psychology and neurology appear to interact in a unique fashion. Consider this: Some early cases of HIV included symptoms of cognitive impairment, dementia, and depression (Gorman & Kertzner, 1990). A number of studies have shown that HIV invades the central nervous system and the brain in the early stages of the disease during the virus's dormant stage (Gabuzda & Hirsch, 1987; Grant, Atkinson, & Hesselink, 1987; Levy, Shimabukuro, & Hollander, 1985), apparently giving rise to cognitive deficiencies. In addition, studies by Levy and colleagues (1985) and Grant and colleagues (1987) suggest that if the brain and other regions of the central nervous system are also affected by HIV the resulting symptoms resemble or are consistent with psychological disorders that occur also in the later stages of the illness.

What does this mean for psychologists? Actually, the question pertains to all health providers who address HIV. The research suggests that the progression of HIV, its speed, and its impact on daily functioning may affect a person's mental, psychological, and physiological state. Some psychologists point to increased suicide rates among HIV-positive individuals as one of a number of psychological or emotional factors that can affect the progression of HIV (Atkinson, Grant, & Kennedy, 1988; Marzuk, Tierney, & Tardiff, 1988). The point is, because psychological factors are likely contributors to the progression of the disease, treatment for HIV requires a holistic approach that involves psychological as well as physiological treatment.

Personal Postscript

"COULD I HAVE HIV?" "SHOULD I BE WORRIED?"

Very often when reading about a disease or illness, we may ask ourselves, "Do I have that symptom? Could I be showing signs of the disease?" The questions may occur more often if the disease is easily transmitted as in the case of sexually transmitted diseases like HIV.

Two important facts will help you put the discussion about HIV into perspective, especially when considering the risk to you. First, HIV is transmitted primarily through risky sexual behavior or unclean instruments. Risky sexual behavior includes any activities in which you were exposed to another person's body fluids without protection. Condoms, specifically latex condoms, are the best barrier to HIV transmission when you are engaging in sexual behaviors. If you believe that you have engaged in risky, that is, unprotected, sexual behaviors, you may want to talk with a counselor to discuss whether HIV testing is recommended. Similarly, if you have experiences with drugs, specifically intravenous drugs, and suspect that you may have been exposed to unclean equipment or "works," you will want to consult with a counselor for possible HIV testing.

Second, you cannot determine the HIV status of other individuals by looking at them and observing their overall health or demeanor. Because many individuals may be unaware of their HIV status, the best way to protect yourself from the risk of HIV infection is to use protection when engaging in sexual behavior.

Finally, if you have questions about your HIV status, take a simple, quick, and reliable HIV test. HIV tests are the only definitive way to determine your status, and it takes only 20 minutes—about the same amount of time to buy and eat lunch at your school cafeteria.

Important Terms

acquired immunodeficiency syndrome (AIDS)   255
adaptive, or acquired, immunity   255
amoebic dysentery   262
antenatal clinics   278
antibody-producing cells   258
antigenic specificity   256
antigens   258
antiretroviral drugs   283
asymptomatic   255
B cells   258
B lymphocytes   258
CD4 cells   259
cell differentiation   260
cell proliferation   260
cytokines   258
cytotoxicity   260
deoxyribonucleic acid (DNA)   260
dermis   255
diversity   258
drug cocktail   283
dual infections   277
efavirenz   283

ELISA (enzyme-linked immunosorbent assay) test   280
epicenter   270
epidermis   255
epithelial cells   255
generic drugs   276
hemophilia   252
high-risk behaviors   269
human immunodeficiency virus (HIV)   254
immunologic memory   258
incidence rates   267
innate, or natural, immunity   255
Kaposi sarcoma   255
keratin   255
lymphocytes   258
lymphoid organs   258
microorganisms   256
mortality rates   267
mother-to-child transmission (MTCT)   265
nevirapine   283
onset   265

opportunistic infection   255
Pan troglodytes troglodytes   262
parenteral transmission   265
perinatal transmission   265
pneumocystic carinii pneumonia   255
point-of-care facilities   282
prevalence rates   267
psychoneuroimmunology   253
retrovirus   260
ribonucleic acid (RNA)   260
sebaceous glands   255
self/nonself process   256
seroconversion   260
sex workers   269
T cells   259
T cytotoxis (T_C)   259
T helper (T_H)   259
T lymphocytes   259
T suppressor (T_S)   259
viral RNA   260
virus   254
zidovudine   283

Cardiovascular Disease

Chapter Objectives

After studying this chapter you will be able to:

1. Identify the principal structures of the heart and describe their functions.
2. Identify and describe the four types of cardiovascular disease associated with health behaviors.
3. Identify the six main risk factors for cardiovascular disease.
4. Describe the contributions of carbohydrates, fats, cholesterol, vitamins, and minerals to heart disease.
5. Explain the risks of heart disease for men and women.
6. Explain the risk of heart disease for ethnic groups.
7. Explain the effects of family, community, and environment on risk factors for heart disease.
8. Explain the effect of access to healthcare on risks for cardiovascular disease.

OPENING STORY: TIM RUSSERT

Television news commentator Tim Russert was known for many things. He was a respected jour-nalist, a tenacious reporter, a challenging interviewer, and the well-regarded moderator of a popular Sunday morning talk show, Meet the Press. *But one thing not widely know was that he had* **coronary artery disease (CAD)**, *a disease caused by* **plaque**—*a composite made up of fat, cholesterol, calcium, and other substances—that builds up in the arteries (National Heart, Lung and Blood Institute [NHLBI], 2008b).*

On June 13, 2008, Tim Russert collapsed at work and later died from a heart attack due to coronary artery disease. According to his doctors, Russert had been diagnosed earlier with **asymptomatic** *CAD, meaning that he had experienced no warning signs of his illness. He did not experience pressure in the chest or pain in the shoulders, neck, arm, or back—symptoms that usually accompany CAD—caused by a reduced flow of blood and oxygen to the heart or the brain (NHLBI, 2008b). Doctors determined that when Russert collapsed on June 13, part of the plaque buildup in one of the arteries broke off. The dislodged plaque blocked the supply of blood and oxygen from one artery and reduced the flow of blood to the heart. The blockage caused a heart attack and, eventually, Russert's death.*

Russert's sudden death shocked many people. But more shocking was the fact that his CAD was said to be under control. He was taking medication for the disease and even passed a **stress test**, *a test that measures the electrical activity of the heart while an individual exercises on a treadmill or another type of exercise machine (NBC News, 2008). And, although not confirmed, we might speculate that Russert was also monitoring his health behaviors: limiting the con-sumption of foods high in fats and cholesterol and increasing his exercise. Unfortunately, in Russert's case, monitoring, medication, and health behavior changes did not prevent the very thing doctors were working to avoid: a heart attack that could prove fatal.* ■

Tim Russert's case is sobering. After all, how many times have we indicated in previous chapters that early detection and treatment of an illness, in addition to adopting healthy behaviors, will contribute to good health outcomes?

Without a full medical history, we cannot speculate about the distal causes (see Chapter 2, Research Methods) of Russert's death. But, we do know that he was overweight, suggesting that at some point his diet may have contained high levels of fats or cholesterol. Thus, in spite of the fact that Russert was receiving medical care for CAD, the medical treatment may not have been sufficient to reverse the effects of years of poor diet, lack of exercise, or other unhealthy behaviors.

Typical of a chronic disease, the behaviors that contributed to the development of CAD in Tim Russert did not lead to death in the short term. Rather, the combined effects over time contributed to a heart attack, listed as the proximal cause of death. CAD and other forms of cardiovascular disease associated with lifestyles are, therefore, an excellent example of the health consequences of risky health behaviors. This is one reason that cardiovascular disease is of interest to health psychologists.

This chapter is the first of three chapters that examine a chronic illness relevant to the field of health psychology. In this chapter, we examine diseases of the heart that are highly correlated with health behaviors and lifestyles including coronary artery disease (CAD), cardiac arrests, cerebrovascular disease (stroke), and hypertension (high blood pressure).

Before proceeding it is important to note that most forms of cardiovascular disease are preventable. Why do we refer to these illnesses as preventable? In earlier chapters we learned that lifestyles and health behaviors will affect health outcomes. Diet, alcohol consumption, use of tobacco, stress and stress management, and physical exercise can singly or in combination increase or decrease the risk of heart disease. And, as we will soon see, even the dietary habits of children as young as five years of age, if left unchanged, can predispose them to cardiovascular disease in adulthood. For this reason, and others, we view cardiovascular diseases as highly preventable illnesses. The question for health psychologists is how to encourage individuals to adopt and maintain healthy behaviors that limit the risk of avoidable diseases.

We begin the chapter with an overview of the cardiovascular system to identify the important components and functions of the heart and circulatory system and to understand how they work (Section I). Next, we use our understanding of the heart and its functions to examine, in Section II, the development of cardiovascular diseases, such as coronary artery disease (CAD), cardiac arrests, stroke, and hypertension, that are associated with lifestyle choices. We continue in Section III with an exploration of the risk factors that lead to each of these diseases, including behavioral, genetic, individual, familial, environmental, and health policy factors. Finally, in Section IV we explore the psychological impact of heart disease on individuals, demonstrated in new research that reveals the role of depression on the onset of and recovery from cardiovascular disease. As you may be able to tell by now, new discoveries of the relationship between emotional health and physiological outcomes increase the role of health psychologists in individual health management.

At the conclusion of this chapter you will be able to explain the role of the heart in sustaining life, identify and describe the major cardiovascular diseases associated with unhealthy behaviors, describe how various health risk factors negatively affect our heart health, and identify health-enhancing behaviors that minimize the risk of heart disease.

One reminder before we begin. Our opening story introduced Tim Russert, a person who died of CAD. While cardiovascular diseases of all types can cause death, it is important to keep in mind that these diseases are classified as chronic diseases. As we indicated earlier, chronic diseases are illnesses that may linger for months or years. Although they may contribute to death, they rarely cause immediate death. We do not know how long Russert suffered from CAD. But, as we will see later in the chapter, his coronary artery disease was probably in formation for several years: too many, in fact, to be reversed by a relatively recent change in diet, exercise, and medication.

SECTION I. THE HEART AND ITS FUNCTIONS

Structure

The heart can be described many ways: a muscular bag made up of two pumps, the body's transport system (Kunz, 1982), and an upside-down pear among other things. All of these descriptions accurately characterize the heart, including its shape.

The heart is a very strong muscle that is the focal point of the body's circulatory system. It is a vital muscle because the heart circulates blood to all parts of the body. The blood carries necessary "food," here meaning oxygen and other nutrients, needed by other organs and systems to function properly. In addition to carrying "food" to other organs, blood also carries carbon dioxide, a waste product, for the lungs to expel, thus eliminating a substance that is harmful to the body.

How does the heart work? The heart muscle has two sides and a total of four chambers (two per side): the right and left *atria* (the plural of *atrium*) and the right and left *ventricles*. The blood enters the right side of the heart through one of two upper chambers. In general, the right side of the heart receives and transports "used" blood, or deoxygenated blood, from the organs. Other organs in the body extracted oxygen (their "food") from the blood before returning the blood to the heart.

Figure 9.1 shows that used blood enters the right atrium, is passed to the right ventricle, and then goes through the *pulmonary arteries* to make its way to the lungs. The lungs *reoxygenate* the blood, meaning that the lungs resupply blood with new oxygen. The oxygen-rich blood is then pumped from the lungs into the heart through the left pulmonary veins and enters the heart's left atrium (NHLBI, 2008a). The blood, now with a fresh supply of oxygen, passes through the *aorta* to provide oxygen-rich blood to the organs.

One group of critical structures that connects the *arteries*, vessels carrying blood to other organs and *veins*, is the *capillaries*, small blood vessels with very thin walls. The capillaries' thin walls allow oxygen and other nutrients in the blood to pass through the walls to other parts of the

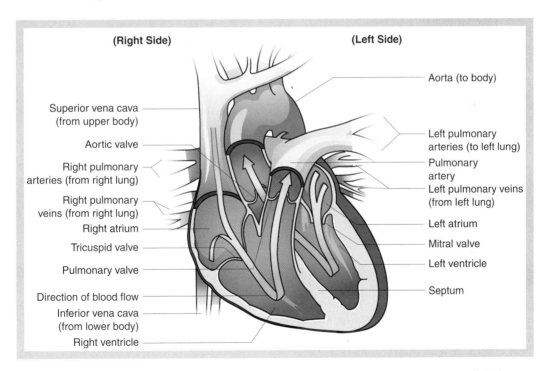

FIGURE 9.1 Heart Interior. The heart circulates "food" in the form of blood and oxygen to all vital organs of the body.

Source: Recreated with permission. © Link Studio, LLC and the National Heart, Lung, and Blood Institute (2008a).

body. In addition, capillaries allow waste products like carbon dioxide to pass through their walls into the blood to be carried to the lungs for removal.

Function

The four chambers, the arteries, and the veins are critical structures that facilitate blood flow. Yet, as we mentioned earlier, the heart is a complex muscle, and the circulation process involves more than chambers, arteries, and veins. It requires a process to move the blood from one chamber to the next. One function that helps move the blood into the correct chambers is the heartbeat. Consider this: Blood is a liquid. When moving a liquid from one area to another, there is the risk of backward flow. A backward flow of blood would be dangerous to our circulatory system. Therefore, the heartbeat and a system of *inlet valves* that open and close help to direct the blood flow in and around the heart and to prevent backward flow. The heartbeat works with the valves to complete the movement.

You have heard the sound of a heartbeat many times, whether it was your own or someone else's. The sound that characterizes the heartbeat is "lub-DUB." What you may not know is that each part of the sound corresponds to a specific function of the heart. We take a moment to explain the process here because it is important when discussing hypertension, a form of cardio-vascular disease, later in the chapter.

The "lub" sound of the heartbeat is produced when either the *tricuspid valve*, one of the inlet valves on the right side of the heart, opens to permits the blood to flow between the right atrium and ventricle, or when the *mitral valve*, another type of inlet valve on the left side of the heart, opens to permit the blood to move between the left atrium and ventricle. Remember, on the right side of the heart, oxygen-poor blood is en route to the lungs to be resupplied with oxygen. On the left, the oxy-genated blood is moving to other organs in the body. This process, represented by the lub sound, measures the *diastolic* blood pressure, or the pressure when the atria and the ventricles relax and fill with blood. It is sometimes referred to as the heart's resting or relaxation state.

The second part of the heartbeat, the "DUB" sound, occurs when the atria and ventricles contract to force the blood out. This process is called systole. It corresponds to the *systolic* mea-sure of blood pressure and measures the heart's pressure when actively pumping blood. This occurs when the *pulmonary valves* on the right side of the heart open and the ventricles contract to move the blood from the right ventricle to the pulmonary arteries, assisting the process of get-ting the blood to the lungs for oxygenation. On the left side of the heart, the *aortic valves* open, and the ventricles contract to move the blood from the left ventricle to the aorta, once again send-ing oxygenated blood to the organs.

Thus, blood pressure, one measure of heart health, assesses both the heart's resting and working states as blood is moved to and from the heart. We will discuss the importance of blood pressure in the section on hypertension. For now, however, it is sufficient to note that blood pres-sure is reported using the systolic and diastolic pressure, the amount of pressure exerted when the heart is pumping blood (systolic) versus resting (diastolic).

Summary

In sum, the heart is a complex muscle and critical to the body's circulatory system. It provides oxygen and nutrients (transported by blood) to the body's organs. It also receives the "used" blood from the organs in order to resupply it with needed oxygen.

SECTION II. CARDIOVASCULAR DISEASE

As we mentioned in the beginning of the chapter, the term ***cardiovascular disease*** refers to a group of disorders of the heart (*cardio*) or the circulatory system. The name for our circulatory system, ***vascular***, comes from the Latin word *vasculum,* meaning small vessels. In this case, the small vessels are the arteries, veins, and capillaries that transport blood throughout the body.

In general, cardiovascular disease refers to a number of diseases that damage the heart or its vessels as a result of ***atherosclerosis***, a Greek word that means hardness (*sclerosis*) of gruel or paste (*athero*) (see Figure 9.2). When used in connection with cardiovascular disease, the term *atherosclerosis* describes a process by which deposits of fats, cholesterol, calcium, and other

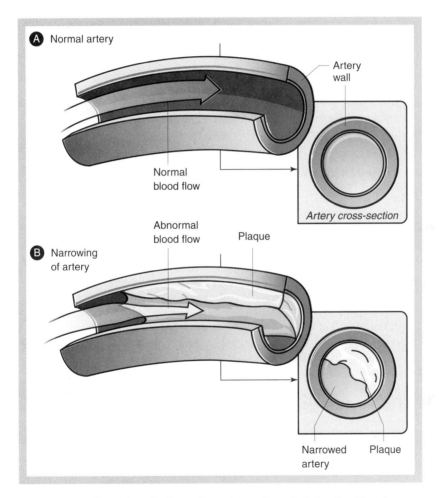

FIGURE 9.2   Atherosclerosis. Normal arteries are free of obstruction like plaque (B), which impedes blood flow and causes the heart muscle to work harder.

Source: Recreated with permission. © Link Studio, LLC and the National Heart, Lung, and Blood Institute (2008b).

substances called plaque line the arteries (vessels) of our circulatory system and cause the normally flexible arteries to harden (American Heart Association, 2008).

There are three key points to remember about cardiovascular disease. First, plaque narrows the passageway of arteries and reduces the volume of blood flowing to or from the heart. A reduction in blood flow can cause damage to the heart. Remember Tim Russert, from our opening story? In his case, plaque, dislodged from an artery, blocked the flow of blood from one artery and resulted in a heart attack and later death.

Second, a normal artery is flexible, allowing blood to flow easily through the vessel. When plaque forms in the arteries, it hardens the vessels, thereby reducing flexibility and causing another impediment to blood flow.

The final key point is particularly relevant for health psychologists. In the majority of cases, a buildup of plaque is caused by a diet high in fats and cholesterol and low in fiber. In other words, plaque buildup is preventable. And so are heart disease, heart attack, and death associated with atherosclerosis. Motivating individuals to adopt healthy eating habits is one way health psychologists can help prevent cardiovascular disease and possibly death. We review the important elements of a healthy diet in Section III of this chapter.

Although there are six principal types of cardiovascular disease, we will focus our attention on the four most directly linked to lifestyle choices: coronary artery disease, cardiac arrests, cerebrovascular disease, and hypertension.

Coronary Artery Disease (CAD)

Coronary artery disease (CAD), perhaps the most common type of cardiovascular disease, is the leading cause of heart attacks. We explained earlier that coronary artery disease is a condition in which the arteries that pump blood to and from the heart muscle become partially or completely obstructed. Less blood flowing through the arteries means less blood for the heart or other vital organs. The reduced volume of blood can damage heart tissues and produce a range of outcomes from chest pain and shortness of breath, often associated with *angina*, to heart attacks, also known as ***myocardial infarction***.

We mentioned previously that CAD and atherosclerosis, the condition that causes CAD, are largely preventable. Yet cardiovascular disease is the leading cause of death both in the United States (see Figure 9.3) and internationally (Kung, Hoyert, Xu, & Murphy, 2008; World Health Organization, 2008a). How is it possible that a disease that is linked to lifestyles and is very preventable is the leading cause of death worldwide?

As we noted in Chapter 5, Risky Health Behaviors, knowledge of health-enhancing behaviors does not ensure that people will adopt the healthy behaviors. For example, many people know that poor diet, lack of exercise, smoking, and alcohol consumption increase the risks for cardiovascular disease. Such behaviors sometimes are referred to as ***modifiable risk factors***. As the name implies, individuals can modify (increase or decrease) their risk of having a cardiovascular disease by changing behaviors: eating high-fiber and low-fat foods, exercising regularly (about 30 minutes a day), avoiding smoking, and limiting alcohol consumption.

Yet it may be difficult to change eating behaviors when fast foods and junk foods are marketed widely in a culture as the preferred cuisine, and video games, a sedentary activity, pass for recreational sport. As we noted when discussing health behavior change models in Chapter 4, Theories and Models of Health Behavior Change, environmental factors like social norms and

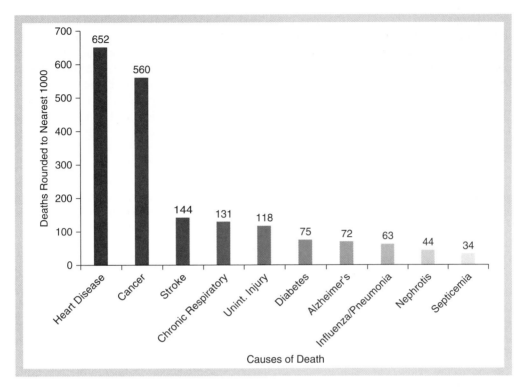

FIGURE 9.3   Ten Leading Causes of Death in the United States in 2005.

Source: Adapted from Kung et al., 2008.

cultures, in addition to individual differences and familial practices, can reinforce unhealthy diets and behaviors and serve as impediments to change.

It is also the case, however, that many individuals have insufficient knowledge of nutrition, exercise, and the effects of stress on heart health. Clearly knowledge and access to information needed to make informed choices will increase the likelihood of adopting healthy behaviors. We explore in detail the effects of nutrition on heart health in Section III. What is important to note here is that many individuals overestimate their knowledge of nutrition and healthy eating behaviors: an error that can increase the incidences of unhealthy behaviors that can lead to heart disease.

Cardiac Arrest

We first introduced cardiac arrests in Chapter 2, Research Methods. Briefly, a ***cardiac arrest*** is caused by ***ventricular fibrillation***, an abnormal heart rhythm that occurs when the heart fails to pump blood to other organs (Becker, 1996; Eisenberg, 1995; Ragin et al., 2005a). The heart's rhythm is determined in part by electrical impulses that begin with ***sinus nodes***, a cluster of cells in the right atrium that serves as a pacemaker for the heart. The nodes send electrical currents through the heart, synchronizing the heart rate and pumping blood to other organs. When the signal is interrupted, the result is a sudden cardiac arrest.

In more than 80% of cases, cardiac arrest is accompanied by a prior history of CAD. The interruption of blood flow to the heart due to CAD can interfere with the heart's ability to send electrical impulses (Mayo Clinic, 2006). Plaque-clogged arteries are the most common cause of obstruction. And, as we have said numerous times before, plaque buildup is directly related to dietary habits, lack of exercise, smoking, excessive alcohol consumption, and even stress.

It is important to note that the term *cardiac arrest* is not a synonym for a heart attack. Rather, a cardiac arrest is a condition that renders a person unconscious and is fatal unless the heart is jolted back into its normal rhythm. Remember, the heart controls the body's circulatory system. When it fails, blood cannot be supplied to the other organs.

Cardiac arrests are not always fatal. If the heart can be restarted in a timely way so that it may resume circulation of blood and oxygen to the body, an individual's chances of survival are good. However, time is the key. While many researchers suggest that a cardiac arrest victim can survive for 10 minutes without medical care, in truth, medical care providers note that after seven minutes without medical attention, a person will suffer irreparable brain damage due to the loss of oxygen to the brain. The chance of surviving a cardiac arrest after eight minutes is poor (American Heart Association, 2004; Pell, 2003).

Without a doubt you have seen, either on television, in movies, or in actual practice, at least one of two processes used to restart the heart of a cardiac arrest victim: *cardiopulmonary resuscitation (CPR)* or *automated external defibrillators (AEDs)*. CPR, most often used by emergency medical technicians and other trained persons, does two things. First, it stimulates the heart of the unconscious person to restart the body's vital circulation process. Second, it provides oxygen to the unconscious person to ensure that the lungs remain inflated and oxygen can enter the blood. This procedure involves no equipment, just a trained person who knows how to perform heart massages and to administer oxygen.

In comparison, automated external defibrillators (AEDs) are portable electrical devices with two pads that send an electric charge to the heart when placed on a person's chest (see Figure 9.4). The charge is meant to mimic the electrical charge of the heart and to restart the circulation process. Studies have shown that AEDs are more effective and work more quickly than CPR in restoring the heart's normal rhythm (Ragin et al., 2005a).

It is important to repeat that although the precipitating factor (see Chapter 2, Research Methods) for a cardiac arrest is an interruption in the electrical impulses sent by the sinus nodes, the predisposing factor (again, see Chapter 2, Research Methods) is usually coronary artery disease, a condition that comes about as a result of lifestyle behaviors that increase the risks for heart disease.

Stroke

A third type of preventable cardiovascular disease is stroke or *cerebrovascular disease*. Cerebrovascular diseases affect the vessels that carry blood and oxygen to the brain (*cerebro*). A stroke can be either an *ischemic stroke*, an interruption of blood flow to the brain, or a *hemorrhagic stroke*, here meaning a rupture of a blood vessel in the brain.

How are strokes related to other cardiovascular diseases that are caused by modifiable risk factors? By now it is clear that most interruptions in blood and oxygen flow, whether to the heart or the brain, are due to plaque buildup in the vessels or, as in Tim Russert's case, dislodged plaque that impedes blood flow. In the case of an ischemic stroke, the same agent can cause a disruption of blood flow to the brain.

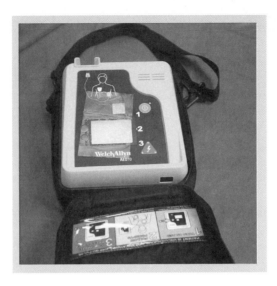

FIGURE 9.4   Fully Automated External Defibrillators. AEDs buy time when a person suffers an "out-of-hospital" cardiac arrest.

Source: Adapted from Erdine & Ari, 2006.

The role of modifiable risk factors may be clear for an ischemic stroke, but how do they apply to hemorrhagic stroke, when a blood vessel in the brain suddenly ruptures? The answer: This happens indirectly. *Hypertension*, the excessive force of blood pumping through the blood vessels, can prompt a hemorrhagic stroke.

Hypertension

Hypertension, also called *high blood pressure (HBP)*, is a descriptive name that characterizes the effect of the illness on the heart. Hypertension means that the systolic pressure (see page 294), the amount of pressure exerted when the atria and ventricles are contracting to force blood out of the heart's chamber, and the diastolic pressure, the amount of pressure exerted when the atria and ventricles relax and fill with blood, are higher than normal blood pressure ranges, as defined by medical standards (see Table 9.1). Normal blood pressure is indicated by a systolic pressure of 120 or fewer millimeters of mercury, and a diastolic pressure of 80 millimeters or fewer of mercury. Mercury, contained in a column, is the substance used in the original blood pressure devices to measure diastolic and systolic pressure readings. The catch here is that the systolic and diastolic pressures cannot be too high. Too much can damage the heart muscle.

It is important to point out that a hypertensive person will show signs of an enlarged heart. Enlarged hearts present new health problems because the heart is no longer able to work as efficiently as it did when at a normal size. When the heart muscle is enlarged it has reached its threshold of efficiency and cannot push blood through the chambers as efficiently as before. The increased pressure readings that signal hypertension indicate greater resistance by the heart when performing its normal functions.

TABLE 9.1	Normal and Abnormal Blood Pressure Ranges	
Category	**Systolic**	**Diastolic**
Optimal	<120	<80
Normal	120–129	80–84
High normal	130–139	85–89
Grade 1 hypertension (mild)	140–159	90–99
Grade 2 hypertension (moderate)	160–179	100–109
Grade 3 hypertension (severe)	>180	>110

A clue to the dangers of hypertension is its nickname: "the silent killer." High blood pressure is almost always a disease that escapes detection. One reason is that the symptoms associated with high blood pressure are often nonspecific, meaning that the symptoms are so general that they could be associated with any number of illnesses. It is often the case than an individual with hypertension becomes aware of the problem only when a medical provider measures his or her blood pressure as part of an annual physical or sick visit, or when previous exams have indicated high blood pressure. If the latter, a collection of symptoms commonly associated with hypertension may occur, including painful headaches, heart palpitations, sudden and unexplained nosebleeds, and a general feeling of ill health. Untreated elevated blood pressure can cause severe damage to the heart, the kidneys, the brain, and the arteries. In the most severe cases it can lead to sudden heart attack or death.

Hypertension can be assessed using a number of techniques. The most common test involves a *sphygmomanometer*, an instrument that consists of an inflatable rubber cuff and an air valve attached to a meter that measures heart pressure. Physicians use a *stethoscope* with this instrument to listen for the lub-DUB sound of the heartbeat to obtain the systolic and diastolic readings. Individuals can use modified home versions of blood pressure instruments to obtain a quick assessment of current blood pressure.

ESSENTIAL AND SECONDARY HYPERTENSION   The most common form of hypertension, called *essential* or *primary hypertension*, has no known or identifiable causes. Individuals with essential or primary hypertension have consistently high blood pressure over time, as determined through multiple blood pressure readings over months or years. More than 95% of current cases of hypertension worldwide are diagnosed as essential hypertension. For this reason, researchers believe that one contributing factor for essential hypertension may be genetics (Kunz, 1982; Penn State, 2008). Other potential factors include generalized stress and stressful events occurring over time.

We explain secondary hypertension more fully in the next section. Briefly, secondary hypertension is caused largely by health inhibiting behaviors, such as high fat, high calorie diets, lack of exercise, and smoking: behavioral health factors known to increase the risk of high blood pressure.

SECTION III. PSYCHOSOCIAL FACTORS AND CARDIOVASCULAR DISEASE

Up to this point we have identified several nonbiological factors that contribute to the development of cardiovascular disease, including poor diets, lack of exercise, and smoking. We also characterized these as modifiable risk factors because individuals can change their behaviors and, by doing so, modify or reduce their risk of heart disease.

Research shows, however, that there are other psychosocial factors that also contribute significantly to the development of heart disease. A review of the extensive literature on the relationship of cardiovascular disease and psychosocial factors is beyond the scope of this chapter. Yet in this section we can summarize the principal findings on the effects of psychosocial factors on one type of heart disease, hypertension.

Stress

In Chapter 6, Emotional Health and Well-Being, and Chapter 7, Stress and Coping, we explained the role of stress on disease. Specifically we noted that some psychological and biological illnesses are attributable to stress. One such illness is hypertension (Heine & Weiss, 1987). Current research suggests that the association between stress and hypertension is strongest when the stressful is persistent, meaning either repeated exposures to stressful situations or that the effects of one particular event are long-lasting (Markovitz et al., 2004; Radi et al., 2005; Schnall, Landsbergis, & Baker, 1990). For example, Radi and colleagues' study of job constraints in approximately 200 French workers revealed that job strain, which they define as a psychologically demanding environment with little ability to affect decisions or outcomes, was associated with high levels of hypertension, especially among women. They note that it is the prolonged effect of psychological stress with little ability to change the environment that increased hypertension rates in the female study participants.

On the other hand, Dorn, Yzermans, Guiju, and Zee (2007) demonstrated the association between stress and hypertension from a single stressful event with long-lasting effects. In their study, parents of adolescents who, together with other adolescents, were seriously injured in a large-scale fire, experienced stress both at the time of the event and later as they coped with the medical and psychological consequences of the disaster for their children. Dorn and colleagues demonstrated that although only one stressful event occurred, one or both parents of adolescents reported ongoing hypertension due to the long-term effect of stress stemming from the accident. Thus, results from studies like Radi and colleagues' (2005) and Dorn and colleagues' show that stress experienced over time in response to recurring stress-inducing situations and the stress experienced as a result of a one-time event can both lead to hypertension.

Ethnicity

It is the case, however, that some illnesses occur with higher frequency in specific populations. For example, hypertension is prevalent among African Americans. In fact, in 16 studies comparing hypertension rates of African Americans and whites, the majority found significantly higher hypertension rates among African Americans (Kurian & Cardarelli, 2007). Do significantly higher rates of hypertension among African Americans suggest a genetic predisposition (see Chapter 2, Research Methods) to the disease? Apparently it does not. Rather, what these and similar studies show is that, for many African Americans, common culture behaviors such as preferred foods and individual factors such as weight and environmental stressors contribute significantly to hypertension. Consider this: Foods such as baked macaroni and cheese, candied yams, and collard greens seasoned with pork are part of the cultural cuisine for many African Americans. Such foods have high fat and cholesterol content. You may remember that fats and cholesterol are two substances that contribute to the buildup of plaque in the arteries, a precursor for many types of cardiovascular diseases, including hypertension. The important point here is that it is not ethnicity, per se, that increases a group's risk for hypertension or other heart diseases but the behaviors or the traditions, including culinary delights, associated with specific ethnic groups that put them at higher risk. It is worth noting, however, that such diets also tend to increase weight levels. Hence, a cultural practice can put African Americans at higher risk directly by the food consumed and indirectly through weight gain associated with diet. When behavioral factors cause hypertension, we refer to the disease as ***secondary hypertension***, suggesting that the illness is the result of other primary behaviors, in this case high-risk dietary habits that predispose individuals to hypertension.

Perceived Racism

Recently researchers have explored the effects of ***perceived racism***, an environmental factor, on hypertension, especially among African Americans (Brindoli, Rieppi, Kelly, & Gerin, 2003). The term *perceived racism* refers to the belief that another person's actions or words are intended as prejudicial, discriminatory, or demeaning toward people of a specific race or ethnicity. It qualifies as a persistent and stressful factor for the recipients because minority groups are likely to experience racism as both single and repeated occurrences.

The persistent nature of racism can be compared to the persistent stressful environments in workplace settings. And a number of studies examining exposure to perceived racism in the workplace suggest that here, too, there is a relationship between perceived racism and hypertension. James, La Croix, and Kleinbaum (1984) examined the reports of perceived racism, job success, and blood pressure among African American men and found that while there was no direct association between blood pressure and perceived racism, there was an interactive effect among racism, coping, and blood pressure. Specifically, James and colleagues noted that men with greater success in their jobs who reported perceived racism at work and who used persistent coping strategies to address the racism in the environment were significantly more likely to have higher diastolic (or resting state) blood pressure than were men who reported no perceived workplace racism. This, then, is similar to the findings reported by Radi and colleagues (2007). The perception of a stressor that is beyond one's control, and in James and colleagues' case, the continual effort to cope with this stressor, appears to elevate diastolic blood pressure rates.

It is important to note, however, that findings from studies that examine the specific impact of perceived racism on blood pressure appear to yield mixed findings (Williams & Neighbors, 2001). For example, in one laboratory-based study, African American participants were exposed to racial stimuli in one of four conditions: videos, films, speech or debate tasks, or harassment from a white experimenter. African American participants showed increased systolic and diastolic blood pressures rates shortly after all tasks (Armstead et al., 1989; Gentry, 1972; Guyll, Matthews, & Bromberger, 2001). But in other similar studies, no notable changes were associated with perceived racism (Bowen-Reid & Harrell, 2002; Clark, 2006).

One problem with a number of the studies on racism and blood pressure is the difficulty in measuring precisely an individual's reaction to a perceived racial event. However, studies that examine *cardiovascular reactivity (CVR)*, or the body's return to a baseline blood pressure and heart rate at the conclusion of a stressful event, appear to offer more reliable measures of the impact of perceived racism on physiological health (Schwartz, Landsbergis, & Baker, 1990).

Lepore and colleagues' (2006) study of cardiovascular reactivity in black versus white women compared differences in blood pressure and heart rate after no stimulus, after a nonracial or neutral stimulus (a talk about a college tour), and after a perceived racial stimulus (discussion of differential treatment while shopping). The no-stimulus condition was the baseline, the college talks provided the reactivity measure, and the differential treatment condition represented the experimental condition yielding a recovery measure. Lepore and colleagues found that measures of heart rate and blood pressure for black women after the perceived racism condition were significantly higher than those of the white female participants in the study. Putting this into perspective, we noted in Chapter 7, Stress and Coping, that the body contains systems that help it return to its normal or resting state after stressors. The same is true for the heart. After exposures to stress, the heart must be able to return to a normal resting state. A higher than normal diastolic or resting state causes continued stress to the heart and can increase risks of damage to the heart.

Similar studies of hypertension and perceived racism also suggest that repeated exposure to perceived racism increased the instances of elevated blood pressure that can, over time, erode health (Merritt et al., 2006). Thus, while studies that examine the association between racism and elevated blood pressure report mixed findings, research that examines cardiovascular reactivity (CVR) shows that the more relevant measure for assessing the effect of racism and blood pressure is the cardiovascular reactivity rate (Fang & Myers, 2001). Lepore and colleagues' (2006) study suggests that cardiovascular recovery can lead to early onset and long-term hypertension, especially in African Americans' response to perceived racism (Christenfeld, Glynn, & Gerin, 2000; Knox, Hausdorff, & Markovitz, 2002).

Personality

Friedman (1991) and Friedman (1989) introduced yet another psychological factor thought to be associated with heart disease: type A personality. We first identified the impact of type A personality on stress and illness in Chapter 7, Stress and Coping. Recall that we noted that people with type A personality are described as individuals who are aggressive, ambitious, and impatient and who easily and frequently become angry or hostile (Johnsen, Espnes, & Gillard, 1998; Watson, Minzenmayer, & Bobler, 2006).

Although early research supported the association between type A behaviors and heart disease (Allan & Scheidt, 1992; Cohen & Reed, 1985), later research refined the association, showing that it is actually anger and cynicism that together predicted a higher risk of cardiovascular disease (Dembroski et al., 1985). For example, Kawaichi and colleagues (1998) reported that individuals who had greater difficulty controlling their anger increased their risk factor for coronary heart disease by a factor of three. It is not the experience of anger, per se, that appears to increase risk for heart disease. Rather, researchers suggest that it is the expression of that anger that causes a physiological reaction that increases cardiovascular risks. For example, Williams and colleagues (2000) found that anger can disrupt and dislodge atherosclerosis plaque that can build up in the linings of the arteries. In other words, anger can be considered an acute risk factor that can trigger heart disease.

Summary

The research on hypertension suggests that a number of factors contribute to high blood pressure. Some of the causes are unknown to us and result in essential or primary hypertension. Other factors such as diet, exercise, and smoking are clearly associated with hypertension and lead to secondary hypertension (Erdine & Ari, 2006; Sparrenberger et al., 2008). Finally, research indicates that environmental stimuli can also trigger hypertension. This appears to be true whether the trigger is a job-related stressor or perceived racism.

SECTION IV. CARDIOVASCULAR DISEASE AND HEALTH DETERMINANTS

Most researchers agree that there are six principal risk factors for cardiovascular disease: excessive alcohol consumption, tobacco, high blood cholesterol levels due to diet, physical inactivity, overweight/obesity, and diabetes. These factors are often referred to as ***moderating risk factors*** because, when controlled, they can lessen the risk of contracting cardiovascular disease. We will explore some of these factors in the current section.

In addition, however, other factors—factors that we have referred to as health determinants in previous chapters—are often associated with heart disease. They include gender, age, race/ethnicity, environment, and health systems. In this section we explore the relative importance of each of these factors when compared with lifestyles. Finally, we will explain in greater detail why race/ethnicity is not a risk factor for heart disease and explore the role of health care systems on health outcomes.

Individual Determinants

EATING BEHAVIORS AND NUTRITION   Levy, Fein, and Stephensson (1993) and Suter and Burton (1996) suggest that many individuals have, at best, a minimal understanding of daily nutritional requirements and that this lack of knowledge adversely affects food choices. As Jacoby, Chestnut, and Silberman (1977) found, many participants in their study on nutrition claimed to have a high level of knowledge about nutrition. But when testing their knowledge on a 19-item questionnaire, respondents answered, on average, fewer than half of the questions correctly. Similarly, Levy and colleagues found that study participants had a particularly poor level of knowledge about the fat content in foods But, even among individuals with greater than average knowledge of nutrition, incomprehensible information labels on prepared and processed foods can be confusing at best and meaningless at worst (Suter & Burton, 1996).

Health psychologists seek to improve an individual's knowledge about nutrition and food content and determine how to make the information more accessible and useful. We will address the knowledge question first.

For years, nutritionists and health practitioners used a "food pyramid" to instruct people on the components of a healthy diet. The pyramid was intended, in part, to guide an individual's food choices. For example, the pyramid identified foods that should be consumed in smaller

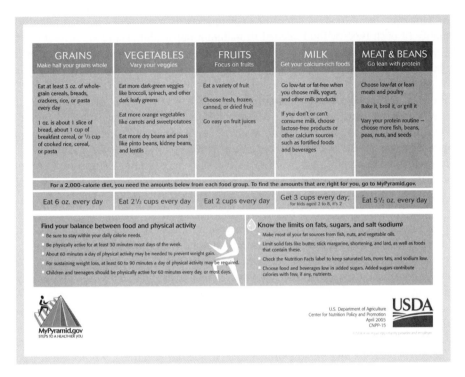

FIGURE 9.5 Food Pyramid. The revised food pyramid provides useful information that defines "portions" and suggests physical activity as part of a healthy diet.

quantities than others due to their high fat and cholesterol content. Yet the pyramids were confusing. For example, an earlier version of the guidelines indicated that individuals need three to five servings of vegetables a day. But many people had no idea what was meant by a "serving." How much was in a serving? If you have a meal consisting entirely of vegetables, is that one serving or multiple servings?

The revised food pyramid provides clearer guidelines on appropriate and healthy food quantities and food choices (see Figure 9.5). It avoids ambiguity by explaining the quantity of food to be consumed each day using measures that are understood by the average person. For example, the new pyramid explains that individuals need 2.5 cups of vegetables per day. Half a cup of food is more readily understood than a "serving." Clearer, less confusing guidelines increase the probability that individuals understand the information and will use it correctly.

The new pyramid also provides additional helpful information. For example, it explains clearly the types of "good" versus "bad" fats and the role of exercise in preventing weight gain. In essence, the revised pyramid presents a more user-friendly guide to nutrition. It is, however, still an abbreviated guide to nutrition. For this reason, we add a few more details about nutrition here to complete the picture.

Five Food Elements   The pyramid categorizes foods into five groups: meats and beans, grains, dairy products, fruits, and vegetables. These are commonly referred to as "the five food groups." However, these foods can also be explained by their elements, another factor to guide the quantity of each type of food needed to maintain our health. There are a total of five elements: proteins, carbohydrates, fats, vitamins, and minerals. We add to these elements a sixth component—water—an essential ingredient for health.

Proteins   *Proteins* are chemical compounds that form the basis of all living organisms. They are essential because proteins help to repair damaged body tissues and to promote new tissue growth. Protein is found in animal products, beans, peas, and some grains. Thus, proteins are contained in the "meat and beans" food group as well as in some of the grains in the "grain" food group. It supplies approximately 10 to 15% of our energy source. However, if consumed in excess of the body's needs, protein will be stored in the body as fat. Thus, while protein is needed, it is not needed in large supply.

Carbohydrates   *Carbohydrates* are often thought of as one of the "villains" of any diet. Why? Carbohydrates include starches and sugars and are found in foods such as breads, pastas, potatoes, and cereals, among others. The main component of carbohydrates is a sugar molecule. Thus, when consumed in excess, carbohydrates are taken in as sugar and stored in the body as fat, an ingredient that is needed only in small quantities. This leads to another reason why carbohydrates are thought of as villains. Foods high in sugars and starches are so tasty that they are often consumed in excess of the body's needs. This almost ensures added storage of fat in the system.

Current research suggests, however, that not all carbohydrates are bad. In fact, foods such as whole grains, cereals and breads, brown rice (instead of potatoes), whole wheat pasta, and especially beans are good sources of carbohydrates (Harvard School of Public Health, 2008). Recent studies even suggest that low levels of carbohydrates, especially the "good" carbohydrates, can be helpful and more effective for long-term weight loss than are carbohydrate-free diets (Harvard School of Public Health, 2008). And relevant to our discussion on cardiovascular disease, a recently concluded study of women's eating habits over 20 years reported than women who consumed a low-carbohydrate, high-vegetable-fat diet had a 30% lower risk of heart disease than women who reported a high-carbohydrate, low-fat diet (Hulton, Willett, & Liu, 2006). In essence, we do not need large quantities of carbohydrates; however, low levels of good carbohydrates, in combination with other healthy elements, can help protect our heart health.

Other "villains" in diets are *fats* and *cholesterol*. Found in both plants and animals, fats provide energy and also aid the body in repair. But, here, as with carbohydrates, there are "bad" fats, which include *saturated fats*, and "good" fats, which include *monounsaturated* and *polyunsaturated fats*, each of which has a direct impact on cardiovascular diseases.

Saturated fats include *trans fatty acids* (sometimes called trans fat). These fats are a problem for health, and hence are thought of as "bad" fats, because they tend to raise the levels of *low-density lipoproteins (LDL)* in the system. LDLs are commonly referred to as "artery-clogging cholesterol agents." They carry cholesterol from the liver to the rest of the body. Excessive amounts of LDL in the system will adhere to the arteries, lining the walls of the arteries with cholesterol. Remember plaque? The substance that clogs the arteries is made from fats and cholesterols, specifically the LDL cholesterol found in trans fatty acids and saturated fats.

The problem with trans fatty acids can be seen more clearly in the following concrete examples: A 2% increase in trans fatty acids a year—approximately a medium order of fast-food French fries each day for one year—will increase the risk of coronary artery disease by 23%.

Yet, if individuals would eliminate trans fatty acids from their diet, researchers estimate that deaths related to coronary artery disease would decrease by 200,000 per year (Mozaffarin et al., 2006). These research findings led to New York City, Boston, and other cities across the nation requiring restaurants to eliminate trans fats from all foods.

We indicated that there are, in fact, good fats. These include the monounsaturated fats, which include oils from peanuts, olives, and canola oil, and polyunsaturated fats, such as the oils found in sunflowers, corn, and walnuts, and the omega-3 oils found in fish and plants. Monounsaturated and polyunsaturated fats help to decrease the LDL levels in the blood and to increase the level of ***high-density lipoproteins (HDL)***. The nickname for HDL is the "good cholesterol" or the "garbage truck of the blood system." Like mono- and polyunsaturated fats, HDL helps to clean the cholesterol from the blood and the walls of arteries, sending them to the liver for disposal.

Fruits and Vegetables   The last two elements of the food group, ***vitamins*** and ***minerals***, are contained in vegetables and fruits. Fruits and vegetables are a natural source of vitamins that convert food into energy. Thus, lettuce, spinach, and the cruciferous vegetables like broccoli, cauliflower, bok choy, and cabbage also supply vitamins such as vitamin A, C, and E and minerals such as calcium, sodium, and zinc.

Just how essential are vitamins and minerals to healthy outcomes? Consider this: Studies suggest that individuals who consume at least 2.5 to 5 cups of fruits and vegetables daily are at lower risk for heart disease. Furthermore, in a study involving over 110,000 Harvard-affiliated nurses and health professionals, researchers found that study participants who consumed at least eight servings (approximately four cups) of fruits and vegetables daily over 14 years were 30% less likely to have a heart attack or stroke (Hung, Joshipura, & Jiang, 2004). Thus, while the expression "an apple a day keeps the doctor away" may not literally be correct, it captures the essence of the beneficial role of fruits and vegetables as necessary to improve health outcomes.

Studies have demonstrated the long-term effects of poor diet and physical inactivity on cardiovascular disease. In particular, two studies involving military personnel illustrate the relationship between poor dietary choices and atherosclerosis, even among children.

There is a general assumption that men and women serving in armed forces are at low risk for CAD because of the intense exercise regimen in the military and the need to be physically fit for combat. However, early research by Enos, Holmes, and Beyer (1953) and a later study by McNamara, Molot, Stremple, and Cutting (1971) suggest that even the intense physical training in the military cannot counteract the effects of soldiers' poor diet and lack of exercise during their childhood and adolescence.

Enos and colleagues' (1953) study of 300 American soldiers injured during the Korean War revealed a surprisingly high frequency of CAD or atherosclerosis among active military personnel at the time of their injury. They found that of the 300 soldiers surveyed (their average age was 22.1 years), more than 77% had evidence of atherosclerosis, and 65% showed signs of plaque buildup, an unexpected outcome given the rigorous physical training in preparation for combat. In a related study of heart disease in the military, McNamara and colleagues (1971) found that 45% of American soldiers in their sample, who had fought in Vietnam, similarly showed signs of atherosclerosis. Although a somewhat smaller percentage than that obtained in Enos and colleagues' study, McNamara and colleagues' results confirmed that the risk for heart disease among active military may be higher than expected.

The studies hold several implications for the average citizen as well. First, the studies seems to suggest that CAD and atherosclerosis begin forming early in an individual's life. As illustrated by these studies, the high risk for some military personnel is due to the distal factors of poor diet and lack of sufficient exercise earlier in life. Furthermore, the high rates of atherosclerosis and CAD found in soldiers, due presumably to eating behaviors as children and adolescents, are supported by similar outcomes in studies on nonmilitary study participants, including children (Bao et al., 1997; Berenson et al., 1998). Collectively, the studies suggest that nutritional programs, specifically those designed to help maintain healthy heart functions, should include children and adolescents as a primary target audience. While such programs may also benefit adults, introducing such programs to children may help avoid the plaque buildup that creates the conditions for coronary artery disease later in life.

A second and somewhat troubling point of the military studies is that, for individuals with a predisposition to CAD based on lifestyle behaviors, vigorous physical activity without medical supervision and monitoring may be harmful (Burke et al., 1999; McGraw et al., 2008). Indeed, in a study of deaths in the military between 1996 and 1999, 39% of exercise-related deaths were attributed to CAD (Gutmann, Gardner, Potter, & Kark, 2002; McGraw et al., 2008). Undoubtedly, with the exception of athletes, few people engage in the type of regular and strenuous exercise performed by soldiers. Yet even civilians may unknowingly embark on an exercise regimen that is too strenuous for their heart condition.

Clearly, most researchers would support a program of exercise and diet for individuals at risk for CAD. Yet the key is moderate exercise with supervision to prevent undue stress to the heart. In addition, a physical exam to evaluate a person's ability to engage in the type of exercise being considered is certainly recommended. Consider this: Routine physicals are usually required for soldiers and even for adolescents who wish to participate in extracurricular sports teams in their high school or college. However, these findings might suggest that a more thorough exam may be required if atherosclerosis cannot be detected through the routine physical examination.

GENDER   Which gender is at higher risk for cardiovascular disease? If you guessed men, your answer would be consistent with the outcomes from early research that showed higher rates of cardiovascular disease for men than women (Gillum et al., 1983; Public Health Agency of Canada, 2002; Yu, Wong, Lloyd, & Wong, 1995). In fact, during the 1960s and 1970s, the prevailing wisdom that men were at higher risk for CAD was so overwhelming that researchers and practitioners helped to significantly decrease the mortality (death) rates of cardiovascular disease for men (Lee & Foody, 2008) by targeting them as study participants. At the same time, women's risk for CAD was not systematically explored. We now know from data obtained through the Framingham Heart Health Study (see Chapter 2, Research Methods) that mortality rates for women due to CAD exceed that for men. Approximately 25% of men but 38% of women die within one year of having an initial and identified heart attack (Hurst, 2002).

Do you wonder why researchers missed this distinction? One reason for the missed finding is that women either were not regularly included as study participants or were not included in large enough numbers in research examining the likelihood of developing CAD. As we learned in Chapter 2, Research Methods, researchers need a representative sample to generalize their findings to the larger population. Due to the overrepresentation of men in earlier studies, the research accurately captured the incidences of heart disease among men but significantly underestimated the incidences of heart disease among women.

An additional factor that reinforced the mistaken belief that women were less susceptible to heart disease than men was the common belief in many industrialized countries that women did not experience as much stress, especially job-related stress, as men. Here, *job-related* refers to paid employment outside of the home. Admittedly, this is a difficult concept to grasp today because changes in employment opportunities for women have, in fact, placed them in a greater variety of paid positions in the workplace. For example, it is not uncommon to see many women employed in managerial and senior management-level positions that entail high stress, such as chief executive officers of major corporations, judges on the U.S. Supreme Court and lower courts, as well as senators and congresswomen in federal and state legislatures. (We will hold aside for the moment any discussion of the stress related to child rearing and managing a household. Research studies on the stress related to those tasks are far fewer in number.) Thus, not surprisingly, the new studies of cardiovascular disease show that women, too, are at high risk for heart disease in part as a function of their more demanding and responsible positions in the workforce.

Finally, the symptoms associated with heart disease differ by gender. We explain these differences more fully in the next section. For the moment, it is sufficient to note that the different symptoms often caused physicians to overlook early signs of heart disease among women. Now that we know that women, too, are susceptible to heart disease, researchers regularly assess incidences of heart disease and differences in rates of disease in both genders. The surprising results of current studies is that women are at high risk for heart disease and that cardiovascular disease is the leading killer of women nationally and globally (Agency for Healthcare Research & Quality [AHRQ], 2003; Gorodeski, 2002).

Women and Heart Disease   To put things in perspective, the number of cases of cardiovascular disease in the United States as of 2003 was 89,700,000, with hypertension or high blood pressure accounting for approximately 72.5% of all cardiovascular diseases (Thom et al., 2006). The prevalence and mortality statistics for women, however, show that the number of women diagnosed with heart disease is higher than that of men, although the percentages are comparable.

The biggest difference in health outcomes for men and women with heart disease emerges in the mortality statistics (see Table 9.2). Here, both in number and percentage, more women (53.1%) die of heart disease than do men (46.9%).

How could researchers and medical providers miss the greater health impact of heart disease on women? We identified one reason previously. A cultural bias in the research on cardiovascular disease lead researchers to believe that this disease primarily affected men. Another

TABLE 9.2	Prevalence and Mortality of Cardiovascular Diseases by Gender (2003)			
Population	Prevalence of CVD (N)	Prevalence of CVD (%)	Mortality due to CVD (N)	Mortality due to CVD (%)
Total	71,300,000	34.2	910,614	
Males	33,100,000	34.4	426,772	46.9
Females	38,200,000	33.9	483,842	53.1

Source: Thom, Hause, Rosamond, Howard, Rumsfeld & Manolio (2006).

reason for overlooking the prevalence of heart disease among women is the difference in symptoms and the age of first onset.

Women and Age of Onset   Recent studies reveal that heart disease for women first appears at a later point in life than men. On average, men report the first signs of cardiovascular health problems in their 40s. The same is not true for women. Twenty- to forty-year-old women report far fewer incidences of heart disease than men (Anderson, Kochanek, & Murphy, 1995). On average, only after age 50 do we see rates of heart disease for women that are comparable to men (Thom et al., 2006).

One reason for the higher incidences of heart disease in women after age 50 appears to be physiological. On average, until age 45, women's bodies produce high levels of ***estrogen***, a vital hormone for reproduction. It appears from research findings that estrogen plays two essential roles in women's health. It is crucial for reproduction, but it is also a protective factor that helps minimize the risk of cardiovascular disease for women who are ***premenopausal***, that is, women who are still potentially reproductively active. In fact, some research suggests that estrogen helps to lower the LDL cholesterol level in the blood, a specific function that contributes to lower rates of heart disease in premenopausal women (Lee & Foody, 2008; Kalin & Zumoff, 1990). Between the ages of 45 and 55, however, estrogen levels decrease substantially. It is during this time that rates of heart disease show marked increases that continue in the succeeding years.

If estrogen protects women from cardiovascular disease, then it seems logical to reason that by replacing the lost estrogen women should continue their trend of lower rates of heart disease. Unfortunately, the research does not support this assumption. Studies testing the effectiveness of ***hormone replacement therapy***, a process that restores estrogen to premenopausal levels, found no significant difference in the rate of cardiovascular disease in menopausal women who received the hormone replacement therapy when compared with women in the control group who did not receive the therapy (Barrett-Connor & Stuenkel, 1999). While estrogen may help protect women in the earlier years, it does not appear to reduce the risk of heart disease when used in replacement therapy approaches.

Gender and Symptoms   One additional difficulty in diagnosing heart disease in women is the difference in symptom profiles between men and women. Studies show that women report different, and in some cases milder, symptoms than men (Kessler, 1992). Men generally report tightness in the chest, shortness of breath, and possibly pain in the left arm. These symptoms have come to represent the "classic" symptoms of heart disease. We now know that the classic symptoms of heart disease in women are pain in the neck and shoulder, lower back pain, and possibly shortness of breath. Medical providers trained to look for the symptoms specific to men will miss or misinterpret the symptoms reported most often by women.

The delay in recognizing the symptoms of heart disease in women often leads to a delay in diagnosis. And a delayed diagnosis increases the likelihood that the heart disease will worsen, leading eventually to more severe cardiovascular disease and death. Given the assumptions about risk factors for cardiovascular disease, the later onset of heart disease in women, and the difference in illness-related symptoms between men and women, it is not surprising that researchers and medical providers overlooked women as a population at high risk for heart disease. These differences also explain, in part, the higher mortality rate from heart disease for women versus men that we mentioned earlier.

BOX 9.1   The Red Dress Campaign: Raising Awareness of Heart Disease among Women

FIGURE 9.6   Educational Advertisement for the Red Dress Campaign. The educational poster about women and heart disease is one part of the successful campaign.

Source: NHLBI, 2008c.

The Heart Truth®, a national awareness campaign for women about heart disease sponsored by the National Heart, Lung, and Blood Institute (NHLBI), part of the National Institutes of Health, created and introduced the Red Dress as the national symbol for women and heart disease awareness in 2002. Seeking to advance the Red Dress symbol, *The Heart Truth*® forged a groundbreaking collaboration between the federal government and the fashion industry, an industry intrinsically tied to female audiences (see Figure 9.6).

The purpose of *The Heart Truth*® campaign is to give women a personal and urgent wake-up call about their risk of heart disease. The campaign is especially aimed at women ages 40 to 60, the age when a woman's risk of heart disease starts to rise. But its messages are also important for younger women, since heart disease develops gradually and can start at a young age—even in the teenage years.

But, now that we know that women also are at risk for cardiovascular disease, the question for health psychologists is how to minimize the risk. We know from discussions earlier in the chapter that smoking is one behavior that increases the risk for heart disease. Fortunately for women, cigarette smoking has been called the single most preventable risk factor for heart disease (Gorodeski, 2002). In a recent study, Sclavo (2001) showed that women who smoke are two to four times more likely than men to be at risk for heart disease. What is more, research also indicates that the risk decreases *immediately* when women stop smoking. In fact, the decrease is so substantial that in just three to five years after smoking, former female smokers have a risk profile for heart disease that is comparable with that of women who never smoked (Manson, Tosteson, & Ridker, 1992; Rosenberg, Palmer, & Shapiro, 1990; Sclavo, 2001).

AGING   Without a doubt, an individual's age also affects risk for heart disease. The statistics show that the prevalence rates for cardiovascular diseases, including coronary artery disease, heart failure, stroke, and hypertension, increase almost 30% from the age group 40 to 59 (group 2) to the prevalence for ages 60 to 79 (group 3) (Rosamond et al., 2007). In addition, all major statistical sources of data on cardiovascular disease report that, among people 65 years of age or older, cardiovascular disease is the leading cause of death (National Academy on an Aging Society, 2000; Rosamond et al., 2007; Thom et al., 2006) (see Figure 9.7).

What causes the higher rates of cardiovascular disease among older adults? There appear to be several causes, three of which we highlight here: the body's aging process, co-occurring chronic diseases, and women's longer life spans. We consider first the body's aging process. Think of it this way: The human body can be compared with an automobile. While this is not the most elegant example, the body, like most automobiles, is constantly in operation. The older the car, the more likely it is to develop mechanical problems. Similarly, over time, the toll placed on the body by regular daily activities, stressful events, physically or mentally demanding tasks, or health-compromising behaviors such as smoking or excessive consumption of fats, cholesterol, or alcohol will cause damage to the organs. The accumulated damage will result in less effective functioning of the organs including the heart (Laurent & Bautouyrie, 2007; Nicita-Mauro, Maltese, Nicita-Mauro, & Basile, 2007).

In addition to wear and tear, other factors such as co-occurring chronic diseases and medications for non-heart-related illnesses can also impair the heart's functions over time. The impact of these factors can be seen specifically in cardiovascular reactivity (Priebe, 2000). We mentioned earlier that cardiovascular reactivity is the rate at which the heart returns to its resting state. The more quickly it can return to a resting state, the less wear and tear there is on the heart.

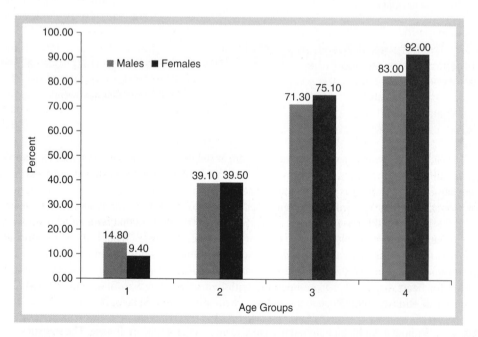

FIGURE 9.7   Cardiovascular Disease, by Age and Gender. As the population ages, women are at higher risk for cardiovascular disease than are men.

Source: Rosamond et al. (2007).

Other health conditions and medications may slow cardiovascular reactivity, a problem that can, over time, cause excessive wear, possibly damaging heart tissue.

Finally, we noted that women not only have a higher risk of cardiovascular disease than men, they also have higher prevalence rates for the same disease. Research suggests that the higher prevalence rates are influenced by the fact that women live longer than men (Kalin & Zumoff, 1990). Thus, a third age-related factor for heart disease is that, among older persons, women outnumber men. And, among the population of older women, there may also be a greater percentage of women living with CAD.

The aging process, in addition to compromising health behaviors, would seem to paint a somewhat bleak prognosis for the cardiovascular health of older persons. In truth, it is not quite that grim. Many older adults have limited or no heart problems, and others manage their heart disease with appropriate medications and lifestyle adjustments. However, the research is clear about one thing: Adoption of a healthy and nutritional diet, maintaining a moderate weight, regular exercise, moderate consumption of alcohol (see Chapter 5, Risky Health Behaviors, for a definition of moderate alcohol use), and refraining from smoking will help maintain and restore heart health. This is the first step to improving longevity.

RACE/ETHNICITY   In previous chapters we identified race/ethnicity as one of several individual characteristics that affect health and health outcomes. But, unlike gender or age, there is little evidence in the literature to suggest that there is a physiological difference between people of different races or ethnic groups such that one race or ethnic group is predisposed to heart disease based on genetic or inherited traits. Instead, it appears that high-fat and high-cholesterol diets, smoking, and greater exposure to stressful situations among some ethnic groups contribute to higher rates of cardiovascular disease.

To what extent can research rule out race/ethnicity as a factor in heart disease? Simply put, current research shows that risk factors for heart disease are not race- or ethnic-specific. But, many racial and ethnic groups do share risk factors. Consider these two examples. In several studies comparing risk factors for heart disease among African, Mexican, and Native American populations, researchers found that all three groups shared a number of factors, including obesity and hypertension among Mexican and African Americans and smoking among Mexican and Native Americans (Kurian & Cardarelli, 2007; Mensah et al., 2005; Sharma, Malarcher, Giles, & Myers, 2004). In the majority of these studies the three groups shared at least two of six risk factors that put them at higher risk for cardiovascular disease.

Because behavioral risk factors account for the preponderance of cardiovascular disease, studies that demonstrate shared risk factors among ethnic groups help dispel the notion that any single group is predisposed to heart disease because of its ethnicity. Rather, specific risk factors are directly attributable to health behaviors that are common to many of the groups.

A second example that highlights the role of risk factors in heart disease is found in the comparison of two samples of populations, both of which are white but which practice very different lifestyles. Research by Bielak and colleagues (2007) examined the risk factors for cardiovascular disease among the Amish, a population that resides in a rural setting, and an urban/suburban-based population from the Rochester metropolitan area in Minnesota.

Bielak and colleagues (2007) chose the Amish as one of two groups for their study because Amish lifestyle in the United States is characterized by the high levels of physical activity associated with farming and less reliance on modern technologies. For example, they do not use

BOX 9.2   Do Some Heart Medications Work Better for One Racial/Ethnic Group than Another?

Years of research have convinced health researchers and medical care providers that race/ethnicity is not, in and of itself, a risk factor for heart disease. The behaviors associated with some groups may increase risk, but being a member of a specific ethnic group is not a factor.

If that is true, then why did some medical researchers advocate the use of a heart medication for use specifically with African Americans?

In 1997, the U.S. Food and Drug Administration (FDA) was prepared to withdraw a new heart drug for use on patients who experienced heart failure. They believed that studies did not show conclusively that the drug was effective. Yet the drug appeared to be effective when used with African Americans.

Mindful of the historic legacy and negative repercussions pertaining to medical experimentation on African Americans (see Chapter 2, Research Methods, the Tuskegee study), a number of scientists were leery of efforts to show that the proposed medication, BiDil, was effective on African Americans who experienced heart failure (Saul, 2005). Some disbelieved the claim while others suggested that there was reason to believe that there was no ethnic group difference in the drug's effectiveness.

To test the drug's effectiveness, NitroMed, the manufacturers of BiDil, solicited the help of African American politicians and physicians, including the Association of Black Cardiologists, to cosponsor a new trial in 2001 to test the effectiveness of BiDil among a study sample of African Americans (Saul, 2005). All participants in the study were African Americans who had a history of heart failure that had been unsuccessfully treated with other heart therapies. The results of the study on the 1,051 self-identified African American heart failure patients were stunning. They showed that the patients who received BiDil had a 43% decrease in deaths due to heart failure and a 39% decrease in hospitalizations for the case cause—a significant difference from patients who received the placebo (U.S. Food and Drug Administration, 2005).

The findings were so impressive that the FDA and NitroMed suspended the study and approved the drug for use, in combination with other heart therapies, among African Americans with diagnosed cases of heart failure.

It is not clear exactly why the drug appears to be effective among this group. And others have questioned the methodology of the study, which, apparently, did not include trials using other ethnic groups. Certainly the reason for its effectiveness remains an unanswered question. Most researchers contend that the underlying genetic differences among racial/ethnic groups are small, and therefore they would argue against different treatment outcomes based solely on race/ethnicity. However, it is not the first time that a drug has been more or less effective on one group. The FDA has noted that a cholesterol-lowering drug appears to cause serious side effects for Asians, an outcome not obtained when used with other racial/ethnic groups.

The general consensus is that there are few major differences among racial/ethnic groups. Yet, on occasion, there may be a drug that appears to be more or less beneficial for a specific group. Initial reports suggest that BiDil may be such a drug for the treatment of heart failure among African Americans.

automobiles, and the absence of modern appliances in their homes and on their farms means it takes considerably more physical labor to perform the daily tasks of maintaining both. The Amish were compared with a nonrelated group of whites in Rochester whose urban lifestyle entailed less physically demanding work. The researchers purposively chose a white comparison group to ensure that race did not affect the study's outcomes.

Bielak and his coauthors found that, although the Amish did not engage in health-compromising behaviors such as smoking or drinking, as was the case with the Rochester group, they had significantly higher levels of coronary artery calcification than the Rochester group. This was true even though their lifestyles were more physically demanding than the Rochester group. On further analysis, Bielak and colleagues (2007) found that the higher calcification rates of the Amish was due principally to their diets, which contained significantly higher levels of calories, fats, and proteins than that of the Rochester group. The Amish diet is high in energy as needed for a very physical lifestyle, but may still cause risk factors for heart disease.

A second and equally interesting finding was that more than one-third of the Rochester group used prescription medicine for lowering cholesterol or blood pressure levels. Thus, although the Amish diet led to higher rates of artery calcification, it was not, apparently, high enough to require medication. In comparison, many participants from the Rochester group had already been diagnosed as being at high risk, enough so that they needed medical intervention.

This study by Bielak and coauthors (2007) seems to support the notion that physical exercise may help mitigate the risks of heart disease. But the study appears to suggest that exercise, in combination with low-fat, low-cholesterol diets, could indeed improve heart health and lower rates of heart disease.

Community/Environment

The term *community* can be defined many ways, including geography (neighborhood, city or region, state or country), close friends and family, work colleagues, or those who share professional or leisure time interests (Ragin et al., 2008). Indeed, in the current computer age, we can even include cyber communities such as MySpace or Facebook.

For the purpose of health behaviors, however, we define *community* as the people with whom an individual feels most connected or a place in which an individual feels a sense of belonging. Most individuals can identify multiple communities, including communities of both people and places. For example, for a 10-year-old boy, community could include his family, his closest friends, his Boy Scout troop, his softball team, his school classmates or his geographic neighborhood. Others may have a larger network of community that would include their religious community, work associates, colleagues from professional associations, and more. The number of communities one associates with is unimportant. More important is the level of influence a community exerts on each individual.

For many people, immediate family members are a very influential community. Immediate family members usually share cultural and behavioral beliefs that may influence health outcomes. Consider this: Thanksgiving is a favored holiday in many American homes. Central to the holiday is the Thanksgiving meal that includes favorite foods prepared by one or several family members. At such an occasion, it may be very difficult to avoid Grandma's special gravy for the turkey, or Aunt Carole's baked macaroni and cheese with three types of cheeses, or Uncle Ken's homemade sausages, and of course Cousin Sarah's homemade sweet potato pie à la mode.

In fact, declining to sample some of these treats might be taken as an insult. Unintentionally, families may encourage the consumption of foods that increase risk of heart disease or that contribute to someone's already dangerously high risk of cardiovascular disease.

We can see the effects of community on health also when community is defined as geographic space. In Chapter 5, Risky Health Behaviors, we explored the impact of community violence on overall health. We noted that, in neighborhoods where violence is prevalent, individuals may not make use of public recreational facilities in their neighborhoods for fear that violent acts by others in the community could increase the risk of injury to themselves or other family members when using the public facilities. Thus, children and adults may not engage in activities such as bicycling in the park, Rollerblading, or perhaps participating in organized sports in local parks such as softball or basketball. And because physical inactivity can increase incidences of heart disease, residents in high-crime neighborhoods may be putting themselves at higher risk of poor health outcomes in an effort to protect themselves from another source of harm.

Health Systems and Access to Care

Several times in this and other chapters we explored the health profiles of individuals in different countries. A new study also exploring differences in health outcomes of two communities, non-Hispanic whites in England and non-Hispanic whites in the United States, reveals significant health differences between groups in these two countries that do not appear to be related to age, gender, or education and perhaps only nominally related to socioeconomic class or health behavior risk factors.

The study by Banks, Marmot, Oldfield, and Smith (2006) examined self-report data and biological measures of health for 4,386 Americans and 3,681 English study participants, aged 55 to 64, from comparable, established databases in both countries. The study examined specifically the prevalence rates for two chronic diseases, heart disease and diabetes. Their findings were surprising. Banks and colleagues (2006) found that overall Americans were less healthy than the English. The American sample reported higher rates of hypertension, heart disease, heart attack, and stroke. They also reported higher rates of other chronic illnesses, including diabetes, lung disease, and cancer.

Having controlled for differences due to age, gender, or education, Banks and colleagues (2006) found that the difference also could not be attributed to health behaviors. On average, the English reported higher levels of smoking and drinking behaviors than Americans. What could account for the difference?

Banks and colleagues (2006) suggest two possible explanations: first, an early onset for disease based on early dietary habits; and, second, access to health care. With regard to early onset, these researchers suggest that, as we indicated earlier, diseases that become evident in adulthood may have their origins in childhood (Case, Lubotsky, & Paxson, 2002; Winkleby, Robinson, Sundquist, & Kraemer, 1999). Thus the dietary behaviors one adopts as a child or adolescent can, if unaltered, predispose a person to chronic illnesses.

Second, Banks and colleagues (2006) found an effect of access to care on health outcomes. Now, you may recall that in this and earlier chapters we identified access to health care as a determinant of health status. Why, therefore, are Banks and colleagues' findings considered interesting? Put simply, they found that access to care was not tied to socioeconomic class, at least not in England. Specifically, Banks and colleagues showed that lower- and middle-income Brits have better health outcomes than upper-income Americans. What is more, they found the disparity in health outcomes even though the British study subjects reported engaging more frequently in health-risk behaviors such as smoking and drinking. What can explain this unexpected finding? The only significant difference between the two groups (British and Americans) was their access to health care. Put simply, these researchers concluded that long-term and continued access to care contributed to overall better health outcomes for the British over the Americans regardless of either groups' socioeconomic status. We review the health care systems of the United States and other countries in Chapter 12, Health Care Systems and Health Policy. Briefly, however, in England, people at all socioeconomic income levels have the same level of initial access to care through the National Health Service. It appears, therefore, that, when controlling for the effects of the usual individual (age, gender, education) and social (socioeconomic status) factors and recognizing that the English sample engaged in more risk behaviors associated with smoking and drinking, the only significant predictor for disparities in health outcome is a health systems and health policy issue: access to care.

The important point about Banks and colleagues' (2006) study is that health outcomes can be and are influenced by access to care . This is particularly true when examining issues of heart disease and other chronic illnesses. Banks and colleagues' study comparing outcomes from individuals exposed to two different health care systems and health policies demonstrates the point.

Personal Postscript

MEASURING YOUR RISK LEVEL FOR CARDIOVASCULAR DISEASE

By now you may have a mental checklist of the behaviors that can put you at high risk for cardiovascular disease. They include diets high in fats and cholesterol, smoking, excessive alcohol consumption, inactivity, overweight/obesity, and diabetes. All of this means little if you do not have a way to measure your current activities against a standard.

The best way to measure your heart risk is through a complete physical exam, which should include a stress test and an electrocardiogram. The stress test will measure your heart's performance while under exertion. For example, walking on a treadmill tests your heart's performance when engaging in physical activity. The electrocardiogram measures the electrical activity of the heart. It measures activity of different parts of the heart muscle. It can help identify any abnormal heart rhythms in need of further examination.

If you are reading this textbook as part of a class assignment, you may wonder why you should be concerned about your heart health. But, if you remember the studies we reviewed on the long-term effects of diet and physical inactivity on later incidences of atherosclerosis and CAD, you may be able to answer your own question. In addition, the following questions may help you to think about your health behaviors and identify needed changes.

Where do you stand on the following health indicator?

1. Vital measurements
   - Normal blood pressure is 120/80. What is your blood pressure?
   - Desirable cholesterol levels are 200 overall and HDL over 60. What is your cholesterol level?
   - Desirable body mass index is under 25, but certainly under 30. What is your BMI?

2. Physical activity
   - Thirty minutes of moderate to vigorous exercise per day are recommended. This can include walking or any activity that you will maintain. What is your plan in consultation with your doctor?

3. Nutrition
  • Eat at least 2.5 cups of fruits and vegetables daily. What is your current consumption? How can you increase your intake?
  • Drink no soda unless it is diet soda. What do you usually drink? What changes are possible here?
  • Limit snacks high in fats and cholesterol. What are your favorite snacks? What low-fat and low-cholesterol snacks do you like?
4. Smoking
  • No smoking! Immediate effects can be seen in three to five years, especially for women. Are you a smoker? What can you do to limit or end this behavior?
5. Drinking
  • If you drink, consume a moderate amount of alcohol. What is your alcohol consumption pattern? Should you reduce your consumption?

Important Terms

angina   296
aorta   293
aortic valve   294
artery   293
atherosclerosis   295
asymptomatic   291
atrium (plural, atria)   293
automated external
   defibrillator (AED)   298
capillary   293
carbohydrate   306
cardiac arrest   297
cardiopulmonary resuscitation (CPR)   298
cardiovascular disease   295
cardiovascular reactivity
   (CVR)   303
cerebrovascular
   disease   298
cholesterol   306
coronary artery disease
   (CAD)   291
diastolic   294

essential or primary
   hypertension   300
estrogen   310
fat   306
hemorrhagic stroke   298
high blood pressure
   (HBP)   299
high-density lipoproteins
   (HDL)   307
hormone replacement
   therapy   310
hypertension   299
inlet valves   294
ischemic stroke   298
low-density lipoproteins
   (LDL)   306
minerals   307
mitral valve   294
moderating risk factor   309
modifiable risk factor   296
monounsaturated fat   306
myocardial infarction   296
perceived racism   302

plaque   291
polyunsaturated fat   306
premenopausal   310
protein   306
pulmonary artery   293
pulmonary valve   294
reoxygenate   293
saturated fat   306
secondary hypertension   302
sinus node   297
sphygmomanometer   300
stethoscope   300
stress test   291
systolic   294
trans fatty acids   306
tricuspid valve   294
vascular   295
vein   293
ventricle   293
ventricular fibrillation   297
vitamins   307

Chapter Ten

Chronic Pain Management and Arthritis

Chapter Objectives

After reading this chapter you will be able to:

1. Define and explain chronic pain.
2. Identify and explain three pain measurement scales and their functions.
3. Identify and describe the three major types of arthritis.
4. Explain ankylosing spondylitis.
5. Identify and define three pharmacological therapies for arthritis.
6. Define exercise therapy.
7. Explain the benefits of exercise therapy for people with arthritis.
8. Explain the role of psychological therapies for the treatment of arthritis.

OPENING STORY: JUVENILE ARTHRITIS

The day began just like all others for the past seven years. Caitlin awoke, and as she got out of bed she felt the familiar pain, stiffness, and soreness in her fingers, toes, elbows, knees, and shoulders (Stahl, 2008). Caitlin has arthritis.

*Aches and pains may seem usual for a person with arthritis. In fact, many older persons experience these symptoms daily. But Caitlin is only 10 years old. She was first diagnosed at age three with **juvenile rheumatoid arthritis**, a form of arthritis that affects children usually before age 16. Caitlin's arthritis began with knee pain. But because it is rare to find arthritis in 3-year-olds, Caitlin's doctors looked for other possible and likely explanations for her pain: a fall from a bicycle, cancer, meningitis, or another infectious disease. After ruling out each of these and other possible illnesses, doctors settled on the one most likely explanation, even if the patient seemed a little young: juvenile arthritis (Stahl, 2008). According to doctors, juvenile arthritis can be treated and even go into **remission**, that is, show no signs or symptoms of illness. But it is more likely that Caitlin, like other children diagnosed with the disease, will carry it into adulthood.* ∎

Caitlin's case calls attention to the fact that there are almost 295,000 children in the United States with juvenile arthritis, a statistic that reminds us that arthritis is not just an older person's disease (Abramson, 2004; Arthritis Foundation, 2008a). *Juvenile arthritis* is an umbrella term that includes many different forms of the disease that affect children under 16 years of age (Centers for Disease Control [CDC], 2008). And, while more than one-quarter of a million children have been diagnosed with some form of arthritis, it remains a poorly understood and even less well-researched illness, especially for children.

Researchers have described current demographic trends in juvenile arthritis. Based on their research, we know that more female children are diagnosed with the disease, and it appears to be more common among non-Hispanic white children (see Figure 10.1). For children, the average age of onset is between one and six years of age (CDC, 2008).

The research also shows that children with arthritis experience some of the same sensations of achiness in the *joints*—for example, elbows, knees, and knuckles—as do adults. Like adults, children complain of pain and stiffness after prolonged periods of sitting or lying in one position. Children with arthritis also can experience discomfort when engaging in physical activity. Consider this: Ten-year-old Caitlin participates in team sports. She will take a few minutes to do additional stretching exercises before playing to minimize possible physical discomforts or limitations due to her disease.

Similar to adults with arthritis, Caitlin will most likely alternate forms of treatment, using a combination of drug treatments, exercise therapies, and psychological approaches to maximize the relief from the pain and inflammation caused by the illness. As we will see later in the chapter, there is no single treatment for arthritis that is used to control pain, reduce inflammation, and halt the degeneration of bone and tissue. Therefore, people with the disease change therapeutic approaches often to obtain better or more effective pain relief. For Caitlin and for many adults, changing treatments to improve pain management is part of life.

Arthritis is only one of many illnesses that results in chronic pain. Therefore, in this chapter, we begin with a brief overview of chronic pain and pain management. Considerable attention has

FIGURE 10.1 Water Exercises for Children with Juvenile Arthritis.
Swimming and other exercises in water are excellent ways to work
joints affected by arthritis.

Source: Arthritis Foundation (2010).

been given to chronic pain, pain management, and pain medicine in the past 20 years. Beginning in the early 1990s, health care providers as well as federal and some state legislators called attention to the numerous documented cases of undertreatment of pain. In 1999, the Joint Commission on Accreditation of Healthcare Organizations determined that pain management was a priority for medical practitioners (JCAHO, 1999). In fact, the 106th session of the U.S. Congress passed a resolution (Title VI, Section 1603) declaring the period from January 1, 2001, through December 31, 2010, the "Decade of Pain Control and Research" (Loeser, 2003; Weiner, 2003)).

Research on pain clearly shows that there are numerous illnesses that report chronic pain as a major symptom including arthritis, cancer, cardiovascular disease, ***musculoskeletal*** pain that affects muscles, ligaments, or tendons around the bone, as well as other illnesses. Therefore in Section II of the chapter we select one chronic condition, arthritis, through which to examine chronic pain and pain management. As with other illnesses, managing the chronic pain associated with arthritis requires attention to the physiological origins and its psychological health consequences. Together, the physical and psychological impact of the disease can cause depression and other mental health problems that negatively affect overall well-being. As such, arthritis is a particularly fitting illness to examine in the context of a holistic approach to health.

We begin the section on arthritis with an overview of three of the most common types of arthritis: rheumatoid arthritis, osteoarthritis, and gout. We add to this, however, one less common form of arthritis, ankylosing spondylitis, which, even though it appears to be largely ***congenital***, or hereditary, improves with some forms of psychological interventions. We also review in

Section II the ***pharmacological*** or drug treatments traditionally used as the first choice of therapy for arthritis and explore reasons for their ineffectiveness.

The inability of drug therapies to efficiently treat many forms of chronic pain, specifically arthritis pain, led researchers and practitioners to explore multidisciplinary treatment options, including psychological therapies. In Section III we introduce three psychological interventions used in the treatment of arthritis pain: cognitive-behavioral therapy/pain coping skills training, biofeedback/stress management, and emotional disclosure. While the psychological therapies can be used alone, they are more commonly used in combination with drug or exercise therapies to provide maximum pain relief and to reduce inflammation. Whether used alone or in combination with other approaches, psychological therapies appear to play a major role in the more successful treatment options for the illness. As such, health psychologists may be well suited to assist people with illnesses that entail chronic pain management.

SECTION I. CHRONIC PAIN MANAGEMENT

It is abundantly clear to medical providers and health psychologists that many illnesses produce chronic pain. Injuries, too, often involve chronic pain long after the physical site has healed.

Generally, individuals experience pain when an illness or injury causes inflammation or changes to the nervous system. The changed states are then relayed to the brain, resulting in a physical sensation that a change has occurred (National Institute of Neurological Disorders and Stroke, 2010). Often the pain subsides or goes away. When it does not, however, an individual can experience either episodic or continued sensations of pain that may be characterized as ***chronic pain***.

Chronic pain is a common reason why people seek medical care. In fact, medical providers report that over 80% of all patient visits list pain as the primary symptom. It affects nearly 76.2 million Americans, more than three other chronic illnesses—diabetes, heart disease, and cancer—combined (American Pain Foundation, 2009). Global estimates suggest that as many as 30% of adults in developed countries suffer from some form of chronic pain (Verbaak et al., 1998).

Efforts to more effectively study and address pain and pain management have been hampered by four factors: accurate measures of pain, the changing characteristics of pain, pain management versus pain elimination, and gender and cultural differences in the classification of pain. We address each of these issues in depth in the following sections and illustrate how they apply to chronic arthritis pain. We begin with a brief overview of research on chronic pain.

Measuring Pain

In Chapter 3, Global Communicable and Chronic Disease, we noted that chronic illnesses were defined as long-term (three to six months or longer), complex illnesses that can be controlled but not cured. Similarly, chronic pain is defined as long-term pain that can be controlled but not eliminated completely.

One reason efforts to assess an individual's level of pain have been hampered is the absence of reliable measures of pain. Of the over 80 pain assessment measures currently in use, most measure pain along one dimension, either pain intensity or duration, or measure a specific type of pain (Hjermstad et al., 2008). While pain and intensity are important components for understanding pain, research shows that eight other factors (in addition to intensity or duration) may help present a fuller understanding of the factors that contribute to the general perception of pain: temporal pattern, treatment effect (including relief/exacerbating factors), pain quality, location, interference, affect, pain history, and beliefs about pain, including attitudes, coping, and beliefs about causes and consequences of pain (Hjermstad et al., 2008). Presently, few assessment measures include all 10 factors. For this reason, a health provider's ability to fully characterize an individual's pain is limited often to one factor and the individual's own descriptive abilities.

Changing Characteristics of Pain

The long-term nature of chronic pain suggests that the sensation of pain may differ over time. For example, chronic lower back pain is a common complaint among older adults (see Figure 10.2). The National Center for Health Statistics, a division of the Centers for Disease Control and Prevention (CDC), estimates that approximately 30% of people 65 years of age or older, and another 30% of persons between the ages of 45 and 64, report frequent occurrences of lower back pain (National Center for Health Statistics, 2006) (again see Figure 10.2). Yet a person's pain experienced over weeks or months can appear different each day. For example, a person complaining of chronic lower back pain may characterize the pain as dull but persistent one day and as sharp but intermittent on another. The original source of the pain remains unchanged, yet the perception of pain can change based on a person's subjective assessment of the sensation at the time. Factors that may influence the variable perception include a person's psychological state, mood, and general affect.

Varying manifestations of lower back pain within one individual may lead a health care provider to conclude incorrectly that the pain has no identifiable physical cause and will eventually cease; that the pain is minor, perhaps resulting from a minor injury, and will also cease; or that the individual is unreliable in reporting pain. Although understandable, the medical provider's inability to diagnose the cause of the pain or to prescribe treatment almost assuredly means the individual will continue to suffer often for extended periods of time. It is important to note that reports of pain that exceeds one year in duration are common, especially among older adults. Health statistics data for the United States show that fully 57% of older Americans report pain that has endured for more than one year, while approximately 37% of younger adults reported

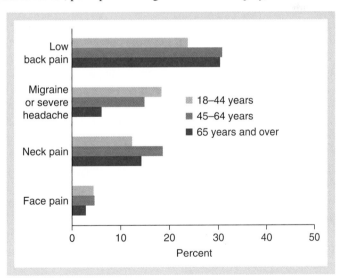

FIGURE 10.2 Low Back, Migraine, Neck, and Face Pain in the Past Three Months, 2004.

Source: National Center for Health Statistics (2006).

similar pain duration. What is more, previous notions that pain and disability caused by injuries are short-lived and end once the injury heals are now widely discredited. Instead, researchers find that injury-related pain and disability show rapid improvement for the first three months. After that time, however, progress on both fronts is slow. In many cases an individual may never be fully free of pain due to injury or return to full and normal functional ability (Tunks, 2008).

In essence, pain can be an enduring problem. The chronic and unremitting nature of pain is one reason why it is of interest to health psychologists. And, because chronic pain will certainly affect a person's perceived quality of life and overall well-being, it is also an example of a physiological health problem that has a direct impact on an individual's emotional and psychological health.

Clearly, pain and pain management are also relevant topics for health psychologists when addressing the needs of people with terminal illnesses. Most health care professionals would also agree that one goal of health providers when caring for terminally ill patients is to provide *palliative care* or maximal relief from pain, suffering, and stress due to the illness, to improve an individual's quality of life for as long as possible. A review of the unique problems encountered when providing palliative care for terminally ill individuals is beyond the scope of this chapter. We address selected issues concerning end-of-life care in Chapter 13, Health Psychologists' Role: Research, Application, and Advocacy. For now, it is sufficient to note that end-of-life care presents a host of medical, psychological, and ethical challenges for health care providers which include chronic pain management.

Pain Management versus Pain Elimination

Much of the research on chronic pain focuses on two main processes, *pain management* and *pain elimination*. The research on and intervention for the type of chronic pain related to illnesses emphasizes pain minimization, or management, because there is no proven, effective treatment that offers total and complete relief from chronic pain (Crombez, Eccleston, Van Hamme, & De Vlieger, 2008). In addition, as Tunks (2008) points out, injury-related pain also focuses on management because often pain due to injury lingers well beyond the point of treatment—in some cases, for years afterward. Consider this: There are millions of high school, college, and professional athletes. These athletes suffer sports-related injuries often; so often, in fact, that there is a special branch of medicine known as sports medicine. Initially, some sports injuries may be treated with drug therapies. Others require surgery to repair torn or broken elements, and still others are addressed through some form of physical therapy, which could include exercise and strength-building techniques. Whatever the injury, you can be sure that the injury itself, as well as the process of repair, will entail some level of pain: pain at the point of injury, pain during the repair and healing process, and possibly intermittent or persistent pain once the injury is determined to be resolved.

Yet severe athletic injuries will require more than medical and exercise treatments. For some individuals, healing from sports-related injuries will also include psychotherapy. Consider another example: A baseball pitcher or a champion butterfly swimmer who injures his or her *rotator cuff*, one of four muscles in the shoulder, will experience severe pain and be unable to rotate the arm as needed to perform his or her sport (see Figure 10.3). The damage may be severe enough to warrant surgical repair. However, even after surgery and physical therapy, the pitcher or competitive swimmer may face additional challenges. In some instances, surgery and physical therapy will be sufficient to return the athlete to full or near full form. But, in other instances, the damage may be too severe. Even though surgery may repair the shoulder muscle sufficiently to allow the pitcher or swimmer to perform most daily activities, it may not permit the type of taxing and strenuous exertion required in either sport. In such cases, the individual must learn more than how to cope until the shoulder muscle heals. The athlete may need to learn to cope with feelings of loss, disappointment, or dismay as he or she adjusts to a life without a favorite pastime or a preferred career.

FIGURE 10.3 Butterfly Stroke. Swimming requires a full range of arm movements that use the rotator cuff.

There is little doubt that such a change will present significant psychological health consequences in addition to likely ongoing challenges to pain management. It is in such situations that health psychologists can assist people with their feelings of loss and perhaps depression following their inability to perform an important and favorite activity. Using coping strategies, cognitive-behavioral therapies, or other psychotherapeutic techniques described in Chapter 7, Stress and Coping, and Chapter 11, Cancer, health psychologists can aid athletes in adapting to their new limitations. They may find productive ways to use their limited athletic skills or adopt new interests. Whatever their choice, they will find that the healing process requires both physical and psychological adjustments.

Differences in Pain Perception

Researchers and health providers have noted that women often report more pain than men. Interestingly, however, the higher frequency of reports of pain by women does not result in higher frequencies of treatments for the complaints. Rather, women are more likely to receive prescriptions for sedatives to suppress the sensation of pain than analgesics to relieve pain. The same is not true for men.

In addition, researchers, and some providers, report that perceptions of pain may differ among ethnic groups. There is a considerable body of research on the difference in pain perception and pain treatment, specifically among African Americans, Latinos, and whites. While some findings suggest no ethnic differences in pain perception, others suggest that there are differences in the epidemiology of pain, access to pain care, and assessment and treatment of pain, as well as pain outcomes (Cintron & Morrison, 2006; Edwards, Fillingim, & Keefe, 2001).

Differences in pain threshold and sensitivity to experimental pain stimuli among ethnic groups have been reported as early as 1944. An early report by Chapman and Jones (1944) suggested that African Americans showed lower thresholds for heat pain than did non-Hispanic whites. Additional non-laboratory-based research on perception of acute (sudden) and chronic pain tolerance showed similar ethnic differences. For example, Faucett, Gordon, and Levine's (1994) study of postoperative pain suggested that Latinos and African Americans reported greater postoperative pain than did whites in their sample. Other studies of acute pain perception by Sheffield, Kirby, Bites, and Ships (1999) also reported ethnic differences when assessing pain related to angina (chest and heart pain) when African Americans and white study participants performed treadmill exercise.

Finally, many studies examining chronic pain or pain associated with chronic health conditions reported similar outcomes. In these studies, African Americans were more likely than whites to report persistent pain related to AIDS (Breitbart et al., 1996), arthritis (Creamer, Lethbridger-Cejku, & Hochberg, 1999), and severe low back pain (Selim et al., 2001).

These studies appear to document differences in pain perception and pain sensitivity, but why would there be an ethnic difference in pain perception? To date, few studies have reported that there are biological causes that can explain the apparent ethnic differences. Some researchers speculate that ethnic factors could play a role in triggering activity in the nervous centers of the body that modulate pain (Edwards et al., 2001). However, there appears to be greater support for the belief that social factors, such as limited access to care due to socioeconomic factors or lack of insurance; provider limitations, such as lack of knowledge and training or beliefs about minority patients; and even ethnic differences in coping styles may contribute to the differences in perception.

Consider this: Research by Todd, Samaroo, and Hoffman (1993) and Todd, Lee, and Hoffman (1994) has shown that minority patients are more likely to be undertreated for pain and are less likely to receive a comprehensive diagnosis and treatment for their complaints of pain. In a study comparing pain treatment for Latinos, African Americans, and whites in the emergency department, Todd and colleagues (1993) found that Latinos were twice as likely as whites to receive no pain medication for a bone fracture while African Americans were 66% less likely than whites to receive medication. Such studies suggest that one reason for higher ratings on pain perception by ethnicities is the inadequate treatment of pain when it occurs. If inadequately treated, minorities may be exposed to longer periods of unrelieved pain. The reasons for the inadequate treatment could be rooted in inadequacies of health insurance or other socioeconomic limitations that prevent patients from receiving the care needed to address their medical condition. Still other researchers suggest that attitudes or biases that providers hold about their patients may interfere with effective treatment (Diesfled, 2008). Post, Blustein, Fordon, and Neveloff (1996) suggest the following explanation:

> The multiplicity of factors that influence the perception and expression of pain take on special importance in the health care setting, where pain becomes an interpersonal experience between the sufferer and reliever. How pain is signified by the patient and understood by the provider determines in large measure how it is valued and, ultimately, how it is treated. (p. 348)

While we explore disparities in pain treatment more thoroughly in the following sections on arthritis, it is important to point out here that researchers have also noted differences in pain coping strategies. For example, some research suggests that while African Americans are more likely to rely on support systems and religious coping (praying) to manage through the pain, whites are more likely to implement techniques such as ignoring the pain or to believe in a greater ability to control the pain themselves (James, Hartnett, & Kalsbeek, 1983; Jordan, Lumly, & Leisen, 1998; McNeilly & Zeichner, 1989). Researchers suggest that the differences in strategies may be learned within ethnic groups or cultures and that such differences may affect an individual's awareness of and level of comfort with the pain.

Caregivers, Pain Management, and Psychological Distress

Chronic pain, regardless of the source, may have a long-term psychological effect on the sufferer. As we will see later in the section on arthritis, pain can also impair a person's ability to be self-sufficient and to accomplish basic tasks such as prepa ing a meal, eating, or getting dressed. As a result, a person may find that the chronic pain carries with it the psychological disadvantage of being dependent on others for basic necessities.

An increase in functional disability and dependency on others, together with chronic pain, is dispiriting to many individuals. Research on chronic pain indicates that depression, worry, avoidance behavior, and a sense of helplessness are common psychological reactions for people with chronic pain, another reason health psychologists can be instrumental in helping people with pain management issues (Samwel et al., 2009). We explore specific psychological outcomes and methods of treatment when exploring chronic pain and arthritis later in the chapter.

Yet, like those with other chronic conditions, people who suffer from chronic pain do not suffer alone. Family members and caregivers of chronic pain sufferers also experience psychological and emotional health problems when caring for someone with a chronic condition. Consider this: A study by Simon, Kumar, and Kendrick (2009) measured the psychological distress of live-in caregivers of stroke victims (see Chapter 9, Cardiovascular Disease) in England, to determine whether the role of caregiver to first-time stroke survivors would increase levels of psychological distress among the caregivers. These researchers measured the caregiver's psychological health and social well-being before the stroke victim was discharged from the hospital, six weeks after discharge, and again 15 months after the stroke. They found that not only was caregiver distress commonly reported among the 105 people sampled but that it started quite early in the care process.

What is more, when comparing the psychological health and social well-being of caregivers with a matched sample of noncaregivers near the same time period, caregivers were 2.5 times more likely to evidence significant psychological distress (Simon et al., 2009). They even found gender differences in caregiver distress. Women were more likely than men to develop stress in anticipation of the caregiving role. Men, on the other hand, were more likely to first evidence stress when the caregiving responsibilities began.

Research by Ho and her colleagues (2009) similarly reports that caregivers suffer negative psychological health. In their study, 246 caregivers of elderly persons were compared with approximately 490 noncaregivers. These researchers found that caregivers reported more doctor visits to tend to their own health needs than did noncaregivers. Caregivers were also at higher risk for anxiety, depression, and reported increases in weight loss. And, once again, females seemed to fare worse than males, reporting greater incidences of chronic disease and insomnia.

Thus, the research on caregivers in general clearly shows that the task of providing ongoing assistance and aid to someone with a chronic illness, including chronic pain, can cause emotional, psychological, and physical harm to the caregiver. Thus, this research suggests that, when examining chronic health problems, it is as important to address the health needs of the caregiver as those of the person afflicted with the illness (see Chapter 6, Emotional Health and Well-being).

INTERVENTIONS FOR CAREGIVERS   There is hope for the caregivers. Research on interventions for caregivers report a number of strategies that have been used with varying levels of success. For example, Folkman and Moskowitz (2000) examined the emotional and psychological health of caregivers for people with late-stage AIDS (see Chapter 8, HIV and AIDS). The slow physical deterioration and social stigma still experienced by some people with HIV/AIDS presents additional psychological stressors for both the sufferer and his or her caregiver. Yet Folkman and Moskowitz found that caregivers who were able to set and accomplish small, goal-specific tasks each day—for example, to mail a package at the post office or purchase needed groceries at the supermarket—were more likely to report better overall psychological health in the short term and in the longer term once their responsibilities ended.

Similarly, other studies examining interventions for caregivers report less long-term psychological distress when caregivers employ psychotherapy or psychoeducational interventions. We explain these interventions in more detail later in the chapter and in Chapter 11, Cancer. For now it is important only to note that social support assistance, such as respite care that allows the caregiver time away from care responsibilities, or specialized care training prove helpful to a caregiver of persons with chronic or debilitating diseases (Pinquart & Sorensen, 2005). Arthritis, a chronic but not life-threatening illness, can present similar challenges for caregivers.

SECTION II. ARTHRITIS DEFINED

We began the chapter with a story about Caitlin, a 10-year-old girl diagnosed with juvenile arthritis. We noted that Caitlin was only one of almost 295,000 children with the disease. More than a quarter of a million may seem like a large number of sufferers, but it is small when compared to the over 44 million adults diagnosed with a similar form of the disease. Research on the characteristics and forms of arthritis for adults presents a somewhat clearer picture of the disease and its health outcomes. For adults, three characteristics define arthritis. First, *arthritis* is a physiologically based disease caused either by *degeneration*, or gradual wearing away or erosion, of the bones near the joints, or by *inflammation*, a swelling of the tissue surrounding the bones and joints.

Second, arthritis is a *progressive disease*, meaning that the degeneration or inflammation worsens over time. As we will see later in the chapter, there are no cures for arthritis, and no treatments have proven effective in halting or reversing the degenerative effects of the disease.

Finally, arthritis is a chronic disease. We have discussed chronic diseases numerous times, most recently in Chapter 9, Cardiovascular Disease. Applying the definition of *chronic* to arthritis, we can conclude that arthritis is a long-term progressive disease that can be a contributing factor to mortality. It is the proximal (Chapter 2, Research Methods) cause of mortality (death).

For many, the term *arthritis* immediately conjures thoughts of pain (see Figure 10.4). Again, think about Caitlin. Her arthritis meant pain from the moment she awoke. It also evokes thought of wear and tear on the body. In fact, many people think that arthritis is the result of gradual wear and tear on the body due to old age. Clearly, pain and wear and tear are components of arthritis, but they do not fully describe the illness.

The word *arthritis* derives from the Greek words *arthro* meaning joints, such as elbows, knees, shoulders, and fingers, and *itis* meaning inflammation, hence inflammation of the joints (Pisetsky, 2007). Yet even this is a somewhat narrow definition of the disease. *Arthritis* describes a class of diseases that refer to any joint condition or disease causing inflammation, pain, and stiffness in the joint or in connective tissues (Harvard Medicine, 2007; Pisetsky, 2007). Therefore, arthritis can describe inflammation of the joints, as is common in rheumatoid arthritis, but also may refer to the degeneration of the joints commonly found in osteoarthritis. As with juvenile arthritis, the broader category of arthritis is an umbrella term that we use here to describe a painful joint condition due to one of a number of underlying conditions. We begin by examining rheumatoid arthritis.

Rheumatoid Arthritis (RA)

Research on *rheumatoid arthritis (RA)* is still evolving; however, at present RA is classified as a chronic, inflammatory, *autoimmune disease* for which the exact cause is unknown (Tedesco et al., 2009). It is classified as an inflammatory disease because one characteristic of RA is inflammation, or swelling of the joints and of the *synovium*, the thin layer of tissue that covers the joints.

We also refer to RA as an autoimmune disease because it appears that RA is triggered by the body's immune system. We explored the body's immune system in Chapter 6, Emotional Health and Well-Being; Chapter 7, Stress and Coping; and Chapter 8, HIV and AIDS. The immune system is also relevant to understanding arthritis because inflammation

FIGURE 10.4   Painful Arthritis of the Hands. Painful arthritis limits functions and causes emotional distress.

is the body's normal response to injury. For example, when the body detects an infection or experiences damage to tissue, white blood cells are sent to the affected areas to attack and destroy foreign organisms. The inflammation is an autoimmune system response, designed to protect the body. RA, however, triggers inflammation in the absence of infection or injury, a kind of "false alarm" that causes an immune system malfunction, resulting in unnecessary inflammation in addition to possible damage to tissues, blood vessels, and other organs, as well as pain, stiffness, and swelling of the inflamed joints (Goldbach-Mansky et al., 2002; Pisetsky, 2007; Tedesco et al., 2008).

Like other forms of arthritis, rheumatoid arthritis is a progressive disease, meaning that the inflammation, tissue damage, and functional limitations usually become worse over time. In advanced stages of the disease, the joints and the surrounding areas may become deformed, as shown in Figure 10.5. Approximately 1.3 million people have been diagnosed with some form of RA (Arthritis Foundation, 2008a).

In addition to the physiological damage, studies show that RA also affects psychological health. The physiological damage to the joints and the pain caused by RA frequently are well known. They often result in physical disabilities. Inflamed, swollen, and stiff joints that are painful and sometimes difficult to move reduce an individual's ability or desire to perform tasks that involve the affected joints. For example, arthritis of the hand and finger joints can cause stiffness

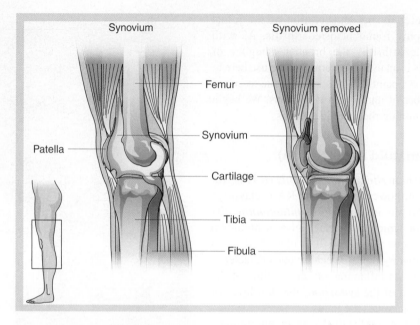

FIGURE 10.5   Effects of Rheumatoid Arthritis. Swelling of the joints and of the synovium is common in RA.

Source: U.S. National Library of Medicine & National Institutes of Health (2010).

that limits a person's ability to bend his or her fingers or grasp objects securely (see Figure 10.6). As a result, it can limit a person's ability to perform simple tasks that we take for granted, such as picking up a fork to eat.

People with RA often identify emotional and psychological health problems as part of the disease. Included in this list are depression, excessive worry, avoidance behavior, and helplessness (Samwel et al., 2009). Consider again our eating example: How frustrating would it be for you if eating took much longer and resulted in spillage or dropped food, or if you were unable to perform daily hygiene tasks, such as brushing your teeth, because inflamed finger joints made movement difficult and painful?

People who suffer from RA may face such challenges on a daily basis. It is not difficult to imagine that the aggravation or, as Lazarus calls it, the "daily hassles" (see Chapter 6, Emotional Health and Well-Being) caused by the physical limitations can result in feelings of incompetence or helplessness when an individual is unable to independently perform routine hygiene or self-help activities that he or she successfully performed in the past. Thus, as we indicated earlier, the *functional limitations*, or inability to perform daily tasks independently, associated with arthritis can contribute to depressive symptoms.

Ankylosing Spondylitis (AS)

A specific type of RA that affects the spinal joints is ***ankylosing spondylitis (AS)***. Also of Greek origin, the word *ankylos* means bent, and *spondylitis* means inflammation of the spinal column.

FIGURE 10.6 **Late-Stage Rheumatoid Arthritis of the Hands.** Advanced stages of RA can impair normal functioning of hands and distort their appearance.

Today, the diagnosis of AS does not suggest a bent, inflamed spinal column but a rigid or stiff spine. The disease usually causes the spinal column to fuse, limiting an individual's ability to pivot or turn his or her back or neck, a movement that people without AS do effortlessly and without thinking. It may also cause a stooped appearance if the spinal column fuses or stiffens in accordance with poor body posture (see Figure 10.7).

AS is largely genetic in origin. Many individuals with AS also carry a gene—the *HLA-B27 gene*—that appears to be a marker that predisposes individuals to AS. Remember, however, that having a predisposition does not mean that a person will, in fact, develop the disease or its associated symptoms. In this case, the HLA-B27 gene indicates that a person is more likely than those without the marker to be at high risk for AS.

Research also reveals that AS is closely associated with specific ethnic/racial groups. Studies of individuals with the HLA-B27 gene reveal that approximately 90% of northern Europeans who are diagnosed with AS and 80% of Mediterranean individuals with AS carry the gene. However, only about 50% of African Americans with AS also have the marker (Khan, 2006). Thus, it appears that HLA-B27 and AS are more prevalent in some ethnic groups than others.

Consistent with the characteristics of RA, AS is a progressive, inflammatory disease that advances over time. It first appears during adolescence, usually in individuals 15 to 24 years of age (Khan, 2006; Sieper et al., 2002). Unlike RA, which occurs more frequently in women than in men, AS appears to be more prevalent in males (Hamilton-West & Quine, 2007). Note, however, that as was also the case in the early research on cardiovascular disease (see Chapter 9, Cardiovascular Disease, page 308), early studies on AS tended to focus primarily on men. It may

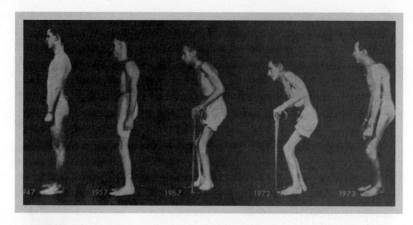

FIGURE 10.7   Progressive Effects of Ankylosing Spondylitis. AS can cause a change in posture due to fusion of the spinal column.

Source: Little, Swinson, & Cruckshank (1976).

be that future studies that include a more representative sample of women will show an increase in the rates of AS among women also. Unfortunately, the difficulty in diagnosing AS—a lag time that can take up to six years—means that there are few instances of early diagnosis of the disease for women or men.

We include AS here primarily because it is an interesting genetic version of rheumatoid arthritis that, in spite of its origins, responds well to psychological therapy when added to medical regimens. We will explain the effects of psychological therapy on arthritis more fully in Section III.

Osteoarthritis (OA)

Approximately 27 million people in the United States suffer from some form of Osteoarthritis (Arthritis Foundation, 2008b). *Osteoarthritis (OA)* is the oldest known form of arthritis and is commonly associated with wear and tear on the body. Specifically, the *cartilage*, the part of the joint that cushions the end of the bones and enables easy movement of the joints, is worn away (see Figure 10.8). As a result, new bones may form *bone spurs* that rub against each other, causing pain and further deterioration of both the cartilage and bones (Arthritis Foundation, 2008b; Pisetsky, 2007). The erosion process is one reason OA is considered a *degenerative joint disease*, here meaning one that causes the permanent deterioration of the cartilage.

What causes OA? Like RA, the cause of degeneration is not well understood (Kidd, 2006). Researchers suggest that several factors may play a role in the development and progression of OA, including genetic abnormality, developmental defects, trauma that alters or disrupts the body's normal biomechanics, and obesity (Goldring, 2006).

OA is most commonly reported in the hand, knee, hip, or foot joints. Unlike RA, which often affects multiple joints simultaneously, OA usually affects a smaller number, perhaps one or two joints. Most often OA targets the larger joints, such as the knee or hip (Pisetsky, 2007), which are more easily repaired by surgery to replace the kneecap or hip joints with artificial devices.

Gout

Gout is an increasingly common disease among men and women, specifically in the United States (Roddy, Zhang, & Doherty, 2007). Research suggests that gout is caused by crystal deposits in joints and tissues (Doherty, 2009).

Sometimes called "gouty arthritis," gout is commonly associated with older adults and the elderly. But, while it is strongly associated with age, other factors such as environment, behavior, genetics, and gender have been cited in studies as major contributors also (Doherty, 2009; Roddy et al., 2007)

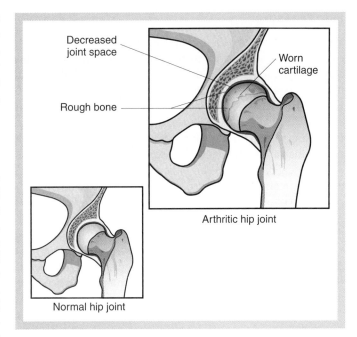

FIGURE 10.8 Effects of Osteoarthritis OA wears away the cartilage causing painful joint movement.

Source: U.S. National Library of Medicine and National Institutes of Health (2009).

One proximal cause of gout is behavioral, in the form of foods consumed. A buildup of *uric acid*, a by-product of foods eliminated from our bodies as waste products, becomes lodged in the joints and causes inflammation, redness, and soreness (National Institute of Arthritis & Musculoskeletal & Skin Diseases [NIAMS], 2006). Other behavioral factors such as overeating, excessive consumption of red meat, excessive alcohol consumption (especially beer), and nutrition are also known contributors to the condition (Annemans, Spaepen, & Gasken, 2008; Choi et al., 2004a, 2004b; NIAMS, 2006). Therefore, some types of gout are preventable with changes in health behaviors or lifestyles, an important contributing factor that can be addressed by health psychologists.

Some research suggests that gout may also be caused by genetic factors. Genetic disorders associated with an overproduction of uric acid, though rare, have been found primarily among males and within families (Doherty, 2009).

To review, arthritis is a painful disease that causes inflammation and deformities in joints, appendages, or even the torso, as in the case of ankylosing spondylitis. It is not a life-threatening disease and rarely is a proximal cause of death. It is, however, a painful, chronic condition that has a significant impact on daily functioning, psychological health, and overall well-being. For many arthritis sufferers, addressing this health condition means primarily reducing the pain to manageable levels to improve overall quality of life.

Pain Measures

We noted earlier that pain is a challenging concept to measure, largely because it is influenced by an individual's subjective perception of discomfort and by a provider's assessment of the physiological symptoms and of the patient's accurate recall. In addition, some researchers contend that pain is a private and internal sensation that cannot be observed directly (McDowell & Newell, 1996). Consequently, researchers attempt to identify pain either by using an individual's self-reported pain levels or by measuring behavioral limitations that can be attributed to discomfort. Using this approach, pain is best understood as the combined influence of a painful stimulus (biological or environmental) experienced by the body; the characteristics of the individual experiencing pain, such as his or her age, gender, and coping strategies; and finally the social and environmental circumstances, such as cultural upbringing, that may proscribe an individual's perception of or response to pain (McDowell & Newell, 1996).

We also noted in the earlier section that, while there are many pain measures, they are thought to be largely inadequate for accurately quantifying pain levels. Wide discrepancies in the variables used to define pain and the criteria for classifying mild, moderate, or severe pain have prevented researchers from arriving at a consensus on the definition and measurement of pain (Hjermstad et al., 2008). Yet, researchers and practitioners must employ some method to assess the level of discomfort caused by chronic pain. Therefore they use one of three types of measures: verbal or written questionnaires, behavioral observations, or visual analogue pain ratings. The ***verbal or written questionnaires*** measure an individual's self-assessment of his or her pain. As is the case with many pain measures, such questionnaires allow respondents to characterize their pain (dull, sharp, throbbing); describe its duration (minutes, hours, weeks); rate its intensity, usually on a scale of one to ten; and explain any functional limitations resulting from the pain. The Brief Pain Inventory (Box 10.1) is an example of an assessment instrument that focuses primarily on level of severity of pain as well as related functional limitations.

By comparison, Melzack's (1975) McGill Pain Questionnaire uses 102 items to assess pain along three dimensions: the sensory quality of the pain ("cool," "cold," or "hot"), the affective qualities of pain (pain or exhaustion), and the subjective intensity of the experience (pain that is annoying, intense, or unbearable). Individuals rate their pain experience by selecting the appropriate word or by indicating pain intensity on a scale of one to ten.

To be sure, both the Brief Pain Inventory and the McGill Pain Questionnaire provide subjective assessments of pain. But an individual's perception of pain will influence his or her likely participation in activities of daily living or dependence on others for assistance. What is more, as we indicated earlier, a person who perceives him- or herself to be dependent on others due to chronic pain may feel helpless or become depressed as a result of the inability to function independently. For these reasons, some of the pain questionnaires also assess an individual's psychological state. For example, the Brief Pain Inventory includes three questions intended to assess an individual's emotional state. While more would be preferred, the questions can identify psychological health issues due to pain that will contribute to a person's overall sense of well-being.

A second technique obtains ***behavioral observations*** of pain in one of two ways: during a health care visit with a medical or other health care professional, or during the execution of daily activities as observed by relatives, friends, or caregivers. When conducted as part of a health care visit, the observed individual performs assigned tasks that test the flexibility or maneuverability of the affected joints. For example, when assessing the pain levels associated with arthritis, health care

BOX 10.1   Verbal or Written Pain Questionnaire

B1. Brief Pain Inventory (Short Form)

Study ID#_____   Hospital#_____

Do not write above this line

Date:____/____/____

Time:_____

Name:_____

    Last   First   Middle Initial

1. Throughout our lives, most of us have had pain from time to time (such as minor headaches, sprains, and toothaches). Have you had pain other than these everyday kinds of pain today?
    1. yes   2. no

2. On the diagram, shade in the areas where you feel pain. Put an X on the area that hurts the most.

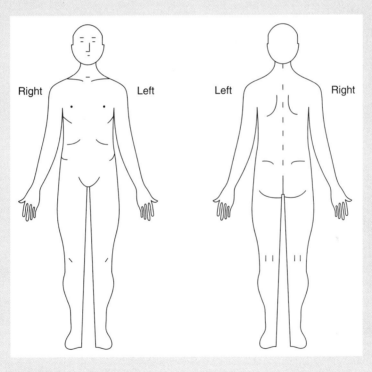

FIGURE 10.9   Documenting Pain on the Brief Pain Inventory (Short Form).

(continued)

3. Please rate your pain by circling the one number that best describes your pain at its **WORST** in the past 24 hours.

0	1	2	3	4	5	6	7	8	9	10
No pain								Pain as bad as you can imagine		

4. Please rate your pain by circling the one number that best describes your pain at its **LEAST** in the past 24 hours.

0	1	2	3	4	5	6	7	8	9	10
No pain								Pain as bad as you can imagine		

5. Please rate your pain by circling the one number that best describes your pain on the **AVERAGE**.

0	1	2	3	4	5	6	7	8	9	10
No pain								Pain as bad as you can imagine		

6. Please rate your pain by circling the one number that tells how much pain you have **RIGHT NOW**.

0	1	2	3	4	5	6	7	8	9	10
No pain								Pain as bad as you can imagine		

7. What treatments or medications are you receiving for your pain?

8. In the past 24 hours, how much **RELIEF** have pain treatments or medications provided? Please circle the one percentage that most shows how much.

0%	10%	20%	30%	40%	50%	60%	70%	80%	90%	100%
No relief									Complete relief	

9. Circle the one number that describes how, during the past 24 hours, **PAIN HAS INTERFERED** with your:

A. General Activity:

0	1	2	3	4	5	6	7	8	9	10
Does not interfere									Completely interferes	

B. Mood

0	1	2	3	4	5	6	7	8	9	10
Does not interfere									Completely interferes	

C. Walking ability

0	1	2	3	4	5	6	7	8	9	10
Does not interfere									Completely interferes	

D. Normal work (includes both work outside the home and housework)

0	1	2	3	4	5	6	7	8	9	10
Does not interfere									Completely interferes	

E. Relations with other people

0	1	2	3	4	5	6	7	8	9	10
Does not interfere									Completely interferes	

F. Sleep

0	1	2	3	4	5	6	7	8	9	10
Does not interfere									Completely interferes	

G. Enjoyment of life

0	1	2	3	4	5	6	7	8	9	10
Does not interfere									Completely interferes	

providers document the limitations of movement and any associated expressions of pain, using a standard assessment form such as the Patient Evaluation Conference System Form (Harvey & Jellinek, 1981) to score the person on his or her functional and psychological status. The assessment measures physical mobility, activities of daily living (hygiene, dressing), use of devices (crutches, cane, or wheelchair), and pain behavior and psychology, among others.

The functional assessment, conducted by family, friends, or caretaker, identifies any diminished capacity on tasks of daily living, including but not limited to preparing a meal, playing a game, various writing tasks, and attention to ongoing events such as a television program or current events. Recall that in Chapter 7, Stress and Coping, we noted that Lazarus and Folkman (1984) theorized that diminished functional capacity created the type of daily hassles that may lead to depression. Thus, according to their theory, functional assessment of an individual should include an assessment of his or her psychological state.

Finally, researchers may choose to use *visual analogue measures* to rate pain severity. Scott and Huskisson (1976) popularized the visual analogue measures in the 1970s (McDowell & Newell, 1996). The typical scale includes a straight, vertical line capped at each end with words that describe pain severity (see Figure 10.10). For example, Huskisson chose "pain as bad as it could be" to appear at the top of the vertical line and "no pain" to appear at the bottom (Scott & Huskisson, 1976). Here, individuals are instructed to place a mark along the vertical continuum to indicate the pain level experienced as a result of a specific injury or illness.

One property of all three types of pain assessment instruments described here is that they all measure an individual's tolerance for pain. For example, researchers note that many individuals with arthritis can function adequately with low levels of persistent pain (Pisetsky, 2007). However, there are perceptual differences in the definition of "low levels" of pain.

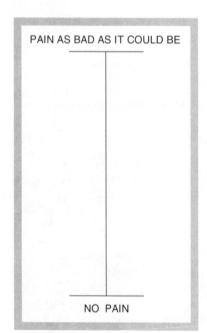

FIGURE 10.10   Visual Analogue Pain Assessment Instrument. Pain assessment using a vertical rating scale.

Source: Scott & Huskisson (1976).

Several research studies suggest that pain tolerance and perception of pain severity vary due to demographic and cultural factors such as gender or ethnicity. For example, Tsai (2007) found gender differences in perceptions of pain among Chinese men and women. Similar findings were reported by Mince and Stewart in their study of gender differences and depression in chronic pain conditions (2007).

Gender difference in pain tolerance appears even among adolescents with juvenile arthritis. In a study comparing pain perception and tolerance by gender and age, Sallfors, Hallberg, and Fasth (2003) found that girls reported more pain, a greater number of affected joints, and more morning pain than boys. Remember Caitlin? The stiffness and soreness she experienced every morning appears consistent with this study's findings.

With respect to ethnicity, however, the findings from arthritis research are less clear. For example, research by Bolen and colleagues (2005) reports a higher frequency of severe joint pain and activity limitations among African American and Hispanic adults with doctor-diagnosed arthritis than among other ethnic groups (Table 10.1). Yet other studies report that these same groups tend to underreport pain levels (Green et al., 2003). Additional research by Cintron and Morrison

TABLE 10.1	Estimated Proportion of Adults with Doctor-Diagnosed Arthritis Who Reported Limitations and Severe Joint Pain in the United States in 2002				
Characteristics	White (%)	African American (%)	Hispanic (%)	Other (%)	Total (%)
Activity limitations	34.1	44.2	39.7	44.0	35.9
Work limitations	28.0	39.5	38.8	35.1	30.3
Severe joint pain	22.6	34.0	32.5	25.5	24.6

Source: Adapted from Bolen et al. (2005).

(2006) supports the finding of underreported pain, adding that African American and Hispanic groups are also more likely to have their pain underestimated by providers and are less likely to receive opioids for treatment of pain.

To review, measures of pain are obtained using three principal approaches: self-reported questionnaires or interviews, behavioral observations conducted by health care providers or individuals with frequent contact with the observed individual, or visual analogues. Research suggests that pain reports are, for the most part, subjective and vary as a function of gender and ethnicity. It appears that reports of pain from some ethnic groups are frequently underestimated and undertreated, but for such groups, research findings are inconclusive with regards to differences in the perceived severity of pain.

SECTION III. MEDICAL AND PSYCHOTHERAPEUTIC TREATMENTS

In this section we continue our discussion of pain and pain management by exploring a sample of medical and psychological treatments used to address arthritis pain. The methods used to treat most forms of arthritis include pharmacological measures (drugs), exercise, and, more recently, psychological therapies. But, as we noted earlier, treatments for the pain associated with arthritis have met with very mixed results. In this section, we explore the pharmacological, psychological, and exercise therapies; their outcomes; and the psychosocial factors that also influence healthy outcomes.

Medical Therapies for Arthritis

Medically, health care providers use one of three types of treatments, either alone or in combination with other therapies: nonsteroidal anti-inflammatory drugs (NSAIDs), drugs that reduce the

BOX 10.2 *Behavioral Assessment of Pain by Nonmedical Professionals:* The Functional Activities Questionnaire

TABLE 10.2 Excerpts from The Functional Activities Questionnaire

Activities questionnaire to be completed by spouse, child, close friend, or relative of the participant.

Instructions: The following pages list ten common activities. For each activity, please read all choices, then choose the one statement which best describes the current ability of the participant. Answers should apply to that person's abilities, not your own. Please check off a choice for each activity; do not skip any.

1. **Writing checks, paying bills, balancing checkbook, keeping financial records.**
   - _____ A. Someone has recently taken over this activity completely or almost completely.
   - _____ B. Requires frequent advice or assistance from others (e.g., relatives, friends, business associates, banker), which was not previously necessary.
   - _____ C. Does without any advice or assistance, but more difficult than used to be or less good job.
   - _____ D. Does without any difficulty or advice.
   - _____ E. Never did and would find quite difficult to start now.
   - _____ F. Didn't do regularly but can do normally now with a little practice if they have to.

2. **Shopping alone for clothes, household necessities, and groceries.**
   - _____ A. Someone has recently taken over this activity completely or almost completely.
   - _____ B. Requires frequent advice or assistance from others.
   - _____ C. Does without any advice or assistance, but finds more difficult than used to or does less good Job.
   - _____ D. Does without any difficulty or advice.
   - _____ E. Never did and would find quite difficult to start now.
   - _____ F Didn't do routinely, but can do normally now should they have to.

3. **Playing a game of skill such as bridge, other card games, or chess, or working on a hobby such as painting, photography, woodwork, stamp collecting.**
   - _____ A. Hardly ever does now or has great difficulty.
   - _____ B. Requires advice, or others have to make allowances.
   - _____ C. Does without advice or assistance, but more difficult or less skillful than used to be.
   - _____ D. Does without any difficulty or advice.
   - _____ E. Never did and would find quite difficult to start now.
   - _____ F. Didn't do routinely, but can do normally now should they have to.

4. Heating the water, making a cup of coffee or tea, and turning off the stove.

_____ A. Someone else has recently taken over this activity completely, or almost completely.

_____ B. Requires advice or has frequent problems (for example, burns pots, forgets to turn off stove).

_____ C. Does without advice or assistance but occasional problems.

_____ D. Does without any difficulty or advice.

_____ E. Never did and would find quite difficult to start now.

_____ F. Didn't usually, but can do normally now, should they have to.

---

5. Keeping track of current events, either in the neighborhood or nationally.

_____ A. Pays no attention to, or doesn't remember, outside happenings.

_____ B. Some idea about major events (for example, comments on presidential elections, major events in the news or major sporting events).

_____ C. Somewhat less attention to, or knowledge of, current events than formerly.

_____ D. As aware of current events as ever was.

_____ E. Never paid much attention to current events, and would find quite difficult to start now.

_____ F. Never paid much attention, but can do as well as anyone now when they try.

---

6. Paying attention to, understanding, and discussing the plot or theme of a one-hour television program; get something out of a book or magazine.

_____ A. Doesn't remember, or seems confused by, what they have watched or read.

_____ B. Aware of the general idea, characters, or nature while they watched or read, but may not recall later; may not grasp theme or have opinion about what they saw.

_____ C. Less attention, or less memory than before, less likely to catch humor, points which are made quickly, or subtle points.

_____ D. Grasps as quickly as ever.

_____ E. Never paid much attention to or commented on T.V., never read much and would probably find very difficult to start now.

_____ F. Never read or watched T.V. much, but reads or watches as much as ever and gets as much out of it as ever.

---

7. Remembering appointments, plans, household tasks, car repairs, family occasions (such as birthdays or anniversaries), holidays, medications.

_____ A. Someone else has recently taken this over.

_____ B. Has to be reminded some of the time (more than in the past or more than most people).

_____ C. Manages without reminders but has to rely heavily on notes, calendars, schemes.

_____ D. Remembers appointments, plans, occasions, etc. as well as they ever did.

_____ E. Never had to keep track of appointments, medications, or family occasions, and would probably find very difficult to start now.

_____ F. Didn't have to keep track of these things in the past, but can do as well as anyone when they try.

Source: Pfeffer et al. (1982).

pain and inflammation associated with arthritis; opioid analgesics, narcotic substances generally used to treat noncancer pain; or the newest agent in the arsenal of NSAIDs, antitumor necrosis factor (TNF) drugs.

NONSTEROIDAL ANTI-INFLAMMATION DRUGS (NSAIDS)   Aspirin is the mildest *nonsteroidal anti-inflammatory drug (NSAIDs)* available to control mild, arthritis-related symptoms of inflammation and pain. When taken in low doses, aspirin is a relatively safe medication. However, to relieve the inflammation and stiffness associated with arthritis, aspirin must be taken frequently and in high doses (Kunz, 1982), a dosing practice that can cause other health problems. Research has shown that aspirin in high doses causes disruptive effects on the urinary and digestive tract, and can result in stomach ulcers. To understand the limitations of an aspirin regimen for arthritis, consider stomach ulcers. An ulcer is essentially a hole in the stomach's lining. Ulcers present a problem because the hole allows the gastric juices from the stomach to irritate other body systems. If severe, the hole may not be repaired, but only treated with medication and a restricted diet. Such a diet would exclude aspirin and other medications that similarly can irritate the stomach. Therefore, a high-dose aspirin therapy needed to control arthritis pain and inflammation has risky side effects, can limit the effective use of other medications, and must be used only with medical supervision.

Other NSAIDs that are more effective in reducing inflammation include *ibuprofen*, a generic drug more commonly known by the brand names Motrin, Advil, or Excedrin. Yet, ibuprofen, regardless of the manufacturer, can also cause stomach distress and thus pose similar risks as aspirin regimens. Somewhat stronger NSAIDs include *naproxen*—brand name Aleve—and *ketoprofen*, brand name Acton (Khan, 2006). Naproxen and ketoprofen are believed to be more effective because they block the body's natural production of *COX-1* and *COX-2 inhibitors*, enzymes that help protect the stomach lining (COX-1) and that produce inflammation (COX-2).

The advantage of nonaspirin NSAIDs is that they appear to be more effective than aspirin in minimizing pain. They also may cause fewer gastrointestinal or digestive problems (Bjordal, Klovning, Ljunggren, & Slordal, 2007). Yet they are considered inadequate pain relievers because they do not totally relieve pain and stiffness (Grond, Zech, & Lynch, 1992). In fact, individuals who use NSAIDs report relief from, at best, 80% of pain (Khan, 2006)—adequate to allow someone to resume daily functions while tolerating a reduced level of pain. What is more, NSAIDs do not appear to slow or reverse the progression of the disease (Scott et al., 2000). They are, therefore, moderate pain relievers that manage symptoms and minimize pain but do not address the underlying disease.

OPIOID ANALGESICS   *Opioid analgesics*, commonly known as opium, are a second type of drug therapy that researchers and practitioners believe to be more effective than NSAIDs in alleviating pain. In fact, opium is the most potent pain reliever known to medicine. This powerful pain-killing substance was used as early as 4000 BCE when the Sumerians of Mesopotamia (current-day Iraq and parts of Iran) discovered that opium could suppress pain and put an individual in a calm, somewhat sedate state of consciousness.

Yet opium is rarely used. The reason? Opium is a highly addictive drug. The addictive nature of the drug prohibits its use as a long-term treatment option either alone or in combination with other therapies.

ANTITUMOR NECROSIS FACTOR (ANTI-TNF) DRUGS   The newest NSAIDs drug treatment for arthritis, ***antitumor necrosis factor (anti-TNF) drugs***, also has positive and negative effects. Antitumor necrosis factor drugs are unique because, unlike other pharmacological therapies, they significantly reduce pain and stop the progression of the disease. Far more effective than other NSAIDs and free of the addictive properties of opioid analgesics, anti-TNF drugs work quickly and are effective in a variety of arthritic conditions, including ankolosing spondylitis, the genetic form of arthritis mentioned earlier. Current versions of this drug are known as ***infliximab*** (brand name Remicade) and ***etanercept*** (Enbrel).

By now you may be asking, "What is the catch?" If anti-TNFs are the most effective treatment for arthritis, why are they not the drug of choice for arthritis? The problem is that TNFs fight the body's natural inflammation process. We mentioned earlier that inflammation is a natural immune system process for fighting infections. But anti-TNFs lower the body's natural production of inflammation, leaving an individual vulnerable to infections. And because the drug is new, researchers have not yet determined whether the drugs' benefits—reducing inflammation—outweigh the costs—increased risk of infections.

An additional limitation of anti-TNFs is the administration process. The drug must be given by injection. While etanercept (Enbrel) can be injected at home by an individual, infliximab (Remicade) is taken intravenously, meaning an injection by needle into the veins, a procedure that must be done by a medical provider.

Finally, anti-TNF drugs are expensive. The full retail cost (assuming no health insurance supplement) of a year's supply of either drug is approximately $18,000. Clearly, without health insurance to offset the costs, anti-TNF drugs may be unaffordable. We explore the role of health insurance companies in providing or restricting access to medicines in Chapter 12, Health Care Systems and Health Policy.

In sum, drug treatment approaches to arthritis are less than optimal. Only the opioids control pain totally, but the addictive properties of opioids make them an unacceptable long-term treatment option for chronic arthritic pain. NSAIDs, while safer, are less effective for pain management, and anti-TNFs, the newest drugs available, carry higher risk of susceptibility to infection and are likely to be unaffordable without health insurance that reimburses some of the cost of the medication. It is no surprise, therefore, that researchers and physicians look to additional therapies to treat arthritis.

Exercise Therapy

In earlier chapters we indicated that exercise is an effective treatment for some illnesses. We noted the beneficial effects of exercise for cardiovascular health (Chapter 9) and for emotional health and overall well-being (Chapter 6). Exercise is beneficial for individuals with arthritis also, but for somewhat different reasons.

The inflammation and stiffness that result from arthritis can make movement of the affected joints very painful. Yet, as arthritis sufferers know, exercise will, in the long term, both minimize pain and improve functionality. Therefore, we have a dilemma: How do we convince someone to engage in daily exercise regimens that will be very painful in the short term but beneficial in the long term? And how do we make exercise a sustainable behavior that individuals will continue for the rest of their lives?

This is precisely the type of problem best suited to the work of health psychologists. Exercise therapies for individuals with arthritis are one form of behavioral intervention designed by health psychologists. The therapies may be one-on-one interventions administered by a *physical therapist*, an individual trained in methods to provide maximum movement and flexibility, or group programs, again with physical therapists or athletic directors. Individual therapies may be customized to work on specific regions of the body and to improve specific motor functions. They usually include stretching and weight-bearing exercises to improve both mobility and strength (see Figure 10.11).

By comparison, group exercise programs aim to improve range of movement or to target specific regions of the body that are often cited as painful or problem sites. Thus, the goal of individual as well as group exercise therapy programs is to increase an individual's range of movement while decreasing his or her pain levels.

For health psychologists, however, the goals of such programs are somewhat different. They, too, want to increase movement and decrease pain. However, they also seek to motivate individuals to do something that is not immediately gratifying and that will increase their pain burdens in the short term but will have long-term benefits. In many ways, the problem is analogous to healthy eating intervention programs introduced in Chapter 9 (Cardiovascular Disease). Such programs identified the difficulty convincing individuals with cardiovascular disease to forego the sweet, starchy, and high-fat foods that are tasty and easy to obtain, substituting them with high-fiber foods that may be less appealing but that will improve cardiovascular health in the near future. Likewise, research by health psychologists on chronic arthritic pain show that while long-term adherence to an exercise regimen is one of the best methods for reducing the pain, stiffness, and inflammation caused by arthritis, in the beginning the exercises are painful and may be a disincentive (Brosseau et al., 2004; Minor et al., 2003; Pelland et al., 2004; Petrella & Bartha, 2000).

In general, studies on exercise therapy for arthritis show that individuals report significant decreases in pain after short-term exercise regimens regardless of the type of exercise or the intensity (Baker et al., 2001; Hughes et al., 2004; Petrella & Bartha, 2000). For example, studies of individuals enrolled in aerobic exercise classes show that participants were as likely to report significant pain reduction and improved movement as were individuals enrolled in strength training classes. Similar outcomes were obtained when comparing individuals in high- versus low-intensity exercise programs (Deyle et al., 2000; Mangione et al., 1999; Messier et al., 2000).

One impediment to the success of such programs is barriers to participation. If normal movement if painful, it will be challenging to convince people with arthritis that more intense movement or exercise will hurt less in the long run. To overcome such barriers, health psychologists can match individuals with exercises that appeal to their interests. For example, people who usually enjoy recreational or competitive swimming may be more likely to participate in water aerobic programs, something they can enjoy while reaping the therapeutic benefits of exercise at the same time. Likewise, individuals who enjoy exercising with free weights might find that working with a physical trainer on a program of strength building may have a similar appeal (again see Figure 10.11).

The goal of exercise programs is to connect people with arthritis to a program that is both therapeutically beneficial and enjoyable. By matching an individual to his or her preferred physical activity, health psychologists may be more likely to improve retention rates in programs and to obtain good immediate as well as long-term outcomes. As we noted in Chapter 4 (Theories and Models of Health Behavior Change), theories and models of health behavior change, together with social marketing techniques, may offer health psychologists tools to encourage initiation of exercise regimes and to improve adherence in the longer-term.

FIGURE 10.11   Weight Workout. Weight-bearing exercises help strengthen muscles and improve mobility.

Psychotherapeutic Treatments

Drug and exercise therapies each provide limited relief for the pain and discomfort of arthritis. But the perception of pain, the frustrations associated with limitations of movement, and their consequences for daily functioning affect the psychological well-being of persons with arthritis. What is more, researchers have shown that an individual's psychological state can and does affect their disease progression. Therefore, it is logical that therapies that address the psychological effects of the disease must be included as part of a holistic health approach to chronic diseases.

PSYCHOLOGICAL INTERVENTIONS   It bears repeating that arthritis is a physiological illness. However, the effects of arthritis on the daily activities of individuals, in addition to the continual pain and discomfort, often lead to feelings of frustration, helplessness, and depression as people feel less able to exert control over themselves and their environments. Clearly, then, in addition to posing physiological limitations, arthritis also diminishes psychological health and negatively affects overall well-being.

The inability of drug and exercise therapies to address the psychological factors that also affect arthritis offers a strong rationale for including psychological interventions in all arthritis treatment plans (Turk, Swanson, & Tunks, 2008). Such arguments have been proposed by a number of researchers. For example, recently Dixon and colleagues (2007) examined the effectiveness of psychological therapies on arthritis management and outcomes. These researchers conducted a *meta-analysis*, a review of the findings of relevant studies, of the psychological interventions used most often as part of a combination therapy for individuals with arthritis. Their study revealed five frequently used treatments: cognitive-behavioral therapy for pain management/pain coping skills training, biofeedback, stress management, emotional disclosure, and *psychodynamic therapy*.

Of the five modalities, they found cognitive-behavioral therapy (CBT) to be the most frequently used and most successful technique in addressing arthritic pain.

Cognitive-Behavioral Therapy (CBT)   *Cognitive-behavioral therapy (CBT)* involves four key components: education, skills acquisition, skills consolidation, and generalization and maintenance (Turk et al., 2008). The aim of CBT is to help individuals remove self-imposed inhibitions to independent functioning based on their fear of pain and feelings of helplessness (Turk et al., 2008). If this seems similar to the concept of self-efficacy introduced in Chapter 4 (Theories and Models of Health Behavior Change), it is. CBT encourages individuals to realize that they can manage their pain independently by mastering their pain, their fear of pain, and their feelings of frustration and hopelessness. Thus, self-efficacy is central to this approach (see Table 10.3).

It is important to note, however, that while CBT is recognized as the most successful form of psychological intervention for the management of arthritis pain, it can and often does include elements of other psychological techniques such as stress management, biofeedback, and hypnosis (Turk et al., 2008).

Biofeedback   A second commonly used psychotherapeutic approach to pain management is *biofeedback*, a self-regulatory technique in which individuals learn to voluntarily control their responses to pain to minimize its sensations (Arena & Blanchard, 2002). The goal is to teach people to control the physiological process and to reregulate the autonomic nervous system (Turk et al., 2008). You may remember from Chapter 6, Emotional Health and Well-Being, that the autonomic nervous system includes two subsystems, the sympathetic nervous system and the parasympathetic nervous system, both of which are essential in our response to stress. Some researchers contend that stress is another major contributing factor to arthritis pain. Thus, the biofeedback approach uses *stress management* techniques to manage pain. The assumption is that management of pain will lead to improved control of arthritic pain symptoms (Dixon et al., 2007).

Emotional Disclosure   The third technique, *emotional disclosure*, is used less frequently than either CBT or biofeedback. Emotional disclosure therapy is based on the assumption that current and past unresolved issues create stressors that are poorly managed. It supports the notion that stress contributes to arthritic pain. Like biofeedback, therefore, emotional disclosure includes stress management as a critical component in minimizing the pain of arthritis.

In emotional disclosure, individuals talk or write about traumatic experiences and associated emotions over three or four consecutive days. Researchers believe that, by releasing suppressed feelings about traumatic events, people with arthritis also obtain relief from the stress and other related pain that aggravates arthritis.

Emotional disclosure therapy has been tested on individuals with RA and those with ankylosing spondylitis. Findings suggest that both groups report an improvement in immune functions and lower levels of pain and disease progression than individuals in control groups who were not given emotional disclosure conditions (Hamilton-West & Quine, 2006; Wetherell et al., 2005).

Emotional disclosure may be conceptually similar to psychodynamic techniques that also seek to address unresolved conflicts that contribute to pain (Weisberg & Keefe, 1999). There is one main difference in the two theories: Psychodynamic therapies assume that the underlying emotions contributing to the arthritic discomfort are unknown, whereas in emotional disclosure the traumatic events may be known but not discussed or resolved previously.

TABLE 10.3	Assumptions of the Cognitive-Behavioral Perspective

- People are active processors of information and not passive reactors.
- Thoughts (for example, appraisals, expectancies, beliefs) can
  - Elicit and influence mood.
  - Affect physiological processes.
  - Have social consequences.
- Thoughts also serve as an impetus for behavior.
- Conversely, mood, physiology, environmental factors, and behaviors can influence the nature and content of thought processes.
- Behavior is reciprocally determined both by individual and by environmental factors.
- People can learn more adaptive ways of
  - Thinking.
  - Feeling.
  - Behaving.
- People should be active collaborative agents in changing their
  - Thoughts.
  - Feelings.
  - Behavior.
  - Physiology.

Source: Turk, Swanson, & Tunks (2008).

In general, whether using CBT alone or in combination with other psychological techniques, researchers found that individuals using psychological interventions report improvements in pain coping, pain self-efficacy, anxiety, depression, and physical and psychological disability (Claudpierre, 2005; Dixon et al., 2007). In essence, psychological interventions contribute significantly to the emotional and physical well-being of individuals with arthritis and are a necessary component of care for chronic arthritis. It goes without saying, therefore, that health psychologists can and have made significant contributions to the treatment and management of arthritis through the psychological intervention techniques that now are a standard part of many treatment regimens for arthritis.

In sum, arthritis is a chronic condition that affects quality of life and overall well-being. Although it is a physiological condition, a significant component of treatment for arthritis is pain management. In fact, the pain associated with arthritis is often cited as the most irritating and troublesome part of the disease. Pharmacological (drug) and exercise treatments alone are insufficient remedies for the pain caused by arthritis. Current treatments recommend an interdisciplinary approach that includes medical, exercise, and psychological interventions.

The three-therapy approach to arthritis, however, does not mask the fact that no current treatment can eliminate arthritis pain entirely. The point here is that the combination therapy approach can and does reduce pain levels more effectively than any single therapeutic technique.

Remember, absent a cure for arthritis, the goal remains to reduce pain levels so that arthritis sufferers are able to function independently.

We need to add one more point: A number of studies suggest that several psychosocial factors also appear to manage arthritis. These include coping strategies, gender, and social support. Thus, to conclude this chapter we review the effects of these factors on chronic pain, specifically arthritic pain.

COPING STRATEGIES   *Coping strategies* are not meant to solve a problem, rather to help an individual manage the consequences of the problem (Helder et al., 2002). Yet studies that examine coping strategies of men and women show significant differences in their choice of techniques that directly impact pain. Specifically, research findings appear to suggest that women use less effective coping strategies, which result in perceptions of greater and less-controlled pain.

In Chapter 7, Stress and Coping, we explored theories on coping styles. Therefore we will only briefly review coping strategies here. The research on coping suggests essentially two principal coping styles: problem- or emotion-focused versus engagement/disengagement. ***Problem- or emotion-focused coping*** includes two levels, problem-focused and emotion-focused, where problem-focused involves seeking information to generate solutions to address the issue or problem. Conversely, an emotion-focused coping approach seeks solace or emotional support from others for emotional reasons.

The second type of coping, ***engagement/disengagement***, also includes two levels. Engagement is a hybrid of the two levels in the problem- or emotion-focused coping approach. It includes both problem solving and emotional support. Finally, as the name suggests, disengagement is best characterized as withdrawal or a denial of the problem. For example, individuals with arthritis who experience a pain flare-up and who use a disengagement coping strategy may continue with their activities, tolerating the pain as best they can but not seeking treatment or acknowledging that the pain is related to arthritis. Other disengagers may resort to substances (drug or alcohol), also to disengage from the pain (Helder et al., 2002). Researchers have demonstrated that, of the four coping styles, the problem-focused approach appears to be the most effective strategy for addressing a problem, whereas, predictably, the disengagement approach is the least effective (Garver, Weintraub, & Scheier, 1989; Lazarus & Folkman, 1984).

In a study testing coping strategies among adults with osteoarthritis pain, France and colleagues (2004) found a gender difference in pain coping strategies that resulted in a difference in perceived pain. These researchers compared postmenopausal women and similarly aged men and found that women were more likely to use emotion-focused strategies than were men. Moreover, individuals who used the emotion-focused approach were significantly more likely to report more arthritis pain and a lower pain tolerance than were individuals who used another strategy.

Finally, research on coping also suggests that the coping techniques individuals adopt for a specific illness are related to the coping strategies they use when dealing with everyday life (Helder et al., 2002). In essence, coping strategies appear to be linked to an individual's own disposition toward handling stress of any sort, and are not limited to approaches to address pain or to one's gender.

Earlier we identified studies that suggest there are gender differences in the perception of severity of pain associated with arthritis. It appears that the effects of gender on arthritis can be seen in two ways: the effects of coping styles of women versus men when managing pain, and the incidence and prevalence of arthritis among women.

The main point is that women are more likely to use emotion-focused strategies to cope with arthritic pain, an approach that results in lower pain tolerance and higher overall perception of pain.

With regards to incidence and prevalence rates, we mentioned earlier in the chapter that women experience higher rates of rheumatoid arthritis than men. They also report higher levels of osteoarthritis than men. Studies reveal that women are three times more likely to be diagnosed with RA and 1.5 times more likely to be diagnosed with OA than men (Anderson et al., 1985; Godfrey & Felson, 2008; Suh et al., 2000). The reason for the gender difference in prevalence rates of RA and OA is unclear; however, it appears that hormonal changes and weight gains that occur in women over 50 years of age are correlated with the increased rates and may offer one possible explanation for the difference.

SOCIAL SUPPORT   Essentially, researchers agree that individuals are able to achieve better overall outcomes when they receive support from others. The most beneficial form of support is *tangible assistance*, such as materials or help with issues that directly address the problem. For individuals with arthritis, tangible support could include help with daily tasks such as cooking or getting dressed or assistance with transportation—getting to a doctor's office or to the bank—when needed. Other forms of support include information, guidance, or emotional support. While all forms of support are helpful, research suggests that tangible support that assists an individual in accomplishing specific goals is most beneficial.

While both genders benefit from social support, research suggests that women with arthritis who receive strong social support are less likely to experience depressive symptoms. Consider this: Women often report feelings of guilt when they are unable to perform household or family responsibilities due to the restricted movements associated with arthritis. To illustrate this point, research by Hwang, Kim, and Jun (2006) offer transcripts of interviews in a case study of five Korean women with RA that revealed many expressions of guilt or anxiety because they were unable to attend to their children's needs or to perform household tasks as expected. In addition, Hwang and colleagues (2004) report that in more traditional societies women with RA who do not receive strong social support from their spouses are not only at greater risk of functional disabilities over time but also at greater risk of depression.

Such outcomes appear to hold for women in general. Other researchers similarly suggest that women's feelings of anxiety or guilt due to their inability to perform their expected family roles often lead to depression (Escalante, del Rincon, & Mulrow, 2000). And, as noted previously, arthritis sufferers' inability to perform simple daily tasks for themselves or for others, such as dressing, cooking, and eating or feeding others, or involving themselves in social activities, also leads to a sense of helplessness that can promote depressive symptoms (Katz, 1995; Katz & Yelin, 1994).

Social support for the management of osteoarthritis and rheumatoid arthritis has also been linked to improvements in an individual's coping process and daily functioning as well as his or her perceptions of pain over time. In a study of 78 individuals with RA, researchers found that both coping styles and social support predicted overall well-being. Patients who reported passive coping strategies to deal with pain, here meaning avoiding or restricting activities due to pain, reported greater functional disability over three years (Evers et al., 2003). In addition, those with fewer social support networks, here meaning fewer support groups, or individuals who could not count on others for emotional support when facing physical challenges also showed greater functional disability and poorer pain tolerance when followed up three and five years later (Evers et al., 2003).

Similar findings by other researchers strengthen the claim that social support, in addition to coping strategies, contributes to health outcomes and overall well-being of arthritis sufferers (Keefe et al., 2002; Linton, 2000; Martire et al., 2003).

It is important to observe that cultures may help shape the coping strategies individuals choose. Women may be supported in their use of emotion-focused coping because seeking solace and emotional support for problems is consistent with the roles assigned to women in many societies. On the other hand, emotion-focused coping is not encouraged among men. Rather, men may receive messages that society expects them to work through the pain and stiffness, neither focusing on nor calling attention to their limitations and discomfort. Individuals who receive such messages may perceive greater pain and less tolerance associated with the illness and less effective management of their arthritis than others who take a more problem-centered coping style.

The social support literature leaves little doubt that assistance of whatever sort and from a variety of support groups is an essential element in the effective management of the illness and the mental health status of individuals with arthritis. In addition, these findings demonstrate a need for health psychologists in interventions and therapies developed for arthritis management. Group-structured interventions may offer a support group for individuals without such resources. In addition, exercise therapy groups, discussion groups that address relationship issues, and arthritis self-management techniques may be particularly helpful as part of the disease management process (Barlow et al., 2002).

The psychosocial impacts on arthritis, therefore, support the need for psychosocial therapies as part of the process of treating and managing arthritis (American Pain Society, 2002; Dixon et al., 2007).

Personal Postscript

Many times family members comment that parents, grandparents, or aunts and uncles are often "grouchy" or in a bad mood for no apparent reason. If you have made similar observations, you may wonder why also. Are these relatives just grouchy people, or is something wrong?

Chances are if any of the relatives are experiencing a form of arthritis there will be times when the pain and discomfort make them very uncomfortable. Certainly you would agree that when a person is uncomfortable, it is very difficult to be pleasant.

If you suspect that a parent or relative suffers from arthritis, there are a number of things you can do to help without calling attention to their illness or discomfort. Consider the following suggestions:

1. Invite your relative to join you on an outing that will provide that person with a low-stress form of exercise. Bicycling, swimming, and even walking are excellent forms of exercise that help to move and stretch the painful joints.
2. Offer to draw his or her bath. Soaking in a warm bath provides relief to the inflamed and swollen joints.

3. If your relative has been given a physical exercise regimen by a physical therapist, offer to do the exercises with him or her. Having someone as an "exercise buddy" can make the task more enjoyable.
4. Offer to help with tasks when the inflammation or pain is particularly bothersome.

No doubt, there will be times when the relative refuses your offers. In fact, he or she may do so the first several times. But just knowing that someone has offered support and understands his or her disease will provide emotional comfort even if your relative does not accept your assistance.

Important Terms

ankylosing spondylitis (AS) 330

antitumor necrosis factor (anti-TNF) drugs 343

arthritis 328

autoimmune disease 329

behavioral observations 334

biofeedback 346

bone spur 332

cartilage 332

chronic pain 322

cognitive-behavioral therapy (CBT) 346

congenital 321

coping strategy 348

Cox-1 inhibitor 342

Cox-2 inhibitor 342

degeneration 328

degenerative joint disease 332

emotional disclosure 346

engagement/disengagement coping 348

etanercept 343

functional limitations 330

gout 333

HLA-B27 gene 331

ibuprofen 342

inflammation 328

infliximab 343

joints 320

juvenile rheumatoid arthritis 320

ketoprofen 342

meta-analysis 345

musculoskeletal 321

naproxen 342

nonsteroidal anti-inflammatory drug (NSAID) 342

opioid analgesic 342

osteoarthritis (OA) 332

pain elimination 324

pain management 324

palliative care 324

pharmacological therapy 322

physical therapist 344

progressive disease 328

psychodynamic therapy 345

remission 320

rheumatoid arthritis (RA) 329

rotator cuff 324

stress management 346

synovium 329

tangible assistance 349

uric acid 333

verbal or written questionnaires 334

visual analogue measures 338

Chapter Eleven

Cancer

Chapter Objectives

After reading this chapter you will be able to:

1. Define benign and malignant tumors.
2. Identify and define the four major types of cancer.
3. Compare mortality rates for cancer with those of other major illnesses.
4. Identify and give examples of five risk factors for cancer.
5. Describe how nutrition and exercise help prevent cancer.
6. Identify the benefits of and barriers to breast self-examination.
7. Explain the benefits of psychotherapeutic interventions for cancer treatment.
8. Explain the benefits of problem-focused coping as a psychological intervention for cancer management.
9. Explain the benefits of social support as a psychological intervention for cancer management.

OPENING STORY: CAN CELL PHONES CAUSE CANCER?
CONSIDER THE CASE OF REGINALD LEWIS

Reginald Lewis's death in 1993 was unexpected. The 50-year-old successful lawyer, business-man, and chief executive officer of TLC Beatrice International—a major international foods company—developed a brain tumor, an abnormal growth of cells in the brain. The tumor was malignant, meaning that the mass of cells grew and spread, crowding the adjacent brain tissue.

Malignant tumors are usually life threatening. When doctors were asked about Lewis's apparently sudden illness and death, some offered a shocking conclusion. Some proposed that Lewis's constant use of his cell phone caused the malignant tumor, resulting in a diagnosis of cancer, the proximal cause of death.

The cell phone was vital for Lewis. By most estimates, Lewis used his mobile phone extensively over 10 years, beginning in 1983 when he first purchased TLC Limited. He relied on the mobile phone as he expanded the business into a successful and major international food corporation.

The view of some doctors that cell phones contribute to the development of brain tumors is based on studies that report that cell phones emit radio waves that, over time, promote the growth of tumors. As you might imagine, such views have been met with a mixture of support and skepticism in the research community. Support for the belief is based, in part, on studies on individuals who used the first generation of cell phones, those produced and sold between 1980 and 1990. The studies showed that, for first-generation cell phone users who developed brain cancer, tumors usually grew on the side of the head that was in contact with the cell phone. Thus, participants in these studies who routinely placed a cell phone next to their left ear usually developed brain tumors on the left side of the head. (The late Senator Ted Kennedy of Massachusetts is a recent example.)

What is more, the studies also suggest that the tumors were usually the same size and occurred at the same place on the brain that paralleled the location of the antennas on the first-generation cell phones.

Opponents of the theory that cell phone waves may promote tumors cite the extremely low levels of radio waves emitted from cellular phones, as well as the hundreds of millions of people who use mobile phones without developing brain cancers, as proof that cell phones do not cause tumors.

Both sides continue to examine incidences of brain tumors among mobile phone users to determine whether a relationship exists. It is clear, however, that the health outcomes of Reginald Lewis and Senator Kennedy, among others, raise concerns among some scientists about the safety of cell phones. ■

Could any of the 1.6 billion current cellular phone users worldwide be at risk for developing a brain tumor due to cell phones (ICNIRP et al., 2004)? More specifically, are you putting yourself in danger if you use a cell phone?

It is important that we state clearly that, to date, the association between cell phones and brain tumors is unclear. The research findings are inconclusive. You have heard that expression before. Simply put, it means while some studies show a relationship, or a correlation, between

FIGURE 11.1   Analog Cell Phone from the 1980s.
Early cell phone technology may be associated with brain tumors.

the two factors, others do not. There are two major reasons for the inconclusive findings. First, cell phone technology has changed considerably over the past 30 years. The early, or first-generation, phones introduced in the 1980s used an analog technology that emitted low-frequency radio waves, a technology that some researchers believe is harmful after prolonged exposure (ICNIRP et al., 2004) (see Figure 11.1). The newer phones use a digital technology that emits higher-frequency radio signals in pulses, posing fewer health risks.

Second, and perhaps most important, researchers note that heavy use of cell phones, here meaning ten or more years of use, is a critical factor that contributes to the development of brain tumors. While there are studies of the effects of long-term use of analog cellular phones, no such research is available yet on the effects of long-term use of digital cell phones (Christensen et al., 2004; Hardell, Mild, & Carlberg, 2002). Therefore, researchers are unable to determine whether long-term use of the newer digital cellular phones present the same health hazards as does heavy use with the analog mobile phones.

Applying this information to Reginald Lewis, some scientists would argue that the earlier technology analog phone, the low-frequency radio waves, and the ten or more years of consistent use were essential factors that lead to the development of Mr. Lewis's malignant tumor.

The late Senator Kennedy's diagnosis, however, is more puzzling. Far less information is available to the research community about his condition, the type of phone he used, and the behaviors that may have contributed to the outcome. However, one thing is known. According to reports, Kennedy had been diagnosed with ***glioma***, a malignant, cancerous tumor that some scientists attribute to cell phone use (National Public Radio, 2008; Parker-Pope, 2008). Kennedy's diagnosis reignited the cell phone and cancer debate in the scientific community and brought it once again to the attention of the public.

We will discuss the current research on the relationship between cell phone use and brain tumors in more detail in the following section. For the moment, however, it is important to remember two points. First, the question about cancer and cell phones highlights the potential impact of environmental agents, here specifically radio waves, on health. Certainly some argue that the waves emitted from cell phones can be hazardous to one's health. But the way individuals use the mobile phones (individual behaviors) appears to affect health outcomes as well. An individual's decision to use a cell phone frequently throughout the day, and daily for prolonged periods, may affect the likelihood of a tumor developing as much as the emission of radio waves. Thus, individual behaviors together with unknown environmental risks may increase an individual's risk of cancer when using a mobile phone.

Second, the results of research and medical treatments have led us to reclassify cancer as a chronic, rather than a terminal, illness. After more than 60 years of research, medical science has developed life-prolonging and, in some cases, lifesaving treatments for many, though not all, forms of cancer. Now, a diagnosis of cancer no longer means imminent death. Instead, people with cancer can live one or two decades past the diagnosis, sometimes dying of other, wholly unrelated causes. Therefore, we include cancer as the third of three chronic diseases for review.

Improved cancer survival rates also allow researchers more time to learn about and understand cancer, the causes as well as effective prevention strategies and treatments. Thus, in this chapter, we focus the discussion of cancer on the same three areas: the causes of cancer and its prevention and treatment. Like the preceding chapters on cardiovascular disease and chronic pain and arthritis, we begin by reviewing basic information about the disease, its definition, and its origins. Like arthritis, cancer is an umbrella term used to describe a collection of diseases. There are many different types of cancer; therefore, we will focus on the five most frequently occurring forms of the illness in the United States: lung, prostate, breast, colorectal, and cervical cancers.

In Section II, we explore risk factors for cancers. In particular, we discuss the role of gender, genetics, race/ethnicity, environment, and health risk behaviors (individual behaviors) on cancer. We will also explore the interaction of some of these factors because, as we saw when discussing cell phones, two or more factors may collectively increase the relative risk of cancer to individuals.

In Section III, we explore cancer treatments. The diagnosis, treatment, and management of cancer have physiological as well as psychological effects on the individual and his or her family and friends. Thus, we examine the effects of depression, one of many possible psychological reactions to the disease. Specifically we examine the impact of depression as a deterrent to improved health outcomes after treatment and as a possible contributing factor to the illness. Finally, we explore the vital role of social support and support networks in cancer treatment. We will see that health psychologists can and do play a significant role in cancer treatments.

SECTION I. DEFINING CANCER

Like arthritis, the term *cancer* represents a number of diseases. In fact, some cite over 200 different types of cancers, many with different origins (Agency for Toxic Substances and Disease Registry, 2002).

A cancer is a collection of cells that reproduce in an uncontrolled, or some say "rebellious," manner, forming a mass of cells. In our discussions of the immune system in Chapters 6, 7, and 8, we noted that cells are the essential ingredients for life. Cells reproduce in the body as needed to perform the myriad functions we require to live. However, cell reproduction is usually controlled and regulated by the body, producing only the type and number of cells needed. Cancerous cells are the result of unregulated or uncontrolled cell reproduction. In other words, something went wrong.

The exact cause of any specific cancer is difficult to determine. However, research has shown that chemical agents (tobacco smoke or asbestos), biological agents (viruses like HIV or bacterial parasites), and environmental factors (ultraviolet light and radiation), in addition to genetic factors, may contribute to abnormal or uncontrolled cell growth (American Cancer Society, 2008; Moadei & Harris, 2008; World Health Organization, 2008a). In addition, some individual health behaviors also increase the risk of cancer. These include poor nutrition, smoking, obesity or overweight, physical inactivity, exposure to sexually transmitted diseases, and HIV (Moadei & Harris, 2008; World Health Organization, 2008a).

Some of the health behaviors associated with cancer should sound very familiar because, as we have indicated in earlier chapters, they contribute to other illnesses as well. For health psychologists, changing an individual's unhealthy behaviors, particularly those behaviors that increase the risk of cancer, is an important objective that may lead to improved health status and longer life expectancy.

Tumors

We explained in the opening story that when cells reproduce in an uncontrolled manner they form a *mass* or *tumor*. Two types of tumors are possible, benign and malignant. A *benign tumor* is a large mass of overgrown cells. The important point about benign tumors, however, is that they are not usually life threatening. While they may grow in size, they do not reproduce, nor do they spread to other parts of the body. In most cases, benign tumors can be removed safely and without damage to other body tissues or organs.

Malignant tumors, on the other hand, are life threatening (see Figure 11.2). They consist of a large mass of cells that grow and multiply uncontrollably and interfere with other body organs and functions. In addition, malignant tumors are cancerous. Undetected, the tumors can *metastasize*, or spread to other parts of the body, making it virtually impossible to locate and remove all of the tumors. A cancer that has metastasized is unlikely to be contained or effectively treated, so the outcome usually is fatal.

Categories of Cancer

Only malignant tumors are considered cancerous. There are four principal categories of cancer: carcinomas, sarcomas, leukemia, and lymphomas. *Carcinomas* are cancers derived from epithelial cells. As dissussed in to Chapter 8 (HIV and AIDS), epithelial cells are found in many parts

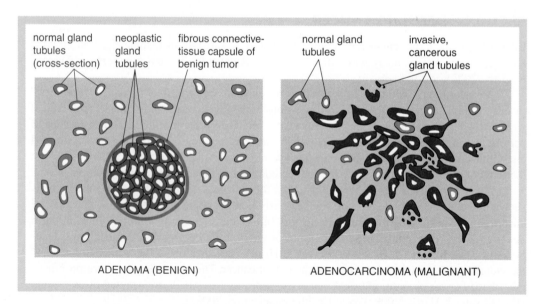

FIGURE 11.2 Benign versus Malignant Tumor. Benign tumors do not spread to other parts of the body, unlike malignant cells which do.

Source: Bruce, Bray, Lewis, Raff, Roberts & Watson (2002).

of the body, including skin, glands, and organs such as the liver or bladder. The skin and breasts, for example, contain large quantities of epithelial cells that are susceptible to cancer.

One well-known form of carcinoma is ***basal cell carcinoma***, commonly called skin cancer (see Figure 11.3). Basal cell carcinoma occurs more frequently in people over age 40 but can occur in anyone who has repeated, prolonged, and unprotected exposure to the harmful ultraviolet rays of the sun. Skin cancer is the most frequently occurring yet the least deadly form of cancer in the United

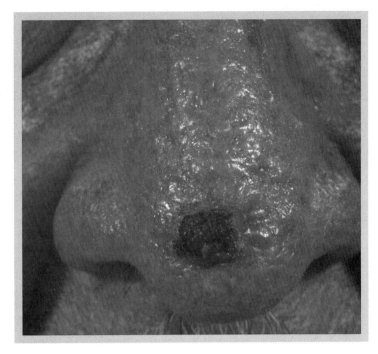

FIGURE 11.3 Basal Cell Carcinoma. Basal cell carcinoma may be unattractive but is rarely life threatening.

States. To put this in perspective, the American Cancer Society estimated that over 1 million cases of skin cancer would be diagnosed in the United States in 2008, of which fewer than 100 cases would be fatal (ACS, 2008).

Other forms of carcinomas include breast, liver, bladder, and prostate cancer. We will discuss some of these forms of cancer more fully in the following section. For now, it is important to note that these cancers are more likely to be fatal forms of cancer than basal cell carcinoma. The mortality rates associated with each of the four exceed those for skin cancer even though the incidence rate for breast, liver, bladder, and prostate cancers are much lower than skin cancers. Thus, carcinomas illustrate one property of cancer: The most frequently occurring form of the disease is not necessarily the deadliest (see Figure 11.4).

SARCOMAS   The name *sarcoma* may sound familiar because we introduced Kaposi's sarcoma in Chapter 8, HIV and AIDS. *Sarcomas* are soft-tissue cancers that can occur in a number of sites in the body, including fat, muscle, nerves, tendons, and other tissues that support organs (University of Minnesota, 2008). Sarcomas often spread to other places in the body. Therefore, sarcomas are usually malignant tumors.

Sarcomas can be caused by genetic diseases, exposure to chemicals like herbicides or arsenic, and some infectious viruses such as the virus that causes Kaposi's sarcoma. There appear to be, however, other causes of sarcoma that are as yet unidentified (Brennan, Singer, Maki, & O'Sullivan, 2004; Yarchoan & Little, 2004).

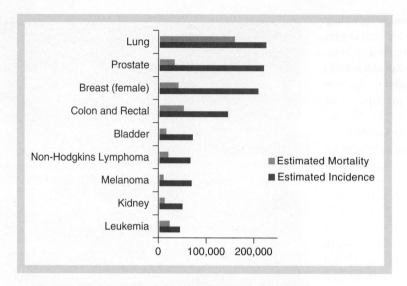

FIGURE 11.4 Comparison of Estimates of Incidences of Cancer with Mortality Statistics for the United States, 2008. Cancer statistics show that the most frequently occurring forms of cancer have the lowest mortality rates.

Source: American Cancer Society (2010).

LEUKEMIA *Leukemia* develops in blood-producing tissues, most commonly in the bone marrow. *Bone marrow* produces most of the body's blood cells, including all of the red and most of the white blood cells (Kunz, 1982).

The disease known as leukemia is best characterized as an uncontrolled growth of white blood cells. While the uncontrolled growth of cells is, in itself, a problem, leukemia presents additional problems because the cells produced as a result of the disease are abnormal, sometimes characterized as "immature" cells.

You will remember from Chapter 8, HIV and AIDS, that white blood cells are critical to the body's immune system. The white blood cells include the T cells, responsible for killing microorganisms or producing the antibodies that fight microorganisms, and B cells, a second type of white cell that also produces antibodies to attack microorganisms. Leukemia produces an abundance of white cells, but they are abnormal. They are unable to perform the protective function of the body's more mature white blood cells. Because of a smaller than needed supply of mature white blood cells, the body's immune system weakens over time, leaving the body vulnerable to infections.

Leukemia generally is a rare disease; however, among children in the United States and in Europe it is the most common form of cancer. Approximately one in 450 U.S. children are diagnosed with leukemia before 15 years of age (Agency for Toxic Substances and Disease Registry, 2002). Similar statistics are reported in Europe, where leukemia is the most common malignant disease reported for the same demographic (Kaatsch & Mergenthaler, 2008).

The research on childhood leukemia suggests that several factors are linked to its development, including genetic predisposition, nutrition, drug use, infections, and environmental factors

(Bunin, 2004; Schüz et al., 2003). For example, one environmental contributor, especially for children under 5 years of age, is exposure or proximity to nuclear power plants (Kaatsch & Morgenthaler, 2008; Kaatsch et al., 2008). We will explore the effects of environmental factors on cancer in more detail in the following sections.

Although the disease is rare, the mortality rates associated with leukemia are high. People with leukemia may be treated with bone marrow transplants from bone marrow donors. Similar in concept to blood donation, donors agree to the removal of a small portion of their marrow, which is injected into the individual with leukemia. The transplanted marrow helps to replace the diseased cells, here meaning cells damaged by cancer.

Unfortunately, more than 70% of individuals in need of bone marrow transplants are unable to find suitable non-related donors with compatible bone marrows (Columbia Presbyterian Medical Center, 1992). Within families, approximately 40% of whites but only 15% of African Americans find matches from their own siblings (Nosheen, 2009). This fact helps to explain the high mortality rates associated with this infrequent but deadly form of cancer.

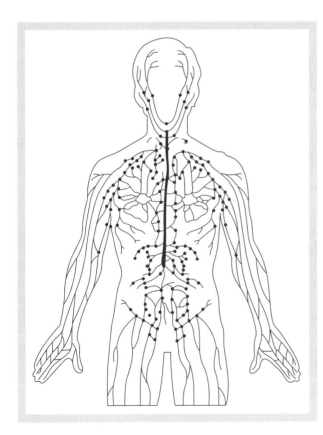

FIGURE 11.5 The Lymphatic System. This diagram of the lymphatic system shows lymph nodes.

LYMPHOMAS The fourth category of cancers, *lymphomas* are malignant and form in the lymphatic system. Recall from Chapter 8, HIV and AIDS, that the lymphatic system consists of lymph vessels (glands) and organs that produce white blood cells needed by the body's immune system (see Figure 11.5). The white blood cells, called lymphocytes, which serve as the "security patrol" for the body, produce the T cells and B cells that search for and destroy invading microorganisms (see Chapter 8, HIV and AIDS). Put another way, they defend against infection.

When the white blood cells in the lymph glands, called *lymphocytes*, become abnormal, they cannot perform the needed protective functions for the body and will not be able to adequately destroy invading viruses or other infections. What is more, one function of the lymph glands is to act as a barrier to infections by preventing them from spreading to other parts of the body through the extensive lymphatic system. If lymphocytes are transformed into abnormal cells, they cannot control the spread of microorganisms. Thus, like the immature cells developed as a result of leukemia, the abnormal lymphocytes also leave the body vulnerable to infections or other illnesses.

Lymphomas are usually classified as either ***non-Hodgkin's lymphoma*** or ***Hodgkin's disease***. Non-Hodgkin's lymphoma is frequently a fatal form of lymphoma because the tumors are usually malignant. And, although the incidence rates for non-Hodgkin's lymphoma are low, the mortality rates associated with the disease are high. By comparison, Hodgkin's disease is less severe. Although it also infects the lymph glands, it is less likely to spread to other organs. Therefore, it is more easily controlled and treated.

To summarize, benign tumors are not cancer forming and are not life threatening. Malignant tumors, however, are often cancerous and have varying mortality rates, depending on the type of cancer. Generally, basal cell carcinoma, the most frequently occurring form of cancer, has the lowest mortality rate, while other forms of cancers, such as leukemias and lymphomas, are less commonly occurring but have higher mortality rates.

Comparing Global and U.S. Incidences of Cancer

In Chapter 3, Global Communicable and Chronic Disease, we noted that chronic diseases disproportionately affect people in developing countries. Lack of access to health care for many in developing countries often results in higher death rates for illnesses that are curable or easily controlled in developed countries. Cancer is an example of such a disease. The statistics in Figure 11.6 show that, while the incidence and mortality rates of cancer are high for both developed and developing countries, in general people in developing countries experience higher mortality rates from cancer than do those in developed countries. There are, however, a few important differences.

A global comparison on types of cancer by country status (developed versus developing, see Figure 11.6) shows that three types of cancer—colorectal cancer, prostate cancer (for men), and breast cancer (for women)—have higher incidences and mortality rates in developed countries. Conversely, developing countries report a higher prevalence of stomach and liver cancer for men and uterine cancer for women.

As we will see in following sections, individual health behaviors, including diet and nutrition, may explain some of the between-country differences in types, prevalence, and mortality rates of cancer. We will explore the effects of health behaviors on cancer more fully in the following section. For now, it is important to note that developed countries such as the United States, England, and Canada report high rates of colorectal and other cancers associated with lifestyle behaviors. For example, the preference for high-fat, high-cholesterol foods, sometimes referred to as "the Western diet," is linked to such cancers. By comparison, lack of access to health care is associated with higher mortality rates due to cancer in regions where health care is unaffordable or there are few available health care providers. In such settings, individuals' likelihood of receiving timely and potentially lifesaving or life-prolonging treatments for their cancers is low.

SECTION II. RISK FACTORS FOR CANCER

Cancer and Gender

Do women have higher incidence and mortality rates for cancer than men? Educational campaigns in the United States in the early 1900s suggested that women were, in fact, at higher risk (Reagan, 1997; Wood, 1924).

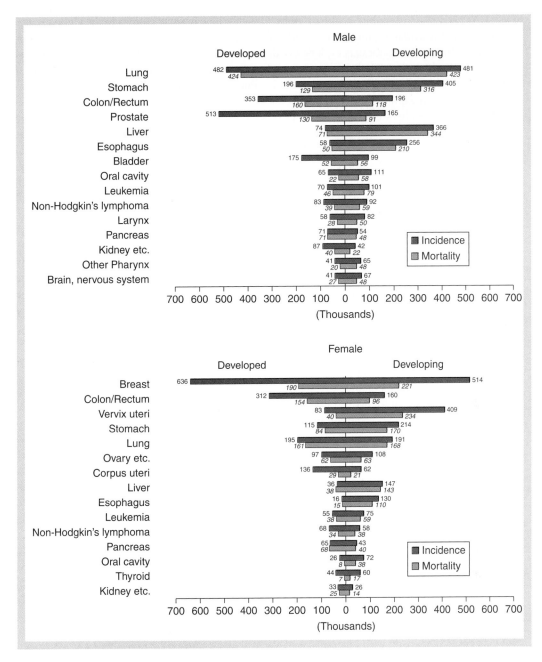

FIGURE 11.6 Global Cancer Rates by Country Status and Gender. Mortality rates for cancer in developing countries exceed those in developed countries due in large measure to a lack of access to care.

Source: Parkin, Bray, Ferlay, & Pisani (2005).

As early as 1913, public health officials and other health organizations in the United States produced and distributed public service advertisements, mainly print and radio advertisements, to educate the public about cancer, a newly discovered and somewhat feared disease. Many of the early ads either identified women as a high-risk group for cancer, focusing on the types of cancers most common to women, or identified women as the caregivers, responsible for overseeing the health and welfare of their family.

Some researchers contend that both types of advertisements led men as well as some women to believe that women were at higher risk for cancer (Reagan, 1997). In fact, the belief that cancer largely affected women was so pronounced that, in the early 1950s, the American Cancer Society changed their educational campaign to state clearly that men were also at high risk for cancer (Reagan, 1997). Still, decades of misperception were difficult to correct. Even today, women continue to misperceive their risks of cancer. For example, American women still overestimated the incidence rates of breast cancer and their mortality risks from the disease. Today, some misperceptions may be due to the large volume of ads that continue to stress women's risk for cancer, specifically breast cancer.

So what is the truth? Statistics do show a gender difference in cancer incidence and mortality rates; however men, not women, have higher relative risks. One reason for the dramatic difference between men and women is the relationship between smoking and lung cancer. We will examine the impact of smoking on cancer later in this chapter. The important point to note, however, is that before the 1960s few women smoked or smoked regularly. Thus, the incidences of cancer linked to smoking were higher for men than for women. After 1960, the number of female smokers and the frequency of smoking increased substantially. The increased smoking behavior lead to an increase in the incidence rates of cancer in women as well as an increase in cancer-related mortality.

In general, women continue to lag behind men on incidence and mortality rates of cancer, a surprising finding given the focus on women and cancer in the early to mid-1900s. Current data, however, show a new and disturbing trend. Death rates due to cancer have declined 1.5% for men from 1992 to 2000. For women, however, while the death rates declined 1.3% between 1995 and 1998, they remained steady between 1998 and 2000, essentially showing no change in the three-year period. This is a disturbing trend because, given current innovations in cancer prevention, detection, and treatment, we would expect the mortality rates for women to show declines similar to those for men. Instead, the current data may suggest that women are not benefiting from new prevention, detection, and treatment approaches as much as men. We explore possible reasons for this trend in the section on breast cancer later in this chapter.

Cancer is an important illness, but we need to put it in perspective. Cancer can lead to death, but it is not the leading cause of death for either gender. Chapter 9, Cardiovascular Disease, revealed that heart disease is, in fact, the leading cause of death for men and women. Yet, even today, when asked, many women believe that breast cancer claims more women's lives. In fact, many are surprised to learn that heart disease is the leading killer for women. This is, literally, a life-and-death issue, so it is important that we take a moment to review the statistics to clarify the mortality risks of cancer in comparison with other diseases. We will also examine the mortality risks associated with various forms of cancer within and across genders in the United States.

Recent U.S. mortality statistics show that, as of 2004, cancers were the second leading cause of death. Worldwide, cancer accounts for approximately 13% (7.9 million) deaths and is also the second leading cause of death (World Health Organization, 2008a). Only heart disease (all forms) surpassed cancer as the leading cause of death for both males and females (Heron, 2007).

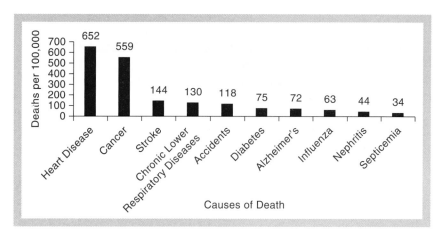

FIGURE 11.7   The 10 Leading Causes of Death in the United States, 2005. In the United States heart disease, not cancer, is the leading cause of death.

Source: Kung, Hoyert, Yu, & Murphy (2008).

When examining U.S. cancer mortality rates, data from the Centers for Disease Control (CDC) suggest that lung and bronchial cancer are the leading types of cancer that result in mortality for both men and women (CDC, 2004c). Together, they account for approximately 53.5 deaths per 100,000 of the population. The association between smoking, a lifestyle issue, and cancer, which we explore later in this section, helps to explain the high mortality rates associated with lung cancer.

The statistics show that, except for gender-specific cancers, the leading causes of cancer deaths are similar for both men and women. For men, the three leading causes of deaths due to cancer are lung, prostate, and colorectal cancer (see Figure 11.8). For women, lung and colorectal cancers are also the first and third leading causes of cancer deaths. But breast cancer is the second leading cause for women's cancer deaths (see Figure 11.9).

To review, the answer to the question posed at the start of this section is no, women do not have a higher relative risk for cancer than men. Efforts to educate the U.S. public about the new disease in the early 1900s appear responsible for the misperception. The newest data on cancer incidence and mortality rates show that there is a gender difference, but that it is men, not women, who are at high risk. We even find gender-based differences in incidence and mortality rates of cancer when exploring the association between genetics, race, and ethnicity.

Genetic Factors

GENETIC MARKERS FOR BREAST CANCER   Current estimates suggest that fully 5 to 10% of breast cancer incidences are due to cancer-susceptible genes or other hereditary factors (Claus et al., 1996; DeGreve et al., 2008). Medical researchers agree that in some racial and ethnic populations, two mutated genes, BRCA1 and BRCA2, have been linked with increased risk for and incidences of early breast cancer. ***Mutated genes*** experience a change in their genetic material. The reason for the change is unclear but is usually attributed to a genetic error.

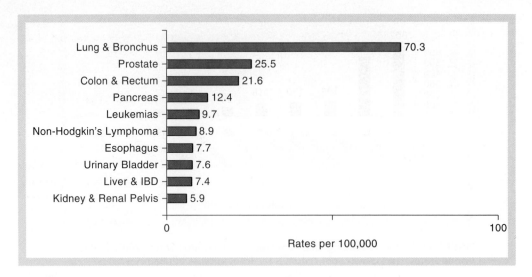

FIGURE 11.8   The Top 10 Cancer Sites, 2004: U.S. Men, All Races. For men, the second most frequently occurring cancer is prostate cancer.

Source: U.S. Cancer Statistics Working Group (2005).

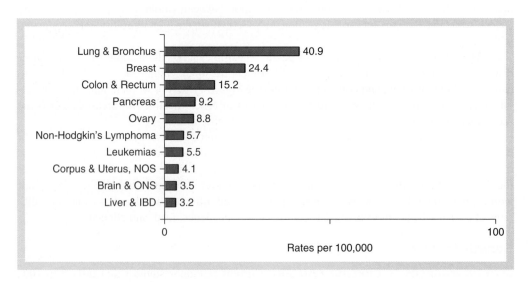

FIGURE 11.9   The Top 10 Cancer Sites, 2004: U.S. Women, All Races. For women, the second most frequently occurring form of cancer is breast cancer.

Source: U.S. Cancer Statistics Working Group (2005).

The link between BRCA1 and BRCA2 and breast cancer has been identified in groups of British and Icelandic women (Anglican Breast Cancer Study Group, 2000; Tryggvadottir et al., 1998). Yet the ethnic group that shows the strongest association between BRCA1 and BRCA2 and breast cancer is Ashkenazi Jewish women. In several studies of breast cancer examining the mutated BRCA1 gene in women of various ethnic groups, Ashkenazi Jewish women accounted for between 12 and 20% of early incidences of the disease (Neuhausen et al., 1996; Warner et al., 1999).

The association is more pronounced in studies examining *lifetime risk* of breast cancer, meaning the likelihood of developing breast cancer over the course of one's lifetime. In these studies, Ashkenazi women with mutated BRCA1 or BRCA2 had an 82% chance of developing breast cancer (King et al., 2003). It is important to note, however, that the risk of developing breast cancer increases with age. Therefore, statistics on lifetime risk must include the effects of age in addition to genetic factors.

Other studies show that a woman's chance of contracting breast cancer is influenced also by the number of female family members with prior early onsets of breast cancer (Ford et al., 1998; King et al., 2003), a phenomenon that occurs with other types of cancer as well.

We add one final note about breast cancer. Early studies that identified a genetic link for breast cancer also found a correlation between breast and *ovarian cancer*, or cancer that forms in the ovaries. In fact, many studies of breast cancer also include women with high risk factors or incidences of ovarian cancer. What is more, it appears that the mutated BRCA1 and BRCA2 genes are risk factors for both forms of cancer (Miki et al., 1994; Wooster et al., 1995).

GENETIC MARKERS FOR COLON CANCER   Gene mutation may also explain some forms of colon and rectal cancer, sometimes referred to as *colorectal cancer*. Some studies have linked a small percentage of colorectal cancers to Lynch syndrome, an inherited disease (Uhrhammer & Bignos, 2008), while others note a higher risk of colon and rectal cancers among relatives (Potter, 1999).

Although genetic testing for colorectal cancer is still exploratory, some preliminary results suggest that Lynch syndrome may be due to the mutation of one of five genes. Studies suggest that individuals with Lynch syndrome caused by gene mutation have a lifetime risk of 80% for colorectal or other forms of cancer. Current data suggest that between one in 500 and one in 1,000 individuals carry the Lynch syndrome, putting them at increased risk of gene-determined colorectal cancer (Aaltoner, Salovaara, & Kristo, 1998; Wijnen et al., 2008).

The incidences of colorectal cancer in families suggest that an individual's lifetime risk of colorectal cancer is increased when *first-degree relatives*, here meaning parents, siblings, or children, have been diagnosed with the disease (St. John, McDermott, & Hopper, 1993). In instances where a first-degree relative is diagnosed with colorectal cancer before age 55, an individual's own risk of contracting the disease is two to four times higher than someone without a familial risk factor (Fuches et al., 1994; St. John et al., 1993). Such studies also conclude that the familial risk factor for colorectal cancer decreases when the affected person is a *second-degree* (grandparent, aunt, or uncle), or *third-degree* (cousin) relative. Taken together, the studies strongly suggest a genetic component to colorectal cancer.

Of the few studies that examine genetic links for rectal cancers only, a study by Maul, Burt, and Cannon-Albright (2007) offers the clearest association between rectal cancer and familial risk factors. Working with a population of family members in Utah, these researchers used the extensive genealogical database in Utah to find participants with clear genealogical information on at least three generations of family members. They found a significant increase in the risk of rectal and colon cancers among the first-degree relatives of those diagnosed with the disease, here meaning the children of a diagnosed parent. Interestingly, they also found a significant risk of rectal cancer among second-degree and third-degree relatives. Maul and colleagues' findings suggest a strong familial or possibly a genetic risk factor for rectal cancers also.

It is important to point out, however, that much more research on colorectal cancers is needed. It will be important for researchers to determine whether the early findings of genetic and familial links to colorectal cancer are replicated in later studies. In the meantime, we point out that researchers have established an important link between individual risk behaviors, particularly nutrition, diet, and exercise, and colon cancer that could mitigate some of the proposed genetic determinants identified in current studies. We will explore the link between risk factors and colorectal cancers in more depth in the coming sections.

Race/Ethnicity and Cancer

The relationship between race/ethnicity and cancer can be examined from two perspectives: genetics and health outcomes and treatments. We mentioned earlier that several genetic studies suggest a higher likely occurrence of breast cancer among Ashkenazi Jewish women than among other ethnic/racial groups. This is true especially when examining the prevalence of BRCA1 and BRCA2 mutations, a breast cancer susceptibility gene. By comparison, there are fewer incidences of breast cancer due to gene mutation in other ethnic groups. Studies of African American and non-Jewish white American women with breast cancer report only a 0 to 3% chance of gene mutation. In addition, white women of Spanish descent show a 10% chance (de Sanjose et al., 2003; Newman et al., 1998). In essence, to date studies suggest a possible genetic factor for breast cancer that appears to affect specific ethnic groups.

When we are examining the mortality rates due to breast cancer, there emerges another and somewhat contradictory effect of race/ethnicity on cancer. Without a doubt, studies conducted in the United States show greater incidences of breast cancer among white women than African American or Latina women (Eley et al., 1994; Jacobellis & Cutter, 2002; Smith et al., 2008). However, these same studies and others cite the reverse trend in cancer survival rates. African American and Latina women have higher mortality rates from breast cancer than whites (Delgado, Lin, & Coffey, 1995; Eley et al., 1994). In fact, African American women are five times more likely to die from breast cancer than white women, whereas Latinas are 1.5 times more likely than whites to die of the same disease (Eley et al., 1994).

How is it possible that some groups of women have a lower incidence rate but a higher mortality rate attributed to the same disease (see Figure 11.10)? There appear to be a number of possible explanations. Some studies point to access to health care to explain the discrepancies. They note that African American and Hispanic women are far less likely to undergo routine *mammograms*, a screening procedure to detect early stages of breast cancer. Mammograms accurately identify 83 to 95% of all early-stage breast cancers (Joy, Penhoet, & Petitti, 2004). One reason cited for the failure to obtain early testing is the lack of either health insurance or of a regular medical provider who alerts the women to the need for such tests, or both (Jacobellis & Cutter, 2002; Wells & Horn, 1992). Whatever the reason, the result is that African American and

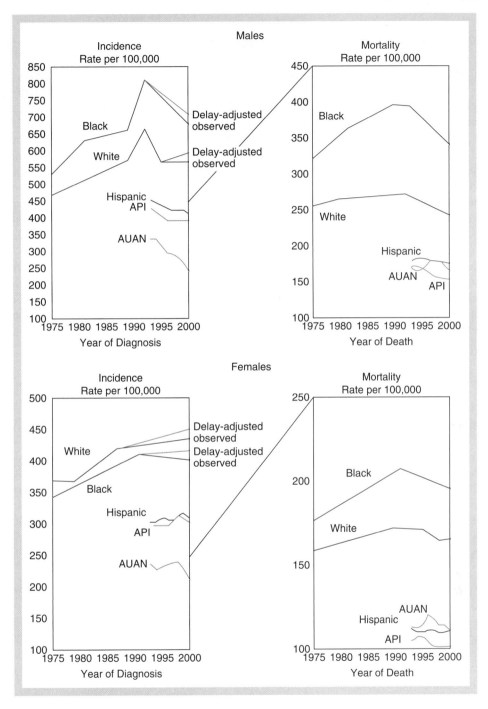

FIGURE 11.10 Male and Female Cancer Incidence and Mortality Rates by Race, 1975–2000.
Statistics reveal marked differences in incidence and mortality rates for cancer by ethnicity.

Source: Weir et al. (2003).

Latina women are less likely than whites to obtain the screening test that can help detect early stages of breast cancer. And, as we noted earlier, one strategy proven effective in reducing mortality rates due to cancer or other diseases is early detection and treatment (Joy et al., 2004).

Some researchers note that socioeconomic class also explains, in part, the disparity in access to care and to potentially lifesaving tests like mammograms. Working-class and low-income women appear to experience greater delays between detection of breast abnormalities and a doctor's diagnosis and treatment than do middle- and upper-middle-class women (Smith et al., 2008). Because race/ethnicity is correlated highly with socioeconomic status in the United States, African American and Latina women—who are overrepresented in the lower socioeconomic groups—are more likely to experience delays in diagnosis and treatment than women in higher socioeconomic groups. Thus socioeconomic status may also contribute to the apparent racial/ethnic disparities in cancer diagnosis and treatment (Taplin, Ichikawa, & Yood, 2004).

It is important to note that the disparity in incidences and survival rates for cancer between ethnicities is true for all cancers, not just breast cancer. On average, African Americans (63%) are more likely to die five years or less after a diagnosis of cancer of any type than are white Americans (52%) (Bach et al., 2002). In sum, while African Americans and Latinos report lower incidences of cancer than do whites, they have higher overall mortality rates, suggesting a disparity in access to timely and good-quality health care. And, as we noted in previous chapters, access to health care is an individual, health systems, and health policy issue that will determine a person's health outcomes. In the case of cancer, it can also influence early mortality rates.

Environment and Cancer Mortality

Environmental factors (exposure to pesticides, air pollutants, and contaminants) and cultural or behavioral practices, specifically diet and exercise, also appear to contribute to the disparity in cancer survival rates for ethnic groups.

In Chapter 4, Theories and Models of Health Behavior Change, we identified hazardous waste sites as one of the environmental triggers for leukemia and lung and breast cancers. Other environmental agents similarly have been identified as *carcinogens*, or cancer-causing agents. For example, we noted earlier that research in Germany demonstrated significantly higher incidences of leukemia among children 5 years old or younger living near nuclear power plants (Kaatsch et al., 2008) (see Leukemia, page 358). But the list of possible environmental carcinogens is long. For that reason, we choose to focus on just two possible factors: cellular phones, an environmental and individual factor introduced in the opening story, and asbestos.

CELLULAR PHONES AND CANCER?   As noted in the opening story, some scientists propose that radio waves from cellular phones contribute to the growth of tumors in the brain. The strongest support for a link between mobile phones and tumors was reported in Sweden, where nearly 80% of the population own and use mobile phones (Lonn, Ahlbom, Hall, & Feychting, 2004). In a population-based study of all 20- to 69-year-olds in three Swedish geographical areas, Lonn and colleagues compared the relationship between long-term cell phone use and *acoustic neuroma*, a benign tumor. They report that individuals who reported heavy cell phone use were almost four times more likely to be diagnosed with an increased risk of developing acoustic neuroma than were infrequent or non–cell phone users. Similar findings were reported by Hardell, Mild, and Carlberg (2003), who also studied cell phone use and incidences of cancer in a Swedish population.

By comparison, other research appears to contradict the findings of Lonn and colleagues (2004) and Muscat et al. (2000). But consider this: Even though Muscat and colleagues (2000, 2002) conclude that their results do not support the association between mobile phones and cancer, their findings still show a trend in tumor development among cell phone users. Fully 63% of the participants in their study developed cerebral tumors. Even more interesting, the tumors also occurred on the same side of the head participants used for their cell phones.

What should we make of the different study findings? We reiterate that the results are inconclusive. But we indicated in the beginning of the chapter that both frequency and duration of cell phone use are important behavioral factors that may affect tumor development (Inskip, et al., 2001; Johansen, Boice, McLaughlin, & Olsen, 2002). Remember Reginald Lewis? One factor in the development of his brain tumor is believed to be the type of cell phone used. The duration of use was another significant factor. We know from earlier studies that short-term use, that is less than ten years, is considered a low-risk factor for tumor development. Yet, 63% of participants in Muscat and colleagues' study developed tumors after just three years or less of continued cell phone use. We could argue that the trend toward cerebral tumors in Muscal and colleagues' study, even with such short use, suggests that even shorter cell phone exposure can increase the frequency and severity of tumor development in users.

Finally, several studies on cellular phone use, including those showing no association between cell phones and brain tumors, note that study participants report *subjective symptoms*, or symptoms that are self-identified and self-reported, after increased use of the phones. The most frequently occurring subjective symptoms include fatigue, headaches, dizziness, and sensations of warmth or burning at the site where the phone is held (Chia, Chia, & Tan, 2000; Sandstrom et al., 2001). Such symptoms appear to pose no immediate health risks but do alert researchers that the radio signals may result in minor or short-term health symptoms at the same site of the brain where tumors occur that may be related to cell use.

In essence, most studies on digital cellular phones suggest no danger of brain tumors from short-term use. However, it is important to restate that studies examining the effects of digital cell phone have reported on short-term (less than ten years) rather than long-term use as did earlier studies with the analog phones. To fully examine the impact of the newer technology phone, more longitudinal research is needed. For the moment, researchers must be content to monitor and report if or when health risks occur.

ASBESTOS   Another environmental agent classified as a carcinogen is *asbestos*. Asbestos is a bundle of fibers made of natural minerals. It was used commercially in the United States beginning in the 1800s, principally because of its natural properties as an insulator for heat and sound. As such, it was frequently used in buildings to insulate boilers, steam pipes, or hot water pipes or for fireproofing because of its fire-retardant properties.

In spite of its useful, natural properties, a health policy regulation issued by the U.S. Consumer Product Safety Commission banned the use of asbestos in 1970, especially in situations where the fibers could be dislodged and released into the environment. Subsequently, in the late 1980s, the U.S. Environmental Protection Agency ordered the removal or encasement of all damaged asbestos insulation to prevent the release of the fibers into the air. Clearly the health risks of asbestos must have been considerable if two U.S. agencies issued health policies that banned its use and required its removal or containment (Agency for Toxic Substances and Disease Registry, 2001). In fact, research showed that asbestos was a dangerous health hazard.

Airborne asbestos can become trapped in lung tissues in the body, causing inflammation of the lungs and complicating breathing (Darton, McElvenny, & Hodgson, 2006; Frost et al., 2008). In extreme cases asbestos can cause cancer of the lung tissues, also called *mesothelioma*, a rare form of cancer affecting the membranes that line the chest and abdomen.

Health Behaviors and Cancers

Up to this point we have focused on nonbehavioral risk factors for cancer. We turn our attention now to the relationship between health compromising behaviors and selected types of cancer. And, as indicated earlier, health psychologists focus on health problems caused, even in part, by individual voluntary behaviors because one goal of health psychologists is to motivate individuals to increase their healthy and health-enhancing behaviors. Therefore, in this section we explore health behaviors linked to cancer.

SMOKING AND CANCER   Smoking causes cancer. We can make this causal statement because evidence from research supports such a strong declaration.

Studies over the past 30 years have demonstrated a causal link between cigarette smoke and lung tumors, the leading cause of cancer deaths in the United States (International Agency for Research on Cancer, 2004). Specifically, the studies show that cancer is responsible for 90% of all deaths due to lung cancer and 75% of deaths from oral and pharyngeal cancer (CDC, 2004d). Statistics show that 85 to 90% of individuals with lung cancer in the United States are, or were, smokers (Harvard Medical School, 2006).

Why is cigarette smoke so harmful? Consider this: Cigarettes introduce over 4,000 chemicals into the body. Researchers have not yet determined how many of the 4,000 agents contribute to the growth of lung tumors; however, information on three of the agents—tar, nicotine, and carbon monoxide—demonstrates the deadly effects of some of the ingredients. Of these three elements, most attention had been focused on the damaging effects of tar.

Most smokers report that they inhale and swallow the smoke when using cigarettes. The act of swallowing moves the smoke containing tar through the esophagus to the lungs. The tar and the inhaled smoke damage the cells of the bronchial tubes. Over time, the damaged cells can form into tumors that spread from the bronchi to the lungs. From there, the cancerous tumors can metastasize to other parts of the body.

The effect of tar on the system is dangerous by itself, even without the other 3,999 elements. When added to addictive elements such as nicotine, or carbon monoxide, a poisonous substance when ingested in high quantities, it is no wonder that tobacco smoke is a deadly element.

Other studies provide additional evidence of the dangers of smoking. Individuals who smoke one or more packs of cigarettes a day are 20 to 25% more likely to develop lung cancer than are individuals who never smoked. And, while cigar and pipe smokers also face an increased risk of cancer, the fact that cigar and pipe smoke is not swallowed appears to significantly decrease the risk of lung cancer among those groups. Cigarette smoke also presents health hazards for the nonsmoker. A Harvard Medical School study (2006) shows that approximately 3,000 people have been diagnosed with lung cancer who are not smokers themselves but have been exposed on a regular basis or at least frequently to secondhand smoke. The discovery that nonsmokers can develop smoking-related cancers elevated cigarette smoking to a major public health risk in many city and regional public health departments in the United States. It is one reason why city and regional authorities sought to curb exposure to secondhand smoke by banning smoking in public areas (see Table 11.1). Put another way, municipal and regional health policies were enacted to limit the health-compromising behaviors of smokers in order to enhance the health status of both smokers and nonsmokers, with an emphasis on protecting the health of nonsmokers.

Finally, current research by Peto and colleagues (2000) show the benefits of not smoking. These researchers found that the lifespan of former smokers increases by 5 to 10 years after they stop smoking. In fact, the effect is so dramatic that women who stop smoking for three to five years appear to have life expectancies that are comparable to women who have never smoked.

DIET AND EXERCISE   Diet and exercise are another type of health behaviors linked to some forms of cancer. But, as you will remember we also discussed the effects of diet and exercise on other diseases, such as cardiovascular disease and chronic pain and arthritis, in earlier chapters. Clearly these are critical health-enhancing or health-inhibiting behaviors.

One compelling argument for the effect of diet on cancer is found in the data on incidences of colon cancer in developed versus developing countries. Parkin and colleagues (2002) demonstrated that in developed countries the incidences of colon cancer among men were 80% higher than incidences for the same disease among men in developing countries. What is more, when individuals immigrate from countries with low incidence of colon cancer—for example, China— to countries with high incidences of the disease—like the United States—the immigrants' risk profiles for colon cancer change and approximate that of their adopted country (Flood et al., 2000). In other words, immigrants adopt the health behaviors of their new country that increase their risk of colon cancer.

In the United States and other developed countries, fully 60 to 70% of colorectal cancers are attributable to diet (Bingham, 2000). What does this mean? We return for a moment to the food pyramid charts and nutritional guidelines introduced in Chapter 9, Cardiovascular Disease. The charts identified a number of foods and ingredients that contributed to heart disease. Recall that foods with high levels of fats, especially trans fatty acids, and that contain high levels of cholesterol increase risks for cardiovascular disease. By comparison, diets that include a recommended average of three to five cups of fruits and vegetables and foods high in fiber decrease cardiovascular risks. The point here is that the same guidelines that minimize the risk of heart disease also minimize risks of developing colon cancers.

If diet is associated with colon cancers it should be logical that weight is also a contributing factor. Consider the research by Lee and Paffenberger. In 1992, these researchers conducted a longitudinal study to examine the relationship between weight and colon cancer among undergraduate men at Harvard College. The researchers weighed the study participants when they entered Harvard as freshmen in 1962 and again when they graduated in 1966.

When reevaluating the health and weight of the same group 22 years later (in 1988), Lee and Paffenberger found 302 cases of colon cancer among the study participants. Furthermore, there was a relationship between colon cancer and overweight or obese BMI levels in the study samples. Researchers determined that the incidences of colon cancer in their sample were linked to weight gain caused primarily by unhealthy eating habits.

TABLE 11.1	Statewide Smoking Bans in the United States	
State	**Year adopted**	**Smoking banned in:**
Arizona	2006	Bars, restaurants, workplaces
California	2008 1998 1994	In presence of minor Bars Restaurants
Colorado	2006	Bars, restaurants, enclosed workplaces, indoor public places, casinos
Connecticut	2004	Bars, restaurants, indoor public places
Delaware	2002	Bars, restaurants, workplaces, public buildings, casinos
Florida	2003	Restaurants
Hawaii	2006	Bars, restaurants, enclosed or partially enclosed workplaces
Idaho	2004	Restaurants
Illinois	2008	Bars, restaurants, enclosed workplaces, casinos
Iowa	2008	Restaurants (indoors only), enclosed workplaces
Louisiana	2007	Restaurants and workplaces
Maine	1985 1999 2004	Nonpublic workplaces Restaurants Bars
Maryland	2007	Bars, restaurants, enclosed workplaces, clubs
Massachusetts	2004	Bars, restaurants, workplaces

TABLE 11.1	(Continued)	
State	**Year adopted**	**Smoking banned in:**
Minnesota	2007	Bars, restaurants, public and home workplaces, public transportation
Montana	2005	Bars, restaurants, workplaces, all public buildings
Nebraska	2008	Bars, workplaces, enclosed public spaces
Nevada	2007	Restaurants and workplaces
New Hampshire	2007	Bars and restaurants
New Jersey	2006	Bars, restaurants, bowling alleys, workplaces
New Mexico	2007	Bars, restaurants (indoor only), indoor workplaces, public places
New York	2003	Bars, restaurants, workplaces, bowling alleys, pool halls, company cars
North Carolina	2009	Bars and restaurants
North Dakota	2005	Workplaces
Ohio	2006	Bars, restaurants, workplaces
Oregon	2007	Bars, restaurants, enclosed public places, taverns, workplaces
Pennsylvania	2008	Workplaces
Puerto Rico	2007	Bars, restaurants, Indoor locations, workplaces
Rhode Island	2005	Bars, restaurants, indoor workplaces

(continued)

TABLE 11.1	(Continued)	
State	**Year adopted**	**Smoking banned in:**
South Dakota	2002	Workplaces
Utah	2007 2006	Private clubs Bars, taverns, workplaces
Vermont	2005	Bars, restaurants, public workplaces, public places
Washington	2005	Bars, restaurants, workplaces, bowling alleys, nontribal casinos, bus stops

Source: American Nonsmokers' Rights Foundation (2010).

Additional evidence for the link between diet and colon cancer is found in a six-year longitudinal study in Europe conducted among approximately 370,000 men and women. The results of the large-scale European study also revealed a significant correlation between BMI and colon cancer (Pischon, Lehmann, & Boeing, 2006). Interestingly, while Pischon and colleagues found a strong correlation between BMI and colon cancer for men, the correlation was less strong for women.

Finally, researchers have found an inverse relationship between physical activity and cancer. In a second European study of approximately 400,000 individuals, Friedenreich, Norat, and Steindor (2006) found that two hours of moderate physical activity or one hour of vigorous physical activity daily reduces the risk of colon cancer by 20 to 25%, especially for premenopausal women. After menopause, however, the beneficial effects of lifelong physical activity disappear.

SECTION III. CANCER: TREATMENTS AND PREVENTIONS

By now it is clear that some forms of cancer are caused by genetic or other unknown factors while others are attributable to specific health-compromising behaviors, usually the same behaviors that increase risks for other types of chronic diseases. In some respects, therefore, prevention and treatment for cancers linked to lifestyle behaviors is similar to preventive strategies for other illnesses.

It is tempting to suggest that the health-enhancing behaviors that minimize risks for cardiovascular disease and cancer, among other chronic illnesses, would be readily adopted by many people. After all, this seems like a perfect example of a one-size-fits-all solution: Changes in diet and exercise will reduce the risks for cardiovascular diseases, diabetes, and cancer. But, as we saw earlier when discussing motivation to change behaviors, sustaining changes in health behaviors can be difficult. Consider this: Many health promotion and healthy living programs report good initial behavior chance and maintenance for the first six months but poor adherence thereafter. It is far more difficult to change unhealthy habits than to establish and maintain healthy behaviors. Logically, therefore, when attempting to maximize an individual's ability to adopt to and maintain healthy lifestyles, health psychologists and other health professionals should emphasize programs that teach children to adopt healthy behaviors. Indeed many schools, city and regional health departments, and health professionals are doing just that. In the meantime, health professionals still need to attempt to change the poor health habits of adolescents and adults as well.

In the following section we briefly review three types of health behavior change programs designed to reduce risks or incidences of cancer: diet and exercise to minimize colon cancer; breast self-examination (BSE) for early detection and treatment of breast cancer; and immunization, the newest medical approach to prevent cervical cancer. Although the interventions address three distinct behaviors, they share one thing in common: All interventions were either initiated or strongly supported by health policy.

Preventive Health Behaviors

DIET, EXERCISE, AND COLON CANCER   Consider this: When going to the movie theater, it is common for customers to purchase a snack to eat while watching the movie. The first problem with snacking at the movies is that consuming between-meal snacks while sitting passively for two or more hours adds fats, calories, and cholesterol—substances that increase fat deposits in the body and that contribute to weight gain. As if that were not enough, the types of snacks offered compound the problem. Popcorn saturated with artificial oils high in trans fatty acids, candies, sodas (admittedly diet sodas are available), and nacho chips with melted cheese are inconsistent with the food pyramid's recommended healthy eating behaviors. And, consistent with the "supersize" Western diet culture, movie theaters often promote extra-large servings of their snacks for a nominal increase in cost. For the moviegoers' convenience, some even offer package deals: Get a large bag of popcorn, a box of candy, and a soda for a special low price. By featuring snacks high in fats and cholesterol, is it possible that snacking at the theater contributes to an increased risk of cancer, especially cancer of the colon?

The concession stand at movie theaters is just one example of the prevalent snack and fast-food culture, especially in industrialized nations. Fast-food chains that offer limited or no vegetables, fruits, or fiber-rich foods on their menus also promote poor nutrition and dietary habits that increase risks for colon cancer. Thus, to answer the question, yes, the ready availability of high-fat, high-cholesterol foods in movie theaters and at fast-food places do contribute to increased risk of cancer. Yet, psychologists know that it is difficult to encourage individuals to give up the "good stuff" in favor of healthier dietary habits in part because of the heavily promoted junk food culture. Challenges aside, health psychologists continue to promote and advocate for healthy alternatives.

Researchers have learned that eating habits are often developed early, usually during childhood. Therefore, to teach healthy habits, health promotion programs must also begin early and may need to use health policy regulations to effect change. For example, new public health regulations that restrict the types of snacks and drinks sold in school vending machines are one example of a health policy initiative designed to shape early healthy eating habits (see Chapter 5, Risky Health Behaviors). Instead of selling sodas and high-calorie juices, many school vending machines in New York City, Boston, and other cities now restrict beverages sold in schools to 2% white and chocolate milk. In addition, rather than filling vending machines with candies, cookies, and potato chips, schools in the same cities replace these snack items with fruits and sometimes granola or low-fat nuts. The changes are due to health policy initiatives proposed or adopted in over 16 states, including California, Connecticut, Mississippi, and Louisiana. These policies mandate changes in the marketing and selling of foods to adolescents in schools. Specifically, they aim to limit children's and adolescents' consumption of such snacks in an effort to reduce weight gain and decrease incidences of obesity among school children (National Conference of State Legislatures, 2005), The effects of the new policies, if enforced and maintained, could help lower rates of many chronic illnesses such as Type 2 diabetes (see Chapter 3, Global Communicable and Chronic Diseases) and colon cancer for which diet and nutrition are contributing factors. Unfortunately, it may take several decades before the long-term outcomes of the recently enacted health policies are realized.

BREAST SELF-EXAMINATION   Prior to the introduction of *breast self-examinations (BSE)*, women relied on their physician or on diagnostic tests to detect possible cancerous tumors. But in the interval between annual physical exams, a small and undetected lump could grow to an appreciable size.

One solution, therefore, was to teach women to use the same breast examination technique used by their physician. Women could then perform the exams monthly, rather than yearly. Increasing the frequency of breast exams would, theoretically, increase women's ability to detect irregularities and receive treatment well before the next physical exam.

Unfortunately, the mass social marketing campaign to promote breast cancer self-examination (BSE) (see Chapter 4, Theories and Models of Health Behavior Change) was only partially successful. Some women were able to detect lumps before they became larger in size, but the early detection did not lead to a reduction in mortality rates due to breast cancer. Why?

In Chapter 4 we noted that one barrier to successful health behavior change is health maintenance. The easy part of health behavior change is initiation. Once an individual decides to change behaviors, the enthusiasm for beginning a new behavior and the expectation of improved or changed health status is a motivator in itself. Once the newness wears off, however, it is difficult for many individuals to maintain the interest and consistently continue the behavior. While some women did detect small lumps before they became problematic, the majority of women decreased the frequency of their BSE well before the development or detection of any lump

TABLE 11.2	Age-Related Chance of Diagnosis of Breast Cancer
Women's Age	**Probability of Diagnosis**
30–39 years	1 in 229
40–49 years	1 in 68
50–59 years	1 in 37
60–69 years	1 in 26

Source: National Cancer Institute (2007).

BOX 11.1   Do Breast Self-Examinations (BSE) Prevent Deaths Due to Breast Cancer?

With the increased incidences of breast cancer and growing concern over the number of **mastectomies**, medical surgeries to remove breasts infected with malignant tumors, health care providers and researchers have searched for ways to detect breast tumors earlier and reduce the number of breast removal surgeries.

Mammograms, a diagnostic test that uses X-rays or lasers to identify potential tumors in the breast, are effective in detecting precancerous and malignant tumors approximately 80% of the time (National Cancer Institute, 2007). Yet, an 80% detection rate is considered low by most medical standards, with 90 to 95% as the minimum accepted success rate.

Medical providers and health professionals realized that, to increase the probability of early breast cancer detection, they needed another tool. This time, however, the tool was not a sophisticated piece of equipment or even a highly trained specialist. Rather, the most effective tool, according to health specialists, was women, the same women who regularly schedule screening mammograms and annual visits to their gynecologists for preventive care reproductive health visits (Rutledge, 1987).

The new strategy involved teaching women to perform the same breast examinations done in offices by their physician. Researchers and health providers proposed that if women were taught to perform breast self-examinations (BSE) every month, they would be better able to detect small growths or irregularities in their breasts between annual visits or annual diagnostic tests (Weiss, 2003). They may even identify some of the 20% of growths that are missed by the mammograms. Because the key to reducing mortality due to breast cancer is early detection, an increase in detection through monthly BSEs would help to reduce mortality rates.

Armed with the new tool, researchers, health psychologists and physicians began teaching women BSE techniques. They conducted intervention studies to determine how many women reported performing the tests monthly at home. They also sought to determine whether the tests were successful in increasing the rate of early detection of breast cancers and to identify barriers to successful BSE. The results of the study were both heartening and disappointing. Researchers found that the number of women who conducted BSE monthly as required ranged from 14 to 40% (Rutledge, 1987), somewhat fewer than hoped. The barriers to self-examination included embarrassment, perceived unpleasantness (of the examination), difficulty conducting the examination, concerns about the reliability of the exam, lack of confidence in their ability to conduct the exam, lack of knowledge about BSE procedures, and anxiety about discovering a lump at home during the BSE (Erlbich, Boubjerg, & Valdimarsdottir, 2000; Lindberg & Wellisch, 2001).

To address some of these concerns, researchers tested a new strategy for BSE. Using a concept known as **protection motivation theory**, Milne, Orbell, and Sherran (2002) designed a study to determine if self-regulatory, or planned, behaviors might

(continued)

increase the frequency of the BSE and also increase maintenance of the behavior. Essentially, Milne and colleagues (2002) and Gollurtzer (1993) contend that by planning in advance when and where to do the examinations, women may view the examinations as a habitual behavior, much the same way someone thinks of paying monthly bills or other monthly tasks as habitual.

To test their hypothesis, Milne and colleagues (2002) measured female undergraduate students' intent to conduct BSEs and compared their stated intent with their actual behaviors. They found that, while the students were compliant in the first several months of the study, they were less reliable in performing monthly BSE by the sixth month of the study.

What went wrong? There may be several explanations. However, Prestwich and colleagues (2005) point to one possible factor. They contend that in such studies, researchers may overlook the role of social context on the behavior. More specifically, they suggest that a behavior such as BSE, which is embarrassing to some and challenging to others, may be especially difficult to perform at home where a woman may be more self-conscious about the behavior than when in a doctor's office. In other words, researchers suggest that psychological factors of inhibition may undermine the success of the program. Perhaps what is needed is a social marketing campaign to convince women and their families that BSEs are positive health-enhancing behaviors that must be supported.

small or large. Like other intervention programs that require long-term maintenance, many BSE programs reported a drop-off in self-examinations after six months. Thus, in the short term the programs are successful. However, if women are to be effective in performing early detection procedures, they must continue beyond the six-month period.

IMMUNIZATIONS FOR CERVICAL CANCER   One of the newest "weapons" in the war on cancer is a vaccine that appears to protect women from infection by the ***human papillomavirus (HPV)***, the virus that causes cervical cancer. Tested both in the United States and internationally, the new vaccine appears to prevent infections from human papillomavirus (HPV) for at least five years (Stanley, 2008).

You may remember from our discussion about vaccines and immunizations in Chapter 3, Global Communicable and Chronic Disease, that vaccines are the most effective strategy to protect individuals from harmful diseases. Because vaccines prevent infections, they represent a new approach to cancer interventions. Recall that for other forms of cancer the only effective prevention is behavioral intervention, a strategy that varies considerably based on an individual's adherence to healthy lifestyles. And, if there is one thing we have learned from our study of theories and models of health behavior, it is that health maintenance behavior is variable at best. Thus, for the moment, a vaccine is available as a preventive measure for only one type of cancer, cervical cancer.

As we explain in Box 11.2, in spite of the excitement in the medical community for a vaccine to protect against cervical cancer, the public is less enthusiastic. The principal reason for the

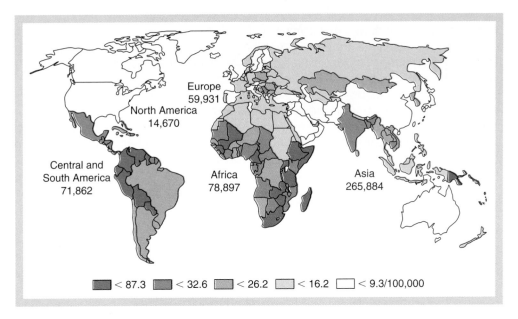

FIGURE 11.11   Estimated Number of Cases and Incidence of Cervical Cancer. Cervical cancer rates are highest in developing countries where access to health care is limited.

Sources: Ferlay, Bray, Pisani, & Parkin (2004); RHO (2008).

lack of support for the vaccine appears to be cultural and social norms. Consider this: For the vaccine to achieve maximum effectiveness, medical researchers advise that it be given to adolescent girls before they are sexually active. Essentially, parents are asked to vaccinate their 9- to 13-year-old daughters. For many parents, the idea of vaccinating pre- and early teenage girls against a sexually transmitted disease is contrary to their values of delaying discussions about sexual behaviors with their daughters until well after they turn 13. Thus, the beneficial effects of the vaccine are colliding with social norms. For the moment, the social norms are winning.

BOX 11.2   Why the Hurry? Is There a Rush to Vaccinate Teens against Human Papillomavirus?

Finally, there is good news in the war on cancer. Researchers discovered that **cervical cancer,** a form of cancer that is prevalent throughout the world, although somewhat less so in the United States, is caused by a virus (see Figure 11.11).

Why is that good news? Knowing the cause of a disease is a big step forward in the search for a cure or prevention. With cervical cancer, researchers found a cause and were able to develop a vaccine, known as **Gardisil,** to prevent HPV infection, thereby preventing the cancer. It is important to point out that the vaccine is not a cure. That is

(continued)

to say, it is not a treatment that is applied after an individual has been diagnosed with the disease. Rather, it is a protective agent that prevents likely individuals from contracting the disease in the first place. It works in the same way that childhood immunizations protect children from diseases like measles, mumps, and chicken pox.

The discovery marks the first time in the history of cancer research that scientists have developed a vaccine to prevent the onset of a cancer. Because cervical cancer affects women, the vaccine has been tested for effectiveness on women. So far results indicate that the vaccine is very effective in preventing HPV infection and protecting against cervical cancer for five years after the vaccine (Cutts et al., 2007; Stanley, 2008).

There is, however, not so good news. To maximize the effectiveness of the vaccine, researchers and health care providers strongly recommend that girls receive the vaccine before they become sexually active. Because cervical cancer is a sexually transmitted disease, researchers suggest that girls must be vaccinated before exposure, or before becoming sexually active to prevent the risk of infection which would increase their risk of contracting the cancer. Specifically, they recommend that girls 9 to 13 years of age be vaccinated because current statistics suggest that a significant minority of adolescents are sexually active by age 13.

To that end, researchers and health care providers engaged in an active public health campaign to convince parents to vaccinate their 9- to 13-year-old daughters against the virus. The campaign informs parents about the risks posed by HPV, and increases awareness of the vaccine as an effective protection from a disease that infected over 11,000 U.S. women in 2008 and resulted in the death of more than 3,500 that same year (Cutts et al., 2007).

If you are wondering why the recommendation presents a problem, consider this: Most parents of 9- to 13-year-old adolescent girls discourage their daughters from becoming sexually active. Furthermore, studies suggest that parents are concerned that, by giving girls the vaccine, they will be promoting promiscuity (Davis, Dickman, Ferris, & Dias, 2004). In essence, they are concerned that by giving early and preteens a vaccine against HPV, a sexually transmitted disease, they may send the wrong messages to their daughters. What is more, some medical care providers also express concern, noting that they would be comfortable giving the vaccine to adults and older adolescents but not to younger teens (Washam, 2005). Medical providers may be aware of research that shows that early initiation into sexual behaviors predisposes girls to other high-risk behaviors. Therefore, for some, it may be preferable to minimize the likelihood that young adolescents would engage in this or other health risk behaviors.

For some parents, however, the push to vaccinate young teen girls went too far when 20 U.S. states proposed a health policy mandating HPV vaccinations for girls 9 to 13 years of age. In the face of great opposition from parents, advocacy groups, and public officials, most states abandoned that health policy initiative (Savage, 2007).

Where do things stand currently with HPV vaccination? At present, most U.S. states have voluntary vaccination, relying on physicians, public health experts, and other health practitioners to make the case to parents for the need to vaccinate. Currently, approximately 25% of adolescent girls in the United States have been vaccinated. This rate compares less favorably with vaccination rates worldwide, which includes 50% in Canada and 80% in Australia (Cassels, 2007). However, it seems clear that unless and until researchers, medical professionals, and, yes, health psychologists make a convincing case for the need to vaccinate young teens that is consistent with parents' beliefs about adolescent sexual behaviors, a policy mandate to vaccinate young teens will remain unpopular and unsuccessful.

SECTION IV. MEDICAL AND PSYCHOLOGICAL TREATMENTS

Earlier we explored interventions designed to prevent the onset of cancer—for example, diet and exercise—or to protect individuals from infection, such as vaccination. The truth is, however, that the interventions are only minimally successful. Incidence rates for cancer are still quite high, especially in the United States. Thus, many people still contract cancer. When faced with a diagnosis, a person will confront a number of psychological and physical health problems, treatment decision dilemmas, and endless posttreatment follow-ups. For years, health psychologists have intervened, assisting people with cancer as they attempt to manage with cancer-related psychological and physical issues. Therefore, in this section, in addition to reviewing the medical therapies for cancer, we also identify psychological treatments and interventions often incorporated as part of the overall health care of cancer patients. As with treatments for arthritis, medical providers and health psychologists have found that psychological interventions and therapies can enhance the overall effectiveness of medical treatments and contribute to the recovery process.

The Diagnosis: A Psychological Process

The scene is portrayed often in movies or television series: A person makes an appointment with a health care provider to determine the cause of a recent illness or to understand why he or she is experiencing feelings of general ill health. In a follow-up visit, that person learns that he or she has a life-threatening illness, in this case cancer. What happens next?

In the immediate moments after the revelation, the person may experience a range of emotions, including shock, disbelief, denial, despair, and anger. At the same time he or she may be asked to consider a number of treatment options to control or, optimally, to eradicate the cancer. But, how likely is it that after receiving such news a person will be able to engage in a rational and logical decision-making process about the best course of medical treatment? For most individuals, accepting the diagnosis of cancer is difficult enough. Yet psychological research shows that how someone responds to a diagnosis may have a long-term impact on that person's psychological as well as physiological health.

Consider this: In a study examining psychological disorder among women diagnosed and treated for breast cancer, Paez, Luciano, and Gutierrez (2007) studied 12 women randomly assigned to one of two psychological treatment outcomes postdiagnosis: acceptance and commitment therapy or cognitive-based therapy that provided cognitive control strategies for adjusting to the new diagnosis. The 12 women were assessed on anxiety, depression, and life quality before the intervention and again three, six, and twelve months postintervention. Paez and colleagues found that the acceptance and commitment therapeutic approach was more effective, especially in coping long term with the discomfort and suffering due to the illness. Thus, results from this study suggest that acceptance therapy is directly associated with a patient's increased ability to cope with the inevitable discomfort and difficulties inherent in cancer treatment and recovery.

In addition, much of the research on successful treatment interventions for chronic illnesses, like cancer, also suggests that early detection and early treatment increases the likelihood of good health outcomes. Therefore, early acceptance of a diagnosis not only suggests an improved capacity to withstand the disease-related discomforts, but also improves the chances for recovery. Here we see that research as well as intervention programs conducted by psychologists can help cancer patients with the first step in a long process of treatment for cancer.

Medical Therapies

Having accepted the diagnosis, the patient's next step is deciding on treatment options. The standard medical treatment options for individuals diagnosed with cancer are well known. Generally, medical treatments include surgery to remove the malignant tumor and any infected lymph nodes to prevent the spread of the disease to other parts of the body. However, it is also generally recommended that individuals who elect surgery receive either chemotherapy or radiation to kill remaining cancerous cells that were undetected during surgery or that could not be removed during the procedure.

The benefits of a successful surgery and follow-up treatment are clear. The removal of the life-threatening tumor and the destruction of potentially dangerous cells reduce the probability that additional cancerous tumors will grow in the near future. The drawbacks of the treatment, however, are also well known.

Chemotherapy is a drug therapy that kills cancerous cells. In the process of killing the "bad" cells, however, it also kills healthy cells, usually white blood cells that are needed to boost the immune system (see page 358 and Chapter 8, HIV and AIDS, for a discussion of the immune system). In other words, chemotherapy drugs work indiscriminately, killing all cells in the targeted area. Yet chemotherapy is beneficial because it can either kill or slow the growth of cancer cells, thereby prolonging the life of an individual with cancer while minimizing discomfort or, when unable to do either, simply minimize the discomfort due to the disease.

With few exceptions, individuals who receive chemotherapy experience a number of side effects from the drug that adversely affect their quality of life. These include nausea, vomiting, diarrhea, a change in appetite, hair loss, excessively dry skin, fatigue, and pain (Moadei & Harris, 2008). And, because chemotherapy kills the healthy white blood cells that are critical for the immune system, more serious complications include a severely depressed immune system. As we noted often in the current and previous chapters, a suppressed immune system increases the risk of infection and, in rare cases, can enable fatal opportunistic infections (see Chapter 8, HIV and AIDS).

The medical effectiveness of chemotherapy notwithstanding, there are significant psychological and well-being consequences to the treatment. For example, limitations in cognitive functioning, such as memory loss or sexual dysfunction, are common complaints. While short-term memory loss and sexual dysfunction are physiological health issues, the effects of these changes often create psychological distress (Jansen et al., 2005; Muscari, Lin, Aikin, & Good, 1999). For some, the cognitive limitations and sexual dysfunction create psychological or other psychological comorbidity problems including depression.

Psychological Comorbidity

COMORBID DEPRESSION   Researchers note that approximately 20 to 30% of cancer patients suffer from depression (Sellick & Crooks, 1999; Streltzer, 1983). (Higher rates of depression appear to be linked to greater levels of disability, pain, or more advanced stages of the disease; Breitbart, 1995.) While it is true that some people diagnosed with depression will have preexisting depressive conditions or are predisposed to depressive responses following diagnosis, the incidences of depression among cancer patients still exceed the average rate of depression (6% of population) in the country (Sellick & Crooks, 1999). As such, depression or depressive symptoms appear to be a common psychological health side effect for people diagnosed with cancer.

Depression that occurs as a result of a diagnosis of a severe or life-threatening illness is called *comorbid depression*. Depression suggests a poor overall psychological state of well-being that has both physiological and psychological consequences. Specifically, depression can complicate medical treatments. Studies suggest that depressed individuals may be less likely to comply with medication regimens needed to effectively treat the disease (Speigel & Giese-Davis, 2003). Noncompliance undermines the effectiveness of the medical treatments and can exacerbate depression when, as a result of a depression-initiated noncompliance, the cancer treatments are minimally successful. Given the dual impact of depression on health, it is clear that health psychologists can play a major role in improving the mental and the physical health outcomes of people with cancer.

FEAR, ANXIETY, AND PATIENT–PROVIDER COMMUNICATION   Health psychologists may intervene also to help patients with other psychological or emotional responses to cancer. For example, psychologists may address a patient's anxiety or fear when first learning of the diagnosis. Individual counseling or support groups may be particularly helpful to persons managing through the initial shock and the fear of the unknown. Uncertainties about what will happen to them or their families may be more effectively managed using psychological support systems such as individual or group therapies.

Health psychologists can also help improve the patient–provider communication process. As we will see in Chapter 12, Health Care Systems and Health Policy, studies show that patients often misunderstand the medical diagnosis or treatment recommendations given by their medical provider, even when discussing routine or non-life-threatening health concerns. It is only reasonable to conclude that the quality of the patient–provider communication will deteriorate, and patients may be more likely to misunderstand the information given when discussing life-threatening conditions. Such misunderstandings can also negatively affect a patient's ability to make sound treatment decisions.

Finally, psychologists can also assist patients with efforts to adhere to their medical regimen and to cope with the troubling psychological side effects of the medication, such as fatigue, loss of appetite, loss of sexual desire, and cognitive impairment. Such symptoms can and do disrupt a person's daily functions and independence. Recall the work by Lazarus and Folkman (1984) on daily hassles and stress in Chapter 7, Stress and Coping. Any illness that profoundly changes a person's daily functioning, even in the short term, increases the risk of depression as the person seeks new ways to function while coping with the limitations of his or her disease. It is no surprise, therefore, that health psychologists can play a critical role in the health treatments of individuals with cancer and that such treatments are integral to the holistic health and overall well-being of the person.

Psychotherapeutic Approaches

COGNITIVE-BEHAVIORAL THERAPIES   In the previous chapter on Chronic Pain Management and Arthritis (Chapter 10), we introduced three psychological intervention therapies used to treat arthritis pain and the resulting psychological problems: cognitive-behavioral therapies, biofeedback, and emotional disclosure. We noted that, with respect to arthritis pain, cognitive-behavioral therapies were the most widely used and consequently thought to be a more successful therapy in combination with medical or drug therapies. It should come as no surprise, therefore, that cognitive-behavioral therapies (CBT) are considered effective intervention techniques for coping with the discomforts and limitations of cancer and its medical treatments. For example, cognitive-behavioral therapy has been shown to reduce reports of depression or depressed moods for individuals at all stages of the disease (Uitterhoeve et al., 2004). With cancer, CBT helps manage the discomfort of vomiting and pain, two frequently cited side effects of chemotherapy (Redd, Montgomery, & DuHamel, 2001; Tatrow & Montgomery, 2006).

Cognitive-behavioral therapies can also be employed to teach individuals about their illness and treatment as well as the psychological consequences (Moadei & Harris, 2008). The goal of the educational techniques in CBT is to inform the individual and prepare that person for potential problems and difficulties. In some respects, it takes the approach that "to be forewarned is to be forearmed." Thus, educational intervention programs such as the one developed and implemented by Fawzy and Fawzy (1994) which focus on health education, stress management awareness, stress management training, coping skills, and psychological support, help to both reduce emotional distress and improve an individual's problem-focused coping skills (see Chapter 10, Chronic Pain Management and Arthritis).

EDUCATIONAL INTERVENTIONS   There are two general types of educational therapy. One focuses on providing information about cancer and its treatments. Such support can be offered immediately, that is, as soon as the diagnosis has been shared, and can continue throughout the treatment and posttreatment phases. It can also serve as a useful means of support for patients when making decisions about their treatment options (Moadei & Harris, 2008).

The second type of intervention, psychoeducational intervention, focuses on the psychological aspects of cancer. The goal of this therapeutic approach is to help patients cope with the stress and emotional strain caused by the diagnosis. Pioneers of the psychoeducational approach, Fawzy and Fawzy (1994) focus on providing health education, stress management awareness, coping skills training, and psychological support (Moadei & Harris, 2008).

SUPPORTIVE-EXPRESSIVE THERAPY   A third psychotherapeutic option addresses the patient's emotional and social support needs by also encouraging the individual's emotional expression. The specific focus of programs that employ *supportive-expressive therapy* may vary. Generally they include spiritual themes, religion, and faith, or they address existential questions, in this case the meaning of cancer (Moadei & Harris, 2008).

Early research by David Spiegel suggested that, for cancer patients, intensive group psychotherapy like that offered in supportive-expressive therapy lowered pain levels, improved coping mechanisms, improved moods, and ultimately increased survival rates (Spiegel et al., 1989; Spiegel, Bloom, & Yalom, 1981). In their early studies, Spiegel and colleagues (1981, 1989) found that women with cancer who participated in support groups for one year reported less depression, fatigue, confusion, or maladaptive coping skills. In addition, they reported an 18-month survival advantage, which Spiegel and colleagues (1981) attributed to the group psychotherapy offered through their supportive-expressive therapy.

In light of more than a dozen studies that reported conflicting findings, some showing psychological and survival benefits resulting from Spiegel's therapeutic approach and others not, Spiegel and colleagues (2007) attempted to replicate their original randomized control trial to determine whether their original findings still held. Somewhat surprising, they were not able to replicate the outcomes from their original study. Spiegel and colleagues found no significant differences in survival rates between women who received supportive-expressive therapy versus women assigned to the control group. Yet Spiegel and colleagues (2007) and other researchers contend that even though supportive-expressive therapy does not enhance survival rates, it is emotionally beneficial for breast cancer patients as they struggle with ways to confront their fears and to address their emotions.

COMPLEMENTARY AND ALTERNATIVE MEDICINES Sometimes used interchangeably, the terms ***complementary medicine*** and ***alternative medicine*** refer to different concepts. The term *complementary medicine* generally describes techniques, practices, or methods that are used alongside modern (Western) medical approaches. Yoga, acupuncture, meditation, and arts such as music or dance are now considered complementary forms of medicine (Moadei & Harris, 2008). Many researchers agree that these techniques help to address emotional or stressful situations, but there are few studies that suggest these complementary medicines can retard disease progression or change the course of an illness.

The term *alternative medicine* refers to the use of herbal medicines (see Chapter 1, An Interdisciplinary Approach) in lieu of modern (Western) medicines. As we noted in Chapter 1 and in Chapter 6, Emotional Health and Well-Being, herbal medicines have a long history. For example, Chinese traditional medicines and Native American medical practices have long employed plants and other natural elements to create herbal remedies to address chronic and acute illnesses. In fact, proponents of traditional medicines believe that alternative medicines are preferable to Western medicines when addressing long-term or chronic illnesses.

Both forms of treatment may well be effective for certain illnesses. The paucity of research on complementary medicine (although the number of studies in this area is growing) limits our ability to assess its effectiveness compared with other medical approaches. On the other hand, while there is also limited research on the success of alternative medicines, centuries of history that documents the use of herbal and other forms of traditional medicine suggest that this field has met with some success in addressing health concerns. And although we noted in Chapter 6 that alternative or traditional medicines are preferred by many practitioners when addressing chronic illnesses, to date there have been no alternative medical agents found to effectively retard, reverse, or eliminate the tumors that cause cancer.

COPING STRATEGIES   For a refresher on the importance of social support systems and effective techniques when managing a life-threatening illness we turn again to Chapter 10, Chronic Pain Management and Arthritis. We will address, first, the issue of coping strategies.

Research on coping strategies of individuals with a terminal illness examines two principal factors: the choice of coping techniques and the presence or absence of social support networks. In Chapter 7 we introduced four principal types of coping techniques. Briefly, they are problem- or emotion-focused versus engagement/disengagement. A problem-focused individual identifies the problem and works to find a solution to the problem with little emotional involvement in the coping process. On the other hand, an emotion-focused individual puts a premium on the emotional response, seeking comfort and solace from others, with less attention given to finding a solution.

Engagement/disengagement is similarly divided. Engagement-focused individuals actively work on the problem, using a combination of problem-centered and emotion-centered approaches. Here, however, the emotional response will be productive because the engagement-focused individual may experience emotional moments as part of the process but will obtain valuable information during the process to help address the issue. The disengagement-focused individual seeks neither to address the problem nor to obtain emotional support. This person appears to avoid the problem and does not attempt to find solutions.

Similar to the research in the field of stress and coping, research on coping and cancer suggests that individuals who employ a problem-centered approach to coping not only manage more effectively through the illness process, they also present healthier mental health profiles after the crisis subsides.

Two studies offer examples. In a study of 146 women with breast cancer, Ransom, Jacobson, Schmidt, and Andrykowski (2005) instructed women in an experimental group on problem-focused techniques they could use to address their diagnosis and treatment for breast cancer. They compared the women in the treatment group (problem-centered coping) with those in the control group (no special coping strategies) to assess women's perceived changes in quality of life after six months. These researchers found that the women in the control group reported focusing more on their cancer symptoms and reported a poorer physical and mental quality of life. Women in the experimental group, however, reported a better physical quality of life with less attention and focus on their symptoms. Interestingly, the experimental group's improved quality of life neither enhanced nor hindered their mental quality of life. The control group, however, reported setbacks in the quality of their mental health.

A second study of the coping strategies of adolescents and young adults with cancer also shows a stronger tendency to report problem-focused and appraisal-focused coping as helpful strategies in working through cancer. It should be noted, however, that in this group of 14 study participants, emotion-focused coping was also mentioned as an additional resource (Kyngas et al., 2001).

Coping through Spirituality

Coping through Spirituality   An additional form of coping that we have not addressed previously is the use of spirituality as a coping mechanism. Psychologists appeared reluctant at first to include spirituality in studies of psychological coping. For some, spirituality is a difficult concept to quantify in the context of the social sciences. However, increasingly, researchers have noted the importance of spirituality, particularly in studies of coping that address an individual's overall emotional state.

While many studies focus on the role of spirituality among minority groups, specifically African American and Latino populations, it is important to state that the impact of spirituality on coping has been cited for all racial/ethnic groups. For example, in the previously cited study of coping styles of adolescents and young adults with cancer, all participants cited the importance of their faith as a coping aid (Kyngas et al., 2001). The study, conducted among Finnish adolescents in Finland, did not include minority populations.

In a study of the role of religion and spirituality on coping with cancer, Bowie, Sydnor, Granot, and Pargament (2004) conducted focus groups with 38 men with cancer. Fourteen of the men were African American, and the remaining 24 were white. The researchers found that all participants agreed on four principal themes regarding the role of religion and spirituality on coping with cancer: the beneficial effects of faith and religious belief in coping, the multiple functions of church social events and spiritual support, the durability of their faith in God, and the distinction between religion and spirituality. While these researchers did find that African American men scored higher on measures of religiosity than did white males, as measured by church attendance, both groups strongly endorsed spirituality as an important factor in coping with cancer.

SOCIAL-EMOTIONAL SUPPORT   There are numerous studies that report the benefits of social and emotional support when managing through episodic crises as well as life's daily hassles. Consistent with those findings, the research on cancer also shows that people with social support networks report numerous benefits from their support networks when confronting the physical and psychological stressors of the illness.

For example, turning once again to research on breast cancer, Holland and Holahan (2003) found in their study of 56 women with breast cancer that individuals who relied on social support together with an active, problem-solving coping style reported a better adjustment to the illness and an improved outcome than those with limited support networks. Conversely, studies that examine either an absence of social support or an unsupportive social network suggest that such networks, together with an avoidance or a disengagement style of coping, lead to increased levels of mental distress among women with breast cancer (Manne et al., 2005; Manne, Taylor, Dougherty, & Kemeny, 1997).

In essence, the studies suggest that effective coping strategies, together with social support, provide the strongest assistance for individuals struggling with a serious or life-threatening condition. The composition of the social support network appears to be less important than the fact that one exists and is perceived to be helpful when managing through crises.

Teaching coping strategies and establishing or maintaining social support networks are two ways in which health psychologists complement the medical treatment regimens for cancer. Health psychologists can provide such services on an individual basis or as group sessions, much like the group programs for individuals with cardiovascular or chronic pain and arthritic conditions. The most effective coping strategy, social support networks, or programs that address both are largely dependent on the individual's needs.

CANCER AND INTERPERSONAL RELATIONSHIPS   Social support networks comprise just one type of social relationship that may be affected by cancer. Consider this: We explored the effects of social support networks on an individual diagnosed with a chronic or terminal disease. But what about the effects of the chronic illness on others, such as the family and friends in the network? Interpersonal relationships and intimate partner relationships also may be affected by the diagnosis and a person's ability or inability to cope with the disease, its symptoms, and the new limitations. Consider this: Women diagnosed with breast cancer have reported a number of new relationship challenges, including the need to renegotiate family roles and responsibilities, communication behaviors, less sexual and social engagement, and greater psychological distress (Fergus & Gray, 2009; Hilton, Crawford, & Tarko, 2000; Lindholm, Rehnsfeldt, Arman, & Hamrin, 2002; Walsh, Manuel, & Avis, 2005).

In addition to changes in relationship roles and communication, researchers note that for married women with breast cancer, the support from her spouse during the cancer diagnosis and treatment phase outweigh support from other networks, including family and friends (Pistrang & Barker, 1995). Specifically, women who perceive that their spouse is emotionally involved, is empathetic, acknowledges the existence of the cancer, and fosters open communication report better adaptation to their cancer diagnosis (Manne et al., 2004; Zunkel, 2002).

Unfortunately, the emotional support many women with breast cancer seek from their spouse is the most difficult form of support for men to provide. Research by Fergus and Gray (2009) and by Bolger, Foster, Vinoker, and Ng (1996) show that men married to women with breast cancer report being better able to cope with the requests for instrumental or tangible support than with emotional needs. Bolger and colleagues found that men increased their support to their spouse in response to physical symptoms of pain but decreased support in response to emotional or psychological distress. According to Fergus and Gray, their findings along with Bolger and colleagues' suggest a role for health psychologists to assist men and women in communicating and providing the support needed to cope with breast cancer. As important, psychologists can help validate the difficulties males experience by showing that such experiences are common challenges for couples recovering from breast cancer.

It is important to note that research on males with cancer reveal similar challenges to interpersonal relationships. As we noted earlier in the chapter, for males prostate cancer is the second most prevalent form of cancer. In spite of its frequency, however, it appears that there is considerably less information about the psychosocial support needs or programs for men with prostate cancer than for women with breast cancer. Unlike women, male cancer survivors are reportedly less likely to reveal their diagnosis and treatment or to discuss their symptoms. In addition, men are less likely than women to attend cancer support groups. Not surprisingly, therefore, male cancer patients are far less likely to receive the emotional support or assistance needed to communicate with others about their illness.

Do men refuse emotional support because they are better able to address their own emotional needs? Unlikely. Rather, researchers propose that men encounter a number of barriers to seeking emotional support including embarrassment, social stigma based on gender roles or gender expectations, and fear of appearing weak (Sanders, Thompson, Bazile, & Akbar, 2004).

And, as we learned in Chapter 4, Theories and Models of Health Behavior Change, barriers to seeking emotional or psychological support can have a negative impact on health outcomes. A recent pilot study to teach coping skills to African American men treated for prostate cancer illustrates this point. Working with 40 couples, Campbell and colleagues (2006) provided coping skills training for the couples to determine whether it improved emotional, physiological, and psychological problems related to the diagnosis and treatment of prostate cancer. They reported that coping skills training helped improve men's perceived quality of life. Specifically, participants reported reduced levels of depression and fatigue and an improvement in vigor and sexual responsiveness. Campbell and colleagues concluded that men's barriers to seeking help to overcome their emotional distress can be addressed using coping skills training.

Summary

Without a doubt, cancer is a physiological illness that requires treatments that address the physiological properties of the disease. From the research presented here, however, we see that psychological therapies when used in conjunction with a medical regimen appear to enhance the treatment's effectiveness and also to improve perceived quality of life and overall well-being. In sum, cancer is yet another illness that may yield better outcomes for the individual when a coordinated medical and psychological treatment approach is used. As such, this chapter identifies yet another important role for health psychologists in addressing individual health status.

Personal Postscript

There is much more good news about cancer and cancer treatments today than there was 50 or 60 years ago. First, advances in modern medicine make it easier to detect early stages of cancer. Second, there are many more treatment options that have been proven effective either in prolonging life or in curing the cancer completely.

Similar advances have been made in the treatment of the psychological and emotional health issues that often accompany the illness. These developments aside, it still may be a daunting task to assist a close friend or relative who is coping with cancer. The research we explored on coping strategies suggests that problem-focused coping is the most effective strategy for working with challenging and emotionally difficult issues. We agree. But remember the lessons learned in Chapter 6, Emotional Health and Well-being. Caregivers or people who are called upon to assist people with chronic or debilitating diseases must remember to take good care of themselves as well. Caregivers must realize that the illness takes a toll on everyone, including them. Therefore, it is important that when assisting someone with such an illness, you take time to engage in activities that allow you to think, reflect, or enjoy a few moments free of the responsibilities you assumed. To that end, the coping strategies discussed here and in earlier chapters, as well as other forms of relaxation, including music therapy, aromatherapy, and spirituality, all have been shown to be effective. But here is the key: Coping strategies are most effective with people who have prior exposure with and appreciation for those experiences. In other words, continue to make time to use those coping strategies that have been effective for you in other situations. Together, problem-focused coping and other coping support elements may be your most effective strategy.

Important Terms

acoustic neuroma 368
alternative medicine 385
asbestos 369
basal cell carcinoma 357
benign tumor 356
bone marrow 358

breast self-examination (BSE)
    376
carcinogen 368
carcinoma 356
cervical cancer 379
chemotherapy 382

colorectal cancer 365
comorbid depression 383
complementary medicine 385
first-degree relative 365
Gardisil 379
glioma 354

Chapter Twelve

Health Care Systems and Health Policy: Effects on Health Outcomes

Chapter Objectives

After reading this chapter you will be able to:

1. List and describe the four major health care systems in the United States.
2. Identify three major barriers to access to health care.
3. Explain the relationship between consumer satisfaction and health outcomes.

4. Explain the importance of communication on health outcomes.
5. Identify three communication challenges for health care providers.
6. Describe single-payer versus multipayer health care systems.

OPENING STORY: MICHELLE'S DILEMMA

*Michelle often thought about changing her primary care physician. Dr. B., Michelle's doctor, was one of several physicians in her **health maintenance organization (HMO)**, a managed-care health insurance company that offers a variety of health services by physicians, hospitals, and other health providers. Michelle chose Dr. B. because he had over 20 years' experience in medicine and because he was affiliated with one of the best teaching hospitals in Michelle's city. Given his background she believed that Dr. B. could handle her routine health needs. But over the years Michelle began to doubt her assumptions.*

Increasingly, Michelle felt that Dr. B. minimized her health complaints. For example, for several years she complained to Dr. B. about pain in her left ear and above her left eye. One time she remembered telling her doctor that if someone could just remove the left side of her face she would feel much better. Each time, after listening to Michelle's complaint Dr. B. would do the same thing: look in her left ear, probe the sinus regions of her face, and say, "There is nothing wrong here."

On the advice of a friend, Michelle asked Dr. B. for a referral to a neurologist. She thought a specialist could help determine the cause of her headaches. Dr. B. referred Michelle to a neurologist at the same hospital, and she went the following week. After what was, in Michelle's opinion, a very basic exam, the neurologist told her that 50-year-old premenopausal women, like Michelle, often experience such discomforts. She was stunned and angry that a doctor would essentially dismiss her complaints, blaming her age and gender. When she asked the neurologist about specific tests that could confirm or rule out a reason for her pain, he indicated that there was no need for further tests. In addition, he doubted that her HMO would authorize tests based on Michelle's complaints.

One week later, Michelle had a bizarre accident that convinced her that both doctors were wrong. While at home, Michelle fainted and hit her head on a piece of furniture. The blow to her head caused several deep gashes on her face requiring emergency medical attention. Emergency department physicians repaired the wounds with 22 sutures. But, after learning of Michelle's prior complaints of head and ear pain, the doctors suspected that neurological problems may have caused her loss of consciousness. They decided to admit Michelle to the hospital for two days to conduct neurological tests. You can imagine Michelle's surprise and feelings of relief when she learned that her complaints were finally being taken seriously. She was also thrilled to learn that her HMO approved all requested tests.

The two-day stay in the hospital gave Michelle plenty of time to think about the years she suffered with headaches, earaches, and facial pain. She also thought about her doctors' response— or lack thereof. If emergency department physicians could determine, in less than 12 hours, that she may be experiencing neurological problems and that additional tests were needed, she wondered why her own doctors could not have done the same. Thus, after ten years with the same provider, Michelle decided that she had to change physicians to protect her health.

This time, instead of choosing a doctor from a list, Michelle asked her ophthalmologist for a recommendation. Michelle respected the ophthalmologist's professional judgment and knew that she would choose someone who would listen carefully to her concerns.

Michelle's first appointment with the new physician confirmed that she had made a good choice. There was no doubt that her new doctor was competent, as evident from the referral, a quick

Internet search of her credentials, and the initial visit. The new doctor thoroughly reviewed the emergency department tests and identified the likely neurological cause for the loss of consciousness. Finally, Michelle had reason to hope that her bouts with headaches and pain would soon come to an end.   ∎

It may seem strange to begin a chapter on health care systems and health policy with a story about choosing and changing ***health care providers***, here meaning not just doctors, but nurses, nurse practitioners, and physician assistants as well. But health providers are often an individual's first or only point of contact with the large and sometimes daunting ***health care system*** (see Figure 12.1). Health providers serve as intermediaries between the individual and the system, helping to interpret the rules and regulations governing the types of services and treatments available to individuals from their health care system. As we will see, however, while serving as intermediaries, health providers can control an individual's access to additional medical care on the belief that they are acting in ways consistent with the system's rules. Michelle's problems with her health providers illustrate this point.

The opening story identified two additional problems: first, a consumer–provider communication problem between Michelle and both physicians; and second, an inability to access quality care. Michelle felt that neither Dr. B. nor the neurologist believed that her chronic pain was physiological. When they discounted her complaints, Michelle felt her doctors did not understand the effect of the pain on her overall well-being and were not sensitive to her continual discomfort.

The second problem involved an inability to obtain additional tests to identify or rule out possible causes for her illness. Specifically, after her experience in the emergency department, Michelle realized that the neurologist was restricting her access to additional medical services. But why would a doctor refuse to request a test that could help diagnose a problem?

We will explore both issues—consumer–provider communication and limited access to health services—and their effects on individual health outcomes more fully in the current chapter. For the moment, however, it is

FIGURE 12.1   Patient–Doctor Communication.

important to note that the opening story also illustrates that often both health systems and individuals interact to shape health outcomes. Michelle's health care system allows consumers to change health providers when and if necessary. However, the decision to change is left to the individual. That is to say, a person must know that a change is possible and must take the initiative to obtain a new primary care provider. Given Michelle's dissatisfaction, it seems logical that she would change physicians. But, remember, it took her more than ten years to come to that decision. While some people would have changed physicians sooner, others never do, in spite of the fact that they are dissatisfied with their care. In essence, in some instances health care system rules and a knowledgeable and motivated individual can work jointly to improve quality of care.

In the current chapter, we will explore health care systems, health providers, and individual consumers as factors that contribute to an individual's health status. In earlier chapters we noted that one factor that enhances or impedes good health outcomes is access to timely and good quality care. Therefore, we begin Section II with a brief overview of the structure of health care systems in the United States because, as we will see, for many people the health care structure also regulates access to care. In the process we will identify examples of structural impediments to access to care.

We continue in Section III by examining frequently cited problems encountered by individuals when interacting with their health care system. Remember, by health care system we mean the organization or structure that provides and regulates the type and frequency of services available to people in the heath care group. We pay particular attention to the interaction between the individual, whom we refer to as the *consumer*, and the health care provider. Remember, in many cases the provider may be the consumer's first or only contact with the health system. We will review the research on *consumer–provider communication*, sometimes called patient–physician communication and *consumer (patient) satisfaction*, to explore their effects on individual health status.

In Section IV we examine the health care system from the perspective of the health care provider. Here, too, research on the interaction between the consumer and the provider suggests that the provider's response, independent of the consumer, can also affect an individual's health.

Finally, in Section V we examine the impact of health care systems and health policies on an individual's health status. Recently, health psychologists have determined that both factors are critical to the health status of individuals. We begin by exploring the effect of regulations on an individual's access to care. As we have said many times, access to timely and good-quality health care will affect a person's overall well-being. Michelle's story demonstrates this point. We conclude by exploring two health systems that have been shown to improve health outcomes but are not widely practiced in the United States.

SECTION I. ACCESS TO THE HEALTH CARE SYSTEM

Health Care: An Unnecessary Expense?

It may be difficult for 25-year-old recent college graduates, employed in their first "serious" or career-track job, to think about health insurance. At 25, most young adults feel great. Many believe they are in the best of health and may view health insurance as an unnecessary expense.

These perceptions are confirmed by many studies that show that young adults are the least likely age group to have health insurance. For example, a study by the Commonwealth Foundation (Kriss et al., 2008) revealed that 46% of young working adults between the ages of 24 and 29 were likely to be uninsured over a three-year period of time. Thus, young adults in good physiological health, who have no immediate need for ongoing health care, may not consider health insurance necessary for their overall well-being.

What many young adults do not know is that individuals ages 21 through 29 have a higher incidence of emergency medical care and higher rates of unintended pregnancies than any other age group (Burt & Overpeck, 2001; Todd, Mountvarner, & Lichenstein, 2005). Given their high rates of unexpected medical problems or mishaps, they are, medically speaking, a high-risk group.

Being in a high-risk group for unanticipated medical care is one of the best reasons for purchasing health insurance. In fact, health insurance is designed for just such people because they cannot accurately anticipate when or whether they will need medical attention. Rather than paying unexpected and expensive medical charges when an emergency occurs, health insurance allows individuals to pay a fixed rate, considerably less than what one would pay in emergency situations, for access to all necessary care whenever needed. Consider this: When purchasing a car, drivers are required by many U.S. states to have motor vehicle insurance. The insurance protects drivers from paying expensive repair or medical bills in the event of an accident. The same principle applies to health insurance. While it is true that car owners are only required to carry liability insurance, defined as coverage to pay for the medical or material damage to other drivers, passengers, or vehicles, such coverage still protects car owners from expensive and unanticipated repair bills or medical costs, regardless of the person. In essence, health insurance protects people from large financial responsibilities due to medical emergencies.

Studies also show that, without health insurance, individuals are less likely to seek and obtain needed health care on a timely basis. A study by Kriss and colleagues (2008) reveals that without insurance, people are less likely to obtain needed medications, make and keep appointments with medical specialists, or seek health care when needed than are individuals with health insurance (Figure 12.2). Why would an individual neglect to obtain needed medical care? In the following sections we identify several compelling reasons, one of which is the cost of care.

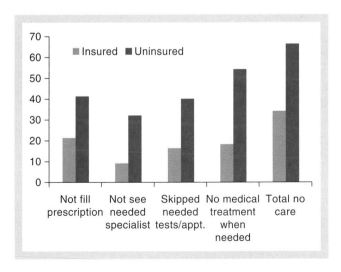

FIGURE 12.2   Health Care Behaviors of Insured versus Uninsured Adults, Aged 19 to 29. Uninsured individuals are less likely to engage in health-enhancing behaviors.

Source: Adapted from Kriss et al. (2008).

Health Care: An Unaffordable Expense?

Many young adults believe that health care is an unaffordable expense, especially when compared with other items thought to be essential for daily living, such as rent, car loan payments, or Internet and phone access. In fact, Kriss and colleagues' study (2008) indicates that fully 66% of young adults who do not have health insurance cited cost as the principal reason.

Unfortunately, the benefits of health insurance are often unappreciated until faced with a medical emergency. The out-of-pocket cost of emergency medical care is always greater for the uninsured than for insured individuals. We explain the payment arrangements of health insurance organizations later in the chapter. Briefly, however, the uninsured bear the full cost of all medical services at the time of treatment whereas, for insured individuals, the cost of care is subsidized or paid for entirely by their insurance company.

One additional problem for uninsured individuals is the quality of care. When faced with a medical problem that requires immediate attention, there is no time to search for the best physician or the best medical care facility to address the need. Thus, uninsured individuals are a little like gamblers, taking a chance on whomever they are assigned much the same way a poker player takes a chance with the cards that are dealt. If lucky, the uninsured person will get a good hand, a skilled doctor or medical provider with experience treating the medical problem. An unlucky hand could result in an inexperienced or less-skilled health provider and perhaps a number of ongoing, long-term medical problems.

In this chapter we focus on young adults because, as statistics show, they are more likely to be uninsured than other age groups. However, uninsured young adults represent only one group that may underestimate the need for full-time and unlimited access to care. It is important to state that many individuals in all age groups prioritize other important, and sometimes not so important, issues over health care. In the following section we make the case for unlimited access to health care for all individuals. But, as we will see, in the United States cost is only one of the many barriers to care.

Let us return for the moment to our analogy of a car to emphasize the point that obtaining health care is as important as purchasing any other goods or services. Before buying a car, individuals usually consider their needs. For our purposes, we will assume that a car is necessary for transportation to and from work or school, and for performing other basic daily activities. Exactly what type of car to purchase will depend on three main factors: the reliability and dependability of the car and its manufacturers, desired amenities, and, of course, costs. We contend that the same three main factors apply when choosing a health care plan. (We acknowledge that another minor factor—a nice-looking car that attracts attention—can influence one's choice. But few health plans are chosen on the basis of looks.)

SECTION II. OVERVIEW OF HEALTH CARE SYSTEMS IN THE UNITED STATES

In the Beginning

Prior to 1929, health insurance did not exist. When people became ill, they had two options. If financially able, they requested a doctor who made house visits or went to the doctor's office to avoid the additional charge for a house call. Those who could not afford to pay a doctor's fee may have relied on traditional medicines or home remedies.

In 1929, ***indemnity insurance***, the first form of health insurance, was introduced in the United States (Paharia, 2008). *Indemnity* is a legal term that, when used in the context of health insurance, simply means that a person makes a contract with a company that allows the individual to be reimbursed all or part of the cost they incur as a result of their medical injury or need. With an indemnity insurance policy, an individual pays a fixed monthly or annual amount, called a ***premium***, to the insuring company. The company then reimburses the individual for, usually, 50 to 80% of the usual and customary medical charges. (We will return to this phrase later in the chapter.) In most instances, the monthly or annual premium for insurance is less than the actual cost of care.

Blue Cross/Blue Shield was the nation's earliest national private health insurance company, offering indemnity health insurance. It now insures approximately 80 million people nationwide (Gapenski, 2003). Today, in addition to Blue Cross/Blue Shield there are a number of other private insurance companies as well as public or government-sponsored insurance programs available to eligible U.S. citizens or legal residents. As we will see later in the chapter, public health systems are also quite common in many industrialized or developed countries. Together, private and public insurance programs provide access to health care for approximately 85% of the U.S. population. The remaining 15% constitute the approximately 45.7 million people who are commonly referred to as the "uninsured."

Health Plans: Gatekeepers to Health Care

Today, health care systems in the United States include many different private and public plans. We will explain the differences among these plans later in this section. For the moment, it is important to know that most health care systems offer a number of different health plans, essentially a choice of insurance options that address the various health needs of individuals, couples, and families.

BOX 12.1 How Expensive Is Health Insurance?

Answering the question how expensive is health insurance could require a cost-benefit analysis. Monthly health insurance premiums that may range from $150 to $500 for a single person may seem unnecessary and expensive for a person who is currently healthy, who tries to "eat right," who exercises, and who neither drinks nor smokes. In fact, some would contend that the insurance premiums on a health plan could be put to better use paying housing costs, transportation expenses, and other necessities.

On the other hand, what would happen if the healthy person just described fell while bicycling and fractured his or her leg? Would the cost of health insurance premiums be more or less expensive than the cost of emergency health care? Consider this: The cost associated with doctors' fees, the use of the hospital's facilities, tests to determine the extent of the fracture, and medicines could exceed $70,000. Remember this is the cost of treatment for just one day. Included in this figure would be approximately 12 hours in a hospital emergency department, X-ray tests to identify the fracture, consultations by orthopedic, specialists, and the surgeon's time to repair the damaged leg. Yet this does not include the cost of follow-up care or physical therapy to regain full use of the leg. Now we ask again, just how expensive is health insurance?

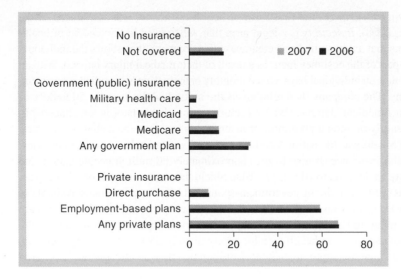

FIGURE 12.3
Percent of U.S. Residents with Private, Public, and No Insurance Plans, 2006 versus 2007. Employer-offered health plans enroll the largest number of insured people.

Source: Adapted from U.S. Census Bureau (2007).

PRIVATE INSURANCE PLANS   Private health insurance plans in the United States consist of either indemnity, commonly called *fee-for-service,* plans or *managed-care* plans. Collectively, the private plans insure approximately 68% of the U.S. population (U.S. Census Bureau, 2007). As mentioned earlier, Blue Cross/Blue Shield was the first national private indemnity plan. In part for that reason it is referred to as *traditional indemnity health insurance* (see Figure 12.3).

Traditional Indemnity Plans   Individuals enrolled in traditional indemnity plans receive their health care from any provider they choose and are reimbursed 50 to 80% of the usual and customary cost of the service. The term *usual and customary* is critical to the plan and to understanding the cost of health care. Usual and customary means that the indemnity plan pre-determines the cost for each medical service, including the provider's fee, tests, medicines, and other costs. Thus, reimbursement of 50 to 80% of usual and customary costs does not mean reimbursement of 50 to 80% of the actual billed costs, since reimbursement rates for the same procedure can vary depending on the fee charged by the provider.

Indemnity plans impose no restrictions on individuals when choosing a care provider and similarly impose no limits on the provider for the type or frequency of health services offered (Fang & Rizzo, 2008). What does that mean? Consider, again, the case of Michelle in the opening story. If Michelle had been insured through a traditional indemnity plan rather than a managed care plan, she would not have encountered resistance from her neurologist when asking for tests to diagnose her problem. Indemnity plans allow for unlimited access to and use of medical services—limited only by the consumer's willingness to pay.

A health system that offers an unlimited choice of health care providers and services would seem optimal. Yet traditional indemnity plans are the most expensive of all health plans and are prohibitively expensive for the average wage earner. For that reason, traditional indemnity plans in the United States are used by only a small percentage of the insured population.

Managed-Care Plans   Private managed-care plans were first introduced in the 1970s by the Kaiser Corporation for its employees. Kaiser proposed the new system of health care as an alternative to the rising cost of health care under the traditional indemnity plans (Getzen, 2004). Unlike fee-for-service plans, managed care uses a system of tight controls to reduce the cost of health treatments. By reducing the cost of medical care, Kaiser passed the savings to members enrolled in their managed-care plan. Thus, the low costs made managed care an appealing and affordable health insurance option.

Consider again Michelle in the opening story. The neurologist denied Michelle's request for additional tests. The restriction on services is, in part, consistent with a managed-care company's goal of limiting their own financial risks and reducing the cost of care (Paharia, 2008). Yet, there are times when medical services, albeit costly, are necessary. In such instances health plans require either preauthorization or preapproval from plan administrators for the specific test. The preapproval process allows the system to limit unnecessary expenses. It also leads to managed-care plans being called "gatekeepers," monitoring and controlling the delivery of services.

Following the lead by the Kaiser Corporation, many managed-care organizations were subsequently established. Today, private managed-care plans take the form of either *health maintenance organizations (HMOs)*, *preferred provider organizations (PPOs)*, or *point of service (POS)* (see Box 12.2). All plans use similar methods of financial incentives and controls to encourage its members to use the health care providers associated with the plans and to encourage health care providers to avoid unnecessary health services (Gold et al., 1995).

For example, consumers are given financial incentives that encourage them to use managed-care providers or services. Consumers pay lower *copayments*, the part of the provider's fee paid by the individual, when using HMO or PPO providers or services. Managed-care plans also incentivize the provider. The incentives given to physicians are often unspecified, but in general, the plans encourage physicians to direct medical referrals to providers or services employed or owned by the HMO or PPO (Fang & Rizzo, 2008) and to limit the number of "unnecessary" medical procedures. As we saw in the opening story, however, the definition of "unnecessary" can be somewhat subjective.

Problems with Private Managed Care   Encouraging or even requiring providers and customers to use managed-care sponsored services is essential to contain health care costs. So is denying medical procedures thought to be unnecessary to treat an individual's health problem. Yet, research has shown that the practice of denying services introduced medical conflicts of interest between physicians and their consumers that caused problems for some managed-care systems and appeared to jeopardize individual health outcomes.

Specifically, research suggests that such incentives encouraged physicians to provide fewer medical services to the consumer even when such services were medically justified (Reschovsky, Hadley, & Landon, 2006). Consequently, the incentives cause two problems. First, a physician who knowingly refuses to authorize necessary medical services for a patient to maximize the provider's own incentives from an HMO or PPO is providing substandard or inadequate health care to the consumer, a violation of medical ethics. Second, if a consumer is denied needed health service, the physician's decision may contribute to that person's diminished heath status and, over a longer term, a diminished quality of life.

In the case of Michelle, while we cannot claim that the neurologist refused additional tests because of incentives from the HMO, we can state that without such tests Michelle would have continued to suffer with chronic head and ear pain, undoubtedly leading to a poorer quality of life. Research by Reschovsky and colleagues (2006) shows that a decrease in medical services negatively affects patients' perceived quality of care and also lowers their overall satisfaction with

BOX 12.2 Sample of Managed Health Care Systems in the United States

Name	Characteristics
Managed care	Private or public organizations
	Individual consumers must be members
	Health care provided by medical and mental health providers
	Fixed or reduced fee for service
	Monthly or annual health insurance premiums
Private managed care organizations	
Health maintenance organizations (HMO)	Health care providers employed by organization
	Hospitals, laboratories, and supplies owned or purchased by organization
	Individual consumers must be members
	Fixed or reduced fee when using HMO services
	Increased cost for non-HMO services
	Monthly or annual health insurance premium
	Additional services, tests, hospitalizations require preauthorization or preapproval
Preferred provider organizations (PPO)	Subcontract with health care providers
	Providers negotiate reduced fee to be paid by organization
	Individual consumers must be members
	Fixed or reduced fee when using PPO providers
	Increased cost for non-PPO
Point of service (POS)	Hybrid HMO and PPO
	Allows members to use out-of-network providers
	Higher copayments apply
Public Managed-Care Organizations	
Medicaid	U.S. federal- and state-funded program
	Eligibility restrictions apply
	Membership based on income, disability, or related factors
Medicare	U.S.-sponsored program
	Care generally restricted to individuals 65 years or older with U.S. citizenship or permanent resident status. Exceptions may be granted depending on the medical condition or type of care required.

their health care. Thus, as we will see shortly, decreased satisfaction also has a direct impact on an individual's overall well-being.

No one would disagree with managed care's efforts to limit increases in health care costs, especially now when spending on health care is escalating. The incentive system, however, put health care providers in a difficult position: They could either request medical services for the consumer in spite of strong messages from the system to eliminate "unnecessary" medical services or deny services and receive an incentive. Current research suggests, however, that changes to the managed-care systems that resulted in new procedures beginning in 2004 now show no difference in access to additional health services for individuals in managed care compared with those in fee-for-service plans (DeLaet, Shea, & Carrisquillo, 2002; Haas et al., 2002).

PUBLIC (GOVERNMENT) HEALTH PLANS   People who cannot afford private plans may qualify for public health insurance programs sponsored by federal and state governments. As of 2007, approximately 20% of the U.S. population was insured through a government-sponsored health insurance program, such as ***Medicaid*** for low-income and disabled individuals; ***Medicare*** for individuals over 65 years of age who also qualify; and health coverage for military personnel and veterans (again, see Box 12.2).

Publicly sponsored and funded plans are also called single-payer plans because one agency, in this case the U.S. government, provides the sole financial support. For the moment it is important to note that in all other developed countries, including Canada, England, France, and Sweden, a single-payer health care model is the norm for the majority of the populations. While private insurers also offer health insurance in these countries, the vast majority of people in the industrialized countries mentioned above and others rely on the government-sponsored managed-care plans for their primary source of care. We discuss the single-payer system in the section on health policy later in the chapter.

THE UNINSURED   With access to either public or private health insurance plans in the United States, it would seem inconceivable that anyone would be without health insurance. But, as of 2007, approximately 45.7 million people were not insured by either system. How is that possible? Consider this: Some of the uninsured earn too much to qualify for public insurance plans, but they make too little to afford the annual premiums required by private health companies. And, there are some who, as we noted previously, believe that health insurance is not necessary. We demonstrated earlier that the absence of health insurance poses real health and economic problems for the individual. But, it poses unique problems for the community and the country as well. When uninsured people forego timely and necessary medical care they pose potential health risks to the larger community.

Consider this: An individual without health insurance may postpone medical care for a painful sore throat lasting almost two weeks. Chances are that by delaying treatment the person will inadvertently share the illness with others, regardless of whether others have insurance or not. Untreated illnesses, especially contagious illnesses, increase the risks of illness for other people.

If the sore throat remains untreated, the infected individual may also find that what was once a simple bacterial streptococcal infection that could have been easily treated with antibiotics has become rheumatic fever, a disease that could lead to problems of the heart valves. Now, instead of simple treatments with antibiotics, the uninsured individual is in for a much longer course of treatment and possible hospitalization.

Who pays for the treatment or hospitalization for the uninsured? In short, everyone. Hospitals are required to treat and even admit, if necessary, all individuals who present themselves in need of care, regardless of ability to pay. But, when a patient is unable to pay, hospitals must shoulder the cost of the treatment. Some of the cost is absorbed by the hospital, but some is also borne by individuals through higher insurance premiums that are paid to institutions such as hospitals to pay for unreimbursed medical care for uninsured individuals.

THE COMPONENTS OF COST   We noted earlier that Kaiser introduced managed-care plans in response to the high cost of health care. Yet, current statistics show that health care costs are rising again. Merlis, Gould, and Mahato (2006) report that, between 2001 and 2002, 13 million U.S. families (approximately 11% of all families) noted that their direct, out-of-pocket medical cost met or exceeded 10% of their annual incomes, an increase from 8% of incomes in 1996–1997. Ten percent of one's annual income may indeed lead some individuals to view health care as a luxury.

Others access affordable health plans through the workplace, that is, through employers. Although individuals may purchase health insurance plan for themselves or their families independent of their workplace, such plans are considerably more expensive than employer-sponsored plans. Consider this: If purchasing health insurance independently, not through an employer, the monthly *health care premiums* for a 30-year-old single female with no health problems, no outstanding health conditions, and no history of smoking can range from $300 to $850 per month. The higher end of the range equates to 21% of an average individual's monthly income before taxes. And, the monthly premiums only provide access to a network of health care providers. They do not include copayments or the additional out-of-pocket costs such as medicines that, as we noted earlier, accounted for 10% of some families' incomes in 2002.

Yet, even the price of health insurance plans obtained through the workplace is increasing. According to the Kaiser Family Foundation Report (2008), health insurance plans offered by employers rose from an average annual fee of $5,791 for a family plan (two adults and children) in 1999 to $12,680 in 2008, an increase of approximately 120%. The point here is that while workplace insurance plans are more affordable, they are not inexpensive. A comparable plan purchased outside of the workplace, however, would cost approximately twice as much or approximately $25,000, an unlikely prospect for many middle-income workers.

Before concluding that workplace health plans are the best solution for providing health insurance for all workers, consider this: There are three fundamental problems with employer-sponsored health plans. First, not all employers offer health insurance plans. Federal, state, and local agencies, and private businesses are under no obligation to provide health insurance benefits to their employees. What is more, many businesses cannot afford to offer health insurance plans. As explained in Box 12.3, rising health insurance premiums adversely affect both the employer and the employee. When available, many workers consider employer-sponsored health care plans to be both convenient and economical. It is important to restate, however, that workplace health insurance plans are not available to all.

A second limitation to workplace-sponsored health programs is that many employers set eligibility requirements. Employers may require employees to complete a minimum number of days or months of work before qualifying for the benefit. Others maintain waiting lists. Being employed does not ensure that an employee will be eligible to enroll in workplace-sponsored health insurance plans.

Finally, for some individuals the cost of the employer-sponsored health benefit is beyond their means. While eligible for health benefits they, like the young adults described earlier in

BOX 12.3   Businesses Cannot Afford Health Care Plans?

The Kaiser Employee Health Benefits Survey estimates that approximately 63% of the employees included in their study worked for private corporations that offered health benefits. And, of those companies, approximately 90% of the employees are enrolled in managed-care plans. If the plans are so popular, then why do businesses claim they cannot afford the plans?

The issue of affordability of plans pertains largely to small, private businesses that employ fewer than 50 people. When employers provide health benefits, the employer as well as the employee contribute to the monthly premiums. For example, the total cost of health care premiums for one year for an employee and his or her family could be approximately $12,600 (Figure 12.4). Typically the employer will pay two-thirds to three-quarters of that cost, approximately $9,300 per year, while the employee pays the balance of $3,300 per year. It may be apparent by now that in order for the employer to pay annual premiums for all eligible employees, in addition to employees' annual salaries, the company's gross income must be sufficient to afford the added expense. Many small businesses do not have gross incomes large enough to pay the employer part of the health premiums. Therefore, many small companies cannot afford to offer health care insurance.

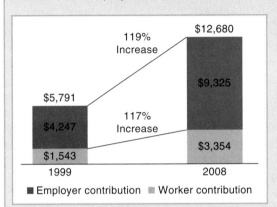

FIGURE 12.4   Average Health Insurance Premium and Worker Contribution for Family Coverage, 1999 to 2008. The cost of health care has risen for both employer and employee, in some cases more than 230%.

Source: Adapted from Kaiser Family Foundation (2008).

the chapter, may determine that health insurance is an unaffordable luxury given the mandatory costs associated with daily living expenses. In such instances, health care may be viewed as an unaffordable option.

In sum, the most affordable health care plans are offered through employers. But, some of the 45.7 million uninsured are employed at businesses that do not or cannot afford to offer health care, or that set eligibility criteria that exclude some employees. Still others cannot afford the employer-sponsored health plan even if they are eligible.

The employed but uninsured, together with the unemployed and self-employed who cannot afford health care insurance, account for the approximately 15.3% of the U.S. population without a health plan (U.S. Census Bureau, 2007). In light of the large number of uninsured, many health care professionals ask whether a single-payer system such as those offered in Canada, England, or France might help solve the health care crisis in the United States. Remember, lack of access to care often leads to future long-term and chronic health problems.

SECTION III. NEGOTIATING THE SYSTEM

Undoubtedly Michelle, the woman in the opening story, is pleased that she has a health care plan that gives her access to a network of health providers and health services, all of which comprise the health system. But her story demonstrates that access to care does not insure quality care. In fact, at times it is necessary to negotiate with providers or others in the system to obtain the expected quality of care. To improve her quality of care, Michelle tried to negotiate two important changes. First, she asked for a referral and for neurological tests, and second, she requested a change of doctors. By requesting specific health services, Michelle became an active participant in her own health care rather than a passive recipient of services. Later in this section we will see that individuals who are active participants in their own care tend to have better health outcomes.

Michelle also negotiated to change her health care providers when it was apparent that her original providers were not responding to her as an active partner. Thus, by being an active participant, someone involved in the decision-making process, Michelle also improved her quality of care.

Transitioning from a passive to an active participant in one's care and changing one's care provider requires that an individual knows the rules of the system and can effectively negotiate the system to his or her advantage. Consider this analogy: After selling a car, the dealer or seller usually reminds the new owner to read the manual cover to cover. Few people actually do; many flip through the thick handbook to familiarize themselves with the features they will need and a few other interesting details. In the same way, individuals should flip through the health care system "handbook" to learn how to use the system effectively, particularly when encountering problems. Michelle may not have reviewed the health care manual for her HMO in its entirety before her dilemma, but no doubt she referred to the manual after her stay in the emergency department, to determine how to change service providers.

By comparing the body to a car, we intend only to reinforce the point that we should give our body the same quality of care and attention that we give other things, such as the cars we rely on for our daily functioning. A poorly maintained car will not start reliably or when needed. Similarly, a body in poor repair will not allow us to function appropriately. We should take care to select, obtain, and maintain the services needed to function. As part of our self-servicing, we may need to negotiate for improved care.

All negotiations involve communication. Studies on the ***consumer–provider communication*** process show that two factors, the quality of the communication and consumer satisfaction, significantly influence health outcomes. We begin this section, therefore, with a review of the research on consumer satisfaction, followed by a discussion of the effect of consumer–provider communication on health outcomes.

We add one note before continuing. In health, many researchers and providers refer to "patient satisfaction" and "patient–provider communication." We substitute "consumer" for patient in this section to reinforce the concept of the individual as an active participant in his or her health process. By redefining the individual as a consumer of health services, rather than the passive recipient of health care ("patient"), we conceptualize the consumer as someone who must be engaged and satisfied (Vouri, 1991). As we will see, engaging consumers in the care process increases their understanding of the problem and increases adherence to the recommended procedures, a process that should improve health outcomes.

Consumer Satisfaction

DEFINING SATISFACTION   Consumer satisfaction has been defined variably by health psychologists and medical researchers. For our discussion, we adopt Johannson, Oleni, and Fridlund's (2002) definition of *consumer (patient) satisfaction* as a comparison between a person's subjective assessment of his or her expectations regarding care and that person's perceptions of the actual care received. The actual care received is measured by the consumer's emotional and cognitive interaction with the provider.

Michelle expected to receive high-quality care from her first doctor given his years of experience, his affiliation with an excellent teaching hospital, and his ten years serving as her primary care provider. As a result of poor consumer–provider communication with Dr. B. (discounting Michelle's complaints), and her dissatisfaction with the neurologist (unwillingness to authorize additional medical tests), it seems accurate to characterize Michelle as an unsatisfied consumer.

MEDICAL PROVIDER, EMOTIONAL INTELLIGENCE, PERSONALITY, AND DEMOGRAPHICS
Studies examining consumers' satisfaction with medical care providers focus primarily on satisfaction with physicians. Research suggests that consumers assess three factors when determining their degree of satisfaction: physician characteristics, physicians' interpersonal skills, and overall service. Of these factors, however, the studies also show that consumer satisfaction is most strongly influenced by one physician characteristic—the physician's emotional intelligence—and by the consumer's trust in the physician (Thom, Hall, & Paulson, 2004; Weng, 2008).

It may seem strange to include emotional intelligence as a relevant factor in consumer satisfaction, but consider this: When ill, individuals may believe that a doctor's ability to understand and manage people is critical to their belief that the doctor is able to address their concerns. In this way, the concept of emotional intelligence is similar to earlier notions of social intelligence (Mayer & Salovey, 1997). Another example may help illustrate the point. Consider this scenario: A consumer phones her physician complaining of sinus pain. When she walks into the office, the doctor notes immediately that she walks slowly, as if stepping lightly, and that her head is tilted to one side. The doctor comments to her, " It is easy to see that you are uncomfortable even if you had not phoned." The doctor's expression of emotion conveys to the consumer an understanding that something is wrong and that it is causing pain. It appears that the expression of emotion increases the consumer's satisfaction with the provider.

Looking again at Weng's (2008) study of emotional intelligence and consumer satisfaction we find that physicians who were rated high on four factors—appraisal (here meaning assessment of the situation or the consumer), expression of emotion in oneself and others, regulation of emotion, and the use of emotion to facilitate performance—were more likely to be rated higher on trust and on consumer satisfaction. We can test part of Weng's findings using our opening story with Michelle. Clearly, the neurologist showed limited appraisal when he determined that Michelle's head pain was consistent with her gender and age. Put it this way: Telling a 50-year-old woman that her pains are age related may be easily understood. Saying, however, that one's gender explains head pain is illogical. It may also seem insensitive, because it could be viewed as a gender-biased view of women.

Michelle's primary physician was deficient in emotional expression when he performed the same basic examination each time Michelle complained of head pain. He offered no response that would indicate he was aware of the lingering problem or the distress it was causing Michelle.

It is not every day that a physician hears someone say that removing one side of her head would make her feel better. Perhaps, then, some expression of emotion is an appropriate part of a doctor's medical treatment.

Other studies suggest that aspects of the provider's personality also contribute to consumer satisfaction. Duberstein and colleagues (2007) used several measures of patient satisfaction in addition to consumer's assessment of physician's personality, to assess health care consumers' perception of their physicians. With respect to personality, consumers used McCrae and Costa's (1987) five-factor personality model to rate their physicians on neuroticism, extraversion, openness to new experiences, agreeability, and conscientiousness. Duberstein and colleaues (2007) found that those physicians who were rated high on openness to new experiences and conscientiousness were rated higher also on trust and were more likely to have consumers who were highly satisfied with both their physician and their health care.

Finally, two specific demographic factors add to consumers' satisfaction with their health care provider: age and experience. In point of fact, the two factors may be related. Experience is, in part, a function of age. Studies by Malcolm, Wong, and Elwood-Martin (2008) in Canada suggest that some patients consider level of experience of medical providers when determining whom to consult. Consider this: At teaching hospitals in Canada (in the United States also), medical residents often accompany the primary care physician when seeing patients. Malcolm and colleagues report that one reason, albeit a minor reason, why patients refuse to allow medical residents to be present during the visit is the residents' inexperience. Thus, experience for some is an important prerequisite to determining whether another doctor should even be present during the visit. Similar findings were reported in Pakistan. Saleem, Khalid, and Qidwai (2009) noted that among geriatric patients, physicians' knowledge was one of several factors that predicted patients' satisfaction with their medical care provider. We must point out that these two demographic factors also governed Michelle's initial choice of Dr. B. as her primary care physician. But, her case demonstrates that a provider's age and experience may not always enhance consumer satisfaction.

HEALTH PROVIDER AND SERVICE FACTORS The provider's characteristics affect consumer satisfaction, but so does the health care setting. Here, we define "setting" as the physical environment as well as the health management process. Studies suggest that setting factors such as consumer wait times, efficiency of medical staff, and the range of services provided all contribute to the perception of satisfactory care (Kendro, 2008). What is more, efficiency and range of services are determined to be important regardless of whether they are provided in a physician's private practice offices or in hospital emergency departments. In a nationwide study conducted in 28 hospital emergency departments, Ragin and her colleagues (2005) found that one reason why consumers sought care from a hospital emergency medical service for a nonmedical emergency was because they preferred the emergency department over other health care facilities. Participants further explained their preference by noting that they perceived they received better medical care, and had access to a range of services and to staff who spoke their language (if applicable). They also believed that the emergency department offered a better overall health environment.

In sum, consumers assess a range of factors when determining their level of satisfaction with their health care provider. Some, like Michelle, focus on the personal characteristics of the provider, like age or experience, while others may include the provider's emotional intelligence, personality, and the setting of the health services as critical to overall satisfaction.

Consumer–Provider Communication

Consider the following scenario: A medical care provider walks into an examining room preparing to treat a young man who injured his shoulder lifting heavy crates. When the health provider enters, she does not make eye contact, mutters her name, and begins examining the man's eyes, nose, throat, and ears before asking what brings him to the office today. What is wrong with this approach?

No doubt a thorough physical exam should include the eyes, nose, and ears. But, it seems strange, perhaps even unnecessary, to begin an examination by examining the senses (eye, nose, ears) especially when the medical problem appears to be a shoulder injury. If the process seems strange to us, what might the young man think? No doubt he would wonder why the health provider is looking in all the wrong places. In addition, however, he might wonder what happened to "Hello" or "How are you feeling?" the more customary opening greetings one expects when initiating a conversation. Finally, the young man may wonder whether the health provider will pay attention to his specific problem or whether his care will be routine and indistinguishable from other consumers that day.

A greeting followed by a minute or less of general conversation can offer providers more information about the consumer's physical and emotional state of health and the reason for the visit than carefully scripted and practiced clinical questions or lab tests (Kreps, 2002). While it is true that the ability to engage well with individuals may evidence good manners, another reason for establishing a rapport with consumers is to maximize the likelihood that a positive interaction will help both the health provider and the consumer identify the health problem and agree on a course of action that will improve the health status of the consumer. Health psychologists, with their combined knowledge of interpersonal interactions and health issues, are well prepared and able to establish a good rapport for the purpose of advancing individual health outcomes. Health psychologists can also assist health care providers in developing the interpersonal skills that improve consumer–provider communication.

Studies on consumer–provider communication also identify psychosocial factors, similar to the consumer satisfaction variables we reviewed earlier, as critical to good communication. For example, in their study of Latina and Asian domestic abuse victims, Rodriguez, Bauer, Flores-Ortiz, and Szkupinski-Quiroga (1998) found that women preferred physicians who listened attentively, offered advice and support, demonstrated understanding, and were kind hearted. Their results showed that psychological and emotional support was essential for establishing trust in the provider, allowing women to communicate openly with their provider, and for improving the likelihood of the women adhering to medical advice.

Other studies examining consumer–provider communication in the context of medical decision making find that here, too, psychosocial factors are important. For example, in a study involving cardiovascular disease and decision making, Collins, Clark, Petersen, and Kressin (2002) identified four areas of communication that were critical for patients to maximize their comfort and to select a cardiac treatment procedure: trust; belief in the necessity of the procedure; full, complete, and clear information; and, finally, consistent recommendations (Collins et al., 2002). Trust in the physician, a psychosocial factor, was important for all patients but particularly for African American patients, who preferred to build a trusting relationship with their provider before agreeing to any procedure.

Remember Michelle, from the opening story? Researchers list active participation as yet another factor that is instrumental to establishing good consumer–provider communication and that also affects health outcomes. Studies show that patients who are less involved in the consultation process and who receive less information and support from their physician tend to be less satisfied with their care, tend to understand less about their health and possible treatment options, and tend to be less likely to follow medical advice (Esch, Marion, Busato, & Heusser, 2008). We pause for a moment to underscore that less involvement in each of these areas means that a person is less likely to accept and use the medical advice given by the provider. It is not surprising that the combination of these factors leads to poorer health outcomes (Bullman & Svarstad, 2000; Gordon et al., 2005; Ong, deHess, Hoos, & Lammes, 1995) (see Figure 12.5).

One final point: Although we are told many times to ask questions when we do not understand something, studies show that remarkably few consumer ask questions about their most pressing health concerns. Kirscht (1977), in reviewing the early literature on "patient"–provider communication, noted that consumers avoided asking questions either for fear of being seen as ignorant or due to concerns that they may delay a busy physician with their questions.

Other research on consumer–provider communication suggests that another reason individuals may not ask questions may be that they are not aware that they do not understand the information given. Sounds incredible? Consider this: In a study of consumers' understanding of the discharge information and medical care instructions given after a visit to a hospital emergency department, researchers discovered that fully 78% of the persons discharged indicated that they did not understand the discharge care instructions. What is more, over 50% did not know that they did not understand the instructions (Health & Hospitals Network, 2008). Even when individuals are in less emotionally charged environments, receiving information about their health condition in nonemergency medical settings, researchers suggest that individuals still

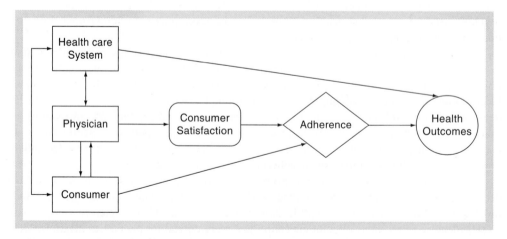

FIGURE 12.5 The Impact of Communication on Health Outcomes. Health outcomes are influenced directly by the health care system and the consumer, but also indirectly by psychosocial factors including consumer satisfaction.

have a limited ability to process and recall negative news about their health (Hadlow & Pitts, 1992; Lerner, Jehle, & Janicke, 2000).

It is important to state that communication is a two-way street, and misunderstandings concerning medical diagnosis and care instructions involve the physician also. We will address the physician-related communication issues in the following section. For now, however, the main point is that consumers are subjected to a number of psychosocial factors that inhibit their ability to be fully conversant about and to understand aspects of their health condition. Whether consumers are self-conscious of their lack of medical knowledge, lack self-efficacy in becoming an active participant in their health, or are reacting to the personality characteristics or style of the provider, if they do not understand their condition or the medical advice given are less likely to follow medical advice and therefore have poorer health outcomes. Improving communication, from both ends of the process, is essential to enhancing health (again, see Figure 12.5).

We need to add one final point about consumer–provider communication. Many studies identify racial/ethnic background as a contributing or inhibiting factor in the communication process between consumer and provider (Ashton et al., 2003; Cooper-Patrick et al., 1999). A number of studies cite race/ethnicity as barriers to effective communication between consumer and physician (Institute of Medicine, 2002; LaVeist & Nuru-Jeter, 2002; Saha, Komaromy, Koepsell, & Bindman, 1999), while others suggest no significant effect (Lasser et al., 2005; Stevens et al., 2005). But studies that cite race/ethnicity as a barrier note specific differences in the communication patterns between consumers and providers of different race/ethnicities that interfere with the communication process. For example, Gordon and colleagues (2005) demonstrated that white physicians initiated less sharing of information with African American consumers, while African American consumers were less likely to initiate active participation in their own medical care than did white patients. A passive communication style both by physicians and consumers in cross-racial interactions will result in overall poorer health status due, in part, to the consumers' inability to understand their health problems and consequently their reluctance to adhere to the recommended health regimen.

Trust

An additional and important factor regarding race/ethnicity and consumer–physician relationships (including communication) is trust. Collins and colleagues (2002) stated that, before making decisions about their health care, African Americans in their study felt it essential to establish a level of trust with their health provider. When introducing that study, we did not mention that for many minorities, African Americans in particular, there is a long and deep-seated mistrust of the medical community and of medical providers (see Figure 12.6).

Much of the mistrust is rooted in a history of medical malpractice or questionable medical procedures conducted on African Americans. The Tuskegee experiment, explained in Chapter 2, Research Methods, is one of the worst examples of medical malpractice. Yet other and more recent examples continue to fuel the sense of mistrust of the health community by African Americans.

The Institute of Medicine's (2002) report on the unequal treatment of minorities by the health professions adequately documents the current experiences. While there is no immediate remedy for the decades of medical mistrust, this psychological factor cannot be overlooked when addressing the health needs of African American consumers. For health psychologists, the challenge

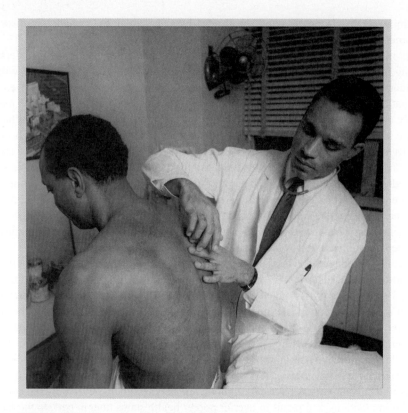

FIGURE 12.6   Consumer–Provider Relations. Trust in one's health care provider is an essential ingredient for improving health outcomes.

is to use our considerable knowledge of psychology and health to rebuild the lost trust and to help both groups work together to improve the health status of African Americans.

SECTION IV. CHALLENGES FOR HEALTH CARE PROVIDERS

We have identified several consumer-related factors that may contribute poor consumer–provider communication. Some of these factors involved an interaction between the consumer and the physician. Here, however, we focus on the providers and their unique contributions that directly or indirectly affect outcomes. And, although the focus is on the health provider in this section, it is important to remember that the physician is often the "face" of the health care system to the consumer. Thus, the physician also represents the health system.

Physicians' Three "Fatal" Communication Errors

The "fatal" communication problems we address in this section rarely cause the death of a consumer. They may cause some health setbacks or delay the recovery process. At worse, they may end a consumer's relationship with their care provider, as in the case with Michelle and her primary care physician in the opening story. In this section we focus on three physician-related communication errors and their consequence not only for the consumer–provider relationship but also for the consumer's health outcomes. The errors addressed here are medspeak, limited face time with consumers, and nonverbal communication miscues.

Medspeak, a term first coined by Christy (1979), describes health providers' use of medical terminology, sometimes called medical jargon, when speaking with consumers. It is important to point out that there is nothing problematic with medical providers using medspeak among themselves. It serves as an effective shorthand for communication among providers. The problem occurs when medical providers use the same medical jargon when communicating with patients. Are medical providers oblivious to the medical knowledge gap between providers and consumers, or do they use medspeak purposely in those encounters?

Some researchers suggest that physicians may use medical jargon when speaking with consumers as a way of demonstrating their knowledge. Without a doubt, most consumers want a knowledgeable medical professional, but using medspeak is not the best way to demonstrate knowledge. Medspeak leaves patients confused about their own medical condition, intimidated about asking questions for fear they would appear ignorant in the face of such knowledge, and unwilling to converse freely with a provider. While medspeak allows a medical provider to demonstrate his or her superior medical vocabulary–not a very difficult task because many patients are clueless when they hear words such as *protein* or *sutures* (McKinley, 1975)—it increases the likelihood that the provider will miss opportunities to develop a rapport with his or her patient. In particular, when demonstrating their medical knowledge, the provider may be less inclined to demonstrate the emotional intelligence and understanding that contribute to individuals' feelings of satisfaction with their health provider and their health care. In sum, the negatives of medspeak outweigh any positives as a communication tool.

Interestingly, some research suggests that, in fact, the negative impact of medspeak may benefit the doctor who has limited time for each consumer or who would prefer not to explain an illness or procedure that challenges even the doctor's understanding. With consumers arriving for appointments throughout the day, providers compress the time spent with each person. Researchers suggest that providers in managed-care settings spend, on average, 13 minutes per person (Gottschalk & Flocke, 2005). Think about it. Can you explain your medical problems, fears, and concerns adequately in 13 minutes? And how much time does that leave the doctor to respond to your concerns? If pressed for time, some doctors may use medspeak to quickly express their observations and conclusions to the consumer. Having communicated the information, and with no questions from the confused but likely intimidated consumer, the provider can conclude the visit and move on to the next patient.

A more charitable explanation for the use of medspeak is that physicians overestimate consumers' knowledge. As we noted previously, consumers' medical vocabulary is usually limited. And, rather than indicate they do not understand, consumers may remain silent, giving the impression that they grasp both the diagnosis and the medical care instructions (McKinley, 1975; Mechanic, 1972). In such cases, medspeak may represent a misjudgment by the physician of the consumer's knowledge. Without questions from the consumer, physicians may be unaware that they are ineffectively communicating with the consumer. The lapse in communication may become apparent only later, when the individual does not comply with medical advice or delays returning for visits because of the lack of rapport with the physician. By now you know the health consequences of such outcomes.

Physician Miscommunication or Patient Inattentiveness

Some consumers leave a doctor's office believing that they did not receive a diagnosis. Is it possible the doctor did not tell the consumer his or her medical problem? Did the consumer forget, or is this another example of medspeak?

According to several studies there is real disagreement between physicians and consumers over the issue of effective communication of diagnoses. Early studies by Ley and Spelman (1965) and more recent work by Fried, Bradley, and O'Leary (2003) suggest that consumers often do not remember or misremember, meaning that individuals make mistakes when recalling the information or their diagnosis. Ley and Spelman compared participants' recollection of a recent health care visit with the provider's summary of the visit. Approximately 63% of the time, consumers accurately recalled the overall statement. However, 56% of the participants misremembered the doctor's specific instructions, and 27% erroneously reported the diagnosis. Thus, while consumers recalled the general gist of the visit, important details like instructions and specific diagnoses were not recalled or were recalled incorrectly between one-quarter and one-half of the time. If consumers misremember diagnoses about half of the time, then how likely is it they will adhere to the provider's instructions? Consequently, the likelihood for improved health outcomes is slim.

Current research by Fried and colleagues (2003) also suggests high error rates in individuals' recall. But even more telling, these researchers found that providers and consumers disagreed over whether a discussion about diagnosis ever took place. When comparing the consumer's and provider's recall concerning a poor health diagnosis, Fried and colleagues found that, in 46% of the cases, clinicians reported telling the individual about his or her poor prognosis, but the same individuals claimed not to recall the discussion.

Realizing that it may be difficult to hear distressing news about oneself, the researchers also tested the agreement in recall between providers and caregivers for the patient. The outcomes were marginally worse, with only 38% of clinicians and caregivers agreeing that such discussions took place.

What does all this mean? The lack of agreement about whether discussions occurred and the content of those discussions and the difficulty communicating about health issues and concerns suggest that consumer–provider communication is a complicated process that becomes more difficult when dealing with personal and perhaps emotional issues like one's health. In such instances, good communication skills are essential. This, then, is yet another role for health psychologists as an aid or facilitator in communications between provider and consumer.

The recent attention to interpersonal skills in medicine is due largely to a break from the more traditional, paternalistic approach of medicine in the United States (Teusch, 2003). In that model, the physician was considered the knowledgeable entity, and consumers were expected to comply with all medical directives without question. But, as we indicated earlier in the chapter, modern medical practices have evolved to view individuals as consumers of services and therefore as participants in their own health care. The new approach requires continued training of new health care providers on interpersonal skills, listening skills, and all forms of communication skills. Included in this new approach is a focus on nonverbal communication.

Nonverbal Communication Cues

More than 30 years ago, psychologists established that communication involves more than just the spoken or written word. Nonverbal signals, such as facial expressions, a touch, a gaze, or even a tone of voice also communicate information to the listener. Early research on ***nonverbal communication*** by psychologist Robert Rosenthal and his colleagues (1979) demonstrated that, in psychotherapy settings, counselors who were more sensitive to their own body's nonverbal communication were more effective with their clients than were counselors who were unaware of their nonverbal communication. Thus, according to this study, facial, body, and voice cues all conveyed information to the clients that was interpreted along with the counselor's verbal message.

Applying this research to medicine, researchers have concluded that nonverbal cues may also affect a physician's ability to establish a rapport with consumers. For example, a provider's body language can suggest impatience or an intention to leave imminently, which can be interpreted as a physician's lack of interest in talking with the consumer (Teusch, 2003). Other body language, such as fully facing the consumer when talking, using facilitative nodding, and looking at the consumer while both speaking and listening, are nonverbal body language cues that individuals attend to when rating a physician's interest in them and their health issues (Ishikawa, Hashimoto, Kinoshita, & Fujimori, 2008).

BOX 12.4   Introducing Difficult Topics

We indicated that communication is a two-way street. But who is responsible for introducing difficult or unanticipated topics, such as risky health behaviors or illicit behaviors that also affect an individual's health? For example, who should raise the subject of illicit drug use, dependence on sleeping pills, or unprotected sexual behaviors? Additionally, should the physician or the consumer raise concerns about an intimate relationship that is causing emotional distress (see Figure 12.7)?

Topics such as these tend to be avoided by many physicians. They are sensitive and can be embarrassing to both the consumer and the provider, not to mention just awkward to discuss. As we have discussed, however, health is more than one's physiological state. Emotional health, psychological health, and risky health behaviors all affect physiological functioning.

Research on adolescent health reveals that among that age group physicians rarely asked about teens' exposure to or experience with risky health behaviors. Fewer than half of physicians who treat adolescents initiated discussions or sought to counsel teens about risky sexual or substance use behaviors, although, as we saw in Chapter 5, Risky Health Behaviors, experimental risk behaviors begin early in the adolescent years. Studies by Klein, Wilson, and McNulty (1999) and Ziv, Boulet, and Slap (1999) suggest that less than 3% of adolescents report ever being asked about STDs or HIV/AIDS and less than one-quarter of adolescent boys or girls were asked or counseled about pregnancy prevention. More surprisingly, less than one-third of adolescents discussed mental health issues at their last physical health visit, a disturbing finding given our current understanding of the role of mental and emotional health issues on adolescents' overall well-being.

In truth, few would expect adolescents to initiate such discussions with an adult, especially if the adult is an authority figure or a virtual stranger. After all, adolescents are reluctant to admit to behaviors that are viewed negatively by society or that are illegal. Therefore, physicians or other medical care providers need to broach the topic to signal

(continued)

to adolescents that health settings are the appropriate place to talk about any—literally any—behaviors that influence health.

Current research by Mulvihill and colleagues (2005) suggests that adolescents who are given regular access to a health care provider trained to address such topics report a significant increase in discussions on risky and mental health behaviors. In their study on the SCHIP program, these researchers reported a 50% increase in discussions about mental health and even greater gains in discussions about STDs, HIV/AIDS, and other health risk behaviors. If the goal of health care providers is to reduce health-compromising behaviors and to increase the likelihood of health-enhancing behaviors, they should raise such topics even in the absence of physical or psychological symptoms. Raising the question indicates to adolescents that the provider not only expects to discuss such topics, but that such topics are appropriate in the context of a health care visit and that the provider is prepared to provide information and guidance on these issues in a confidential setting.

Training medical students and other health professionals about the importance of interpersonal communication style, including nonverbal communication, is one way health psychologists can contribute to more effective consumer–provider communication, a first step on the road to enhancing consumer health outcomes.

FIGURE 12.7 Good interpersonal communication, including non-verbal communication skills, are essential for everyone when addressing difficult topics.

In sum, consumer–provider communication is a complex process with many factors and many possibilities for error. Research by social and health psychologists suggests that provider characteristics and demographics (age and experience), consumer characteristics (active participant versus passive recipient), consumer demographics (ethnicity and gender), as well as the health care setting can contribute to miscommunication. A good rapport and good communication with one's health provider will improve a consumer's level of satisfaction with their health care. More important, it will increase trust and the likelihood that the consumer will adhere to the medical advice given: all of which ultimately affects health outcomes.

SECTION V. HEALTH POLICY

The term *health policy* can describe the system of rules and regulations that apply to managed-care organizations. In this section, however, we define *health policy* as the regulations on health behavior and health services designed to improve an individual's or community's health status. Government agencies, including regional and federal agencies, rather than health systems, are responsible for establishing and enforcing such policies.

In earlier chapters we identified a number of health policy initiatives by local and state governments. For example, the decision by over 24 states to prohibit smoking in restaurants, bars, and other public places is an example of a state health policy regulation to limit exposure to secondhand smoke, a known carcinogen. Additionally, new regulations introduced in New York City and California to post the calorie content of foods on menus in national chain restaurants with more than 11 establishments is a health policy initiative to educate individuals about the nutritional content of foods. The goal of this initiative is to decrease the rates of obesity and diabetes by increasing consumers' knowledge of the fats and calorie content of foods.

In this section, we focus on local and federal health policy that could affect health care delivery rather than changes in individual behaviors. Specifically, we examine two policy initiatives that, if adopted, could help improve access to and quality of care: preventive care–focused health plans, and single-payer health care systems.

Preventive Care

As we noted in Chapter 6, Emotional Health and Well-Being, Western medicine is based on the biomedical model, a reactive approach to health and illness. The model responds to illnesses or dysfunctions after they have occurred, but does not address, nor is it designed to address, ways of preventing illness or dysfunction.

Admittedly, many illnesses are unanticipated or unforeseen, and we will always need a system for responding to the unexpected. However, as we have seen in earlier chapters, other illnesses, especially chronic illnesses, are wholly preventable. Currently much of the responsibility for preventing illnesses such as obesity (see Chapter 5) or specific forms of cancer (see Chapter 11) lies with the individual. It is the case, however, that many individuals are unaware of the behaviors that put them at risk for chronic illnesses. Others may not understand that their preventive behaviors are insufficient to avoid the onset of illnesses. Take smoking, for example. Many smokers were unaware of the dangers of secondhand smoke until public health advertisements appeared in print media and on radio and television. When realizing the potential harm to family members who were nonsmokers, many smokers tried to make adjustments in their smoking habits. For example, when smoking in a car, the smoker would take pains to lower the window even in the coldest of weather. While admirable, their self-initiated efforts to reduce risks would have minimal effects. Educating consumers about the benefits and limitations of individually initiated preventive health behaviors is one way to achieve health behavior change.

It is important to note that some managed care plans do, in fact, provide continuing education to their members as part of a preventive care campaign. Pamphlets and informational brochures sent to managed-care plan members provide information about general health-enhancing behaviors as well as information about specific behaviors to improve knowledge. In addition, some managed care plans now offer *wellness visits*, annual physical exams to review the health status of an individual and to identify problems or potential problems in their early stages before they become severe.

The operative word here is *some*. Preventive care programs and wellness visits have not been implemented by all health systems. Without a health policy mandate that requires preventive care services, it is unlikely that all health care systems will adopt such a strategy. In addition, changing from the reactive health model (biomedical model) most prevalent in the United States to a preventive model requires more than voluntary change on the part of a few willing systems. Such a change requires concerted effort by government and private businesses.

Single-Payer Health Care System

In this section we explore differences in *single-payer* versus *multipayer health care systems*. Briefly, however, one difference between the single-payer health care system found in many developed countries versus the multipayer system in the United States is the conceptual difference in the concept of health care. A single-payer system fits a preventive approach to health care whereas, as we noted previously, multipayer systems are rooted more closely to a reactive approach to health and wellness.

We mentioned earlier that Canada, the United Kingdom (England, Scotland, Wales, and Northern Ireland), and France, along with all other developed countries, use single-payer health care systems that serve the health needs of the majority of their populations. But the system is implemented somewhat differently in each country.

The general concept of the single-payer system is shared by all countries. They seek to offer universal and comprehensive care without impediment to access (Munn & Woznick, 2007). A critical part of the goal, however, is to offer services at a low cost, all the while maximizing productivity of health care workers in the system. Yet in each country the administration of the universal system, even the supervision of medical services, differs.

In England, the National Health Service (NHS) is responsible for the administration of the universal system. The NHS owns the health care facilities and employs the doctors who work in the system. However, the delivery of care is managed by physicians clustered in primary care groups. The groups are organized according to geographic region and are located throughout the United Kingdom. Thus, the process of deciding and delivering medical care is made at the local level by physicians (Klein, 2001). Even though the majority of the population in the United Kingdom are registered with the National Health Service, there are also private physicians for individuals who prefer to receive their medical care from health care providers not affiliated with the national system.

By comparison, in the Canadian system, control of both the administrative and medical portions of the service are managed by local agencies, in other words, the territories and provinces in Canada. Each territory is able to establish its own set of procedures as long as they are consistent with the Canada Health Act, the national governing document that sets the general guidelines for the system (Munn & Wozniak, 2007). In Canada, while approximately 95% of the physicians are in private practice, about the same proportion of the health care facilities—such as hospitals—are publicly owned.

The point here is that there are many different variations of universal care. Each country developed the system that fits best with its larger government and culture. But, when examining the benefits of a universal, or single-payer system, one fact is quite clear: Preventive health care as a concept appears more consistent with single-payer rather than multipayer systems. Consider this: Multipayer systems of care, like the many managed-care organizations in the United States, assume that individuals will change health care systems several times over a 10- to 20-year period. For this reason, they are less vested in establishing and promoting wellness and preventive care programs because they assume some level of turnover in their membership (Hussey, 2005). Put another way, they focus on the short-term health needs of their members.

On the other hand, single-payer systems show less turnover in membership during the same period of time. Once enrolled in a single-payer system, members tend to stay for 20 or more years. It is important to note that the lack of turnover may be due, in part, to the lack of other good or affordable options. Whatever the reason, the absence of turnover encourages such single-payer systems to introduce and promote preventive care services because they will serve a relative stable population of clients for several decades. By focusing on preventive care the single-payer system also reduces health costs by early detection and early treatment of health problems.

When considering the two options, therefore, it appears that single-payer systems have two strong advantages. First, they provide unfettered low-cost access to care for all eligible individuals. Those truly in need of care, with urgent or emergency medical needs, are covered. It is true, however, that in some systems, like England, individuals may be placed on a waiting list for some services. Usually, however, these waiting lists are maintained for nonessential or elective care such as elective surgeries. Second, because individuals in universal health care systems remain for several decades on average, the system strongly promotes preventive health care as a concept and offers preventive care services as a regular feature of the system.

Does the system work? In an earlier chapter we cited a study by Banks, Marmot, Oldfield, and Smith (2006) comparing the health status of individuals in the United States versus those in England. The researchers were surprised to learn that English residents were reported to be in better overall health relative to Americans. Specifically, the study found that even the wealthiest Americans in the study had poorer health profiles than the average working-class English person. While there are many possible explanations, one conclusion proposed by the researchers was that the national health system in England, which provides individuals with unfettered access to care, gives even those of limited socioeconomic status better and more consistent health care and better health outcomes than comparable or even higher-income Americans. It would appear from this study that there may be some benefits to a universal health care system.

To be sure, the single-payer system has some disadvantages. We noted that consumers may be placed on a waiting list for some procedures deemed nonurgent or elective. Remember, however, that nonurgent can be a subjective judgment. Recall the research on knee replacement surgery in Chapter 6, Emotional Health and Well-Being. Researchers Toye, Barlow, Wright, and Lamb (2006) found that participants, decision to have knee replacement surgery was based primarily on their discomfort with being dependent on others and with their limited mobility. This is not to negate the psychological and emotional health consequences of the loss of one's independence. (We addressed these issues as critical to overall health in previous chapters.) Yet, in single-payer systems, these issues of psychological or emotional discomfort may not elevate the physical health problem to a level of urgent or necessary treatment. In countries with single-payer systems, it may be difficult to convince some individuals that their psychological or emotional health does not result in a higher placement on the waiting list.

Personal Postscript

HOW IS THIS CHAPTER RELEVANT TO COLLEGE AND UNIVERSITY STUDENTS?

If you are attending college or university, you may have thought that this chapter is not relevant to you at the moment. Many students are required to enroll in their university's health care plan, so you may feel that you are covered, at least for now. But what does "covered" mean? You may know where to go if you are feeling ill, but do you know what services are offered and whether any require a copayment from you?

You may want to take a few moments to review your school's health manual to acquaint yourself with the provisions of the health care service at your university. Pay specific attention to the answers to the following questions:

HOURS OF OPERATION

What are the hours of the health service?
Do you need an appointment for service or can you be a walk-in?
Are there emergency hours?

MEDICAL STAFF

What medical specialties are represented at the health service?
Are referrals possible if you have a medical condition not covered at the university's health service?
Are dental and optical care available through the health service?
Can you choose one physician as your primary care provider while at the university or are you randomly assigned to whomever is available?
Are mental health care visits included in the plan?

PAYMENT FOR SERVICES

Is there a copayment for services?
Can the copayment be billed to your term bill?
If you need a prescription, does the health service have a preferred pharmacist who fills prescriptions for students covered under the university's health plan?

HEALTH CARE SERVICES DURING VACATION

Is the health service open during vacations and semester breaks?

If you are away from campus but need medical care, are you still covered under the university's health policy?

This is not an exhaustive list of questions, but it will help you to begin the process of understanding the rules and regulations of your current health plan. Chances are you will have very few occasions to use your university's health services. When you do, however, you will be better prepared if you know the answers to these basic questions.

Important Terms

consumer   394
consumer–provider
   communication   404
consumer (patient) satisfaction
   394
copayments   399
fee-for-service plans   398
health care premiums   402
health care providers   393
health care system   393

health maintenance organization
   (HMO)   392
health policy   415
indemnity insurance   397
managed-care plans   398
Medicaid   401
Medicare   401
medspeak   411
multipayer health care
   system   416

nonverbal communication   413
point of service (POS)   399
preferred provider organization
   (PPO)   399
premium   397
single-payer health care
   system   401
traditional indemnity health
   insurance   398
wellness visits   416

Chapter Thirteen

The Health Psychologist's Role: Research, Application, and Advocacy

Chapter Objectives

At the conclusion of this chapter you will be able to:

1. Describe the health psychologist's likely role in developing the four education strategies used with individuals.
2. Identify and define six self-advocacy behaviors to monitor health.
3. Define and explain the health psychologist's role in developing program evaluations.
4. Define euthanasia.
5. Explain the ethical arguments supporting and countering euthanasia.

6. Define and explain community-based participatory research and programs.
7. Define the role of community advocates in improving individual health status.
8. Explain why health policy is a form of self-advocacy.
9. Identify and describe two health policies influenced by research on health and health behaviors.
10. Describe how health psychologists contribute to healthy workplace environments.
11. Identify two ways in which health psychologists can be health advocates.

OPENING STORY: JOHN AND AHMED: ASPIRING HEALTH PSYCHOLOGISTS

John and Ahmed share a common goal: Both want to pursue a career in health psychology. But when talking about the field they realized they had very different concepts of what health psychologists do. For example, John understood that health psychologists work directly with people, offering education and health intervention programs to improve an individual's health status. John is particularly interested in cardiovascular disease. He would like to work in a hospital out-patient clinic or community-based center, providing health information and guidance to individuals with heart disease.

For Ahmed, health psychology means health policy. His views on health psychology were influenced by his father, a public health advocate who worked closely with researchers to change their city's policy on free school lunches for high school students. Roughly 50% of the high school students in Ahmed's small town qualified for free lunches because their families' household incomes were below the poverty level. Yet on average less than 10% of students took school lunch daily.

A change in the city's policy made school lunches available to all students. School officials reported that since the change, 80% of students consumed a school lunch daily. Health researchers suggested that by removing the eligibility restrictions on school lunches, they unknowingly removed another barrier: the perceived stigma based on socioeconomic class associated with school lunches. Ahmed is fascinated by the complex interaction of human motivation and human behavior, particularly when it involves health. The response to the change in the school lunch policy is an example of just such interactions. His ideal job would be working in a department of health to develop policies that improve the health status of communities.

Are John and Ahmed thinking about the same profession? ∎

Although John and Ahmed seem to have different concepts of what health psychologists do, they are both correct. As John observed, some health psychologists work with individuals and small groups to improve health outcomes or to help people manage their health problems. John's concept is consistent with the work performed by health psychologists in the early years of the profession when the field focused primarily on individual and community health issues. They addressed the relationship between diseases and the ***psychosocial***, here meaning psychological and sociological, needs of individuals (Smith & Suls, 2004).

Recently, however, the scope of the field was expanded. As we explained in Chapter 1, An Interdisciplinary View of Health, consistent with changes in the concept of health, psychologists now also examine the effects of external factors such as the environment, health policies, and health systems on health outcomes. Currently, many health psychologists take an ***ecological*** view of health, consistent with the belief that an individual's health cannot be evaluated independent of his or her environment.

You have heard the term *ecological* before. In earlier chapters we explained that the ecological model examined the social, systemic, and environmental factors that contribute to health (Merzel & D'Afflitti, 2003). An ecological perspective also requires an interdisciplinary approach to the study and practice of health, drawing on work from epidemiology, medicine, psychology, public health, and sociology (McLeroy, Bibeau, Steckler, & Glanz, 1988).

The American Psychological Association's Division of Health Psychology has also adopted a view of health psychology that approximates the ecological perspective. In 2002, the Division of Health Psychology revised their mission statement to reflect the changed perspective. They now note that psychology serves as a "means for promoting health, education and human welfare" (American Psychological Association, 2004). In this context, "human welfare" refers to the cultural, economic, and organizational influences that contribute to an individual's health status (Smith & Suls, 2004).

Why is this relevant for individuals interested in health psychology? The expanded field has created more professional opportunities. As we will see in the current chapter, health psychologists now work in a variety of capacities, including working directly with patients with medical conditions, working with research teams designing health intervention programs or evaluating such programs, and working with health policy professionals. And this range of options is available to people who are trained as clinicians as well as researchers. For example, as part of their work on health policy, psychologist—clinicians as well as researchers—may advocate for the health needs of specific communities. Both types of training can be used also as preparation for careers in more specialized health or *allied health professions*, including physical or occupational therapy, social work, or even medicine.

In the current chapter we examine health psychologists' roles in four domains of health: individual, community, health care systems, and health policy. Through specific examples of the type of work health psychologists do in each of the major areas, we describe the breadth of the field and perhaps help you identify your area of interest in health psychology.

SECTION I. WORKING WITH INDIVIDUALS

Consider this example: a 45-year-old woman suddenly experiences extreme fatigue, excessive weight loss, and blurry vision. She makes an appointment with her physician to determine the cause of the symptoms. She learns she has type 2 diabetes (see Chapter 3, Global Communicable and Chronic Disease). She is instructed by her physician to change her diet. She also must check her blood sugar levels regularly and begin taking *insulin*, a hormone that helps release glucose (sugar) for the body's cells. The woman's doctor starts her on a regimen of oral medication but warns that if that is not effective in reducing her blood sugar levels she many need to receive daily injections of insulin. In effect, the woman is told to make major changes in her daily health habits immediately.

This is a large undertaking. And as is often the case, her physician is not able to devote the time needed to guide her through the many health behavior changes. Will the woman be able to significantly change years of health behaviors by herself to control the progression of type 2 diabetes?

Change is possible; however, effective change, one that slows disease progression or reverses the adverse effects, is almost impossible without the help of knowledgeable and trained professionals. In this case, the woman could seek assistance from an allied health professional, such as a therapist or nutritionist who works with patients to change their diet (Association of Schools of the Allied Health Professions, 2009). But health psychologists who also focus on nutrition and diet may be another resource for the woman. Health psychologists would use their knowledge about nutrition and diet along with their understanding of the psychosocial issues that influence health behavior change to assist the women in setting and maintaining her required new behaviors. Both health psychologists and allied health professionals, however, would be sure to devote time to educating the woman about her new condition.

Education

Working with an ***interdisciplinary*** team of health professionals, here meaning individuals from other fields, health psychologists often design education, training, and support programs to help individuals make and sustain changes to their health behaviors. There are, however, many types of education, training, and support programs. For example, education programs can be conducted through mass media advertisements; formal education programs in schools, clinics, or health seminars; or informal information sessions. It should come as no surprise that health psychologists can and do contribute to the development of all forms of health education programs.

MASS MEDIA ADVERTISEMENTS Mass media advertisements help raise awareness about a specific disease among large groups of potentially at-risk individuals. In fact, raising awareness is one of the principal goals of mass advertisements.

Remember social marketing, introduced in Chapter 4, Theories and Models of Health Behavior Change? Social marketing campaigns often begin with mass media advertisements. Consider, for example, a media campaign to increase awareness of diabetes. In such campaigns, brochures and posters may be used to identify the problem and the behaviors that control or prevent diabetes. The advertising campaign helps to provide basic information about the illness—such as symptoms, risk factors, or behavior modification—to large numbers of people in specific target groups who may be at risk for the identified health problem (see Figure 13.1).

What role do health psychologists play in developing such materials? First, it is important to state that psychologists often work on all types of advertising campaigns. Using their knowledge of human motivation, they contribute to advertising campaigns that motivate

FIGURE 13.1 Health Promotion Advertisement. This ad cautions parents on sudden infant death syndrome (SIDS).

individuals to purchase a product—perhaps a piece of clothing—or engage in a specific activity, like taking a trip. You encounter examples of advertisements that are intended to influence your behaviors every day.

Similarly, health psychologists involved in advertising campaigns to improve heath outcomes integrate their knowledge of human motivation, health behaviors, and health to design ads that motivate the targeted group to change behaviors or to purchase healthy products. Many health promotion ads are found in print media and television commercials. The number of health promotional ads has increased in the past three decades due, in part, to a growing emphasis on health-enhancing behaviors.

FORMAL EDUCATION PROGRAMS   Health education is also delivered in small group presentations in schools, clinics, or seminars (see Figure 13.2). The programs usually provide in-depth information about the disease and an individual's risk of contracting the disease, details not usually offered in advertisements.

Formal educational programs may be designed as a one-time event or may include multiple presentations spanning weeks or months. For example, Walter and colleagues (1992, 1993) designed and implemented an eight-week educational program to teach HIV/AIDS prevention to adolescents in a high school health class. The goal of the program was to educate adolescents about HIV/AIDS and the risky health behaviors that transmit the virus. Included in the eight-week program were role-playing exercises to help adolescents develop skills to abstain from sexual behavior or to negotiate safer sexual practices.

Educational programs that impart skills usually require more than a single session. It is not surprising, therefore, that Walter and colleagues (1992, 1993) chose to deliver their program over

FIGURE 13.2   School-Based Health Education Programs. Formal health education programs housed in schools may address many factors that influence individual health outcomes.

Source: Centers for Disease Control (2009).

several weeks. And, because the goal of the intervention study was to educate and to impart skills, it is also not surprising that the research team who developed the program included health psychologists, adolescent medicine physicians, cognitive psychologists, health educators, psychiatrists, and biostatisticians (see Box 13.1).

INFORMAL EDUCATIONAL PROGRAMS   Educational programs may also take place in informal settings (see Figure 13.3). For example, when Kelly and colleagues (1991) developed an educational program to teach gay men about HIV/AIDS and HIV prevention, Kelly chose to conduct the education campaign in a neighborhood bar patronized largely by gay men (see Chapter 4, Theories and Models of Health Behavior Change).

The researchers asked bar patrons to identify the "group leaders" or individuals most influential with regular bar customers. Kelly then recruited and trained the leaders to be health educators. The leaders were trained to use social marketing techniques (see Chapter 4) to initiate discussions about HIV/AIDS. They then used the discussions to promote the benefits of condom use as a form of effective prevention against HIV/AIDS.

The point here is that there are many ways to educate people about health, including mass media advertisements, formal group instruction in schools or other settings, or informal instruction like the conversations conducted in Kelly's study. Regardless of the educational approach or setting, health psychologists are often involved in developing health education, health research, or programs. Their research methods skills (see Chapter 2, Research Methods), together with their knowledge of human behaviors and health, are valuable when planning and implementing such programs.

FIGURE 13.3   Informal Health Education and Health Promotion. Informal health programs can be conducted in any setting, including a book store.

BOX 13.1   The Art of Negotiation

Consider the following scenario: Two adolescent boys, James and Eric, are at a party at a friend's house. They managed to join the party even though it was restricted to varsity sports team members and their guests. Because no one questioned them when they arrived, they decided to stay and look as if they fit in.

In one corner, a group of adolescents was chugging beer, another group nearby was playing video games, and a third group was outside smoking. James decided to watch and possibly play a video game. He did not drink and was not interested in smoking. Eric preferred to go outside. Before separating, they agreed to meet at the end of the party and drive home together.

When the party ended, Eric found James sitting on a sofa staring blankly into space. It was clear that James was drunk, something Eric did not expect. When he asked James what happened, James told him about feeling coerced to participate in a drinking game because two of the captains of the football team told him he had to drink if he wanted to stay at the party. Eric faced similar pressure from another group who teased him about not smoking, but he was not persuaded to smoke.

Do adolescents succumb easily to pressure from friends or acquaintances to experiment with health-compromising behaviors? Apparently so, according to studies by Walter and colleagues (1992, 1993). In an intervention project designed to teach student negotiating skills to avoid or negotiate safer sexual behaviors, Walter and colleagues delivered an eight-week course on HIV/AIDS prevention. Students received information about HIV/AIDS, its modes of transmission, signs and symptoms, and skills training to negotiate safer sexual behaviors. The students watched vignettes that depicted successful and failed negotiation scenarios on video. They also participated in role-play scenarios in the class to practice their negotiation skills.

At the conclusion of the class, most students believed they significantly improved their negotiation skills and were confident that they could use them effectively. They believed they would be able either to withstand pressure to engage in risky sexual behaviors or to negotiate safer sexual behaviors—with one exception. Responding in postintervention surveys, students indicated that they would not be able to effectively use their new negotiation techniques if they had consumed alcohol or other substances prior to the attempted negotiation. What is more, students reported that the pressure to engage in risky sexual behaviors greatest when attending parties where drinking and consuming other substances was the norm.

Is it realistic to tell students not to use substances at a party? Perhaps as realistic as assuming that James could withstand pressure to drink from varsity sports team captains, a group with whom he wanted to fit in. Walter and colleagues' findings clearly showed a willingness on the part of students to practice health-enhancing behaviors. It also identified real barriers that effectively limit students' ability to perform the safer behaviors.

SUPPORT GROUPS Support groups are another type of educational program in which the groups provide much of the health information (see Figure 13.4). Consider this: Weight Watchers, a well-known national organization that guides and advises individuals striving to lose weight, uses formal and informal group sessions to help individuals achieve and maintain weight loss. They contend that supportive networks are an important feature of any behavior change program because the groups contribute to the long-term success of the intended outcome.

Weight Watchers uses both traditional support groups as well as web-based assistance when working with people to attain their goals. For example, a person can elect to attend weekly Weight Watchers meetings at which participants weigh in at the beginning of the meeting and then

FIGURE 13.4 Aerobic Exercise as Part of a Weight Loss Maintenance Program. Running is a great individual aerobic exercise, but gym workouts work well in both individual and group exercise programs.

Source: www.pro.corbis.com/images/AX061044.jpg

share stories about successful or unsuccessful efforts to address their weight challenges. However, for people who either prefer not to or cannot attend sessions in person, Weight Watchers has created an online support service. Using the computer, people can still weigh in by reporting their weight online (note this is a self-report versus monitored and observed reporting) and receive immediate feedback of congratulations, encouragement, or helpful hints for doing better. In addition, online participants have access to a wealth of recipes and helpful suggestions from other members who also use the Web to share their experiences.

If this concept sounds familiar, it may be because in earlier chapters we reviewed research that explained the relationship between support groups and health behavior change (see, for example Chapter 10, Chronic Pain Management and Arthritis). Specifically, we explained that individuals who must adopt new health behaviors—such as increased exercise regimens to control joint stiffness due to arthritis—usually are more successful in initiating and maintaining such behaviors when they have supportive networks (Keefe et al., 2002; Martire et al., 2003). Research suggests that the psychological support from the groups enhance the chances of success in changing and maintaining the targeted behavior (Evers et al., 2003; Holland & Holahan, 2003).

Weight Watchers' support networks may be premised on such research. Through monthly meetings or online exchanges using the program's web page, Weight Watchers provides its members with information and support through social networks as well as other sources.

A reasonable question at this point might be, How are health psychologists involved in educational programs that involve social support? They contribute in two ways. First, they may help design and facilitate formal support groups, such as the Weight Watchers' group meetings. Second and equally as important, some of the research we identified earlier concerning the contributions of support networks was conducted by health psychologists. The research may be used by organizations that include support networks as part of their program's plan to achieve behavior change.

Evaluation of Interventions

We noted that health psychologists contribute to the design and implementation phase of health programs. Yet programs must be evaluated to determine their effectiveness in changing health outcomes. Here, too, we may find health psychologists working as members of a research evaluation team. For example, to determine whether 30 minutes of an aerobic exercise program will help individuals achieve weight loss, researchers would design an evaluation of the intervention that measures the program's stated goals (weight loss), the exercise techniques employed to reach the goals (aerobic exercise), individuals' adherence to the goal, and individual outcomes at the conclusion of the program. As trained researchers, health psychologists can use their research design and analysis skills to assess an intervention program's overall effectiveness in achieving its goals.

Most effective health intervention programs develop the evaluation plan at the outset. What is more, it is common to find that health psychologists who conduct evaluations are involved in the initial design of the study as well as the evaluation and planning process. When health psychologists design intervention programs, they pay close attention to the variables needed to measure change and to assess the program's success.

Consider the following example: Bayne-Smith and colleagues (2004) tested the effectiveness of the PATH Program, a new cardiovascular health program developed for adolescent girls in New York City. Their program consisted of vigorous aerobic and strength-building exercises, health and nutrition education, and lessons in physiology that emphasized the cardiovascular system. The goal of the study was to determine whether education, exercise, and dietary changes would result in improved cardiovascular health for the adolescents.

Bayne-Smith and colleagues (2004) measured the adolescents' weight, body mass index (the percentage of body fat to height; see Chapter 5, Risky Health Behaviors), blood pressure, and cholesterol level two weeks prior and two weeks after the 12-week program. Their results showed improvements in cholesterol levels, dietary habits, blood pressure, cardiovascular knowledge, and percent of body fat, all essential factors for improving cardiovascular health. The variables included as part of the program design are the same factors used to demonstrate the program's effectiveness in reaching its goal. Program evaluation is a task well suited to health psychologists.

Promoting Individual Self-Advocacy

Health psychologists also work with individuals on ways to monitor and enhance their own outcomes independently. The ability to effectively address one's own health needs is the first step in health advocacy. Thus, in this section we explore simple self-advocacy health techniques.

To be an effective health advocate for ourselves we must know our health history. Here we mean not just our own history, but the illness and disease histories of our first-degree (father, mother, siblings) and second-degree (grandparents, aunts, uncles) relatives.

Does this sound easy? It really is not. For example, perhaps someone told you that your maternal grandmother had heart problems. But does that mean that she had coronary artery disease (see Chapter 9, Cardiovascular Disease) or a birth defect of the heart? Or, if your paternal grandfather had a weight problem, was it caused by obesity or a thyroid disorder? The medical histories of family members may be incomplete. The origins of the problems can be misidentified. In some instances health histories may be unknown. For example, someone who is adopted may not know the medical histories of his or her biological parents. Finally, in some families, medical histories are considered personal information and therefore not to be shared.

While family members have the right to privacy concerning their health, information about common or recurring family health problems may help others in the family understand the health outcomes or anticipate potential problems. Consider this example: A 33-year-old woman experiences irregular bowel symptoms. She consults her physician who refers her to a colon specialist. The specialist performs a ***colonoscopy***, an examination of the large colon using a fiber optic camera. The exam reveals several small ***polyps***, small growths on the lining of the colon. The doctor removes the polyps and examines them to determine whether they are cancerous (see Chapter 11, Cancer). The polyps are benign, meaning noncancerous, but the doctor advises the woman to return in five years for a follow-up colonoscopy.

When relaying her experiences to her mother, the woman learns that her father, who died when she was a young child, had colon cancer. After telling her doctor about her father's illness, the doctor shortened the interval for colonoscopies to every three years from every five. Is there a connection between the health outcomes of the woman and her father's illness that led the doctor to change health care plans?

Given the genetic nature of some forms of cancer, there could be an association between the two health conditions. Most likely, the woman will be considered to be at higher risk for colon cancer given her father's illness and her own symptoms. In the absence of a family history of cancer, her risk levels would be lower. What is important here is that the father's disease and the woman's new symptoms signal a need for regularly scheduled colonoscopies at frequent intervals. Thus, family histories can inform the type or frequency of health care other family members should receive.

SELF-MONITORING   Family health history is one type of health advocacy activity. Another activity of involves self-monitoring, meaning a systematic process of checking health indicators such as weight, blood pressure, cholesterol, and other measures that could signal impending health problems. We discussed many of the risky behaviors that could create negative health outcomes in Chapter 5, Risky Health Behaviors. Here, we focus on simple and easy-to-obtain measures that allow individuals to monitor their own health status.

Weight Scales   In earlier chapters we discussed body weight management as one health-enhancing behavior. Weight management helps reduce the likelihood of obesity, diabetes, cardiovascular disease, and even some forms of cancer. Because weight management is an important health-enhancing activity, we might assume that many people would weigh themselves regularly. In fact, they do not. In an international study of scale obsessions, fast-food addictions, and obesity, researchers examined the self-weighing behaviors of individuals in 13 countries: Australia, Brazil, Canada, the Czech Republic, France, Hong Kong, Malaysia, Romania, Saudi Arabia, Singapore, the United Arab Emirates, the United Kingdom, and the

BOX 13.2   Modified Family Health History Form

Do you know your family's health history? See how many of the following questions you can answer about your family members.

Health condition	Mother	Father	Maternal grandmother	Maternal grandfather	Paternal grandmother	Paternal grandfather
Medical health conditions						
Alzheimer's disease						
Allergic rhinitis (hay fever)						
Anemia						
Anesthesia problems						
Arthritis (rheumatoid)						
Arthritis (osteoarthritis)						
Asthma						
Birth defects						
Bleeding problems						
Cancer (breast)						
Cancer (lung)						
Cancer (melanoma)						
Cancer (prostate)						
Cancer (skin, other than melanoma)						
Cancer (ovarian)						
Cancer (other)						
Depression						
Diabetes, type 1						
Diabetes, type 2						
Epilepsy						
Eye condition						
Glaucoma						

(continued)

Health condition	Mother	Father	Maternal grandmother	Maternal grandfather	Paternal grandmother	Paternal grandfather
Heart problems						
Heart disease						
High cholesterol						
High blood pressure						
Kidney disease						
Lungs						
Mental retardation						
Migraine headaches						
Miscarriages						
Stroke						
Thyroid disorder						
Tuberculosis						
Ulcer						
Other						
Behavioral health conditions						
Alcoholism						
Drug use						
Obesity						
Smoking						

United States. The results revealed that very few study participants reported frequent weight monitoring. While approximately 50% of American and French participants reported weighing themselves on average once per week, more than 37% of Singaporeans reported *never* weighing themselves (Amerinfo, 2008).

Because research suggests that frequent weighing is associated with better weight loss and improved weight management (O'Neil & Brown, 2005), infrequent monitoring poses at least two disadvantages. In the short term it results in less weight loss. In the long term it leads to a higher likelihood of chronic disease.

Exercise   The 13-country international study also noted that when asked about weight loss strategies, most individuals (for example, approximately 57% of Americans) choose controlling food intake as their preferred weight loss strategy. Indeed, limiting the intake of foods high in fats and calories will contribute to weight loss. Yet studies also stress the role of exercise in sustained weight loss. A 2005 study by Carels and colleagues revealed that individuals who monitored their exercise frequency reported increased and sustained weight loss.

The beneficial effects of exercise can be seen also in chronic diseases such as arthritis. Exercise minimizes the discomfort and stiffness often associated with forms of arthritis and increases mobility. Aquatic exercises and other water sports are particularly helpful for arthritis sufferers because they facilitate joint movement while minimizing discomfort. While some avid exercisers boast "no pain, no gain," for people with arthritis, water-based exercises take away the pain and ensure gain.

Self-Examinations   We discussed the benefits of breast self-examinations as a form of early detection for breast cancer in Chapter 11, Cancer. What we did not mention at the time, however, was the benefits of self-examination to monitor other forms of illnesses or diseases. Take for example skin cancer. Many individuals who enjoy sunbathing may not notice sudden discolorations or moles on their face or other parts of the body as they perform their regular hygiene. However, periodic self-examinations for skin irregularities could help detect early symptoms of skin cancer, should they appear.

We learned that while there will be an estimated 1 million cases of skin cancer in the United States, fewer than 100 cases will result in death (see Chapter 11, Cancer). Yet, with early detection, some of those 100 incidences might be prevented. In other words, self-examination for irregularities of any form is recommended to detect early warning signs of health problems. Self-examination, therefore, is another form of health self-advocacy.

Self-Review   Assume for the moment that you have carefully gathered information about your family's health history. You try to monitor your weight and make an effort to exercise regularly. You are reasonably observant of your health status, taking note of things that may signal a health problem. What else can you do?

Consider having an independent assessment of your health. An annual physical examination to confirm your opinion of your health or to explore any unusual findings is another form of individual health advocacy. An annual physical exam, or *wellness examination*, may help prevent unexpected health problems or detect and treat new problems as early as possible. Thus, annual exams are checkups: checking to ensure that all is well or to address new problems quickly.

There is one additional benefit of annual checkups: the opportunity to learn new strategies for improving one's current health. If asked, physicians will share information about new medical findings or recommendations that may help maintain or improve one's health status. For example, some individuals who exercise regularly may not see a change in their stamina or endurance within four to six weeks, as suggested by many exercise experts. Thus, in the annual exam, an individual might ask the physician for recommendations for new or different exercises.

Annual checkups also allow patients to learn about the risk of contracting illnesses or diseases common to family members. For example, if learning that two relatives, a first cousin and an aunt, both contracted breast cancer, the annual exam could be an opportunity for the individual to determine, in consultation with her health provider, whether the changed health status of relatives increases her own risks of contracting breast cancer. In essence, the annual checkup should be viewed as an opportunity to do two things: check on one's current health status and improve one's knowledge about health-enhancing behaviors and health risks.

We need to make one additional point. In Chapter 12, Health Care Systems and Health Policy, we noted that some individuals are reluctant to ask questions of their health care providers. They may be concerned about appearing medically uninformed or taking too much of the busy provider's time. Questions are a necessary part of learning about one's health. No health provider should be too busy to respond to questions. But, if a provider is truly too overwhelmed on a given day to respond to specific questions at that time, an individual should ask for a time when the provider would be available to have a fuller discussion, perhaps by phone. Physicians know that timely medical advice is also a form of health advocacy.

FINAL SELF-ADVOCACY   Irrespective of health habits and behaviors, there may be times when individuals experience debilitating physical health problems. For some, the problem occurs suddenly and without warning. Others may have experienced a gradual deterioration of their health over weeks or months.

Each person's response to debilitating illnesses or accidents will differ according to the person, their lifestyle, and their coping styles. Some may explore new studies about their illness, hoping that new treatments may better control or cure it. For such individuals, one strategy for coping with terminal or debilitating illnesses is to advocate for continued research on their specific illness. One well-known health advocate for a debilitating disease is Christopher Reeve (see Box 13.3).

Some know Christopher Reeve best for his role as Superman. Whatever name is used, it is a fact that Reeve became an active and effective advocate for stem cell research, a new and controversial research technique believed to be a vital tool for repairing spinal cord injuries. Reeve not only advocated for stem cell research, but he also established a foundation to help people who, like him, were disabled due to an injury to the spinal cord that resulted in paralysis.

OTHER ADVOCATES FOR ENDING LIFE WITH DIGNITY   Consider the following scenario:

> Every morning Emily awakes to the same thought: "I did not expect my life to end this way."
>
> Emily used to be an active, energetic, 67-year-old grandmother of two. She fondly described herself as "healthy as a horse." She was rarely sick, traveled frequently, and enjoyed regular outings to the pool and to the tennis courts. All that changed, however, when Emily was in a near-fatal car accident.
>
> Emily remembers little about the accident. She recalls driving home alone from an evening out with friends. It began to rain. At one point it was raining so hard that it was difficult to see the road. But Emily's biggest problem that night was neither the roads nor the rain: It was another driver. An oncoming car swerved suddenly as if to avoid an object in the road. As a result of the shift in direction the car was headed straight for her. There was no time to react. Emily remembers the head-on collision, but everything else is a blur.
>
> Now, six weeks after the accident, Emily is paralyzed from the neck down. She is unable to move her arms or legs. She spends her days either in bed or in a

BOX 13.3 Superman to the Rescue

Christopher Reeve may be best known for his Hollywood portrayal of the fictional character Superman (see Figure 13.5). In real life, however, his advocacy work on behalf of individuals with spinal cord injuries made him a true superman for many with the same disorder.

An avid equestrian, Reeve was performing in a sporting competition in May of 1995 when he fell from his horse. Reeve broke two vertebrae, which appeared at first to result in permanent paralysis, a loss of sensation and voluntary movement of his body below his neck (Christopher & Dana Reeve Foundation, 2009). Consistent with spinal cord injuries that originate at the neck region, Reeve was unable to move his legs or arms. Such conditions also compromise breathing functions. Therefore Reeve also relied on a ventilator to breathe (Mayo Clinic, 2009).

Many feared that Reeve would be dependent on a ventilator for the duration of his life. Many also predicted a poor overall quality of life for Reeve. It seemed, however, that Superman had other ideas. Having honed his skill as an advocate for many other causes, Reeve seemed determined to this time use his advocacy skills to improve health outcomes for him and others similarly afflicted.

After six months, Reeve was able to breathe for 15 minutes at a time without the respirator. But, according to reports, even before these signs of notable improvements, Reeve was beginning to work to advocate for research on spinal cord injuries.

From 1995 to his death in 2004, Christopher Reeve became the public face of advocates for spinal cord research. Specifically, Reeve and others pushed for increased funding for stem cell research, which appeared to be a vital link to understanding and repairing spinal cord injuries.

While spearheading the charge for research on stem cell, Reeve also championed causes to accommodate the needs of people with disabilities. For example, he worked with TEAM Sport to create athletic competitions that challenged athletes like him who

FIGURE 13.5 **Christopher Reeves as Superman.** A superhero on the "silver screen" and in real life.

(continued)

became disabled as a result of an accident. And he lobbied U.S. senators to enable people with disabilities to continue receiving disability benefits after returning to work.

Almost 10 years after his accident Reeve died of heart failure, one of several complications he developed in the aftermath of his fall. However, his legacy of promoting research with potentially lifesaving and life-enhancing benefits continues.

Reeve will remain a superhero in the hearts and minds of millions who benefited from his advocacy.

wheelchair and depends on her home health care assistants, who are with her 24 hours a day, to help her with all basic and bodily needs. Because speaking is difficult, Emily often prefers to communicate with a slight nod of the head. Most of the time she is silent.

Nighttime is perhaps the worse for Emily. Alone and lonely, she thinks about the active life she once led: the social gatherings, the tennis teams, and the summer parties. And although her family visits regularly, their visits are short due to Emily's limited communication ability. This is not the life Emily envisioned for herself. Emily feels the best outcome would be to end her life, but she is unable to communicate her strong desire because she cannot write and speaks only with great difficulty.

Like many others suffering from debilitating or terminal illnesses, Emily is having difficulty coping with her current existence (few who experience such paralysis call it a "life"). It appears that Emily is thinking about *euthanasia*, a word adopted from the Greek word *euthanatos,* which means "the good death." Euthanasia has been called "mercy killing" by some who see it as a dignified end to life. For others it is "another form of murder." To be sure, it is a controversial issue.

Dr. Jack Kevorkian is perhaps one of the better known advocates for euthanasia. And he, too, is controversial. Nicknamed "Dr. Death," Dr. Kevorkian pioneered a process that enabled patients suffering from an interminable illness or pain to end their life with the assistance of a physician. The procedure became known as *physician-assisted suicide*. He also developed a method which allowed patients to participate in the act without the assistance of others, known as *active euthanasia*. Kevorkian is credited (or accused, depending on your point of view) of assisting or enabling more than 45 patients to end their lives. While many question Kevorkian's motives, others support his belief that individuals should have the right to end their life in dignity. Emily's condition and her strong desire to end her suffering may be similar to many other patients who sought Dr. Kevorkian's help.

Euthanasia may seem like an unusual topic for a section on health advocacy. Most discussions of health advocacy focus on ways to improve one's state of health by, for example, improving access to good-quality health care or improving environmental conditions in communities, such as air or water quality. But advocates like Dr. Kevorkian suggest that an individual's ability to choose a dignified end to life is inherent in the definition of quality of life. He and others who hold similar beliefs support the right of individuals to choose not to endure years of pain, clinical depression, or other psychological problems that contribute to a poor quality of life.

The principal question concerning euthanasia appears to be whether it is ethical to require a person to live life in constant pain or suffering or whether it is ethical to permit that person to painlessly end his or her life. Consider this: In the majority of euthanasia cases, an individual is either terminally ill or, like Emily, suffers from a debilitating injury for which there are few, if any, life-enhancing treatments. According to advocates of euthanasia, the physical suffering together with the mental and emotional "pain" that accompanies the illness are sufficient reasons to allow individuals to choose a dignified end to their suffering. Others contend, however, that individuals can be helped to overcome the pain, discomfort, and depression by learning and using appropriate coping techniques.

It is impossible to determine which group has the more compelling claim. For the moment, however, we make the following two points. First, the right of individuals to die with dignity or for individuals to cope and live with challenging physical and mental health problems are two examples of health advocacy at work.

Second, health psychologists can contribute to the research and debate on euthanasia. Many psychologists would agree that anyone considering an early termination to his or her life, even those with terminal or painful illnesses, should first seek psychological and emotional support and counseling. Health psychologists working with such individuals can introduce coping techniques that may marginally improve a person's overall health and well-being. But they can also address the holistic health needs of a person considering euthanasia.

Advocates for euthanasia are aware that the act is illegal in most U.S. states. In fact, fully 47 states have passed laws that expressly prohibit physician-assisted suicide. Oregon is the only state to have passed a law allowing doctors to engage in physician-assisted suicide. In such cases, however, the physician can prescribe, but not administer, a lethal dose of medication for the patient. And the patient must be shown to be mentally competent to make the request (Public Broadcast Service, 1999).

Some see Oregon's law as precedent setting, potentially influencing other states to consider a similar law. Oregon's law also is an example of advocacy using public policy. We will discuss other uses of public policy to advocate for health later in the chapter.

EUTHANASIA AND MEDICAL ETHICS   The issue of euthanasia also raises concerns about medical ethics. Specifically, some wonder whether it is ethical for physicians to participate in such acts given their Hippocratic oath, an oath taken by many physicians in which essentially they promise to "first do no harm" to any individual or patient. It also raises questions about who is best equipped to make such judgments, the afflicted individual or someone with medical training.

Research on the ending of life suggests that, if needing to consider such requests, both laypersons and medical professionals prefer to hear the request from the individual with the illness, not the medical doctor (Guedi et al., 2005). What is more, research on physicians who respond to requests for end-of-life assistance indicate that they were significantly more likely to respond with assistance when the patient him- or herself made the request and when the requests were made repeatedly (Meier et al., 2003).

Finally, both laypersons and medical professionals are more inclined to accept such requests when the reason for euthanasia is to end *intractable physical suffering* (Guedi et al., 2005), here meaning severe pain, seizures, delirium, or other painful or disorienting symptoms.

It is important to note that other research also shows that the most commonly cited reasons for euthanasia in fact are not related to intractable physical suffering. Instead, patients most often cite loss of autonomy, loss of ability to control bodily functions, loss of enjoyment of life, and a preference to control their manner of death when terminally ill (Sullivan, Hedberg, & Flemming, 2000). Does this mean that individuals who request euthanasia due largely to severe psychological or emotional distress are considered less credible than those in clear physical pain? Perhaps not. The research suggests that when making difficult decisions that involve ethical judgments, it may be easier for medical persons to accept a request for euthanasia when they can readily see and understand the extent of someone's pain and discomfort. We must add, however, that the mental and psychological distress associated with illnesses, something that may be less apparent to another individual, must be considered also because such factors influence overall health and well-being. Once again, health psychologists can contribute to the important decisions pertaining to euthanasia by examining both the physical and emotional health of a person to assess the overall well-being.

Can an individual considering euthanasia also be an advocate for him- or herself? The answer appears to be "sometimes." But this, too, is highly controversial. Remember we noted that in Oregon physicians can assist only someone who is mentally competent to make such a request. Some health care providers believe that patients suffering from terminally ill or debilitating conditions can be lucid and are able to distinguish between momentary discomfort and intractable discomfort that shows no hope of abating. Others contend that the pain and suffering can be so intense that the wish to die is more likely an intense desire to remove the immediate pain or discomfort and to regain the part of the quality of life the individual enjoyed previously.

This highly controversial topic will continue to engage health professionals. Questions about the ethics of living with unremitting pain versus the right to choose to end such suffering will not be resolved easily. An embedded issue in this debate is whether individuals can advocate for and win the right to choose to end a painful existence.

SECTION II. WORKING WITH COMMUNITIES

We described the ways in which health psychologists help design health programs and research to change individual health behaviors. They use some of the same techniques when working in community settings. Each of the educational approaches explained earlier—mass advertisement campaigns, formal and informal educational programs, and support groups—can be used, with some modifications, when working with communities. One important difference is the need to involve the community in the planning and implementation process of the health program.

Community Needs Assessment

When working in communities, many health care workers understand that the community, not the individual, is the focus. But, like individuals, a community will be more responsive to new behavior change programs if the members of the community believe the program addresses their perceived health needs.

Consider this: In southern Africa, health professionals labeled the growing HIV/AIDS epidemic the most important health issue in the region. Yet many of the residents in southern Africa did not agree. They understood the potential long-term impact of such a disease. Many villagers and government health officials, however, were more concerned about other health problems that they believed posed a greater and more immediate risk to the community. For example, in South Africa incidence rates of HIV were increasing rapidly for several years. Yet the health department (or ministry as it is called there) was struggling to address the need to expand a health care system, which provided easy access to care for white South Africans, into a system that provided health services to more than 24 million blacks, colored, and Indians who were denied basic care under the apartheid regime (Schenider & Stein, 2001). In this case, the health department's first concern was providing immediate, basic health services to 24 million neglected individuals. It took precedence over treating the rapid escalation of HIV/AIDS.

Similar problems were encountered by health workers in other countries where the need to focus on basic survival, including food, shelter, or attention to other diseases such as cholera or malaria that result in death in the short-term, were determined to be more immediate and more critical to improving the health status of the community (Loewenson, 2007).

Conflicting views on the most important health concerns often pit health researchers against the community. Such problems have been noted in the United States as well and have led to similar "turf wars" when attempting to identify a community's most pressing health need (Merzel & D'Afflitti, 2003).

How do health psychologists introduce and implement a specific education and intervention program in a community when the community is focused on other pressing concerns? As public health workers know, programs are most effective when using a community-based approach to program intervention. Health psychologists will be more effective in identifying and developing successful health programs if they first assess the needs of the community from the community's perspective. Most important, psychologists must include community residents, especially the community's own health professionals, in the assessment. Thus, the first job of health psychologists when working in communities is to assist the community members in conducting their own needs assessment.

Many health care workers understand that when working in communities, individuals and their behaviors must be evaluated in their *social milieu*, or social context (Merzel & D'Afflitti, 2003). By social context we mean the community values, norms, and behaviors that shape the attitudes that help shape the behaviors (Thompson & Kinne, 1990). You may recall that in Chapter 4, Theories and Models of Health Behavior Change, several theories proposed that a society's norms and values influence an individual's behavior (Thompson & Kinne, 1990). Similarly, any effort to change health outcomes at the community level must consider the community norms, here meaning behavioral practices and beliefs, in addition to the social environment (Goodman et al., 1996).

Let us put this in perspective. Earlier we mentioned an intervention program by Walter and colleagues (1992, 1993) designed to teach adolescents techniques for negotiating safer sexual behaviors to prevent the risk of HIV infection. Unfortunately, these researchers did not anticipate the social context that gives rise to the high-risk sexual behaviors. In a posttest analysis, Walter and colleagues (1993) noted that the adolescents felt able to use the training and negotiation skills learned in the intervention program to negotiate safer sexual behaviors. But they noted that they would be less able to use the newly acquired skills after drinking or using drugs.

Why is this relevant? In most instances, adolescents report a higher risk of engaging in sexually risky behaviors after consuming alcohol or other substances. In essence, they identify

FIGURE 13.6   "Kegs and Eggs" Party. Social context may help shape an individual behavior.

substance use as an important context in which the risky behavior occurs, a context that was not tested by Walter and colleagues (1993). Their intervention program did not consider the social context of adolescents. Community-based participatory research offers one method for overcoming similar obstacles.

Program Implementation

There is, currently, an emphasis on ***community-based participatory research*** or ***programs***, here meaning research or programs that involve the community from the inception through to the conclusion. Community-based participatory programs usually include community members as part of the planning team. Their knowledge of the community's values and belief systems, together with their interest in the health problem, facilitates the researcher's or practitioner's introduction into the community as well as the effective delivery of the program. Examples of successful community-based programs or studies exist for a range of health issues throughout the world. They include participatory programs to improve the cardiovascular health of Latina residents in a community of Los Angeles (Kim, Koniak-Griffin, Fluskerund, & Guarnero, 2004), a program to increase women's physical activity and cardiovascular health in the Persian Gulf (Pazoki, Nabipour, Seyednezami, & Imami, 2007), and programs to promote weight loss among Turkish and Moroccan women to promote healthy lifestyles (Wagemakers et al., 2008).

The common factor in all of the studies is a partnership between the community and the health practitioner or health researcher in designing, conducting, and evaluating the program's effectiveness. Such programs are based on the assumption that individuals are inextricable from their context and that a supportive context will reinforce and sustain the behavior. Community-based participatory programs may use as their foundation theories of health behavior that include social context as one factor that shapes behavior.

In sum, the current work of community-based health intervention programs recognizes that an individual is linked to his or her context. Efforts to improve a community's—and therefore an individual's—health will be more successful if health professionals carefully study the community and its perceived needs, take account of community's values and attitudes in the proposed health behavior, and include the community as partners in the project. Health psychologists often work on such community-based participatory programs.

We must make one final observation. Some researchers suggest that, when working in communities, health psychologists need to change the community's social norms or attitudes to obtain the targeted behavior change. We caution that changing social norms and values is a process that occurs slowly if at all. Programs that require substantial changes to norms and attitudes may be successful only for the duration of the program. Once the program ends, or the health professionals leave, it is unlikely that the health behaviors will be self-sustaining. In essence, a community-based health behavior change must be a community-led initiative if it is to be effective and enduring.

Selecting Populations within Communities

An effective strategy for changing a health behavior involves selecting a specific (or target) population and a health problem or behavior prevalent in that population. As we noted in Chapter 4, Theories and Models of Health Behavior Change, social marketing programs demonstrate that effective behavior change programs focus on one target group, even though the behavior may be evident in other groups in the community.

Targeting one group to receive a health intervention is troublesome to some in the health field. It means that others with similar health behaviors may not benefit from the intervention program. In point of fact, health professionals and researchers regularly segment populations to develop and deliver effective health intervention programs. Consider this: What advertising message would you use to inform all audiences, including adolescents, about the dangers of smoking (see Figure 13.7)? Would a warning about the dangers of cigarette smoke to pregnant women and their fetus be equally as effective with adolescents as with women contemplating pregnancy? We contend that it would not. Rather, a campaign that derides smoking as "uncool" among popular students or that suggests that smoker's breath is a turnoff when speaking up close with someone attractive may have more impact for teens than messages about the dangers of smoking for the unborn child. Thus, health psychologists, like marketers, must select and work with specific groups in communities to increase the likelihood of effective message communication and successful behavior change.

Promoting Community Advocates

After participating in the community needs assessment and assisting with program development to address the health needs of the community, health psychologists may also advocate for the needed changes on behalf of the community. Health issues of interest to *community health advocates* include ensuring access to nutritious and fresh produce, access to clean water, environments that are free of toxic waste sites, and violence reduction in neighborhoods. As we indicated in earlier chapters, each of these issues affect the health of the community as well as the individual.

Recent research by nursing students from a university in southern Georgia provides an example of community advocacy by health researchers and community members. The university

FIGURE 13.7   **The Impact of Health Behaviors on Others.** Matching the message with the target audience is fundamental to changing health behaviors.

students chose to work in a community adjacent to their university that also included family members and friends of some of the students. No doubt the students' familiarity with the community and their existing social networks increased the community's receptivity to the health advocates and their proposed health programs.

The students and the community conducted a community needs assessment and identified five health problems, one of which was lack of fluoridation in the water (Wold et al., 2008). Fluoride in water helps to prevent dental cavities, especially in small children (Adain et al., 2001; Truman et al., 2002). Together, the community and students developed programs to address the individual and community dental health needs of the children. They then develop a teaching plan on preventive dental care that was adopted by and implemented at a local elementary school. The educational program was geared to elementary school children because they are the most susceptible to tooth decay when fluoride is in short supply.

The resulting program provided a benefit to the individual children and the community. Each child received immediate dental health care and learned preventive dental hygiene habits that could help to arrest future tooth decay. In addition the community gained a dental health program that could be incorporated into the school's health program and used annually to educate future elementary school students. Thus, it will provide ongoing dental health benefits for children in the community.

SECTION III. WORKING WITH HEALTH CARE SYSTEMS

When health psychologists work with health care systems (see Chapter 12), most often they are engaged in research to explain patterns of health care–seeking behaviors or barriers to using the health care systems. Yet, studies of health care behaviors must also consider the effects of the regulations and restrictions of the health care system on individual health behaviors.

As we noted in Chapter 12, Health Care Systems and Health Policy, health care systems include many components that offer a prescribed set of services and that specify the frequency of services to be provided to individuals who subscribe to or use the plan. A system that regulates access to care by defining when, what, and how frequently health services can be provided will certainly affect an individual's health outcomes.

Assessing Access to Health Care

What is more likely to influence a person's decision to obtain needed health care: the individuals, their families/communities, or the health care system—including physicians—from which they usually obtain medical care? There is broad agreement that all three factors—individuals, family and community, and health care systems—influence individuals' decisions to seek care. Yet there is little agreement about the relative contribution of each of the factors. Simply stated, we do not know which factor is more instrumental in affecting an individual's health or health-seeking behaviors. Consider this example: An individual with a chronic cough but no other cold symptom decides not to obtain medical advice. If the cough evolves into bronchitis, it would be fair to assume that the individual's own inattention to his or her health contributed to the poorer health status.

Now, assume that the same individual with the same cough condition calls his or her physician for an appointment but is told that the next available appointment is in three weeks. While the consumer is waiting three weeks, the cough worsens and progresses to bronchitis. In this instance, the worsening health condition can be attributed to a delay in medical care. This time, however, the delay is caused by the physician, not the individual.

Finally, assume that the same individual with the same cough condition calls and receives an appointment with the physician within 48 hours. The doctor determines that a chest X-ray is needed to check for possible pneumonia. Unfortunately, the individual's managed care plan (see Chapter 12) denies authorization for the X-ray, and the individual cannot afford to pay for the test out-of-pocket. Once again, the cough evolves into bronchitis. In this instance, it is clear that the delay in diagnosis and treatment is the fault of the health care system, not the health care provider or the individual.

The examples cited are simplistic and clearly link the cause of the worsening health condition to a specific factor. In most instances, however, the causes of the poor health outcomes are not so easily determined. What is more, there are a number of characteristics imbedded in each of the three factors (individual, provider, or health system) that also influence health outcomes.

Early studies suggested that individual factors largely explained why individuals delayed obtaining health care. For example, some studies report that people in lower socioeconomic classes, males, and less educated individuals tend to delay care (Baker, Stevens, & Brook, 1994; Wilson & Klein, 2000; Zuckerman & Shen, 2004). Yet, a recent study by Lowe and his colleagues (2005) suggests that the type of health services and the structure of the services provided by primary care physicians also contribute to an individual's decision to delay medical care.

Lowe and his coauthors (2005) examined patients' decisions to obtain medical care in a hospital emergency department rather than from their primary care physician for nonemergency medical needs. Results of their study showed that three factors influenced an individual's likelihood of seeking care from someone other than his or her primary care physician: patient volume, here meaning the number of patients in a doctor's private or group practice, a factor that affects the amount of time patients have to wait to be examined; availability of evening appointments; and the range of medical services available in office. These researchers found that physicians with a large number of patients; physicians who allocated fewer than 12 hours per week for evening appointments; physicians who reported no support services available through their office, such as nurse practitioners; and those who reported no special equipment available for special needs, such as asthma, were more likely to have patients who sought medical care from hospital emergency departments than were physicians who reported some or all of the above services (see Table 13.1).

Why is Lowe's research important to health psychology? His research suggests that the quality of services provided by the doctor is not the most significant factor when explaining patients' decisions to postpone or find alternative sources of medical care. Rather, they found that the packet of services, such as hours of operation or volume of patients—in other words, psychosocial factors—is critical to explaining the health care–seeking behaviors of individuals. Lowe's research suggests additional reasons that individuals may choose alternative care options even when they have a relationship with one physician. It may also help explain decisions to delay seeking care altogether.

In essence, Lowe and colleagues' (2005) research identifies a new area of inquiry relevant to health psychology: the effect of psychosocial variables on patient's delay in obtaining health care.

Promoting Access to Health Care through Advocacy

Lowe and coauthors' (2005) research on factors affecting access to care identify a number of factors that, if addressed, would improve patients' access and also satisfaction with their care. In fact, recently, many providers have changed their office practices taking these psychosocial

TABLE 13.1	Influences on Health Status: Individual, Provider, and Health Service Characteristics	
Individual	**Provider**	**Health Services**
Age	Hours of operation	Number of providers in network
Gender	Evening hours	Out-of-network option
Ethnicity	Weekend hours	Covered medical test
Socioeconomic status	Telephone advice	Referrals available
Level of education	Returns patient calls	Preauthorization needed for tests and referrals
Inner city versus rural	Urgent appointments	Limits on additional services
Health insurance	Practice type (office, hospital, clinic)	
Medicaid eligibility	Hospital inpatient care	
Prior medical condition	Availability of special equipment	
Current health status		

factors into account. The most common change has been adding evening appointments and expanding staff to include other health providers who may address a variety of special needs. Thus, Lowe and colleagues' research (2005) and that of other psychologists offer one way to advocate for changes to the health care system to improve access to care (Goin, Hays, Landeman, & Hobbs, 2009; Prentice & Pizer, 2007).

DeVoe (2009) offers another approach for advocating greater access to health care by offering an interesting glimpse into the problems with access to health care in the United States. DeVoe developed a hypothetical scenario in which access to education was regulated in the same manner as access to health care. His example, which refers specifically to publicly funded health care (such as Medicaid or Medicare), illustrates the unexpected and for many unacceptable consequences of such a system.

In DeVoe's (2009) scenario, access to education for children would require insurance, as does health care. Children without insurance would be denied access to a school and consequently to daily instruction. Proof of insurance would be required before admission is granted. Once in the educational arena, parents and children might find that their access to various educational experiences is limited by restrictions imposed by their education insurance carrier. For example, some education insurance companies may restrict access to foreign language instruction or art or music, holding those as special services available only to parents enrolled in enhanced education programs. Furthermore, they may also find that many teachers refuse to accept the children's educational insurance (called educaid by DeVoe), making it difficult to find a teacher who will enroll the child in his or her class.

Educational insurance would be linked to employment. Thus, parents who are employed and who work for an employer that offers insurance would be able to acquire educational insurance for their child. In the event of parental job loss, the child's educational insurance would be terminated as well. What is more, should the parent find employment that would allow him or her to restart the educational insurance, children may find educators doubtful that they could bridge the months or years of missed educational experience.

Sound incredible? Perhaps so. But DeVoe's (2009) hypothetical story helps to illustrate the problems with access to health care in the United States. Few parents would willingly accept the limitations to access to education for their children posed by DeVoe's scenario. Yet these very restrictions to access to health care exist for both children and adults. DeVoe's approach of analogizing education insurance to health insurance clarifies the need for changes in the health care system in the United States.

SECTION IV. WORKING IN HEALTH POLICY

It may seem unlikely, at first, that health psychologists would have much involvement with health policy. But think back to the opening story. Ahmed's father, a public health professional, worked with health researchers, some of whom could be health psychologists, to change policies that directly affect health. Such a pairing is indeed quite common. Some health psychologists work directly with policy makers while others conduct research that helps inform the development of new regulations that also shape or, in some cases, restrict behaviors that affect health. Examples of health policies influenced by research include smoking restrictions in public places, workplace safety regulations, and healthy workplace rules.

Smoking Bans as Health Policy

The ban on smoking on all U.S. domestic airline flights (GPO Access, 2008) and the ban on smoking in public places, including bars, restaurants, and bowling alleys, are two examples of health policy regulations initiated to reduce the incidences of a health-compromising behavior, smoking, and its health implications for individuals.

We have discussed the association between smoking and respiratory illnesses and cancer in Chapter 11, Cancer, so we will not review it here. The fact that cigarette smoke harms the smoker has long been accepted in the research community. What is new, however, is that nonsmokers face some of the same health hazards from *secondhand smoke*, or smoke from another individual's cigarette. Overwhelming evidence of the dangers of secondhand smoke was the basis for the ban on smoking in many public places, including workplaces, by 27 states, as well as the federal ban on smoking in airplanes (see Figure 13.8).

Health psychologists conducted and contributed to the vast research literature on the effects of smoking.

Workplace Safety

Another health policy influenced by researchers is workplace safety. The concept of workplace safety in the United States, specifically the employer's role in creating a safe work environment, is relatively new. It began with the concept of behavioral safety introduced by Herbert Heinrich in the 1930s. Heinrich's research examining the causes of workplace injuries and accidents suggested that the actions of the workers, not the work environment, were responsible for the

FIGURE 13.8   The Dangers of Passive Smoking.

Source: www.cartoonstock.com/lowres/ggu0024l.jpg

majority of injuries on the job (Heinrich, Petersen, & Roos, 1980; Wirth & Sigurdsson, 2008). In other words, Heinrich suggested that individual, not environmental determinants contributed to workplace injury. Recent studies on workplace safety, however, criticize Heinrich's assessment that the worker bore the greatest responsibility for workplace accidents and injuries (Cooper, 2003). Instead, the later studies determined that workplace hazards caused by the environment and by poor safety guidelines contributed significantly to injuries and accidents at work sites.

Can psychologists contribute to the research on workplace safety? Absolutely! In fact, B. F. Skinner, the famous behavioral psychologist, demonstrated that psychologists could contribute to efforts to improve employees' safe behavior in the workplace.

Skinner, as you may recall, was the psychologists who developed the principle of *operant conditioning*, a process by which individuals and animals could learn to perform a specific behavior by gradual shaping of their behavior. Skinner demonstrated that, through operant conditioning, individuals can learn to adopt and maintain behaviors, such as safety behaviors. Key to Skinner's theory is the principle of reinforcement or reward. When individuals are appropriately rewarded, Skinner showed that they will not only perform but will retain the desired behavior.

Using Skinnerian principles, industrial/organizational (I/O) psychology, a new discipline in psychology, was developed to identify and test strategies that would motivate employees to adopt and maintain desired work related behaviors. Consider this: Employees at a magazine company may be told that if they sell at least 20 magazine subscriptions they will receive a bonus. The bonus is the incentive or reward offered to shape the work behavior, selling 20 magazine subscriptions. Would the same operant conditioning process work to shape workplace safety behaviors? It is reasonable to conclude that if Skinner's operant conditioning principles can shape workplace behavior and enhance productivity, they can be effective also in shaping and reinforcing safe workplace habits. Thus, health psychologists can also use Skinner's operant conditioning theory to shape and reinforce safe workplace behaviors.

Earlier in the chapter we demonstrated how health psychologists can work in communities to identify and develop health-enhancing behaviors. The same techniques can be used with employees in a business or work environment to introduce and reinforce workplace safety behaviors. For example, health psychologists can work with employees to identify workplace safety behaviors unique to their environments. Together with the employees, health psychologists can introduce safety plans and procedures through small group presentations or seminars, and use posters to reinforce the message (a Skinnerian principle again) and to remind workers of the goal. Some of the most effective posters reminding employees of workplace safety behaviors are cartoons. Humorous posters can attract attention and are easy to recall while reminding workers of the safety goals.

Currently, the U.S. Occupational Safety and Health Administration (OSHA), together with divisions of workplace safety administered by state agencies, conducts evaluations of workplace sites to identify potential and specific job hazards (OSHA, 1989). U.S. regulations mandate that state workplace safety plans must include both management leadership and employee participation when developing and maintaining a safe and hazard-free workplace. Thus, it appears that the federal regulations support the view that the environment, the management company (policy), and the worker all contribute to establishing and maintaining a safe workplace environment.

In spite of the regulations, U.S. workplaces still report accidents in the millions. In 2006, the U.S. Bureau of Labor Statistics reported more than 3.9 million nonfatal workplace injuries and approximately 5,700 fatalities (Wirth & Sigurdson, 2008). The injuries and fatalities included in the statistics represent a mix of all three causal factors: individual, company policy, and environment. As the statistics suggest, much more work is needed to establish and ensure a safe work environment for employees.

A Healthy Workplace

Some work environments have few physical hazards or hazardous jobs. For example, the average office worker or employee in educational institutions is not required to work with dangerous chemicals or heavy machinery. Yet even in office or educational settings, many employers are establishing healthy workplace rules.

Work environments that promote a healthy workplace do so for two reasons. First, they consider the productivity loss when one person is ill. If an employee is absent from work due to illness, that worker's work production may be lost for the duration of the illness. His or her lost productivity can result in lost earnings for both the employer and the employee. Second, employers consider the potential impact on other workers. Consider the effect on work productivity when several employees are absent due to illness. The potential loss of revenue when several employees are absent could financially strain some employers.

Programs that promote healthy workplace environments offer potential benefits to both the workers and to the employer. For the worker, less absenteeism may mean less lost income or, equally as important, overall good health. We already noted the benefits to the employer of no loss of productivity and therefore no loss of potential revenue due to illness.

For those reasons, healthy workplace programs, sometimes called worksite health promotion programs, are being implemented in many businesses (see Figure 13.9). Studies that evaluate the effect of healthy workplace programs on worker absenteeism and worker productivity

FIGURE 13.9   **Maintaining a Healthy Workplace through Exercise.** Exercise during the work day is one component of healthy workplace programs.

demonstrate the dual benefit of these programs. Kuoppala, Lamminpaa, and Husman (2008) showed that workplace health promotion programs were credited with decreasing absenteeism, increasing the mental well-being of the workers, and increasing the productivity of the workers. Similarly, Mills, Kessler, Cooper, and Sullivan (2007) studied the effects of a workplace health intervention program in the U.K. office of a multinational company, a company with major office operations in more than one country. They compared workers' responses to questionnaires before the program and 12 months after the program. Mills and coauthors' (2007) results showed that workers reported a decrease in health risk factors and an increase in productivity as a result of the healthy workplace program.

Clearly, a healthy workplace benefits workers by increasing the likelihood that they will remain in good physical health with less exposure to and risk of physical illness. However, as these studies suggest, they also improve employees' mental health and overall well-being. It appears, therefore, that some healthy workplace programs address the holistic health of individuals.

Advocating for New Health Policies

Can health policy be a form of health advocacy? In the current and prior chapters we provided examples of health policy developed and implemented for the purpose of improving the health status of individuals, communities, special populations, and workplace environments. And, according to our definition of health advocacy stated in the beginning of the chapter, a principal goal of health advocacy is to promote behavior and practices that improve an individual's or a community's state of health.

Consistent with the definition, therefore, health policy can be a form of health advocacy. Consider this: A state mandate that requires all passengers and drivers to wear seat belts when riding in automobiles is a health policy. Most would agree that the policy is also a form of health advocacy that promotes automobile safety. Similarly, state regulations that ban the use of hand-held cell phones while driving is a health policy intended to reduce accidents rates due to cell phone use.

In most cases, health policies are developed and implemented to improve health or at least remove health hazards. There are times, however, when health policies appear to jeopardize, rather than enhance, the health outcomes of individuals. Consider the case of childhood immunizations. In Chapter 3, Global Communicable and Chronic Disease, we described the benefits of vaccines that, when given to children by age 5, help to reduce incidences of serious illnesses and death primarily of children. Recently, however, parental concern about the measles, mumps, rubella (MMR) vaccine routinely given to children in most developed and many developing countries has raised questions about the safety of the vaccine.

Specifically, parents raised concerns about the likelihood that the MMR vaccine increases the risk of autism in young children. Results from a study in 1998, in addition to increased levels of *ethyl mercury* in the vaccine between 1987 and 1995, led some researchers, but mostly parents, to see a causal link between the higher levels of ethyl mercury and alarmingly higher rates of autism in children within the past 10 to 15 years (Fombonne et al., 2006; Wakefield et al., 1998). More important, parents who participated in the original study with Wakefield and colleagues and who learned of the increased level of ethyl mercury also believed that the MMR vaccine resulted in developmental delays associated with autism (see Box 13.4).

BOX 13.4   Does the Measles Mumps Rubella (MMR) Vaccine Cause Autism?

According to approximately 40 parents and some researchers, the MMR vaccine is the cause of a new variant of autism that involves severe gastrointestinal symptoms.

Claims of the new variant of autism took many researchers by surprise. The reports of a new strain of autism were first published by Wakefield and colleagues in 1998. They noted that, in their initial study of 12 children, parents reported that the children's severe gastrointestinal symptoms and progressive developmental disorders began within days of their child receiving an MMR vaccine. The symptoms included abdominal pain, diarrhea, bloating, and food intolerance. Wakefield and colleagues determined that because previous studies showed that children with autism also reported intestinal disorders, it was possible and perhaps likely that the gastrointestinal problems and other behavioral disorders evidenced in 12 children could be related to autism (Reichert et al., 1993; Shattock, Kennedy, Powell, & Berney, 1991). Some earlier studies even suggested a link between gastrointestinal disorders and disruption of normal brain development. Wakefield and colleagues believed that their study had indeed identified a link between the vaccine and autism when an additional 27 children were identified whose parents reported the same symptoms shortly after their children were administered an MMR vaccine. With a total of 39 cases, these researchers believed they identified a health policy problem: The MMR vaccine appeared to cause a new variant of autism.

This claim by Wakefield and colleagues (1998) puzzled health psychologists. Up to this point, most researchers believed autism to be a largely genetic and neurological disorder, a defect that occurred in embryonic development. Few were able to understand how a vaccine given after the first year of life could be responsible for a disorder that up to now was thought to occur in utero (DeStefano & Chen, 2008). Even more puzzling to some were the statistics on the increased rates of autism in California used to support the association between MMR vaccines and autism.

It is true that between 1980 and 1994 California saw its rates of diagnosed cases of autism increase by over 373%. In 1980 incidence rates of autism were 44 per 100,000 children. By 1994, however, the incidence rates had increased to 208 per 100,000 children. But, at the same time, the rates of MMR vaccine only increased 14%, far too little to explain the dramatic increase of over 300% in autism (Dales, Hammer, & Smith, 2001).

In the face of numerous studies that refuted the association between autism and MMR vaccines, and earlier research demonstrating that autism was a neurological disorder that occurred in utero, how could researchers explain the dramatic increase in rates?

For many researchers the answer lay with improvements in medical knowledge. DeStefano and Chen (2008) and Fombonne and colleagues (2006) suggest that the most likely reason for the dramatic rise in autism rates is broader diagnostic criteria used to identify the illness and better detection of early indicators of autism. Broader diagnostic criteria allowed health professionals to classify children as autistic who, in the past, would not have been identified as such. In addition, physicians and other medical providers are now better able to detect early signs of the disease, leading to earlier diagnosis. Together, both may account for some, though not all, of the dramatic increase in cases of autism.

One thing appears to be clear, however. The fear that a childhood immunization may cause autism in one's child is sufficient to deter many parents from an otherwise safe and effective vaccine. It will no doubt take time for the public to review the evidence showing no clear link between the MMR vaccine and autism and to lose their fear of the vaccine. In the meantime, however, unvaccinated children are at increased risk of contracting measles, a potentially fatal and wholly preventable childhood illness.

Numerous studies that attempted to replicate Wakefield and colleagues' (1998) claim of an increase in autism rates linked to the MMR vaccine found no such link (Dales, Hammer, & Smith, 2001; Fombonne & Chakvabarti, 2001; Smith, Ellenberg, Bill, & Ruben, 2008). They argue for the maintenance of the health policy that requires children to receive the MMR vaccine by the time they enter elementary school. Unfortunately, public opinion on the issue appears to favor the proposed link. As a result, a growing number of parents in the United States and in England are choosing to refuse the MMR vaccine for their children (Jansen et al., 2003). The effect of even a small number of parents refusing to vaccinate their children caused a spike in the incidence rates of measles in England in 2001 and 2002 (Jansen et al., 2003). Some researchers and health workers fear that, should parents continue to refuse the vaccine for their children, new cases of measles will result in a significant increase in serious illness and even death to children. And remember, as we noted in Chapter 3, Global Communicable and Chronic Disease, measles is one of the deadliest diseases for children under 5 years of age worldwide.

Are researchers' fears exaggerated? Perhaps not. Consider again the consequences of Nigeria's decision to end its polio vaccine program, explained in Chapter 3, Global Communicable and Chronic Disease. That decision resulted in an escalation of polio in Nigeria and in eight neighboring countries in West Africa. Researchers and health care providers worry that a similar escalation in measles may occur if more parents refuse the vaccine for their children.

Health Psychologists as Health Advocates

We explained how individuals can become their own advocates for health. We also explained how nursing students with a connection to a community can become community advocates. But how can health psychologists serve as health advocates and inspire change?

By addressing euthanasia, we saw how health psychologists may demonstrate their ability to serve as advocates for terminally ill or debilitated patients for one of two outcomes: ending life in dignity or coping with debilitating illnesses or injuries. In addition, throughout the book and indeed throughout this chapter we identified ways in which social determinants affect health outcomes. Some of the effects of social determinants on health are known due to the research of health psychologists. And, through that same research, the health psychologists can integrate their expertise in research design, their knowledge of health and the health problems of a community, and their understanding of social determinants of health to present a carefully designed and carefully executed study that can advocate for health change.

Some health psychologists will use their research or that of others to work closely with policy professionals to implement the changes recommended by the research. When implementing policy, health psychologists will evaluate the effects of the policy in much the same way they evaluate the impact of an intervention program designed to change behaviors.

These are only a sample of the ways in which health psychologists may use their own work or that of others to advocate for improved health outcomes for individuals and communities.

Personal Postscript

WHAT ARE YOUR CAREER PLANS?

Are you considering a career as a health psychologist? If so, after reading this chapter you may see that there are a number of options available to you.

Before deciding on one approach, or "domain," as identified in the chapter, we suggest a few things to help you learn more about the field in general and to help you make an informed choice.

First, consider volunteering in areas where health psychologists work. For example, health psychologists can be found in many hospital outpatient clinics that provide support programs for individuals with chronic health issues. Teaching hospitals, particularly those affiliated with major universities, are more likely to employ health psychologists in such settings.

Second, health psychologists also work as researchers in major teaching hospitals. Research directors are often willing to have volunteers work on their research teams. By volunteering you will gain valuable experience to help you determine whether you enjoy working as part of a research team with other health psychologists. In addition, you may have an opportunity to identify a health issue of interest to you.

Third, explore the role of health psychologists in public health settings, such as departments of health or community health settings, in your city or town. In such settings health psychologists could be involved in either research or policy making or in designing or administering public health programs.

Finally, consider the work of health psychologists in community-based intervention projects. Community-based participatory research is fast becoming the preferred method of conducting community health research or intervention programs. Volunteering with a community-based participatory project may provide opportunities to test both the research and the direct service side of health psychology.

Important Terms

active euthanasia   435
allied health professions   422
colonoscopy   429
community-based participatory
   research or programs   439
community health
   advocates   440

ecological   421
ethyl mercury   448
euthanasia   435
insulin   422
intractable physical
   suffering   436
interdisciplinary   423

operant conditioning   446
physician-assisted suicide   435
polyp   429
psychosocial   421
secondhand smoke   445
social milieu   438
wellness examinations   432

REFERENCES

Aaltoner, L. A., Salovaara, R., & Kristo, P. (1998). Incidence of heredity nonpolyposis colorectal cancer and the feasibility of molecular screening for the disease. *New England Journal of Medicine,* 21, 1481–1487.

ABC/Associated Press (2007). Andrew Speaker. Retrieved on June 7, 2008, from: http://www.cbc.ca/health/story/2007/06/06/tuberculosis.travel.html.

Abel, E. (2007). Women with HIV and stigma. *Family and Community Health,* 30 (supplement), pS104–S106.

Abel, M. H. (2002). Humor, stress and coping strategies. *Humor: International Journal of Humor Research,* 15, 4, 365–381.

Abrams, K. K., Allen, L. R., & Gray, J. J. (1993). Disordered eating attitudes and behaviors, psychological adjustment, and ethnic identity: A comparison of black and white female college students. *International Journal of Eating Disorders,* 14, 49–58.

Abril, I. F. (1977). Mexican-American folk beliefs. *American Journal of Maternal Child Nursing.* May-June, 168–173.

Abu-Raddad, L. J., Patnaik, P., & Kublin, J. G. (2006). Dual infection with HIV and malaria fuels the spread of both diseases in sub-Saharan Africa. *Science,* 314, 1603–1606.

Adain, S. M., Bowen, U. H., Bent, B. A., Kumer, J. V., Levy, S. M., & Pendrys, D. G. (2001). Recommendation for using fluoride to prevent and control dental caries in the US. *MMWR,* 50 (RR14), 1–42.

Adams, T. D., Heath E. M., Lamonte, M. J., Gress, R. E., Pendleton, R., Strong, M., et al. (2007). The relationship between body mass index and percent of body fat in the obese. *Diabetes Obesity Metab.,* 9(4), 498–505.

Adewuya, A. O., Afolabi, M. O., Ola, B. A., Ogundele, O. A., Ajibare, A. O., Oladipo, B. F., et al. (2010). The effects of psychological distress on medication adherence in persons with HIV infection in Nigeria. *Psychosomatics,* 51, 1, 68–73.

Adler, I., & Kandel, D. B. (1981). Cross-cultural perspectives on developmental stages in adolescent drug use. *Journal of Studies on Alcohol,* 42, 701–715.

Adler, N. E., Boyce, W. T., Chesney, M., Cohen, S, Folkman, S., Kahn, R., et al. (1994). Socioeonomic status and health: The challenge of the gradient. *American Psychologist,* 49, 15–24.

Africa First. (2008). *Report of the Second Global Summit on HIV/AIDS, Traditional Medicine & Indigenous Knowledge,* March 10–14, 2008. Retrieved from: www.africa-first.com/final510version%20of%20report%20re%202nd%20global%20summit.pdf.

Afrol News (2003). *President Museveni explains Uganda's success in combating AIDS.* December 8, 2003. Retrieved from: http://www.afrol.com. success.htm.

Agency for Healthcare Research and Quality. (2003). *Results of systematic review of research on diagnosis and treatment of coronary heart disease in women.* Evidence Report/Technology Assessment: Number 80. AHR! Publication No. 03-E035. Rockville, MD: Agency for Healthcare Research & Quality.

Agency for Toxic Substances and Disease Registry. (2001). *Public health statement for asbestos.* Retrieved from: www.atsdr.cdc.gov/tocprofiles/phs61.html.

Agency for Toxic Substances and Disease Registry. (2002). Cancer fact sheet. Department of Health and Human Services. Retrieved from: www.atsdr.cdc.gov/com/cancer-fs.html.

Ahola, K., Toppinen-Tanner, S., Huuhtanam, P., Koskien, A., & Vaananen, A. (2009). Occupational burnout & chronic work disability: An eight-year cohort study in pensioning among Finnish forest industry workers. *Journal of Affective Disorders,* 115, 1–2, 150–159.

AIDSPAC. (2007). Ryan White. Retrieved from: www.aidspac.org/atstake/ryan.asp.

Ajzen, I. (1985). From intentions to actions: A theory of planned behavior. In K. Kuhland & J. Beckman (eds.) *Action control: From cognitions to behavior (11–39).* Heidelberg: Springer.

Ajzen, I., & Fishbein, M. (1980). *Understanding attitudes and predicting social behavior.* Englewood Cliffs, NJ: Prentice-Hall.

Ajzen, I., & Madden, T. J. (1986). Prediction of goal-directed behavior: Attitudes, intention and perceived behavioral control. *Journal of Experimental Social Psychology,* 22, 453–474.

Akers, R. (1996). A longitudinal test of social leaning theory: Adolescent smoking. *Journal of Drug Issues,* 26, 2, 317–343.

Albert, T. (2004). Doctors protest 400% price hike in HIV medication. *Amednews.com,* the newspaper for America's physicians. March 8, 2004. Retrieved from: www.ama-assn.org/amednews/2004/03/08/gvsc0306.htm.

Albert, M. A., Ravenell, J., Glynn, R. J., Khera, A., Halevy, N., & de Lemon, J. A. (2008). Cardiovascular risk indications & perceived race/ethnic discrimination in the Dallas Heart Study. *American Heart Journal,* 156, 6, 1103–1109.

Alegria, D., Guerra, E., Martinez, C., & Meyer, G. (1977). *El hospital* invisible: A study of *curanderismo. Archives of General Psychiatry,* 34, 11, 1354–1357.

Allan, R., & Scheidt, S. (1992). Is coronary heart disease a lifestyle disorder? A review of psychological & behavioral factors. *Cardiovascular Research Reports,* 13–53.

Allen, P. (1979). The Justinian Plague. *Byzantion,* 49, 14.

Allen, K., & Blascovich, J. (1994). Effects of music on cardiovascular reactivity among surgeons. *Journal of the American Medical Association,* 272, 22, 882–884.

American Cancer Society. (2006). Cancer facts and figures 2006. Atlanta, GA: American Cancer Society.

American Cancer Society. (2008). *Cancer facts & figures, 2008.* Retrieved from: www.acs.org.

American Diabetes Association (2007). All about diabetes. Retrieved on December 6, 2007, from: www.diabetes.org/about-diabetes.org.

American Heart Association (2004). *Automated external defibrillation funding fact sheet.* Retrieved from: www.americanheart.org.

American Heart Association (2008). Atherosclerosis. Retrieved on July 15, 2008, from: www.american heart.org/presenter,jhtml?identifier=4440.

American Non-Smoker's Rights Foundation. (2010). State, commonwealth & municipalities with 100% smokefree laws in workplace, restaurants & bars. Retrieved from: www.nosmoke.org/pdf/100ordlist.pdf.

American Pain Foundation. (2009). Pain facts & figures. Retrieved on September 4, 2009, from: www.pain foundation.org/newsroom/reporter-resources/pain-facts-figures.html.

American Pain Society. (2002). *Guidelines for the management of pain in osteoarthritis, rheumatoid arthritis and juvenile chronic arthritis.* Glenview, IL: Author.

American Psychological Association (APA). (1992). Ethical principles of psychologists and code of conduct. *American Psychologist,* 47, 1597–1611.

American Psychological Association (APA). (2004). Bylaws of the American Psychological Association, Article I, 1. Retrieved from: www.apa.org/governance/bylaws/art1.html.

American Rhetoric (2001). Press conference announcing HIV infection and retirement. Retrieved on November 1, 2008, from: www.americanrhetoric.com/speeches/magicjohnsonhivRetirement.html.

Amerinfo.com. (2008). Global weight survey look at scale obsession, fast food addiction, and obesity. Retrieved from: www.anmerinf.com/143020.html.

AMFAR. (2006). Statistics Worldwide. Retrieved from www.amfar.org/abouthiv/article.aspx?id=3592&terms=latin+america

Anderson, G. F., & Chu, E. (2007). Expanding priorities: Confronting chronic diseases in countries with low income. *The New England Journal of Medciine,* 356(3), 209–211.

Anderson, K. O., Bradley, L. A., Young, L. D., McDaniel L. K., & Wise, C. M. (1985). Rheumatoid arthritis: review of psychological factors related to etiology, effects and treatment. *Psychological Bulletin,* 98, 358–387.

Anderson, R. N., Kochanek, K. D., & Murphy, S. L. (1995). Report on final mortality statistics. *Monthly Vital Statistics Report,* 45 (Supplement 2), 23–33.

Anderson, K. M., Odell, P. M., Wilson, P. W., Kannel, W. B. (1991). Cardiovascular disease risk profiles. *American Heart Journal,* 121, 293–298.

Andreasen, A. R. (1995). *Marketing social change: Changing behavior to promote health, social development, and the environment.* San Francisco: Jossey-Bass Publishers.

Andrews, J. A., Tildesley, E., Hops, H., & Li, F. (2002). The influence of peers on young adult substance use. *Health Psychology,* 21(4), 349–357.

Anglican Breast Cancer Study Group. (2000). Prevalence and penetration of BRCA1 and BRCA2 mutations in a population-based series of breast cancer cases. *British Journal of Cancer,* 83, 1301–1308.

Annals of Internal Medicine. (2008). Health consequences. *Annals of Internal Medicine,* 149, 7, 14.2–14.3.

Annemans, L., Spaepen, E., Gaskin, M., et al. (2008). Gout in the UK & Germany; Prevalence, comorbidities & management in general practice 2000–2005. *Annals of Rheumatoid Disease,* 67, 960–966.

Anteghini, M., Fonseca, H., Ireland, M., & Blum, R. W. (2001). Health risk behaviors and associated risk and protective factors among Brazilian adolescents in Santos, Brazil. *Journal of Adolescent Health,* 2001 (28), 295–302.

Arena, J. G., & Blanchard, E. B. (2001). Biofeedback training for chronic pain disorders: A primer. In Loeser, J., Turk, D., Chapman, R., & Butler, S. (eds.) *Bonica's Management of Pain* (3rd ed.), pp. 1755–1763. Baltimore: Williams and WIlkins.

Armstead, C. A., Lawler, L. A., Gordon, G., et al. (1989). Relationship of racial stressors to blood pressure responses and anger expression in black college students. *Health Psychology,* 8, 541–556.

Armstrong, D. (2002). Theoretical tensions in biopsychosocial medicine. In Marks, D. (ed.) *The Health Psychology Reader.* London: Sage Publications.

Arroyo, C., Hu, F. B., Ryan, L. M., Kawachi, I., Colditz, G. A., Speizer, F. E., et al. (2004). Depressive symptoms and risk of type 2 diabetes in women. *Diabetes Care,* 27, 129–133.

Arthritis Foundation. (2008a). *Arthritis Prevention, Control and Cure.* Retrieved on August 22, 2008, from: www.arthritis.org/apcca.php.

Arthritis Foundation. (2008b). Osteoarthritis. Retrieved from: www.arthritis.org.

Arthritis Foundation. (2010). Juvenile arthritis. Retrieved on February 2, 2010, from: www.arthritis.org/chapters/north-central/juvenile-arthritis.php.

Ashley, C. D., Smith, J. F., Robinson, J. B., & Richardson, M. T. (1996). Disordered eating in female collegiate athletes and collegiate females in an advanced program of study: A preliminary investigation. *International Journal of Sport Nutrition,* 6, 391–401.

Aspinwall, L. G., & Staudinger, U. M. (2003). A psychology of human strengths: Some critical issues

of an emerging field. In L. G. Aspinwall &
U. M. Staudinger (eds.), *A psychology of human
strengths: Fundamental questions & future directions
for a positive psychology* (9–22). Washington, DC:
American Psychological Association.

Association of Schools of the Allied Health Professions.
(2009). Allied health professions. Retrieved from:
www.explorehealthcareers.org/en/Field.1aspx.

Atkinson, J. H., Grant, I., & Kennedy, C. J. (1988).
Prevalence of psychiatric disorders among men
infected with human immunodeficiency virus.
Archives of General Psychiatry, 45, 859–864.

Aubel, J., Touré, I., & Diagne, M. (2004). Senegalese grand-
mothers promote improved maternal and child nutrition
practices: The guardians of tradition are not averse to
change. *Social Science & Medicine,* 59, 945–959.

Australian Institute of Health & Welfare (2002). *Australia's
Health.* AIWA: Cat. No. AUS 25. Canberra: AIHW.

Avery, C. (1991). Native American medicine: Traditional
healing. *Journal of American Medical Association,*
265, 17, 2271–2273.

Ayouba, A. J., Nerrienet, A., Menu, E., Lobe, M.,
Thonnon, J., & Leke, R. (2003). Mother-to-child
transmission of human immunodeficiency virus type
1 in relation to the season in Yaounde, Cameroon.
American Journal of Tropical Medicine and Hygiene,
69(4), 447–449.

Azjen, I. (1985). From intentions to actions: A theory
of planned behavior. In K. Kuhland & J. Beckman
(eds.), *Action control: From cognitions to behavior
(11–39).* Heidelberg: Springer.

Bach, P. B., Schrag, D., Brawley, O. W., Galaznik, A.,
Yakren, S., & Begg, C. B. (2002). Survival of blacks
and whites after a cancer diagnosis. *JAMA,* 287,
2106–2113.

Bagley, C., & Mallick, K. (2000). Prediction of sexual,
emotional, and physical maltreatment and mental
health outcomes in a longitudinal cohort of 290 adolescent women. *Child Maltreatment,* 5, 218–226.

Baker, D. W., Stevens, C. D., & Brook, R. H. (1994).
Regular source of ambulatory care and medical care
utilization by patients presenting to a public hospital
emergency department. *Journal of the American
Medical Association,* 271, 1909–1912.

Baker, K. R., Nelson, M. E., Felson, D. T., Layne, J. E.,
Sarno, R., & Roubenoff, R. (2001). The efficacy of
home based progressive strength training in older
adults with knee osteoarthritis: A randomized controlled trial. *Journal of Rheumatology,* 18, 1655–1665.

Bandura, A. (1977). Self-efficacy: Towards a unifying
theory of behavioral change. *Psychological Review,*
84(2), 191–215.

Bandura, A. (1982). Self-efficacy mechanism in human
agency. *American]Psychologist,* 37(2), 122–147.

Bandura, A. (1986). *Social foundations of thought &
action: A social cognitive theory.* Englewood Cliffs,
NJ: Prentice-Hall.

Banks, J., Marmot, M., Oldfield, Z., & Smith, J. P.
(2006). Disease and disadvantage in the United States
and in England. *Journal of the American Medical
Association,* 295(17), 2037–2045.

Banks, S. M., & Kerns, R. D. (1996). Explaining high
rates of depression in chronic pain: A diathesis–stress
framework. *Psychological Bulletin,* 119, 95–110.

Bao, W., Srinivasan, S. R., Valdez, R., Greenlund, K. J.,
Wattigney, W. A., & Berenson, G. S. (1997).
Longitudinal changes in cardiovascular risk from
childhood to young adulthood in offspring of
parents with coronary artery disease. *JAMA,* 278,
1749–1754.

Barksdale, D. J., Farrug, E. R., & Harkness, K. (2009).
Racial discrimination & blood pressure: Perceptions,
emotions, and behaviors of black American adults.
Issues of Mental Health Nursing, 30, 2, 104–111.

Barlow, J. H., Cullen, L. A., & Rowe, I. F. (2002).
Education preferences, psychological well-being and
self-efficacy among people with rheumatoid arthritis.
Patient Education and Counseling, 46, 11–19.

Barrett, B., Shadick, K., Schilling, R., Spencer, L., del
Rosario, S., Moua, K., et al. (1998). Hmong/medicine
interactions: Improving cross-cultural health care.
Family Medicine, 30(3), 179–184.

Barrett-Connor, E., & Stuenkele, C. (1999). Hormones &
heart disease in women's health and estrogen/
progesterone replacement studies in perspective.
Journal of Clinical Endocrinology & Medicine,
84(6), 1848–1853.

Bashour, H., & Mamaree, F. (2003). Gender differences
and tuberculosis in the Syrian Arab republic:
Patients' attitudes, compliance and outcomes. *East
Mediterranean Health,* 9(4), 757–768.

Baum, A., & Posluszny, D. M. (1999). Health psychology:
Mapping biobehavioral contributions to health &
illness. *Annual Review of Psychology,* 50, 137–163.

Bayne-Smith, M., Farder, P. S., Azzollini, A., Magel, S.,
Schmitz, K. H., & Agin, D. (2004). Improvements in
heart health behaviors, reduction in coronary artery
disease risk factors in urban teenage girls through a
school-based intervention. *American Journal of
Public Health,* 94(9), 1538–1543.

Beaglehole, R., Ebrahim, S., Reedy, S., Voute, J.,
Leeder, S., & Chronic Disease Action Group. (2007).
Prevention of chronic diseases: a call to action. *The
Lancet,* 370, 9605, 2152–2157.

Beck, L. F., Dellinger, A. M., & O'Neil, M. E. (2007).
Motor vehicle crash injury rates by modes of travel,
United States: Using exposure-based methods to
quantify differences. *American Journal of
Epidemiology,* 166(2), 212–218.

Becker, L. B. (1996). The epidemiology of sudden death.
In N. A. Paradis, H. R. Halperin, & R. M. Nowak
(eds.), *Cardiac arrests: the science and practice of
resuscitation medicine* (28–47). Baltimore: Williams &
Wilkins.

Beenstock, M., & Rahav, G. (2002). Testing gateway theory: Do cigarette prices affect illicit drug use? *Journal of Health Economics,* 21(4), 679–698.

Belknap, R. A., & Cruz, N. (2007). When I was in my home I suffered a lot: Mexican women's description of abuse in family of origin. *Health Care for Women International,* 28(5), 506–522.

Bell, D., Ragin, D. F., & Cohall, A. (1999). Cross-cultural issues in prevention, health promotion, and risk reduction in adolescence. *Adolescent Medicine: Prevention Issues in Adolescent Health Care. State of the Art Reviews,* 10(1), 57–70.

Bennington, D., Tetsch, N., Kunzendorf, S., & Jantschek, G. (2007). Body image in patients with eating disorders and their mothers' and the role of family functioning. *Comprehensive Psychiatry,* 48, 118–123.

Bentacourt, J. R. (2006). Eliminating racial and ethnic disparities in health care: What is the role of academic medicine? *Academic Medicine,* 81(9), 788–794.

Bentley, M. (1988). The household management of childhood diarrhea in rural north India. *Social Science & Medicine,* 27, 75–85.

Berenson, G. S., Srinivasan, S. R., Bao, W., Newman, W. P., Tracy, R. E., & Wattigney, W. A. (1998). Association between multiple cardiovascular risk factors and atherosclerosis in children and young adults. *New England Journal of Medicine,* 338, 1650–1656.

Bethel, J. W., & Schenker, M. B. (2005). Acculturation and smoking patterns among Hispanics: A review. *American Journal of Preventive Medicine,* 29(2), 143–148.

Bielak, L. F., Yu, P. F., Ryan, K. A., Rumberger, J. A., Sheedy, P. F., Turner, S. T., et al. (2007). Differences in prevalence and severity of coronary artery calcification between two non-Hispanic white populations with diverse lifestyles. *Artherosclerosis,* e-release before publication.

Biglan, A., Metzler, C. W., & Wirt, R. (1990). Social and behavioral factors associated with high-risk sexual behaviors among adolescents. *Journal of Behavioral Medicine,* 13, 245–261.

Bingham, S. A. (2000). Diet and colorectal cancer prevention. *Biochemical Social Transmission,* 28, 12–16.

Binkin, N. J., Vernon, A. A., Simone, P. M., McCray, E., Miller, B. I., & Schieffelbein, C. W. (1999). Tuberculosis prevention and control activities in the US: An overview of the organization of TB screening. *International Journal of Tuberculosis Lung Disease,* 3(8), 663–674.

Bjorck, J. P., Hopp, D. P., & Jones, L. W. (1999). Prostate cancer and emotional functioning: Effects on mental adjustment, optimism and appraisal. *Journal of Psychosocial Oncology,* 17(1), 71–85.

Bjordal, J. M., Klovning, A., Ljunggren, A. E., & Slordal, L. (2007). Short-term efficacy of pharmapsychotherapeutic interventions in osteoarthritic knee pain: A meta-analysis of randomized placebo-controlled trials. *European Journal of Pain,* 11, 125–138.

Blake, L. V. (1992). Hemophilia and HIV—A hidden majority. Paper presented at the International Conference on AIDS. July 19, 1992.

Bledsoe, G. H., Schexnayder, S. M., Carey, M. J., Dobbins, W. N., Gibson, W. D., Hindman, J. W., et al. (2002). The negative impact of the repeal of the Arkansas motor cycle helmet law. *Journal of Trauma,* 53(6), 1078–1086.

Blossner, M., & deOnis, M. (2005). Malnutrition: Quantifying the health impact at national and local levels. WHO Environmental Burden of Disease Series, No, 12. Geneva: WHO.

Blum, R. W., Beuhring, T., Shew, M. L., Beavinger, L. H., Sieving, R. E., & Resnick, M. D. (2000). The effects of race/ethnicity, income and family structure on adolescent risk behaviors. *American Journal of Public Health,* 90(12), 1879–1884.

Boddington, P. (2009). Theoretical & practical issues in the definition of health: Insight from Aboriginal Australia. *Journal of Medicine and Philosophy,* 34(1), 49–67.

Boehmer, T. K., Lovegreen, S. L., Haire-Joshu, D., & Brownson, R. C. (2006). What constitutes an obesogenic environment in rural communities? *American Journal of Health Promotion,* 20(6), 411–421.

Bolen, J., Sniezek, T., Theis, K., Helmich, C., Hootman, J., Brady, T., et al. (2005). Racial/ethnic differences in the prevalence and impact of doctor-diagnosed arthritis: United States, 2002. *Morbidity & Mortality Weekly Report,* 54, 119–123.

Bolger, N., Foster, M., Vinoker, A. D., & Ng, R. (1966). Close relationships & adjustments to a life crisis: The case of breast cancer. *Journal of Personal & Social Psychology,* 70, 283–294.

Bolland, J. M. (2003). Hopelessness and risk behavior among adolescents living in high-poverty inner-city neighborhoods. *Journal of Adolescence,* 26, 145–158.

Boney, F. H. (1967). Doctor Thomas Hamilton: Two views of a gentleman of the old South. *Phylon,* 28, 288–292.

Borders, A. (2004). Predicting problem behaviors with multiple expectancies: Expanding expectancy-value theory. *Adolescence,* 39(155), 539–550.

Bosswell, G. H., Kahana, E., & Dilworth-Anderson, P. (2006). Spirituality and healthy lifestyle behaviors: Stress counter-balancing effects on the wellbeing of older adults. *Journal of Religion and Health,* 45, 4, 587–602.

Bourgeois, A. P. (1980). Kakungu among the Yaku and Suku., *African Arts,* 14(1), 42–46.

Bourne, P. A. (2009). Health inequalities in Jamaica, 1988–2007. *Australian Journal of Basic and Applied Science,* 3, 3, 3040–3052.

Bowen-Reid, T. L., & Harrell, J. P. (2002). Racist experiences and health outcomes: An examination of spirituality as a buffer. *Journal of Black Psychology, 28,* 18–36.

Bowie, J. V., Sydnor, K. D., Granot, M., & Pargament, K. J. (2004). Spirituality and coping among survivors of prostate cancer. *Journal of Psychosocial Oncology,* 22(2), 41–56.

Boyd, B., & Wandersman, A. (1991). Predicting undergraduate condom use with the Fishbein and Azjen and the Triandis attitude-behavior models: Implications for public health intervention. *Journal of Applied Social Psychology,* 21, 1810–1830.

Brady, S. S., & Donenberg, G. R. (2006). Mechanisms linking violence exposure to health risk behavior in adolescence: Motivation to cope and sensation-seeking personality. *Journal of the American Academy of Child and Adolescent Psychiatry,* 45, 673–680.

Brady, S. S., Dolcini, M. M., Harper, G. W., & Pollack, L. M. (2009). Supportive friendships moderate the association between stressful life events and sexual risk taking among African American adolescents. *Health Psychology,* 28, 2, 238–248.

Bratberg, E., Dahl, S. A., & Risa, A. E. (2002). The double burden. Do combinations of career and family obligations increase sickness absence among women? *European Sociological Review,* 18(2), 233–249.

Braun, S., Mejia, R., Ling, P. M., & Perez-Stable, E. J. (2008). Tobacco industry target youth in Argentina. *Tobacco Control,* 17, 2, 111–117.

Breitbart, W. (1995). Identifying patients at risk for a treatment of major psychiatric complications of cancer. *Supportive Cancer Care,* 3, 45–60.

Breitbart, W., McDonald, M. V., Rosenfield, B., Passic, S. D., Hewitt, H. D., Thaler, H., et al. (1996). Pain in ambulatory AIDS patients I: Pain characteristics and medical correlates. *Pain,* 68, 315–321.

Brender, N. D., & Collins, J. L. (1998). Co-occurrence of health-risk behaviors among adolescents in the United States. *Journal of Adolescent Health* 22, 209–213.

Brendgen, M., & Vitaro, F. (2008). Peer rejection and physical health problems in early adolescence. *Journal of Developmental and Behavioral Pediatrics,* 29, 3, 183–190.

Brendgen, M., Vitaro, F., Bukowski, W. M., Doyle, A. B., & Markiewicz, D. (2001). Developmental profiles of peer social preference over the course of elementary school: associations with trajectories of externalizing and internalizing behaviors. *Developmental psychology,* 37, 308–320.

Brennan, M., Singer, S., Maki, R., & O'Sullivan, B. (2004). Sarcomas of the soft tissue and bone. In V. T. DeVita, S. Hellman, & S. A. Rosenberg (eds.), *Cancer: Principle & practice of oncology,* Vol. 2 (7th ed.). Philadelphia: Lippincott, Williams & Wilkins.

Brentlinger, P. E., Behrens, C. B., & Kublin, J, G. (2007). Challenges in the prevention, diagnosis & treatment of malaria in human immunodeficiency virus infected adults in sub-Saharan Africa. *Archives of Internal Medicine,* 167(17), 1827–1836.

Breslau, N., Fenn, N., & Peterson, E. L. (1993). Early smoking initiation and nicotine dependence in a cohort of young adults. *Drug and Alcohol Dependence,* 33, 129–137.

Britto, M. T., Klostermann, B. K., Bonny, A. E., Altum, S. A., & Hornung, R. W. (2001). Impact of a school-based intervention on access to healthcare for underserved youth. *Journal of Adolescent Health,* 29, 116–124.

Broadhead, W. E., Kaplan, B. H., James, S.A., Wagner, E. H., Schoenback, V. J., & Grumson. R., et al. (1983). The epidemiologic evidence for a relationship between social support and health. *American Journal of Epidemiology,* 117, 521–537.

Brondolo, E., Rieppi, R., Kelly, K. P., & Gerin, W. (2003). Perceived racism and blood pressure: A review of the literature and conceptual and methodological critique. *Annals of Behavioral Medicine,* 25, 55–66.

Broome, B., & Broome, R. (2007). Native Americans: Traditional healing. *Urologic Nursing,* 27(2), 161–173.

Brosseau, L., Pelland, L., Wells, G., Macleay, L., Lamothe, C., Michaud, G., et al. (2004). Efficacy of aerobic exercises for osteoarthritis (Part II): A meta-analysis. *Physical Therapy Review,* 9, 125–145.

Brown, L. K., & DiClemente, R. J. (1992). Predictors of condom use in sexually active adolescents. *Journal of Adolescent Health,* 13(8), 651–657.

Bruce, A. Bray, D., Lewis, J., Raff, M., Roberts, K., & Watson, J. D. (2002). *The molecular biology of the cell.* Bunin, G. R. (2004) Nongenetic causes of childhood cancer: evidence from international variation, time trends, and risk factor studies. *Toxicology & Applied Pharmacology,* 199, 91–103.

Bruce, A., Bray, D., Lewis, J., Raff, M., Roberts, K., & Watson, J. D. (2002). *The molecular biology of the cell.* Retrieved on February 26, 2010: www.ncbi.nlm.nih.gov/bookshelf/br.fcgi?book=mboc4&part=A4419&rendertype=figure&id=A4427.

Bruce, K. R., & Steiger, H. (2005). Treatment implications of Axis-II comorbidity in eating disorders. *Eating Disorders,* 13, 93–108.

Bucko, R. A., & Cloud, S. I. (2008). Lakota health and healing. *Southern Medical Journal,* 101(6), 596–598.

Bullman, D. C., & Svarsted, B. L. (2000). Effects of physician communication style on client medication beliefs and adherence with antidepressant treatment. *Patient Education and Counseling,* 40, 2, 173–185.

Burke, A. P., Farb, A., Malcom, G. T., Liang, Y., Smialek, J. E., & Virmani, R. (1999). Plaque rupture and sudden death related to exertion in men with coronary artery disease. *JAMA,* 281(10), 921–926.

Burnam, A. M., Telles, C. A., Karno, M., & Hough, R. I. (1987). Measurement of acculturation in a community of Mexican Americans. *Hispanic Journal of Behavioral Science,* 9, 105–130.

Burt, W., & Overpeck, M. D. (2001). Emergency visits for sports-related injuries. *Annals of Emergency Medicine,* 37(3), 301–308.

Burton, L. E., Smith, H. H., & Nichols, A. W. (1980). *Public Health and Community Medicine,* 3rd ed. Baltimore: Wiliams & Wilkins.

Caban, A. J., Lee, D. J., Fleming, L. E., Gomez-Martin, O., Leblanc, W., & Pitman, T. (2005). Obesity in U.S. workers: The national health interview survey 1986–2002. *American Journal of Public Health,* 95(9), 1614–1622.

Calcagni, E., & Elenkov, I. (2006). Stress system activity, innate & T helper cytokines & susceptibility to immune-related diseases. Annals of the New York Academy of Science, 1069, 62–76.

Caminero Luna, J. A. (2003). *Guia de la tuberculosis para medicos especialistas.* France: International Union Against Tuberculosis and Respiratory Disease.

Campbell, L. C., Keefe, F. J., Scipio, C., McKee, D. C., Edwards, C. L., & Herman, S. H. (2006). Facilitating research participation & improving quality of life for African American prostate cancer survivors & their intimate partners. *Cancer,* Suppl, 109, 2, 414–424.

Campsmith, M. L., Rhodes, P. H., Hall, H. I., & Green, T. A. (2010). Undiagnosed HIV prevalence among adults & adolescents in the US at the end of 2006. *Journal of Acquired Immune Deficiency Syndrome,* 53, 3, 619–624.

Cannon, W. B. (1929). *Body changes in pain, hunger, fear & rage.* New York: Appleton.

Cantor, D. (2000). The diseased body. In R. Cooter & J. E. Pickstone (eds.), *Medicine in the 20th Century.* London: Harwood Press.

Capaldi, D. M., & Clark, S. (1998). Prospective family prediction of aggression towards female partner for at-risk young men. *Developmental Psychology,* 34, 1175–1188.

Carels, R. A., Darby, L. A., Ryder, S., Douglas, O. M., Cacciapaglia, H. M., & O'Brien, N. H. (2005). The relationship between self-monitoring, outcome expectations, difficulty with eating and exercise and physical activity and weight loss treatment outcome. *Annals of Behavioral Medicine,* 30(3), 182–190.

Carroll, D., Smith, G. D., & Bennett, P. (2002). Some observations on health and socio-economic status. In D. F. Marks (ed.), *The health psychology reader.* London: Sage Publications.

Carstensen, L. I., & Charles, S. T. (2003). Human aging: Why is even good news taken as bad? In L. G. Aspinwall & U. M. Staudinger (eds.), *A Psychology of human strengths* (75–86). Washington, DC: American Psychological Association.

Cartwright, M., Wardle, J., Steggles, N., Simon, A. E., Croker, J. E., & Jarvis, M. J. (2003). Stress and dietary practices in adolescents. *Health Psychology,* 22, 362–369.

Case, A., Lubotsky, D., & Paxson, C. (2002). Economic states and health in childhood: The origins of the gradient. *American Economic Review,* 92, 1308–1334.

Cassels, A. K. (2007). Vaccination against human papillomavirus. *Canadian Medical Association Journal,* 177, 1526.

Cavanagh, S. E. (2007). Peers, drinking, and the assimilation of Mexican American youth. *Sociological Perspectives,* 50, 3, 393–416.

Centers for Disease Control (CDC). (1992). 1993 Revised classification system for HIV infection and expansion of surveillance case definition for AIDS among adolescents and adults. *Mortality and Morbidity Weekly Reports,* Dec.18, 41(RR-17).

Centers for Disease Control (CDC). (1993). Arthur Ashe, tennis star, is dead at 49. HIV/AIDS, STD, TB Prevention Update. Retrieved from: www.aegis.com/news/ads/1993/ad930239.html/.

Centers for Disease Control (CDC). (1999). National Center for Health Statistics. National Vital Statistics.

Centers for Disease Control (2000). Boy's Growth Chart: weight vs. Height. CDC: National Center for Health Statistics. Retrieved on February 24, 2009, from: http://www.cdc.gov/growthcharts/data/set1clinical/cj41c025.pdf.

Centers for Disease Control. (2004a). Dracunculiasis, parasites and health. Retrieved on May 12, 2007, from: www.dpd.cdc.gov.dpdx/HTML/Frames/A-F/Dracunculiasis/body.

Centers for Disease Control (CDC). (2004b). Excite: An Introduction to epidemiology. Retrieved on March 23, 2009, from: www.cdc.gov/excite/classroom/intro-epi.htm.

Centers for Disease Control (CDC). (2004c). *National program of cancer registry: United States cancer statistics.* Retrieved on July 15, 2009, from: www.apps.nccd.cdc.gov/uscs/Table.aspx?group=3f&year=2004&Display=n.

Centers for Disease Control (CDC). (2004d). *Tobacco use in the US.* Washington, DC: National Centers for Disease Control and Prevention and Health Promotion, Tobacco Information & Promotion Source.

Centers for Disease Control (CDC). (2004e). West Nile Virus Background: Virus History and Distribution. Retrieved on May 15, 2007, from: www.cdc.gov/ncidod/dvbid/westnile/background/html.

Centers for Disease Control (2004f). National Center for Occupational Safety & Health. Worker's Health Chartbook.

Centers for Disease Control. (2005). Surveillance for illnesses and injury after Hurricane Katrina—New

Orleans, Louisiana, September 8–25. *Morbidity & Mortality Weekly Report.*

Centers for Disease Control. (2006a). Avian influenza infections of humans. Retrieved on May 30, 2008, from: www.cdc.gov/flu/avian/gen-info/avian-flu-humans.htm.

Centers for Disease Control (CDC). (2006b). Racial/ethnic disparities in diagnoses of HIV/AIDS. *Morbidity and Mortality Weekly Report,* 55, 121–125.

Centers for Disease Control (2007a). Prevention of specific infectious diseases. Chapter 4. Retrieved on September 26, 2007, from: www.cdc.gov/travel/yellow BookCh4-TB.aspx.

Centers for Disease Control. (2007b). *Tuberculosis Factsheet.* Division of Tuberculosis and Elimination. Retrieved on February 10, 2010, from: http://www.cdc.gov/tb/publications/factsheets/statistics/TB Trends.htm.

Centers for Disease Control (CDC). (2007c). HIV/AIDS Basics. Retrieved on April 27, 2008, from: www.cdc.gov/hiv/resources/qa/qa5.htm.

Centers for Disease Control (CDC). (2008). Arthritis Types—Overview: Childhood arthritis. Retrieved from: www.cdc.gov/arthritis/arthritis/childhood.htm.

Centers for Disease Control (CDC). (2009a). HIV mortality (through 2006). Retrieved on February 26, 2010, from: www.cdc.gov/hiv/topics/surveillance/resources/slides/mortality/index.htm.

Centers for Disease Control (CDC). (2009b). HIV, statistics and surveillance: Basic statistics. Retrieved from: www.cdc.gov/hiv/topics/surveillance/basic.htm#hivaidsexposure.

Centers for Disease Control. (2009c). Overweight and Obesity. CDC: National Center for Health Statistics. Prevalence of Overweight Children and Adolescents US 2003_2004. Retrieved on February 24, 2010, from: http://www.cdc.gov/mmwr/preview/mmwr html/mm5408a6.htm; www.cdc.gov/nchs/data/hestat/overweight/overwght_child_03.htm.

Centers for Disease Control. (2009d). Travelers' Yellowbook. Retrieved on February 19, 2010, from: www.cdc.gov/travel/yellowbook/2010/Chapter-5/tuberculosis.aspx#1315.

Centers for Disease Control (2009e). Health promotion and Healthy Schools. Retrieved on September 1, 2009, from: http://www.cdc.gov/healthyyouth/images/school_health_ model.jpg.

Centers for Disease Control. (2010). FluView: A Weekly Influenza Surveillance Report. Prepared by Influenza Division, Week ending January 8, 2010 Retrieved on June 2, 2010, from: http://www.cdc.gov/h1n1flu/updates/us/011510.htm.

Centers for Disease Control and Prevention (CDC). (2001). *Sexually transmitted disease surveillance, 2000.* Atlanta, GA: U.S. Department of Health and Human Services.

Centers for Disease Control and Prevention (CDC). (2005a). Avian flu: Transmission of influenza A virus between animals and people. Retrieved on March 1, 2007, from: www.cdc.gov/flu/avian/gen-into/transmission/htm.

Centers for Disease Control and Prevention (CDC). (2005b). Web-based injury statistics querie and reporting system. WISQARS 2005. National Center for Injury Prevention and Control, CDC. Retrieved from: www.cdc.gov/ncipc/wisqars/default/htm.

Centers for Disease Control and Prevention (CDC). (2006). Multi-state outbreak of E-coli 0157 infections. November–December, 2006. Foodborn & Diarrheal Disease Branch. Retrieved on May 23, 2007, from: www.cdc.gov/ecoli/2006/december/121406.htm.

Centers for Disease Control and Prevention (CDC). (2008a). Alcohol. Retrieved on May 22, 2009, from: www.cdc.gov/alcohol.

Centers for Disease Control and Prevention (CDC). (2008b). Alcohol & public health. Retrieved on May 23, 2009, from: www.cdc.gov/alcohol/.

Centers for Disease Control and Prevention (CDC). (2008c). *Quick stats: General information on alcohol use and health,* alcohol and public health. Retrieved from: www.cdc.gov/alcohol/quickstats/general_info.htm.

Centers for Disease Control and Prevention (2008d). Surveillance Summaries, 57, No. SS-12, 1–60. Retrieved on July 12, 2010, from: http://www.cdc.gov/mmwr/pdf/ss/ss5712.pdf.

Centers for Disease Control & Prevention (CDC). (2008e). Quick Stats: General Information on alcohol use & health, alcohol & public health. Retrieved on May 22, 2009, from: www.cdc.gov/alcohol/quickstats/general/info.htm.

CERD Working Group on Health & Environmental Health. (2008). *Unequal health outcomes in the United States: Racial & ethnic disparities in health care treatment & access, the role of social & environmental determinants of health & the responsibilities of the state.* A Report to the U.N. Committee on the Elimination of Racial Discrimination. Accessed on September 22, 2009, from: http://www.prrac.org/pdf/CERDhealthEnvironmentReport.pdf.

Chafin, S., Roy, M., Gerin, W., & Christenfeld, N. (2004). Music can facilitate blood pressure recovery from stress. *British Journal of Health Psychology,* 9, 3, 393–403.

Chambers, D. W. (2001). A brief history of conflicting ideals in health care. *Journal of the American College of Dentists,* 68(3), 48–51.

Chamorro, R., & Florez-Ortiz, Y. (2000). Acculturation and disordered eating patterns among Mexican American women. *International Journal of Eating Disorders,* 28, 125–129.

Chapman, W. P., & Jones, C. M. (1944). Variations in cutaneous & visceral pain sensitivity in normal subjects. *Journal of Clinical Investigations, 23*, 81.

Chapple, A., Ziebland, S., & McPherson, A. (2004). Qualitative study of men's perceptions of why treatment delays occur in the UK for those with testicular cancer. *British Journal of General Practice, 54*, 25–32.

Chaves, S. S., Gargiullo, P., Zhang, J. X., Civen, R., Guris, D., Mascola, L, et al. (2007). Loss of vaccine-induced immunity to varicella over time. *The New England Journal of Medicine,* 356:1121–1129.

Checkland, K., Harrison, S., McDonald, R., Grant, S., Campbell, S., & Guthrie, B. (2008). Biomedical, holism & general medical practice: responses to the 2004 general practitioner contract. *Sociology of Health & Wellness, 30*(5), e-journal prepublication.

Chee, V. A. (1991). Medicine men. *Journal of the American Medical Association,* 265, 17, 2276.

Chesney, M. A., Darber, L. A., Hoerster, K., Taylor, J. M., Chambers, D. B., & Anderson, D. E. (2005). Positive emotions: Explaining the other hemisphere in behavioral medicine. *International Journal of Behavioral Medicine, 12,* 2, 50–58.

Chia, S. E., Chia, H. P., & Tan, J. S. (2000). Prevalence of headache among handheld cellular telephone users in Singapore: A community study. *Environmental Health Perspective,* 108, 1059–1062.

Chida, Y., & Steptoe, A. (2008). Positive psychological well-being and mortality: A qualitative review of prospective observational studies. *Psychosomatic Medicine, 70,* 741–756.

Chida, Y., & Vedhara, K. (2009). Adverse psychosocial factors predict poorer prognosis in HIV disease: A meta-analytic review of prospective investigations. *Brain, Behavior, and Immunity, 23,* 434–445.

Child Trends Data Bank. Teen Births. Retrieved on February 2, 2009, from: www.childtrendsdatabank.org/pdf/13_PDF.pdf.

Chisuwa, N., & O'Dea, J. A. (2010). Body image and eating disorders amongst Japanese adolescents: A review of the literature. *Appetitie,* 54, 1, 5–15.

Choi, H. K., Atkinson, K., Karlson, L. W., Willett, W., & Curhan, G. (2004a). Alcohol intake & risk of incident of gout in men: A prospective study. *Lancet,* 363, 1277–1281.

Choi, H. K., Atkinson, K., Karlson, L. W., Willett, W., & Curhan, G. (2004b). A purine-rich foods, dairy & protein intake & the risk of gout in men. *New England Journal of Medicine,* 350, 1093–1103.

Christensen, P. (2003). "In these perilous times": Plagues and plague policies in early modern Denmark. *Medical History,* 47(4), 413–450.

Christenfeld, N. Glynn, L. M., & Gerin, W. (2000). On the reliable assessment of cardiovascular recovery: An application of curve-fitting techniques. *Psychophysiology,* 37, 543–550.

Christensen, H. C., Schuz, J., Kosteljanetz, M., Poulsen, H. S., Thomsen, J., & Johansen, C. (2004). Cellular telephone use and risk of acoustic neuroma. *American Journal of Epidemiology,* 159, 277–283.

Christopher and Dana Reeve Foundation (2009). The history of the Reeve foundation. Retrieved on November 27, 2009, from: http://www.christopherreeve.org/site/c.ddJFKRNoFiG/b.4506337/apps/s/content.asp?ct=5856133.

Chua, J. L., Touyz, S., & Hill, A. J. (2004). Negative mood-induced overeating in obese binge eaters: An experimental study. *International Journal of Obese Related Metabolism Disorders, 28,* 606–610.

Cintron, A., & Morrison, R. S. (2006). Pain & ethnicity in US: A systematic review. *Journal of Palliative Medicine,* 9(6), 1454–1473.

Clark, R. (2006). Perceived racism and vascular reactivity in black college women: Moderating effects of seeking social support. *Health Psychology,* 25(1), 20–25.

Claudpierre, P. (2005). Spa therapy for ankylosing spondylitis: Still useful? *Joint, Bone Spine,* 72, 283–285.

Claus, E. B., Schildkraut, J. M., Thompson, W. D., & Risch, N. J. (1996). The genetic attributable risk of breast and ovarian cancer. *Cancer,* 77, 2318–2324.

Clauss-Ehlers, C. C. C. (2003). Promoting ecological health resilience for minority youth: Enhancing health care access through the school health center. *Psychology in the Schools,* 40, 3, 265–278.

Clay, R. (1977). Prevention is theme of the '98 presidential year. *The American Psychological Association Monitor.* December, 35. Washington, DC: The American Psychological Association.

Coburn, D. (2004). Beyond the income inequality hypothesis: Class, neo-liberalism, and health inequalities. *Social Science & Medicine,* 58, 41–56.

Cockerham, W. C. (2001). *Medical sociology.* Upper Saddle River, NJ: Prentice Hall.

Cohen, M. (2006). Jim Crow's drug war: Race, Coca Cola and the southern origins of the drug prohibition. *Southern Cultures,* 12, 3, 55–79.

Cohen, S. (2004). Connecting social relationships and health. *Monitor on Psychology,* 35, 14–15.

Cohen, S. (2005). Keynote presentation at the Eighth International Congress of Behavioral Medicine: The Pittsburgh common cold studies: Psychosocial predictors of susceptibility to respiratory infectious illness. *International Journal of Behavioral Medicine,* 12, 3, 123–131.

Cohen, S., & McKay, G. (1984). Social support, stress & the buffering hypothesis: A theoretical analysis. In Baum, A., Singer, J. E., & Taylor, S. E. (eds.) *Handbook of Psychology and Health,* Vol. 4 (pp. 253–267). Hillsdale, NJ: Erlbaum.

Cohen, J. B., & Reed, D. (1985). Type-A behavior & coronary heart disease among Japanese men in Hawaii. *Journal of Behavioral Medicine,* 8, 343–352.

Cohen, S., & Williamson, G. M. (1991). Stress & infectious diseases in humans. *Psychological Bulletin,* 109, 5–24.

Cohen, S., & Wills, T. A. (1985). Stress, social support & the buffering hypothesis. *Psychological Bulletin,* 98, 2, 310–357.

Cohen, S., Doyle, W. J., Skoner, D. P., Fireman, P., Gwaltney, J. M., & Newsom, J. T. (1995). State and trait negative affect as predictors of objective and subjective symptoms of respiratory viral infections. *Journal of Personality and Social Psychology,* 68, 159–169.

Cohen, D., Farley, T. A., Bedimo-Etam, J., Scribner, R., Ward, W., Kendall, C., et al. (1999). Implementation of condom social marketing in Louisiana. *American Journal of Public Health,* 89, 204–208.

Cohen, S., Kaplan, G. A., & Salonen, J. T. (1999). The role of psychological characteristics in the relations between socioeconomic status and perceived health. *Journal of Applied Social Psychology,* 29, 445–268.

Cohen, S., Tyrrell, D. A. J., & Smith, A. P. (1991). Psychological stress and susceptibility to the common cold. *New England Journal of Medicine,* 325, 606–612.

Cohen, S., Tyrrell, D. A. J., & Smith, A. P. (1993). Life events, perceived stress, negative affect and susceptibility to the common cold. *Journal of Personality and Social Psychology,* 64, 131–140.

Cold, J., Petruckevitch, A., Feder, G., Chung, W., Richardson, J., & Moorey, S. (2001). Relation between childhood sexual and physical abuse and risk of revictimization in women: A cross- sectional survey. *Lancet,* 258, 450–454.

Collins, T. C., Clark, J. A., Petersen, L. A., & Kressin, N. R. (2002) Racial differences in how physicians communication regarding cardiac testing. *Medical Care,* 40 (1 Suppl.), 127–134.

Columbia Presbyterian Medical Center. (1992). Bone marrow transplant. *Bone Marrow Transplant Newsletter.* Retrieved from: http://cpmcnet.columbia.edu/ dept/medicine/Bonemarrow/bminfo.html.

Committee on Ethical Standards of Psychologists. (1958). Standards of ethical behavior for psychologists. Report of the committee on ethical standards of psychologists. *American Psychologists,* 13, 266–271.

Committee on Injury, Violence, and Poison Prevention and Committee on Adolescence. (2006). The teen driver. *Pediatrics,* 118, 2570–2581.

Compston, A. (2000). The genetics of multiple sclerosis. *Journal of Neurovirology,* Suppl 2, S5–S9.

Connolly, M. A., Gayer, M., Ryan, M. J., Salama, P., Spiegel, P., & Heymann, D. L. (2004). Communicable diseases in complex emergencies: Impact and challenges. *Lancet,* 364, 1974–1983.

Cooke, B., & Ernst, E. (2000). Aromatherapy: A systematic review. *British Journal of General Practice,* 50, 493–496.

Cooke, M., Holzhauser, K., Jones, M., Davis, C., & Finucan, J. (2007). The effect of aromatherapy massage with music on stress & anxiety levels of emergency nurses: Comparison between summer and winter. *Journal of Clinical Nursing,* 16, 9, 1695–1703.

Cooper, M. D. (2003). Behavior based safety still a viable strategy. *Safety and Health,* 46–48.

Cooper, D. C., Mills, P. J., Bardwell, N. A., Ziegler, M. G., & Dimsdale, J. E. (2009). The effect of ethnic discrimination and socioeconomic status on etidothelin-1 among blacks and whites. *American Journal of Hypertension,* 22, 7, 698–704.

Cooper-Patrick, L., Gallo, J. J., Gonzalez, J. J., Vu, H. T., Powe, N. R., Nelson, C., et al. (1999). Race, gender and partnership in the patient–physician relationship. *Journal of the American Medical Association,* 282, 6, 583–589.

Coovadia, H. M., Rollins, N. C., Bland, R. M., Little, K., Coutsoudis, A., Bemis, N. L., et al. (2007). Mother-to-child-transmission of HIV-1 infection during exclusive breastfeeding in the first 6 months of life: an intervention cohort study. *Lancet,* 369, 1107–1116.

Corso, P. S., Mercy, J. A., Simon, T. R., Finkelstein, E. A., & Miller, T. R. (2007). Medical costs and productivity losses due to interpersonal and self-directed violence in the United States. *American Journal of Preventive Medicine,* 32(6), 474–482.

Coursen, C. C. (2009). Inequalities affecting access to healthcare: A philosophical reflection. *International Journal for Human Caring,* 13, 1, 7–15.

Cressey, T. R., & Lallemant, M. (2007). Pharmacogenetics of antiretroviral drugs for the treatment of HIV-infected patients: An update. *Infection, Genetics and Evolution,* 7, 333–342.

Crombez, G., Eccleston, C., Van Hamme, G., & De Vlieger, P. (2008). Attempting to solve the problem of pain: A questionnaire study in acute and chronic pain patients. *Pain,* 137(3), 556–563.

Cruz-Coke, R. M. (2007). Peregrinaciones a las Fuentes de la medicina clasica. *Revista Medica De Chile,* 135, 8, 1076–1081.

Cummings, K. M., Hyland, A., Giovino, G. A., Hastrup, J. L., Bauer, J. E., & Bansal, M. A. (2004). Are smokers adequately informed about the health risks of smoking and medicinal nicotine? *Nicotine Tobacco Research,* 6 (Suppl 3), S333–S340.

Cutts, F. T., Franceschi, S., Golden, S., Castellasque, X., de San Jose, G., & Garnet, G. (2007). Human papillomavirus and HPV vaccines: A review. *Bulletin of the World Health Organization,* 85(9), 719–726.

Dabelea, D. (2007). The predisposition to obesity and diabetes in offspring of diabetic mothers. *Diabetes Care,* 30:S, 169–174.

Dageid, W., & Duckert, F. (2008). Balancing between normality and social death: Black, rural, South African women coping with HIV/AIDS. *Quantitative Health Research,* 18, 2, 182–195.

D'Alberto, A. (2006). The withering of yin: A mid-life crisis? *Positive Health,* September, 18.

Dales, L., Hammer, S. J., & Smith, N. J. (2001). Time trends in autism and in MMR immunization coverage in California. *Journal of the American Medical Association,* 285, 1183–1185.

Daniel, T. M. (2006) The history of tuberculosis. *Respiratory Medicine,* 100(11), 1862–1870.

Dariotis, J. K., Sonenstein, F. L., Gates, G. J., Astone, N. M., Pleck, J. H., Sifakis, F., & Zeger, S. (2008). Changes in sexual risk behaviors as young men transition into adulthood. *Perspectives on Sexual and Reproductive Health,* 40, 4, 218–225.

Darton, A. J., McElvenny, D. M., & Hodgson, J. T. (2006). Estimating the number of asbestos related lung cancer deaths in GB from 1980–2000. *Annals of Occupational Hygiene,* 50(1), 29–38.

Dassow, P. (2005). Setting educational priorities for women's preventive health: Measuring beliefs about screening across disease states. *Journal of Women's Health,* 14(4), 324–330.

Daughtery, J. D., & Houry, D. E. (2008). Intimate partner violence screening in the emergency department. *Journal of Postgraduate Medicine,* 54(4), 301–305.

Davis, A. L. (1996). History of the sanatorium movement. In W. N. Rom & S. M. Garay (eds.), *Tuberculosis.* Boston: Little Brown.

Davis, K., Dickman, E. D., Ferris, D., & Dias, J. K. (2004). Human papillomavirus among parents of 10–15 year old adolescents. *Journal of Lower Genital Track Disease,* 8(3), 188–194.

Dawber, T. R., & Kannel, W. B. (1966). The Framingham study: An epidemiological approach to coronary heart disease. *Circulation,* 34(4), 553–555.

de Sanjose, S., Leone, M., Berez, V., Izquierdo, A., Font, R., Brunet, J. M., et al. (2003). Prevalence of BRCA1 and BRCA2 germline mutations in young breast cancer patients: A population-based study. *International Journal of Cancer,* 106, 588–593.

De Smet, P. A. G. M. (1998). Traditional pharmacology and medicine in Africa: Ethnopharma-cological themes in sub-Saharan art objects and utensils. *Journal of Ethnopharmacology,* 63, 1–175.

DeGreve, J., Sermijn, E., De Brakeleer, S., Ren, Z., & Tengels, E. (2008). Heredity breast cancer: From bench to bedside. *Current Opinoins in Oncology,* 20(6), 605–613.

DeLaet, D. E., Shea, S., & Carrisquillo, O. (2002). Receipt of preventive services among privately insured minorities in managed care versus fee-for-service insurance plans. *Journal of General Internal Medicine,* 17(6), 451–457.

DelBocca, F. K., Darkes, J., Goldman, M. S., & Smith, G. T. (2002). Advancing the expectancy concept via the interplay between research and theory. *Alcoholism: Clinical and Experimental Research,* 26, 926–935.

Delgado, D. J., Lin, W. Y., & Coffey, M. (1995). The role of Hispanic race/ethnicity and poverty in breast cancer survival. *Puerto Rican Health Science Journal,* 14, 103–116.

Delucchi, K. L., Matzger, H., & Weisner, C. (2008). Alcohol in emerging adulthood: 7-year study of problem and dependent drinkers. *Addictive Behaviors,* 33(1), 134–142.

Dembroski, J. M., MasDougall, J. M., Williams, R. B., Haney, T. L., & Blumenthall, J. A. (1985). Components of type-A, hostility & anger in relationship to angiographic findings. *Psychosomatic Medicine,* 47, 219–233.

Denollet, J., Pedersen, S. S., Vrints, C. J., & Conraads, V. M. (2006). Usefulness of Type D personality in predicting five-year cardiac events above and beyond concurrent symptoms of stress in patients with coronary heart disease. *American Journal of Cardiology,* 97, 970–973.

Derlega, V. J., Winstead, B. A., Oldfield, E. C., & Barbee, A. P. (2003). Close relationships and social support in coping with HIV: a test of sensitive interaction systems. *AIDS Behavior,* 7, 119–129.

DeStefano, F., & Chen, R. T. (2008). Autism and measles-mumps-rubella vaccination: Controversy laid to rest? *CNS Drugs,* 15, 11, 831–837.

DeVoe, J. E. (2009) Educaid: What if the US systems of education and healthcare were more alike? *Family Medicine,* 41, 9, 652–655.

Diaz, D. P. (1993). Foundations for spirituality: establishing the variables of spirituality within the disciplines. *Journal of Health Education,* 24(6), 24–326.

DiClimente, R. J., Lodico, M., Grinstead, O. A., Harper, G., Rickman, R. L., Evans, P. E., et al. (1996). African American adolescents residing in high-risk urban environments do use condoms: Correlates and predictors of condom use among adolescents in public housing developments. *Pediatrics,* 98, 269–278.

Diener, E. (2000). Subjective well-being: The science of happiness and a proposal for a national index. *American Psychologist,* 55, 34–43.

Diener, E., & Suh, E. M. (2000). *Culture & subjective well-being.* Cambridge, MA: MIT Press.

Diesfled, K. (2008) Interpersonal issues between pin physicians and patient: Strategies to reduce conflict. *Pain Medicine,* 9, 8, 1118–1124.

DiFranza, J. R., Richards, J. W., Paulman, P. M., Wolf-Gillespie, N., Fletcher, C., Jaffe, R. D., et al. (1991). RJR Nabisco's cartoon panel promotes camel cigarettes. *JAMA,* 266(22), 3149–3153.

Dinh, N. M. H., & Groleau, D. (2008). Traumatic amputation: A case of Laotian indignation and injustice. *Culture, Medicine & Psychiatry,* June 17, e-publication ahead of print.

DiSpezio, M. (1997) *The science of HIV.* A National Science Teachers' Association Publication. U.S.A: Automated Graphic Systems.

Distefan, J. M., Pierce, J. P., & Gilpin, E. A. (2004). Do favorite movie stars influence adolescent smoking initiation? *American Journal of Public Health, 94*, 7, 1239–1244.

Dixon, K. E., Keefe, F. J., Scipio, C. D., Perri, L. M., & Abernethy, A. P. (2007). Psychological interventions for arthritis pain management in adults: A meta-analysis. *Health Psychology, 26*(3), 241–250.

Doctors without Borders. (2006) Malnutrition. Retrieved on January 7, 2008, from: http://www.doctorswithout-borders.org/news/malnutrition/background.cfm.

Dodds, C. (2006). HIV-related stigma in England: Experiences of gay men & heterosexual African immigrants living with HIV. *Journal of Community & Applied Social Psychology, 16*(6), 472–480.

Dodgen, C. E. (2005) *Nicotine dependence: Understanding and applying the most effective treatment Interventions.* Washington, DC: American Psychological Association.

Doherty, M. (2009). New insights into the epidemiology of gout. *Rheumatology, 48*, Suppl 2, ii1–ii8.

Dorn, T., Yzermans, C. J., Guiju, H., & Zee, J. (2007). Disaster-related stress as a prospective risk factor for hypertension in parents of adolescent fire victims. *American Journal of Epidemiology, 165*, 410–417.

Downing, R. G., Otten, R. A., Marem, E., Biryahwaho, B., Alwano-Edyegu, M. G., & Sempala, S. D. (1998). Optimizing the delivery of HIV counseling and testing services: The Ugandan experience using rapid HIV antibody test algorithms. *Journal of Acquired Immune Deficiency Syndromes and Human Retroviorology, 18*(4), 384–388.

Duberstein, P., Meldren, S, Fiscella, K., Shields, C. G., & Epstein, R. M. (2007). Influences on a patient's ratings of physicians: Physician demographics & personalities. *Patient Education & Counseling, 65*, 270–274.

Dunbar, H. F. (1943). *Psychosomatic Diagnosis.* New York: Hoeber Press.

Duncan, C. J., & Scott, S. (2005). What caused the Black Death? *Postgraduate Medical Journal, 81*, 315–320.

Dunkel-Schetter, C., Feinstein, L. G., Taylor, S. E., Falke, & L. R. (1992). Patterns of coping with cancer. *Health Psychology, 11*, 79–87.

Dusek, J. A., & Benson, H. (2009). Mind–body medium: A model of the comparative clinical impact of the acute stress & relaxation response. *Minnesota Medicine, 92*, 5, 47–50.

Dushoff, J., Plotkin, J. B., Viboud, C., Earn, D. J. D., & Simonsen, L. (2006). Mortality due to influenza in the US. An annualized regression approach using multiple cause mortality data. *American Journal of Epidemiology, 163*, 2, 181–187.

Duterte, E. E., Bonomi, A. E., Kernic, M. A., Schiff, M. A., Thompson, R. S., & Rivara, F. P. (2008). Correlates of medical and legal helpseeking among women reporting intimate partner violence. *Journal of Women's Health, 17*(1), 85–95.

Easton, D., Iverson, E., Cribbin, M., Wilson, E., Weiss, G., & the Community Intervention Trial for Youth Group. (2007). *AIDS Education & Prevention, 19*(6), 465–478.

Ebrahim, A. H., & Atrash, H. (2006). Managing persistent preventable threats to safer pregnancies and infant health in the United States: Beyond silos and into integration, early, intervention, and prevention. *Journal of Women's Health, 15*(9), 1090–1092.

Eby, C. H., & Evjen, H. D. (1962). The plague at Athens: A new oar in muddied waters. *Journal of the History of Medicine*, 258–263.

Eggleston, P. A. (1999). The environment and asthma in US inner cities. *Environmental Health Perspectives, 107*(3), 439–450.

Eisenberg, M. S. (1995). The problem of sudden cardiac death. In R. W. Alexander, R. C. Sclant, & Fuster (eds.) *Vol I. Hurst's the heart, arteries and veins*, 9th ed. (1081–1112). New York: McGraw-Hill.

Eisenberg, M. S. (1995). The problem of sudden cardiac death. In M. S. Eisenberg, L. Bergner, & A. P. Hallstrom (eds.), *Sudden cardiac death in the community* (1–16). New York: Praeger.

Eisner, M. D., Klein, J., Hammond, S. K., Koren, G., Lactao, G., & Iribarren, C. (2005). Directly measured second hand smoke exposure and asthma health outcomes. *Thorax, 60*, 814–821.

Eley, J. W., Hill, H. A., Chen, V. W., Austin, D. F., Wesley, M. N., Muss, H. B., Greenberg, R. S., et al. (1994). Racial differences in survival from breast cancer. Results of the National Cancer Institute Black/White Cancer Survival Study. *JAMA, 272*(12), 947–954.

El-Sadig, M. M., Sarfraz, A. M., Carter, A. O., Fares, K., Al-Tanueiji, H. O., Romilly, P., et al. (2004). Evaluation of effectiveness of safety seatbelt legislation in the United Arab Emirates. *Accident Annals Prevention, 36*(3), 399–404.

Engel, G. L. (1977). The need for a new medical model: a challenge for biomedicine. *Science* 196, 129–136.

Engel, G. L. (2002). The need for a new medical model: A challenge for biomedicine. In D. L Marks (ed.), *The health psychology reader.* London: Sage Publications.

Enos, W. F., Holmes, R. H., & Beyer, J. (1953). Coronary disease among United States soldiers killed in action in Korea; preliminary report. *JAMA, 152*(12), 1090–1093.

Environmental Health Information Services. (2000). *Ninth report on carcinogens.* Washington, DC: U.S. Department of Health and Human Services, Public Health Service, National Toxicology Program.

Environmental Protection Agency (EPA). (2007a). Clean Air Act 42 U.S.C. s/s 7401 et. seq. (1970). Retrieved on July 15, 2007, from: www.epa.gov/region5/defs/html/caa/htm.

Environmental Protection Agency (EPA). (2007b). Climate change basic information. Retrieved on

July 15, 2007, from: www.epa.gov/climatechange/basicinfo.html.

Epel, E., Lapidus, R., McEwen, B., & Brownell, K. (2001). Stress may add bite to appetite in women: A laboratory study of stress-induced cortisol & eating behaviors. *Psychoneuroendocrinology,* 26, 1, 37–49.

Erdine, S., & Ari, O. (2006). ESH-ESC guidelines for the management of hypertension. *Herz,* 31, 331–338.

Erlbich, J., Boubjerg, D. H., & Valdimarsdottir, R. B. (2000). Psychosocial distress, health and beliefs and frequency of breast self-examination. *Journal of Behavioral Medicine,* 23, 277–292.

Escalante, A., del Rincon, I., & Mulrow, C. D. (2000). Symptoms of depression and psychological distress among Hispanics with rheumatoid arthritis. *Arthritis Care and Research,* 13(3), 156–167.

Esch, B. M., Marion, F., Busato, A., & Heusser, P. (2008). Patient satisfaction with primary care: An observational study comparing anthroposophic and conventional care. *Health Quality Life Outcomes,* 30, 6, 74.

Eskenazi, B., Bradman, A., & Castorina, R. (1999). Exposures of children to organophosphate pesticides and their potential adverse health effects. *Environmental Health Perspectives,* 107(S3), 409–414.

Essajee, S. M. (1999). Immunologic and virologic responses to HAART in severely immunocompromised HIV-1 infected children. *AIDS,* 13, 2523–2532.

Ethnicity and body dissatisfaction: Are Hispanic and Asian girls at increased risk for eating disorders? *Journal of Adolescent Health,* 19, 384–393.

Evans, J. J. (1997). Oxytocin in the humans-regulation of derivations & destinations. *European Journal of Endocrinology/European Federation of endocrine Societies,* 137, 559–571.

Evers, A. W. M., Kraaimaat, F. W., Geenen, R., Jacobs, J. W. G., & Bijlsma, J. W. J. (2003). Pain coping and social support as predictors of long-term functional disability and pain in early rheumatoid arthritis. *Behavioral Research and Therapy,* 41, 1295–1310.

Ezzati, M., Vander-Hoorn, S., & Lowes, C. M. M. (2005). Re-thinking the disease of affluence paradigm: Global patterns of nutritional risks in relation to economic development. Public Library of Science and Medicine, 2(5), e133.

Falagas, M. E., Zarkadoulia, E. A., & Samonis, G. (2006). Arab science in the golden age (750–1258 CE) and today. *The FASEB Journal: Official Publication of the Federation of American Society for Experimental Biology,* 20, 10, 1581–1586.

Falagas, M., Vardakas, K., & Paschalis, V. (2007). Underdiagnosis of common chronic disease prevalence and impact on human health. *International Journal of Clinical Practice,* 61, 1569–1579.

Famularo, R., Kinscherff, R., & Fenton, T. (1992). Parental abuse and the nature of child maltreatment. *Child Abuse and Neglect,* 16, 475–483.

Fang, C. Y., & Myers, H. F. (2001). The effects of racial stressors and hostility on cardiovascular reactivity in African American and Caucasian men. *Health Psychology,* 20, 64–70.

Fang, H., & Rizzo, J. A. (2008). The changing effect of managed care on physicians. *American Journal of Managed Care,* 14, 653–660.

Farnill, D., & Robertson, M. F. (1990). Sleep disturbance, tertiary-transition stress & psychological symptoms among young first-year Australian college students. *Australian Psychologist,* 25, 2, 178–188.

Faucett, J., Gordon, N., & Levine, J. (1994). Differences in postoperative pain severity among four ethnic groups. *Journal of Pain Symptom Management,* 9, 383–389.

Fawzy, F. L., & Fawzy, N. W. (1994). A structured psycho-educational intervention for cancer patients. *General Hospital Psychiatry,* 60, 100–103.

Fekete, E. M., Antoni, M. H., Duran, R., Stoelb, B. L., Kumar, M., & Schneiderman, N. (2009). Disclosing HIV serostatus to family members: effects on psychological and physiological health in minority women living with HIV. *International Journal of Behavioral Medicine,* 16, 4, 367–76.

Fekete, E. M., Antoni, M. H., Lopez, C. R., Duran, R. E., Penedo, F. J., Bandiera, F. C., et al. (2009). Men's serostatus disclosure to parents: Associations among social support, ethnicity & disease status in men living with HIV. *Brain, Behavior, and Immunity,* 23, 5, 693–699.

Fergus, K. D., & Gray, R. E. (2009). Relationship vulnerabilities during breast cancer: Patient & partner perspectives. *Psycho-Oncology,* 18, 1311–1322.

Ferlay, J., Bray, F., Pisani, P., & Parkin, D. M. (2004). International Agency for Research on Cancer (IARC). GLOBOCAN 2002: Cancer incidences and prevalence worldwide. Lyon, France: IARC Press, Cancer Base, No. 5, version 2.0.

Field, T., Morrow, C., Valedon, C., Larson, S., Kuhn, C., & Schanberg, S. (1992). Massage reduces anxiety in child and adolescent psychiatric patients. *Journal of the American Academy of Child and Adolescent Psychiatry,* 31, 125–131.

Finch, E. A., Linde, J. A., Jeffery, R. W., Rothman, A, J., King, C. M., & Levy, R. L. (2005). The effects of outcome expectations and satisfaction on weight loss and maintenance: Correlational and experimental analyses—a randomized trial. *Health Psychology,* 24, 608–616.

Finer, L. B., Darroch, J. E., & Singh, S. (1999). Sexual partnership patterns as a behavioral risk factor for sexually transmitted diseases. *Family Planning Perspective,* 31, 3, 228–236.

Fischer, P. M., Schwartz, M. P., Richards, J. W., Goldstein, A. O., & Rojas, T. H. (1991). Brand logo recognition by children aged 3 to 6 years. Mickey

Mouse and Old Joe the Camel. *Journal of the American Medical Association,* 266(22), 3185–3186.

Fishbein, M., & Ajzen, I. (1975). *Beliefs, attitudes, intentions and behaviour: An introduction to theory and research.* Reading, MA: Addison-Wesley.

Flood, D. M., Weiss, N. S., Cook, L. S., Emerson, J. C., Schwartz, S. M., & Potter, J. D. (2000). Colorectal cancer incidences in Asian immigrants to the US and their descendants. *Cancer Cause and Control,* 11, 403–411.

Flores, G., & Vega, L. (1998). Barriers to health care access for Latino children: A review. *Family Medicine,* 30(3), 196–205.

Folkman, S., & Greer, S. (2002). Promoting psychological well-being in the face of serious illness: When theory, research and practice inform each other. *Psycho-oncology,* 9, 11–19.

Folkman, S., & Moskowitz, J. T. (2000). Positive affect and the other side of coping. *American Psychologist,* 55, 6, 647–654.

Fombonne, E., & Chakvabarti, S. (2001). No evidence for a new variant of measles-mumps-rubella-induced autism. *Pediatrics,* 108(11), e58.

Fombonne, E., Zakanan, R., Bemuth, A., Meny, L., & McLean-Heywood, D. (2006). Pervasive developmental disorders in Montreal, Quebec, Canada: Prevalence and links with immunization. *Pediatrics,* 118, 1,1 e139–e150.

Ford, D., Easton, D. F., Stratton, M., Nurod, S., Goldgar, D., & Devilee, P. (1998). Genetic heterogeneity and penetrance analysis of the BRCA1 and BRCA2 genes in breast cancer families. *American Journal of Human Genetics,* 62, 676–689.

France, C. F., Keefe, F. J., Emery, C. F., Affleck, G., France, J. L., Waters, S., et al. (2004). Laboratory pain perception & clinical pain in post-monopausal women & age-matched men with osteoarthritis: Relationship to pain coping & hormonal status. *Pain,* 112, 3, 274–281.

Franco-Paredes, C., Tellez, I., & delRio.C. (2006). Rapid HIV testing: A review of the literature and implications for the clinician. *Current HIV/AIDS Report,* 3(4), 169–175.

Fried, T. R., Bradley, E. H., & O'Leary, J. (2003) Prognosis communication in serious illnesses: Perceptions of older patients, caregivers & clinicians. *Journal of the American Geriatrics Society,* 51, 1398–1403.

Friedenreich, C., Norat, T., & Steindor, F. K. (2006). Physical activity and risk of colon and rectal cancer: The European prospective investigation into cancer. *Cancer Epidemiology Biomarkers Prevention,* 15, 2398–2407.

Friedman, E. H. (1991). Role of Type A behavior pattern (TABP) in the pathogenesis of coronary heart disease (CHD). *Social Science and Medicine,* 32, 11, 1317–1318.

Friedman, M. (1989). Type A behavior, its diagnosis, cardiovascular relation and the effects of its modification on occurrences of coronary artery disease. *American Journal of Cardiology,* 64, 6, 12c–19c.

Friedman, H., Newton, C., & Klein, T. W. (2003). Microbial infections, immunomodulation and drugs of abuse. *Clinical Microbiology Review,* 16(2), 209–219.

Friedman, M., & Rosenman, R. H. (1959). Association of specific over behavior pattern with blood and cardiovascular findings. *Journal of the American Medical Association,* 169, 1286–1296.

Frost, G., Hurdany Darnton, A., McElvenny, D., & Morgan, A. H. (2008). Occupational exposure to asbestos and mortality among asbestos removal workers: A Poisson regression analysis. *British Journal of Cancer,* 99(5), 822–829.

Fry, W. F. (1994). The biology of humor. *Humor: International Journal of Humor Research,* 7, 111–126.

Fuches, C., Giovanucci, E., Colditz, G., Hunter, D., Speizer, F., & Wittell, W. (1994). A prospective study of family history of risk of colorectal cancer. *New England Journal of Medicine,* 3331, 1669–1674.

Gable, S. L., & Haidt, J. (2005). What (& why) is positive psychology? *Review of General Psychology,* 9, 2, 103–110.

Gabuzda, D. H., & Hirsch, M. S. (1987). Neurological manifestations of infection with human immunodeficiency virus. *Annals of Internal Medicine,* 107, 383–391.

Galdas, P. M., Cheater, F., & Marshall, P. (2005). Men and health help-seeking behaviour: Literature review. *Journal of Advanced Nursing,* 49(6), 616–623.

Gallo, L. C., & Matthews, K. A. (2003). Understanding the association between socioeconomic status and physical health. Do negative emotions play a role? *Psychological Bulletin,* 129, 10–51.

Gao, F., Bailes, E., Robertson, D. L., Chen, Y., Rodenberg, C. M., & Michael, S. F. (1999). Origins of HIV-1 in the chimpanzee Pan troglodytes troglodytes. *Nature,* 397, 436–441.

Gapenski, L. C. (2003). *Understanding healthcare financial management* (4th ed.). Washington, DC: Health Administration Press.

Garfinkel, P. E., Lin, E., Goering, C., Spegg, C., Goldbloom, D. S., Kennedy, S., et al. (1996). Should amenorrhea be necessary for the diagnosis of anorexia nervosa? Evidence from a Canadian community sample. *British Journal of Psychiatry,* 168, 500–506.

Garrett, M. T. (1998). *Walking on the wind: Cherokee teachings for harmony and balance.* Santa Fe, NM: Bear & Co.

Garver, C. S., Weintraub, J. K., & Scheier, M. E. (1989). Assessing coping strategies: A theoretically based approach. *Journal of Personality and Social Psychology,* 56, 267–283.

Gaugler, J. E., Mittleman, M. S., Hepburn, K., & Newcomer, R. (2009). Predictors of change in caregiver burden & depressive symptoms following nursing home admissions. *Psychology of Aging,* 24, 2, 385–396.

Gaugler, J. E., Zarit, S. H., & Perlin, L. I. (1999). Caregiving & institutionalization: Perceptions of family conflict & socioemotional support. *International Journal of Aging & Human Development,* 49, 1, 1–25.

Gee, G. C., & Payne-Sturges, D. C. (2004). Environmental health disparities: A framework integrating psychosocial and environmental concepts. *Environmental Health Perspectives,* 112(17), 1645–1653.

Geller, E. S. (1989). Applied behavior analysis and social marketing: An integration for environmental preservation. *Journal of Social Issues,* 45, 17–36.

Gellert, G. A., Weismuller, P. C., Higgins, K.V., & Maxwell, R. M. (1992). Disclosure of AIDS in celebrities. *New England Journal of Medicine,* 327, 1389.

Gentry, W. D. (1972). Biracial aggression; I. Effect of verbal attack and sex of victim. *Journal of Social Psychology,* 88, 75–82.

Gergen, P. J., Fowler, J. A., Maurer, K. R., Davis, W. W., & Overpeck, M. D. (1998). The burden of environmental tobacco smoke exposure to the respiratory health of children 2 months through 5 years of age in the United States: Third national health and nutrition examination study, 1988 to 1994. *Pediatrics,* 101(2), E8.

Getzen, T. E. (2004). *Health economics: fundamentals and flows of Funds* (2nd ed.). Danvers, MA: Wiley & Sons.

Gili, M., Roca, M., Ferrer, V., Obrador, A., & Cabeza, E. (2006). Psychosocial factors associated with the adherence to a colorectal cancer screening program. *Cancer Detection & Prevention,* 30(4), 354–360.

Gillum, R. F., Folsom, A., Luepker, R. V., Jacobs, D. R., Kottle, T. E., & Gomez-Martin, O. (1983). Sudden death and acute myocardial infarction in a metropolitan area, 1970–1980. The Minnesota Heart Survey. *New England Journal of Medicine,* 309(22), 1353–1358.

Ginzler, J. A., Cochran, B. N., Domenech-Rodriguez, M., Cauce, A. M., & Whitbeck, L. B. (2003). Sequential progression of substance use among homeless youth: An empirical investigation of gateway theory. *Substance Use and Misuse,* 38(1–6), 725–758.

Glantz, S. A., & Parmley, W. W. (1991). Passive smoking and heart disease: Epidemiology, physiology and biochemistry. *Circulation,* 83, 1–12.

Glassman, A. H., & Shapiro, P. A. (1998). Depression and the course of coronary artery disease. *American Journal of Psychiatry,* 155, 4–11.

Gobodo-Madikizela, P. (2002). *A human being died that Night: A South African story of forgiveness.* New York: Houghton Mifflin.

Gobodo-Madikizela, P. (2003). Remorse, forgiveness & rehumanization: Stories from South Africa. *Journal of Humanistic Psychology,* 42, 1, 7–32.

Godfrey, J. R., & Felson, D. T. (2008). Toward optimal health: Managing arthritis in women. *Journal of Women's Health,* 17, 5, 729–734.

Goin, R. T., Hays, J. C., Landeman, D. R., & Hobbs, G. (2009). Access to healthcare and self-rated health among community-dwelling older adults. *Journal of Applied Gerontology,* 20, 3, 307–321.

Gold, M. R., Hurley, R., Lake, T., Ensor, T., & Berenson, R. (1995). A national survey of the arrangements managed care plans make with physicians. *New England Journal of Medicine,* 333(25), 1678–1683.

Goldbach-Mansky, R., Lee, J., McCoy, A., Hoxworth, J., Yarboro, C., Smolen, J. S., et al. (2002). Rheumatoid arthritis associated auto antibodies in patients with synovitis of recent onset. *Arthritis Research,* 3, 236–243.

Goldring. (2006). Update on the biology of the chondrocyte & new approaches to treating cartilage disease. *Best Practices & Research in Clinical Rheumatology,* 20, 5, 1003–1025.

Goldsby, R. A., Kindt, T. J., Osborne, B. A., & Kuby, J. (2003). *Immunology.* New York: W. H. Freeman and Co.

Goldsmith, S. K., Pellmar, T. C., Kleinman, A. M., & Bunney, W. E. (2002). *Reducing suicide: A national imperative.* Washington DC: National Academy Press.

Gollurtzer, P. W. (1993). Goal achievement: The role of intentions. In W. Strobe and M. Hewstone (eds), *European Review of Social Psychology,* Vol. 4 (141–188). Chichester, UK: Wiley & Sons.

Goodman, R. M., Wandersman, A., Chinman, M., Imm, P., & Morrissey, E. (1996). An ecological assessment of community-based interventions for prevention and health promotion: Approaches to measuring community coalitions. *American Journal of Community Psychology,* 24(1), 33–61.

Goodnough, A. (2003). Schools cut down on fat and sweets in menus. *The New York Times,* June 25.

Goodwin, A. H., Wells, J. K., Foss, R. D., & Williams, A. F. (2006). Encouraging compliance with graduated driver licensing restrictions. *Journal of Safety Research,* 37, 343–351.

Goodyear, I. M., Herbert, J., Tamplin, A., & Altham, P. M. (2000). First-episode major depression in adolescents: affective, cognitive and endocrine characteristics of risk status and predictors of onset. *British Journal of Psychiatry,* 176, 142–149.

Gordillo, V., del AMo, J., Soriano, V., & Gonzalez-Lahoz, J. (1999). Sociodemographic and psychological variables influencing adherence to antiretroviral therapy. *AIDS,* 13, 13, 1763–1769.

Gordon, H. S., Street, R. L., Kelly, P. A., Souchek, J., & Wray, N. P. (2005). Physician-patient communication following invasive procedures: An analysis of post-angiogram consultations. *Social Science & Medicine,* 61(5), 1015–1025.

Gorman, J. M., & Kertzner, R. (1990). Psychoneuro-immunology and HIV infection. *Neurosciences, 2,* 241–252.

Gorodeski, G. (2002). Update on cardiovascular disease in post-menopausal women. *Best Practice & Research Clinical Obstetrics and Gynecology,* 16(3), 329–355.

Gottschalk, A., & Flocke, S. A. (2005). Time spent in face-to-face patient care and work outside the examination room. *Annals of Family Medicine,* 3(6), 488–493.

GPO Access (2008). Electronic code of federal regulations. Title 14: Aeronautics & Space. National Archives & Records Administration. Retrieved on October 2, 2009, from: http:ecfr.gpoaccess.gov/egi/t/text/text-idx?c.

Grant, I., Atkinson, J. H., & Hesselink, J. R. (1987). Evidence for early central nervous system involvement in the acquired immunodeficiency syndrome (AIDS) and other human immunodeficiency virus (HIV) infections: studies with neuropsychological testing and magnetic resonance imaging. *Annals of Internal Medicine,* 107, 828–836.

Green, C. R., Anderson, K. O., Baker, T. A., Campbell, L. C., Decker, S., Fillingin, R. B., et al. (2003). The unequal burden of pain: Confronting racial and ethnic disparities in pain. *Pain,* 4(3), 277–294.

Greenberg, D. R., & LaPorte, D. J. (1996). Racial differences in body type preferences of men for women. *International Journal of Eating Disorders,* 19, 275–278.

Greenblatt, R. M., & Hessol, N. A. (2001). Epidemiology and natural history of HIV infection in women. In R. J. Anderson (ed.), *A guide to the clinical care of women with HIV* (1–32). Washington, DC: U.S. Department of Health and Human Services, Health Resources and Services Administration.

Greenlund, K. J., Johnson, C. C., Webber, L. S., & Berenson, G. S. (1997). Cigarette smoking attitudes and first use among third- through sixth-grade students: The Bogalusa heart study. *American Journal of Public Health,* 87(8), 1345–1348.

Greeno, C. G., & Wing, R. R. (1994). Stress-induced eating. *Psychological Bulletin,* 115, 444–464.

Greenwald, J. L., Burstein, G. R., Pincus, J., & Branson, B. (2006). A rapid review of rapid antibody tests. *Current Infections Disease Reports,* 8, 125–131.

Grond, S., Zech, D., Lynch, J., et al. (1992). Tramadol-a weak opioid for relief of cancer pain. *Pain Clinic,* 5, 241–247.

Grunbaum, J. A., Kann, L., Kinchen, S. A., Williams, B., Ross, J. G., Lowry, R. et al. (2002). Youth risk behavior survey: Surveillance summaries. *MMWR,* 51, (ss04), 1–64.

Grunberg, N. E., & Straub, R. O. (1997). The role of gender and taste class in the effects of stress on eating. *Health Psychology,* 11, 2, 97–100.

Guay, L. A., Muskoe, P., Fleming, T., Bagenda, D., Allen, M., & Nakabiito, C. (1999). Intrapartum and neonatal single-dose nevirapine compared with zidovudine for prevention of mother-to-child transmission of HIV-1 in Kampala, Uganda. *Lancet,* 354, 795–802.

Guedi, M., Gilbert, M., Maudet, A., Munoz-Sastre, M. T., Mullet, E., & Sorun, P. C. (2005). The acceptability of ending of patient's life. *Journal of Medical Ethics,* 31, 311–317.

Gutmann, F. D., Gardner, J. W., Potter, R. N., & Kark, J. A. (2002). Nontraumatic exercise related deaths in the U.S. military, 1996–1999. *Military Medicine,* 167(12), 964–970.

Guyll, M., Matthews, K. A., & Bromberger, J. T. (2001). Discrimination and unfair treatment: Relationship to cardiovascular reactivity among African American and European American women. *Health Psychology,* 20, 315–325.

Haas, C. (2006). The Antonine plague. *Bulletin Academie National Medicine,* 190(4–5), 1093–1098.

Haas, J. S., Phillips, A. S., Sonneborn, D., McCulloch, C. E., & Liang, S. Y. (2002). Effects of managed care insurance on the use of preventive care for specific ethnic groups in the U.S. *Medical Care,* 40(9), 743–751.

Hadlow, J., & Pitts, M. (1992). The understanding of common health terms by doctors, nurses and patients. *Social Science and Medicine,* 32, 193–196.

Hale, H. I., Song, R., Rhodes, P., Prejean, J., An, Q., & Lee, L. M. (2008). Estimates of HIV incidences in the US. *Journal of the American Medical Association,* 300(5), 520–529.

Haller, E. (1992). Eating disorders: A review and update. *Western Journal of Medicine,* 157, 658–662.

Halpern-Felsher, B. L., & Rubinstein, M. D. (2004). Clear the air: adolescents' perceptions of the risks associated with secondhand smoke. *Preventive Medicine,* 41(1), 16–22.

Halpern-Felsher, B. L., Biehl, M. A., Kropp, R. Y., & Rubenstein, M. D. (2004). Perceived risks and benefits of smoking: differences among adolescents with different smoking experiences and intentions. *Preventive Medicine,* 39(3), 559–567.

Hamilton, B. E., Martin, J. A., & Ventura, S. J. (2007). Births: Preliminary data for 2006. *National Vital Statistics Reports,* 56(7). U.S. Department of Health and Human Services. Centers for Disease Control and Prevention.

Hamilton-West, K. E., & Quine, L. (2007). Effects of written emotional disclosure on health outcomes in patients with ankylosing spondylitis. *Psychology and Health,* 22(6), 637–757.

Hamlin, C., & Sheard, S. (1998). Revolutions in public health: 1848–1998. *British Medical Journal,* 317, 587–591.

Hammonds, E. M. (1994). Your silence will not protect you: Nurse Eunice Rivers and the Tuskegee Syphilis Study. In E. C. White (ed.), *The Black Woman's Health Book: Speaking for Ourselves,* 323–331. Seattle, WA: Seal Press.

Handel, A. E., Handrennetthi, L., Giovannoni, G., Ebers, G. C., & Ramagopalan, S. V. (2010). Genetic & environmental factors & the distribution of multiple sclerosis in Europe. *European Journal of Neurology,* March 22, epublication ahead of print.

Haney, C., & Zimbardo, P. (1998). The past and future of U.S. prison policy: Twenty-five years after the Stanford prison experiment. *American Psychologist,* 53(7), 709–727.

Haney, C., Banks, W., & Zimbardo, P. (1973). Interpersonal dynamics in a simulated prison. *International Journal of Criminology and Penology,* 1, 69–97.

Hardell, L., Mild, K. H., & Carlberg, M. (2003). Further aspects on cellular and cordless telephones and brain tumors. *International Journal of Oncology,* 22, 339–407.

Hardell, L., Mild, K. H., & Carlberg, M. (2002). Case-control study on the use of cellular and cordless phones and the risk for malignant brain tumors. *International Journal of Radiation Biology,* 78, 931–935.

Hargreaves, M. K., Schundt, D. G., Buchowaki, M. S., Hardy, R. E., Rossi, S. R., & Rossi, J. S. (1999). Stages of change and the intake of dietary fat in African-American women: Improving stage assignment using the eating styles questionnaire. *Journal of the American Dietetic Association,* 99(11), 1392–1399.

Harlow, L. L., Prochaska, J. O., Redding, C. A., Rossi, J. S., Velicer, W., Snow, M. G., et al. (1999). Stages of condom use in a high HIV-risk sample. *Psychology & Health,* 14, 143–157.

Harrell, Z. A. T., & Karim, N. M. (2008). Is gender relevant only for problem alcohol behaviors? An examination of correlates of alcohol use among college students. *Addictive Behaviors,* 33(2), 359–365.

Harris, P. G., & Siplon, P. (2001). International obligation and human health: Evolving policy responses to HIV/AIDS. *Ethics & International Affairs,* 15(2), 29–52.

Harvard Medicine. (2007). What is arthritis? Retrieved on August 20, 2008, from: www.hms.harvard.edu/oublic/disease/arthritis/arthritis.html.

Harvard School of Public Health. (2008). *The nutrition source*: Carbohydrates: Good carbs guide the Way. Retrieved from: www.hsph.harvard.edu/Nutritionsources/what-should-you-eat/carbohydrates-full-story/index.html.

Harvard University Library Open Collections Program, 2008. Contagions: Historical Views of Diseases and Epidemics. The Boston Smallpox Epidemic, 1721.

Retrieved on March 6, 2009, from http://ocp.hul.harvard.edu/contagion/smallpox.html.

Harvey, R. F., & Jellinek, H. M. (1981). Functional performance assessment: A program approach. *Archives of Physical Medicine & Rehabilitation,* 62, 9, 456–460.

Haynes, C., Lee, M. D., & Yeomans, M. R. (2003). Interactive effects of stress on dietary restraint & disinhibition on appetite. *Eating Behavior,* 4, 4, 369–383.

He, K., Kramer, E., Houser, R. F., Chomitz, V. R., & Hacker, K. A. (2004). Defining and understanding healthy lifestyles choices for adolescents. *Journal of Adolescent Health,* 35(1), 26–33.

Healing, R. (2003). Testament of Richard F. Healing of the National TransportatioSafety Board before the Wisconsin State Assembly, Committee on Transportation on Primary Enforcement. Madison, WI, April 24, 2003.

Health & Hospitals Network. (2008). ED patients don't understand instructions about their care. *Health and Hospitals Network,* 82, 2, 54.

Health Resources & Service Administration. (2009). A living history. Retrieved on February 26, 2010, from: http://hab.hrsa.gov/livinghistory/timeline/1986-1990/1990.html.

Hecker, M. H., Chesney, M. A. B., & Frautschi, N. (1988). Coronary-prone behaviors in the Western Collaborative Group Study. *Psychosomatic Medicine,* 50, 153–164.

Heijmans, M., Rijken, M., Foets, M., de Ridder, D., Schreurs, K., & Bensing, J. (2004). The stress of being chronically ill: From disease-specific to task-specific aspects. *Journal of Behavioral Medicine,* 27, 3, 255–271.

Heine, H., & Weiss, M. (1987). Life stress and hypertension. *European Heart Journal,* 8 (Suppl B), 45–55.

Heinrich, H. W., Petersen, D., & Roos, N. (1980). *Industrial accident prevention* (5th ed.) New York: McGraw Hill.

Held, B. S. (2005). The "virtues" of positive psychology. *Journal of Theoretical & Philosophical Psychology,* 25, 1, 1–34.

Helder, D. I., Kaptein, A. A., VanKempen, G. M. J., Weinman, J., VanHouwelinger, J. C., & Roos, R. A. C. (2002) Living with Huntington's disease: Illness perception, coping mechanisms & spouse's quality of life. *International Journal of Behavioral Medicine,* 9, 1, 37–52.

Helder, D. I., Kaptein, A. A., vanKempen, G. M. J., Weinman, J., van Houwelinden, H. C., & Roos, R. A. C. (2002). Living with Huntington's disease: Illness perceptions, coping mechanisms, and patient's well-being. *British Journal of Health Psychology,* 7, 449–462.

Herd, J. A. (1991). Cardiovascular response to stress. *Physiological Reviews,* 71, 305–330.

Heron, M. (2007). Deaths: Leading causes for 2004. *National Vital Statistics Reports, 56,* 5.

Herrnstein, R. J. (1961). Relative and absolute strength of response as a function of frequency or reinforcement. *Journal of the Experimental Analysis of Behavior, 4,* 267–272.

Herrnstein, R. J. (1970). On the law of effect. *Journal of the Experimental Analysis of Behavior,* 13, 243–266.

Herz, R. S. (2009). Aromatherapy facts and fiction: A scientific analysis of olfactory effects on mood, physiology & behavior. *International Journal of Neuroscience,* 119, 2, 263–290.

Hilbert, A., & Tuschen-Caffier, B. (2007). Maintenance of binge eating through negative moods: A naturalistic comparison of binge eating disorder and bulimia nervosa. *International Journal of Eating Disorders,* 40, 521–530.

Hilton, B. A., Crawford, J. A., & Tarko, M. A. (2000). Men's perspectives on individuals & families coping with their wife's breast cancer & chemotherapy. *Western Journal of Nursing Research,* 22, 438–459.

Hjermstad, M. J., Gibbons, J., Haughen, D. F., Caraceni, A., Loge, J. H., Kaasa, S., et al. (2008). Pain assessment tolls in palliative care: an urgent need for consensus. *Palliative Medicine,* 22, 895–903.

Ho, S. C., Chan, A., Woo, J., Chang, P., & Sham, A. (2009). Impact of caregiving on health & quality of life: A comparative population-based study of caregivers for elderly persons & noncaregivers. *The Journal of Gerentology; Series A: Biological Sciences & Medical Sciences,* 64, A8, 873–879.

Hoek, H. W. (1991). The incidence and prevalence of anorexia nervosa and bulimia nervosa in primary care. *Psychological Medicine,* 21, 455–460.

Hoek, H. W., & van Hoeken, D. (2003). Review of the prevalence and incidence of eating disorders. *International Journal of Eating Disorders,* 34, 383–396.

Hoffman, B. R., Sussman, S., Unger, J. B., & Valente, T. W. (2006). Peer influences on adolescent cigarette smoking: A theoretical review of the literature. *Substance Use & Abuse,* 41, 103–155.

Hoffman, D., Brunnemann, K. D., & Gori, G. B. (1975) On the carcinogenicity of marijuana smoke. In V. C. Runeckles (ed.), *Recent Advances in Phytochemistry.* New York: Plenum.

Holland, K. D., & Holahan, C. K. (2003). Relations of social support and coping to positive adaptation to breast cancer. *Psychology and Health,* 18(1), 15–29.

Holm, J. E., & Holroyd, K. A. (1992). The daily hassles scale (revised): Does it measure stress or symptoms? *Behavioral Assessment,* 14, 465–482.

Holmes, T. H., & Rahe, R. H. (1967). The Social Readjustment Rating Scale. *Journal of Psychosomatic Research,* 11, 2, 213–218.

Holohan, C. J., & Moos, R. H. (1990). Life stressors, resistance factors & psychological health: An extension of the stress-resistance paradigm. *Journal of Personality and Social Psychology,* 58, 909–917.

Holohan, C. J., & Moos, R. H. (1991). Life stressors, personal & social resources & depression: A 4-year structural model. *Journal of Abnormal Psychology,* 100, 337–340.

Holt, J. Warren, L., Wallace., & Neher, J. (2006). Clinical inquiries: What behavioral interventions are safe and effective for treating obesity. *Journal of Family Practice,* 55(6), 536–538.

Hon, K. L. E., Leung, T. F., Tse, H. M., Lam, L. N., Tam., K. C., & Chu, K. M. (2005). A survey of attitudes to traditional Chinese medicine among Chinese medical students. *American Journal of Chinese Medicine,* 33(2), 269–279.

Hopkins, D. R. (2006). Health: A global goal. The Carter Center. Retrieved on August 9, from: www.carter center.org/news.

Hout, M., Brooks, C., & Manzay, J. (1993). The persistence of classes in post-industrial societies. *International Sociology,* 8, 259–277.

Howard, S., & Hughes, B. M. (2008). Expectancies, nor aroma, explain impact of lavender on aromatherapy or psychophysical indices of relaxation in young healthy women. *British Journal of Health Psychology,* 13, 4, 603–617.

Hu, D., Hannah, J., Gray, R. S., Jablonski, K. A., Henderson, J. A., Robbins, D. C., et al. (2000). Effects of obesity and body fat distribution on lipids and lipoproteins in non-diabetics American Indians: The strong heart study. *Obesity Research,* 8(6) 411–421.

Hudson, J. I., Hiripi, E., Pope, H. G., & Kessler, R. C. (2007). The prevalence and correlates of eating disorders in the national comorbidity survey replication. *Biological Psychiatry,* 61, 348–358.

Hughes, S. L., Seymour, R. B., Campbell, R., Pollak, N., Huber, G., & Sharma, L. (2004). Impact of the fit and strong intervention on older adults with osteoarthritis. *Gerontologist,* 44, 217–228.

Hulton, T. L., Willett, W. C., & Liu, S. (2006). Low carbohydrate-diet score & the risk of coronary heart disease in women. *New England Journal of Medicine,* 355, 1991–2002.

Human Disease and Condition. (2010). The central and autonomic nervous systems. Retrieved on June 1, 2009, from: www.humanillnesses.com/Behavioral-Health-A-Br/The-Brain-and-Nervous-System.html.

Hung, H. C., Joshipura, K. J., Jiang, R., et al. (2004). Fruit & vegetable intake & risk of major chronic diseases. *Journal of National Cancer Research,* 96, 1577–1584.

Hur, M.-H., Oh, H., Lee, M.-S., Kim, C., Choi, A.-N., & Shin, G.-R. (2007). Effects of aromatherapy massage on blood pressure & lipid profile in Korean climacteric women. *International Journal of Neuroscience,* 117, 9, 1281–1287.

Hurst, W. (2002). *The Heart, arteries & veins.* (10th ed.) New York: McGraw-Hill.

Hussey, P. (2005). A comparison of single and multi-payer health insurance systems and options for reform. *Health Policy, 66,* 3, 215–228.

Hwang, E. J., Kim, Y. H., & Jun, S. S. (2004). Lived experience of Korean women suffering from rheumatoid arthritis: A phenomenological approach. *International Journal of Nursing Studies, 41,* 239–246.

Ibrahim, S. A., Whittle, J., Mayberry, B., Kelley, M. E., Good, C., & Conigliaro, J. (2003). Racial /ethnic variation in physician recommendations for cardiac resvacilariztion. *American Journal of Public Health,* 93, 10, 1689–1693

ICNIRP, Ahlbom, A., Green, A., Kheifets, L., Savitz, D., & Swerdlow, A. (2004). Epidemiology of health effects of radiofrequency exposure. *Environmental Medicine,* 112, 1741–1754.

Inskip, P. D., Tarone, R. E., Hatch, E. E., Wicosky, T. C., Shapiro, W. R., Selker, R. G., et al. (2001). Cellular-telephone use and brain tumors. *New England Journal of Medicine, 344,* 79–86.

Institute of Medicine. (2000). *American's health care safety net: Intact but endangered.* Washington, DC: National Academy Press.

Institute of Medicine. (2002). *Unequal Treatment: Confronting Racial & Ethnic Disparities in Health Care.* Washington, DC, National Academy Press.

International Agency for Research on Cancer. (2004). Tobacco smoke and involuntary smoking. *IARC monograph on the evaluations of carcinogenic risks to humans* (83). Lyon, France: Author.

International on Line (IOL). (2004). SA approves law to recognize sangomas. Retrieved on June 30, 2008, from: www.int.iol.co.za.

Ironson, G., & Hayward, H. (2008). Do positive psychosocial factors predict disease progression in HIV-1? A review of the evidence. *Psychosomatic Medicine, 70*(5), 546–554.

Ironson, G., O'Cleirigh, C. Fletcher, M. A., Laurenceau, J. P., Balbin, E., Klimas, N., et al. (2005). Psychosocial factors predict CD4 and viral load change in men and women with human immunodeficiency virus in the era of highly active antiretroviral treatment. *Psychosomatic Medicine, 67,* 1013–1021.

Ironson, G., Stuetzle, R., & Fletcher, M. A. (2006). An increase in religiousness/spirituality occurs after HIV diagnosis & predicts slower disease progression over four years in people with HIV. *Journal of General Internal Medicine, 21*(Suppl. 5), S62–S68.

Irving, M., & Schweiger, A. (1991). Individual and family characteristics of middle class adolescents hospitalized for alcohol & other drug abuses. *British Journal of addictions, 86*(11), 1435–1447.

Ishikawa, H., Hashimoto, H., Kinoshita, M., & Fujimori, S. (2008). Evaluating medical students non-verbal communication during the objective structured clinical examination. *Medical Education, 40*(12), 1180–1187.

Jacobellis, J., & Cutter, G. (2002). Mammography screening and differences in stage of disease by race/ethnicity. *American Journal of Public Health, 92*(7), 1144–1150.

Jacobs, G. D. (2001). The physiology of mind–body interactions: The stress response and the relaxation response. *Journal of Alternative & Complementary Medicine, 7,* S83–92.

Jacoby, J., Chestnut R. W., & Silberman, W. (1977). Consumer use and comprehension of nutritional information. *Journal of Consumer Research, 4,* 119–128.

James, S. A., Hartnett, S. A., & Karlsbeek, W. D. (1983). John Henryism & blood pressure differences among black men. *Journal of Behavioral Medicine, 6,* 259–278.

James, S. A., La Croix, H. Z., Kleinbaum, D. G. et al. (1984). John Henryism & blood pressure differences among black men: II. The role of occupational stressors. *Journal of Behavioral Medicine, 7,* 259–275.

Jansen, C. E., Miaskowski, C., Dodd, M., Dowling, G., & Kramer, J. (2005). A meta-analysis of studies of the effects of cancer chemotherapy on various domains of cognitive functions. *Cancer, 104*(10), 2222–2233.

Jansen, V. A. A., Stollenwerk, N., Jensen, H. J., Ramsay, M. E., Edmunds, W. J., & Rhodes, C. J. (2003). Measles outbreak in a population with declining vaccine uptakes. *Science Magazine,* 804.

Janz, N. K., & Becker, M. H. (1984). The health belief model: A decade later. *Health Education Quarterly,* 11, 1–47.

Jessor, R., Donovan, J. E., & Costa, F. M. (1991). *Beyond adolescence: Problem behavior and young adult development.* Cambridge, UK: Cambridge University Press.

Johannson, P., Oleni, M., & Fridlund, B. (2002). Patient satisfaction with nursing care in the context of health care: A literature study. *Scandinavian Journal of Caring Science,* 16, 4, 337–344.

Johansen, C., Boice, J. D., McLaughlin, J. K., & Olsen, J. H. (2002). Cellular telephone and cancer: A nationwide cohort study in Denmark. *Journal of the National Cancer Institute, 93,* 203–207.

Johns Hopkins University. (2001). *Report of internal investigation into the death of a volunteer research subject.* Retrieved on January 15, 2007, from: www.hopkinsmedicine.org/Press/2001/july/report_of_internal_investigarion.html.

Johnsen, K., Espnes, G. A., & Gillard, S. (1998). Associations between type A/B behavioral dimensions & type 2/4 personality patterns. *Journal of Personality & Individual Differences, 25,* 937–945.

Johnson, G. (2006). Successful folk healing course returning for 5th summer at University of New Mexico. Retrieved on March 30, 2009, from: www.unm.edu/news/06JunNewsRelease/06-05-folk healing.htm.

Johnston, K. L., White, K. M., & Norman, P. (2004). An examination of the individual-difference approach to the role of norms in the theory of reasoned action. *Journal of Applied Social Psychology, 34*(12), 2524–2549.

Joint Commission Focus on Pain Management (JCAHO). (1999). *Report of the Joint Commission on Accreditation of Healthcare Organizations.* Washington, DC: Author.

Jones, J. (1981). *Bad blood: The Tuskegee syphilis experiment: A tragedy of race and medicine.* New York: The Free Press.

Jordan, M. S., Lumly, M. A., & Leisen, J. C. (1998). The relationship of cognitive coping & pain control beliefs to pain & adjustment among African American & Caucasian women with rheumatoid arthritis. *Arthritis Care Research,* 11, 80–88.

Joseph, A. M., Muggli, M., & Pearson, K. C. (2005). Cigarette manufacturers' efforts to promote tobacco in the U.S. military. *Military Medicine,* 10, 874–880.

Joy, J. E., Penhoet, E. E., & Petitti, D. B. (2004). *Saving women's lives: Strategies for improving breast cancer detection and diagnosis.* Washington, DC: National Academic Press.

Jukkala, T., Makinen, I. H., Kislitsyna, O., Ferlander, S., & Vagero, D. (2008). Economic strain, social relations, gender and binge drinking in Moscow. *Social Science and Medicine,* 66(3), 663–674.

Kaatsch P., Spix C., Schulze-Rath, R., Schmiedel, S., & Blettner M. (2008). Leukaemia in young children living in the vicinity of German nuclear power plants. *International Journal of Cancer,* 122, 721–726.

Kaatsch, P., & Mergenthaler, A. (2008). Incidence, time trends & regional variations in childhood leukaemia in Germany and Europe. *Radiation Protection Dosimetry,* 10. Published online.

Kagee, A., & van der Merwe, M. (2006). Predicting treatment adherence among patients attending primary heath care clinics; The utility of the theory of planned behaviors. *South African Journal of Psychology,* 36(4) 699–714.

Kahn, J. A., Huang, B., Gillman, M. U., Field, A. E., Austin, S. B., & Colditz, G. A. (2008). Patterns & determinants of physical activity in US adolescents. *Journal of Adolescent Health,* 42, 4, 369–377.

Kaiser Family Foundation. (2008). *Employees health benefits 2008 annual survey.* Retrieved from: http://ehbs.kff.org/pfd/7790.pdf.

Kalichman, S. C., DiMarco, M., Austin, J., Luke, W., DiFonzo, K. (2003). Stress, social support & HIV status disclosure to family and friends among HIV-positive men and women. *International Journal of Behavioral Medicine,* 26, 315–332.

Kalin, M. F., & Zumoff, B. (1990). Sex hormones and coronary disease: A review of the clinical studies. *Steroids,* 55, 330–352.

Kandel, D. B., Kessler, R. C., & Margulies, R. Z. (1978). Antecedents of adolescent initiation into stages of drug use: A developmental analysis. In D. B. Kandel (ed.), *Longitudinal research on drug use: Empirical findings and methodological issues* (137–156). Washington, DC: Hemisphere Press.

Kandel, D. B., Simcha-Fagan, O., & Davies, M. (1986). Risk factors for delinquency and illicit drug use from adolescence to young adulthood. *Journal of Drug Issues,* 16, 67–90.

Kandel, D. B., Yamaguchi, K., & Chen, K. (1992). Stages of progression in drug involvement from adolescence to adulthood: Further evidence for the gateway theory. *Journal of Studies on Alcohol,* 53, 447–457.

Kannel, W. B., Dawber, T. R., Friedman, G. D., Glennon, W. E., & McNamara, P. H. (1964). Risk factors in coronary heart disease. *Annals of Internal Medicine,* 61(5), 888–900.

Kapke, B. (2004). Yin & yang: Energy medicine. *Massage & Bodywork.*

Kaplan, H. B., Martin, S. S., & Robbins, C. (1984). Pathways to adolescent drug use: Self-derogation and adolescent drug use. *Journal of Health and Social Behavior,* 25, 270–285.

Katz, P. P. (1995). The impact of rheumatoid arthritis on life activities. *Arthritis Care & Research,* 8(4), 272–278.

Katz, P. P., & Yelin, E. H. (1994). Life activities of persons with rheumatoid arthritis with and without depressive symptoms. *Arthritis Care & Research,* 7(2), 69–77.

Kaur, S., Cohen, A., Dolor, R., Coffman, C. J., & Bastian, L. A. (2004). The impact of environmental tobacco smoke on women's risk of dying from heart disease: A meta-analysis. *Journal of Women's Health,* 13(8), 888–897.

Kawaachi, I., Sparrow, D., Kubzansky, L. D., Spiro, A., Vokones, P. S., & Weiss, S. T. (1998). Prospective study of a self-report type-A scale & risk of coronary heart disease. *Circulation,* 98, 405–412.

Kawano, Y. (2008). Association of job-related stress factors with psychological and somatic symptoms among Japanese hospital nurses: Effects of departmental environment in acute care hospitals. *Journal of Occupational Health,* 50(1), 79–85.

Keefe, F. J., Smith, S. J., Buffington, A. L. H., Gibson, J., Studts, J. L., & Caldwell, D. S. (2002). Recent advances and future directions in the biopsychosocial assessment and treatment of arthritis. *Journal of Consulting and Clinical Psychology,* 70, 640–655.

Kelley, E., Moy, E., Stryer, D., Burstin, H., & Clancy, C. (2005). The national healthcare quality and disparities reports: An overview. *Medical Care,* 43 (3 Suppl), I3–I8.

Kelly, J. A., St. Lawrence, J. S., Diaz, Y. E., Stevenson, L. Y., Hauth, A. C., Brasfield, T. L., et al. (1991). HIV risk behavior reduction following intervention with key opinion leaders of population: An experimental analysis. *American Journal of Public Health,* 81(2), 168–171.

Kendro, W. (2008). Canadian disparities in access to healthcare. *Canadian Medical Association Journal,* 179(9), 892.

Kenya, P. R., Gatiti, S., Muthami, L. N., Agwanda, R., Mwensi, H. A., Katsivo, M. N., et al. (1990). Oral rehydration therapy and social marketing in Kenya. *Social Science and Medicine,* 31, 979–987.

Kershau, S., Mood, D. W., Newth, G., Ronis, D. L., Sanda, M. G., Vaishampayan, U., et al. (2008). Longitudinal analysis of a model to predict quality of life in prostate cancer patients and their spouses. *Annals of Behavioral Medicine,* 36, 2, 117–128.

Kessler, K. M. (1992). Syndrome X: The epicardial view. *Journal of the American College of Cardiology,* 19, 32–33.

Keyes, K. M., Grant, B. F., & Hasin, D. S. (2008). Evidence for a closing gender gap in alcohol use, abuse, and dependence in the United States population. *Drug and Alcohol Dependence,* 93(1–2), 21–29.

Khan, M. A. (2006). The facts: Ankylosing spondylitis. Oxford, UK: Oxford University Press.

Khan, A., & Hussain, R. (2008). Violence against women in Pakistan: Perceptions and expressions of domestic violence. *Asian Studies Review,* 32(2), 239–253.

Kidd, B. L. (2006). Topical review: Osteoarthritis and joint pain. *Pain,* 123, 1–6. New York: Random House.

Kidder, T. (2003). *Mountains beyond mountains.* New York: Random House.

Kiecolt-Glaser, J. K., & Glaser, R. (1988). Psychological influences on immunity: Implications for AIDS. *American Psychologist,* 43, 892–898.

Kiecolt-Glaser, J. K., & Glaser, R. (1995). Psychoneuro-immunology and health consequences data & shared mechanism. *Psychosomatic Medicine,* 57, 269–274.

Kiecolt-Glaser, J. K., Fisher, L. K., & Ogrocki, P. (1987). Marital quality, marital disruption, and immune function. *Psychosomatic Medicine,* 49, 13–33.

Kiecolt-Glaser, J. K., Gouin, J. P., & Hanstoo, L. (2009). Close relationship inflammation & health. *Neuroscience & Biobehavioral Review,* Sept. 12.

Kim, S., Koniak-Griffin, D., Fluskerund, J. H., & Guarnero, P. A. (2004). The impact of lay health advisors on cardiovascular health promotion: Using a community-based participatory approach. *Journal of Cardiovascular Nursing,* 19, 3, 192–199.

Kimball, C. P. (1981). *The Biopsychosocial Approach to the Patient.* Baltimore: Williams & Wilkins. Kunz, J. (1982). *American Medical Association Family Medical Guide.* Random House: New York.

King, E., DeSilva, M., Stein, A., & Patel, V. (2009). Interventions for improving the psychosocial well-being of children affected by HIV and AIDS. *Cochrane Database System Review,* 15, 2, 733.

King, M. C., Marks, J. H., Mandell, J. B., & New York Breast Cancer Study Group. (2003). Breast and ovarian cancer risks due to inherited mutations in BRCA1 and BRCA2. *Science,* 302, 643–646.

Kirscht, J. P. (1977). Communication between patient and physician. *Annals of Internal Medicine,* 86(4), 499–500.

Klatsky, A. L. (2007). Alcohol cardiovascular diseases and diabetes mellitus. *Pharmacological Research,* 55(3), 237–247.

Klein, J. D., & St. Clair, S. (2000). Do candy cigarettes encourage young people to smoke? *British Medical Journal,* 321, 362–365.

Klein, J. D., Thomas, R. K., & Sutter, E. J. (2007). History of childhood candy cigarette use is associated with tobacco smoking by adults. *Preventive Medicine,* 45(1), 26–30.

Klein, J. D., Wilson, K. M., & McNulty, M. (1999). Access to medical care for adolescents: Results from the 1997 Commonwealth Fund study of the health of adolescent girls. *Journal of Adolescent Health,* 25, 120–130.

Klein, R. (2001). What's happening to Britain's national health service? *New England Journal of Medicine,* 345(4), 305–308.

Knox, S. S., Hausdorff, J., & Markovitz, J. H. (2002). Reactivity as a predictor of subsequent blood pressure: Racial differences in the coronary artery risk development in young adults (CARDIA) study. *Hypertension,* 40, 6, 914–919.

Knussen, C., Tolson, D., Swan, I. R. C., Slott, D. J., & Brogan, C. A. (2005). Stress proliferation in caregivers: The relationship between caregiving stressors & deterioration in family relationships. *Psychology & Health,* 20, 2, 207–221.

Kohler, C. L., Grimley, D., & Reynolds, K. (1999). Theoretical approaches guiding the development and implementation of health promotion programs. In J. Raczynski & R. DiClemente, *Handbook of health promotion and disease prevention* (23–44). New York: Kluwer Academic/Plenum Publishers.

Krassner, M. (1986). Effective features of therapy from the healer's perspective: A study of *curanderismo.* *Smith College Studies in Social Work,* 56, 157–183.

Kreps, G. L. (2002). Consumer/provider communication research: A personal plea to address issues of ecological validity, relational, development, message diversity, and situational constraints. In D. F. Marks (ed.), *The health psychology reader.* London: Sage Publications.

Kriss, J. L., Collins, S. R., Mahato, B., Gould, E., & Schoen, C. (2008). Rite of passage: Why young adults become uninsured & how new policies can help. 2008

Update. The Commonwealth Fund. Retrieved on October 3, 2009, from: http://www.common wealthfund.org/~/media/Files/Publications/Fund%20Report/2008/May/Rite%20of%20Passage%20%20Why%20Young%20Adults%20Become%20Uninsured%20and%20How%20New%20Policies%20Can%20Help%20%202008%20Update/Kriss_riteofpassage2008_1139_ib%20pdf.pdf.

Kropp, R. Y., & Halpern-Felsher, B. L. (2004). Adolescents' beliefs about the risks involved in smoking "light" cigarettes. *Pediatrics,* 114(4), 445–451.

Kublin, J. G., & Steketee, R. W. (2006). HIV infection and malaria: Understanding the interactions. *Journal of Infectious Diseases,* 193, 1, 1–3.

Kulbok, P. A., & Cox, C. L. (2002). Dimensions of adolescent health behavior. *Journal of Adolescent Health,* 31, 294–400.

Kumpfer, K. L., & Turner, C. W. (1990–1991). The social ecology model of adolescent substance abuse: Implications for prevention. *International Journal of the Addictions,* 25, 435–463.

Kung, H.-C., Hoyert, D. l., Yu, J., & Murphy, S. L. (2008). Death: Final data for 2005. Centers for Disease Control and Prevention, *National Vital Statistics Reports,* 56(10), 1–121.

Kunz, J. R. M. (1982). *The American Medical Association family medical guide.* New York: Random House.

Kuoppala, J., Lamminpaa, A., & Husman, P. (2008). Work health promotion, job well-being & sickness absences: A systematic review and meta-analysis. *Journal of Occupational and Environmental Medicine,* 50, 11, 1216–1227.

Kupper, N., & Denollet, J. (2007). Type D personality as a prognostic factor in heart disease. *Journal of Personality Assessment,* 89, 265–276.

Kurian, A. K., & Cardarelli, K. M. (2007). Racial and ethnic differences in cardiovascular disease risk factors: a systematic review. *Ethnic Diseases,* 17(1), 143–152.

Kyngas, H., Mikkonen, B., Nousianinen, E.-M., Rytilahti, M., Seppanes, P., Vaatlovaara, R., & Jamsa, T. (2001). Coping with the onset of cancer: Coping strategies and resources of young people with cancer. *European Journal of Cancer Care,* 10(1), 6–11.

Labbe, E., Schmidt, N., Babin, J, & Pharr, M. (2008). Coping with stress: the effectiveness of different types of music. *Applied Psychophysiology and Biofeedback,* 32(3–4), 163–168.

Lace, M. (2009). From Edgar, 5, coughs heard around the world. *The New York Times,* April 29, A1 and A10.

Lacey, J. H., & Dolan, B. M. (1988). Bulimia in British blacks and Asians: A catchment area study. *British Journal of Psychiatry,* 152, 73–79.

Lallemant, M., Jourdain, G., Le Coeur, S., Mary, J. Y., Ngo-Giang-Huong, N., & Koetsawang, S. (2004).

Single-dose perinatal nevirapine plus standard zidovudine to prevent mother-to-child transmission of HIV-1 in Thailand. *The New England Journal of Medicine,* 351, 217–228.

Lam, T. P. (2001). Strengths and weaknesses of traditional Chinese medicine and Western medicine in the eyes of some Hong Kong Chinese. *Journal of Epidemiological and Community Health,* 55, 762–762.

Lando, A. M., & Labiner-Wolfe, J. (2006). Helping consumers make more healthful food choices: Consumer views on modifying food labels and providing point-of-purchase nutritional information at quick-service restaurants. *Journal of Nutritional education and Behavior,* 39(3), 157–163.

Lane, D. A., Langman, C. M., Lip, G. Y. H., & Nouwen, A. (2009). Illness perceptions, affective responses, health-related quality-of-life in patients with atrial fibrillation. *Journal of Psychosomatic Research,* 66, 3, 211–220.

Lasser, K. E., Mintzer, I. L., Lambert, A., Cabral, H., & Bor, D. H. (2005). Missed appointment rates in primary care: The importance of site of care. *Journal of Health Care of the Poor and Underserved,* 16(3), 475–486.

Lasserm, K. E., Himmelstein, D. U., & Woolhandler, S. (2006). Access to care, health status & health disparities in the United States and Canada: Results of a cross-national population-based survey. *American Journal of Public Health,* 96, 7, 1300–1307

Laurent, S., & Bautouyrie, P. (2007). Arterial stiffness: a new surrogate and end-point for cardiovascular disease? *Journal of Nephrology,* 20(Suppl), 12, S45–S50.

LaVeist, T. A., & Nuru-Jeter, A. (2002). Is doctor-patient race concordance associated with greater satisfaction with care? *Journal of Health and Social Behavior,* 43(3), 296–306.

Lawrence, C. (2007). *Teens drive distracted.* CNN Transcript. Retrieved from: www.Cnn.com/2007/EDUCATION/01/25/transcript.fri/index.html#first.

Lazarus, R. S., & Folkman, S. (1984). *Stress, Appraisal and Coping.* New York: Springer.

Lazarus, R. S., & Folkman, S. (1984). Coping and adaptation. In W. D. Gentry (ed.), *Handbook of Behavioral Medicine* (282–325). New York: Guilford Press.

Lazarus, R. S., DeLonges, A., Folkman, S., & Gruen, R. (1985). Stress & adaptation outcomes: The problem of confounded measures. *American Psychologists,* 40, 1, 770–779.

Lea, E. J., Crawford, D., & Worsley, A. (2006). Public views of the benefits and barriers to the consumption of a plant-based diet. *European Journal of Clinical Nutrition,* 60(7), 828–837.

Lechner, S. C., Carver, C. S., Antoni, M. H., Weaver, K. E., & Phillips, K. M. (2006). Curvilinear associations between benefit finding & psychosocial adjustment to breast cancer. *Journal of Consulting & Clinical Psychology,* 74, 5, 828–840.

Lee, I. M., & Paffenberger, R. S. (1992). Quetelet's index and risk of colon cancer in college alumni. *Journal of the National Cancer Institute,* 84, 1326–1331.

Lee, J., Pomeroy, E., & Bohman, T. (2007). Intimate partner violence & psychological health in a sample of Asian and Caucasian women: The roles of social support and caring. *Journal of Family Violence,* 22(8), 709–720.

Lee, L. V., & Foody, J. M. (2008). Cardiovascular disease in women. *Current Atherosclerosis Report,* 10(4), 295–302.

Lefcourt, H. M., Davidson, K., Shepherd, R., Phillips, M., Prkachin, K., & Mills, D. (1995). Perspective-taking humor: Accounting for stress moderation. *Journal of Social and Clinical Psychology,* 14, 373–391.

LeMaster, P. J., Beub, J., Novins, D. K., & Manson, S. M. (2004). The prevalence of suicidal behaviors among Northern Plains American Indians. *Suicide & Life Threatening Behavior,* 34, 242.

Lepore, S. T., Revenson, T. A., Weinberger, S. L., Weston, P., Pasquale, G., & Frisina, M. A. (2006). Effects of social stressors on cardiovascular reactivity in black and white women. *Annals of Behavioral Medicine,* 31(2), 120–127.

Lerner, E. B., Jehle, D. H. V., & Janicke, D. M. (2000). Medical communication: Do our patients understand? *American Journal of Emergency Medicine,* 18, 764–766.

Leserman, J. (2008). Role of depression, stress and trauma in HIV disease progression. *Psychosomatic Medicine,* 70, 539–545.

Lesiuk, T. (2008). The effects of preferred music listening on stress levels of air traffic controllers. *The Arts in Psychotherapy,* 35, 1, 1–10.

Levy, A. S., Fein, S. B., & Stephenson, M. (1993). Nutrition knowledge levels about dietary fats & cholesterol: 1983–1988. *Journal of Nutritional Education,* 25, 60–66.

Levy, J. A., Shimabukuro, J., & Hollander, H. (1985). Isolation of AIDS-associated retrovirus from the cerebrospinal fluid and brain of patients with neurological symptoms. *Lancet,* 2, 580–586.

Lewin, K. (1935). *A dynamic theory of personality.* London: McGraw-Hill.

Ley, P., & Spelman, M. S. (1965). Communications in an out-patient setting. *British Journal of Clinical Psychology,* 4, 2, 114–116.

Liberatos, P., Link, B. G., & Kelsey, J. L. (1988). The measurement of social class in epidemiology. *Epidemiologic Review,* 10(1), 87–121.

Lindberg, N. M., & Wellisch, B. (2001). Anxiety and compliance among women at risk for breast cancer. *Annals of Behavioral Medicine,* 23, 298–303.

Lindegger G., & Richter, L. (2000). Relationships between science and ethics in HIV/AIDS prevention trials. *South African Journal of Science,* June, 96, 313–317. July 13.

Lindholm, L., Rehnsfeldt, A., Arman, M., & Hamrin, E. (2002). Significant other's experience of suffering when living with women with breast cancer. *Scandinavian Journal of Care Science* (Special Issue: The Challenging Complexity of Cancer Care Research), 16, 248–255.

Linton, S. J. (2000). A review of psychological risk factors in back and neck pain. *Spine,* 25, 1148–1156.

Little, H., Swinson, D. R., & Cruickshank, B. (1976). Upward subluxation of the axis in ankylosing spondylitis. *American Journal of Medicine,* 60, 2, 279–285.

Littman, R. J., & Littman, M. L. (1973). Galena and the Antonine plague. *American Journal of Philology,* 94, 254–255.

Lock, J., & Fitzpatrick, K. K. (2009). Anorexia nervosa. *Clinical Evidence (Online),* Nov. 10, 2009, 1011.

Locke, S. E., Kraus, L., & Lesserman, J. (1984). Life change stress, psychiatric symptoms, and natural killer cell activity. *Psychosomatic Medicine,* 46, 441–453.

Loeser, J. D. (2003). The Decade of pain control and research. *American Pain Society Bulletin, 13,3.* Retrieved on July 20, 2010, from: http://www.ampainsoc.org/pub/bulletin/may03/article1.htm.

Loewenson, R. (2007). Exploring equity and inclusion in the responses to AIDS. *AIDS Care,* 19 (Supplement 1), S2–S11.

Lonn, S., Ahlbom, A., Hall, P., & Feychting, M. (2004). Mobile phone use and the risk of acoustic neuroma. *Epidemiology,* 15, 653–659.

Lopez, R. A. (2005). Use of alternative folk medicine by Mexican American women. *Journal of Immigrant Health,* 7, 1, 23–31.

Lopez-Velez, M., Martinez-Martinez, E., & Del Valle-Rebes, C. (2003). The study of phenolic compounds as natural antioxidants in wine. *Critical Review of Food Science and Nutrition,* 43(3), 233–244.

Lowe, R. A., Localio, A. R., Schwartz, D. F., Williams, S., Tuton, L. W., Maroney, S., et al. (2005). Association between primary care practice characteristics and emergency department use in a Medicaid managed care organization. *Medical Care,* 43, 8, 792–800.

Lowry, R., Holtzman, D., & Truman, B. (1994). Substance use and HIV-related sexual behaviors among US high school students: Are they related? *American Journal of Public Health,* 84, 1116–1120.

Luna, E. (2003). Nurse-*curanderas: Las que curan* at the heart of Hispanic culture. *Journal of Holistic Nursing,* 21(4), 326–342.

Luszczynska, A., & Schwarzer, R. (2003). Planning and self-efficacy in the adoption and maintenance of breast self-examination: A longitudinal study of self-regulatory cognition. *Psychology & Health,* 18(1), 93–108.

Macharia, W. M., Shiroya, A., & Njeru, E. K. (1997). Knowledge, attitudes and beliefs of primary caretakers towards sickle cell anaemia in children. *East African Medical Journal,* 74(7), 416–419.

Madden, T. J., Ellen, P. S., & Ajzen, I. (1992). A comparison of the theory of planned behaviors and the theory of reasoned action. *Personality & Social Psychology Bulletin,* 18(1), 3–9.

Mai, P. L., Sullivan-Hally. J., & Ursin, G. (2006). Activity and colon cancer risk among women in the California teachers study. *Cancer Epidemiology Biomarkers Prevention,* 16, 517–525.

Malaria No More (2010). Learn the Facts. Retrieved on July 6, 2010, from: www.malaria nomore.org/get_involved.php.

Malcolm, C. E., Wong, K. K., & Elwood-Martin, R. (2008). Patient's perceptions of experiences of family medicine residents in the office. *Canadian Family Physician,* 54, 4, 570–571.

Manary, M. J. (2005). Local production and provision of ready-to-use therapeutic food for the treatment of severe child malnutrition. Technical Background Paper. Geneva: WHO.

Manderson, L., & Kokanovic, R. (2009). "Worried all the time": Distress and the circumstances of everyday life among immigrant Australians with type 2 diabetes. *Chronic Illness,* 5, 1, 21–32.

Mangione, K. K., McCully, K., Gloviak, A., Lefebvre, I., Hoffman, M., & Craik, R. (1999). The effects of high-intensity and low-intensity cycle ergometry in older adults with knee osteoarthritis. *Journals of Gerontology: Biological Sciences and Medical Sciences,* 59, 86–93.

Manne, S. L., Ostroff, J., Rini, C., Fox, K., Goldstein, L., & Granna, G. (2004). The interpersonal process model of intimacy; the role of self-disclosure, partner-disclosure & partner responsiveness in interactions between breast cancer patients & their partners. *Journal of Family Psychology,* 18, 589–599.

Manne, S. L., Ostroff, J., Winkel, G., Grana, G., & Fox, K. (2005). Partner unsupportive responses, avoidant coping, and distress among women with early stage breast cancer: Patient and partner perspective. *Health Psychology,* 24(6), 635–641.

Manne, S. L., Taylor, K. L., Dougherty, J., & Kemeny, N. (1997). Supportive and negative responses in the partner relationship: Their association with psychological adjustment among individuals with cancer. *Journal of Behavioral Medicine,* 20, 101–125.

Manson, J. E., Tosteson, H., Ridker, P. M., et al. (1992). The primary prevention of myocardial infarction. *New England Journal of Medicine,* 326, 1406–1416.

Marcus, R. F. (2008). Flight-seeking motivation in dating partners within an aggressive relationship. *Journal of Social Psychology,* 148(3), 261–276.

Markel, H., Gostin, L. O., & Fidler, D. P. (2007). Extensive drug-resistant tuberculosis: An isolation order, public health powers, and a global crisis. *JAMA,* 298(1), 83–86.

Markovitz, J. H., Matthews, K. A., Whooley, M., Lewis, C. E., & Greenlund, K. L. (2004). Increases in job strain are associated with incident hypertension in the CARDIA study. *Annals of Behavioral Medicine,* 28, 4–9.

Marks, David. (2002). Theories in health psychology. In D. Marks (ed.), *The Health Psychology Reader,* 90–93. London, UK: Sage Publications.

Martin, R. A. (2001). Humor, laughter, and physical health methodological issues and research findings. *Psychological Bulletin,* 127, 4, 504–519.

Martin, R. A., Kuiper, N. A., Olinger, L. J., & Dance, K. A. (1993). Humor, coping with stress, self-concept, and psychological well-being. *Humor: International Journal of Humor Research,* 6, 89–104.

Martire, L. M., Schulz, R., Keefe, F. J., Starz, T. W., Osial, T. A., Dew, M. A., et al. (2003). Feasibility of a dyadic intervention for management of osteoarthritis: a pilot study with older patients and their spousal caregivers. *Aging & Mental Health,* 7(1), 53–60.

Marzuk, P. M., Tierney, H., & Tardiff, K. (1988). Increased risk of suicide in persons with AIDS. *Journal of American Medical Association,* 259, 1333–1337.

Masalu, J. R., & Astrom, A. N. (2003). The use of the theory of planned behavior to explore beliefs about sugar restriction. *American Journal of Health Behavior,* 27(1), 15–25.

Mason, J. W., Maher, J. T., Hartley, L. H., Mougey, E., Perlow, M. J., & Jones, L. G. (1976). Selectivity of corticosteroid & catecholamine response to various natural stimuli. In G. Serban (ed.), *Psychopathology of human adaptation.* New York: Plenum Press.

Matarazzo, J. D. (1980). Behavioral health and behavioral medicine: Frontiers for a new Health psychology. *American Psychologist,* 35, 807–817.

Mathews, K. A., & Gump, B. B. (2002). Chronic work stress and marital dissolution increase risk of posttrial mortality in men from the multiple risk factor intervention trial. *Archives of Internal Medicine,* 162, 309–315.

Maul, J. S., Burt, R. W., & Cannon-Albright, L. A. (2007). A familial component to human rectal cancer, independent of colon cancer risk. *Clinical Gastroenterology & Hepatology,* 5(9), 1080–1084.

Mayer, J., & Salovey, P. (1997). *What is emotional intelligence?* New York: Basic Books.

Mayhew, D. R., Simpson, H. M., & Pak, A. (2003). Changes in collision rates among novice drivers during the first months of driving. *Accidents Annals of Prevention,* 35, 683–691.

Mayne, T. J. (1999) Negative effect and health: The importance of being earnest. *Cognition and Emotion,* 13, 5, 601–635.

Mayo Clinic. (2006). Heart disease: Sudden cardiac arrests. Retrieved from: www.mayo clinic.com/health/sudden-cardiac-arrest/0500764/Dsection=causes.

Mayo Clinic. (2008). Leukemia. Retrieved from: http://www.mayoclinic.com/health/leukemia/DS00351.

Mayo Clinic (2009). Spinal cord injuries: symptoms. Retrieved on November 27, 2009: from: http://www.mayoclinic.com/health/spinal-cord-injury/DS00460/DSECTION=symptoms.

McCrae, R. R., & Costa, P. T. (1987). Validation of the five-factor model of personality across instruments & observers. *Journal of Personality & Social Psychology,* 52, 81–90.

McDowell, I., & Newell, C. (1996). *Measuring health: A guide to rating scales and questionnaires* (2nd ed.). Oxford, UK: Oxford University Press.

McEwen, B. S., & Winfield, J. C. (2003). The concept of allostasis in biology and biomedicine. *Hormones and Behavior,* 43, 2–15.

McGinley, A. M. (2004). Health beliefs & women's rise of hormone replacement therapy. *Holistic Nursing Practices,* 18(1), 18–25.

McGinnis, J. M., & Foege, W. H. (1993). Actual causes of death in the United States. *Journal of the American Medical Association,* 270, 2207–2212.

McGraw, L. K., Turner, B. S., Stotts, N. A., & Dracup, K. A. (2008). A review of cardiovascular risk factors in US military personnel. *Journal of Cardiovascular Nursing,* e-release prior to publication.

McGuire, P. A. (1999). More psychologists are finding that discrete uses of humor promote healing in their patients. *American Psychological Association Monitor,* 30, 1.

McKenna, M. T., & Hu, X. (2007). Recent trends in the incidence and morbidity associated with perinatal human immunodeficiency virus infection in the United States. *American Journal of Obstetrics and Gynocology,* 197, 3, Suppl 1, S10–S16.

McKenzie-Mohr, D. (2000). Fostering sustainable behavior through community-based social marketing. *American Psychologist,* 5, 531–537.

McKeowan, T. (1988). *The origins of human disease.* Oxford, UK: Blackwell Press.

McKinley, J. B. (1975). Who is really ignorant—physicians or patient? *Journal of Health and Social Behavior,* 16, 3–11.

McLeroy, K. R., Bibeau, D., Steckler, A., & Glanz, K. (1988). An ecological perspective on health promotion programs. *Health Education Quarterly,* 15, 351–377.

McNamara, J. J., Molot, M. A., Stremple. J. F., & Cutting, R. T. (1971). Coronary artery disease in combat causalities in Vietnam. *JAMA,* 216(7), 1185–1187.

McNeilly, M. D., & Zeichner, A. (1989). Neuropeptid & cardiovascular response to intravenous catheterization in normotensive & hypertensive blacks and whites. *Health Psychology,* 8, 487–501.

Means, R. K. (1975). *A History of Health Education in the United States.* Thorofare, NJ: Charles B. Slack.

Mechanic, D. (1972). Social psychological factors affecting the presentation of bodily complaints. *New England Journal of Medicine,* 286, 1132–1139.

Mehler, P. S., Lasater, L., & Padillo, R. (2003). Obesity: Selected medical issues. *Eating Disorders,* 11, 317–330.

Meier, D., Emmons, C. A., Litke, A., Wallenstein, S., & Morrison, S. (2003). Characteristics of patients requesting and receiving physician assisted death. *Archives of Internal Medicine,* 163, 1537–1542.

Mellor, D., McCabe, M., Ricciardelli, L., Yeow, J., Daliza, N., & Hapidzal, N. F. B. M. (2009). Sociocultural influences on body dissatisfaction and body change behaviors among Malaysian adolescents. *Body Image,* 6, 2, 121–128.

Melzack, R. (1975). The McGill pain questionnaire: major properties and scoring methods. *Pain,* 1, 277–299.

Menezes Succi, D. (2007). Mother-to-child transmission of HIV in Brazil during the years 2000 & 2001: Results of a multi-centric study. *Cadernos de Saude Publica,* 23 (Suppl 3), S379–S389.

Mensah, G. A., Mokdad, A. H., Ford, E. S., Greenlund, K. J., & Croft, J. B. (2005). State of disparities in cardiovascular health in the United States. *Circulation,* 111(10), 1233–1241.

Merlin, A., Jager, J., & Schulenberger, J. E. (2008). Adolescent risk factors for adult alcohol use and abuse: Stability & change of predictive values across early and mid-adolescence. *Addiction,* Suppl 103, 84–99.

Merlis, M., Gould, D., & Mahato, B. (2006). Rising out-of-pocket spending for medical care: A growing strain on family budgets. *The Commonwealth Fund.* Retrieved from: www.commonwealthfund.org/publicaions/publications_show.htm?doc_id=347500&#doc347500.

Merritt, M. M., Bennett, G. G., Williams, R. B., Edwards, C. L., & Sollers, J. J. (2006). Perceived racism and cardiovascular reactivity and recovery to personally relevant stress. *Heath Psychology,* 25(3), 364–369.

Merzel, C., & D'Afflitti, J. (2003). Reconsidering community-based health promotion: Promise, performance and potential. *American Journal of Public Health,* 93, 4, 557–580.

Messier, S. P., Loeser, R. F., Mitchell, M. N., Valle, G., Morgan, T., Rejesk, W. J., & Ettinger, W. H. (2000). Exercise and weight loss in obese older adults with knee osteoarthritis. *Journal of the American Geriatrics Society,* 48, 1062–1072.

Metzer, W. S. (1989). The Caduceus and Aesculapian staff: Ancient Eastern origins and Western parallels. *Southern Medical Journal,* 82, 743–748.

Meyer, A. J., Nash, J. D., McAlister, A. L., Maccoby, N., & Farquhar, J. W. (1980). Skills training in cardiovascular health education campaign. *Journal of Consulting and Clinical Psychology,* 48, 2, 129–142.

Mickalide, A. D. (1990) Sociocultural factors influencing weight among males. In A. Anderson (ed.) *Males with eating disorders* (30–39). Philadelphia, PA: Brunner/Mazel.

Migneault, J. P., Pallonen, U. E., & Velicer, W. F. (1997). Decisional balances and stages of change for adolescent drinking. *Addictive Behaviors,* 22(3), 339–351.

Miki, Y., Swenson, J., Shattuck-Eidens, D., Futreal, P. A., Harsham, K., Tavtigian, S., et al. (1994). A strong candidate for the 17-linked breast and ovarian cancer susceptibility gene BRCA1. *Science,* 266, 66–71.

Miles, T. (2008). Neighborhood disorder, perceived safety and readiness to encourage use of local playgrounds. *American Journal of Preventive Medicine,* 34(4), 275–281.

Miller, B. A., Maguin, E., & Downs, W. (1997). Alcohol, drugs and violence in children's lives. In M. Galanter (ed.), *Recent developments in alcoholism: Vol 13, Alcoholism and Violence* (357–385). New York: Plenum.

Miller, M. N., & Pumariega, A. J. (2001). Culture and eating disorders: A historical and cross-cultural review. *Psychiatry,* 64, 2, 93–110

Mills, E. A. (2006). From the physical self to the social body: Expression & effects of HIV-related stigma in South Africa. *Journal of Community & Applied Social Psychology,* 16(6), 498–503.

Mills, P. R., Kessler, R. S., Cooper, J., & Sullivan, S. (2007). Impact of health promotion program on employee health risks and worker productivity. *American Journal of Health Promotion,* 22(1), 45–53.

Milne, S., Orbell, S., & Sherran, P. (2002). Combining motivational and volitional interventions to promote exercise participation: Protection motivation theory and implementational Intentions. *British Journal of Health,* 7, 163–184.

Mince, S. E., & Stewart, D. E. (2007). Gender differences and depression in chronic pain conditions in a national epidemiological survey. *Psychosomatics,* 48(5), 394–399.

Ministry of Health, Ukraine (2000). HIV/AIDS epidemic in Ukraine: Social and demographic aspects. New York: United Nations Development Program. New York, NY.

Minor, M., Stenstrom, C. H., Klepper, S. E., Hurley, M., & Ettinger, W. (2003). Work group recommendations: 2002 exercise and physical activity conference. *Arthritis Care and Research,* 49, 453–454.

Misra, V. H. (2001). Prehistoric human colonization of India. *Journal of Biosciences,* 26, 4, (Suppl.), 491–531.

Mittleman, M. A., Lewis, R. A., & Maclure, M. (2001). Triggering myocardial infarction by marijuana. *Circulation,* 103(23), 2805–2809.

Mittleman, M. A., Maclure, M., Sherwood, J. B., Mulry, R. P., Tofler, G. H., Jacobs, S. C. et al. (1995). Triggering of acute myocardial infarction onset by episodes of anger: Determinants of myocardial infarction onset study investigators. *Circulation,* 92, 1720–1725.

Mizrachi, N. (2001). From causation to correlation: The story of psychosomatic medicine, 1939–1979. *Culture, Medicine & Psychiatry,* 25, 317–343.

MMWR. (1984). CDC update: Acquired Immunodeficiency Syndrome (AIDS), United States, 32, 688–691.

MMWR. (2002). Youth risk behavior surveillance— United States 2001, 51(SS04), 1–64. Retrieved on January 3, 2009, from: www.cdc.gov/mmwr/preview/mmwrhtml/ss5104a1.htm.

MMWR. (2004). Alcohol use among adolescents and adults—New Hampshire, 1991–2003. *MMWR* 53(08), 174–175.

MMWR. (2005). Annual smoking-attributable mortality, years of potential life lost & productivity losses, United States 1997–2001, 55(25), 625–628. Retrieved on February 24, 2010, from: www.cdc.gov/mmwr/preview/mmwrhtml/mm5425a1.htm#tab.

MMWR. (2008a). HIV prevalence estimates—United States, 2006. *MMWR,* 57, 39, 1073–1076.

MMWR. (2008b). Subpopulation Estimates from the HIV Incidence Surveillance System, United States 2006. *MMWR,* 57(36), 985–989.

Moadei, A. B., & Harris, M. S. (2008). Cancer. In B. A. Boyer & M. I. Paharia (eds.), *Comprehensive handbook of clinical health psychology.* Hoboken, NJ: John Wiley Sons.

Moerman, D. (1998) *Native American Ethnobotany.* Timber Press.

Mokdad, A. H., Marks, J. S., Stroup, D. F., & Gerberding, J. L. (2004). Actual Causes of death in the United States. *Journal of the American Medical Association,* 291, 1238–1245.

Mokdad, A. H., Serdula, M. K., Dietz, W. H., Bowman, B. A., Marks, J. S., & Koplan, J. P. (2000). The continuing epidemic of obesity in the United States. *Journal of the American Medical Association,* 282, 1353–1358.

Molnar, B. E., Gortmaker, S. C., Bull, F. C., & Buka, S. L. (2004). Unsafe to play? Neighborhood disorder and lack of safety predict reduced physical activity among children and adolescents. *American Journal of Health Promotion,* 18(5), 378–386.

Moore, A. A., Gould, R., Reuben, D. B., Greendale, G. A., Carter, M. K., & Zhou, Z. (2005). Longitudinal patterns and predictors of alcohol consumption in the

United States. *American Journal of Public Health,* 95(3), 458–465.

Morales, A. L. (1998). *Remedios: Stories of earth and iron from the history of Puertorriquenas.* Boston: Beacon Press.

Morgaine, K. (2007). Domestic violence and human rights: Local challenges to a universal framework. *Journal of Sociology and Social Welfare,* 34, 1, 109–129.

Mosbach, P., & Leventhal, H. (1988). Peer group identification and smoking: implications for intervention. *Journal of Abnormal Psychology,* 97(2), 238–245.

Moscowitz, J. T., Epel, E. S., & Acree, M. (2008). Positive affect uniquely predicts lower risk of mortality in people with diabetes. *Health Psychology,* 27 (1Suppl.), S73–82.

Moskowitz, J. T., Folkman, S., Colette, L., & Vittinghoff, E. (1996) Coping with mood: AIDS related caregiver bereavement. *Annals of Behavioral Medicine,* 18, 1, 49–57.

Mozaffarin, D., Katan, M. B., Ascherio, A., Stampfer, M. J., & Willett, W. C. (2006). Trans fatty acids and cardiovascular disease. *New England Journal of Medicine,* 354, 1601–1613.

Mullen, K. D., McDermott, R. S., Gold, R. J., & Belcastro, P. A. (1996). *Connections for Health,* 4th ed. Madison, WI: Brown & Benchmark.

Mulvihill, B. A., Jackson, A. J., Mulvihill, F. X., Romaire, M., Gyaben, S., Telfair, S., et al. (2005). The impact of SCHIP enrollment on adolescent-provider communication. *Journal of Adolescent Health,* 37(2), 94–102.

Munck, A., & Guyre, P. M. (1986). Glucocorticoid physiology, pharmacology & stress. *Advanced Experimental Medical Biology,* 196, 81–96.

Munck, A., & Maray-Fejes-Toth, A. (1994). Glucocorticoids & stress: Permissive and suppressive actions. *Annals of the New York Academy of Science,* 746, 115–130.

Munn, J. D., & Woznick, L. (2007). Single payer health care systems: The roles and responsibilities of the public and private sector. *Benefits Quarterly,* 23(3), 7–17.

Munoz, A., Kirby, A. J., He, Y. D., Margolick, J., Visscher, B., Rinaldo, C., et al. (1995). Long-term survivors with HIV-1 infection: Incubation period and longitudinal patterns of CD4+ lymphocytes. *Journal of Acquired Immune Deficiency Syndromes & Human Retrovirology,* 8, 496–506.

Muscari Lin, E., Aikin, J. L., & Good, B. C. (1999). Premature menopause after cancer treatment. *Cancer Practice,* 7(3), 114–121.

Muscat, J. E., Malkin, M. G., Shore, R. E., Thompson, S., Neugut, A. I., Stellmann, S. D., et al. (2002). Handheld cellular phones and the risk of neuroma. *Neurology,* 58, 1304–1306.

Muscat, J. E., Malkin, M. G., Thompson, S., Shore, R. E., Stellman, S. D., McRee, D., et al. (2000). Handheld cellular telephone use and risk of brain cancer. *JAMA,* 284, 3001–3007.

Myers, D. G. (2000). The funds, friends, and faith of happy people. *American Psychologists,* 55(1), 56–67.

Myslakidou, K., Tsilika, E., Parpa, E., Hatzipli, I., Smyrnioti, M., Galanos, A., et al. (2008). Demographic and clinical predictions of spirituality in advanced cancer patients: A randomized control study. *Journal of Clinical Nursing,* 17(13), 1779–1785.

Naar-King, S., Templin, T., & Wright, K. (2006). Psychosocial factors and medication adherence in HIV-positive youth. *AIDS Patient Care, STDS,* 20, 44–47.

Naar-King, S., Wright, K., Parsons, J. T., Frey, M., Templin, T., & Ondersma, S. (2006). Transtheoretical model and condom use in HIV-Positive youths. *Health Psychology,* 25, 648–652.

National Academy on an Aging Society. (2000). *Heart disease: A disabling yet preventable condition* (No. 3). Washington, DC. Retrieved from: www.agingsociety.org/agingsociety/pdf/heart/pdf.

National Biological Information Infrastructure (2009). Northeastern US- EPA Superfund sites. Retrieved on February 22, 2010, from: http://beta.nbii-nin.ciesin.columbia.edu/documents/NINWater_EPA Superfundsites.pdf.

National Cancer Institute. (1996). The FTC cigarette tests methods for determining tar, nicotine & carbon monoxide yields in US cigarettes: Report of the NCI Expert Committee. Bethesda, MD: National Institutes of Health publication No. 96-4028.

National Cancer Institute. (2001). Risks associated with smoking cigarettes with low machine measured yields of tar and nicotine: Monograph 13. Retrieved on March 1, 2007, from: http://cancercontrol.cancer.gov/tcbr/nci_monographs.

National Cancer Institute. (2007). Screening Mammograms: Questions and answers factsheet. Retrieved on January 23, 2010, from: www.cancer.gov/cancer topics/types/breast.

National Center for Health Statistics (2006). Healthy United States in Chartbook on Trends in The Health of Americans. Retrieved on August 7, 2009, from: http://www.cdc.gov/nchs/data/hus/hus06.pdf.

National Conference of State Legislatures. (2005). *Vending machines in schools.* Retrieved on November 1, 2008, from: www.ncsl.org/programs/health/vending.htm.

National Health & Hospitals Reform Commission. (2009). A healthier future for all Australians: An overview of the final report of the National Health & Hospitals Reform Commission. *The Medical Journal of Australia,* 191, 7, 383–387.

National Heart, Lung and Blood Institute. (1986). *Public perceptions of high blood pressure and sodium.* (National Institute of Health Publication No. 86-2730). Bethesda, MD: National Heart, Lung and Blood Institute.

National Heart, Lung and Blood Institute. (2007). Hemophilia. Retrieved from: www.nhlbi.gov/health/dci/diseases/hemophilia/hemophilia_what.html.

National Heart, Lung, and Blood Institute (NHLBI). (2008a). Heart valve disease. Retrieved on October 10, 2008, from: www.nhlbi.nih.gov/health/dci/Diseases/hvd/hvd_whatis.html.

National Heart, Lung, and Blood Institute (NHLBI). (2008b). High blood cholesterol. Retrieved on October 10, 2008, from: www.nhlbi.nih.gov/health/dci/Diseases/Hbc/HBC_WhatIs.html.

National Heart, Lung, and Blood Institute (NHLBI). (2008c). NHLBI health information network e-Bulletin. Retrieved on February 15, 2010, from: http://hp2010.nhlbihin.net/joinhin/news/HowToNWRD08.htm.

National Heart, Lung & Blood Institute. (2009). COPD. Retrieved on January 4, 2010, from: www.nhlbi.nih.gov/health/dci/diseases/COPD/copd_WhatIs.html.

National Heart, Lung, and Blood Institute (NHLBI). Previous red dress collection. Retreived on February 1, 2010, from: http://www.nhlbi.nih.gov/educational/hearttruth/events/red-dress-collection.htm.

National Highway Traffic Safety Administration. (2005a). Traffic safety facts: 2004 data-speeding. Washington DC: National Highway Traffic Safety Administration, U.S. Department of Transportation Publication HS 809–915.

National Highway Traffic Safety Administration. (2005b). Traffic Safety Facts 2005: Alcohol. Washington, DC: National Highway Traffic Safety Administration, U.S. Department of Transportation. Retrieved from: http://www.nhtsa.gov/Research/Human+Factors/Alcohol+Impairment.

National Highway Traffic Safety Administration. (2006). Traffic safety facts: Research notes. Washington, DC: National Highway Traffic Safety Administration, U.S. Department of Transportation, NHTSA's national Center for Statistical Analysis.

National Institute of Arthritis & Musculoskeletal & Skin Diseases. (2006). Questions and answers about gout. NIH Publications No. 07-5027. Washington, DC: U.S. Department of Health and Human Services.

National Institute of Health (NIH). (2004). Guidelines for the conduct of research involving human subjects at the Institutes of Health. Washington, DC: U.S. Department of Health and Human Services, Public Health Services, 00-4783.

National Institutes of Health, Number NIH07-5605. Washington. DC: U.S. Department of Health and Human Services.

National Public Radio. (2008). Understanding Sen. Kennedy's cancer diagnosis. Retrieved from: www.npr.org/templates/story/story/php?storyId=90645054.

National Tuberculosis Center. (1966). *A Brief History of Tuberculosis.* Retrieved on August 9, 2008, from: www.umdnj.edu/-ntbcweb/history/htm.

NBC News. (2008). NBC's Tim Russert dies of heart attack at 58. Retrieved from: www.msnbc.msn.com/id/25145431.

Nelson, M. C., Newmark-Strainer, D., Hannan, P. J., Sirard, J. R., & Story, M. (2006). Longitudinal and secular trends in physical activity and sedentary behavior during adolescence. *Pediatrics,* 118, 6, 1627–1634.

Nelson, T. F., Naomi, T. S., Brewer, R. D., & Wechsler, H. (2005). The state sets the rate: The relationship among state-specific college binge drinking, state binge drinking rates, and selected state alcohol control policies. *American Journal of Public Health,* 95(3), 441–446.

Neria, Y. (2009). Posttraumatic stress disorder. *Psychotic Annals,* 39, 6, 317–318.

Neuhausen, S., Gilewski, T., Norton, L., Tran, T., McGuire, P., & Swenson, J. (1996). Recurrent BRCA2 617delT mutations in Ashkenazi Jewish women affected by breast cancer. *Nature Genetics,* 13, 126–128.

Newman, B., Mu, H., Butler, L. M., Millikan, R. C., Moorman, P. G., & King, M. C. (1998). Frequency of breast cancer attributable to BRCA1 in population-bases series of American women. *JAMA,* 279, 915–921.

Nicita-Mauro, V., Maltese, G., Nicita-Mauro, C., & Basile, G. (2007). Vascular aging and the geriatric patient. *Minerva Cardioangiologica,* 55(4), 497–502.

NIDA. (2002). *Marijuana: Facts for teens.* Retrieved March 2008, from: www.drugabuse.gov/MarijBroch/teenpg9-10.html.

NIDA. (2006a). *NIDA InfoFacts: Crack and cocaine.* Retrieved, March 2008, from: http://nida.gov/info-Facts/Cocaine.html.

NIDA. (2006b). *NIDA InfoFacts: Marijuana.* Retrieved March 2008, from: www.nida.gov/infofacts/Marijuana.html.

NIDA. (2006c). *NIDA InfoFacts: Methamphetamine.* Retrieved from: www.nida.nih.Gov/infofacts/methamphetamine.html.

NIDA. (2006d). *NIDA InfoFacts: Prescription pain and other medications.* Retrieved from: www.nih.Gov/infofacts/PainMed.html.

NIDA. (2007a). *Drugs, brains, and behavior: The science of addiction.* NIDA Report.

NIDA. (2007b). NIDA InfoFacts: High school and youth trends. Retrieved from: NIDA (2010) InfoFacts: Heroin. Retrieved on July 12, 2010, from: http://www.drugabuse.gov/infofacts/heroin.html; www.nida.nih.gov/infofacts/hsyouthtrends.html.

Nikelly, A. G. (2005). Positive health outcomes of social interests. *Journal of Individual Psychology,* 61(4), 329–342.

Nilsson, U. (2009). Soothing music can increase oxytocin levels during bed rest and after open-heart surgery: a randomized control trial. *Journal of Clinical Nursing,* 18, 2153–2161.

Nolen-Hoeksema, S., Larson, J., & Grayson. C. (1999). Explaining the gender difference in depressive symptoms. *Journal of Personality and Social Psychology,* 77, 1061–1072.

Noormohamed, S. E., Ferguson, K. J., Baghair, A., & Cohen, L. G. (1994). Student's knowledge base and attitudes on safer sex, condoms & AIDS: A study of three colleges of pharmacy. *American Journal of Pharmacological Education,* 58, 269–273.

Norem, J. K. (2001). Defensive pessimism, optimism & pessimism. In E. D. Chang (ed.), *Optimism & pessimism: Theory research & practice* (77–100). Washington, DC: American Psychological Association Press.

Norring, C., & Sohlberg, S. (1988). Eating disorder inventory in Sweden: Description, cross-cultural comparison, and clinical utility. *Acta Psychiatrica Scandinavica,* 78, 567–575.

Northridge, M. E., & Sclar, E. (2003). A joint urban planning and public health framework: Contributions to health impact assessment. *American Journal of Public Health,* 93(1), 118–121.

Nosheen, H. (2009). Blacks face bone marrow donor shortage. *National Public Radio.* Retrieved on July 20, 2010, from: http://www.npr.org/templates/story/story.php?storyId=128173149.

Nouwen, A., Gingras, J., Talbot, F., & Bouchard, S. (1997). The development of an empirical taxonomy for patients with diabetes. *Health Psychology,* 16, 263–271.

Nuechlerlein, K. H., Dawson, M.E., Gitlin, M., Ventura, J., Goldstein, M. J., Snyder, K. S., et al. (1992). Developmental processes in schizophrenic disorders: Longitudinal studies of vulnerability and stress. *Schizophrenic Bulletin,* 18, 3, 387–425.

O'Halloran, J., Miller, G. C., & Britt, H. (2004). Defining chronic conditions for primary care in ICPC-2. *Family Practice,* 21(4), 381–386.

O'Neil, P. M., & Brown, J. D. (2005). Weighing the evidence: Benefits of regular weight monitoring for weight control. *Journal of Nutrition, Education & Behavior,* 37(6), 319–322.

Oetting, E. R., & Beauvis, R. (1987). Peer cluster theory, socialization characteristics, and adolescent drug use: A path analysis. *Journal of Counseling Psychology,* 34, 205–213.

Office for Human Research Protection (OHRP) (2001). Suspension letter to Johns Hopkins University Jul 19: 2. Retrieved on March 23, 2007, from: http://ohrp.osophs.dhhs.gov/detrm_letrs/july01a.pdf.

Ogata Jones, K., Denham, B. E., & Springston, T. K. (2006). Effects of mass and inter-personal communication on breast cancer screening: Advancing agenda-setting theory in a health context. *Journal of Applied Communication Research,* 34(1), 94–113.

Olivardia, R., Pope, H. G., Mangweth, B., & Hudson, J. I. (1995). Eating disorders in college men. *American Journal of Psychiatry,* 152, 1279–1285.

Oliver, G., & Wardle, J. (1999). Perceived effects of stress on food choice. *Physiology and Behavior,* 66, 511–515.

Olson, L. M., & Wahab, S. (2006). American Indian & suicide: A neglected area of research. *Trauma Violence Abuse,* 7, 19–33.

Ong, L. M., deHess, J. C., Hoos, A. M., & Lammes, F. B. (1995). Doctor-patient communication: A review of the literature. *Social Science and Medicine,* 40, 7, 903–918.

OSHA. (1989). Safety and health program management guidelines: Insurance of voluntary guidelines. 54 Federal Regulations, 3904–3916, January, 26.

Ouedraogo, A., Ouedraogo, T. L., Ouoba, D. E., & Sawadogo, J. P. (2000). The current situation with regard to nicotine addiction in Burkina Faso: tobacco supply and data from the KAB-P survey of young people in Ouagadougou. *Sante,* 10(3), 177–181.

Paez, M. B., Luciano, C., & Gutierrez, O. (2007). Psychological treatment to cope with breast cancer. A comparative study between strategies of acceptance and cognitive control. *Psicooncologia,* 4, 1, 75–95.

Paharia, M. I. (2008). Insurance, managed care and integrated primary care. In B. A. Boyer & M. I. Paharia (ed.), *Comprehensive handbook of clinical health psychology* (31–51). Hoboken, NJ: John Wiley & Sons.

Paharia, M. I. (2008). Tobacco cessation. In B. A. Boyer and M. I. Paharia (eds.) *Comprehensive handbook of clinical health psychology.* Hoboken, NJ: John Wiley & Sons.

Pain Research Group (2009). Brief Pain Inventory (Short Form). Retrieved online on September 15, 2009, from: http://www.painresearch.utah.edu/cancerpain/attachb1.html. Department of Neurology, University of Wisconsin-Madison.

Palmgreen, P. (1984). Uses and gratifications: A theoretical perspective. In R. N. Bomstrom (ed.), *Communication yearbook,* 8, 61–72. Beverly Hills, CA: Sage Publication.

Paltiel, A. D., Weinstein, M. C., Kimmel, A. D., Seage, G. R., Losina, E., & Zhang, H., et al. (2005). Expanded HIV screening in the United States: Effect on clinical outcomes, HIV transmission and costs.*Annals of Internal Medicine,* 145, 11, 797–806.

Pan, J., Barbeau, E. M., Levenstein, C., & Balbach, E. D. (2005). Smoke-free airlines and the role of organized labor: A case study. *American Journal of Public Health,* 195, 3, 398–404.

Pape, J. W., Farmer, P., Koenig, S., Fitzgerald, D., Wright, P., & Johnson, W. (2008). The epidemiology of AIDS in Haiti refutes the claims of Gilbert et al. *PNAS,* 105, 10, E13.

Pargament, K. I. (1997). *The psychology of religion and coping.* New York: Guilford Press.

Park, N., Peterson, C., & Seligman, M. E. P. (2004). Strengths of character & well-being. *Journal of Social and Clinical Psychology,* 23(5), 603–619.

Park, S. Y., Murphy, S. P., Sharmay, S., & Kolonel, L. N. (2005). Dietary intakes and health-related behaviors of Korean American women born in the USA & Korea: The multiethnic cohort study. *Public Health Nutrition,* 8(7), 904–911.

Parker-Pope, T. (2008). Experts revive debate over cell phones and cancer. *The New York Times,* June 3.

Parkin, D. M., Bray, F., Ferlay, J., & Pisani, P. (2005). Global cancer statistics, 2002. *CA: A Cancer Journal for Clinicians,* 55, 74–108.

Parks, S. H., & Pilisuk, M. (1991). Caregiver burden: Gender & the psychological cost of caregiving. *American Journal of Orthopsychiatry,* 61, 4, 501–509.

Parran, T. (1937). *Shadow on the land: Syphilis.* New York: Reynal & Hitchcock.

Pasteur, L., Chamberland, & Roux. (2002). Summary report of the experiments conducted at Pouille-le-Fort, near Melun, on the anthrax vaccination. T Dasgupta (trans.). *Yale Journal of Biology and Medicine,* 75, 1, 59–62.

Pate, J. E., Pumariega, A. J., Hester, C., & Gardner, D. (1992) Cross-cultural patterns in eating disorders: A review. *Journal of the American Academy of Child and Adolescent Psychiatry,* 31, 802–809.

Patel, D. R., Philips, E. L., & Pratt, H. D. (1998). Eating disorders. *Indian Journal of Pediatrics,* 65, 4, 487–494.

Pawlyk, A. C., Morrison, A. R., Ross, R. J., & Brennan, F. X. (2008). Stress-induced changes in sleep in rodents: Model & mechanism. *Neuroscience & Biobehavioral Review,* 32, 1, 99–117.

Pazoki, R., Nabipour, I., Seyednezami, N., & Imami, S. R. (2007). Effects of a community-based health heart program in increasing healthy women's physical activity: A randomized controlled trial guided by community-based participatory research (CBPR). *BMC Public Health,* 7, 216. Published online, August 23. Doi.10.1186/1471-2458-7-216.

Pederson, L. L., & Lefcoe, N. M. (1987). Short- and long-term predictions of self-reported cigarette smoking in a cohort of later adolescents: Report of an 8-year follow-up of public school students. *Preventive Medicine,* 16, 432–447.

Pell, J. P. (2003). The debate on public place defibrillators: Charged but shockingly ill informed. *Heart,* 89, 1375–1376.

Pelland, L., Brosseau, L., Wells, G., Macleay, L., Lambert, J., Lamothe, C., et al. (2004). Efficacy of strengthening exercises for osteoarthritis (Part I): A meta-analysis. *Physical Therapy Review,* 9, 77–108.

Pendry, B. (2001). *Stigma and HIV/AIDS in South Africa.* Presentation at the 21st United Nations General Assembly, Special Session on HIV/AIDS, June 2001.

Penn State. (2008). Health and disease information: Essential hypertension. Milton S. Hershey Medical Center, College of Medicine. Retrieved from: www.hmc.psu.edu/healthinfo/e/essentialhypertesion.htm.

Perez-Pena, R. (2003). Obesity on rise in New York public schools. *The New York Times,* July 9.

Perrin, K. M., & McDermott, R. J. (1999). The spiritual dimension of health: A review. *American Journal of Health Studies,* 13(2), 90–99.

Peterson, C. B., Thuras, P., Ackard, D. M., Mitchell, J. E., Berg, K., Sandager, N., et al. (2010). Personality dimensions in bulimia nervosa, binge eating disorder & obesity. *Comprehensive Psychiatry,* 51, 31–36.

Peterson, C., & Seligman, M. E. P. (2004). *Character strengths & virtues: A handbook & classification.* New York: Oxford University Press.

Petersson, M., & Uvnas-Moberg, K. (2007). Effects of an acute stressor on blood pressure and heart rate in rats pretreated with intercerebroventricular oxytocin injections. *Psychoneuroendrocrinology,* 32, 959–965.

Peto, R., Darby, S., Deo, H., Silcocks, P., Whitley, E., & Doll, R. (2000). Smoking, smoking causation and lung cancer in the UK since 1950: Combination of national statistics with two case controlled studies. *British Medical Journal,* 321, 323–329.

Petraitis, J., Flay, B. R., & Miller, T. O. (1995). Reviewing theories of adolescent substance Use: Organizing pieces in the puzzle. *Psychological Bulletin,* 117(1), 7–86.

Petrella, R. J., & Bartha, C. (2000). Home-based exercise therapy for older patients with knee osteoarthritis: A randomized clinical trial. *Journal of Rheumatology,* 27, 2215–2221.

Pfeffer, R. I., Kurosaki, T. T., Harrah, C. H., et al. (1982). Measurement of functional activities in older adults in the community. *Journal of Gerontology, 37,* 323–329.

Phillips, T. (2007). Everyone knew she was ill. The other girls, the model agencies . . . Don't believe it when they say they didn't. *The Observer.* Retrieved on May 28, 2009, from: www.guardian.co.uk/life andstyle/2007/jan/14/fashion.feature4.

Philpott, D. (2009). An ethic of political reconciliation. Ethics and International Affairs, 23, 4, 398–407.

Picket, G., & Hanlon, J. J. (1990). *Public Health: Administration and Practice,* 9th ed. St. Louis, MO: Times Mirror/Mosby.

Pinquart, M., & Sorensen, S. (2005). Caregiving distress & psychological health in caregivers. In K. V. Oxington (ed.), *Psychology of stress* (165–206). New York: Nova Biomedical Books.

Pischon, T., Lehmann, P. H., & Boeing, H. (2006). Body size and risk of colon and rectal cancer in the European Prospective Investigation for Cancer and Nutrition (ERIC). *Journal of the National Cancer Institute,* 98, 920–931.

Pisetsky, D. S. (2007). Clinician's comment on the management of pain in arthritis. *Health Psychology,* 26(6), 657–659.

Pistrang, N., & Barker, C. (1995). The partner relationship in psychological response to breast cancer. *Social Science & Medicine,* 40, 789–797.

Poage, E. D., Kitzenberger, K. E., & Olsen, J. (2004). Spirituality, contentment & stress in recovering alcoholics. *Addictive Behaviors,* 29, 9, 1857–1862.

Pope, H. G., Gruber, A. J., & Hudson, J. I. (2001). Neuropsychological performance in long-term cannabis users. *Archives of General Psychiatry,* 58(10), 909–915.

Portman, T. A. A., & Garrett, M. T. (2006). Native American healing traditions. *International Journal of Disability, Development & Education,* 53, 4, 453–469.

Poss, J. E. (2001). Developing a new model for cross-cultural research: Synthesizing the health belief model and the theory of reasoned action. *Advanced Nursing Science,* 23(4), 1–15.

Post, F. L., Blustein, J., Gordon, E., & Neveloff, D. N. (1996). Pain: Ethics, culture, and informed consent to relief. *Journal of Law and Medical Ethics,* 24, 328–359.

Potter, J. D. (1999). Colorectal cancer, molecules and populations. *Journal of the National Cancer Institute,* 91, 916.

Poulsen, L. H., Osler, M., Roberts, C., Becker, S. L., & Lauer, R. M. (2002) Exposure to teachers smoking and adolescent smoking behaviour: analysis of cross-sectional data from Denmark. *Tobacco Control,* 11, 246–251.

Prentice, J. C., & Pizer, S. D. (2007). Delayed access to care and mortality. *Health Services Research,* 42, 2, 644–662.

Prentice-Hall, Inc. (1995–2002a). Chapter 2: The biological basis of behavior, Chapter Review. The nervous system. Retrieved on February 25, 2010, from: http://cwx.prenhall.com/bookbind/pubbooks/morris5/chapter2/custom1/deluxe-content.html.

Prentice-Hall, Inc. (1995–2002b). Chapter 2: The biological basis of behavior, Chapter Review. The sympathetic and parasympathetic systems. Retrieved on February 25, 2010, from: http://cwx.prenhall.com/bookbind/pubbooks/morris5/chapter2/custom1/deluxe-content.html.

Pressman, S. D., & Cohen, S. (2005). Does positive affect influence health? *Psychological Bulletin,* 131, 925–971.

Prestwich, A., Conner, M., Baisley, W., Letman, J., & Molyneau, V. (2005). Individual and collaborative implementation, intention and the promotion of breast self-examination. *Psychology and Health,* 20(6), 743–760.

Priebe, H. J. (2000). The aged cardiovascular risk patient. *British Journal of Anaesthesiology,* 85(5), 763–778.

Prince, R. (1983). Is anorexia nervosa a culture-bound syndrome? *Transcultural Psychiatric Research Review,* 20, 299–300.

Prochaska, J. O., & DiClemente, C. C. (1983). Stages and processes of self-change of smoking: Towards an integrative model of change. *Journal of Consulting and Clinical Psychology,* 51, 390–395.

Prochaska, J. O., Velicer, W. F., Rossi, J. S., Goldstein, M. G., Marcus, B. H., Rakowski, W., et al. (1994).

Stages of change and decisional balances for 12 problem behaviors. *Health Psychology,* 13, 39–46.

Public Broadcast Service. (1999). The Kevorkian verdict: The law on assisted suicide. Retrieved on February 9, 2009, from: www.pbs.org/wgbh/pages/frontline/kevorkian/law.

Public Health Agency of Canada. (2002). Heart disease & stroke in Canada 1997. Deaths from cardiovascular disease. Retrieved from: www.phac.aspc.gc.ca/publicat.hdsc97/soz=eng.php.

Pumariega, A. J. (1997). Body dissatisfaction among Hispanic and Asian-American girls. *Journal of Adolescent Health,* 21, 1.

Putman, K. M., Lantz, J. ., Townsend, C. L., Gallegos, A. M., Potts, A. A., & Roberts, R. C. (2009). Exposure to violence, support needs, adjustment and motivation among Guatemalan humanitarian aid workers. *American Journal of Community Psychology,* 44, 1–2, 109–115.

Quah, S. R. (2003). Traditional healing systems and the ethos of science. *Social Science & Medicine,* 57, 1997–2012.

Rabin, B. S., Cohen, S., Ganguli, R., Lyle, D. T., & Cunnick, J. E. (1989). Bidirectional interaction between the central nervous system and immune system. *CRC Critical Reviews in Immunology,* 9(4), 279–312.

Radi, S., Lang, T., Lauwers-Cances, V., Diene, E., Chatellier, G., Larabi, L., et al. (2005). Job constraints and arterial hypertension: different effects in men and women: the IHPAF II case-control study. *Occupational and Environmental Medicine,* 62, 711–717.

Ragin, D. F., Griffing, S., Sage, R. E., Madry, L., Bingham, L., & Primm, B. J. (2000). Breaking the intergenerational cycle of violence: a social marketing approach to behavior change. In N. De Meillon (ed.), *Creative rescue counselling and assistance for the children in our country: After conference proceedings.* University of South Africa (UNISA). Pretoria, South Africa: Production Printers.

Ragin, D. F., Holohan, J. A., Ricci, E. M., Grant, C., & Richardson, L. D. (2005a). Shocking a community into action: A social marketing approach to cardiac arrests. *Journal of Health & Social Policy,* 20(2), 49–70.

Ragin, D. F., Hwang, U., Cydulka, R. K., Holson, D., Haley, L. L., Richards, C. F., et al. (2005b). Reasons for using the emergency department: Results of the EMPATH Study. *Academic Emergency Medicine,* 12(12), 1158–1166.

Ragin, D. F., Pilotti, M., Madry, L., Sage, R. E., Bingham, L. E., & Primm, B. J. (2002). Intergenerational substance abuse and domestic violence as familial risk factors for lifetime attempted suicide among battered women. *Journal of Interpersonal Violence,* 17, 10, 1027–1045.

Ragin, D. F., Ricci, E. M., Rhodes, R., Holohan, J., Smirnoff, M., & Richardson, L. D. (2008). Defining the "community" in community consultation for emergency research: Findings from the Community VOICES Study. *Social Science and Medicine,* 66(6), 1379–1392.

Rahe, R. H., Mahan, J. L., & Arthur, R. J. (1970). Prediction of near-future health change from subject's preceding life change. *Journal of Psychosomatic Research,* 14, 4, 401–406.

Ramagopalan, S. V., Knight, J. C., & Ebers, G. C. (2009). Multiple sclerosis & the major histocompatibility complex. *Current Opinion in Virology,* 22, 3, 219–225.

Ransom. S., Jacobson, P. B., Schmidt, J. E., & Andrykowski, M. A. (2005). A relationship of problem-focused coping strategies to changes in quality of life following treatment for early stage breast cancer. *Journal of Pain and Symptom Management,* 30(30), 243–253.

Rasmussen, H. B., Clausen J. (2000). Genetic risk factors in multiple sclerosis & approaches to their identification. *Journal of Neurovirology,* Suppl 2, S23–S27.

Rathner, G., & Messner, K. (1993). Detection of eating disorders in a small rural town: An epidemiological study. *Psychological Medicine,* 23, 175–184.

Ray, O. (2004). How the mind hurts and heals the body. *American Psychologists,* 59, 29–40.

Reagan, L. J. (1997). Engendering the dread disease: Women, men and cancer. *American Journal of Public Health,* 87(11), 1779–1787.

Redd, W. H., Montgomery, G. H., & DuHamel, K. N. (2001). Behavioral intervention for cancer treatment side effects. *Journal of the National Cancer Institute,* 93(11), 810–823.

Regan, G., Lee, R. E., Booth, K., & Reese-Smith, J. (2006). Obesogenic influences in public housing: A mixed-method analysis. *American Journal of Health Promotion,* 20, 4, 282–290.

Reichert, K. L., Hole, K., Hamberger, A., et al. (1993). Biologically active peptide-containing fractions in schizophrenia and childhood autism. *Advances in Biochemical Psychopharmacology,* 28, 627–643.

Reid, T. L. B., & Smalls, C. (2004). Stress spirituality & health promoting behaviors among African American college students. *Western Journal of Black Studies,* 28, 1, 283–291.

Reschovsky, J. D., Hadley, J., & Landon, B. E. (2006). Compensation methods and physicians group structure on physician's perceived incentives to alter service to patients. *Health Services Research,* 41 (4 Pt. 1), 1200–1220.

RHO. (2008). About cervical cancer. Preventing cervical cancer: Unprecedented opportunities for improving women's health. Retrieved from: www.rho.org/images/figure/-ooostl.

Richards, H. M., Reid, M. E., & Watt, G. C. M. (2002). Socioeconomic variations in responses to chest pain: Qualitative study. *British Medical Journal,* 324(7349), 1308–1317.

Roa, B. B., Boyd, A. A., Volcik, K., & Richards, C. S. (1996). Ashkenazi Jewish population frequency for common mutations in BRCA1 and BRCA2. *Natural Genetics,* 14, 185–187.

Roberto, C. A., Larsen, P. D., Agnew, H., Baik, T., & Brownell, K. D. (2010). Evaluating the impact of menu labeling on food choices and intake. *American Journal of Pubic Health,* 100, 2, 312–318.

Robinson, T. N., Killen, J. D., Litt, I. F., Hammer, L. D., Wilson, D. M. Haydel, K. F., et al. (1996).

Roddy, E., Zhang, W., & Doherty, M. (2007). The changing epidemiology of gout. *National Clinical Practice of Rheumatology,* 3, 443–449.

Rodriguez, M. A., Bauer, H. M., Flores-Ortiz, Y., & Szkupinski-Quiroga, S. (1998). Factors affecting patient-physician communication for abused Latina and Asian immigrant women. *Journal of Family Practice,* 47(4).

Romero, L. M., Dickens, M. J., & Cyr, N. E. (2009). The reactive scope model: A new model integrating homeostasis, allostasis & stress. *Hormones & Behaviors,* 55, 375–389.

Rosamond, W., Flegal, K., Friday, G., Furie, K., Go, A., Greenlund, K., et al. (2007). Heart disease & stroke statistics—2007 update: A report from the American Heart Association. Statistics Committee & Stroke Statistics Subcommittee. *Circulation,* 115, 5, e69–e171.

Rosenberg, L., Palmer, J. R., & Shapiro, S. (1990). Decline in the risk of myocardial infarction among women who stop smoking. *New England Journal of Medicine,* 322, 213–217.

Rosengren, A., Hawken, S., Ounpuu, S., Sliwa, K., Zubaid, M., Almahmeed, W. A., et al. (2004). Association of psychosocial risk factors with risk of acute myocardial infarction in 11,119 cases and 13,648 controls from 52 countries (the INTER-HEART study): Case–control study. *The Lancet,* 364, 953–962.

Rosenstock, I. M. (2005). Why people use health services. *The Milbank Quarterly,* 83(4), 1–32.

Rosenstock, I. M., Strecher, V. S., & Becker, M. H. (1988). Social learning theory and the health belief model. *Health Education Quarterly,* 15, 2, 175–183.

Rosenthal, R., Hall, J. A., DiMatteo, M. R., Rogers, P. T., & Archer, D. (1979). Sensitivity to non-verbal communications: The PONS Test. Baltimore, MD: Johns Hopkins University Press.

Ross, L., Kohler, C. L., Grimley, D. M., Anderson-Lewis, C. (2007). The theory of reasoned action and intention to seek cancer information. *American Journal of Health Behavior,* 31(2), 123–134.

Rovniak, L. S., Anderson, E. S., Winett. R. A., & Stephens, R. S. (2002). Social cognitive determinants of physical activity in young adults: A prospective structural equation analysis. *Annals of Behavioral Medicine,* 24, 149–156.

Ruch, W., & Carrell, A. (1998). Trait cheerfulness and the sense of humor. *Personality & Individual Differences,* 24, 551–558.

Rutledge, D. N. (1987). Factors related to women's practice of breast self-examination. *Nursing Research,* 36, 117–121.

Ryan, R. M., & Deci, E. L. (2000). Self-determination theory and the facilitation of intrinsic motivation, social development, and well-being. *American Psychologists,* 55(1), 68–78.

Sagrestano, L. M., Rogers, A., & Service, A. (2008). HIV/AIDS. In B. A. Boyer and M. I. Paharia (eds.), *Comprehensive handbook of clinical health psychology.* Hoboken, NJ: John Wiley & Sons.

Saha, S., Komaromy, M., Koepsell, T. D., & Bindman, A. B. (1999). Patient–physician racial concordance and the perceived quality and use of health care. *Archives of Internal Medicine,* 159(9), 997–1004.

Saleem, T., Khalid, U., & Qidwai, W. (2009). Geriatric patient's expectations of their physicians: Findings from a tertiary care hospital in Pakistan. *BMC Health Services Research,* 13, 9, 205.

Salkind, N. J. (2006). *Exploring Research,* sixth edition. Upper Saddle River, NJ: Prentice Hall.

Sallfors, C., Hallberg, L. R., & Fasth, A. (2003). Gender & age difference in pain, coping, and health status among children with chronic arthritis. *Clinical & Experimental Rheumatology,* 21(6), 785–793.

Sallis, J. F., Hovell, M. F., & Hofstetter, C.vR. (1989). A multivariate study of determinants of vigorous exercise in a community sample. *Preventive Medicine,* 18, 20–34.

Salovey, P., Rothman, A. J., Detweiler, J. B., & Steward, W. T. (2000). Emotional states and physical health. *American Psychologist,* 55(1), 110–121.

Samuels, S. E. (1993). Project LEAN—lessons learned from a national social marketing campaign. *Public Health Reports,* 108(1), 45–53.

Samwel, H. J. A., Kraaimaat, F. W., Crul, B. J. P., van Dongan, R. R., & Evers, A. W. M. (2009). Multidisciplinary allocation of pain treatment: Long-term outcome & correlates of cognitive-behavioral processes. *Journal of Musculoskeletal Pain,* 17, 1, 26–36.

Sanden, I., Larson, U. S., & Eriksson, C. (2000). An interview study of men discovering testicular cancer. *Cancer Nursing,* 23(4), 304–309.

Sanders Thompson, V.vL., Bazile, A., & Akbar, M. (2004). African American's perceptions of Psychotherapists. *Professional Psychologists Research and Practice,* 35, 19–26.

Sandovnick, A. D., Baird, P. A., & Ward, R. H. (1988). Multiple sclerosis: Updated risk for relatives. *American Journal of Medical Genetics,* 29, 533–541.

Sandstrom, M., Wilen, J., Oftedal, G., & Hansson Mild, K. (2001). Mobile phone use and subjective symptoms. Comparison of symptoms experienced by users of analogue and digital mobile phones. *Occupational Medicine (London),* 51, 25–35.

Sargent, J. D., Dalton, M. A., Beach, M., Bernhardt, A., Pullin D., & Stevens, M. (1997). Cigarette promotional items in public schools. *Archives of Pediatric and Adolescent Medicine,* 151(12), 1189–1196.

Saris, W. H., Blair, S. N., vanBaak, M. A., Eaton, S. B., Davis, P. S., & DiPeitro L. (2003). How much physical activity is enough to prevent unhealthy weight gain? Outcome of the IASO 1st stock conference & consensus statement. *Obesity Review: An Official Journal of the International Association of the Study of Obesity,* 4(2), 101–114.

Saul, S. (2005). U.S. to review drug intended for one race. *The New York Times,* June 13, 2005.

Savage, L. (2007). Proposed human papillomavirus mandates rile health experts. *Journal of the National Cancer Institute,* 99(9), 665.

Savulescu, J., & Spriggs, M. (2002). The hexamethorium asthma study and the death of a normal volunteer in research. *Journal of Medical Ethics,* 28, 3–4.

Schaefer, S., & Coleman, E. (1992). Shifts in meaning, purpose & values following a diagnosis of human immunodeficiency virus (HIV) infection among gay men. *Journal of Psychology and Human Sexuality,* 5(1–2), 13–29.

Schenider, H., & Stein, J. (2001). Implementing AIDS policy in post-apartheid South Africa. *Social Science and Medicine,* 52, 122–131.

Schliefer, S. J., Keller, S. E., & Meyerson, A. T. (1984). Lymphocyte function in major depressive disorder. *Archives of General Psychiatry,* 41, 5, 484–486.

Schliefer, S. J., Keller, S. E., & Siris, S. G. (1985). Depression and immunity. *Archives of General Psychiatry,* 42, 129–133.

Schmidt, T., Delorio, N. M., & McClure, K. B. (2006). The meaning of community consultation. *American Journal of Bioethics,* 6, 30–32.

Schnall, P. L., Landsbergis, P. A., & Baker, D. (1990). The relationship between "job strain," workplace diastolic blood pressure and left ventricular mass index. *JAMA,* 263, 1929–1935.

Schnoll, R. A., Knowles, J. C., & Harlow, L. (2002). Correlates of adjustment among cancer survivors. *Journal of Psychosocial Oncology,* 20(1), 37–59.

Schoenborn, C. A., & Adams, P. F. (2002). Alcohol use among adults: United States, 1997–1998. *Advanced Data from Vital and Health Statistics: National Center for Health Statistics, CDC,* Number 324.

Schrieber, G. B., Robins, M., Striegel-Moore, R., Obarzanek, E., Morrison, J. A., & Wright, D. J. (1996). Weight modification efforts reported by black and white pre-adolescent girls: National Heart, Lung and Blood Institute Growth and Health Study. *Pediatrics,* 98, 3–70.

Schultz, A. M., Williams, D. R., Israel, B. A., & Lempert, L. B. (2002). Racial and spatial relations as fundamental determinants of health in Detroit. *Milbank Quarterly,* 80(4), 677–707.

Schultz, A., & Northridge, M. E. (2004). Social determinants of health: Implications for environmental health promotion. *Health, Education & Behavior,* 31(4), 455–471.

Schulz, R., Beach, S. R., Ives, D. G., Martire, L. M., Ariyo, A. A., & Kop, W. J. (2000). Association between depression and mortality in older adults: The cardiovascular health study. *Archives of Internal Medicine,* 160, 1761–1768.

Schulz, R., Martire, L. M., Beach, S. R., & Scheier, M. F. (2005). Depression and mortality in the elderly. In G. Miller & E. Chen E. (eds.) *Current Directions in Health Psychology.* Upper Saddle River, NJ: Prentice Hall.

Schüz, J., Morgan, G., Böhler, E., Kaatsch, P., & Michaelis, J. (2003). Atopic disease and childhood acute lymphoblastic leukemia. *International Journal of Cancer,* 105, 255–260.

Schwartz, A. R., Gerin, W., Davidson, K. W., Pickering, T. G., Brosschot, J. F., Thayer, J. F., et al. (2003). Towards a causal model of cardiovascular responses to stress and the development of cardiovascular disease. *Psychosomatic Medicine,* 65, 22–35.

Schwarzer, R., Schuz, B., Ziegelmann, J. P., Lippke, S., Luszczynska, A., & Scholz, U. (2007). Adoption & maintenance of four health behaviors: Theory-guided longitudinal studies on dental flossing, seat-belt use, dietary behaviors and physical activity. *Annals of Behavioral Medicine,* 33(2), 156–166.

Sclavo, M. (2001). Cardiovascular risk factors and prevention in women: similarities and differences. *Italian Heart Journal Supplement,* 2(2), 125–141.

Scott, P. (2007). Chronic diseases: Another challenge for the developing world. *International Journal of Clinical Practice,* 61(9), 1422–1423.

Scott, J., & Huskisson, E. C. (1976). Graphic representation of pain. *Pain,* 2, 2, 175–184.

Scott, D. L., Berry, H., Capell, H., Coppock, J., Dayman, T., Doyle, D. V., et al. (2000). The long-term effects of non-steroidal anti-inflammatory drugs in osteoarthritis of the knee: a randomized placebo-controlled trial. *Rheumatology* (Oxford), 39(10), 1095–1101.

Seaward, B. L. (1991). Spiritual well-being: A health education model. *Journal of Health Education,* 22(3), 166–169.

Seligman, M. E. P. (2002). Positive psychology, positive prevention & positive therapy. In C. R. Snyder & J. Shane J. (eds.), *Handbook of positive psychology* (3–9). New York: Oxford University Press.

Seligman, M. E. P., & Csikszentmihalyi, M. (2000). Positive psychology. *American Psychologist,* 55, 5–14.

Seligman, M. E. P., Park, N., & Peterson, C. (2004). The value in action (VIA) classification of character strength. *Ricechi di Psicologia,* 27, 1, 63–78.

Seligman, M. E. P., Steen, T. A., Park, N., & Peterson, C. (2000). Positive psychology in progress. *American Psychologist,* 60(5), 410–421.

Selim, A. J., FIncke, G., Ren, X. S., Dego, R. A., Lee, A., Skinner, K., et al. (2001). Racial differences in the use of lumbar spine radiographs: Results from the veterans health study. *Spine,* 26, 1364–1369.

Sellick, S. M., & Crooks, D. L. (1999). Depression & cancer: An appraisal of the literature for prevalence detection & practice guideline development for psychological interventions. *Psycho-oncology,* 8, 315–333.

Selye, H. (1936). A syndrome produced by diverse nocuous agents. *Nature,* 138, 32.

Selye, H. (1946). The general adaptation syndrome & the disease of adaptation. *Journal of Clinical Endocrinology,* 6, 2, 117–231.

Selye, H. (1950). Stress & the general adaptation syndrome. *British Medical Journal,* 1, 4667, 1383–1392.

Selye, H., & Fortier, C. (1950). Adaptive reaction to stress. *Psychosomatic Medicine,* 12, 3, 149–157.

Sharma, S., Malarcher, A. M., Giles, W. H., & Myers, G. (2004). Racial, ethnic and socioeconomic disparities in the clustering of cardiovascular disease risk factors. *Ethnic Diseases,* 14(1), 43–48.

Shattock, P., Kennedy, A., Powell, F., & Berney, T. P. (1991). Role of neuropeptides in autism and their relationships with classical neurotransmitters. *Brain Dysfunction,* 3, 328–345.

Sheldon, K. M., & King, L. (2001). Why positive psychology is necessary. *American Psychologist,* 56, 216–217.

Sher, K. J. (1991). *Children of alcoholics.* Chicago: University of Chicago Press.

Sher, L. (2005). Type D personality: The heart, stress and cortisol. *Quarterly Journal of Medicine,* 98, 323–329.

Shiaw-Ling, W., Charron-Prochownik, D., Sereika, S. M., Siminerio, L., & Yookyung, K. (2006). Comparing three theories in predicting reproductive health behavioral intention in adolescent women with diabetes. *Pediatric Diabetes,* 7(2), 108–115.

Shilts, R. (1987). *And the band played on: People, politics and the AIDS epidemic.* New York, NY: St. Martin Press.

Sibbald, B. (2007). Graduated driver licensing in Canada: Slowly but surely. *Canadian Medical Association Journal,* 176, 6, 752.

Siddiqi, A., Zuberi, D., & Nguyen, Q. C. (2009). The role of health insurance in explaining immigrant versus non-immigrant disparities in access to health care: Comparing the United States to Canada. *Social Science and Medicine,* Sept. 18, e-publication ahead of print.

Sieper, J., Bruan, J., Rudewaleit, M., Boonen, A., & Zink, A. (2002). Ankylosing spondylitis: An overview. *Annals of Rheumatic Diseases,* 61 (Suppl. III), iii8–iii18.

Silverman, A. B., Reinhertz, H., & Giaconia, R. M. (1996). The long-term sequelae of child and adolescent abuse: A longitudinal community study. *Child Abuse and Neglect,* 20, 709–723.

Simon, A. E., Chan, K. S., & Forrest, C. B. (2008). Assessment of children's health-related quality of life in the United States with a multidimensional index. *Pediatrics,* 121, 1, e118–e126.

Simon, C., Kumar, S., & Kendrick, T. (2009). Cohort study of informal carers of first-time stroke survivors: Profiles of health and social changes in the first year of caregiving. *Social Science & Medicine,* 69, 3, 404–410.

Simons, R. L., Murry, V., McLoyd, V., Lin, K., Cutrona, C., & Conger, R.dD. (2002). Discrimination, crime, ethnic identity, and parenting as correlates of depressive symptoms among African American children: A multilevel analysis. *Developmental Psychopathology,* 14, 371–393.

Simons-Morton, R., Lerner, N., & Singer, J. (2005). The observed effects of teenage passengers on the risky driving behavior of teenage drivers. *Accident Annals & Prevention,* 37, 973–982.

Skaff, M. M., Mullan, J. T., Almeida, D. M., Hoffman, L., Masharani, U., Mohr, D., et al. (2009). Daily negative mood affects fasting glucose in type 2 diabetes. *Health Psychology,* 28, 3, 265–272.

Slack, P. (1989). The black death past and present, 2. Some historical problems. *Transactions of the Royal Society of Tropical Medicine and Hygiene,* 83, 461–463.

Smith, E. R., Adams, S. A., Dos, I. P., Bottai, M., Fulton, J., & Herbert, J. R. (2008). Breast cancer survival among economically disadvantaged women: The influences of delayed diagnosis treatment on mortality. *Cancer Epidemiology Biomarkers Prevention,* 17(10), 2882–2890.

Smith, M. J., Ellenberg, S. S., Bill, L. M., & Ruben, D. M. (2008). Media coverage of the measles-mumps-rubella vaccine & autism controversy and its relationship to MMR immunization rates in the US. *Pediatrics,* 122, 3, 684–685.

Smith, T. W., & Suls, J. (2004). Introduction to the special section on the future of health psychology. *Health Psychology,* 23, 2, 115–118.

Snider, G. L. (1997). Tuberculosis then and now: A personal perspective in the last 50 years. *Annals of Internal Medicine,* 126, 237–243.

Sobralske, M. (2006). Machismo sustains health and illness beliefs of Mexican American men. *Journal of the American Academy of Nurse Practitioners,* 18(8), 348–350.

Solomon, G. F. (1987). Psychoneuroimmunology: Interactions between central nervous system and immune system. *Journal of Neuroscience Research,* 18: 1–9.

Solomon, G. F., & Moos, R. H. (1964). Emotions, immunity and disease: A speculative theoretical integration. *Archives of General Psychiatry,* 11, 657–674.

Sonel, A. F., Good, C. B., Mulgund, J., Roe, M. T., Gibler, W. B., Smith, C. C., et al. (2005). Racial variations in treatment and outcomes of black and white patients with high risk non-ST- elevation acute coronary syndrome. *Circulation,* 111, 1225–1232.

Sothern, M. S. (2004). Obesity prevention in children: physical activity and nutrition. *Nutrition,* 20, 7–8, 704–708.

South African AIDS Vaccine Initiative (SAAVI). (2007). Ethical issues: HIV/AIDS vaccine ethics group. Retrieved on July 1, 2007, from: www.saavi.org.za/haveg/htm.

Sparrenberger, F., Cichelero, F. T., Ascoli, A. M., Fonseca, F. P., Weiss, G., Berawanger, O. et al. (2008). Does psychosocial stress cause hypertension? A systematic review of observational studies. *Journal of Human Hypertension,* e-release ahead of publication.

Speigel, D., & Giese-Davis, J. (2003) Depression and cancer: Mechanisms and disease progression. *Biological Psychiatry,* 54, 527–531.

Spiegel, D., Bloom, J. R., & Yalom, I. (1981). Group support for patients with metastatic cancer. *Archives of General Psychiatry,* 38, 527–531.

Spiegel, D., Bloom, J. R., Kraemer, H. C., & Gottheil, E. (1989). Effects of psychosocial treatment on survival of patients with metastatic breast cancer. *The Lancet,* 2, 888–891.

Spiegel, D., Butler, L. D., Giese-Davis, J., Koopman, C., Miller, E., DiMiceli, S., et al. (2007). Effects of supportive-expressive group therapy on survival of patients with metastatic breast cancer. *Cancer,* 110, 5, 1130–1138.

Spitalnick, J. S., DiClemente, R. J., Wingood, G. M., Crosby, R. A., Milhausen, R. R., Sales, J. M., et al. (2007). Brief report: Sexual sensation seeking and its relationship to risky sexual behaviors among African-American adolescent females. *Journal of Adolescence,* 30, 165–173.

Splansky, G. L., Corey, D., Yang, Q., Atwood, L. D., Cupples, L. A., Benjamin, E. J., et al. (2007). The third generation cohort of the National Heart, Lung and Blood Institute's Framingham Heart Study: Design, recruitment, and initial examination. *American Journal of Epidemiology,* 165(11), 1328–1335.

St. John, D. J. B., McDermott, F. T., & Hopper, L. J. (1993). Cancer-risk in relatives of patients with common colorectal cancer. *Annals of Internal Medicine,* 118, 785–790.

Stahl, S. (2008). Health: Juvenile Rheumatoid Arthritis. CBS The CW Philly57. Retrieved on August 30, 2009, from: http://cbs3.com/health/Health.Alert.Stephanie.2.788670.html.

Stanley, M. (2008). HPV vaccines: Are they the answer? *British Medical Bulletin,* 88, 1, 59–74.

Stanley, R. O., & Burrows, G. D. (2008). Psychogenic heart disease, stress and the heart: A historical perspective. *Stress and Health,* 24, 181–187.

Stanton, B., Fang, X., Li, X., Feigelman, S., Gallbraith, J., & Ricardo, I. (1997). Evolution of risk behaviors over 2 years among a cohort of urban African American adolescents. *Archives of Pediatric Adolescent Medicine,* 151, 398–406.

Stephens, M. A. P., Norris, V. K., Kinney, J. M., Ritchie, S. W., & Grotz, R. C. (1988). Stressful situations in caregiving: Relations between caregiver coping and well-being. *Psychology of Aging,* 3(2), 208–209.

Sternhell, P. S., & Corr, M. J. (2002). Psychiatric morbidity and adherence to antiretroviral medication in patients with HIV/AIDS. *Australian New Zealand Journal of Psychiatry,* 36, 528–533.

Stetler, H. C., Grenade, T. C., Nunez, C. A., Meza, R., Terrell, S., Amador, L., et al. (1997). Field evaluation of rapid HIV serologic tests for screening and confirming HIV-1 infections in Honduras. *AIDS,* 11(3), 369–375.

Stevens, G. D., Mistry, R., Zuckerman, B., & Halfon, N. (2005). The patient–provider relationship: Does race/ethnicity concordance or discordance influence parent reports of the receipt of high quality basic pediatric preventive services? *Journal of Urban Health,* 82(4), 560–574.

Strating, M., Schuur, W., & Suurmeijer, T. (2006). Contribution of partner support in self-management of rheumatoid arthritis patients: An application of the theory of planned behavior. *Journal of Behavioral Medicine,* 29(1), 51–60.

Streltzer, J. (1983). Psychiatric aspects of oncology: a review of past research. *Hospital Community Psychiatry,* 34, 716–729.

Strickland, O. L., Giger, J. N., Nelson, M. A., & Davis, C. M. (2007). The relationships among stress, coping, social support, and weight class in premenopausal African American women at risk for coronary heart disease. *Journal of Cardiovascular Nursing,* 22, 4, 272–278.

Strode, A., Slack, C. M., & Mushariwa, M. (2005). HIV Vaccine research: South Africa's ethical and legal framework and its ability to promote the welfare of trial participants. *South African Medical Journal,* 95(8), 598–601.

Strong, K., Mathers, C., Leeder, S., & Beaglehole, R. (2005). Preventing chronic diseases: How many lives can we save? *The Lancet,* 366, 9496, 1578–1582.

Substance Abuse and Mental Health Services Administration. (2005). *Results from the 2004 National Survey on Drug Use and Health: National Findings.* Office of Applied Studies, NSDUH Series H-28, DHHS Publication No. SMA 05-4062. Rockville, MD: SAMHSA.

Suh, M. J., Lee, C. H., Kim, Y. S., Lee, H. R., Park, C. J., & Yoo, S. J. (2000). *Adult nursing* (4th ed.) Seoul: Soo Moon Publications.

Sullivan, A. D., Hedberg, K., & Flemming, D. W. (2000). Legalized physician assisted suicide in Oregon: The second year. *New England Journal of Medicine,* 342, 8, 598–604.

Sundararajan, L. (2005). Happiness donut: A Confucian critique of positive psychology. *Journal of Theoretical & Philosophical Psychology,* 25, 1, 35–60.

Suter, T., & Burton, S. (1996). An examination of correlates and effects associated with a concise measure of consumer nutrition knowledge. *Family & Consumer Science Research Journal,* 25(2), 117–136.

Svaldi, J., Caffier, D., & Tuschen-Caffier, B. (2010). Emotion suppression but not re-appraisal increases desire to binge in women with binge eating disorder. *Psychotherapy and Psychosomatics,* 79, 3, 188–190.

Swardh, E., Biguet, G., & Opava, C. H. (2008). Views on exercise maintenance variations among patients with rheumatoid arthritis. *Physical Therapy,* 88, 9, 1049–1060.

Szabo, S. (1998) Hanz Selye & the development of the stress concept. *Annals of the New York Academy of Science,* 30, 851, 19–27.

Tafur, M. M., Crowe, T. K., & Torres, S. E. (2009). A review of *curanderismo* and healing practices among Mexicans and Mexican Americans. *Occupational Therapy International,* 16, 1, 82–88.

Tan, S. Y., & Berman, E. (2008). Robert Koch (1843–1910): Father of microbiology & Nobel laureate. *Singapore Journal of Medicine,* 49, 11, 854–855.

Tandon, P. S., Wright, J., Zhou, C., Rogers, C. B., & Christiakis, D. A. (2010). Nutrition menu labels may lead to lower-calorie restaurant meal choices for children. *Pediatrics,* 25(2), 244–248.

Taplin, S. H., Ichikawa, L., & Yood, M. U. (2004). Reason for late-stage breast cancer: Absence of screening or detection, or breakdown in follow-up? *Journal of the National Institute of Cancer,* 96, 1518–1527.

Tatrow, K., & Montgomery, G. H. (2006). Cognitive behavioral therapy techniques for distress and pain in breast cancer patients: A meta-analysis. *Journal of Behavioral Medicine,* 29(1), 17–27.

Taylor, S. E. (1989). *Positive illusions: Creative self-deception and the healthy mind.* New York: Basic Books.

Taylor, J., & Turner, R. J. (2001). A longitudinal study of the role and significance of mattering to others for depressive symptoms. *Journal of Health and Social Behavior,* 42, 310–325.

Taylor, S. E., Kemeny, M. E., Reed, G. M., Bower, J. E., & Gruenewald, T. L. (2000). Psychological resources, positive illusions, and health. *American Psychologists,* 55(1), 99–109.

Tedesco, A., D'Agostino, D., Soriente, I., Amato, P., Piccoli, R., & Sabatini, P. (2009). A new strategy for the early diagnosis of rheumatoid arthritis: A combined approach. *Autoimmunity Reviews,* 8, 3, 233–237.

Temcheff, C. E., Serebin, L. A., Martin-Storey, A., Stack, D. M., Hodgins, S., & Lendingham, J. (2008). Continuity and pathways from aggression in childhood to family violence in adulthood: A 30-year longitudinal study. *Journal of Family Violence,* 23(4), 231–242.

Teusch, C. (2003). Patient–doctor communication. *Medical Clinics of North American,* 87(5).

Thom, D., Hall, M. A., & Paulson, L. G. (2004). Measuring patient's trust in physicians when assessing quality of care. *Health Affairs,* 23, 124–132.

Thom, T., Hause, N., Rosamond, U., Howard, V. J., Rumsfeld, J., & Manolio, T. (2006). Heart disease & stroke statistics: 2006 update: A report from the American Heart Association Statistics Committee & Stroke Statistics Sub-Committee.*Circulation,* 113, e85–e151.

Thomas, S. H., & Quinn, S. C. (1991). The Tuskegee syphilis study, 1932 to 1297: Implications for HIV education and AIDS risk education programs in the black community. *American Journal of Public Health,* 81(1), 1498–1505.

Thompson, B., & Kinne, S. (1990). Social change theory: Applications to community health. In N. Bracht (ed.), *Health promotion at the community level* (45–65). Newbury Park, CA: Sage.

Thompson, W., & Hickey, J. (2005). *Society in focus.* Boston: Allen & Bacon.

Tickle, J. J., Sargent, J. D., Dalton, M. A., Beach, M. L., & Heatherton, T. F. (2001). Favorite movie stars, their tobacco use in contemporary movies, and its association with adolescent smoking. *Tobacco Control,* 10, 16–22.

Tisdall, S. (1993). US admits years of atomic radiation tests on people. *Guardian,* 11.

Todd, C. S., Mountvarner, G., & Lichenstein, R. (2005). Unintended pregnancy risk in an emergency department population. *Contraception,* 71(1), 35–39.

Todd, K. H., Lee, T., & Hoffman, J. R. (1994). The effects of ethnicity on physician estimates of pain in patients with isolated extremity trauma. *Journal of the American Medical Association,* 271, 925–978.

Todd, K. H., Samaroo, N., & Hoffman, J. R. (1993). Ethnicity ad a risk factor for inadequate emergency department analgesics. *Journal of the American Medical Association,* 269, 1537–1539.

Torres, E., & Sawyer, T. (2005). *Curanderismo: A life in Mexican folk healing.* Albuquerque: University of New Mexico Press.

Tournoud, M., Ecochard, R., Kuhn, L., & Coutsoudis, A. (2008). Diversity of risk to mother-to-child HIV-1 transmission according to feeding practices, CD4 cell counts haemoglobin concentrations in a South African cohort. *Tropical Medicine & International Health,* 13(3), 310–318.

Toye, F. M., Barlow, J., Wright, C., & Lamb, S. E. (2006). Personal meanings in the construction of need for total knee replacement surgery. *Social Science and Medicine,* 63, 43–53.

Trinidad, D. R., Unger, J. P., Chih-Ping, C., & Anderson, J. C. (2005). Emotional intelligence & acculturation to the United States: Interactions on the perceived social consequences of smoking in early adolescence. *Substance Use and Misuse,* 40(11), 1697–1706.

Trotter, R. T. (2001). *Curanderismo*: A picture of Mexican-American folk healing. *Journal of Alternative and Complementary Medicine,* 7(2), 129–131.

Trotter, J. L., & Allen, N. E. (2009). The good, the bad and the ugly: Domestic violence survivors' experience with their informal social networks. *American Journal of Community Psychology,* 43, 3–4, 221–231.

Truman, B. I., Gooch, B. F., Sulemana, I., Gift, H. C., Horowitz, A. M., Evans, C. A., et al. (2002). Reviews on evidence on interventions to prevent dental caries, oral and pharyngeal cancers, and sports-related craniofacial injuries. *American Journal of Preventive Medicine,* 23(1S), 21–54.

Tryggvadottir, S., Struewing, J. P., Hartge, P., Olafsdottir, G. H., Sigvaldason, H., & Tryggvadottir, L., et al. (1998). Population-based study risk of breast cancer in carriers of BRCA2 mutation. *Lancet,* 352, 1337–1339.

Tsai, Y. F. (2007). Gender differences in pain & depressive tendencies among Chinese elders with knee osteoarthritis. *Pain,* 130(1–2), 1881–1894.

Tsiros, M. D., Sinn, N., Coates, A. M., Howe, P. R. C., & Buckley, J. D. (2008). Treatment of adolescent overweight and obesity. *European Journal of Pediatrics,* 167, 1, 9–16.

Tucker, J. S., Ellickson, P. L., & Klein, D. J. (2002). Five year prospective study of risk factors for daily smoking among early nonsmokers and experimenters. *Journal of Applied Social Psychology,* 32, 1588–1603.

Tugwell, B. D., Lee, L. E., Gillette, H., Lorber, E. M., Hedberg, K., & Cieslak, P. R. (2004). Chickenpox outbreak in a highly vaccinated school population. *Pediatrics,* 113(3), 455–459.

Tullis, L. M., Dupont, R., Frost-Pineda, K., & Gold, M. S. (2003). Marijuana and tobacco: A major connection? *Journal of Addictive Diseases,* 22(3), 51–62.

Tunks, E. R. (2008). Chronic pain and the psychiatrist. *The Canadian Journal of Psychiatry,* 53(4), 211–212.

Turk, D. C., Swanson, K. S., & Tunks, E. R. (2008). Psychological approaches in the treatment of chronic pain patients—when pills, scalpels and needles are not enough. *The Canadian Journal of Psychiatry,* 53(4), 213–223.

Tuskegee Syphilis Study Legacy Committee. (1996). Bad blood: Final report of the Tuskegee Syphilis Study Legacy Committee, May 20, 1996. Retrieved from: www.Healthsystem.virginia.edu/internet/library/historical/medical_history/bad_blood/Html.

U.N. Children's Fund (UNICEF). (2002a). *Young people and HIV/AIDS: Opportunity in crisis.* Geneva: UNICEF, UNAIDS, and WHO.

U.N. Children's Fund (UNICEF). (2002b). *Young people and HIV/AIDS: A UNICEF fact sheet.* New York: UNICEF.

U.N. International Drug Control Programme (UNDCP). (1997). World drug report. New York: Oxford University Press.

U.S. Cancer Statistics Working Group. (2005). *United States Cancer Statistics: 1999–2005: Incidence and Mortality Web-based Report.* Atlanta: U.S. Department of Health and Human Services, Centers for Disease Control and Prevention and National Cancer Institute; Retrieved from: www.cdc.gov/uscs.

U.S. Census Bureau. (2007). *Current population survey, 2006 and 2007 annual social and economic supplements.* Retrieved from: www.census.gov/hhes/www/Hlthins/hlthin07/fig07/pdf.

U.S. Department of Health and Human Services. (1994). Preventing tobacco use among young people: A Report of the Surgeon General. Washington, DC: USGPO.

U.S. Department of Health and Human Services. (2000). Reducing tobacco use: A report of the surgeon general. Atlanta, GA: U.S. Department of Health and Human Services, Centers for Disease Control and Prevention, National Center for Chronic Disease Prevention and Health Promotion, Office of Smoking and Health.

U.S. Department of Health and Human Services (2001). Healthy People 2010. 2nd Ed. With Understanding and Improving Health and Objectives for Improving Health. Vol 2. Washington, DC: Government Printing Office.

U.S. Environmental Protection Agency. (2007). Asthma: Indoor environmental asthma triggers: Cockroaches and pets. Retrieved on December 17, 2007, from: www.epa.gov/asthma/pests.html.

U.S. Food and Drug Administration (FDA). (2005). *FDA News. FDA approves BiDil heart failure drug for black patients.* Retrieved from: www.fda.gov/bbs/topics/news/2005/new01190.html.

U.S. Food and Drug Administration. (2007). Expanded access and expedited approvals of new therapies related to HIV/AIDS. Retrieved on June 1, 2007, from: www.fda.gov/oashi/aids/expanded.html.

U.S. National Library of Medicine & National Institutes of Health. (2009). Medline plus. Arthritis in hip.

Retrieved on December 12, 2009, from: www.nlm.nih.gov/medlineplus/ency/imagepages/19678.htm.

U.S. National Library of Medicine & National Institutes of Health. (2010). Medline plus. Knee joint. Retrieved on January 30, 2010, from: www.nlm.nih.gov/medlineplus/ency/imagepages/19309.htm.

UCLA Integrated Substance Abuse Program. (2006). *Methamphetamine: Overview.* Retrieved from: www.methamphetamine.org/html/overview.html.

Uhrhammer, N., & Bignos, Y. J. (2008). Report of a family segregating mutations in both the APC and MSH2 genes: Juvenile onset of colorectal cancer in a double heterozygote. *International Journal of Colorectal Disease,* 23(11), 1131–1135.

Uitterhoeve, R. J., Vernooy, M., Litjens, M., Potting, K., Bensing, J., De Mulder, P. et al. (2004). Psychosocial interventions for patients with advance cancer: A systematic review of The literature. *British Journal of Cancer,* 91, 1050–1062.

Ulmer, R. G., Preusser, D. F., Williams, A. F., Ferguson, S. A., & Farmer, C. M. (2000). Effect of Florida's graduated licensing program on the crashes of teenage drivers. *Accidental Annual of Prevention,* 32, 527–532.

UNAIDS. (2001). *Condom social marketing: Selected case studies.* Best Practices Collection. Geneva: Joint United Nations Programme on HIV/AIDS.

UNAIDS. (2004). Epidemiological fact sheets on HIV/AIDS and sexually transmitted infections. Ukraine. Geneva: World Health Organization Press.

UNAIDS. (2008a). 2008 report on the global AIDS epidemic, July 2008. Joint United Nations Program on HIV/AIDS, Geneva: UNAIDS.

UNAIDS. (2008b). 2008 report on the global AIDS epidemic, July 2008. Joint United Nations Programme on HIV/AIDS, UNAIDS 2008, Executive Summary. Retrieved from: http://data.unaids.org/pub/Global Report/2008/JC1511_GR08_ExecutiveSummary_en.pdf.

UNAIDS. (2010). Global Campaign Against HIV/AIDS. Retrieved June 9, 2010, from: www.unaids.org/en/default.asp.

Unal, B., Critchley, J., & Capewell, S. (2005). Modelling the decline in CHD deaths in England & Wales 1981–2000: Comparing contributions from primary and secondary prevention. *British Medical Journal,* 331, 614–615.

UNICEF. (2001a). Official summary. The state of the world's children 2001. New York: United Nations.

UNICEF. (2001b). Special session on children. Second substantive session of the Preparatory Committee. Item 4. Organizational arrangements for the preparatory process and the special session. Update on reviews and appraisals. New York, January 29–February 2.

UNICEF. (2004). HIV/AIDS menaces progress in Ukraine. Retrieved on February 1, 2007, from: www.unicef.org/infobycountry/media.

UNICEF. (2008). UNICEF nominee Paul Farmer receives CDC foundation hero Award. Retrieved on February 23, 2009, from: www.unicef.org/infobycountry/usa_45896.html.

United Nations. (2006). *Population and Vital Statistics Report*. Geneva: U.N. Department of Economic and Social Affairs.

United Nations. (2007). World population prospects: The 2006 revision highlights. Working Paper No esa/p/wp.202. New York: United Nations, Department of Economic and Social Affairs, Population Division,. Retrieved on December 12, 2009, from: www.un.org/esa/population/publications/wpp2006/WPP2006_Highlights_rev.pdf.

University of Arkansas, Division of Agriculture. (2007). *Natural resources. Uses of other tree species*. Retrieved on June 26, 2008, from: www.arnatural.org/wildfoods/uses_Trees.htm.

University of California, Agricultural and Natural Resources. (2007). UC Study: Teen drivers distracted by passengers "fooling around." News and Information Outreach, Governmental and External Relations. Retrieved on February 1, 2008, from: http://news.ucanr.org/newsstorymain.cfm?story=1049.

University of Minnesota. (2008). Sarcomas. Masonic Cancer Center. University of Minnesota. Retrieved on October 20, 2008, from: www.cancer.umn.edu/cancerinfo/carcoma/index.html.

Urberg, K. A., Degirmencioglu, S. M., & Pilgrim, C. (1997). Close friends and group influences on adolescent cigarette smoking and alcohol use. *Developmental Psychology, 33*(5), 834–844.

Valenzuela, T. D., Roe, D. J., Nichol, G., Clark, L. L. Spaite, D. W., & Hardman, R. G. (2000). Outcomes of rapid defibrillation by security officers after cardiac arrests in casinos. *The New England Journal of Medicine, 343*(17), 1206–1209.

van der Mei, I. A., Ponsonby, A. L., & Dwyer, T. (2003). Past exposure to sun, skin phenotype & risk of multiple sclerosis: Case-control study. *British Medical Journal, 327*, 311–316.

Van geertruyden, J. P., & D'Alessandro, U. (2007). Malaria & HIV: A silent alliance. *Trends in Parasitology, 23*(10), 465–467.

van Wyk, B.-E. (2008). A review of the Khoi-San and Cape Dutch medical ethnobotany. *Journal of Ethnopharmacology, 119*, 331–341.

vanBeurden, E., Zask, A., Brooks, L., & Dight, R. (2005). Heavy episodic drinking and sensation seeking in adolescents as predictors of harmful driving and celebrating behaviors: Implications for prevention. *Journal of Adolescent Health, 37*, 37–43. Vogels, J., van der Vliet, R., Danz, M., & Hopman-Rock, N. (1993). Young people and sex: Behaviour and health risks in Dutch school students. *Adolescent Medicine and Health, 6*(2), 137–147.

VanDervanter, N. L., Messeri P., Middlestadt, S. E., Bleakley, A., Merzel, C. R., Hogben, M. (2005). A community-based intervention designed to increase preventive health care seeking among adolescents: The gonorrhea community action project. *American Journal of Public Health, 95*, 331–337.

Vargas, L. A., & Koss-Chioino, J. D. (eds.). (1992). *Working with culture: Psycho-therapeutic interventions with ethnic minority children and adolescents*. San Francisco: Jossey-Bass.

Vehbaak, P. F., Kersson, J. J., Dekker, J., et al. (1998). Prevalence of chronic benign pain disorder among adults: A review of the literature. *Pain 77*, 231–239.

Vickers, A. (2000). Why aromatherapy works (even if it doesn't) and why we need less research. *British Journal of General Practice, 50*, 455, 444–445.

Vitaliano, P. P., Zhang, J., & Scanlon, J. M. (2003). Is caregiving hazardous to one's physical health? A meta-analysis. *Psychological Bulletin, 129*, 6, 946–972.

Vouri, H. (1987). Patient satisfaction: An attribute or indicator of the quality of care? *Quality Review Bulletin, 13*, 106–108.

Vouri, H. (1991). Patient satisfaction: Does it matter? *Quality Assurance Health Care, 3*, 183–189.

Wachholtz, A. B., & Pargament, K. I. (2008) Migraines and meditation: Does spirituality matter? *Journal of Behavioral Medicine, 31*(4), 351–366.

Wade, D. T., & Halligan, P. W. (2004). Do biomedical models of illness make for good healthcare systems? *British Medical Journal, 329*, 1398–1491.

Wagemakers, A., Corstjens, R., Koelen, M., Vaandrager, L., Van't Reit, H., & Dijkshoor, H. (2008). Participatory approaches to promote health lifestyles among Turkish and Moroccan women in Amsterdam. *Promotion and Education, 15*, 4, 17–23.

Wakefield, A. J., Murch, S. H., Anthony, A., Linnell, J., Casson, D. M., Malik, M., et al. (1998). Ileal-lymphoid-nodular hyperplasia, non-specific colitis and pervasive developmental disorder in children. *Lancet, 351*, 9103, 637–641.

Walda, I. C., Tabak, C., Smit, H. A., Rasanen, L., Fidanza, F., Menotti, A., et al. (2002). Diet & 20 year chronic obstructive pulmonary disease mortality in middle-aged men from three European countries. *European Journal of Clinical Nutrition, 56*(7), 638–643.

Wallace, J. M., Yamaguchi, R., Bachman, J. G., O'Malley, P. M., Schulenberg, J. E., & Johnston, L. D. (2007). Religiosity and adolescent substance use: The role of individual and contextual influences. *Social Problems, 54*(2), 308–327.

Wallis, D. J., & Hetherington, M. M. (2004). Stress and eating: The effects of ego-threat and cognitive demand on food intake in restrained and emotional eaters. *Appetite, 43*, 39–46.

Walsh, B. T. (1997). Eating disorders. In A. Tasman, J. Kay, & J. A. Lieberman (eds.), *Psychiatry, Volume 2* (1202–1216). *London: John WIley & Sons.*

Walsh, S. R., Manuel, J. C., & Avis, N. E. (2005). The impact of breast cancer on younger women's relationships with their partner & children. *Family Systems Health,* 23, 80–93.

Walter, H. J., Vaughan, R. D., Gladis, M. M., Ragin, D. F., Kasen, S., & Cohall, A. T. (1992). Factors associated with AIDS risk behaviors among high school students in an AIDS epicenter. *American Journal of Public Health,* 82(4), 528–532.

Walter, H. J., Vaughan, R. D., Gladis, M. M., Ragin, D. F., Kasen, S., Cohall, A. T. (1993). Factors associated with AIDS-related behavioral intentions among high school students in an AIDS epicenter. *Health Education Quarterly,* 20(3), 409–420.

Walter, H. J., Vaughan, R. D., Ragin, D. F., Cohall, A. T., & Kasen, S. (1994). Prevalence and correlates of AIDS-related behavioral intentions among urban minority high school students. *AIDS Education and Prevention,* 6(4), 339–350.

Wang, Y., & Beydoun, M. A. (2007). The obesity epidemic in the United States—gender, age, socioeconomics, racial/ethnic & geographic characteristics: A systematic review & meta-regression analysis. *Epidemiology Review,* 29, 6–28.

Ward, A., & Mann, T. (2000). Don't mind if I do: Disinhibited eating under cognitive load. *Journal of Personality and Social Psychology,* 78, 753–763.

Ward, C. L., Martin, E., & Distiller, G. B. (2007). Factors affecting resilience in children exposed to violence. *South African Journal of Psychology,* 37, 1, 165–187.

Wardle, J. (1995). Cholesterol & psychological well-being. *Journal of Psychosomatic Research,* 39, 5, 549–562.

Wardle, J., Hasse, A. M., Steptoe, A., Nillapun, M., Jonwutiewes, K., & Bellisle, F. (2004). Gender differences in food choice: The contribution of health beliefs and dieting. *Annals of Behavioral Medicine,* 27, 107–116.

Warner, E., Foulkes, W., Goodwin, P., Meschino, W., Blondel, J., Paterson, C., et al. (1999). Prevalence and penetrance of BRCA1 and BRCA2 gene mutation in unselected Ashkenazi Jewish women with breast cancer. *Journal of the National Cancer Institute,* 91(14), 1241–1247.

Wartik, N. (2003). Rising obesity in children prompts call to action. *The New York Times,* August 26, 2003, 5.

Washam, C. (2005). Targeting teens and adolescents for HPV vaccine could draw fire. *Journal of the National Cancer Institute,* 97(14), 1030.

Watson, W. E., Minzenmayer, T., & Bobler, M. (2006). Type-A personality characteristics and the effects on individual and team academic performance. *Journal of Applied Social Psychology,* 36(5), 1110–1128.

Weiner, K. A. (2003). 2001–2010: The Decade of pain control and research. *The Pain Practitioner,* Spring. Retrieved on July 20, 2010, from: http://www.aapainmanage.org/literature/PainPrac/V13N1_Weiner_DecadeOfPainControl.pdf.

Weir, H. K., Thun, M. J., Hankey, B. F., Reis, L. A. G., Howe, H. L., & Wingo, P. A. (2003). Special article: Annual report to the nation of the state of the union, 1975–2000. Featuring the use of surveillance data for cancer prevention. *Journal of the National Cancer Institute,* 95(17), 1276–1299.

Weir, L. A., Elelson, D., & Brand, D. A. (2006). Parent's perception of neighborhood safety & children's physical activity. *Preventive Medicine,* 43, 3, 212–217.

Weisberg, J. N., & Keefe, F. J. (1999). Personality, individual differences, and psycho pathology in chronic pain. In R. J. Gatchel & D. C. Turk (eds.), *Psychosocial factors in pain: Critical perspectives* (56–73). New York: Guilford.

Weiss, N. S. (2003). Breast cancer mortality in relation to clinical breast examination and breast self-examination. *The Breast Journal,* 9, 586–589.

Wells, B. I., & Horn, J. W. (1992). Stage at diagnosis in breast cancer: Race and socioeconomic factors. *American Journal of Public Health,* 82, 1383–1385.

Weng, H. C. (2008). Does the physician's emotional intelligence matter? Impacts of the physician's relationship and satisfaction. *Health Care Management Review,* 33(4), 280–288.

Wetherell, M. A., Byrne-Davis, P. D., Donovan, J., Brookes, M. B., Vedhara, K., Horne, R., et al. (2005). Effects of emotional disclosure on psychological and physiological outcomes in patients with rheumatoid arthritis: An exploratory home-based study. *Journal of Health Psychology,* 10, 277–285.

Whitfield, C. L. (2003). *The truth about depression: Choices for healing.* Deerfield Beach, FL: Health Communications.

Whitfield, C. L., Anda, R. F., Dube, S. R., & Felitti, V. J. (2003). Violent childhood experiences and the risk of intimate partner violence in adults. *Journal of Interpersonal Violence,* 18(2), 166–185.

Whittle, J., Conigliaro, J., Good, C. B., & Lofgren, R. P. (1993). Racial differences in the use of invasive cardiovascular procedures in the Department of Veterans Affairs medical system. *New England Journal of Medicine,* 329, 621–627.

Wiet, S. (2009). Care for the caregivers: Information, simplification, peace of mind & time. Retrieved on June 2, 2009, from: Access2wellness.com: www.strengthforcaring.com/manual/about-you-the-caregiver-role/care-for-the-caregiver-information-simplification-peace-of-mind-and-time/.

Wijnen, J. T., Brochet, R. M., vanEijk, R., Jagmohan-Changun, S., Middledor, P. A., & Tops, C. M. (2008). Chromosome 8q23.3 and 11q23.1 variants modify colorectal cancer risk in Lynch syndrome. *Gastroenterology,* e-publication ahead of print.

Wilkinson, R. G. (1996). *Unhealthy societies: The afflictions of inequality.* London: Rutledge.

Willi, J., & Grossman, S. Epidemiology of anorexia nervosa in a defined region of Switzerland. *American Journal of Psychiatry,* 140, 564–567.

Willliams, A. F. (2003). Teenage drivers: patterns of risk. *Journal of Safety Research,* 34, 5–15.

Williams, R., & Williams, V. (1993). *Anger kills.* New York: Random House.

Williams, D. M., Anderson, E. S., & Winett, R. A. (2005). A review of the outcome expectancy construct in physical activity research. *Annals of Behavioral Medicine,* 29(1), 70–79.

Williams, D. R., & Neighbors, H. (2001). Racism, discrimination and hypertension: Evidence and needed research. *Ethnicity and Disease,* 11, 800–816.

Williams, J. E., Paton, C. C., Siegler, I. C., EIgnebrodt, M. L., Neito, F. J., & Tyroler, H. A. (2000) Anger proneness predicts coronary heart disease risk. *Circulation,* 101, 2034–2039.

Wills, T. A., Sargent, J. D., Stoolmiller, M., Gibbons, F. X., Worth, K. A., & Cin, S. (2007). Movie exposure to smoking cues and adolescent smoking onset for mediation through peer affiliations. *Health Psychology,* 26(6), 769–776.

Wilson, D. J. (2005). *Living with polio: The epidemic and its survivors.* Chicago: University of Chicago Press.

Wilson, K. M., & Klein, J. D. (2000). Adolescents who use the emergency department as their usual source of care. *Archives of Pediatric Adolescent Medicine,* 154, 361–365.

Winkleby, M. A., Robinson, T. N., Sundquist, J., & Kraemer, H. C. (1999). Ethnic variations in cardiovascular disease risk factors among children and young adults. *Journal of the American Medical Association,* 281(11), 1006–1013.

Wirth, O., & Sigurdsson, S. O. (2008). When workplace safety depends on behavior change: Topics for behavioral safety. *Journal of Safety Research,* 39, 589–598.

Wittstein, I., Thiemann, D., Lima, J., Baughman, K., Schulman, S., Gerstenblith, G., et al. (2005). Neurohumoral features of myocardial stunning due to sudden emotional stress. *New England Journal of Medicine,* 352, 539–548.

Wold, S. J., Brown, C. M., Chastain, C. E., Griffis, M. D., & Wingate, J. (2008). Going the extra mile: Beyond health teaching to political involvement. *Nursing Forum,* 43, 4, 171–176.

Wong, W. C. W., Lee, A., Wong. S. Y. S., Wu, A. C., & Robinson, N. (2006). Strengths, weaknesses, and development of traditional medicine in the health system of Hong Kong: Through the eyes of future Western doctors. *Journal of Alternative and Complementary Medicine,* 12(2), 185–189.

Wood, F. C. (1924). "Must women die of cancer?" *Women Citizen,* 11, (April 1924), 24.

Woodgate, J., & Brawley, L. R. (2008). Self-efficacy for exercise in cardiac rehabilitation: Review and recommendation. *Journal of Health Psychology,* 13(3), 366–387.

Wooster, R., Bignell, G., Lancaster, J., Swift, S., Seal, S., & Mangion, J. (1995). Identification of the breast cancer susceptibility gene BRCA2. *Nature,* 378, 789–792.

World Health Organization. (1947). Constitutions of the World Health Organization. *Chronicle of the World Health Organization,* 1.

World Health Organization. (1992). *World Health Organization Basic Documents,* 39th edition. Geneva: World Health Organization.

World Health Organization (WHO). (1999). *Dracunculiasis or guinea worm.* CEE Documentation Center. Geneva: WHO.

World Health Organization (WHO). (2000a). Guide to drug abuse epidemiology. Department of Mental Health & Substance Dependencies. Non-Communicable Diseases & Mental Health Cluster. Geneva: World Health Organization.

World Health Organization (WHO). (2000b). Uganda, HIV/AIDS, health, a key to prosperity. Success stories in developing countries. Retrieved on March 2, 2010, from: www.who.int/info-new/aids2.htm.

World Health Organization (WHO). (2002). World Health Organization Report: Reducing risk, promoting healthy lives. Geneva: WHO.

World Health Organization (WHO). (2003). *Traditional medicine.* Fact sheet No. 134. Retrieved from: www.who.int/mediacentre/factsheets/fs134/en/.

World Health Organization (WHO). (2004). *Malaria and HIV interactions and their implications for public health policy: Report of a technical consultation.* Geneva: WHO.

World Health Organization (WHO). (2005a). *Facing the Facts #3. Chronic diseases in low and middle income countries.* Geneva: WHO.

World Health Organization (WHO). (2005b). *Malaria.* Roll back malaria department. Geneva: WHO.

World Health Organization (WHO). (2005c). *Preventing chronic diseases: A vital investment.* Geneva: WHO.

World Health Organization (WHO). (2005d). A systematic approach to developing and implementing mental health legislation. Report of a regional meeting of experts, New Delhi, India, December 6–8, 2004. Who Project ICP MNH 001. New Delhi: WHO.

World Health Organization (WHO). (2005e). HIV/AIDS antiretroviral newsletter, No. 11. Manila: World Health Organization.

World Health Organization (WHO). (2006a). Cholera. Retrieved on November 1, 2006, from: www.who.int/mediacentre/factsheet/Fs107/en.

World Health Organization (WHO). (2006b). Measles. Retrieved on November 1, 2006, from: www.who.int/mediacentre/factsheet/Fs286/en.

World Health Organization (WHO). (2007a). Malaria fact sheet No. 94. Retrieved on October 32, 2007, from: www.who.int/mediacentre/factsheets/fs094/en/print.html.

World Health Organization (WHO). (2007b). Tuberculosis fact sheet. Retrieved on April 30, 2007, from: http://www.who.int/mediacentre/factsheets/fs104/en/index.html.

World Health Organization (WHO). (2008a). Cancer. Fact sheet No. 297. Retrieved from: http://www.who.int/mediacentre/factsheets/fs297/en/.

World Health Organization (WHO). (2008b). Cardiovascular disease: Fact sheet. Retrieved on July 10, 2008, from: www.who.int/cardiovascular_diseases/en.

World Health Organization (WHO). (2008c). Cholera fact sheet No. 107. Retrieved on October 31, 2007, from: www.who.int/mediacentre/factsheets/fs/107/en/print.html.

World Health Organization (WHO). (2008d). Global tuberculosis control: Surveillance, planning, finance. Geneva: WHO.

World Health Organization (WHO). (2009a). About dracunculiasis. Retrieved on April 29, 2009, from: www.who.int/entity/dracunculiasis/diseases/en.

World Health Organization (WHO). (2009b). Malnutrition. Retrieved on from: www.who.int/child_Adolescent_healh/topics/prevention_care/child/nutrition/malnutrition.

World Health Organization (WHO). (2009c). Progress towards global immunization goals, 2008: Summary presentation of key indicators. Retrieved on February 23, 2010, from: http://www.who.int/immunization_monitoring/data/SlidesGlobalImmunization.pdf.

World Health Organization (WHO). (2009d). Wild poliovirus 2008. Retrieved on August 9, 2009, from: www.who.int/vaccines-surveillance/graphies/htmls/global_polio_03.html.

World Health Organization (WHO). (2010a). Influenza A(H1N1): Update 42. Retrieved on June 2, 2010, from: http://www.who.int/csr/disease/avian_influenza/phase/en/index.html.

World Health Organization (WHO). (2010b). Suicide prevention. SUPRE Publication, World Health Organization. Retrieved on February 24, 2010, from: www.who.int/mental_health/prevention/suicide/suicideprevent/en/.

World Health Organization (2010c). About WHO. Retrieved on July 9, 2010, from: http://www.who.int/about/en.

World Medical Association (WMA). (2000). *The Declaration of Helsinki: Ethical Principles for Medical Research Involving Human Subjects*. Geneva: World Health Organization. Retrieved on January 15, 2007, from: www.wma.net/e/policy/b3htm.

World Site Atlas. Retrieved on February 24, 2010, from: www.sitesatlas.com/Maps/Maps/714.gif.

Worley, K. D., Walsh, S., & Lewis, K. (2004). An examination of parenting experiences in male perpetrators of domestic violence: A qualitative study. *Psychology and Psychotherapy*, 77(Pt. 1), 35–54.

Yager, J. (1988). The treatment of eating disorders. *Journal of Clinical Psychiatry*, 49(Suppl), 18–25.

Yang, E. J., Chung, H. K., Kim, W. Y., Bianchi, L., & Song, W. O. (2007). Chronic diseases & dietary changes in relation to Korean American's length of residence in the United States. *Journal of the American Dietetic Association*, 107(6), 942–950.

Yellow Horse Brave Heart, M. (2003). The historical trauma response among natives and its relationship with substance abuse: A Lakota illustration. *Journal of Psychoactive Drugs*, 35, 7–13.

Yeo, I. S. (2003). The concept of disease in Galen. *Uisahak*, 12, 1, 54–65.

Yu, J., & Williford, W. R. (1992). The age of alcohol onset and alcohol, cigarette and marijuana use patterns: An analysis of drug use progression of young adults in New York State. *The International Journal of the Addictions*, 279(11), 1313–1323.

Yu, T. S., Wong S. L., Lloyd, O. L., & Wong, T. W. (1995). Ischemic heart disease. Trends in mortality in Hong Kong 1970–1989. *Journal of Epidemiology Community Health*, 49(1), 16–21.

Zanella, M. T., Kohlmann, O., & Ribeiro, A. B. (2001). Treatment of obesity hypertension and diabetes syndrome. *Hypertension*, 38, 705–708.

Zellner, D. A., Loaiza, S., Gonzalez, Z., Pita, J., Morales, J., Pecora, D., et al. (2006). Food selection changes under stress. *Physiology and Behavior*, 87, 789–793.

Zellner, D. A., Saito, S., & Gonzalez, J. (2007). The effect of stress on men's food selection, *Appetite*, 49, 696–699.

Zhang, Z. F., Morgenstern, H., & Spitz, M. R. (1999). Marijuana use and increased risk of squamous cell carcinoma of the head and neck. *Cancer Epidemiology, Biomarker & Prevention*, 8(12), 1071–1078.

Zickler, P. (2007). Methamphetamine evokes and subverts brain protective responses. *NIDA Notes: Research Trends and News from the National Institute on Drug Abuse*, 20(6), 8–9.

Zimbardo, P. G. (1973). On the ethics of intervention in human psychological research: With special reference to the Stanford prison experiment. *Cognition*, 2(2), 243–256.

Zimbardo, P. G. (2007). Revisiting the Stanford prison experiment: A lesson in the power of situation. *Chronicle of Higher Education*, 53(30), B6–B7.

Ziv, A., Boulet, J. R., & Slap, G. B. (1999). Utilization of physicians offices by adolescents in US. *Pediatrics, 104,* 35–42.

Zuckerman, S., & Shen, Y. C. (2004). Characteristics of occasional and frequent emergency department users: Do insurance coverage and access to care matter? *Medical Care, 42,* 176–182.

Zunkel, G. (2002). Relational coping process: Couples' response to a diagnosis of early stage breast cancer. *Journal of Psychosocial Oncology, 20,* 39–55.

Zuskin, E., Lipozencic, J., Pucarin-Cuetkovic, J., Muslajbegovic, J., Schachter, N., & Mucic, Pucic, B. (2008). Ancient medicine: A review. *Acta Dermato-renerological Coratica: ADC, 16*(3), 149–157.

AUTHOR INDEX

SUBJECT INDEX